SO-BTD-466

155.208
V64p

91932

DATE DUE			
Jul 8 77			
Nov 4 78			
Dec 15 78 B			
Jan 11 '82			
Apr 18 '82			
Dec 10 '82			

WITHDRAWN

PERSONALITY THEORY

PERSONALITY

A SOURCE

THE CENTURY PSYCHOLOGY SERIES

Kenneth MacCorquodale, Gardner Lindzey, Kenneth E. Clark

EDITORS

edited by

HAROLD J. VETTER & BARRY D. SMITH
Florida State University   University of Maryland

THEORY
BOOK

APPLETON-CENTURY-CROFTS

Educational Division

MEREDITH CORPORATION   New York

CARL A. RUDISILL LIBRARY
LENOIR RHYNE COLLEGE

PERSONALITY THEORY: A SOURCE BOOK

Copyright © 1971 by
MEREDITH CORPORATION
All rights reserved

This book, or parts thereof, must not be used or reproduced in any manner
without written permission. For information address the publisher,
Appleton-Century-Crofts, Educational Division, Meredith Corporation,
440 Park Avenue South, New York, N.Y. 10016.

7100-1

Library of Congress Card Number: 75-129993

155.208
V64P
91932
Feb.1975

PRINTED IN THE UNITED STATES OF AMERICA
390-89925-9

Contents

Contents

Preface

Following the introductory chapter, this anthology begins with an article published in 1893 by Josef Breuer and Sigmund Freud on psychic mechanisms in hysteria, and concludes with a 1967 paper by H. J. Eysenck on the application of principles derived from the laboratory study of learning phenomena to the alleviation of neurotic symptoms. The juxtaposition of these two papers was fortuitous but provides a convenient and illustrative contrast: not only do they mark a separation in time of more than seven eventful decades in the development of personality theory, but they also represent polar extremities in the conceptualization and study of human experience and behavior, symbolizing the great variation that characterizes personality theories. It would be difficult to imagine a more striking pair of opposites. On the one hand, we have Freud's astute but subjective and intuitive analysis of human behavior; on the other, we have the stringent empiricism of Eysenck's factor analytic work. Again, we have Freud's purposeful development of an elaborate theoretical system, insightful and influential, but based on little data and difficult to examine empirically, versus Eysenck's relatively limited theorizing, based on massive quantities of relatively objective data.

We could go further, and indeed could draw contrasts throughout the realm of personality theory. But such concern with areas of divergence should not supersede the careful study of the numerous areas of progress and, particularly in recent years, considerable convergence in personality theory. For the student of personality, it is far less important to arrive at a knowledge of theoretical contrasts or a judgment of whether Freud was right and Eysenck wrong, or vice versa, than it is to understand the empirical and conceptual processes by which the two theorists reached their conclusions.

The present volume pursues the understanding of personality through the inclusion of three types of papers: original works by theorists and related works by others, research articles, and papers applying theories to specific problems. The reasons for presenting selections from the original works of various theorists are too obvious to require editorial comment. It should be noted, however, that the theorist alone is not always the best introduction to his own work. Where circumstances warranted, we have thus selected, in addition to or in lieu of original works by the theorist, important contributions by experts concerned with the theorist's work. In

ix

addition to primary sources, we have especially sought to include papers which portray the theory within the context of empirical research and application. This aim is scarcely less important than the inclusion of the original selections themselves. The brief introductions to each section are not intended to take the place of the many thorough and detailed critical studies of various theories that are available; rather, they are a concession to the realistic goal of preparing an anthology of something appreciably less than encyclopedic proportions, while at the same time providing some background and guidance concerning the included readings. We might point out that not every section of the book contains all three major types of article, nor are the articles selected the only ones which might have been chosen. In addition, the coverage of personality theories is intended to be not exhaustive but selective.

In preparing the present volume, we established and attempted to meet three major criteria for the inclusion of each article: representativeness, informativeness, and recency. We consider an article to be *representative* if it deals with major concepts or issues of concern to the theorist, with characteristic research related to or deriving from the work of the theorist, or with the application of a major theory to a specific problem. We consider it to be *informative* if it deals systematically with a number of issues or in detail with one or more issues of relevance to a theory, or, in some cases, if it reviews relevant literature. A research paper is most informative when it discusses theoretical constructs, hypotheses, or issues in the context of presenting data relevant to the work of the theorist. An application paper should likewise deal with major theoretical issues in the context of applying the ideas of the theorist to a specific problem. Ideally, a paper of any type is reasonably self-contained, or the section introduction should provide at least minimal information necessary for understanding the paper. The criterion of *recency* reflects our desire to present, where feasible and appropriate, the most current views of the theorist. We have flagrantly violated this criterion in a number of instances where an earlier article is more representative of the theorist's continuing viewpoint (or of a particularly central earlier viewpoint) or more informative than recent works. Recent research is also emphasized, but again violations to permit the inclusion of more characteristic or informative research are frequent.

Finally, we might return for a moment to the contrast of Eysenck with Freud and the fallacy of pursuing too far such divergencies in personality theory. In this regard, it should be noted simply that the principal reason for the construction, empirical testing, and study of personality theory is not to achieve a knowledge of similarities and contrasts, but to gain a greater understanding of human behavior, of the variables that underlie it, and of the constructs that can be inferred from it. It is to the important task of furthering such understanding that the present volume is directed.

For their cooperation in supplying advice and/or relevant materials, including unpublished papers directly utilized in the preparation of this volume, we are indebted to Raymond B. Cattell, Erik H. Erikson, Rudolph M. Loewenstein, Neal E. Miller, Henry A. Murray, Zygmunt A. Piotrowski, Carl R. Rogers, M. Brewster Smith, and Adrian van Kaam. Special thanks are due to the late A. H. Maslow, to Gardner Murphy, and to Zygmunt A. Piotrowski for allowing us to print previously unpublished papers. In addition, we sincerely thank all the authors and publishers, specifically acknowledged in connection with each selection, who permitted us to reprint their works.

To all those who have aided in various ways in the preparation of this volume, we are also deeply grateful. Our wives, Virginia and Elizabeth, were tremendously helpful in the preparation of the manuscript. Irma Nicholson typed the manuscript with skill and patience, and often on short notice. Josephine Shaffer and Rosemary Tofalo rendered valuable assistance, particularly in the obtaining of permissions. Finally, our thanks to Jack Burton and Marjorie Kalins of Appleton-Century-Crofts, without whose assistance and encouragement this volume would not have been possible.

PERSONALITY THEORY

THE ANALYSIS of specific theories and their empirical consequences is considerably enhanced if one begins with a more general orientation to scientific theories as aspects of the system of science. Such an orientation provides knowledge concerning the functions of theories in empirical science, the origins of scientific theories, and the structural properties which are common to many major theoretical treatments.

In the following introductory chapter, Dr. Zygmunt A. Piotrowski elucidates the system of science. He does not merely treat scientific theories as isolated abstractions, but points out the essential relationships of theories to their empirical referents, underlying concepts, and scientific validation. Dr. Piotrowski's article will prove extremely valuable as a basis for greater understanding of the scientific theories and related empirical evidence which are treated in this anthology.

1

1

Basic System of All Sciences

ZYGMUNT A. PIOTROWSKI

The term "system" rather than "theory" is used in order to emphasize the twofold purpose of this chapter: (a) a description of the series of basic, regulated actions that are a prerequisite for the production of ordered and valid knowledge, and (b) an application of this basic system to some problems of personology (i.e., psychology of personality). Moreover, the word "theory" has so many meanings that its use without qualification can only result in ambiguity.

The system does not explain reality but it tells us how we get to know about reality, including the conditions of adequate theory testing. The particulars of validation depend on the type of theory tested, and the theory depends on our purposes. The perceptible reality which is the object of scientific inquiry is not an absolute reality but the reality as it is accessible to our senses and our methods of study. Nevertheless, empirical scientists make the assumption that there is a reality, the manifestations of which are determined not only by man's capacity and means of inquiry, but also by an order which is independent of man; furthermore, experience justifies the assumption that the laws describing the order of events (of perceived physical objects and processes) remains unchanged even when man changes some aspects of these events. We look for recurrences because they are proof that there is order. Even though most scientists show no interest in the science of science, a formalized basic system serves as a valuable aid in the search for strong and weak points in the scientific structure, revealing what needs correction, and thus becoming a device for the reduction of subjectivism, the illusions of "common sense," and the looseness of everyday language. Scientists who do not know the history of their science waste a great deal of time and effort by repeating past failures or rediscovering known facts.

Figure 1-1 is a diagrammatic summary of the basic system of all sciences. The indispensable functions have been reduced to four. All of them are autonomous in the sense that the results of one cannot be inferred

Dr. Piotrowski is Emeritus Professor of Psychiatry (Psychology) at Thomas Jefferson University and Director of Personality Research, Edward N. Hay and Associates of Philadelphia. He is also Adjunct Professor of Psychology at Temple University, and Area Consultant, Veterans Administration. The editors are indebted to Dr. Piotrowski for his efforts in providing an original contribution for this volume.

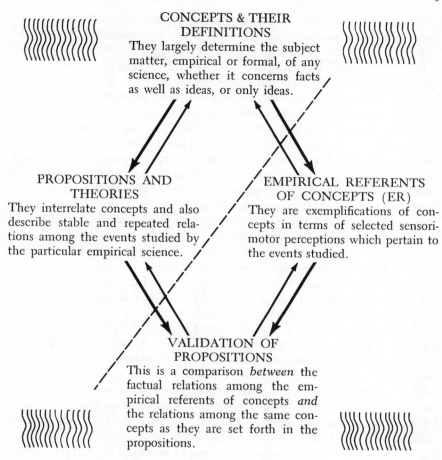

CONCEPTS & THEIR
DEFINITIONS
They largely determine the subject
matter, empirical or formal, of any
science, whether it concerns facts
as well as ideas, or only ideas.

PROPOSITIONS AND
THEORIES
They interrelate concepts and also
describe stable and repeated relations among the events studied by
the particular empirical science.

EMPIRICAL REFERENTS
OF CONCEPTS (ER)
They are exemplifications of concepts in terms of selected sensorimotor perceptions which pertain to
the events studied.

VALIDATION OF
PROPOSITIONS
This is a comparison *between* the
factual relations among the empirical referents of concepts *and*
the relations among the same concepts as they are set forth in the
propositions.

Figure 1-1. Diagram of science structure. The arrows represent the
direction and difference in strength of influence. The wavy
corner lines symbolize the fringes of any science, illustrating the fact that every science deals with events selected
from a much wider area of experiences. The broken diagonal line indicates the fact that formation of concepts
and propositions have more in common with each other
than with the other two functions; also, that the former
two are psychologically and methodologically closer to
concept and theory formation.

from, or substituted by, those of the others. This implies that defects in
any of them cannot be eliminated by improvements in any of the other
functions. On the other hand, only all four together, harmoniously interrelated, constitute an empirical science. To make great advances a science

must improve in all four functions. Every empirical science deals only with some selected aspects of reality and this fact is symbolized by the undulating lines in the corners of the diagram, the lines indicating the fringes of science. The arrows represent the direction and strength of influence of one function upon another and also differentiate between direct and indirect relations among the functions. Changes in basic concepts have by far the greatest influence while the validation of propositions and theories exercises the relatively smallest influence in the sense that theories are hardly ever abandoned because of adverse facts. They are laid to rest only by better theories as the history of sciences plainly demonstrates. A more accurate and comprehensive theory makes the life of the scientist easier by summarizing more relevant observations and ideas in a more precise form and by making possible inferences of a higher degree of validity, thus freeing his energies for new and bolder adventures. The basic system emphasizes the fundamental conditions of scientific advancement.

While any empirical science requires the harmonious integration of all four basic functions, the formal sciences, logic and mathematics, need only two: concepts and propositions. The only validating criterion of logical and mathematical propositions is consistency. Validation of empirical propositions goes beyond logical consistency; it is concerned with the degree of congruence between a conceptual model (the set of propositions) and the relations among the empirical referents of those concepts which appear in the propositional set or conceptual model that is subjected to validation. Such a congruence cannot be determined in the abstract. The reality beyond our selective sensorimotor perceptions will always remain unknown. Science is therefore a confrontation of a mental and verbal set of concepts and propositions, on the one side, with empirical observations, influenced by the same concepts, on the other side.

The nineteenth century was a period of great intellectual revolutions, the effects of which will continue to have a permanent and far-reaching effect. The foundations of traditional logic were revised and a new, formalized logic was developed. The proposition, rather than the concept, became the elements of logical thinking. Mathematics underwent changes and developments previously considered impossible: the concept of order displaced that of quantity in importance. The creation of non-Euclidean geometries dealt the final blow to the belief in the possibility of valid propositions which can be known by reason alone and not through sensorimotor experience, but which nevertheless pertain to perceptible reality and possess universal validity. The proof that atoms disintegrate spontaneously later led to deliberate attempts at atom splitting. These extraordinary changes in man's ways of thinking about reality as well as about his own mental processes brought forth a new science, new criteria of empirical evidence and new habits in creating testable propositions (notice the downgrading of induction as a method of producing knowledge). There exist many versions of the new system of science. Though none of them is identical with our own, none appears incompatible with it. None seems to enclose so many basic functions and their interactions in one simple diagram. Even some features of the historical development of sciences are indirectly referred to by the system. The introduction of a new concept has always been a very great event in any science; in the diagram, too, it is the concepts that are all important. To be sure, modifications in the propositional sets were significant, though in a lesser degree. New empirical referents of concepts, particularly when made possible through the invention of a technique producing new facts (microscope, X rays, etc.), sometimes stimulated the growth of new sciences concerned with previously unsuspected problems. Successful positive validation of propositions usually had the effect of reassuring scientists that they were on the right track. The trail-blazing power of new concepts and the relative unimportance of validation of old theories is revealed by the intellectual revolution in physics which turned against such "unquestionable" scientific "truths" of the day as Euclidean geometry, Aristotelian logic, and the indivisibility of atoms.

Our system suggests that progress in science can be made in any of the four functions, and even at the very fringes of science, without having to be concerned about the other functions at the time of creating something new. The re-integration of the whole system in a new pattern can wait. In fact, scientific work can be made easier by dividing it into natural part-functions which, singly, can be handled with greater efficiency and fruitfulness than the whole integrated system. Formalization of thought processes and of empirical observations is difficult but there is no more potent method of dispelling the secrets of nature.

Although we can know only what is accessible to us and only with means at our disposal, we need not feel discouraged. Human inventiveness makes more and more empirical events and objects accessible to our immediate and repeatable inspection through increasingly more precise instruments. Secondly, we are gradually sharpening our conceptual tools which permit us to extract increasingly more relevant information from our empirical observations. Thus, while absolute and perfectly exact empirical knowledge, expressed in general propositions, will always elude us, we are steadily producing increased amounts of more basic and more accurate knowledge.

Everything in the diagram is meaningful, including the presence or absence of lines connecting the different functions. Propositions and empirical referents are not connected directly with each other. Yet, the empirical referents of concepts make the propositions testable in terms of perceptible reality. There is also no direct connection between validation of propositions and defining of concepts. To proceed from one to the other we must first select empirical referents for the concepts and interrelate the concepts in propositions. The mental operations inherent in concept formation and in validating general propositions are totally unlike. Even the personalities of scientists who prefer either function over the other tend to be dissimilar.

CONCEPTS

Selecting and defining concepts is the crucial operation of any science. The greatest theoretical difficulties, those hardest to detect and to correct, are usually due to inadequate concepts. "Survival of the fittest" had a powerful impact. "Survival" was defined in numbers of descendants. The definition was tautological and thus spurious: it said that the families which survived in largest numbers were the most numerous. Spurious and inaccurate definitions delay the progress of science because concepts determine the direction of scientific investigations. The introduction of a new, and the removal of an antiquated, sterile, concept is a great occurrence. It may even launch a new period of unexpected discoveries, improving science in its three other basic functions as well. A highly creative mind and personal courage are needed to introduce new and productive concepts, and even to remove old and sterile ones, if they are widely accepted. Small wonder that nearly all concepts in personology are more than two thousand years old. Freud's ego, superego and id correspond closely to conscious self-control, conscience, and instincts. While Plato described concepts as timeless and unchanging forms with an existence of their own, the empiricist Aristotle placed them into concrete events and declared that concepts cannot be detached from objects and are modifiable. Timeless or not, concepts last and few scientists ever seriously tackle them. Sensory perceptions and generalizations are frequently questioned, but concepts rarely.

The accidental discovery that undeveloped photographic plates kept in the same drawer with a piece of ore underwent change, prompted a search in carloads of the same ore for the element which provided the energy responsible for the change of the plates. Once spontaneous fission was proved (against great odds, for the skeptics refused to see the evidence), attempts at deliberate atomic fission were made and nuclear physics was born. When the Euclidean postulate that parallels never meet was dropped, mathematicians had to redefine the "straight line." From their endeavor emerged not one but several non-Euclidean geometries which revolutionized mathematics and our ideas about the nature of science. In personology, on the other hand, there is not enough burrowing at the conceptual foundations.

Definitions of concepts can be arbitrary. We can even disregard any reference to empirical reality. In practice, however, the freedom of definition is curbed for the sake of scientific efficiency. Differences in definition have dissimilar effects on research procedures and on the quality of results. Those concepts are preferred by investigators which facilitate quantification of the events grouped together under one concept. Since a modification of definitions and new concepts affect also existing theories, the thought of this possible effect is another serious reason to consider the effects of various possible definitions before deciding which one to use. Since we have at least some idea of the meaning that is to be made precise in a formal definition, we define only what is known to us, although the very attempt at greater precision frequently improves ideas and elicits new ones. The increased precision and consistency clear the mind and facilitate creativeness. However, original and productive concepts are extremely rare. They always mark a new epoch because concepts are the foundation of science. Whenever the aim is a fundamental revision and regeneration of a science, the process of reconstruction begins with a thorough analysis of its concepts.

EMPIRICAL REFERENTS

The chief function of the ER (brief for "empirical referents of concepts") is to establish a direct link between thought and reality. ER are selected empirical sense data which have been chosen by scientists to represent the concepts in terms of sensorimotor experiences. Definitions indicate the meaning of concepts on the conceptual, abstract, or thought level; the ER indicate the meaning of the same concepts on the sensorimotor (mostly visual), concrete, or empirical level. The simplest ER are explained by pointing to a selected and limited qualitative visual sensation and saying in effect: "By red we mean this sort of visual sensation," or "this kind of three dimensional object, so shaped, exemplifies the concept 'sphere,' and this two dimensional object exemplifies a 'circle,' etc." In every ER is an intuitive, non-rational, qualitative element. If "rational" is defined as any process which can be duplicated perfectly by a mechanical device, then "non-rational" is everything that cannot be duplicated by a mechanical device. The "non-rational" is not necessarily anti-rational. It simply is something accessible to our perception and to our understanding (this understanding frequently even being satisfactorily communicable among different observers), but something which defies complete logical analysis. No logical definition will convey the meaning of such simple sensorimotor experiences as "up," "down," "left," "right," "away," "toward," "included," "excluded," "two-dimensional," "three-dimensional," etc., to anyone who does not know already what is meant by these ER. Concepts pertaining to physical reality are relatively simple and their ER are within the grasp of practically everybody. By contrast, the ER of psychological and sociological concepts are usually complex and therefore it is not easy to obtain general agreement regarding the nomenclature of the ER of a given personological concept. One complicating factor is the difference between inner attitudes (or motives) and external behavior. If genuine inner motives influence social behavior in ways which vary because the degree of directness of outward expression varies, the search for reliable ER of the basic motives can become a difficult task. And as is the case with every difficult task, the solutions will be numerous, not comparable, even incompatible.

Depression and anxiety are found in virtually all emotionally and intellectually disturbed individuals. And yet, even the verbal definitions of those concepts vary greatly. No wonder that their ER are diverse and correlate poorly with one another. The ER are understandably the weakest part of personology and for this reason demand the greatest care and improvement if authentic advancement is to be made.

Although our cognitive functions influence the way we perceive reality, we assume on good evidence that the perceived events are related to one another in special and stable ways which we do not influence. We may not know the procedures necessary to discover the laws of an orderly recurrence of events, and they may even be beyond our reach, but we have sufficient reason to believe, on the basis of our success so far, that we can be far more successful. Personology is in its early stages. The best proof of this is its redundancy. Within a sea of diverse terms we find a trickle of truly independent concepts with poor ER. Unless the spurious verbal differences are removed and, more importantly, unless better ER are found, no noticeable advancement can be expected.

It may be argued that the greatest contribution of projective personality techniques, and particularly of perceptanalysis is the improved ER which they provide. Let us take as an example the concept of anxiety. The visual images, freely associated to indeterminate visual stimuli, reveal many forms of anxiety which are easily distinguishable operationally (by specific features of the test responses) and which are at least as valid as any other available anxiety variables (or ER). Each perceptanalytic anxiety sign simultaneously indicates the manner in which anxiety is habitually alleviated. There is one exception to this statement, namely, the uneven pace of responding, especially the delay of the initial meaningful response to an inkblot, for these delays, called "shocks," reveal the so-called free-floating anxiety, unrelieved by reaction formations. Individuals who produce all responses at an evenly normal, or faster than normal, pace throughout the examination experience no conscious anxiety and, if psychotic, have no insight into being seriously ill. Projective tests do not rely on any theory of personality, if by this term we mean an explanation of how individuals have become what they are. It is sensible, of course, to make use of any personality theory, provided that the application of a personality theory to projective test data adds meaningful and significant information about the individual tested. Projective tests, however, need a theory of their own which would explain how and why they give the results they do. Even an incomplete theory of perceptanalysis helped in avoiding blind alleys and pointed the direction in which test development proved to be productive (Piotrowski, 1965, 1966). Psychologists and biologists have a hard time finding empirical equivalents for their concepts because they can hardly isolate their variables and keep them uninfluenced by other variables. Physicists have it much easier. In the first place, they work mostly with events they themselves create artificially and control almost completely, keeping them free from the interference of outside forces. In the second place, they duplicate events rather than predict them. Applications of physical theories consist of adapting laboratory equipment to practical life circumstances without any essential change in the scientific procedures, tested out previously in the laboratory. When physicists try to predict events uncontrolled by their artificial devices (as in meteorology), the accuracy of their predictions drops considerably.

It does not matter whether one begins with abstract concepts and then looks for appropriate ER, or whether one begins with empirical observations and then looks for appropriate concepts to classify the empirical data into meaningful categories. The naturalist or the clinician with his great interest in individual differences usually moves from observations to concepts. Theorists prefer the reverse method of first developing abstract models and then looking for data to which their models could be profitably applied. In most instances it seems impossible to tell which method will be the more fruitful. No doubt, much depends on the ingenuity and adequacy of each in any particular situation.

Science aims at objectivity, which depends, in part, on the consensus of qualified observers. No consensus is possible without adequate ER which make concepts intelligible in terms of repeatable perceptible reality, thus improving genuine communication among experimenters and theorists. Sterile speculations and most arguments end when good ER are available. The insistence of behaviorists that concepts pertaining to human behavior have ER, so to speak, exerted a salutary and lasting influence on personology. This effect has not been weakened by the views of the extremists that concepts be avoided and research concern itself only with reliably selected empirical bits of observation. This extreme view makes generalizations extending beyond the specific conditions of observation—and thus theory construction—impossible. Original and effective ER can be created in a variety of ways. They can be ingenious inventions, lucky discoveries, results of a long and systematic effort, or transplants from other sciences. Here, too, human initiative can aid the search for scientific objectivity.

PROPOSITIONS

Theoretical propositions can be formed with concepts alone without any direct reference to the empirical referents of concepts. With empirical referents as well as their corresponding concepts we can formulate empirical propositions, i.e., generalizations, concerning the regular and orderly recurrence of selected observable events. The act of interrelating concepts and ER in meaningful propositions is a primary intellectual function. It is intuitive and cannot be explained as an inevitable result of other mental functions. Gifted individuals create significant hypotheses. Propositions are hypotheses as long as they are not validated. Propositions are not the end result of a probability count since one cannot compute the probability of a proposition before knowing its content. A set of interrelated propositions constitute a theory. Although we cannot fully explain the origin of theories, we can make them intelligible in terms of empirical observations.

When related to one another in a proposition, concepts usually undergo some changes in meaning, be they ever so small. These amplifications of meaning need not at all be incompatible with the basic definition. In fact, their appearance in a number of different propositions exposes and clarifies the implications of concepts. The Rochefoucauld maxim that "our virtues are disguised vices" points to psychological processes which the definitions of the single concepts "vice" and "virtue" do not imply.

Consistency being the most fundamental requirement of sound thinking and experimenting, the freedom of putting sentences together is limited seriously by the meaning of the concepts related in the same sentence. Not all concepts can be intelligibly combined to express a sound thought. The main concern is to refrain from matching inconsistent concepts. Simplicity of relations among concepts is most desirable because otherwise deductive reasoning is complex and unreliable. On the other hand, it is of little importance whether the concepts themselves are defined in a complex manner or not. In order to simplify laws, we must often complicate the meaning of their terms. Learning theories and perceptanalysis offer many good examples. When the meaning of, say, movement or color responses (elicited by inkblots) is defined in broad and inexact terms, only few general conclusions can be inferred. Conclusions, more numerous, specific, and of a much higher degree of validity, can be deduced when those perceptanalytic responses are subdivided into a number of categories and each category is given its own specific and detailed definition, referring not to one vague but several detailed personality attributes.

In view of the many opportunities for being inexact and making mistakes, predictions of observable events are used in science to test the validity of hypothetical propositions. Predictions involve deductive reasoning, the drawing of references from premises. When deductions are repeatedly supported by factual evidence, we gain assurance that the theoretical system is sufficiently comprehensive and precise to serve the purposes for which it was created. The fact that various scientists obtain essentially the same results gives assurance that, whatever the differences in the meaning which they attach to the proposition and its implications, these differences are negligible. Thus a workable consensus can be reached despite the fact that not every element or part of scientific reasoning is rational and that knowledge is never complete or perfect. If "rational" is defined as "capable of reproduction by a consistently functioning mechanical device," then the empirical referents of concepts, the link between thought and reality, are, at least in part, non-rational.

There are various types of theory. One, which may be called phenomenological, tries to answer questions like the following: When phenomenon or event A occurs, how frequently do other events occur simultaneously, and how frequently are still other events likely to be absent? Such theories are not designed to answer questions about the causes of the events investigated. Etiological theories try to answer such questions as: Why are some events related with one another while others are not; how did objects (including human beings) become what they are; and why do changes take place the way they do? It is important to discriminate clearly between the two types of theory. For example, the question of why and how projective tests of personality obtain the results they do is quite different from, and requires very different procedures than, the question of how individuals develop their particular personalities. Corollary to etiological theories are the technological or applied theories which aim to answer the question: Knowing their causes, how could we produce deliberately certain objects or obtain certain results? Blind trials and errors, needless to say, are not guided by any theory.

VALIDATION OF PROPOSITIONS

The purpose of this function of science is to ascertain to what degree the order of concepts as indicated in the propositions and theories corresponds to the order of the empirical referents of these very concepts when the perceptible events occur uninfluenced by the observing scientist. In other words, the question is: To what degree and in what manner is the set of propositions supported by relevant empirical evidence? Since the validating procedures differ in degree of relevance and reliability, it is more important to use a variety of validating procedures (e.g., diverse control groups) than it is to employ the same validation procedure (e.g., the same control group) repeatedly. Results from a variety of procedures are much more likely to prompt the formulation of alternative and more adequate theories. This is the method which leads to gradual theoretical improvement and constitutes a more decisive test of validity than does the determination of the most reliable probability level of a theory with the aid of only one validation criterion. Diverse validation criteria rely on different ER. A comparison of the results of those diverse procedures gives an opportunity not only to obtain deeper knowledge of the validity and meaning of tested propositions but also of the varying degrees of adequacy of the ER. This is of particular significance to personologists, whose ER leave much to be desired. The multiple validation clearly reveals the qualifications and changes which must be made in the theories to raise their congruence with facts, and points out oversights in the etiology of events encompassed by the theories. Even the selection of appropriate validation procedures then demands the active initiative of the scientist.

Psychopathology has always contributed to the understanding of human personality, normal as well as deviant. There would be no great world literature without psychopathology.

The study of mental disorders in the past one hundred years has contributed far more to personology than have studies of the apparently normal. The reasons for this are methodological. In mental disorders, we deal with personality changes of higher and lower intensities than in the case of normal subjects. Therefore it is possible to obtain very reliable measures of the degree and nature of personality change. Moreover, striking changes in the personality states of disturbed subjects occur much more frequently than do the milder personality changes of the normal individual. Thus, we have more to observe, to record, to explain, and to verify. The greater frankness of overt behavior displayed by the less controlled, more anxious and help-seeking mentally disturbed also contributes to higher reliabilities of observations. Every empirical science began its investigations with the greater deviations (the exceptional or striking) and then moved towards the study of minor deviations, once sound research procedures and some valid generalizations were created. It is sometimes argued that one should start with the average or most frequent phenomena, and then evaluate the deviant cases in terms of the average, the way naturalists do. If feasible, this approach is to be recommended. When limited to a description of static physical features and to a statistical count, the approach is simple and easy. Personologists, however, are concerned with actions, attitudes, and relationships, all complex phenomena which are more effectively investigated when the reverse approach is used, from extremes towards the middle. Most schizophrenics undergo frequent, diverse, and striking personality changes. Therefore he who understands schizophrenia understands any other person. Educationally speaking, schizophrenia should be the focal point of clinical psychology and personology in general.

Sound validation is a far from simple procedure. It should not cease when low validity values are obtained. A search for the reason for a low validity value should be initiated, as the disappointing result may have been due to a vagueness of concepts, inadequacy of the ER, or inconsistency of the theory, or even perhaps to an irrelevant validation procedure.

Highly validated propositions, i.e., general laws, are the aim of science. A scientific law explains unlimited particular empirical observations by one thought, expressed in one sentence. Valid scientific laws save time and effort. They serve as mnemonic devices which remind us of what to expect under certain conditions and provide information how to proceed if this information can be put to practical use. Since we remember words and other symbols better than empirical evidence and the conditions under which the evidence was obtained, it is obviously important that we have valid scientific laws. There is no doubt that there is nothing more practical than a comprehensive and valid theory, and no greater intellectual handicap than clinging to invalid and fragmentary theories. Progress consists in creating theories which explain an ever larger number and variety of empirical observations and which do so on a higher level of validity than the theories which they supersede.

Highly validated propositions or laws can profitably be used as premises in deductive reasoning to discover unknown and unexpected meanings of facts. Such propositions are helpful in research planning or predictions. Anything inconsistent with a valid empirical law or general proposition is physically impossible, thus anything based on it must end in failure. On the other hand, we can never compellingly prove the feasibility of something nonexistent on the basis of abstract laws alone because we can never be certain that the production of the new object or process does not require conditions of which we are ignorant, which we do not control, and which we did not consider in formulating the law. Our knowledge of the world is and always will be incomplete. However, our knowledge of selected aspects of the world can be sound and quite reliable.

FRINGES OF SCIENCES

The wavy lines around the four basic functions of science symbolize the fact that the subject-matter of every science is a result of choice, and that no science deals with the entire empirical reality. The presence of the lines, representing the fringes of a science, reminds us of the limited scope of any particular scientific discipline, and of the possibility that the limits, imposed deliberately or not, may have been chosen poorly, handicapping scientific development. The fringes of a particular scientific discipline may be fixed in such a fashion as to preclude its development towards maturity, by making it incapable of creating significant laws supported by valid empirical evidence. The way out of this impasse is usually the establishment of a logical and experimental alliance with other, related sciences. When this is achieved, great successes follow. Chemistry and physics were separate sciences at one time; now they complement each other. Similarly, biophysics achieves results which biology and physics, operating separately, could not have produced. Psychology, sociology, economics, and anthropology are slowly merging into one integrated discipline which will produce results which those sciences, working independently of each other, could not give us.

One special problem associated with the fringes of sciences is to explain the methodological reasons and particularly the human motives which prompted the creation of the specific science. What were the goals that motivated the particular scientific endeavor, and what stable or changing goals are behind the continuation of the effort? The decision as to which problems to tackle and which promise positive results always involves much guessing. There are good and bad guesses, depending largely on the experience, the habit of independent thinking and the personality of the investigators. By thinking of the "fringes" every scientist may feel encouraged at times to venture "beyond the meaning's edge" and take a close and critical look at his science from the outside. Such an experience may open his eyes to untapped possibilities he would otherwise never discover.

NON-SCIENTIFIC THINKING

All thinking which tries to correspond closely with facts must depend on the four functions indicated in the diagram (Figure 1-1) and consider the possible relevance of the "fringes." Scientific thinking differs from the non-scientific only in degree of care and precision. Scientists are interested primarily in generalizations about impersonal empirical events, in the study of the methods which yielded the evidence, and in modifications of their conceptual and empirical procedures to obtain an ever higher level of agreement among qualified investigators. Non-scientific thinking about practical and personal matters need not be concerned about the approval of others, systematic analysis of evidence, or scientific laws.

Nevertheless, both types of thinking must utilize the same functions to obtain satisfactory results. There is only a difference of degree, not one of essence, between scientific and non-scientific thinking.

Reality-oriented thinking includes two different operations which must be performed harmoniously if sound results are expected. One consists of mobilizing and actuating ideas before intelligent thinking and speech on a given subject can occur, while the other consists of the simultaneous critical evaluation of one's thoughts and words to assure intelligibility, communication, and validity. In well-trained persons who are not under stress, both operations are performed smoothly and complement each other so well that most people are only rarely conscious of the self-evaluation concurrent with their production of ideas. Under stress, and especially in serious psychopathological states, there is a breakdown in the mutual feedback and complementarity of the two operations.

Idea production depends on the concepts and propositions available to the individual. The critical evaluation of a person's ideas relies on his empirical referents of concepts and his skill in validating propositions. The broken diagonal line in the diagram symbolizes the difference between the two operations involved in any individual's thinking.

Both operations usually develop and regress equally. In the early stages of a psychosis (i.e., when standards of reality are qualitatively changed for the worse and primary thought disorders appear), one of the operations frequently is affected more than the other. Mild schizophrenics characteristically display a weakened sense of reality, a lack of concern about the adequacy of their thoughts and reality. This disregard of validity often accompanies a remarkable freedom of imagination which disappears dramatically when the patient improves. When the schizophrenic regression continues over the years, both operations become seriously defective. Patients with demonstrable cerebral disorders, on the other hand, characteristically show an increased concern about making their statements agree with empirical evidence, and they try to adhere to it as much as they can. They try hard to be "right." Needless to say, their achievement in this respect usually falls below their intention. They also like to reduce the unfamiliar to the familiar, suffering a distinct loss in imagination; their supply of ideas decreases. Their desire to adjust despite the intellectual loss makes their thinking dull. The differences between the two groups of psychotics are quite marked in the early phases of their illness. However, those schizophrenics who continue to deteriorate to a permanent low intellectual level increasingly resemble organics.

The difference between being emotionally involved with others and being preoccupied with oneself is best seen in some schizophrenics who are indifferent towards others emotionally but are most sensitive regarding their own person and their physical condition. Emotions can be defined as desires to associate with or dissociate from others with the intent of continuing or discontinuing the exchange of pleasures and pains with them. When primary thought disorders become serious and permanent, emotions gradually weaken and sometimes end in apathy. Even normal subjects need a new concept or a new powerful sensorimotor experience to become aware of new desires and new possibilities of persistent goal striving. This is in keeping with the dominant role of the concepts among the scientific functions. One has to have an idea of what one wants before being able to pursue it persistently. At the beginning of every human activity, including science, is desire. One could define even intellectual curiosity as a desire—

perhaps as a desire for a desire. Despite the subjective or non-rational origin of the search for knowledge, scientific procedures enable us to formulate increasingly objective propositions with increasing degrees of validity.

Repressed conflicts interfere with the optimal functioning of the individual. The ideally normal person is free from such conflicts, is flexible and not fearful of facing reality. His assessment of opportunities and dangers is realistic within the limits of sound knowledge. He is likely to use all thinking functions harmoniously. Not being disposed to wishful or magical thinking, he knows that relevance and effectiveness do not depend on just one or, at best, on several factors. His thinking is multi-causal and his sense of proportion is well developed. He sets up priorities as the need arises. When perplexed by unexpected difficulties, he is likely to give attention to the fringes of thought and planned action. The more he approaches the ideal of normalcy, the less need he has for a deliberate and voluntary self-control. He achieves most of his purposes constructively with a minimal amount of prolonged and effortfully maintained conscious planning. He is attuned to the world around him.

The psychoneurotic, on the other hand, though free of primary thought disorders, is at cross-purposes with himself. He may be unaware of his ambivalence and his spurious fears which interfere with his thinking when problems related to the causes of his anxiety are facing him. Sporadically he does not notice or do what is "obvious" to others. The active search for a gratifying solution of personal difficulties, as well as the inhibitions, result at times in artistic or scientific creations which do not solve the personal problem but are socially useful. The degree of personal happiness seems positively correlated with social usefulness and creativeness but apparently not highly. There are two chief forms of neurosis: hysteria and obsessive–compulsiveness. The outstanding psychological trait of the hysteric is avoidance of unpleasant stimulation which would be experienced as threatening by the neurotic if he became aware of the stimulation. Hysterics are mentally blind to unconsciously selected aspects of interhuman relationships and other circumstances. Dissociation helps to maintain the mental blindness. If the neurotic is incapable of relieving anxiety states, he develops somatic symptoms. These have the added advantage of arousing the pity of others. Not perceiving the meaning of many stimuli and challenges, the patient has a simplified view of the world. His adjustment reveals passivity (at least in certain life areas) and some definite trust that others will help. The thinking of the hysteric is vague in matters pertaining to his neurotic conflicts. He relies a great deal on his intuition and feeling. There is a corresponding neglect of objective and systematic thinking. The system of the four thinking functions is rarely employed. However some hysterics are very sensitive and occasionally excel in penetrating the fringes of thought with interesting results.

The obsessive–compulsive neurotic characteristically distrusts others, is excessively alert, and tries very hard to prevent any impulsive action on his part. He keeps his eyes open for any possible danger. He is rigid and systematic. He spends a lot of time and energy on watching out for up-setting situations and on developing personal habits of restraint in feeling, particularly in overt activities. Extreme obsessive and phobic cases, in fact, concentrate on one or two problems to the neglect of essential tasks in life. The neurotics of this kind tire themselves out in their unconsciously motivated effort to develop inhibitions against the possibility of acting impulsively under any circumstances. This purpose cannot be achieved without a great deal of observing and thinking. The obsessives are constant thinkers. Since their thinking is intensely self-centered, its products are rarely of value to others. The desire to clarify everything prompts them to use the four functions of thinking every day, checking and rechecking the processes of reasoning to avoid mistakes. The exaggerated belief in deter-minism makes them feel that any mistake might expose them to grave dangers; thus their use of the four functions. The fringes of thought do not interest them, probably because the fringes are inevitably vague. Paranoid schizophrenics show interest in the fringes of thought, but not because of any broad and penetrating grasp of the limitations of rational thinking. They manifest that interest when their sense of reality has become defec-tive and they cannot always reason in a clear and consistent manner about relevant factual evidence.

In science, as in everything we do, both emotions and thoughts, subjectivity and objectivity, are involved. New ideas begin as the subjective and personal experiences of unusual individuals. Such personal and sub-jective creations in science influence chiefly the modification of old con-cepts and the introduction of new ones. By giving concepts the most important, top position in the diagram (Figure 1), we have emphasized their role in science. The subjective becomes the objective through the interaction of all science functions. One might say that in the lives of individuals it is the emotions which prompt and lead while intellect follows them. Although the role of the intellect seems secondary, it is actually essential. Intellect can (even though it does not always) make emo-tionally initiated actions personally gratifying and socially constructive. Such a view cannot be maintained, of course, if emotion is believed to be the enemy of thought. One need not share this belief.

CONCLUSION

The fundamental scientific functions of any empirical science have been reduced to four, and those of a formal science (logic and mathe-matics) to two. A further reduction seems impossible. None of the four can be deduced from the rest of them. All four must be integrated into one consistent effort to produce valid generalizations. Noticeable psychological differences exist among scientists who specialize in one or two of the functions in preference to any other. A specialization of this kind seems to depend on individual attitudes, work habits, and talents. The greatest difference can be observed between those who like to develop concepts and theories, on the one hand, and those who prefer to concentrate their effort on the work with and improvement of research equipment, and collect factual data to test theories, on the other hand. Those who formulate new and significant problems are not always good at solving them, and vice versa. New and fertile concepts have often been introduced by individuals who were unable to make them productive. Only a rare and outstanding scientist is a notable contributor in all four of the fundamental functions.

Keeping the diagram of science structure in mind facilitates orientation in the vast psychological literature. It makes it easier to discover the common ideas under apparently different words as well as to discover real differences in seemingly identical terms and statements. Use of the diagram might possibly improve communication and mutual understanding among investigators.

BIBLIOGRAPHY

Broad, C. D. *The mind and its place in nature.* Paterson, N.J.: Littlefield-Adams, 1960.

Caws, P. Science, computers, and the complexity of nature. *Philos. of Science,* 1963, 30, 158–164.

Chwistek, L. *The limits of science.* New York: Harcourt, Brace, 1948.

Nicod, J. *Foundations of geometry and induction.* New York: Harcourt, Brace, 1930.

Peirce, C. S. A *theory of probable inference.* Baltimore: Johns Hopkins U., 1883.

Piotrowski, Z. A. *Perceptanalysis: The Rorschach method fundamentally reworked, expanded and systematized.* Philadelphia: Ex Libris (2217 Spruce St., 19103), 2nd Print., 1965.

Piotrowski, Z. A. Theory of psychological tests and psychopathology. In J. D. Page (Ed.), *Approaches to psychopathology.* New York: Columbia U. Press, 1966, 165–194.

Popper, K. *The logic of scientific discovery.* New York: Basic Books, 1959.

Russell, B. *Our knowledge of the external world.* New York: W. W. Norton, 1929.

Whitehead, A. N. *Essays in science and philosophy.* New York: Philosophical Library, 1947.

PSYCHOANALYTIC THEORY: SIGMUND FREUD

I

Sɪɢᴍᴜɴᴅ ꜰʀᴇᴜᴅ, one of the trio of original thinkers—the others are Karl Marx and Albert Einstein —whose contributions shaped the social, scientific, cultural, and intellectual landscape of the twentieth century, was firmly rooted in the academic and scientific traditions of the nineteenth century. This is unmistakably evident in the introductory article, originally delivered as a lecture by Freud to the Vienna Medical Club in January of 1893 and published in two installments in a professional journal. Although it bears the name of Josef Breuer as senior author, there can be little doubt that the article was actually written by Freud.

By singular coincidence, this article satisfies three major criteria for inclusion in the present anthology: It is a primary source, an example of personality theory in application, and above all, a specimen of theory-generated research. It includes no tabular summaries, list of references, review of the literature, tests of significance, array of *p* values, or cautiously worded summary with its stock plea for further investigation—but it is, nevertheless, an authentic *research report*. It reveals, with remarkable clarity, Freud's understanding in nineteenth-century terms of what research is all about: the distillation of hypotheses from patiently gathered, day-to-day observations of clinical phenomena; the formulation of a theoretical framework to accommodate a series of such hypotheses; the attempts to seek verification for the subsequent modification and revision of theory in the light of insufficient or contradictory evidence.

Among the criticisms that have been leveled at psychoanalysis and its founder, one of the most persistently recurring complaints is the charge that Freud's inferences were drawn primarily from a clinical population, and therefore are suspect on the grounds of biased sampling. Distinctions between the clinic and the laboratory and between the clinic and "real life," always seemed singularly inappropriate to Freud, as the result of a typical nineteenth-century education. Each area of intellectual endeavor—science, philosophy, art, the rest—may reflect its autonomous status in the capital letters which designate independent faculties within our universities today, but the educational practices of Freud's period offered scant hospitality to such specialization and fragmentation.

Whether the quest for knowledge has gained or lost as a consequence of specialization is a question the present volume cannot answer. But the second selection by Gerald Blum and Daniel R. Miller has direct relevance to the more restricted matter of the generality of psychoanalytic postulates derived from observations made on a clinical population. Blum and Miller made a conscientious attempt to provide operational statements of hypotheses derived from the psychoanalytic literature. They then subjected these hypotheses to empirical examination within the context of behavior supplied by normal third-grade children whose responses were evaluated by means of teacher ratings, sociometric techniques, and a variety of other investigatory approaches. Support was obtained for five of the hypotheses; three hypotheses failed to receive support; and two remaining hypotheses received only equivocal support. While the findings and the hypotheses themselves are of considerable interest, it is even more important to note that Blum and Miller were able to validate predictions derived from psychoanalytic theory within a population of normal children.

The paper by Bernard Schwartz is addressed more specifically to theoretical postulates with clinical relevance. Schwartz conducted a two-part study involving, in the first investigation, a comparison of homosexual and normal males on previously validated measures of castration anxiety. In the second investigation, a comparison was made between normal males and females on the same measure. Results supported the hypotheses that: (*a*) homosexual males exhibit more intense castration anxiety than normal males, and (*b*) all males show a higher level of castration anxiety than do females.

In the next selection, Paul Daston investigated the association of homosexual concern and paranoid schizophrenia, a central concept in the psychoanalytic theory of paranoid development. Using paranoid schizophrenics, undifferentiated schizophrenics, and normal subjects, Daston examined comparative levels of recognition for tachistoscopically presented words with neutral, heterosexual, and homosexual connotations. He found that the paranoid and undifferentiated schizophrenics demonstrated slower recognition time than the normal subjects. In the recognition of homosexual words, however, the paranoid schizophrenics significantly exceeded the unclassified schizophrenics; in fact, they approached normal recognition times. Daston concludes that schizophrenics in general are not differentially sensitive to homosexually relevant stimuli, but that responsivity to homosexual stimuli seems to be enhanced in cases where schizophenia shows paranoid involvement.

The selections in Section I span a time period of over seven decades, and marked differences, particularly in methodological sophistication, are clearly evident. Yet one finds himself much less impressed by such differences than by the fact that, despite the numerous inadequacies found in the structure of psychoanalysis, the theories originally formulated by Sigmund Freud retain an astonishing capacity to generate hypotheses and heuristically influence the work of others.

2

On the Psychical Mechanism
of Hysterical Phenomena

JOSEF BREUER
& SIGMUND FREUD

Gentlemen: I am appearing before you today with the object of giving you a report on a work the first part of which has already been published in the *Centralblatt für Neurologie* under the names of Josef Breuer and myself. As you may gather from the title of the work, it deals with the pathogenesis of hysterical symptoms and suggests that the immediate reasons for the development of hysterical symptoms are to be looked for in the sphere of mental life.

But before I enter further into the contents of this joint work, I must explain the position it occupies and name the author and the discovery which, in substance at least, we have taken as our starting point, although our contribution has been developed quite independently.

As you know, gentlemen, all the modern advances made in the understanding and knowledge of hysteria are derived from the work of Charcot. In the first half of the eighties, Charcot began to turn his attention to the "major neurosis," as the French call hysteria. In a series of researches he has succeeded in proving the presence of regularity and law where the inadequate or half-hearted clinical observations of other people saw only malingering or a puzzling lack of conformity to rule. It may safely be said that everything new that has been learnt about hysteria in recent times goes

From Chapter 1 of *Studies on Hysteria* by Josef Breuer and Sigmund Freud. Translated from the German and edited by James Strachey in collaboration with Anna Freud, assisted by Alix Strachey and Alan Tyson. Published in the United States by Basic Books, Inc., by arrangement with The Hogarth Press Ltd., 1957. Acknowledgment is made to Sigmund Freud Copyrights Limited, the Institute of Psycho-Analysis, and The Hogarth Press Limited, for permission to quote "On the Psychical Mechanism of Hysterical Phenomena," in Volume 2 of the Standard Edition of *The Complete Psychological Works of Sigmund Freud.*

(*Footnote to original publication.*) A lecture delivered by Dr. Sigmund Freud at a meeting of the "Wiener medizinischer Club" on 11 January, 1893. Special shorthand report by the *Wiener medizinische Presse*, revised by the lecturer.

back directly or indirectly to his suggestions. But among Charcot's numerous works, none, in my estimate, is of higher value than the one in which he taught us to understand the traumatic paralyses which appear in hysteria; and since it is precisely this work of which ours appears as a continuation, I hope you will allow me to lay this subject before you once again in some detail.

We will take the case of a person who is subjected to a trauma without having been ill previously and perhaps without even having any hereditary taint. The trauma must fulfil certain conditions. It must be severe—that is, it must be of a kind involving the idea of mortal danger, of a threat to life. But it must not be severe in the sense of bringing psychical activity to an end. Otherwise it will not produce the result we expect from it. Thus, for instance, it must not involve concussion of the brain or any really serious injury. Moreover, the trauma must have a special relation to some part of the body. Let us suppose that a heavy billet of wood falls on a workman's shoulder. The blow knocks him down, but he soon realizes that nothing has happened and goes home with a slight contusion. After a few weeks, or after some months, he wakes up one morning and notices that the arm that was subjected to the trauma is hanging down limp and paralysed, though in the interval, in what might be called the incubation period, he has made perfectly good use of it. If the case is a typical one, it may happen that peculiar attacks set in—that, after an aura, the subject suddenly collapses, raves, and becomes delirious; and, if he speaks in his delirium, what he says may show that the scene of his accident is being repeated in him, embellished, perhaps, with various imaginary pictures. What has been happening here? How is this phenomenon to be explained?

Charcot explains the process by reproducing it, by inducing the paralysis in a patient artificially. In order to bring this about, he needs a patient who is already in a hysterical state; he further requires the condition of hypnosis and the method of suggestion. He puts a patient of this kind into deep hypnosis and gives him a light blow on the arm. The arm drops; it is paralysed and shows precisely the same symptoms as occur in spontaneous traumatic paralysis. The blow may also be replaced by a direct verbal suggestion: "Look! your arm is paralysed!" In this case too the paralysis exhibits the same characteristics.

Let us try to compare the two cases: on the one hand a trauma, on the other a traumatic suggestion. The final result, the paralysis, is exactly the same in both cases. If the trauma in the one case can be replaced in the other case by a verbal suggestion, it is plausible to suppose that an idea of this kind was responsible for the development of the paralysis in the case of the spontaneous traumatic paralysis as well. And in fact a number of patients report that at the moment of the trauma they actually had a feeling that their arm was smashed. If this were so, the trauma could really be completely equated with the verbal suggestion. But to complete the analogy a third factor is required. In order that the idea "your arm is paralysed" should be able to provoke a paralysis in the patient, it was necessary for him to be in a state of hypnosis. But the workman was not in a state of hypnosis. Nevertheless, we may assume that he was in a special state of mind during the trauma; and Charcot is inclined to equate that affect with the artificially induced state of hypnosis. This being so, the traumatic spontaneous paralysis is completely explained and brought into line with the paralysis produced by suggestion; and the genesis of the symptom is unambiguously determined by the circumstances of the trauma.

Charcot has, moreover, repeated the same experiment in order to explain the contractures and pains which appear in traumatic hysteria; and in my opinion there is scarcely any point at which he has penetrated into the understanding of hysteria more deeply than here. But his analysis goes no further: we do not learn how other symptoms are generated, and above all we do not learn how hysterical symptoms come about in common, non-traumatic hysteria.

Gentlemen: At about the same time at which Charcot was thus throwing light on hystero-traumatic paralyses, between 1880 and 1882, Dr. Breuer undertook the medical care of a young lady who, with a non-traumatic aetiology, fell ill of a severe and complicated hysteria (accompanied by paralyses, contractures, disturbances of speech and vision, and psychical peculiarities of every kind), while she was nursing her sick father.[1] This case will occupy an important place in the history of hysteria, since it was the first one in which a physician succeeded in elucidating all the symptoms of the hysterical state, in learning the origin of each symptom and at the same time in finding a means of causing that symptom to disappear. We may say that it was the first case of hysteria to be made intelligible. Dr. Breuer kept back the conclusions which followed from this case till he could be certain that it did not stand alone. After I returned, in 1886, from a course of study under Charcot, I began, with Breuer's constant co-operation, to make close observations on a fairly large number of hysterical patients and to examine them from this point of view; and I found that the behaviour of this first patient had in fact been typical and that the inferences which were justified by that case could be carried over to a considerable number of hysterical patients, if not to all.

Our material consisted of cases of common, that is of non-traumatic, hysteria. Our procedure was to take each separate symptom and enquire into the circumstances in which it had made its first appearance; and we endeavoured in this way to arrive at a clear idea of the precipitating cause which might perhaps have determined that symptom. Now you must not suppose that this is a simple job. If you question patients along these lines,

---

[1] This was, of course, Fräulein Anna O., of Case History I in *Studies on Hysteria* (1895d).

you will as a rule receive no answer at all to begin with. In a small group of cases the patients have their reasons for not saying what they know. But in a greater number of cases the patients have no notion of the context of their symptoms. The method by which something can be learnt is a tedious one. It is as follows. The patients must be put under hypnosis and then questioned as to the origin of some particular symptom—as to when it first appeared and what they remember in that connection. While they are in this state the memory, which was not at their disposal in a waking state, returns. We have learnt in this manner that, to put it roughly, there is an affectively coloured experience behind most, if not all, phenomena of hysteria; and further, that this experience is of such a kind that it at once makes the symptom to which it relates intelligible and shows accordingly that the symptom, once again, is unambiguously determined. If you will allow me to equate this affectively coloured experience with the major traumatic experience underlying traumatic hysteria, I can at once formulate the first thesis at which we have arrived: *"There is a complete analogy between traumatic paralysis and common, non-traumatic hysteria."* The only difference is that in the former a major trauma has been operative, whereas in the latter there is seldom a *single* major event to be signalized, but rather a *series* of affective impressions—a whole story of suffering. But there is nothing forced in equating such a story, which appears as the determining factor in hysterical patients, with the accident which occurs in traumatic hysteria. For no one doubts any longer to-day that even in the case of the major mechanical trauma in traumatic hysteria what produces the result is not the mechanical factor but the affect of fright, the *psychical* trauma. The first thing that follows from all this, then, is that the pattern of traumatic hysteria, as it was laid down by Charcot for hysterical paralyses, applies quite generally to all hysterical phenomena, or at least to the great majority of them. In every case what we have to deal with is the operation of psychical traumas, which unambiguously determine the nature of the symptoms that arise.

I will now give you a few instances of this. First, here is an example of the occurrence of contractures. Throughout the whole period of her illness, Breuer's patient, whom I have already mentioned, exhibited a contracture of the right arm. It emerged under hypnosis that at a time before she had fallen ill she was subjected to the following trauma. She was sitting half-dozing at the bedside of her sick father; her right arm was hanging over the back of her chair and went to sleep. At this moment she had a terrifying hallucination; she tried to fend it off with her arm but was unable to do so. This gave her a violent fright, and for the time being the matter ended there. It was not until the outbreak of her hysteria that the contracture of the arm set in. In another woman patient, I observed that her speech was interrupted by a peculiar "clacking" with her tongue, which resembled the cry of a capercaillie.[2] I had been familiar with this symptom for months and regarded it as a *tic*. It was only after I once happened to question her under hypnosis about its origin that I discovered that the noise had first appeared on two occasions. On each of these she had made a firm decision to keep absolutely quiet. This happened once when she was nursing a seriously sick child—nursing sick people often plays a part in the aetiology of hysteria; the child had fallen asleep and she was determined not to make any noise that might wake it. But fear that she might make a noise turned into actually making one—an instance of "hysterical counterwill"; [3] she pressed her lips together and made the clacking noise with her tongue. Many years later the same symptom had arisen a second time, once again when she had made a decision to be absolutely quiet, and it had persisted ever afterwards. A single determining cause is often not enough to fix a symptom; but if this same symptom appears several times, accompanied by a particular affect, it becomes fixed and chronic.

One of the commonest symptoms of hysteria is a combination of anorexia and vomiting. I know a whole number of cases in which the occurrence of this symptom is explained quite simply. Thus in one patient vomiting persisted after she had read a humiliating letter just before a meal and had been violently sick after it. In other cases disgust at food could be quite definitely related to the fact that, owing to the institution of the "common table", a person may be compelled to eat his meal with someone he detests. The disgust is then transferred from the person to the food. The woman with the *tic* whom I have just mentioned was particularly interesting in this respect. She ate uncommonly little and only under pressure. I learnt from her under hypnosis that a series of psychical traumas had eventually produced this symptom of disgust at food. While she was still a child, her mother, who was very strict, insisted on her eating any meat she had left over at her midday meal two hours later, when it was cold and the fat was all congealed. She did so with great disgust and retained the memory of it; so that later on, when she was no longer subjected to this punishment, she regularly felt disgust at mealtimes. Ten years later she used to sit at table with a relative who was tubercular and kept constantly spitting across the table during meals. A little while later she was obliged to share her meals with a relative who, as she knew, was suffering from a contagious disease. Breuer's patient, again, behaved for some time like someone suffering from hydrophobia. During hypnosis it turned out that she had once unexpectedly seen a dog drinking out of a tumbler of water of hers.

<hr />

[2] This was Frau Emmy von N., of Case History II in the *Studies*.—An ornithologist describes the capercaillie's cry as "a ticking ending with a pop and a hiss" (Fisher, *Bird Recognition*, 1955, 3, 46).

[3] Freud had very recently published a paper discussing this phenomenon and this same example of it: "A Case of Successful Treatment by Hypnotism" (1892–3b), *Collected Papers*, 5, 38 ff.

Sleeplessness or disturbed sleep are also symptoms that are usually capable of the most precise explanation. Thus, for years on end a woman could never get to sleep till six in the morning. She had for a long time slept in the adjoining room to her sick husband, who used to rise at six o'clock. After that hour she had been able to sleep in quiet; and she behaved in the same way once more many years later during a hysterical illness. Another case is that of a male hysterical patient who had slept very badly for the last twelve years. His sleeplessness, however, was of a quite special sort. In the summer he slept excellently, but in the winter very badly; and in November he slept quite particularly badly. He had no notion what this was due to. Enquiry revealed that in November twelve years earlier he had watched for many nights at the bedside of his son, who was ill with diphtheria.

Breuer's patient, to whom I have so often referred, offered an example of a disturbance of speech. For a long period of her illness she spoke only English and could neither speak nor understand German. This symptom was traced back to an event which had happened before the outbreak of her illness. While she was in a state of great anxiety, she had attempted to pray but could find no words. At last a few words of a child's prayer in English occurred to her. When she fell ill later on, only the English language was at her command.

The determination of the symptom by the psychical trauma is not so transparent in every instance. There is often only what may be described as a "symbolic" relation between the determining cause and the hysterical symptom. This is especially true of pains. Thus one patient [4] suffered from piercing pains between her eyebrows. The reason was that once when she was a child her grandmother had given her an enquiring, "piercing" look. The same patient suffered for a time from violent pains in her right heel, for which there was no explanation. These pains, it turned out, were connected with an idea that occurred to the patient when she made her first appearance in society. She was overcome with fear that she might not "find herself on a right footing." Symbolizations of this kind were employed by many patients for a whole number of so-called neuralgias and pains. It is as though there were an intention to express the mental state by means of a physical one; and linguistic usage affords a bridge by which this can be effected. In the case, however, of what are after all the typical symptoms of hysteria—such as hemi-anaesthesia, restriction of the visual field, epileptiform convulsions, etc.—a psychical mechanism of this sort cannot be demonstrated. On the other hand this can often be done in respect to the hysterogenic zones.

These examples, which I have chosen out of a number of observations, seem to offer proof that the phenomena of common hysteria can safely be

[4] This was Frau Cäcilie M., whose "symbolic" symptoms are discussed at the end of Case History V in the *Studies*.

regarded as being on the same pattern as those of traumatic hysteria, and that accordingly every hysteria can be looked upon as traumatic hysteria in the sense of implying a psychical trauma and that every hysterical phenomenon is determined by the nature of the trauma.

The further question which would then have to be answered is as to the nature of the causal connection between the determining factor which we have discovered during hypnosis and the phenomenon which persists subsequently as a chronic symptom. This connection might be of various kinds. It might be of the type that we should describe as a "releasing" factor. For instance, if someone with a disposition to tuberculosis receives a blow on the knee as a result of which he develops a tubercular inflammation of the joint, the blow is a simple releasing cause. But this is not what happens in hysteria. There is another kind of causation—namely, *direct* causation. We can elucidate this from the picture of a foreign body, which continues to operate unceasingly as a stimulating cause of illness until it is got rid of. *Cessante causa cessat effectus.* Breuer's observation shows us that there is a connection of this latter kind between the psychical trauma and the hysterical phenomenon. For Breuer learnt from his first patient that the attempt at discovering the determining cause of a symptom was at the same time a therapeutic manoeuvre. The moment at which the physician finds out the occasion when the symptom first appeared and the reason for its appearance is also the moment at which the symptom vanishes. When, for instance, the symptom presented by the patient consists in pains, and when we enquire from him under hypnosis as to their origin, he will produce a series of memories in connection with them. If we can succeed in eliciting a really vivid memory in him, and if he sees things before him with all their original actuality, we shall observe that he is completely dominated by some affect. And if we then compel him to put this affect into words, we shall find that, at the same time as he is producing this violent affect, the phenomenon of his pains emerges very markedly once again and that thenceforward the symptom, in its chronic character, disappears. This is how events turned out in all the instances I have quoted. And it was an interesting fact that the memory of this particular event was to an extraordinary degree more vivid than the memory of any others, and that the affect accompanying it was as great, perhaps, as it had been when the event actually occurred. It could only be supposed that the psychical trauma does in fact continue to operate in the subject and maintains the hysterical phenomenon, and that it comes to an end as soon as the patient has spoken about it.

As I have just said, if, in accordance with our procedure, one arrives at the psychical trauma by making enquiries from the patient under hypnosis, one discovers that the memory concerned is quite unusually strong and has retained the whole of its affect. The question now arises how it is that an event which occurred so long ago—perhaps ten or twenty years—can persist in exercising its power over the subject, and how it is that these memories have not been subject to the processes of wearing away and forgetting.

With a view to answering this question, I should like to begin with a few remarks on the conditions which govern the wearing-away of the contents of our ideational life. We will start from a thesis that may be stated in the following terms. If a person experiences a psychical impression, something in his nervous system which we will for the moment call the sum of excitation is increased. Now in every individual there exists a tendency to diminish this sum of excitation once more, in order to preserve his health.[5] The increase of the sum of excitation takes place along sensory paths, and its diminution along motor ones. So we may say that if anything impinges on someone he reacts in a motor fashion. We can now safely assert that it depends on this reaction how much of the initial psychical impression is left. Let us consider this in relation to a particular example. Let us suppose that a man is insulted, is given a blow or something of the kind. This psychical trauma is linked with an increase in the sum of excitation of his nervous system. There then instinctively arises an inclination to diminish this increased excitation immediately. He hits back, and then feels easier; he may perhaps have reacted adequately—that is, he may have got rid of as much as had been introduced into him. Now this reaction may take various forms. For quite slight increases in excitation, alterations in his own body may perhaps be enough: weeping, abusing, raging, and so on. The more intense the trauma, the greater is the adequate reaction. The most adequate reaction, however, is always a deed. But, as an English writer has wittily remarked, the man who first flung a word of abuse at his enemy instead of a spear was the founder of civilization. Thus words are substitutes for deeds, and in some circumstances (e.g. in confession) the only substitutes. Accordingly, alongside the adequate reaction there is one that is less adequate. If, however, there is no reaction *whatever* to a psychical trauma, the memory of it retains the affect [6] which it originally had. So that if someone who has been insulted cannot avenge the insult either by a retaliatory blow or by a word of abuse, the possibility arises that the memory of the event may call up in him once more the affect which was originally present. An insult that has been repaid, even if only in words, is recollected quite differently from one that has had to be accepted; and linguistic usage characteristically describes an insult that has been suffered in silence as a "mortification" ["*Kränkung*," literally "making ill"]. Thus, if

---

[5] Here was probably the first published statement of the "principle of constancy," on which the whole of Freud's psychological theories were ultimately based. The principle was, strangely enough, not explicitly stated in the "Preliminary Communication," though it appears in a draft for that paper written a month or so earlier but only published posthumously (1940d [1892]), *Collected Papers*, 5, 30. It was discussed at some length in Breuer's theoretical contribution to the *Studies* (1895d).

[6] This is printed "*Effect*" ("effect") in the original German here and again 25 lines lower down. These are probably misprints for "*Affect*."

for any reason there can be no reaction to a psychical trauma, it retains its original affect, and when someone cannot get rid of the increase in stimulation by "abreacting" it, we have the possibility of the event in question remaining a psychical trauma. Incidentally, a healthy psychical mechanism has other methods of dealing with the affect of a psychical trauma even if motor reaction and reaction by words are denied to it—namely by working it over associatively and by producing contrasting ideas. Even if the person who has been insulted neither hits back nor replies with abuse, he can nevertheless reduce the affect attaching to the insult by calling up such contrasting ideas as those of his own worthiness, of his enemy's worthlessness, and so on. Whether a healthy man deals with an insult in one way or the other, he always succeeds in achieving the result that the affect which was originally strong in his memory eventually loses intensity and that finally the recollection, having lost its affect, falls a victim to forgetfulness and the process of wearing-away.

Now we have found that in hysterical patients there are a whole number of impressions which have not lost their affect and whose memory has remained vivid. It follows, therefore, that these memories in hysterical patients, which have become pathogenic, occupy an exceptional position as regards the wearing-away process; and observation shows that, in the case of all the events which have become determinants of hysterical phenomena, we are dealing with psychical traumas which have not been completely abreacted, or completely dealt with. Thus we may assert that *hysterical patients suffer from incompletely abreacted psychical traumas.*

We find two groups of conditions under which memories become pathogenic. In the first group the memories to which the hysterical phenomena can be traced back have for their content ideas which involved a trauma so great that the nervous system had not sufficient power to deal with it in any way, or ideas to which reaction was impossible for social reasons (this applies frequently to married life); or lastly the subject may simply refuse to react, may not *want* to react to the psychical trauma. In this last case the contents of the hysterical deliria often turn out to be the very circle of ideas which the patient in his normal state has rejected, inhibited and suppressed with all his might. (For instance, blasphemies and erotic ideas occur in the hysterical deliria of nuns.) But in a second group of cases the reason for the absence of a reaction lies not in the content of the psychical trauma but in other circumstances. For we very often find that the content and determinants of hysterical phenomena are events which are in themselves quite trivial, but which have acquired high significance from the fact that they occurred at specially important moments when the patient's predisposition was pathologically increased. For instance, the affect of fright may have arisen in the course of some other severe affect and may on that account have attained such great importance. States of this kind are of short duration and are, as one might say, out of communication with the rest of the subject's mental life. While he is in a state of auto-hypnosis such as this, he cannot get rid associatively of an idea that occurs to him, as he can in a waking state. After considerable experience with these phenomena, we think it probable that in every hysteria we are dealing with a rudiment of what is called [in French] *"double conscience,"* dual consciousness, and that a tendency to such a dissociation, and with it the emergence of abnormal states of consciousness, which we propose to call "hypnoid," is the basic phenomenon of hysteria.

Let us now consider the manner in which our therapy operates. It falls in with one of the dearest human wishes—the wish to be able to do something over again. Someone has experienced a psychical trauma without reacting to it sufficiently. We get him to experience it a second time, but under hypnosis; and we now compel him to complete his reaction to it. He can then get rid of the idea's affect, which was so to say "strangulated," and when this is done the operation of the idea is brought to an end. Thus we cure—not hysteria but some of its individual symptoms—by causing an unaccomplished reaction to be completed.

Do not suppose, then, that very much has been gained by this for the therapeutics of hysteria. Hysteria, like the neuroses,[7] has its deeper causes; and it is those deeper causes that set limits, which are often very appreciable, to the success of our treatment.

[7] At this period Freud often used the term "neuroses" to denote neurasthenia and anxiety neurosis.

3

Exploring the Psychoanalytic Theory of the "Oral Character"

GERALD S. BLUM
& DANIEL R. MILLER

In these days of sophisticated discussion on how to study psychoanalytic theory we feel somewhat defensive concerning the methods we are about to describe.[1] Not only did we confine ourselves to conventional techniques in psychology's stockpile but we used as many as we could. This approach was designed to test whether the theory *can* be phrased in operational terms amenable to traditional types of experimentation.

The topic we chose to investigate was the theory of "oral character." On one hand, there is sufficient agreement in the psychoanalytic literature to provide a starting point from which to formulate hypotheses. On the other, this aspect of the theory is admittedly incomplete. The combination made the area seem especially promising for experimental exploration.

Various clinical manifestations of oral passivity are summarized by Fromm in the following selected excerpts describing what he calls the "receptive orientation":

> In the receptive orientation a person feels "the source of all good" to be outside, and he believes that the only way to get what he wants—be it something material, be it affection, love, knowledge, pleasure—is to receive it from that outside source. In this orientation the problem of love is almost exclusively that of "being loved" and not that of loving. . . . They are exceedingly sensitive to any withdrawal or rebuff they experience on the part of the loved per-

From G. S. Blum and D. R. Miller, Exploring the Psychoanalytic Theory of the "Oral Character." *Journal of Personality*, 1952, 20, 287–304. Reprinted by permission of authors and publisher.

This project was supported by a grant from the Rackham School of Graduate Studies at the University of Michigan. The following individuals participated in the planning and execution of the study: Edith B. Bennett, Marvin A. Brandwein, James Chabot, Elizabeth Douvan, Stanley C. Duffendack, Glenn D. Garman, Maizie Gurin, J. Edwin Keller, Louise Morrison, Otto Riedl, E. Robert Sinnett, Ezra H. Stotland, William D. Winter, and Marion P. Winterbottom.

[1] Based on a paper presented at the 1950 American Psychological Association symposium on "Experimental Approaches to Psychoanalytic Theory."

33

son. . . . It is characteristic of these people that their first thought is to find somebody else to give them needed information rather than to make even the smallest effort of their own . . . they are always in search of a "magic helper." They show a particular kind of loyalty, at the bottom of which is the gratitude for the hand that feeds them and the fear of ever losing it. Since they need many hands to feel secure, they have to be loyal to numerous people. It is difficult for them to say "no," and they are easily caught between conflicting loyalties and promises. Since they cannot say "no," they love to say "yes" to everything and everybody, and the resulting paralysis of their critical abilities makes them increasingly dependent on others.

They are dependent not only on authorities for knowledge and help but on people in general for any kind of support. They feel lost when alone because they feel that they cannot do anything without help. . . .

This receptive type has great fondness for food and drink. These persons tend to overcome anxiety and depression by eating or drinking. The mouth is an especially prominent feature, often the most expressive one; the lips tend to be open, as if in a state of continuous expectation of being fed. In their dreams, being fed is a frequent symbol of being loved; being starved, an expression of frustration or disappointment. . . . (Fromm, 1947, pp. 62–63)

COLLECTION OF DATA

Having delimited our field of investigation, we were then faced with decisions concerning subjects and specific techniques. In regard to subjects, we chose to work with humans rather than animals. Generalizations from animal behavior are largely by way of analogy. Furthermore, the complexities of interpersonal relationships cannot be fully duplicated in animal work. A second decision concerned normal versus abnormal subjects. We chose the former because of the frequently heard objection that a theory derived largely from abnormal subjects must be shown to be applicable to normals. A third decision involved the desired age level of the subjects. The selection finally centered on eight-year-olds, since children in the latency period have the double advantage of being relatively free of the rampant psychosexual conflicts of earlier childhood on one hand, and of crystallized adult defenses on the other. The experimental group consisted of the eighteen boys and girls in the third grade at the University of Michigan during 1948–49.

To test the hypotheses formulated from the literature, we first had to select a criterion measure of orality. This operational definition consisted of nonpurposive mouth movements recorded at various times over the three-week period of the research. Trained observers followed the children individually during eight two-minute intervals as part of a time-sampling procedure. They tallied such oral activities as thumb-sucking, licking the lips, tongue-rolling, and bubbling. In addition to these routine classroom observations, the same activities were noted in an experiment on boredom tolerance (see Section X). All children were ranked on both measures and a final average ranking computed.[2]

Data on the dependent variables were collected by the following methods: teacher ratings, time-sampling, sociometrics, and experimental situations. Wherever feasible, we employed several approaches to test each hypothesis. Since the theory postulates that all individuals fall along a continuum of orality, rank-order correlations (corrected for ties) were calculated to measure the association between variable and criterion.

TESTING THE HYPOTHESES

Each of the following sections presents the statement of a hypothesis, the design worked out to test it, and the subsequent results.

I. *Extreme interest in food.*
   A. Hypothesis
      Since the oral character is emotionally involved with eating beyond the dictates of simple hunger, he will consume extreme amounts of oral supplies and evince great interest in related activities. Accordingly, positive correlations are predicted between the orality criterion (mouth movements) and variables measuring interest in food.
   B. Methods
      1. Ice cream consumption. Our measure of consumption of oral supplies was the amount of ice cream eaten after hunger satiation. The children all ate lunch together. The meal, provided by the school, was dietetically planned and ample for all the children. Upon conclusion of a short rest period which followed lunch, they were offered an unlimited supply of vanilla ice cream contained in one-ounce paper cups packaged especially for the study. The carton of ice cream was placed on a table in the center of the room by a female graduate student who supervised the distribution of cups. Each child was allowed to take one whenever he wished. However, only one cup at a time was permitted and that in return for an empty one. No limit was placed on how much a child ate. The carton was kept in the room for the entire forty minutes devoted to arts and crafts, during which period observers recorded the exact number of cups consumed by each child. This procedure was repeated daily over three weeks. From these data averages were computed. The range in any one day's session was quite startling, varying all the way from no cups to thirty-nine for a single child. The absence of any parental complaints concerning

[2] These two measures of mouth movements correlated .61 with each other.

illness or lack of appetite was a pleasant surprise in view of the inability of the observers, even at the end of the most frustrating days of the experiment, to eat more than five or six cups without discomfort.

2. Eagerness at lunch time. The regular teacher and five practice teachers were given a scale describing various kinds of behavior typical of oral children. They were asked to write the names of the children who occurred to them spontaneously as they read each of fourteen items.[3] At the completion of the form they were asked to reconsider each item and to increase all shorter lists of names to five. Among the questions was: "Which children appear most impatient to eat at lunch time, as if eating were particularly important to them?"

C. Results

Mouth Movements

1. Ice cream	.52	$P < .05$
2. Eagerness at lunch time	.51	$P < .05$

These figures strongly support the predicted association between orality (mouth movements) and interest in food.

II. *Need for liking and approval*

A. Hypothesis
In terms of the theory, a significant relationship should be found between degree of orality and the need for liking and approval.

B. Methods
1. "Which children are most eager to have other children like them?" (Teacher item 6)
2. "Which children make a special effort to get the teachers to like them?" (Teacher item 12)
3. Approaches to teachers for approval. (Time-sampling item)
4. Approaches to children for approval. (Time-sampling item)
5. Attention to observers. (Time-sampling item)

---

[3] Following is the complete list of questions: (1) Which children do you think get discouraged or give up most easily when something is difficult for them? (2) Which children do you think are most able to take care of themselves without the help of adults or other children? (3) Which children get the blues most often? (4) Which children would you most like to take with you on a two-week vacation? (5) Which children tend to ask the teacher for help most often, even when they know how to do the task? (6) Which children are most eager to have other children like them? (7) Which children display their affections most openly to the teachers? (8) Which children's feelings seem to be most easily hurt? (9) Which children seem to be always eager to help even when they are inconvenienced? (10) Which children seem to accept the suggestions of others almost without thinking twice? (11) Which children appear most impatient to eat at lunch time, as if eating were particularly important to them? (12) Which children make a special effort to get the teachers to like them? (13) Which children would you least like to take with you on a two-week vacation? (14) Which children seem most concerned with giving and receiving things?

C. Results

Mouth Movements

1. Eagerness for others' liking	.68	$P < .01$
2. Efforts for teachers' liking	.10	N S [4]
3. Approaches to teachers for approval	.44	$P < .10$
4. Approaches to children for approval	.24	N S
5. Attention to observers	.36	$P < .20$

Viewing these correlations as a whole, the hypothesis seems to be fairly well supported. Although only two are significant beyond the 10 per cent level, all are in the positive direction.

III. *Dependency*

A. Hypothesis

Closely allied to the preceding hypothesis is the prediction of a positive correlation between orality and dependency.

B. Methods

1. "Which children do you think are most able to take care of themselves without the help of adults or other children?" (Teacher item 2)

2. "Which children tend to ask the teacher for help most often, even when they know how to do the task?" (Teacher item 5)

C. Results

Mouth Movements

1. Doesn't take care of self	.50	$P < .05$
2. Asks teachers' help	.10	N S

These results tend to be equivocal, with one correlation being significant and the other not.

IV. *Concern over giving and receiving*

A. Hypothesis

Since gifts represent a form of "supplies" to the oral character, it is predicted that concern over giving and receiving varies with degree of orality.

B. Methods

1. "Which children seem most concerned with giving and receiving things?" (Teacher item 14)

2. Generosity without promise of supplies in return. A related prediction held that oral children would be reluctant to give unless attractive supplies were forthcoming. After the distribution of ice cream on the second gift day (see Section 3 immediately following) the class was allowed to use the colored pencils in a drawing period. Shortly before the end of this session, a strange adult wearing a large, yellow badge marked "Pencil Drive" entered the room and made a very stirring appeal to give as many pencils

---

[4] Not significant.

as possible to the poor children of the neighborhood. Each child then went behind a screen and secretly deposited his pencils in the slot of a colorful box marked "Pencil Drive." All the new pencils had been marked with pin points, so that the contributions of each subject were readily identifiable. Unfortunately, this coding system was of little aid since only three in the entire class gave new pencils. The rest of the collection consisted of a variegated assortment of battered, chewed-up stumps with broken points—all without identification marks. In order to locate the pencil contributors, a new procedure was developed which provided the basis for the added experiment described in Section 4 following.

3. Gifts as the equivalent of food. The term "oral supplies" connotes, in addition to food, tokens of personal recognition. It was hypothesized that, if gifts and food are equivalent supplies, receipt of gifts should result in a diminution of ice cream consumption for the group as a whole. On one occasion the children were each given a box of crayons; another time they received seven colored pencils which they had chosen as their most desired gift in a rating session the preceding day.

4. Guilt over not giving. The theory leads to the prediction that guilt, typically experienced as a deprivation of supplies, should bring about an increase in the consumption of ice cream. The day after the pencil drive, the teacher agreed to deliver a stern lecture telling how ashamed she was of their stinginess. She was so effective that, before she finished, one boy blurted out that he had meant to give more new pencils and ran to the box to deposit a few. Next the teacher asked the group to retrieve their donations and observers tallied the number of pencils each pupil took back, which provided the data missing in Section 2 immediately above. Shortly afterward the ice cream was distributed and the number of cups counted as usual.

To relieve the guilt, the pencil solicitor returned later to proclaim happily that the school drive had been 100 per cent successful. He then apologized for not having announced previously that old pencils were not wanted.

C. Results

Mouth Movements

1. Concern over giving and receiving   .46   P < .10
2. Lack of generosity   .22   N S

3. Gifts as the equivalent of food. On the crayon day, 14 of the 16 subjects decreased in the number of cups consumed ($X^2 = 9.00$, $P < .01$); and on the pencil day, 12 out of 15 dropped ($X^2 = 5.40$, $P < .02$).

4. Guilt over not giving. While there were no significant increases in the actual amount of ice cream consumed after the "guilt" lecture, certain qualitative observations were noted. The five most oral

children in the group sat on the table next to the ice cream carton throughout the whole period, in contrast to their usual wandering around the room. Since they had apparently been eating up to maximum physical capacity, it was virtually impossible for them to eat significantly more cups than before. Another exceptional feature was the fact that none of the ice cream was left over this time.

Considering the above experiments as a whole, there seems to be fair support for the hypothesis that orality is related to concern over giving and receiving.

V. *Need to be ingratiating*

A. Hypothesis

The oral character, by virtue of his never-ending search for love and approval, tends to behave towards others in a very ingratiating manner.

B. Methods

1. "Which children display their affections most openly to the teachers?" (Teacher item 7)
2. "Which children seem to be always eager to help even when they are inconvenienced?" (Teacher item 9)
3. Going out of way to do favors. (Time-sampling item)

C. Results

Mouth Movements

1. Displays affection openly	−.28	N S
2. Always eager to help	−.24	N S
3. Goes out of way to do favors	.16	N S

These results clearly negate the predicted association between orality and the need to be ingratiating.

VI. *Social isolation*

A. Hypothesis

According to the theory, the oral character should be infrequently chosen by his peers in view of his passivity, his excessive demands for attention, and his hostility when these demands are not gratified.

B. Methods

In a private interview each child was asked to answer a number of sociometric questions to determine his favorites among his classmates: (1) "Which children in your classroom do you like best?" (2) "Which of the children in your classroom would you most like to invite to a party?" (3) "Which teachers do you like the most?"[5] (4) "Which children in your class are you good friends with?" Class members were then ranked according to the number of times their names had been mentioned.

[5] Included only for use in Section VII.

C. Results
Mouth Movements
1. Social isolation   .68   P < .01

This correlation strongly supports the theoretical deduction that orality and social isolation go hand in hand.

VII. *Inability to divide loyalties*
    A. Hypothesis
        The theory leads to the hypothesis that the more oral child has greater difficulty choosing between two friends, inasmuch as both represent potential sources of supply.
    B. Methods
        Several days after the sociometric ratings a measure of divided loyalty was obtained. Each child was interviewed individually and asked to make a number of choices between his two best friends as noted on the sociometric ratings and also between his two best-liked teachers. The interviewer recorded decision time plus comments, actions, and expressive movements. The protocols were then rated blindly by three judges for degree of indecision.
    C. Results
Mouth Movements
1. Inability to divide loyalties   −.28   N S

The correlation of this variable with the criterion contradicts the hypothesized association between orality and the inability to divide loyalties.

VIII. *Suggestibility*
    A. Hypothesis
        From the theory it was anticipated that the oral child, in view of his excessive need for love and approval, would be suggestible in the presence of a potentially supply-giving adult.
    B. Methods
        1. Upon his arrival in the testing room, the child was told: "We have some things which we want you to help us try out in order to see if they are right for school children of your age." The experiment consisted of three parts: tasting a hypothetical cherry flavor in candy, smelling perfume from a bottle of water, and feeling nonexistent vibrations in a metal rod attached to some apparatus.
        2. "Which children seem to accept the suggestions of others almost without thinking twice?" (Teacher item 10)
    C. Results
Mouth Movements
1. Taste   .50   P < .05
   Touch   .00   N S
   Smell   .03   N S
2. Accepts suggestions   .11   N S

Except for taste, suggestibility does not appear to be related to degree of orality. The discrepancy between results with taste and with the other items is most easily accounted for by the specifically oral quality of the taste measure.

IX. *Depressive tendencies*

A. Hypothesis

Self-esteem in the oral child is presumed to depend upon external sources of love or supplies. Therefore, the unavoidable frustration of oral demands is said to be experienced as a feeling of emptiness or depression.

B. Methods

1. "Which children do you think get discouraged or give up most easily when something is difficult for them?" (Teacher item 1)
2. "Which children get the blues most often?" (Teacher item 3)
3. "Which children's feelings seem to be most easily hurt?" (Teacher item 8)

C. Results

Mouth Movements

1. Get discouraged	.32	$P < .20$
2. Get the blues	.05	N S
3. Feelings easily hurt	.13	N S

The low correlations between mouth movements and personality characteristics relevant to depression do not support the theoretical prediction.

X. *Boredom tolerance*

A. Hypothesis

Boredom is assumed to be especially disturbing to the oral child because it signifies a lack of available supplies. Therefore he would be expected to show very little tolerance for a boring, unrewarded activity.

B. Methods

In this experiment the child was taken into a room where he was shown a large sheaf of papers containing lines of X's and O's. The examiner then said: "Your class is being compared with another class in another town to see which class can cross out the most circles." After giving the instructions, the examiner added: "There are several pages [the examiner leafed through all the sheets]. Don't write your name on the paper. We don't care how much you yourself can do, but how much the class can do. All right, you may begin."

The examiner then left the room. As soon as the child began, an observer casually entered the room, sat at a distance, and recorded all the actions of the subject, such as number of mouth movements and work interruptions. The child was stopped after twenty minutes. Ranks were based on number of lines completed. As mentioned previously, this experiment also contributed to the criterion measure of nonbiting mouth movements, which were tallied throughout.

C. Results

Mouth Movements

1. Boredom Tolerance   .45   P < .10

While not very high, this figure does provide some support for the prediction that orality and boredom tolerance are positively associated.

XI. *Summary of results*

Ten hypotheses concerning oral character structure have been tested. The results can be summarized in tabular form as follows:

Strong Support	Fair Support	Unsupported	Equivocal
1. Extreme interest in food	1. Need for liking and approval	1. Dependency	1. Need to be ingratiating
2. Social isolation	2. Concern over giving and receiving	2. Suggestibility	2. Inability to divide loyalties
	3. Boredom tolerance		3. Depressive tendencies

The goal of this phase of the research is to check the existing status of the theory, and to make revisions wherever dictated by the evidence. The above data represent the initial tests of hypotheses deduced from the psychoanalytic literature on orality. In general, a fair number of predictions have been supported, some remain questionable, and still others are clearly not supported. Before evaluating specific hypotheses, however, we prefer to await the returns from successive attempts to measure the same variables. It is very possible that any one of the significant correlations may still reflect the influence of chance factors. Too, any one of the insignificant findings may be a function of faulty experimentation rather than incorrect theory. Both of these possibilities suggest the necessity for repeated research along similar lines. Apart from the fate of specific hypotheses, the over-all results hold promise for the investigation of psychoanalytic theory by conventional psychological methods.

RELATED EMPIRICAL OBSERVATIONS

Intercorrelations of major variables. In addition to providing data concerning specific hypotheses, the study lends itself to an over-all analysis of correlations among the major variables. This supplementary approach seems worth while in view of the postulated communality of the variables. If each variable really measures oral passivity, the table of intercorrelations should demonstrate positive relationships beyond chance expectancy. These data, grouped according to pure oral measures, experimental situations, and behavioral measures, are shown in Table 3-1.

TABLE 3-1.   Intercorrelations of Major Variables

| | Pure Oral Measures | | | Personality | | | | | | |
| | | | | Experimental Situations | | | | | Behavioral Measures | |
	1. Ice Cream	2. Eagerness at Lunch (T.R.)	3. Mouth Activity (T.S.)	4. Mouth Activity (B.T.)	5. Suggestibility	6. Boredom Tolerance	7. Divided Loyalty	8. Generosity	9. Sociometrics	10. Combined Teacher Ratings [1]	11. Combined Time Samples [2]
1.		19	67‡	32	30	31	−07	−29	40*	−09	43*
2.			41*	50†	11	34	−18	15	44*	20	01
3.				61‡	04	39	−21	19	61‡	15	55†
4.					25	44*	−18	32	71‡	20	17
5.						12	44*	−33	36	07	−11
6.							04	25	35	10	−04
7.								−33	03	04	−31
8.									18	45*	09
9.										23	12
10.											−01

* = P<.10
† = P<.05
‡ = P<.01

[1] Does not include 2 [Eagerness at Lunch (T.R.)]
[2] Does not include 3 [Mouth Activity (T.S.)]

From Table 3-2 we see that the total numbers of significant positive correlations at the 10 per cent, 5 per cent, and 1 per cent levels clearly exceed the chance expectancies. These results suggest the possible existence of a general "factor" of orality.

TABLE 3-2.   Number of Significant Positive Correlations among Major Variables

Probability Level	Number Expected by Chance	Number Obtained
.10	2.75	13
.05	1.38	6
.01	0.28	4

Comparative evaluation of methodological approaches. Table 3-3 presents a breakdown of the personality variables into two general types—experimental situations and behavioral measures. The number of significant

TABLE 3-3. Personality Measures Broken Down by the Type of Approach vs. Major Variables

Personality Measures	Probability Level	Number Positive Correlations Expected by Chance	Number Obtained
Experimental Situations	.10	1.70	3
	.05	0.85	0
	.01	0.17	0
Behavioral Measures	.10	1.35	7
	.05	0.68	3
	.01	0.14	2

correlations for each type with the major variables suggests a probable difference in their relative efficacy. It is true that the same operational variables are not measured in both types. Nevertheless, the large number of significant behavioral correlations warrants speculation concerning possible causes. Three alternative explanations come to mind. One, the experimental designs were adequate and the negative results are a contradiction of the hypotheses. This possibility does not seem very plausible in light of the positive theoretical findings with other techniques. Two, the hypotheses are valid and the designs inadequate. No evidence exists for rejecting this alternative, but the marked discrepancy between results with the two approaches, both of which were carefully designed and pretested, leads us to question the explanation. Three, the difficulty lies, not in experimental design or theory, but in unreliability inherent in the settings in which the experiments were conducted. The number of observations involved in the experiments were necessarily limited to one session, whereas the behavioral measures were usually accumulated over several time periods. Unavoidable and unpredictable obstacles are bound to arise in the course of experimentation in a natural setting, such as a schoolroom, where the success of each design hinges upon the precision and co-operation of a large number of individuals.

Cases in point are the Love Withdrawal and Can't Say No experiments, both of which had to be abandoned. The hypothesis in the former stated that the oral child should be highly sensitive to withdrawal of love. The "ice-cream lady" first asked the children in the class to make drawings using themes of their own choice. When the drawings were finished she circulated around the room, praising them all freely. Then she instructed the group to draw a house, each child individually to bring his drawing to her upon its completion. She lauded half of the drawings, and held them up before the class while commenting on their merits and naming the artists. The other half were received with casual indifference but no criticism. This was the love withdrawal procedure. Finally, she asked the class to draw a picture of a child. The aim of the experiment was to determine the effects of the withdrawal of love upon both drawings and behavior as recorded by observers.

The experiment was to have been repeated several days later, with a reversal of the treatment of the previously praised and ignored halves. In the actual administration it turned out to be impossible to maintain any kind of order in the class. The children were all excited about an Indian play which they had performed that day before the entire school, and their drum-pounding and war-whooping precluded any systematic, experimental procedure.

The Can't Say No hypothesis dealt with the inability of the oral character to refuse requests from adults for fear of losing their approval. Nine observers entered the library while the class was listening to a fascinating record. Each observer approached a child, tapped him on the shoulder, and said in a neutral tone: "Come with me." The reactions to this request were later reported in detail. Like the preceding experiment this one was disrupted by an unforeseen complication. At the last minute the librarian was unable to schedule a record session when the other nine children in the group were to be asked to leave.

In contrast to the above illustrative experiments, the cumulative behavioral measures, on the other hand, were not as susceptible to unforeseen disruptions, since accidental influences on any one day tended to average out in the course of time. For example, differences occurred when ice cream was delivered late, yet this did not seriously alter the final ranking of subjects on the number of cups consumed.

From these speculations, it seems preferable that research designs, when dealing with something as complex as character structure, involve a series of measurements over a period of time.

Exploration of projective instruments. The following four projective techniques were included to explore their suitability as measures of orality: the Rorschach Test (Rorschach, 1942), Thematic Apperception Test (Murray, 1943), Blacky Pictures (Blum, 1949; 1950) and a specially constructed Story Completion Test which had been found to be significantly related to sociometric status in a previous study (Miller & Stine, 1951). Since there had been no previous applications of the techniques to this topic and age range, attempts at explicit prediction were not made.

Table 3-4 presents the correlations of the various projective methods with the major variables. Analysis of the projectives can be grouped under two broad headings, objective and interpretive. The Rorschach, TAT, and Story Completion (Objective) were all scored by counting the number of oral references, e.g., "food," "hunger," "eating," etc. The Blacky and Story Completion (Interpretive) protocols were ranked according to global impressions of oral passivity. While none of the correlations is very high, it should be noted that the "objective" approach yielded 22 negative and 11

TABLE 3-4.   Correlations of Projective Methods with Major Variables

| | Pure Oral Measures | | | | Personality | | | | | | |
| | | | | | Experimental Situations | | | | Behavioral Measures | | |
	1. Ice Cream	2. Eagerness at Lunch (T.R.)	3. Mouth Activity (T.S.)	4. Mouth Activity (B.T.)	5. Suggestibility	6. Boredom Tolerance	7. Divided Loyalty	8. Generosity	9. Sociometrics	10. Combined Teacher Ratings	11. Combined Time Samples
Rorschach (Objective)	28	19	20	−05	11	41	−03	−11	−13	−10	45
TAT (Objective)	−40	−58	−34	−59	01	−37	33	−21	05	−02	−05
Story Completion (Objective)	−11	−45	−29	−36	08	−20	60	−06	−11	−12	−05
Story Completion (Interpretive)	47	06	33	48	40	37	23	−34	19	−12	06
Blacky (Interpretive)	21	−23	16	25	41	−06	16	−20	28	15	21

positive correlations, whereas the "interpretive" produced only 5 negative and 17 positive ($X^2 = 10.1, P < .01$). Whether this difference can legitimately be attributed to type of scoring approach can be answered only by further investigation.

SUMMARY

This project was designed to explore the feasibility of testing psychoanalytic theory by conventional psychological methods. Hypotheses concerning the "oral character," deduced from statements in the literature, were examined by means of teacher ratings, time-sampling, sociometrics, and experimental situations conducted in a third-grade class. The operational definition of orality consisted of nonpurposive mouth movements recorded by observers. The eighteen subjects were ranked on the criterion and on a series of variables related to specific hypotheses.

The resulting correlations lent strong support to hypotheses dealing with (a) extreme interest in food, and (b) social isolation. Fair support was given (*a*) need for liking and approval, (*b*) concern over giving and receiving, and (*c*) boredom tolerance. Unsupported hypotheses were (*a*) need to be ingratiating, (*b*) inability to divide loyalties, and (*c*) depressive tendencies; while remaining equivocal were (*a*) dependency and (*b*) suggestibility. Apart from the currently tentative nature of these specific findings, the over-all results were interpreted as holding promise for the investigation of psychoanalytic theory by traditional techniques.

REFERENCES

Blum, G. S. A study of the psychoanalytic theory of psychosexual development. *Genet. Psychol. Monogr.*, 1949, 39, 3–99.

Blum, G. S. *The Blacky Pictures: A technique for the exploration of personality dynamics*. New York: The Psychological Corporation, 1950.

Fenichel, O. *The psychoanalytic theory of neurosis*. New York: Norton, 1945.

Fromm, E. *Man for himself*. New York: Rinehart, 1947.

Miller, D. R., & Hutt, M. L. Value interiorization and personality development. *J. soc. Issues*, 1949, 5, No. 4, 2–30.

Miller, D. R., & Stine, M. E. The prediction of social acceptance by means of psychoanalytic concepts. *J. Pers.*, 1951, 20, 162–174.

Murray, H. A. *Thematic Apperception Test manual*. Cambridge: Harvard University Press, 1943.

Rorschach, H. *Psychodiagnostics* (translation) Bern: Hans Huber, 1942.

Thompson, C. *Psychoanalysis: Evaluation and development*. New York: Hermitage House, 1950.

Thornton, G. R. The significance of rank-difference coefficients of correlation. *Psychometrika*, 1943, 8, No. 4, 211–222.

4

An Empirical Test
of Two Freudian Hypotheses
Concerning Castration Anxiety

BERNARD J. SCHWARTZ

This paper summarizes two studies that employ a previously developed experimentally validated (Schwartz, 1955) measure of castration anxiety to test derivations from psychoanalytic theory. The first study compares homosexual males and normal males in a search for differences in castration anxiety. The second study makes the same comparison for normal men and women.

STUDY I

Male Homosexuality and Castration Anxiety

Freud, in one of his earliest papers (Freud, 1938), suggests that castration anxiety, because of its role in the resolution of the Oedipus complex, is of crucial importance to subsequent object choice. Later papers (Freud, 1924a, b; 1932) repeat this statement without essential modification. He states: "In extreme cases, this [castration anxiety] inhibits his [the boy's] object choice and, if reinforced by organic factors, may result in exclusive homosexuality," (Freud, 1932, pp. 284–285). Analogously, Horney (1924), states: "We know that in every case in which the castration complex predominates there is without exception a more or less marked tendency to homosexuality." Fenichel (1945, p. 326), whose writings may be considered

From Schwartz, B. J. An Empirical Test of Two Freudian Hypotheses Concerning Castration Anxiety. *Journal of Personality*, 1956, 24, 318–327. Reprinted by permission of author and publisher.

These studies were performed as part of a dissertation submitted in partial fulfillment of the requirements for the degree of Doctor of Philosophy, in the Department of Social Relations, Harvard University. I should like to express my most sincere gratitude to Dr. Gardner Lindzey, who directed this research.

to typify psychoanalytic thinking, states: "Thus castration anxiety (and guilt feelings which are derivatives of castration anxiety) must be the decisive factor" (i.e., in the genesis of perversion). And again (Fenichel, 1945, p. 330), he states: "Whenever the difference in the genitals of the sexes is of outstanding importance to an individual, and whenever his relationships to his fellow human beings are in every respect determined by the sex of the others, such an individual is under the influence of a strong castration complex. This is true of homosexual men, analysis of whom regularly shows they are afraid of female genitals." The above quotations suggest that castration anxiety plays an important role in the personality of the adult male overt homosexual.

PROCEDURE

Subjects

TAT protocols of a group of 20 overt-homosexual males, collected from a college population by another experimenter, were used. This experimenter reported that the Ss demonstrated no other gross psychopathology, were not receiving psychotherapy, and seemed to accept their homosexuality. The experimenter reported further that these Ss were *not* commonly known as homosexuals, and did not seem to be overtly fearful of external punishment for their homosexuality.

Twenty TAT protocols of randomly selected males from a college population constituted the control group data. These protocols as well had been previously obtained by another investigator. The two groups were comparable in age, education, and socioeconomic status.

Administration and Analysis of the Thematic Apperception Test

The TAT was administered individually to Ss of both groups. Different TAT cards were used for the two groups, but they shared in common cards 4, 6BM, 7BM, and 18BM, and only these stories were used in the data analysis.

The TAT data were analyzed by means of the content analysis measure of castration anxiety described more fully by Van Ophuijsen (1924). The measure consists of items (i.e. descriptions of behavior, events, thoughts, or ideas believed related to castration anxiety) which were grouped into nine logically coherent, mutually exclusive categories, as well as into a tenth category dealing with formal characteristics of stories and presumably denotative of nonspecific anxiety. While these items and categories were originally selected on a priori theoretical and clinical grounds, six of the categories discriminated reliably between the TAT protocols of normal Ss who had just seen a film designed to provoke castration anxiety and Ss exposed to a neutral control film. These categories are listed below, and may be considered to be an operationally defined index of castration anxiety:

Category 3: Damage to or loss of extensions of the body image. Items include loss of prized possessions which may symbolize the self or parts of the self, such as weapons, machinery, cameras, etc.

Category 5: Personal inadequacy. These are "lack of competence and strength" items, and include descriptions of the hero as being weak, small, helpless, unable to assert his rights, etc.

Category 6: General repetitive attempts at mastery. These items are concerned with repetitive returning to an area of anxiety in an attempt to master it, and include preoccupation with phallic referents and sexuality, ambivalence (where other items of the measure are involved), exhibitionism, rebellion against threatening authority figures, and repetitive risk-taking.

Category 7: Intrapsychic threat. These items are primarily concerned with guilt, remorse, and expectations of punishment or retaliation.

Category 8: Extrapsychic threat. These items consist in the main of retaliation, punishment, threat, or prohibition from external personal or impersonal sources.

Category 9: Loss of cathected objects. These items are concerned with death, absence, or removal of persons loved by the hero of the story.

The remaining four categories of the measure, though not validated experimentally, are used in these studies because three of these categories (1, 2, 4) are logically and behaviorally closest to the primary representation of castration anxiety, and secondly, these four categories discriminated groups in the validation study, albeit not reliably, in the predicted direction, and the total measure including these unvalidated categories differentiated groups better than did a total score using only the validated categories, and considerably better than any single category. These categories were:

Category 1: Genital injury or loss. Most of these items are unsymbolized representations of actual injury to the genitalia. One item concerns total mutilative destruction of the body.

Category 2: Damage to or loss of other parts of the body. These items include damage to any part of the body other than the genitalia, such as wounds to or operations upon limbs, thorax, or abdomen. Also included are less specific types of damage, such as beating, torture, or illness.

Category 4: Sexual inadequacy. This category includes items such as impotence, sterility, penile inadequacy, renunciation of heterosexuality and equation of sexuality with aggression.

Category 10: Formal characteristics of stories. These items include discontinuities in the stories, misspellings, erasures, and "bad" endings to stories. The items of category 10 are considered indices of anxiety, but are not specific to castration anxiety.

A simple frequency-count system was used in scoring. Each occurrence in the TAT protocol of any item of the measure, or its spontaneous denial, was tallied in one and only one of the first nine categories, but could also be scored in category 10. The number of items of the measure occurring in each story is theoretically unlimited. Only those items of the measure *overtly present* in the stories were tallied: inferences were *not* scored. Interrater reliability of the measure of castration anxiety, using the Pearson coefficient of correlation, was $r = .80$, which compares favorably with reliability indices of other studies using the TAT.

The Link-Wallace method of allowances (Mosteller & Bush, 1954), one-way classification of data, was the statistic used to test the significance of differential occurrence of items between groups. The groups were compared on each category of the measure, on total scores, on the total score of the six validated categories, and on the total score for the nine categories specific to castration anxiety.

RESULTS

Table 4-1 shows the significance of the differences between the overt-homosexual male group and the comparison heterosexual male group on the measure of castration anxiety, as estimated by the method of allowances. Categories 4, 7, 8, and 10 discriminate groups in the predicted direction at the 5-per-cent level of risk. The over-all total score, the total score of valid categories, and the total score of categories specific to castration anxiety discriminate groups at the 1-per-cent level of risk. Differences in categories 5 and 6, though not significant, are in the predicted direction. Category 1 shows no occurrences in either group. Differences in categories 2, 3, and 9 are in a direction opposite to that predicted, and the magnitude of these differences is small. Parallel computations with the more sensitive chi-square technique give analogous results: Categories 4, 7, 8, and 10 are significant at the 1-per-cent level, and category 5, not significant with the method of allowances, proves significant at the 5-per-cent level.

In summary of these results, the psychoanalytic hypothesis that overt homosexual males show more intense castration anxiety than comparable normal males is supported.

TABLE 4-1. Differences Between Overt-Homosexual Male and Normal Male Groups on the Measure of Castration Anxiety

Source		Overt-Homosexual Group Total	Heterosexual Group Total	Differences
	1	0	0	0
	2	12	14	—2
	3	1	3	—2
	4	25	6	19*
	5	74	51	23
Category	6	70	63	7
	7	51	20	31*
	8	92	57	35*
	9	2	5	—3
	10	44	6	38*
Total score		368	225	143**
Total score of previously validated categories (3, 5, 6, 7, 8, 9)		290	198	92**
Total score of categories specific to castration anxiety (1–9)		324	214	105**

* Significant at the 5 per cent level of risk, using the method of allowances.
** Significant at the 1 per cent level of risk, using the method of allowances.

STUDY II

Sex Differences and Castration Anxiety

The weight of psychoanalytic theory suggests castration anxiety is of differential importance in the personalities of normal men and women. Freud (1924a, pp. 274–275), speaking of castration anxiety in the female, states: "She accepts castration as an established fact, an operation already performed. The castration dread thus being excluded in her case. . . ." Deutsch (1930) considers the abandonment of clitoral satisfaction, a function of castration anxiety, to be compensated for by the ability to bear a child, and the hope for one in the future; this has the consequence of reducing the amount of castration anxiety the girl experiences. Fenichel (1945, p. 99) states: "In girls, there seems to be no castration anxiety that could be considered a dynamic force. The idea of having lost an organ cannot condition the same restriction of instinct as the idea that one might lose an organ by instinctual activity. True, many women after their disappointment (i.e., discovery of lack of a penis) have unconsciously built up the fantasy of possessing a penis. But an anxiety concerning a merely fantasied organ cannot have the same dynamic effect as a threat against a real organ. Analysis shows that other and older fears, above all the fear over loss of love, are stronger in women, and in many ways take over the role that castration anxiety plays in men." This quotation suggests, despite a number of qualifications, that castration anxiety should occur more frequently or with greater intensity in men than in women.

PROCEDURE

Subjects

The data for this investigation consisted of TAT protocols of 20 matched pairs of male and female Ss. Pairs of Ss were exactly matched for religion and self-ratings of socioeconomic status: 14 of the pairs were identical in age, six pairs differed by no more than one year. These protocols were selected from data gathered by previous investigators (Lindzey & Goldberg, 1953) in elementary psychology courses at Boston University.

Administration and Analysis of the Thematic Apperception Test

TATs were group administered, with each slide exposed for 20 seconds, and a five-minute time allotment for writing of stories. Cards 1, 2, 4, 5, 10, 13MF, 14, and 15, applicable to both male and female Ss, were used.

The same procedure of analysis was used in this comparison as in the comparison of the TAT protocols of normal and overt-homosexual males.

RESULTS

Table 4-2 shows the significance of the differences between males and females on the measure of castration anxiety, as estimated by the method of allowances. Categories 5 and 6 differentiate groups in the predicted direction at the 5-per-cent level of risks, as do the over-all total score, the total score of valid categories, and the total score of categories specific to castration anxiety. Differences in categories 4, 7, 8, 9, and 10, although in the predicted direction, are not significant. The magnitudes of these differences are small, as are those of categories 1, 2, and 3, which are in direction opposite to that predicted. Parallel statistical analysis with chi-square technique again gives analogous results. Category 6 and the three total scores are significant at the 1-per-cent-level. None of the other categories show change.

These results support the psychoanalytic hypothesis that normal males show more intense castration anxiety than normal females.

TABLE 4-2. Differences Between Male and Female Groups on the Measure of Castration Anxiety

	Source	Male Group Total	Female Group Total	Differences
	1	1	2	−1
	2	11	14	−3
	3	1	3	−2
	4	28	21	7
	5	40	22	18*
Category	6	83	42	41*
	7	33	31	2
	8	72	56	16
	9	14	10	4
	10	5	3	2
Total score		288	203	85*
Total score of previously validated categories (3, 5, 6, 7, 8, 9)		242	162	83*
Total score of categories specific to castration anxiety (1–9)		283	200	80*

* Significant at the 5 per cent level of risk, using the method of allowances.

Though the differences between the group totals are significant, the distributions of total scores show considerable overlap between the two groups. One speculative possibility to account for this finding is that the obtained results may be an accurate representation of the differential intensities of castration anxiety in the personalities of males and females, which are probably not as clear-cut as the hypothesis would suggest. Abraham (1927), for example, considers that some manifestations of castration anxiety occur in all women, as do Freud (1932), Horney (1924, 1932), and Van Ophuijsen (1924). Fenichel qualifies his earlier unambiguous statements by saying (Fenichel, 1924, p. 99): "It is not easy to answer the question about castration anxiety in women. . . . the fear that the state of being castrated, thought of as an outcome of a forbidden activity, might be found out often limits the girl's sexual expressions considerably; the idea of having destroyed one's own body is often encountered, as is that of having lost all possibility of bearing children, or at least of having healthy children, and other anxieties which anticipate that the disgrace is found out . . . . there are anxieties about anticipated retaliatory genital injuries which replace castration fear. Girls often do not know they have a pre-formed hollow organ in their vagina, and this explains the fantastic fear that their genital longings to be penetrated by the father's organ may lead to bodily injury. Despite all this, the analysis of some women still reveals an unconscious fear that an organ will be cut off as punishment for sexual practices."

In summary, the obtained results seem to parallel psychoanalytic thinking about the differential role of castration anxiety in the personalities of normal males and females: the ambiguities, qualifications, and lack of specification of magnitude characteristic of much of psychoanalytic theory are reflected in the overlap of the distributions of total scores.

Content Differences Between the TAT Protocols of Normal Males and Normal Females

The TAT stories told by males seemed to be characterized by frequent descriptions of male heroes as inadequate, weak-willed, stupid, and incapable of fidelity in marriage. Accompanying this were frequent descriptions of women as prostitutes, or as otherwise immoral, or as demanding and dominating. Their stories were also characterized by a prevailing ambivalence and indecisiveness, and by preoccupation with sexuality. Discontinuities in the stories were frequent, as were story endings concerned with illness, debility, death, loss of possessions or status, etc. These "bad" endings sometimes did not seem justified by the content of the stories. Thus, the greater intensity of castration anxiety in males was inferred largely from a tendency toward belittling or questioning the adequacy of male figures, and at the same time representing female figures as threatening or immoral.

DISCUSSION

The findings we have just presented suggested certain conclusions concerning our measure of castration anxiety. In the first place the success we encountered in testing propositions derived from psychoanalytic theory in two different areas not only has implications for psychoanalytic theory, but also strengthens the confidence we have in our measure. In any study where an instrument is used to assess a specific variable in order to test a theoretically derived proposition, and the proposition is verified, this not only confirms the derivation, but also suggests strongly that the instrument is indeed getting at the variable it promised to measure. These two studies may therefore be considered a cross-validation of the results of the experimental validation of the measure of castration anxiety (Schwartz, 1955).

Also of interest is the consistent failure of categories 1 (actual genital injury), 2 (damage to other parts of the body), 3 (damage to extensions of the body image), and 9 (loss of cathected objects) to differentiate the groups at question. For the first two categories this lack of sensitivity is coupled with the earlier failure of the attempt to validate them experimentally, and thus constitutes a rather convincing picture of their lack of validity. However, it seems quite possible that the direct and undisguised nature of the material included in these categories would make their incidence unlikely in normal groups. Whether this would be true in psychotic groups and other groups different from those studied remains a question for the future. Our research does not provide any evidence for the validity of these responses, although their rational link to castration anxiety is sufficiently strong to make their inclusion in future investigations seem justified. A further reason for their inclusion in future investigations is statistical: (1) the total measure, including the unvalidated categories, is itself valid and differentiates groups well, and (2), computed intercorrelations among the experimentally validated categories suggest that the categories are all imperfectly correlated predictors of a single underlying variable.

Thus far we have talked only of the significance of our findings for the measurement of castration anxiety. What of their import for psychoanalytic theory? Granted that many alternative hypotheses could be offered to account for the differences we observed, and granted also that our confirmations are made in terms of group differences with considerable overlap between the differentiated groups, it still seems that the capacity of psychoanalytic theory to predict *in advance* the rather complicated findings we observed is encouraging and provides evidence for the crude power of psychoanalytic theory. The crudity of the theory is made clear by the evident difficulty of making an unambiguous derivation in connection with sex differences in castration anxiety. This difficulty is also implied by the fact that the two derivations we chose to test were among the more straightforward of the many conceivable hypotheses that we might have attempted to extract from psychoanalytic theory.

While we choose to view our findings as supplying some support for one of the more controversial aspects of psychoanalytic theory it is evident that these findings are a mere beginning when the immense number of other statements implied by psychoanalysis concerning castration anxiety is considered. The important consideration seems to be that here we have an instrument that is at least partially validated as a measure of castration anxiety and which is sufficiently manipulable so as to lend itself to many research settings.

SUMMARY

This paper presents the results of a test of two derivations from psychoanalytic theory. TAT protocols of comparable overt-homosexual male and normal male goups were obtained, as were TAT protocols of comparable male and female goups. These protocols were scored with a previously validated measure of castration anxiety. Results support the hypotheses that overt-homosexual males show more intense castration anxiety than normal males, and males show more intense castration anxiety than females.

REFERENCES

Abraham, K. *Selected papers of Karl Abraham*. International Psycho-analytical Library, No. 13. London: The Hogarth Press, 1927.

Deutsch, Helene. The significance of masochism in the mental life of women. *Int. J. Psychoanal.*, 1930, *11*, 48–60.

Fenichel, O. *The psychoanalytic theory of neurosis*. New York: Norton, 1945.

Freud, S. The passing of the Oedipus complex. In *Collected papers*, International Psycho-analytical Library, No. 8. London: The Hogarth Press, 1924, 2, pp. 269–276. (a)

Freud, S. The infantile genital organization of the libido. In *Collected papers*, International Psycho-analytical Library, No. 8. London: The Hogarth Press, 1924. 2, 244–249.

Freud, S. Female sexuality. *Int. J. Psychoanal.* 1932, *13*, 281–297.

Freud, S. Three contributions to a theory of sexuality. In A. A. Brill (Ed.) *The basic writings of Sigmund Freud*. New York: Modern Library, 1938. Pp. 553–632.

Horney, Karen. On the genesis of the castration complex in women. *Int. J. Psychoanal.*, 1924, *5*, 50–65.

Horney, Karen. The dread of women. *Int. J. Psychoanal.*, 1932, *13*, 348–360.

Lindzey, G. & Goldberg, M. Motivational differences between male and female as measured by the Thematic Apperception Test. *J. Pers.*, 1953, *22*, 101–117.

Mosteller, F., & Bush, R. R. Selected quantitative techniques. In G. Lindzey (Ed.) *Handbook of social psychology*. Cambridge, Mass.: Addison-Wesley, 1954. Pp. 289–335.

Schwartz, B. The measurement of castration anxiety and anxiety over loss of love. *J. Pers.*, 1955, *24*, 204–219.

Van Ophuijsen, J. Contributions to the masculinity complex in women. *Int. J. Psychoanal.*, 1924, *5*, 39–49.

5

Perception of Homosexual Words in Paranoid Schizophrenia

PAUL G. DASTON

This study was undertaken to investigate the relationship postulated in psychoanalytic theory between paranoid schizophrenia and homosexuality. The methodological orientation was derived from research in the general area of selective perception.

Psychoanalytic Theory

On the basis of his study of the Schreber case, Freud (1948) postulated that the major factor in all the paranoid disorders was a conflict over inadequately repressed homosexual impulses. The paranoid male unconsciously desires to be the passive recipient of sexual advances from other males. In order to cope with these unacceptable motives which threaten to be expressed at a conscious level, he utilizes the mechanisms of denial and projection. Recognizing that schizophrenic and paranoid phenomena can be combined in any proportion, Freud emphasized that it was the paranoid component which was related to homosexual impulses. In schizophrenia uncolored by paranoid mechanisms, he felt it was extremely unlikely that homosexuality played an equally important etiological role.

From P. G. Daston, Perception of Homosexual Words in Paranoid Schizophrenics. *Perceptual and Motor Skills*, 1956, 6, 45–55. Reprinted by permission of publisher.

The present paper represents a portion of the dissertation presented in partial fulfillment of the requirements for the degree of Doctor of Philosophy at Michigan State College, 1952. The writer wishes to thank Drs. James S. Karslake (committee chairman), M. Ray Denny, Donald M. Johnson, Albert I. Rabin, and Milton Rokeach for their advice and criticism.

A condensed version of this paper was presented at the meeting of the Amer. Psychol. Ass., Cleveland, 1953.

From the Veterans Administration Hospital, Brockton, Massachusetts. This paper is published with the permission of the Chief Medical Director, Department of Medicine and Surgery, Veterans Administration, who assumes no responsibility for the opinions expressed or conclusions drawn by the author.

Research evidence has not provided consistent support for this psychoanalytic interpretation. Observational studies (Alexander & Menninger, 1946; Gardner, 1946; Thorndike & Lorge, 1944) have indicated some relationship between paranoid mechanisms and homosexual impulses, but the findings have been more suggestive than decisive. Correlating response times to a word-association test with recognition times of tachistoscopically-presented pictures, Eriksen (1951) found little evidence for homosexual motives with paranoid or other Ss. More recently, Aronson (1950), using paper and pencil tests as well as projective techniques, found evidence supportive of the Freudian hypothesis. In general, paranoid psychotics gave more homosexually-indicative responses than did either non-paranoid psychotics or normal control Ss. However, Aronson concluded that faulty ego controls as a function of psychosis may also have been instrumental in eliciting a greater number of these responses from both his clinical populations.

Perceptual Theory

The finding that individuals are selectively sensitive in their reactions to various types of environmental stimuli has been accounted for by the postulation of an interaction between perceptual and personality variables (Bruner, 1951; Bruner & Postman, 1948; Frenkel-Brunswick, 1951). Various experiments have tended to show that past experience and current motives influence the S's perception (Bruner, 1951; Bruner & Postman, 1948; Eriksen, 1951; Postman, Bruner, & McGinnies, 1948). The time required for correct verbal recognition of tachistoscopically-presented stimuli has commonly been used as a measure of selective perception. Using recognition times to "neutral" stimuli as a baseline, it has been found that relatively fast recognition times characterize responses to stimuli which are congruent with the S's areas of concern (e.g., values, needs, motives, etc.). This more rapid recognition can be interpreted as a function of greater familiarity with stimuli pertaining to areas of interest or concern for the individual. Conversely, slower recognition times would be related to stimuli reflecting areas of less individual concern or a lesser degree of familiarity. Time required for correct identification was felt to be at least partly determined by response availability.

From the psychoanalytic point of view, the projective defense system and frontal attack on perceived threat by the paranoid is directly related to his underlying concern with homosexual impulses. There is supposedly a greater awareness of and sensitivity toward homosexually-connotative stimuli. Within the perceptual methodology, it was reasoned, this sensitivity should reflect itself in time required for correct recognition of tachistoscopically-presented words connoting homosexuality. For reasons of availability paranoid schizophrenics were employed as the paranoid population, and hypotheses were formulated following these considerations. In the major hypothesis it was predicted that paranoid schizophrenics would verbally identify words with a homosexual meaning relatively more rapidly than would either normal control or non-paranoid schizophrenic Ss. There were also several corollary control hypotheses dealing with recognition times to words other than homosexual, i.e., neutral words and heterosexual words.

METHODOLOGY

Subjects

The Ss consisted of 25 paranoid schizophrenics, 25 unclassified (non-paranoid) schizophrenics, and 25 normals. All were white, American-born, male war veterans, under 45 years of age. None had visual or intellectual deficiencies marked enough to cause undue difficulty in identifying or reporting tachistoscopically-presented words. Each S was required to read above the sixth-grade level on the Jastak-Bijou *Wide Range Achievement Test* (McGinnies, 1950) to minimize the possible effect of reading ability on performance.

The diagnosis of each S in the two schizophrenic groups was established by a staff of hospital psychiatrists and was arrived at by an evaluation of the presenting symptom picture. Differential diagnosis depended almost completely on descriptive nosological features. In addition, information derived from personal interviews and clinical records was examined for corroborative descriptive evidence in each case. The possibility of psychoanalytic considerations having influenced diagnosis and having contaminated the sample was minimal. There were evidences of concern over homosexuality in a number of records, but these appeared in both schizophrenic groups. Apparently in no case had homosexual ideation been a criterion for diagnosis. All Ss were cooperative and showed reality contact good enough to allow them to be tested. The normal group was composed mainly of patients in a general hospital with various medical conditions. None of the latter reported ever having any emotional difficulties severe enough to require either psychiatric consultation or treatment.

Table 5-1 presents a comparison of the groups in terms of age, education, and reading ability. Only in age are there any differences between the groups; the unclassified schizophrenics are slightly, but significantly, younger than the other two groups. The point could be raised that the younger unclassified schizophrenics might develop paranoid symptomatology as they grew older. Such a radical shift in defense systems in a short time interval was deemed unlikely, and the age differences were not considered important.

TABLE 5-1. Comparison of Experimental Ss as to Age, Education, and Reading Ability

	Age		Education		Reading Ability	
	Mean	*t* Value	Mean	*t* Value	Mean	*t* Value
1. Normals	33.32	$t_{12} = 2.91^*$	11.04	$t_{12} = 0.4$	9.52	$t_{12} = 0.82$
2. Unclassified Schizophrenics	28.52	$t_{13} = 0.09$	11.32	$t_{13} = 0.7$	10.02	$t_{13} = 1.71$
3. Paranoid Schizophrenics	33.48	$t_{23} = 3.10^*$	11.56	$t_{23} = 0.3$	10.65	$t_{23} = 0.88$

* Significant at beyond the .01 level of confidence.

Stimulus Words

Such extraneous variables as word length, familiarity, and affective value were controlled in the selection of stimulus words. First, a tachistoscopic study was conducted with 10 Ss, using 30 5- and 6-letter words equated for usage frequency according to the Thorndike-Lorge word counts (Thorndike & Lorge, 1944). Time for correct verbal identification was noted. When the standard error of differences between means was calculated, the *t* value was 0.76. This difference was not significant and indicated 5- and 6-letter words could be considered equivalent for purposes of the study.

Following this, a preliminary list of 200 5- and 6-letter words was constructed. 40 words considered to have homosexual connotation, 40 purportedly heterosexual, and 120 words probably non-sexual in meaning were used. Two forms of this list were presented to 40 judges, a peer group of the experimental populations.

On the first form of the list, judges rated the words on the dimension of affectivity, indicating the emotional value each word had for them. Following this, a re-arranged list of the same words was presented them with instructions to classify only those words with which they were familiar [1] as being homosexual, heterosexual, or non-sexual in meaning. A "Don't Know" category was also provided, in which they placed words with which they had some familiarity but about whose meaning they were unsure. Any word omitted or placed in the "Don't Know" category by 5 raters was considered to be too obscure to be of value and was discarded.

The affective ratings were converted into McCall *T* scores, and interquartile ranges were computed. Percentages of agreement were calculated

[1] It was felt no available frequency of word usage tables would give as adequate a measure of a word's familiarity as would a peer group. This writer felt, with McGinnies (1950), that frequency of usage tables derived from popular periodicals do not list socially taboo words in the frequency with which they are actually used in written and spoken language.

TABLE 5-2. Words Used as Stimulus Variable Along with Judges' Ratings

Word	Affective Rating M_T	$Q_1 - Q_3$	% Agreement on Sexual Meaning	Word	Affective Rating M_T	$Q_1 - Q_3$	% Agreement on Sexual Meaning
Homosexual				*Non-Sexual*			
Pleasant				*Pleasant*			
Fruit	42.9	39 — 46	70	Jolly	40.1	37 — 41	90
Fairy	50.6	44 — 58	85	Alert	41.0	36 — 46	97.5
Pansy	52.0	45 — 60	50	Prize	41.2	38 — 43	90
				Church	38.1	35 — 40	97.5
Neutral				Famous	40.0	37 — 42	92.5
Homos	55.5	51 — 60	82.4	Wealth	41.2	38 — 44	95
Blown	53.6	49 — 59	71.1				
Rectum	56.6	53 — 61	52.5	*Neutral*			
				Cellar	52.1	45 — 60	90
Unpleasant				Turtle	48.8	46 — 51	100
Sissy	59.9	47 — 63	52.6	Tablet	49.2	46 — 51	100
Sucked	59.0	53 — 63	72.5	Swish	50.4	46 — 52	90
Queer	60.4	58 — 63	94.9	Yeast	49.8	47 — 51	97.4
				Ounce	49.0	46 — 51	95
Heterosexual							
Pleasant				*Unpleasant*			
Caress	40.4	35 — 43	100	Murder	61.9	61 — 66	90
Bosom	42.4	38 — 45	90	Nausea	63.1	60 — 66	90
Breast	43.0	39 — 47	92.5	Lynch	61.9	59 — 67	92.5
				Death	63.3	61 — 68	97.5
Neutral				Vomit	63.6	62 — 67	95
Piece	49.1	46 — 51	97.5	Agony	64.5	61 — 68	89.7
Pickup	49.8	46 — 52	95				
Screw	51.4	49 — 55	97.4				
Unpleasant							
Fucked	57.9	51 — 66	100				
Whore	60.1	57 — 64	100				
Rapist	62.4	61 — 66	92.5				

for words in the sexual categories, and the results of both sets of judgments were combined. A list of 36 test words was then selected, made up of those 9 words in each sexual category and those 18 words in the non-sexual category most clearly differentiated by the judges for both sexuality and affectivity. This was the list of words used in the study (see Table 5-2).

It can be seen in Table 5-2 that the judges were less consistent with both affective and sexual ratings for homosexual words than with others, perhaps because few, if any, of these words had an exclusively homosexual meaning. The inclusion of those 9 words in the homosexual category was dictated by practical considerations, although it was recognized that their lack of denotative meaning might work against the principal hypothesis of the study. That is, if words purportedly homosexual were familiar to the experimental populations in contexts other than a homosexual one, then they should be recognized more rapidly by all groups than would be the case if they were related exclusively to homosexuality as an area of concern. It was felt this limiting factor might reduce the size of the hypothesized differences.

Procedure

Each S was tested individually. In a Gerbrands tachistoscope, he was shown a group of 9 pretest words to familiarize him with the apparatus and procedure. Then he was shown the list of test words. Both pretest and test words were capitalized and doubled spaced, electrically typed on individual sheets of white paper.

Each word was presented once at each timer setting; and, wherever possible, the first exposure time for any of the test words was .05 faster than S's quickest recognition time to any of the pretest words.[2] Exposure time was lengthened in even steps of .01 sec. until correct recognition occurred. If, after 25 successive exposures to the same word, S was still unable to recognize it correctly, step-intervals were increased to .05 sec. This was done primarily to reduce feelings of frustration in S. When a word was correctly recognized, the setting of the timer was recorded, and the next word was presented. The procedure was the same for all words with all Ss.

Words were presented in a random order, no two Ss being shown the words in the same order. Participants were requested to maintain silence about the procedure, and there was no evidence to indicate they did otherwise.

RESULTS

In designing the experiment, it was felt the analysis of variance technique would provide a meaningful statistical treatment. Of the requirements to be met for analysis of variance, that of homogeneity of variance in the experimental population was determined by Bartlett's test of homogeneity of variance, as suggested by Edwards (1950). The derived chi-square was 0.537. With a chi-square this small, the null hypothesis could not be rejected. A second requirement, normality of distribution in the experimental population for the variables considered, was assumed. Also, the independence of individual measurements was favored by random presentation of words in the list to each S in the experiment (see procedure). The particular analysis of variance technique used was a modifi-

---

[2] The method was essentially that of a reaction time experiment. The terms "reaction time" and "time for correct recognition" were considered synonymous for the present study.

cation of one found in Edwards (1950, p. 295) for analysis of data involving successive trials. It was chosen because it tended to minimize the effect of practice upon recognition times of Ss to words presented successively in the test list and because it allowed a sharper test of variance between groups of Ss to be made (see Table 5-3).

**TABLE 5-3.   Results of the Analysis of Variance of Times Required
for Correct Recognition of Words**

Source of Variance	df	Mean Square	F	p
Total Variance	2699			
A. *Between Subjects*	74			
1. Between Groups of Subjects	2	229.4	<1	N.S.
2. Residual (within) Variance	72	427.9		
B. *Within Subjects*	2625			
1. Between Words	35	113.0	9.28	.01
2. Between Affective Categories (Holding Subjects and Sexuality Constant)	2*	24.01	1.97	N.S.
3. Between Sexual Categories (Holding Subjects and Affectivity Constant)	2*	367.8	30.2	.01
C. *Interaction Terms*	2590			
Words x Groups**	70	14.5	1.19	N.S.
Affectivity x Sexuality x Groups	8*	10.9	<1	N.S.
Groups x Affectivity (Sexuality Held Constant)	4*	3.3	<1	N.S.
Affectivity x Sexuality (Groups Held Constant)	4*	256.9	21.09	.01
Groups x Sexuality (Affectivity Held Constant)	4*	32.15	2.64	.05
Residual (Pooled Subjects x Groups Interaction) Variance	2520	12.18		

* Degrees of freedom for these variables are from the 70 *df* in the overall interaction term, Words x Groups.
** "Groups," where used in this table, refers to groups of Ss.

From the table it can be seen that there were differences between words, significant at the .01 level of confidence. This finding, that individual Ss reacted differentially to words in the test list, was essential to the proposition that the perceptual technique used in the experiment could yield differences among groups of Ss. Without this finding, further examination of the data would have been superfluous.

Affective connotation of the words did not differentiate. By itself, the emotional quality of the words did not appear to be an important variable. An extremely important item for the hypothesis under test concerned the interaction term, Groups x Sexuality, which was significant at beyond the .05 level of confidence. When this interaction was examined, it was found that the two schizophrenic populations behaved alike with both hetero-sexual and non-sexual words, having slower recognition times to these than did the normal population. On the other hand, with the homosexual words, paranoid schizophrenics and normals behaved alike, both having signifi-cantly faster recognition times to these words than did the unclassified schizophrenics.

It had been planned to use reaction times to non-sexual words as a common baseline from which to make comparisons among the groups of Ss to homosexual and heterosexual words. The finding that statistically signifi-cant differences existed among groups in their recognition times to non-sexual words necessitated statistical treatment of the data beyond that which had been provided for in the original design.

It seemed likely that unknown, uncontrolled variables had affected the groups of Ss differently in terms of their word recognition times. One possible explanation for this disparity may have been lack of concentrative ability on the part of the clinical populations. It is well known that the concentrative attention span of psychotics is limited, and this factor may have operated generally to increase their reaction times to all classes of words. Whatever the explanation, it was necessary to transform the data statistically in such a way as to equate the experimental groups for recogni-tion times to non-sexual words. Analysis of covariance, following McNemar (1949), appeared to be a method of considerable promise for eliminating the effect of these uncontrolled variables on differential word recognition times.

It was also found that differences in recognition times for the various affective categories in the non-sexual words had been well below statistical significance for each experimental group. However, in cognizance of previ-ous research in the area of selective perception, it was decided to use recog-nition times to non-sexual neutral words as the common baseline from which to examine reactions of each experimental group to heterosexual and homosexual words. Two separate analyses of covariance were done: the first comparing experimental groups on reaction times to heterosexual words, the second comparing reaction times to homosexual words. In both analy-ses, recognition times for non-sexual neutral words were held constant.

In the analysis with heterosexual words the derived F with untrans-formed data was not significant, nor did it attain significance following the covariance transformation. This lack of significance indicated there were no appreciable differences among the groups of Ss in their reactions to the heterosexual words in the study, when groups were equated for reactions to non-sexual neutral words.

The second analysis of covariance, with homosexual words, provided definite evidence upholding the major hypothesis of the study. The results of this comparison indicated that, with corrections made for differential reactions to non-sexual neutral words, there was a statistically significant difference among the experimental groups in their reaction times to homosexual words. The derived F with untransformed data was not significant; but with the covariance transformation the F became 4.984, significant at the .01 level of confidence. The means of reaction times were then adjusted, following McNemar (1949, pp. 328–329), and the standard error of the difference calculated. Following this, t tests were applied to determine the sources of the difference implied in the F ratio.

These comparisons, shown in Table 5-4, demonstrated that the paranoid group differed considerably from the normal group. They reacted more

TABLE 5-4.   *t* Tests for Significance of Differences Between Means of Total Recognition Times for all Homosexual Words Following Analysis of Covariance Transformation

Subjects	Adjusted Mean for Total in Hundredths of a Second	t	df	p
Paranoid	40.30			
versus Normal		3.10	71	.01
versus Unclassified		2.21	71	.05
Normal	52.65			
versus Unclassified		0.90	71	N.S.
Unclassified	49.08			

$\sigma\text{Difference} = \sqrt{(\text{Residual Variance})\ (1/n + 1/n)}$
$\sigma\text{Difference} = \sqrt{197.802\ (1/25 + 1/25)}$
$\sigma\text{Difference} = \ 3.98$

rapidly to homosexual words, the difference being significant at the .01 level of confidence. When the two psychotic groups were compared, the difference was significant at the .05 level, with paranoids reacting faster than unclassifieds. The last comparison, normals vs. unclassifieds, was well below statistical significance. It would appear then, from the results of these analyses of covariance, that the major hypothesis was supported.

DISCUSSION

Within the limitations of this study, the results demonstrated a relationship between paranoid schizophrenia and homosexual impulses, as was hypothesized. These findings supported the psychoanalytic proposition. Furthermore, the finding that paranoid schizophrenics correctly recognized homosexual words more rapidly than did unclassified schizophrenics, coupled with the finding that unclassified schizophrenics did not differ from normals in recognition times for homosexual words, indicated that sensitivity to homosexual stimuli was more a function of the paranoid components involved than of schizophrenia itself. This also supported Freud's contention.

Homosexuality appeared to be an area of greater concern for paranoid schizophrenics than for either unclassified or normal Ss. Regardless of their willingness or ability to verbalize overtly their concern with homosexuality, the greater relative sensitivity of paranoid Ss to homosexual words indicated they had more familiarity with these words. Had it been possible to employ words more denotatively homosexual, rather than words with other meanings in addition to a homosexual one, greater sensitivity of paranoid Ss to these stimuli might have been even more clearly demonstrated. Despite this limiting factor, there was fairly clearcut evidence that it was the paranoid component involved in paranoid schizophrenia which was related to concern regarding homosexuality.

There was also some interesting qualitative information. For example, a number of paranoid Ss reacted to the word "queer" with a great deal of feeling, stating how much they hated "queers." One S, a chronic paranoid, recognized the tachistoscopically-presented word "homos" and commented it must be a Latin word, although new to him. Shortly thereafter, he told the examiner about the female psychologist who works with the FBI and who keeps calling him a "homo" over the radio. There were several other indications of high idiosyncratic familiarity with homosexual words among paranoid Ss which undoubtedly influenced time for correct recognition. On the other hand, none of the unclassified schizophrenics gave any overt sign noted by E of overconcern with homosexual words, despite the fact a number of them had histories indicating that homosexuality was an area of conflict. These qualitative findings may be interpreted as indicating that to be "concerned with" or in conflict over homosexual impulses or any other impulses may be important but not sufficient in and of itself in the determination of perceptual response. In fact, the bulk of presently available evidence points up the likelihood of perceptual response reflecting the complex interaction of many stimulus and intraorganismic determinants.

Whether homosexuality is a *major* area of concern for paranoid individuals, or whether it alone is causative of behavior diagnosed as paranoid, could not be determined from the present findings. There was a relationship demonstrated between paranoid mechanisms and homosexual impulses, and it would appear reasonable to infer that homosexuality, as an area of concern, is involved in the determination of paranoid personality components. However, there may well be other areas of concern that serve to differentiate paranoid from other individuals. How and to what degree homosexuality or other areas of concern are related to paranoid aspects of personality functioning is a possible subject for further studies. The perceptual technique used in this research may also be of value in future research of a more general nature. Perceptual tests of hypotheses derived from personality theory might well contribute to existing knowledge in this area.

The findings in the present study agree in general with other findings, with the exception of the experiment by Eriksen (1951). The more direct test of the psychoanalytic postulate in the work reported here may have accounted for the difference in results. Because there were fewer variables extraneous to the psychoanalytic proposition to be considered, these results may be somewhat more indicative than were those of Eriksen.

SUMMARY

The present study was undertaken to investigate the relationship postulated in psychoanalytic theory between paranoid schizophrenia and homosexual impulses. The methodological orientation was derived from research in the area of selective perception. Time required for correct verbal recognition of various classes of tachistoscopically-presented words was used, previous research having indicated that stimuli pertaining to areas of individual concern are recognized more rapidly than "neutral" stimuli, presumably as a function of greater individual familiarity. It was held that motivational variables were involved in the determination of areas of individual concern and that the interaction of motivational with perceptual variables would affect perceptually-mediated response. If homosexuality were an area of concern for paranoid individuals, words reflecting homosexuality would be recognized relatively more rapidly by them than by individuals less concerned with homosexuality. Three groups of Ss were employed: paranoid schizophrenics, unclassified schizophrenics, and normals. Each S's time for correct verbal recognition of tachistoscopically-presented words from a test list was recorded. This test list was composed of words which had been previously judged on the dimensions of affectivity, sexuality, and familiarity. Word length was controlled. It was found that: (a) affective value of the words had little effect on time required for correct verbal recognition; (b) paranoid Ss recognized homosexual words significantly faster than did the other two groups of Ss; and (c) normals and unclassified schizophrenics did not differ significantly in recognition times to homosexual words. In addition, differences in recognition times to heterosexual words were not significant among the groups. These findings supported the psychoanalytic proposition, in that there was a relationship demonstrated between paranoid aspects of personality functioning and homosexuality. Whether homosexuality was a major area of concern for paranoid individuals was not determined.

REFERENCES

Alexander, F., & Menninger, W. C. The relation of persecutory delusions to the functioning of the gastrointestinal tract. In S. S. Tomkins (Ed.) *Contemporary psychopathology*. Cambridge, Mass.: Harvard University Press, 1946. Pp. 381–393.

Aronson, M. L. A *study of the Freudian theory of paranoia by means of a group of psychological tests*. Unpublished Ph.D. dissertation, University of Michigan, 1950.

Bruner, J. S. Personality dynamics and the process of perceiving. In R. R. Blake and G. V. Ramsey (Eds.) *Perception: An approach to personality*. New York: Ronald, 1951. Pp. 121–147.

Bruner, J. S., & Postman, L. An approach to social perception. In W. Dennis (Ed.) *Current trends in social psychology*. Pittsburgh: University of Pittsburgh Press, 1948. Pp. 71–118.

Edwards, A. L. *Experimental design in psychological research*. New York: Rinehart, 1950.

Eriksen, C. W. Perceptual defense as a function of unacceptable needs. *J. abnorm. soc. Psychol.*, 1951, 46, 557–564.

Frenkel-Brunswick, E. *Personality theory and perception*. In R. R. Blake and G. V. Ramsey (Eds.) *Perception: an approach to personality*. New York: Ronald, 1951. Pp. 356–420.

Freud, S. Psycho-analytic notes upon an autobiographical account of a case of paranoia. *Collected papers*, Vol. III. London: Hogarth, 1948. Pp. 387–470.

Gardner, G. E. Evidence of homosexuality in one hundred and twenty unanalyzed cases with paranoid content. In S. S. Tomkins (Ed.) *Contemporary psychopathology*. Cambridge, Mass.: Harvard University Press, 1946. Pp. 394–397.

Jastak, J. *Wide Range Achievement Test*. Wilmington, Del.: Story, 1946.

McGinnies, E. Discussion of Howes' and Solomon's "Note on emotionality and perceptual defense." *Psychol. Rev.*, 1950, 57, 235–240.

McNemar, Q. *Psychological statistics*. New York: Wiley, 1949.

Postman, L., Bruner, J. S., & McGinnies, E. Personal values as selective factors in perception. *J. abnorm. soc. Psychol.*, 1948, 43, 142–154.

Sears, R. R. *Survey of objective studies of psychoanalytic concepts*. New York: Social Science Res. Council, Bulletin 51, 1943.

Thorndike, E. L., & Lorge, I. *The teacher's wordbook of 30,000 words*. New York: Teachers College, Columbia University, 1944.

ANALYTICAL PSYCHOLOGY: CARL G. JUNG

II

Some theorists tend to utilize constructs and postulates which, while unique in their particulars, are largely reflections of the majority of professional opinion concerning the relevant issues and are hence maximally consonant with the current state of the field. Other theorists tend to develop concepts which are relatively unique and often at variance with predominant professional opinion. If we were to classify personality theories on a scale of uniqueness of major constructs, Carl Gustav Jung would stand high on the scale, since certain of his constructs, particularly the concepts of archetype and collective unconscious, are quite unusual and not widely accepted. On the other hand, Jung would fall at quite the opposite end of our scale with respect to his postulation of the attitudes of introversion and extraversion. These latter terms, at least in a general form, are common to everyday usage, to clinical psychologists, and to such empirically oriented individuals as Hans J. Eysenck. In selecting materials relevant to Jung's work, we have attempted to deal with both the unique and the widely accepted concepts in Jungian theory, as well as to acquaint the reader with Jung's applications of his theory to psychotherapy and his approach to psychological research.

The first article by Jung serves to dispel immediately the notion, often held by those newly introduced to Jung's work, that he was a rather "far out" theoretician, who never came to grips with the realities of practical application. The article reprinted here is an extremely straightforward, clear presentation, in his own words, of Jung's approach to psychotherapy. Here he acknowledges his debt to others, particularly Freud and Adler, then proceeds to set forth and relate to his theory of personality what is clearly a Jungian approach to therapy.

When we search Jung's work for examples of his empirical research, we are faced with a dilemma: on the one hand, we have Jung's view that much of the work he reported in support of his theory was research; on the other, we have the view of critics that Jung reported virtually no work which can legitimately be called empirical research. The conflict of opinion represents a difference in viewpoints as to what constitutes research. If research is defined as involving simply careful observation and intensive study, much of Jung's work would certainly qualify. The more widely accepted definition, however, holds that research involves objective observation and measurement under controlled conditions, and, ordinarily, quantification and statistical analysis. Virtually none of Jung's work can be seen as fulfilling the conditions of this latter definition. His research consisted largely of intensive studies of individual cases, utilizing such procedures as dream analysis, active imagination, and spontaneous art. In addition, he has drawn support for such concepts as archetype from his comparative studies in mythology, religion, alchemy, and the occult. In one area, however, the study of the psychology of complexes, Jung did report at least a small amount of quantification and control. In this work, Jung utilized the word association method, recording the subject's verbal response, reaction time, and certain physiological responses to the presentation of each of a series of stimulus words. The method and some of this research are summarized in our second selection, "The Association Method," one of a series of lectures which Jung delivered at Clark University in 1909.

Despite the relative lack of empirical research in Jung's own work, others have entered his constructs into a variety of quantitative (though largely demographic and correlational) investigations. Most of this research has included primarily Jung's conceptualizations involving attitudes (introversion and extraversion) and functions (thinking, feeling, sensing, and intuiting). Though early research on these variables was relatively unsophisticated, involving largely demographic studies of, for example, the relative degrees of introversion and extraversion found as a function of sex, age, or occupation, more recent research has seen the development of reliable inventories which measure the various attitudes and functions. These inventories have been utilized in a wide variety of research, relating the attitudes and functions to numerous demographic, ability, personality and adjustment variables. Two recent reports are particularly relevant. In the third selection, Bradway reports an interesting comparison of the self-typing of Jungian analysts with the typing provided by two major inventories, the Myers-Briggs and the Gray-Wheelwright. In the last article, Stricker and Ross report a series of investigations in which the construct validity of the Myers-Briggs Type Indicator was assessed. Included in this series of studies is a correlational comparison between the Myers-Briggs and the Gray-Wheelwright, indicating the level of concurrent validity of the two instruments as measures of the major Jungian constructs.

6

The Aims of Psychotherapy

CARL G. JUNG

It is generally agreed today that neuroses are functional psychic disturbances and are therefore to be cured preferably by psychological treatment. But when we come to the question of the structure of the neuroses and the principles of therapy, all agreement ends, and we have to acknowledge that we have as yet no fully satisfactory conception of the nature of the neuroses or of the principles of treatment. While it is true that two currents or schools of thought have gained a special hearing, they by no means exhaust the number of divergent opinions that actually exist. There are also numerous non-partisans who, amid the general conflict of opinion, have their own special views. If, therefore, we wanted to paint a comprehensive picture of this diversity, we should have to mix upon our palette all the hues and shadings of the rainbow. I would gladly paint such a picture if it lay within my power, for I have always felt the need for a conspectus of the many viewpoints. I have never succeeded in the long run in not giving divergent opinions their due. Such opinions could never arise, much less secure a following, if they did not correspond to some special disposition, some special character, some fundamental psychological fact that is more or less universal. Were we to exclude one such opinion as simply wrong and worthless, we should be rejecting this particular disposition or this particular fact as a misinterpretation—in other words, we should be doing violence to our own empirical material. The wide approval which greeted Freud's explanation of neurosis in terms of sexual causation and his view that the happenings in the psyche turn essentially upon infantile pleasure and its satisfaction should be instructive to the psychologist. It shows him that this manner of thinking and feeling coincides with a fairly widespread trend or spiritual current which, independently of Freud's

"The Aims of Psychotherapy." from *The Practice of Psychotherapy in The Collected Works of C. G. Jung*, Vol. 16, transl. R. F. C. Hull (copyright 1954 by Bollingen Foundation, Inc.; 2nd. ed., 1966). Reprinted by permission of Princeton University Press and Routledge & Kegan Paul Ltd. [Delivered as a lecture at a congress of the German Society for Psychotherapy, 1929. Published as "Ziele der Psychotherapie" in *Seelenprobleme der Gegenwart* (Zurich, 1931), pp. 87–114. Previously trans. by C. F. Baynes and W. S. Dell in *Modern Man in Search of a Soul* (London and New York, 1933).—Editors.]

theory, has made itself felt in other places, in other circumstances, in other minds, and in other forms. I should call it a manifestation of the collective psyche. Let me remind you here of the works of Havelock Ellis and Auguste Forel and the contributors to *Anthropophyteia;* [1] then of the changed attitude to sex in Anglo-Saxon countries during the post-Victorian period, and the broad discussion of sexual matters in literature, which had already started with the French realists. Freud is one of the exponents of a contemporary psychological fact which has a special history of its own; but for obvious reasons we cannot go into that here.

The acclaim which Adler, like Freud, has met with on both sides of the Atlantic points similarly to the undeniable fact that, for a great many people, the need for self-assertion arising from a sense of inferiority is a plausible basis of explanation. Nor can it be disputed that this view accounts for psychic actualities which are not given their due in the Freudian system. I need hardly mention in detail the collective psychological forces and social factors that favour the Adlerian view and make it their theoretical exponent. These matters are sufficiently obvious.

It would be an unpardonable error to overlook the element of truth in both the Freudian and the Adlerian viewpoints, but it would be no less unpardonable to take either of them as the sole truth. Both truths correspond to psychic realities. There are in fact some cases which by and large can best be described and explained by the one theory, and some by the other.

I can accuse neither of these two investigators of any fundamental error; on the contrary, I endeavour to apply both hypotheses as far as possible because I fully recognize their relative rightness. It would certainly never have occurred to me to depart from Freud's path had I not stumbled upon facts which forced me into modifications. And the same is true of my relation to the Adlerian viewpoint.

After what has been said it seems hardly necessary to add that I hold the truth of my own deviationist views to be equally relative, and feel myself so very much the mere exponent of another disposition that I could almost say with Coleridge: "I believe in the one and only saving Church, of which at present I am the only member." [2]

It is in applied psychology, if anywhere, that we must be modest today and bear with an apparent plurality of contradictory opinions; for we are still far from having anything like a thorough knowledge of the human psyche, that most challenging field of scientific inquiry. At present we have merely more or less plausible opinions that cannot be squared with one another.

---

[1] [Published at Leipzig, 1904–13.—Editors.]
[2] [It has not been possible to trace this quotation and to find the original wording.—Editors.]

If, therefore, I undertake to say something about my views I hope I shall not be misunderstood. I am not advertising a novel truth, still less am I announcing a final gospel. I can only speak of attempts to throw light on psychic facts that are obscure to me, or of efforts to overcome therapeutic difficulties.

And it is just with this last point that I should like to begin, for here lies the most pressing need for modifications. As is well known, one can get along for quite a time with an inadequate theory, but not with inadequate therapeutic methods. In my psychotherapeutic practice of nearly thirty years I have met with a fair number of failures which made a far deeper impression on me than my successes. Anybody can have successes in psychotherapy, starting with the primitive medicine-man and faith-healer. The psychotherapist learns little or nothing from his successes, for they chiefly confirm him in his mistakes. But failures are priceless experiences because they not only open the way to a better truth but force us to modify our views and methods.

I certainly recognize how much my work has been furthered first by Freud and then by Adler, and in practice I try to acknowledge this debt by making use of their views, whenever possible, in the treatment of my patients. Nevertheless I must insist that I have experienced failures which, I felt, might have been avoided had I considered the facts that subsequently forced me to modify their views.

To describe all the situations I came up against is almost impossible, so I must content myself with singling out a few typical cases. It was with older patients that I had the greatest difficulties, that is, with persons over forty. In handling younger people I generally get along with the familiar viewpoints of Freud and Adler, for these tend to bring the patient to a certain level of adaptation and normality. Both views are eminently applicable to the young, apparently without leaving any disturbing after-effects. In my experience this is not so often the case with older people. It seems to me that the basic facts of the psyche undergo a very marked alteration in the course of life, so much so that we could almost speak of a psychology of life's morning and a psychology of its afternoon. As a rule, the life of a young person is characterized by a general expansion and a striving towards concrete ends; and his neurosis seems mainly to rest on his hesitation or shrinking back from this necessity. But the life of an older person is characterized by a contraction of forces, by the affirmation of what has been achieved, and by the curtailment of further growth. His neurosis comes mainly from his clinging to a youthful attitude which is now out of season. Just as the young neurotic is afraid of life, so the older one shrinks back from death. What was a normal goal for the young man becomes a neurotic hindrance to the old—just as, through his hesitation to face the world, the young neurotic's originally normal dependence on his parents grows into an incest-relationship that is inimical to life. It is natural that neurosis, resistance, repression, transference, "guiding fictions," and so forth should have one meaning in the young person and quite another in the old, despite apparent similarities. The aims of therapy should undoubtedly be modified to meet this fact. Hence the age of the patient seems to me a most important *indicium*.

But there are various *indicia* also within the youthful phase of life. Thus, in my estimation, it is a technical blunder to apply the Freudian viewpoint to a patient with the Adlerian type of psychology, that is, an unsuccessful person with an infantile need to assert himself. Conversely, it would be a gross misunderstanding to force the Adlerian viewpoint on a successful man with a pronounced pleasure-principle psychology. When in a quandary the resistances of the patient may be valuable signposts. I am inclined to take deep-seated resistances seriously at first, paradoxical as this may sound, for I am convinced that the doctor does not necessarily know better than the patient's own psychic constitution, of which the patient himself may be quite unconscious. This modesty on the part of the doctor is altogether becoming in view of the fact that there is not only no generally valid psychology today but rather an untold variety of temperaments and of more or less individual psyches that refuse to fit into any scheme.

You know that in this matter of temperament I postulate two different basic attitudes in accordance with the typical differences already suspected by many students of human nature—namely, the extraverted and the introverted attitudes. These attitudes, too, I take to be important *indicia*, and likewise the predominance of one particular psychic function over the others.[3]

The extraordinary diversity of individual life necessitates constant modifications of theory which are often applied quite unconsciously by the doctor himself, although in principle they may not accord at all with his theoretical creed.

While we are on this question of temperament I should not omit to mention that there are some people whose attitude is essentially spiritual and others whose attitude is essentially materialistic. It must not be imagined that such an attitude is acquired accidentally or springs from mere misunderstanding. Very often they are ingrained passions which no criticism and no persuasion can stamp out; there are even cases where an apparently outspoken materialism has its source in a denial of religious temperament. Cases of the reverse type are more easily credited today, although they are not more frequent than the others. This too is an *indicium* which in my opinion ought not to be overlooked.

When we use the word *indicium* it might appear to mean, as is usual in medical parlance, that this or that treatment is indicated. Perhaps this should be the case, but psychotherapy has at present reached no such

---

[3] [Viz., thinking, feeling, sensation, and intuition.—Editors.]

degree of certainty—for which reason our *indicia* are unfortunately not much more than warnings against one-sidedness.

The human psyche is a thing of enormous ambiguity. In every single case we have to ask ourselves whether an attitude or a so-called *habitus* is authentic, or whether it may not be just a compensation for its opposite. I must confess that I have so often been deceived in this matter that in any concrete case I am at pains to avoid all theoretical presuppositions about the structure of the neurosis and about what the patient can and ought to do. As far as possible I let pure experience decide the therapeutic aims. This may perhaps seem strange, because it is commonly supposed that the therapist has an aim. But in psychotherapy it seems to me positively advisable for the doctor not to have too fixed an aim. He can hardly know better than the nature and will to live of the patient. The great decisions in human life usually have far more to do with the instincts and other mysterious unconscious factors than with conscious will and well-meaning reasonableness. The shoe that fits one person pinches another; there is no universal recipe for living. Each of us carries his own life-form within him—an irrational form which no other can outbid.

All this naturally does not prevent us from doing our utmost to make the patient normal and reasonable. If the therapeutic results are satisfactory, we can probably let it go at that. If not, then for better or worse the therapist must be guided by the patient's own irrationalities. Here we must follow nature as a guide, and what the doctor then does is less a question of treatment than of developing the creative possibilities latent in the patient himself.

What I have to say begins where the treatment leaves off and this development sets in. Thus my contribution to psychotherapy confines itself to those cases where rational treatment does not yield satisfactory results. The clinical material at my disposal is of a peculiar composition: new cases are decidedly in the minority. Most of them already have some form of psychotherapeutic treatment behind them, with partial or negative results. About a third of my cases are not suffering from any clinically definable neurosis, but from the senselessness and aimlessness of their lives. I should not object if this were called the general neurosis of our age. Fully two thirds of my patients are in the second half of life.

This peculiar material sets up a special resistance to rational methods of treatment, probably because most of my patients are socially well-adapted individuals, often of outstanding ability, to whom normalization means nothing. As for so-called normal people, there I really am in a fix, for I have no ready-made philosophy of life to hand out to them. In the majority of my cases the resources of the conscious mind are exhausted (or, in ordinary English, they are "stuck"). It is chiefly this fact that forces me to look for hidden possibilities. For I do not know what to say to the patient when he asks me, "What do you advise? What shall I do?" I don't know either. I only know one thing: when my conscious mind no longer sees any possible road ahead and consequently gets stuck, my unconscious psyche will react to the unbearable standstill.

This "getting stuck" is a psychic occurrence so often repeated during the course of human history that it has become the theme of many myths and fairytales. We are told of the Open sesame! to the locked door, or of some helpful animal who finds the hidden way. In other words, getting stuck is a typical event which, in the course of time, has evoked typical reactions and compensations. We may therefore expect with some probability that something similar will appear in the reactions of the unconscious, as, for example, in dreams.

In such cases, then, my attention is directed more particularly to dreams. This is not because I am tied to the notion that dreams must always be called to the rescue, or because I possess a mysterious dream-theory which tells me how everything must shape itself; but quite simply from perplexity. I do not know where else to go for help, and so I try to find it in dreams. These at least present us with images pointing to something or other, and that is better than nothing. I have no theory about dreams, I do not know how dreams arise. And I am not at all sure that my way of handling dreams even deserves the name of a "method." I share all your prejudices against dream-interpretation as the quintessence of uncertainty and arbitrariness. On the other hand, I know that if we meditate on a dream sufficiently long and thoroughly, if we carry it around with us and turn it over and over, something almost always comes of it. This something is not of course a scientific result to be boasted about or rationalized; but it is an important practical hint which shows the patient what the unconscious is aiming at. Indeed, it ought not to matter to me whether the result of my musings on the dream is scientifically verifiable or tenable, otherwise I am pursuing an ulterior—and therefore autoerotic—aim. I must content myself wholly with the fact that the result means something to the patient and sets his life in motion again. I may allow myself only one criterion for the result of my labours: Does it work? As for my scientific hobby —my desire to know *why* it works—this I must reserve for my spare time.

Infinitely varied are the contents of the initial dreams, that is, the dreams that come at the outset of the treatment. In many cases they point directly to the past and recall things lost and forgotten. For very often the standstill and disorientation arise when life has become one-sided, and this may, in psychological terms, cause a sudden loss of libido. All our previous activities become uninteresting, even senseless, and our aims suddenly no longer worth striving for. What in one person is merely a passing mood may in another become a chronic condition. In these cases it often happens that other possibilities for developing the personality lie buried somewhere or other in the past, unknown to anybody, not even to the patient. But the dream may reveal the clue.

In other cases the dream points to present facts, for example marriage or social position, which the conscious mind has never accepted as sources of problems or conflicts.

Both possibilities come within the sphere of the rational, and I daresay I would have no difficulty in making such initial dreams seem plausible. The real difficulty begins when the dreams do not point to anything tangible, and this they do often enough, especially when they hold anticipations of the future. I do not mean that such dreams are necessarily prophetic, merely that they feel the way, they "reconnoitre." These dreams contain inklings of possibilities and for that reason can never be made plausible to an outsider. Sometimes they are not plausible even to me, and then I usually say to the patient, "I don't believe it, but follow up the clue." As I have said, the sole criterion is the stimulating effect, but it is by no means necessary for me to understand why such an effect takes place.

This is particularly true of dreams that contain something like an "unconscious metaphysics," by which I mean mythological analogies that are sometimes incredibly strange and baffling.

Now, you will certainly protest: How on earth can I know that the dreams contain anything like an unconscious metaphysics? And here I must confess that I do not really know. I know far too little about dreams for that. I see only the effect on the patient, of which I would like to give you a little example.

In a long initial dream of one of my "normal" patients, the illness of his sister's child played an important part. She was a little girl of two.

Some time before, this sister had in fact lost a boy through illness, but otherwise none of her children was ill. The occurrence of the sick child in the dream at first proved baffling to the dreamer, probably because it failed to fit the facts. Since there was no direct and intimate connection between the dreamer and his sister, he could feel in this image little that was personal to him. Then he suddenly remembered that two years earlier he had taken up the study of occultism, in the course of which he also discovered psychology. So the child evidently represented his interest in the psyche—an idea I should never have arrived at of my own accord. Seen purely theoretically, this dream image can mean anything or nothing. For that matter, does a thing or a fact ever mean anything in itself? The only certainty is that it is always man who interprets, who assigns meaning. And that is the gist of the matter for psychology. It impressed the dreamer as a novel and interesting idea that the study of occultism might have something sickly about it. Somehow the thought struck home. And this is the decisive point: the interpretation works, however we may elect to account for its working. For the dreamer the thought was an implied criticism, and through it a certain change of attitude was brought about. By such slight changes, which one could never think up rationally, things are set in motion and the dead point is overcome, at least in principle.

From this example I could say figuratively that the dream meant that there was something sickly about the dreamer's occult studies, and in this sense—since the dream brought him to such an idea—I can also speak of "unconscious metaphysics."

But I go still further: Not only do I give the patient an opportunity to find associations to his dreams, I give myself the same opportunity. Further, I present him with my ideas and opinions. If, in so doing, I open the door to "suggestion," I see no occasion for regret; for it is well known that we are susceptible only to those suggestions with which we are already secretly in accord. No harm is done if now and then one goes astray in this riddle-reading: sooner or later the psyche will reject the mistake, much as the organism rejects a foreign body. I do not need to prove that my interpretation of the dream is right (a pretty hopeless undertaking anyway), but must simply try to discover, with the patient, what *acts* for him—I am almost tempted to say, what is actual.

For this reason it is particularly important for me to know as much as possible about primitive psychology, mythology, archaeology, and comparative religion, because these fields offer me invaluable analogies with which I can enrich the associations of my patients. Together, we can then find meaning in apparent irrelevancies and thus vastly increase the effectiveness of the dream. For the layman who has done his utmost in the personal and rational sphere of life and yet has found no meaning and no satisfaction there, it is enormously important to be able to enter a sphere of irrational experience. In this way, too, the habitual and the commonplace come to wear an altered countenance, and can even acquire a new glamour. For it all depends on how we look at things, and not on how they are in themselves. The least of things with a meaning is always worth more in life than the greatest of things without it.

I do not think I underestimate the risk of this undertaking. It is as if one began to build a bridge out into space. Indeed, the ironist might even allege—and has often done so—that in following this procedure both doctor and patient are indulging in mere fantasy-spinning.

This objection is no counter-argument, but is very much to the point. I even make an effort to second the patient in his fantasies. Truth to tell, I have no small opinion of fantasy. To me, it is the maternally creative side of the masculine mind. When all is said and done, we can never rise above fantasy. It is true that there are unprofitable, futile, morbid, and unsatisfying fantasies whose sterile nature is immediately recognized by every person endowed with common sense; but the faulty performance proves nothing against the normal performance. All the works of man have their origin in creative imagination. What right, then, have we to disparage fantasy? In the normal course of things, fantasy does not easily go astray; it is too deep for that, and too closely bound up with the tap-root of human and animal instinct. It has a surprising way of always coming out right in the end. The creative activity of imagination frees man from his bondage to the "nothing but" [4] and raises him to the status of one who plays. As Schiller says, man is completely human only when he is at play.

My aim is to bring about a psychic state in which my patient begins to experiment with his own nature—a state of fluidity, change, and growth where nothing is eternally fixed and hopelessly petrified. I can here of course adumbrate only the principles of my technique. Those of you who happen to be acquainted with my works can easily imagine the necessary parallels. I would only like to emphasize that you should not think of my procedure as entirely without aim or limit. In handling a dream or fantasy I make it a rule never to go beyond the meaning which is effective for the patient; I merely try to make him as fully conscious of this meaning as possible, so that he shall also become aware of its supra-personal connections. For, when something happens to a man and he supposes it to be personal only to him, whereas in reality it is a quite universal experience, then his attitude is obviously wrong, that is, too personal, and it tends to exclude him from human society. By the same token we need to have not only a personal, contemporary consciousness, but also a supra-personal consciousness with a sense of historical continuity. However abstract this may sound, practical experience shows that many neuroses are caused primarily by the fact that people blind themselves to their own religious promptings because of a childish passion for rational enlightenment. It is high time the psychologist of today recognized that we are no longer dealing with dogmas and creeds but with the religious attitude *per se*, whose importance as a psychic function can hardly be overrated. And it is precisely for the religious function that the sense of historical continuity is indispensable.

Coming back to the question of my technique, I ask myself how far I am indebted to Freud for its existence. At all events I learned it from Freud's method of free association, and I regard it as a direct extension of that.

So long as I help the patient to discover the effective elements in his dreams, and so long as I try to get him to see the general meaning of his symbols, he is still, psychologically speaking, in a state of childhood. For the time being he is dependent on his dreams and is always asking himself whether the next dream will give him new light or not. Moreover, he is dependent on my having ideas about his dreams and on my ability to increase his insight through my knowledge. Thus he is still in an undesirably passive condition where everything is rather uncertain and questionable; neither he nor I know the journey's end. Often it is not much more than a groping about in Egyptian darkness. In this condition we must not

---

4 [The term "nothing but" (*nichts als*) occurs frequently in Jung, and is used to denote the common habit of explaining something unknown by reducing it to something apparently known and thereby devaluing it. For instance, when a certain illness is said to be "nothing but psychic," it is explained as imaginary and is thus devalued.—Editors.]

expect any very startling results—the uncertainty is too great for that. Besides which there is always the risk that what we have woven by day the night will unravel. The danger is that nothing permanent is achieved, that nothing remains fixed. It not infrequently happens in these situations that the patient has a particularly vivid or curious dream, and says to me, "Do you know, if only I were a painter I would make a picture of it." Or the dreams are about photographs, paintings, drawings, or illuminated manuscripts, or even about the films.

I have turned these hints to practical account, urging my patients at such times to paint in reality what they have seen in dream or fantasy. As a rule I am met with the objection, "But I am not a painter!" To this I usually reply that neither are modern painters, and that consequently modern painting is free for all, and that anyhow it is not a question of beauty but only of the trouble one takes with the picture. How true this is I saw recently in the case of a talented professional portraitist; she had to begin my way of painting all over again with pitiably childish efforts, literally as if she had never held a brush in her hand. To paint what we see before us is a different art from painting what we see within.

Many of my more advanced patients, then, begin to paint. I can well understand that everyone will be profoundly impressed with the utter futility of this sort of dilettantism. Do not forget, however, that we are speaking not of people who still have to prove their social usefulness, but of those who can no longer see any sense in being socially useful and who have come upon the deeper and more dangerous question of the meaning of their own individual lives. To be a particle in the mass has meaning and charm only for the man who has not yet reached that stage, but none for the man who is sick to death of being a particle. The importance of what life means to the individual may be denied by those who are socially below the general level of adaptation, and is invariably denied by the educator whose ambition it is to breed mass-men. But those who belong to neither category will sooner or later come up against this painful question.

Although my patients occasionally produce artistically beautiful things that might very well be shown in modern "art" exhibitions, I nevertheless treat them as completely worthless when judged by the canons of real art. As a matter of fact, it is essential that they should be considered worthless, otherwise my patients might imagine themselves to be artists, and the whole point of the exercise would be missed. It is not a question of art at all —or rather, it should not be a question of art—but of something more and other than mere art, namely the living effect upon the patient himself. The meaning of individual life, whose importance from the social standpoint is negligible, stands here at its highest, and for its sake the patient struggles to give form, however crude and childish, to the inexpressible.

But why do I encourage patients, when they arrive at a certain stage in their development, to express themselves by means of brush, pencil, or pen at all?

Here again my prime purpose is to produce an effect. In the state of psychological childhood described above, the patient remains passive; but now he begins to play an active part. To start off with, he puts down on paper what he has passively seen, thereby turning it into a deliberate act. He not only talks about it, he is actually doing something about it. Psychologically speaking, it makes a vast difference whether a man has an interesting conversation with his doctor two or three times a week, the results of which are left hanging in mid air, or whether he has to struggle for hours with refractory brush and colours, only to produce in the end something which, taken at its face value, is perfectly senseless. If it were really senseless to him, the effort to paint it would be so repugnant that he could scarcely be brought to perform this exercise a second time. But because his fantasy does not strike him as entirely senseless, his busying himself with it only increases its effect upon him. Moreover, the concrete shaping of the image enforces a continuous study of it in all its parts, so that it can develop its effects to the full. This invests the bare fantasy with an element of reality, which lends it greater weight and greater driving power. And these rough-and-ready pictures do indeed produce effects which, I must admit, are rather difficult to describe. For instance, a patient needs only to have seen once or twice how much he is freed from a wretched state of mind by working at a symbolical picture, and he will always turn to this means of release whenever things go badly with him. In this way something of inestimable importance is won—the beginning of independence, a step towards psychological maturity. The patient can make himself creatively independent through this method, if I may call it such. He is no longer dependent on his dreams or on his doctor's knowledge; instead, by painting himself he gives shape to himself. For what he paints are active fantasies—that which is active within him. And that which is active within is himself, but no longer in the guise of his previous error, when he mistook the personal ego for the self; it is himself in a new and hitherto alien sense, for his ego now appears as the object of that which works within him. In countless pictures he strives to catch this interior agent, only to discover in the end that it is eternally unknown and alien, the hidden foundation of psychic life.

It is impossible for me to describe the extent to which this discovery changes the patient's standpoint and values, and how it shifts the centre of gravity of his personality. It is as though the earth had suddenly discovered that the sun was the centre of the planetary orbits and of its own earthly orbit as well.

But have we not always known this to be so? I myself believe that we have always known it. But I may know something with my head which the other man in me is far from knowing, for indeed and in truth I live as though I did not know it. Most of my patients knew the deeper truth, but did not live it. And why did they not live it? Because of that bias which makes us all live from the ego, a bias which comes from overvaluation of the conscious mind.

It is of the greatest importance for the young person, who is still unadapted and has as yet achieved nothing, to shape his conscious ego as effectively as possible, that is, to educate his will. Unless he is a positive genius he cannot, indeed he should not, believe in anything active within him that is not identical with his will. He must feel himself a man of will, and may safely depreciate everything else in him and deem it subject to his will, for without this illusion he could not succeed in adapting himself socially.

It is otherwise with a person in the second half of life who no longer needs to educate his conscious will, but who, to understand the meaning of his individual life, needs to experience his own inner being. Social usefulness is no longer an aim for him, although he does not deny its desirability. Fully aware as he is of the social unimportance of his creative activity, he feels it more as a way of working at himself to his own benefit. Increasingly, too, this activity frees him from morbid dependence, and he thus acquires an inner stability and a new trust in himself. These last achievements now redound to the good of the patient's social existence; for an inwardly stable and self-confident person will prove more adequate to his social tasks than one who is on bad footing with his unconscious.

I have purposely avoided loading my lecture with theory, hence much must remain obscure and unexplained. But, in order to make the pictures produced by my patients intelligible, certain theoretical points must at least receive mention. A feature common to all these pictures is a primitive symbolism which is conspicuous both in the drawing and in the colouring. The colours are as a rule quite barbaric in their intensity. Often an unmistakable archaic quality is present. These peculiarities point to the nature of the underlying creative forces. They are irrational, symbolistic currents that run through the whole history of mankind, and are so archaic in character that it is not difficult to find their parallels in archaeology and comparative religion. We may therefore take it that our pictures spring chiefly from those regions of the psyche which I have termed the collective unconscious. By this I understand an unconscious psychic functioning common to all men, the source not only of our modern symbolical pictures but of all similar products in the past. Such pictures spring from, and satisfy, a natural need. It is as if a part of the psyche that reaches far back into the primitive past were expressing itself in these pictures and finding it possible to function in harmony with our alien conscious mind. This collaboration satisfies and thus mitigates the psyche's disturbing demands upon the latter. It must, however, be added that the mere execution of the pictures is not enough. Over and above that, an intellectual and emotional understanding is needed; they require to be not only rationally integrated with the conscious mind, but morally assimilated. They still have to be subjected to a work of synthetic interpretation. Although I have travelled this path with individual patients many times, I have never yet succeeded in making all the details of the process clear enough for publication. So far this has been fragmentary only. The truth is, we are here moving in absolutely new territory, and a ripening of experience is the first requisite. For very important reasons I am anxious to avoid hasty conclusions. We are dealing with a process of psychic life outside consciousness, and our observation of it is indirect. As yet we do not know to what depths our vision will plumb. It would seem to be some kind of centring process, for a great many pictures which the patients themselves feel to be decisive point in this direction. During this centring process what we call the ego appears to take up a peripheral position. The change is apparently brought about by an emergence of the historical part of the psyche. Exactly what is the purpose of this process remains at first sight obscure. We can only remark its important effect on the conscious personality. From the fact that the change heightens the feeling for life and maintains the flow of life, we must conclude that it is animated by a peculiar purposefulness. We might perhaps call this a new illusion. But what is "illusion"? By what criterion do we judge something to be an illusion? Does anything exist for the psyche that we are entitled to call illusion? What we are pleased to call illusion may be for the psyche an extremely important life-factor, something as indispenable as oxygen for the body—a psychic actuality of overwhelming significance. Presumably the psyche does not trouble itself about our categories of reality; for it, everything that *works* is real. The investigator of the psyche must not confuse it with his consciousness, else he veils from his sight the object of his investigation. On the contrary, to recognize it at all, he must learn to see how different it is from consciousness. Nothing is more probable than that what we call illusion is very real for the psyche—for which reason we cannot take psychic reality to be commensurable with conscious reality. To the psychologist there is nothing more fatuous than the attitude of the missionary who pronounces the gods of the "poor heathen" to be mere illusion. Unfortunately we still go blundering along in the same dogmatic way, as though *our* so-called reality were not equally full of illusion. In psychic life, as everywhere in our experience, all things that work are reality, regardless of the names man chooses to bestow on them. To take these realities for what they are—not foisting other names on them—that is our business. To the psyche, spirit is no less spirit for being named sexuality.

I must repeat that these designations and the changes rung upon them never even remotely touch the essence of the process we have described. It cannot be compassed by the rational concepts of the conscious mind, any more than life itself; and it is for this reason that my patients consistently turn to the representation and interpretation of symbols as the more adequate and effective course.

With this I have said pretty well everything I can say about my therapeutic aims and intentions within the broad framework of a lecture. It can be no more than an incentive to thought, and I shall be quite content if such it has been.

7

The Association Method

CARL G. JUNG

When you honoured me with an invitation to lecture at Clark University, a wish was expressed that I should speak about my methods of work, and especially about the psychology of childhood. I hope to accomplish this task in the following manner:—

In my first lecture I will give to you the view points of my association methods; in my second I will discuss the significance of the familiar constellations; while in my third lecture I shall enter more fully into the psychology of the child.

I might confine myself exclusively to my theoretical views, but I believe it will be better to illustrate my lectures with as many practical examples as possible. We will therefore occupy ourselves first with the association test which has been of great value to me both practically and theoretically. The history of the association method in vogue in psychology, as well as the method itself, is, of course, so familiar to you that there is no need to enlarge upon it. For practical purposes I make use of the formula shown on page 90.

This formula has been constructed after many years of experience. The words are chosen and partially arranged in such a manner as to strike easily almost all complexes which occur in practice. As shown above, there is a regulated mixing of the grammatical qualities of the words. For this there are definite reasons.[1]

Before the experiment begins the test person receives the following instruction: "Answer as quickly as possible with the first word that occurs to your mind." This instruction is so simple that it can easily be followed. The work itself, moreover, appears extremely easy, so that it might be expected any one could accomplish it with the greatest facility and promptitude. But, contrary to expectation, the behaviour is quite otherwise.

Lectures delivered at the celebration of the twentieth anniversary of the opening of Clark University, September, 1909. From C. G. Jung "The Association Method." In A. A. Brill (Trans.) and C. R. Long (Ed.), *Collected Papers on Analytical Psychology*. London: Baillière, Tindall & Cassell Ltd., 1916. Pp. 94–109. Reprinted by kind permission of Dr. Stanley Hall.

[1] The selection of these stimulus words was naturally made for the German language only, and would probably have to be considerably changed for the English language.

1. head	35. mountain	68. to paint
2. green	36. to die	69. part
3. water	37. salt	70. old
4. to sing	38. new	71. flower
5. dead	39. custom	72. to beat
6. long	40. to pray	73. box
7. ship	41. money	74. wild
8. to pay	42. foolish	75. family
9. window	43. pamphlet	76. to wash
10. friendly	44. despise	77. cow
11. to cook	45. finger	78. friend
12. to ask	46. expensive	79. luck
13. cold	47. bird	80. lie
14. stem	48. to fall	81. deportment
15. to dance	49. book	82. narrow
16. village	50. unjust	83. brother
17. lake	51. frog	84. to fear
18. sick	52. to separate	85. stork
19. pride	53. hunger	86. false
20. to cook	54. white	87. anxiety
21. ink	55. child	88. to kiss
22. angry	56. to take care	89. bride
23. needle	57. lead pencil	90. pure
24. to swim	58. sad	91. door
25. voyage	59. plum	92. to choose
26. blue	60. to marry	93. hay
27. lamp	61. house	94. contented
28. to sin	62. dear	95. ridicule
29. bread	63. glass	96. to sleep
30. rich	64. to quarrel	97. mouth
31. tree	65. fur	98. nice
32. to prick	66. big	99. woman
33. pity	67. carrot	100. to abuse
34. yellow		

I. An Example of a Normal Reaction Type

Stimulus Word	Reaction Time Unit 0.2 second	Reaction	Reproduction
head	9	foot	part of the body
green	11	blouse	
water	14	clear	light
to sing	6	children	
dead	11	do not like	
long	6	short	I, tall
ship	7	forth	
to pay	9	bills	
window	9	room	
friendly	10	children	
table	9	chair	room
to ask	10	all kinds	
cold	7	warm	
stem	6	flower	
to dance	9	I . .	like
lake	8	Zurich	
sick	8	sister	
pride	6	people	
to cook	7	woman	
ink	5	black	
angry	10	children	people
needle	9	to prick	
to swim	10	healthy	
voyage	9	England	
blue	10	pretty	like
lamp	6	light	
to sin	8	much	people
bread	10	good	like, necessary
rich	9	nice	
tree	6	green	
to prick	9	need	

II. An Example of an Hysterical Reaction Type

Stimulus Word	Reaction Time Unit 0.2 second	Reaction	Reproduction
needle	7	to sew	
to swim * †	9	water	ship
voyage	35	to ride, motion, voyager	
blue	10	colour	
lamp	7	to burn	
to sin	22	this idea is totally strange to me, I do not recognize it	

II.   An Example of an Hysterical Reaction Type (*continued*)

Stimulus Word	Reaction Time Unit 0.2 second	Reaction	Reproduction
bread	10	to eat	
rich†	50	money, I don't know	possession
brown	6	nature	green
to prick	9	needle	
pity	12	feeling	
yellow	9	colour	
mountain	8	high	
to die	8	to perish	
salt	15	salty (laughs) I don't know	NaCl
new	15	old	as an opposite
custom	10	good	barbaric
to pray	12	Deity	
money	10	wealth	
foolish	12	narrow minded, restricted	?
pamphlet	10	paper	
despise	30	that is a complicated, too foolish	?
finger	8	hand, not only hand, but also foot, a joint, member, extremity	
dear	14	to pay (laughs)	
bird	8	to fly	
to fall	30	*tomber*, I will say no more, what do you mean by fall?	?
book	6	to read	
unjust	8	just	
frog	11	quack	
to part	30	what does part mean?	?
hunger	10	to eat	
white	12	colour, everything possible, light	
child	10	little, I did not hear well, *bébé*	?
to take care	14	attention	
lead pencil	8	to draw, everything possible can be drawn	
sad	9	to weep, that is not always the case	to be
plum	16	to eat a plum, pluck what do you mean by it? Is that symbolic?	fruit
to marry	27	how can you? reunion, union	union, alliance

* Denotes misunderstanding.
† Denotes repetition of the stimulus words.

The diagrams in Figure 7-1 illustrate the reaction times in an association experiment in four normal test-persons. The height of each column denotes the length of the reaction time.

Figures 7-2, 7-3, and 7-4 show the course of the reaction time in hysterical individuals. The light cross-hatched columns denote the places where the test-person was unable to react (so-called failures to react).

The first thing that strikes us is the fact that many test-persons show a marked prolongation of the reaction time. This would seem to be suggestive of intellectual difficulties,—wrongly however, for we are often dealing with very intelligent persons of fluent speech. The explanation lies rather in the emotions. In order to understand the matter, comprehensively, we must bear in mind that the association experiments cannot deal with a separated psychic function, for any psychic occurrence is never a thing in

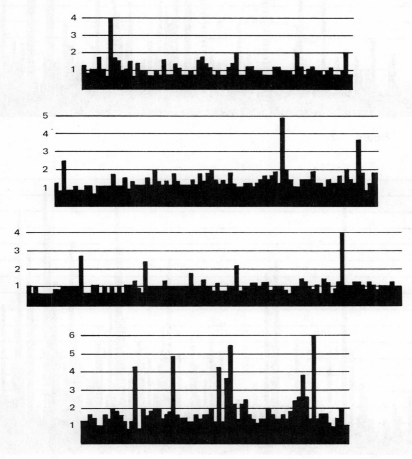

Figure 7-1.

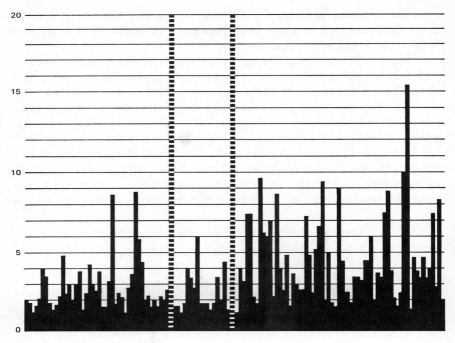

Figure 7-2.

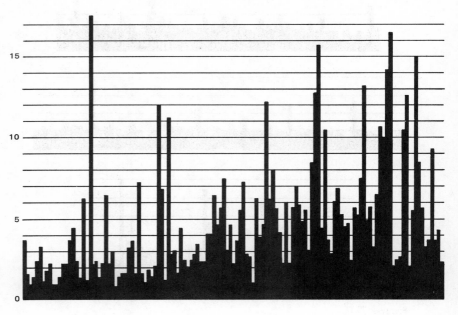

Figure 7-3.

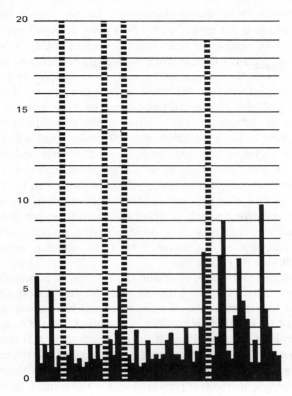

Figure 7-4.

itself, but is always the resultant of the entire psychological past. The association experiment, too, is not merely a method for the reproduction of separated word couplets, but it is a kind of pastime, a conversation between experimenter and test-person. In a certain sense it is still more than that. Words really represent condensed actions, situations, and things. When I give a stimulus word to the test-person, which denotes an action, it is as if I represented to him the action itself, and asked him, "How do you behave towards it? What do you think of it? What would you do in this situation?" It I were a magician, I should cause the situation corresponding to the stimulus word to appear in reality, and placing the test-person in its midst, I should then study his manner of reaction. The result of my stimulus words would thus undoubtedly approach infinitely nearer perfection. But as we are not magicians, we must be contented with the linguistic substitutes for reality; at the same time we must not forget that the stimulus word will almost without exception conjure up its corresponding situation. All depends on how the test-person reacts to this situation. The word "bride" or "bridegroom" will not evoke a simple reaction in a young lady; but the reaction will be deeply influenced by the strong feeling tones evoked, the more so if the experimenter be a man. It thus happens that the test-person is often unable to react quickly and smoothly to all stimulus words. There are certain stimulus words which denote actions, situations, or things, about which the test-person cannot think quickly and surely, and this fact is demonstrated in the association experiments. The examples which I have just given show an abundance of long reaction times and other disturbances. In this case the reaction to the stimulus word is in some way impeded, that is, the adaptation to the stimulus word is disturbed. The stimulus words therefore act upon us just as reality acts; indeed, a person who shows such great disturbances to the stimulus words, is in a certain sense but imperfectly adapted to reality. Disease itself is an imperfect adaptation; hence in this case we are dealing with something morbid in the psyche,—with something which is either temporarily or persistently pathological in character, that is, we are dealing with a psychoneurosis, with a functional disturbance of the mind. This rule, however, as we shall see later, is not without its exceptions.

Let us, in the first place, continue the discussion concerning the prolonged reaction time. It often happens that the test-person actually does *not* know what to answer to the stimulus word. He waives any reaction, and for the moment he totally fails to obey the original instructions, and shows himself incapable of adapting himself to the experimenter. If this phenomenon occurs frequently in an experiment, it signifies a high degree of disturbance in adjustment. I would call attention to the fact that it is quite indifferent what reason the test-person gives for the refusal. Some find that too many ideas suddenly occur to them; others, that they suffer from a deficiency of ideas. In most cases, however, the difficulties first perceived are so deterrent that they actually give up the whole reaction. The example below shows a case of hysteria with many failures of reaction.

In example II. we find a characteristic phenomenon. The test-person is not content with the requirements of the instruction, that is, she is not satisfied with *one* word, but reacts with many words. She apparently does more and better than the instruction requires, but in so doing she does not fulfil the requirements of the instruction. Thus she reacts:—custom—good—barbaric; foolish—narrow minded—restricted; family—big—small—everything possible.

These examples show in the first place that many other words connect themselves with the reaction word. The test-person is unable to suppress the ideas which subsequently occur to her. She also pursues a certain tendency which perhaps is more exactly expressed in the following reaction: new—old—as an opposite. The addition of "as an opposite" denotes that the test-person has the desire to add something explanatory or supplementary. This tendency is also shown in the following reaction: finger—not only hand, also foot—a limb—member—extremity.

Stimulus Word	Reaction Time Unit 0.2 second	Reaction	Reproduction
to sing	9	nice	+
dead	15	awful	?
long*	40	the time, the journey	?
ship†			+
to pay	11	money	
window	10	big	high
friendly	50	a man	human
to cook	10	soup	+
ink	9	black or blue	+
angry			bad
needle	9	to sew	+
lamp	14	light	+
to sin			
bread	15	to eat	+
rich*†	40	good, convenient	+
yellow	18	paper	colour
mountain	10	high	+
to die	15	awful	+
salt†	25	salty	+
new			good, nice
custom†			
to pray			
money†	35	to buy, one is able	+
pamphlet	16	to write	+
to despise†		people	+
finger	22		
dear	12	thing	+
bird	12	sings or flies	+

* Denotes misunderstanding.
† Denotes repetition of the stimulus words.
+ Reproduced unchanged.

Here we have a whole series of supplements. It seems as if the reaction were not sufficient for the test-person, something else must always be added, as if what has already been said were incorrect or in some way imperfect. This feeling is what Janet designates the *"sentiment d'incomplétude,"* but this by no means explains everything. I go somewhat deeply into this phenomenon because it is very frequently met with in neurotic individuals. It is not merely a small and unimportant subsidiary manifestation demonstrable in an insignificant experiment, but rather an elemental and universal manifestation which plays a *rôle* in other ways in the psychic life of neurotics.

By his desire to supplement, the test-person betrays a tendency to give the experimenter more than he wants, he actually makes great efforts to find further mental occurrences in order finally to discover something quite satisfactory. If we translate this observation into the psychology of everyday life, it signifies that the test-person has a constant tendency to give to others more feeling than is required and expected. According to Freud, this is a sign of a reinforced object-libido, that is, it is a compensation for an inner want of satisfaction and voidness of feeling. This elementary observation therefore displays one of the characteristics of hysterics, namely, the tendency to allow themselves to be carried away by everything, to attach themselves enthusiastically to everything, and always to promise too much and hence perform too little. Patients with this symptom are, in my experience, always hard to deal with; at first they are enthusiastically enamoured of the physician, for a time going so far as to accept everything he says blindly; but they soon merge into an equally blind resistance against him, thus rendering any educative influence absolutely impossible.

We see therefore in this type of reaction an expression of a tendency to give more than is asked or expected. This tendency betrays itself also in other failures to follow the instruction:—

to quarrel—angry—different things—I always quarrel at home;
to marry—how can you marry?—reunion—union;
plum—to eat—to pluck—what do you mean by it?—is it symbolic?
to sin—this idea is quite strange to me, I do not recognise it.

These reactions show that the test-person gets away altogether from the situation of the experiment. For the instruction was, that he should answer only with the first word which occurs to him. But here we note that the stimulus words act with excessive strength, that they are taken as if they were direct personal questions. The test-person entirely forgets that we deal with mere words which stand in print before us, but finds a personal meaning in them; he tries to divine their intention and defend himself against them, thus altogether forgetting the original instructions.

This elementary observation discloses another common peculiarity of hysterics, namely, that of taking everything personally, of never being able to remain objective, and of allowing themselves to be carried away by momentary impressions; this again shows the characteristics of the enhanced object-libido.

Yet another sign of impeded adaptation is the often occurring *repetition of the stimulus words*. The test-persons repeat the stimulus word as if they had not heard or understood it distinctly. They repeat it just as we repeat a difficult question in order to grasp it better before answering. This same tendency is shown in the experiment. The questions are repeated because the stimulus words act on hysterical individuals in much the same way as difficult personal questions. In principle it is the same phenomenon as the subsequent completion of the reaction.

In many experiments we observe that the same reaction constantly reappears to the most varied stimulus words. These words seem to possess a special reproduction tendency, and it is very interesting to examine their relationship to the test-person. For example, I have observed a case in which the patient repeated the word "short" a great many times and often in places where it had no meaning. The test-person could not directly state the reason for the repetition of the word "short." From experience I knew that such predicates always relate either to the test-person himself or to the person nearest to him. I assumed that in this word "short" he designated himself, and that in this way he helped to express something very painful to him. The test-person is of very small stature. He is the youngest of four brothers, who, in contrast to himself, are all tall. He was always the *"child"* in the family; he was nicknamed "Short" and was treated by all as the "little one." This resulted in a total loss of self-confidence. Although he was intelligent, and despite long study, he could not decide to present himself for examination; he finally became impotent, and merged into a psychosis in which, whenever he was alone, he took delight in walking about his room on his toes in order to appear taller. The word "short," therefore, stood to him for a great many painful experiences. This is usually the case with the perseverated words; they always contain something of importance for the individual psychology of the test-person.

The signs thus far discussed are not found spread about in an arbitrary way through the whole experiment, but are seen in very definite places, namely, where the stimulus words strike against emotionally accentuated complexes. This observation is the foundation of the so-called "diagnosis of facts" (*Tatbestandsdiagnostik*). This method is employed to discover, by means of an association experiment, which is the culprit among a number of persons suspected of a crime. That this is possible I will demonstrate by the brief recital of a concrete case.

On the 6th of February, 1908, our supervisor reported to me that a nurse complained to her of having been robbed during the forenoon of the previous day. The facts were as follows: The nurse kept her money, amounting to 70 francs, in a pocket-book which she had placed in her cupboard where she also kept her clothes. The cupboard contained two compartments, of which one belonged to the nurse who was robbed, and the other to the head nurse. These two nurses and a third one, who was an intimate friend of the head nurse, slept in the room where the cupboard was. This room was in a section which was occupied in common by six nurses who had at all times free access to the room. Given such a state of affairs it is not to be wondered that the supervisor shrugged her shoulders when I asked her whom she most suspected.

Further investigation showed that on the day of the theft, the above-mentioned friend of the head nurse was slightly indisposed and remained the whole morning in the room in bed. Hence, unless she herself was the thief, the theft could have taken place only in the afternoon. Of four other nurses upon whom suspicion could possibly fall, there was one who attended regularly to the cleaning of the room in question, while the remaining three had nothing to do in it, nor was it shown that any of them had spent any time there on the previous day.

It was therefore natural that the last three nurses should be regarded for the time being as less implicated, so I began by subjecting the first three to the experiment.

From the information I had obtained of the case, I knew that the cupboard was locked but that the key was kept near by in a very conspicuous place, that on opening the cupboard the first thing which would strike the eye was a fur boa, and, moreover, that the pocket-book was between some linen in an inconspicuous place. The pocket-book was of dark reddish leather, and contained the following objects: a 50-franc banknote, a 20-franc piece, some centimes, a small silver watch-chain, a stencil used in the lunatic asylum to mark the kitchen utensils, and a small receipt from Dosenbach's shoeshop in Zürich.

Besides the plaintiff, only the head nurse knew the exact particulars of the deed, for as soon as the former missed her money she immediately asked the head nurse to help her find it, thus the head nurse had been able to learn the smallest details, which naturally rendered the experiment still more difficult, for she was precisely the one most suspected. The conditions for the experiment were better for the others, since they knew nothing concerning the particulars of the deed, and some not even that a theft had been committed. As critical stimulus words I selected the name of the robbed nurse, plus the following words: cupboard, door, open, key, yesterday, banknote, gold, 70, 50, 20, money, watch, pocket-book, chain, silver, to hide, fur, dark reddish, leather, centimes, stencil, receipt, Dosenbach. Besides these words which referred directly to the deed, I took also the following, which had a special effective value: theft, to take, to steal, suspicion, blame, court, police, to lie, to fear, to discover, to arrest, innocent.

The objection is often made to the last species of words that they may produce a strong affective resentment even in innocent persons, and for that reason one cannot attribute to them any comparative value. Nevertheless, it may always be questioned whether the affective resentment of an innocent person will have the same effect on the association as that of a guilty one, and that question can only be authoritatively answered by experience. Until the contrary is demonstrated, I maintain that words of the above-mentioned type may profitably be used.

I distributed these critical words among twice as many indifferent stimulus words in such a manner that each critical word was followed by two indifferent ones. As a rule it is well to follow up the critical words by indifferent words in order that the action of the first may be clearly distinguished. But one may also follow up one critical word by another, especially if one wishes to bring into relief the action of the second. Thus I placed together "darkish red" and "leather," and "chain" and "silver."

After this preparatory work I undertook the experiment with the three above-mentioned nurses. Following the order of the experiment, I shall denote the friend of the head nurse by the letter A, the head nurse by B, and the nurse who attended to the cleaning of the room by C. As examinations of this kind can be rendered into a foreign tongue only with the greatest difficulty, I will content myself with presenting the general results, and with giving some examples. I first undertook the experiment with A, and judging by the circumstances she appeared only slightly moved. B was next examined; she showed marked excitement, her pulse being 120 per minute immediately after the experiment. The last to be examined was C. She was the most tranquil of the three; she displayed but little embarrassment, and only in the course of the experiment did it occur to her that she was suspected of stealing, a fact which manifestly disturbed her towards the end of the experiment.

The general impression from the examination spoke strongly against the head nurse B. It seemed to me that she evinced a very "suspicious," or I might almost say, "impudent" countenance. With the definite idea of finding in her the guilty one I set about adding up the results. You will see that I was wrong in my surmise and that the test proved my error.

One can make use of many special methods of computing, but they are not all equally good and equally exact. (One must always resort to calculation, as appearances are enormously deceptive.) The method which is most to be recommended is that of the probable average of the reaction time. It shows at a glance the difficulties which the person in the experiment had to overcome in the reaction.

The technique of this calculation is very simple. The probable average is the middle number of the various reaction times arranged in a series. The reaction times are, for example,[2] placed in the following manner: 5, 5, 5, 7, 7, 7, 7, 8, 9, 9, 9, 12, 13, 14. The number found in the middle (8) is the probable average of this series.

The probable averages of the reaction are:

A	B	C
10.0	12.0	13.5

No conclusions can be drawn from this result. But the average reaction times calculated separately for the indifferent reactions, for the critical, and for those immediately following the critical (post-critical) are more interesting.

From this example we see that whereas A has the shortest reaction time for the indifferent reactions, she shows in comparison to the other two persons of the experiment, the longest time for the critical reactions.

---

[2] Reaction times are always given in fifths of a second.

CARL A. RUDISILL LIBRARY
LENOIR RHYNE COLLEGE

The Probable Average of the Reaction Time

for	A	B	C
Indifferent reactions	10.0	11.0	12.0
Critical reactions	16.0	13.0	15.0
Post-critical reactions	10.0	11.0	13.0

The difference between the reaction times, let us say between the indifferent and the critical, is 6 for A, 2 for B, and 3 for C, that is, it is more than double for A when compared with the other two persons.

In the same way we can calculate how many complex indicators there are on an average for the indifferent, critical, etc., reactions.

The Average Complex-Indicators for each Reaction

for	A	B	C
Indifferent reactions	0.6	0.9	0.8
Critical reactions	1.3	0.9	1.2
Post-critical reactions	0.6	1.0	0.8

The difference between the indifferent and critical reactions for A = 0.7, for B = 0, for C = 0.4. A is again the highest.

Another question to consider is, the proportion of imperfect reactions in each case.

The result for A = 34 percent, for B = 28 percent, and for C = 30 percent.

Here, too, A reaches the highest value, and in this, I believe, we see the characteristic moment of the guilt-complex in A. I am, however, unable to explain here circumstantially the reasons why I maintain that memory errors are related to an emotional complex, as this would lead me beyond the limits of the present work. I therefore refer the reader to my work *"Ueber die Reproductionsstörungen im Associationsexperiment"* (IX Beitrag der Diagnost. Associat. Studien).[3]

As it often happens that an association of strong feeling tone produces in the experiment a perseveration, with the result that not only the critical association, but also two or three successive associations are imperfectly reproduced, it will be very interesting to see how many imperfect reproductions are so arranged in the series in our cases. The result of computation shows that the imperfect reproductions thus arranged in series are for A 64.7 percent, for B 55.5 percent, and for C 30.0 percent.

Again we find that A has the greatest percentage. To be sure, this may partially depend on the fact that A also possesses the greatest number of imperfect reproductions. Given a small number of reactions, it is usual that

---

[3] "Studies in Word Association." Translator, M. D. Eder. Heinemann.

the greater the total number of the same, the more the imperfect reactions will occur in groups. But this cannot account for the high proportion in our case, where, on the other hand, B and C have not a much smaller number of imperfect reactions when compared to A. It is significant that C with her slight emotions during the experiment shows the minimum of imperfect reproductions arranged in series.

As imperfect reproductions are also complex indicators, it is necessary to see how they distribute themselves in respect to the indifferent, critical, etc., reactions.

It is hardly necessary to bring into prominence the differences between the indifferent and the critical reactions of the various subjects as shown by the resulting numbers of the table. In this respect, too, A occupies first place.

Imperfect Reproductions which Occur

in	A	B	C
Indifferent reactions	10	12	11
Critical reactions	19	9	12
Post-critical reactions	5	7	7

Naturally, here, too, there is a probability that the greater the number of the imperfect reproductions the greater is their number in the critical reactions. If we suppose that the imperfect reproductions are distributed regularly and without choice, among all the reactions, there will be a greater number of them for A (in comparison with B and C) even as reactions to critical words, since A has the greater number of imperfect reproductions. Admitting such a uniform distribution of the imperfect reproductions, it is easy to calculate how many we ought to expect to belong to each individual kind of reaction.

From this calculation it appears that the disturbances of reproductions which concern the critical reactions for A greatly surpass the number expected, for C they are 0.9 higher, while for B they are lower.

Imperfect Reproductions

	Which may be expected			Which really occur		
For	Indifferent reactions	Critical reactions	Post-critical reactions	Indifferent reactions	Critical reactions	Post-critical reactions
A	11.2	12.5	10.2	10	19	5
B	9.2	10.3	8.4	12	9	7
C	9.9	11.1	9.0	11	12	7

All this points to the fact that in the subject A the critical stimulus words acted with the greatest intensity, and hence the greatest suspicion falls on A. Practically relying on the test one may assume the probability of this person's guilt. The same evening A made a complete confession of the theft, and thus the success of the experiment was confirmed.

Such a result is undoubtedly of scientific interest and worthy of serious consideration. There is much in experimental psychology which is of less use than the material exemplified in this test. Putting the theoretical interest altogether aside, we have here something that is not to be despised from a practical point of view, to wit, a culprit has been brought to light in a much easier and shorter way than is customary. What has been possible once or twice ought to be possible again, and it is well worth while to investigate some means of rendering the method increasingly capable of rapid and sure results.

This application of the experiment shows that it is possible to strike a concealed, indeed an unconscious complex by means of a stimulus word; and conversely we may assume with great certainty that behind a reaction which shows a complex indicator there is a hidden complex, even though the test-person strongly denies it. One might get rid of the idea that educated and intelligent test-persons are able to see and admit their own complexes. Every human mind contains much that is unacknowledged and hence unconscious as such; and no one can boast that he stands completely above his complexes. Those who persist in maintaining that they can, are not aware of the spectacles upon their noses.

It has long been thought that the association experiment enables one to distinguish certain *intellectual* types. That is not the case. The experiment does not give us any particular insight into the purely intellectual, but rather into the emotional processes. To be sure we can erect certain types of reaction; they are not, however, based on intellectual peculiarities, but depend entirely on the *proportionate emotional states*. Educated test-persons usually show superficial and linguistically deep-rooted associations, whereas the uneducated form more valuable associations and often of ingenious significance. This behaviour would be paradoxical from an intellectual viewpoint. The meaningful associations of the uneducated are not really the product of intellectual thinking, but are simply the results of a special emotional state. The whole thing is more important to the uneducated, his emotion is greater, and for that reason he pays more attention to the experiment than the educated person, and his associations are therefore more significant. Apart from those determined by education, we have to consider three principal individual types:

1. An objective type with undisturbed reactions.
2. A so-called complex-type with many disturbances in the experiment occasioned by the constellation of a complex.
3. A so-called definition-type. The peculiarity of this type consists in the fact

that the reaction always gives an explanation or a definition of the content of the stimulus word; *e.g.*:

> apple—a tree-fruit;
> table—a piece of household furniture;
> to promenade—an activity;
> father—chief of the family.

This type is chiefly found in stupid persons, and it is therefore quite usual in imbecility. But it can also be found in persons who are not really stupid, but who do not wish *to be taken as stupid*. Thus a young student from whom associations were taken by an older intelligent woman student reacted altogether with definitions. The test-person was of the opinion that it was an examination in intelligence, and therefore directed most of his attention to the significance of the stimulus words; his associations, therefore, looked like those of an idiot. All idiots, however, do not react with definitions; probably only those react in this way who would like to appear smarter than they are, that is, those to whom their stupidity is painful. I call this widespread complex the "intelligence-complex." A normal test-person reacts in a most overdrawn manner as follows:

> anxiety—heart anguish;
> to kiss—love's unfolding;
> to kiss—perception of friendship.

This type gives a constrained and unnatural impression. The test-persons wish to be more than they are, they wish to exert more influence than they really have. Hence we see that persons with an intelligence-complex are usually unnatural and constrained; that they are always somewhat stilted, or flowery; they show a predilection for complicated foreign words, high-sounding quotations, and other intellectual ornaments. In this way they wish to influence their fellow beings, they wish to impress others with their apparent education and intelligence, and thus to compensate for their painful feeling of stupidity. The definition-type is closely related to the predicate-type, or, to express it more precisely, to the predicate-type expressing personal judgment (*Wertprädikattypus*). For example:

> flower—pretty;
> money—convenient;
> animal—ugly;
> knife—dangerous;
> death—ghastly.

In the definition type the *intellectual* significance of the stimulus word is rendered prominent, but in the predicate type its *emotional* significance.

There are predicate-types which show great exaggeration where reactions such as the following appear:

> piano—horrible;
> to sing—heavenly;
> mother—ardently loved;
> father—something good, nice, holy.

In the definition-type an absolutely *intellectual* make-up is manifested or rather simulated, but here there is a very *emotional* one. Yet, just as the definition-type really conceals a lack of intelligence, so the excessive *emotional* expression conceals or overcompensates an emotional deficiency. This conclusion is very interestingly illustrated by the following discovery: —On investigating the influence of the familiar milieus on the association-type it was found that young people seldom possess a predicate-type, but that, on the other hand, the predicate-type increases in frequency with advancing age. In women the increase of the predicate-type begins a little after the fortieth year, and in men after the sixtieth. That is the precise time when, owing to the deficiency of sexuality, there actually occurs considerable emotional loss. If a test-person evinces a distinct predicate-type, it may always be inferred that a marked internal emotional deficiency is thereby compensated. Still, one cannot reason conversely, namely, that an inner emotional deficiency must produce a predicate-type, no more than that idiocy directly produces a definition-type. A predicate-type can also betray itself through the external behaviour, as, for example, through a particular affectation, enthusiastic exclamations, an embellished behaviour, and the constrained-sounding language so often observed in society.

The complex-type shows no particular tendency except the *concealment* of a complex, whereas the definition and predicate types betray a positive tendency to exert in some way a *definite* influence on the experimenter. But whereas the definition-type tends to bring to light its intelligence, the predicate-type displays its emotion. I need hardly add of what importance such determinations are for the diagnosis of character.

After finishing an association experiment I usually add another of a different kind, the so-called *reproduction* experiment. I repeat the same stimulus words and ask the test-persons whether they still remember their former reactions. In many instances the memory fails, and as experience shows, these locations are stimulus words which touched an emotionally accentuated complex, or stimulus words immediately following such critical words.

This phenomenon has been designated as paradoxical and contrary to all experience. For it is known that emotionally accentuated things are better retained in memory than indifferent things. This is quite true, but it does not hold for the *linguistic* expression of an emotionally accentuated content. On the contrary, one very easily forgets what he has said under emotion, one is even apt to contradict himself about it. Indeed, the efficacy of cross-examinations in court depends on this fact. The reproduction method therefore serves to render still more prominent the complex stimulus. In normal persons we usually find a limited number of false reproductions, seldom more than 19–20 percent, while in abnormal persons, especially in hysterics, we often find from 20–40 percent of false reproductions. The reproduction certainty is therefore in certain cases a measure for the emotivity of the test-person.

By far the larger number of neurotics show a pronounced tendency to cover up their intimate affairs in impenetrable darkness, even from the doctor, so that he finds it very difficult to form a proper picture of the patient's psychology. In such cases I am greatly assisted by the association experiment. When the experiment is finished, I first look over the general course of the reaction times. I see a great many very prolonged intervals; this means that the patient can only adjust himself with difficulty, that his psychological functions proceed with marked internal friction, with *resistances*. The greater number of neurotics react only under great and very definite resistances; there are, however, others in whom the average reaction times are as short as in the normal, and in whom the other complex indicators are lacking, but, despite the fact, they undoubtedly present neurotic symptoms. These rare cases are especially found among very intelligent and educated persons, chronic patients who, after many years of practice, have learned to control their outward behaviour and therefore outwardly display very little if any trace of their neuroses. The superficial observer would take them for normal, yet in some places they show disturbances which betray the repressed complex.

After examining the reaction times I turn my attention to the type of the association to ascertain with what type I am dealing. If it is a predicate-type I draw the conclusions which I have detailed above; if it is a complex type I try to ascertain the nature of the complex. With the necessary experience one can readily emancipate one's judgment from the test-person's statements and almost without any previous knowledge of the test-persons it is possible under certain circumstances to read the most intimate complexes from the results of the experiment. I look at first for the reproduction words and put them together, and then I look for the stimulus words which show the greatest disturbances. In many cases merely assorting these words suffices to unearth the complex. In some cases it is necessary to put a question here and there. The matter is well illustrated by the following concrete example:

It concerns an educated woman of thirty years of age, married three years previously. Since her marriage she has suffered from episodic excitement in which she is violently jealous of her husband. The marriage is a

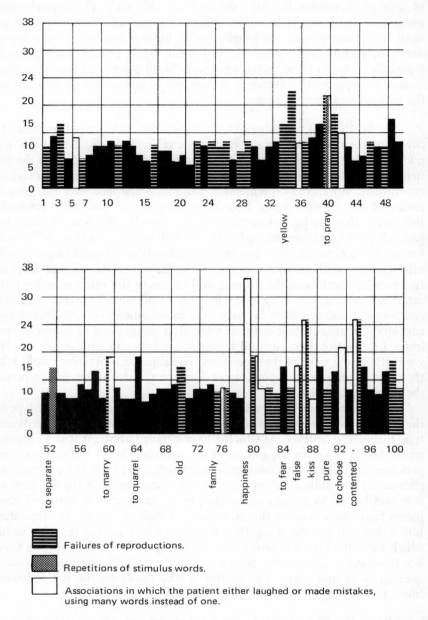

Failures of reproductions.

Repetitions of stimulus words.

Associations in which the patient either laughed or made mistakes, using many words instead of one.

Figure 7-5. The height of the columns represents the length of the reaction time. For the stimulus words corresponding to the numbers, see the list on page 90.

happy one in every other respect, and it should be noted that the husband gives no cause for the jealousy. The patient is sure that she loves him and that her excited states are groundless. She cannot imagine whence these excited states originate, and feels quite perplexed over them. It is to be noted that she is a Catholic and has been brought up religiously, while her husband is a protestant. This difference of religion did not admittedly play any part. A more thorough anamnesis showed the existence of an extreme prudishness. Thus, for example, no one was allowed to talk in the patient's presence about her sister's childbirth, because the sexual moment suggested therein caused her the greatest excitement. She always undressed in the adjoining room and never in her husband's presence, etc. At the age of twenty-seven she was supposed to have had no idea how children were born. The associations gave the results shown in Figure 7-5.

The stimulus words characterised by marked disturbances are the following: yellow, to pray, to separate, to marry, to quarrel, old, family, happiness, false, fear, to kiss, bride, to choose, contented. The strongest disturbances are found in the following stimulus words: *to pray, to marry, happiness, false, fear,* and *contented*. These words, therefore, more than any others, seem to strike the complex. The conclusions that can be drawn from this is that she is not indifferent to the fact that her husband is a protestant, that she again thinks of praying, believes there is something wrong with marriage, that she is false, entertains fancies of faithlessness, is afraid (of the husband? of the future?), she is not contented with her choice (to choose) and she thinks of separation. The patient therefore has a separation complex, for she is very discontented with her married life. When I told her this result she was affected and at first attempted to deny it, then to mince over it, but finally she admitted everything I said and added more. She reproduced a large number of fancies of faithlessness, reproaches against her husband, etc. *Her prudishness and jealously were merely a projection of her own sexual wishes on her husband.* Because she was faithless in her fancies and did not admit it to herself she was jealous of her husband.

It is impossible in a lecture to give a review of all the manifold uses of the association experiment. I must content myself with having demonstrated to you a few of its chief uses.

REFERENCES

Freud. "Die Traumdeutung," II Auflage. Deuticke, Wien, 1909.
Jung. "Diagnostische Associationsstudien," Band I. Barth, Leipzig, 1906.
———. "Die Psychologische Diagnose des Thatbestandes." Carl Marhold, Halle, 1906.
Jung. "Die Bedeutung des Vaters für das Schicksal des Einzelnen." Deuticke, Wien, 1908.
Fürst. "Statistische Untersuchungen über Wortassoziationen und über familiäre Übereinstimmung im Reactionstypus bei Ungebildeten," X Beitrag der Diagnost. Assoc. Studien, vol. II.

8

Jung's Psychological Types: Classification by Test versus Classification by Self

KATHERINE BRADWAY

INTRODUCTION

Despite the fact that Jung presented his theory of psychological types nearly half a century ago (Jung, 1921), American psychology has continued to classify individual differences in personality, almost exclusively, according to psychological theories based upon a normal distribution of personality traits from none to much. This is in contrast to Jung's concept of a pair of opposing attitudes: introversion and extraversion; a pair of opposing perception functions: sensation and intuition; and a pair of opposing judgement functions: thinking and feeling. With the recent appearance of reports of research in which subjects are described or selected in terms of these classifications, the desirability of evaluating available tests of psychological types is apparent. This study was undertaken to evaluate two such tests: the Gray-Wheelwright Questionnaire (Gray and Wheelwright, 1946) and the Myers-Briggs Type Indicator (Saunders, 1958). Each of these tests was to be compared with an outside criterion. The criterion selected was the self-typing of Jungian analysts.

From K. Bradway, Jung's Psychological Types. *Journal of Analytical Psychology,* 1964, 9, 129–135. Reprinted by permission of the *Journal of Analytical Psychology* and the author.

The author wishes to acknowledge her gratitude to the Educational Testing Service, Princeton, New Jersey, for making the Myers-Briggs Type Indicators available for the purposes of this study, and to Dr. Joseph Wheelwright and Dr. Horace Gray for their cooperation with regard to the use of their test. She also wishes to express her appreciation to the members of the Society of Jungian Analysts of Northern California and of the Society of Analytical Psychology of Southern California for their participation; special thanks are due to Dr. Bruno Klopfer and Dr. William Alex for handling the collection of data for the latter society.

SUBJECTS AND PROCEDURE

Twenty-eight practising analysts, members of the two Jungian analytical societies in California, participated in this study. The group consisted
of 17 males and 11 females between the ages of 34 and 70 years (median
chronological age: 50.0 years), either licensed physicians or certified psychologists. The subjects were asked, before taking either test, to indicate
the type to which they thought they belonged in terms of introversion
versus extraversion, sensation versus intuition, and thinking versus feeling.
After so classifying themselves, they were asked to fill out the Gray-Wheelwright Questionnaire (14th draft) and the Myers-Briggs Type Indicator
(Form F) without direction as to sequence.

For those not familiar with these tests, a brief description of them
may be helpful. The Gray-Wheelwright consists of 85 items in the form
of a question with two answers. Item number 22, for example, is: "Do you
prefer to (A) Hear about a thing; (B) Read about a thing?" And item
number 29: "In room decorations, do you prefer (A) Primary colours, (B)
Earthy tones?" The directions for the Gray-Wheelwright ask the subject to
choose the answer which "best describes your original inborn tendency, as
distinguished from what you may wish to do, and from what you have
made of yourself."

The Myers-Briggs is in three parts: Part I consists of 71 items identical in form with those of the Gray-Wheelwright; Part II consists of 52
pairs of words (e.g., who/what; soft/hard; make/create) with the direction
to check which word appeals most; Part III consists of 43 items identical in
form with those of Part I, ending with "Would you have liked to argue
the meaning of (A) a lot of these questions; (B) only a few?"

The self-typing of Jungian analysts provides excellent criterion data
against which to validate tests of psychological types, in that the fact of
their being Jungian analysts specially qualifies them to classify themselves
according to type. The test results of such a group, however, just because of
these qualifications, may be more markedly influenced by the conscious and
unconscious motivations which operate in the taking of such questionnaires.
Our procedure did not provide for studying the nature or extent of this
influence.

RESULTS

The data to be analysed consist of three sets of type indices for each
of the 28 subjects. Table 8-1 shows the frequencies of basic types (without
reference to the superiority of the perception or the judgement function) as

indicated by self-typing, by the Myers-Briggs test, and by the Gray-Wheelwright test, together with the distribution of types within the general population as scored by and reported for the Myers-Briggs (Saunders, 1958, p. 17) and the Gray-Wheelwright (Gray and Wheelwright, 1946, p. 10) tests. Of the percentages shown for the general population, the greatest disparity is for the introvert-sensation-thinking type, which is the largest group on the Gray-Wheelwright scale but one of the smallest on the Myers-Briggs. According to both tests, over 30 per cent of the general population fall into the two extravert-sensation groups: extravert-sensation-feeling and extravert-sensation-thinking.

It will be noted that although the two tests agree in finding the general American population approximately equally divided as between feeling and thinking types and split approximately 75 to 25 per cent as between the sensation and the intuitive types, they do not agree as to the proportion of extraverts and introverts. The Myers-Briggs data show 75 per cent extraverts to 25 per cent introverts, whereas Gray-Wheelwright data show 45 per cent extraverts to 55 per cent introverts, or a roughly equal division. How far this is due to differences in test construction and norms and how far to differences in sampling is not clear from our data. The close agreement of the two tests in the extravert versus introvert classification of our 28 subjects (5 extraverts according to the Myers-Briggs; 4 according to the Gray-Wheelwright) would suggest that the differences for the general population are due rather to sampling than to test differences, but the number of subjects in our study is too small for any definite conclusions to be drawn from it. For our subjects it is in the thinking versus feeling classification that the two tests are most divergent.

A marked contrast between the Jungian analysts and the general population is apparent from Table 8-1. It will be noted that approximately 70 per cent of the analysts fall into the introvert-intuitive-feeling or the introvert-intuitive-thinking groups as classified by themselves or by either test, whereas less than 15 per cent of the general population as classified by either test fall into these groups. Less than 20 per cent of the Jungian analysts, whether classified by themselves or by test, fall into the four sensation groups (introvert-sensation-thinking, introvert-sensation-feeling, extravert-sensation-feeling, or extravert-sensation-thinking), as contrasted with over 70 per cent of the general population according to both tests.

A breakdown by sex of the Myers-Briggs data on the Jungian analysts shows that 15 of the 17 male analysts, or 88 per cent, were classified by the Myers-Briggs test as introverted, compared with 25 per cent of the general male population; 8 of the 11 female analysts, or 73 per cent, were classified by the Myers-Briggs test as introverted, compared with 25 per cent of the general female population. Fifteen of the male analysts, or 84 per cent, were classified by the Myers-Briggs test as of intuitive type, compared with 20 per cent of the general male population; 11 of the female analysts, or

TABLE 8-1.   Self-Typing versus Myers-Briggs and Gray-Wheelwright
for 28 Jungian Analysts and for General Population

Type[1]	Self-typing of analysts N[2]	%	Myers–Briggs Analysts N	%	General population %	Gray–Wheelwright Analysts N	%	General population %
IUF	10	36	13	46	3	12	43	6
IUT	9	32	7	25	2	9	32	8
EUT	4	14			6	3	11	5
IST	3	11			8	2	7	31
ISF	1	4	3	11	12	1	4	10
ESF	1	4			36			15
EST					24			16
EUF			4	14	9	1	4	9
ES[3]			1	4				
Total I	23	83	23	82	25	24	86	55
Total S	5	19	4	15	80	3	11	72
Total T	16	57	7	25	40	14	50	60

[1] I = Introvert; E = Extravert; U = Intuition; S = Sensation; T = Thinking;
F = Feeling.

[2] N = Number of subjects.

[3] The Myers–Briggs score was zero for one subject on the T–F scale, indicating
that neither was superior to the other.

100 per cent, were classified by the Myers-Briggs test as of intuitive type,
compared with 20 per cent of the general female population. Ten of the
male analysts, or 59 per cent, were classified by the Myers-Briggs test as of
feeling type, compared with 40 per cent of the general male population; 10
of the female analysts, or 90 per cent, were classified by the Myers-Briggs
test as of feeling type, compared with 80 per cent of the general female
population. According to these data, classification as to introvert/extravert
and intuitive/sensation is related rather to whether one is an analyst than
to whether one is male or female; whereas classification as to thinking/
feeling is related rather to one's sex. Complete data for making parallel
comparisons for self-typing and for the Gray-Wheelwright test are not
available.

The next comparisons to be made are between self-typing and test
scores. Table 8-2 presents frequencies and percentages of concordance for
each test with the criterion of self-typing and with each other for basic type
(without reference to the superiority of perception or judgement), and for
introversion/extraversion, sensation/intuition, thinking/feeling, and judg-
ing/perceptive. It should be noted that the Myers-Briggs test provides a
score for judging/perceptive, making four indices for four pairs of opposites
rather than the three pairs described by Jung. For the purposes of this study
the Myers-Briggs judging/perceptive score was compared with the analyst's

TABLE 8-2. Comparison of Self-Typing, Myers-Briggs, and Gray-Wheelwright for 28 Analysts on Basic Types and Separate Indices

Comparisons	Basic type N	Basic type %	I–E N	I–E %	S–U N	S–U %	T–F N	T–F %	P–J N	P–J %
Self-typing v. M–B	12	43†	28	100***	19	68*	17	61	15	54
Self-typing v. G–W	17	61†	27	96***	22	79***	22	79***	19	68*
M–B v. G–W	15	54†	27	96***	21	75**	20	72*	14	50

Columns I–E, S–U, T–F, P–J fall under the heading "Identical Indices".

* Significantly different from chance beyond .05 level.
** Significantly different from chance beyond .01 level.
*** Significantly different from chance beyond .001 level.
† Significance of difference from chance not computed because of undetermined effect on chance of the interrelationships among the types.

indication of whether he considered his judgement function (thinking/feeling) or his perception function (sensation/intuition) to be his superior function. Comparable data from the Gray-Wheelwright test were obtained by noting for which function the score showed the largest difference from the mid score of the respective scales and assigning it as the index of the superior function in the judgement/perception classification.

A high congruence is immediately noted for introversion/extraversion: all three comparisons reach or approach 100 per cent. A comparison of the other percentages indicates that the Gray-Wheelwright agrees with the criterion of self-typing more closely than it does with the Myers-Briggs or than the Myers-Briggs does with the criterion.

A question which might be asked is whether the discrepancies between criterion and test classifications reflect large or small discrepancies in scores. We might ask, thus, whether a subject who classified himself as of thinking type and was classified as of feeling type by one of the tests received a score which was well into the feeling range of scores or was close to the mid point between feeling and thinking. The data showed that the Myers-Briggs test differentiated introverts from extraverts, as classified by themselves, with two separate distributions and no overlapping. The separation between introverts and extraverts on the Gray-Wheelwright was not complete, but the one subject who classified himself as extravert and was classified as introvert by the test obtained a score close to the mid point of the scale.

As regards the parallel distributions for the intuitive/sensation scales, it was found that four subjects who classified themselves as intuitive types and were classified as sensation types by the Myers-Briggs test obtained scores which spread over a wide range, with one falling at the upper end of the distribution of sensation scores. The five subjects who typed themselves as sensation and were classified as intuitive by the Myers-Biggs test likewise obtained scores over a wide range. Three of the six subjects who were misclassified as to sensation versus intuitive type by the Gray-Wheelwright test obtained scores within two intervals of the mid point.

It was in the thinking/feeling classification that the largest discrepancies between self-typing and test scores occurred. One of the subjects who classified himself as of thinking type received the highest score of the total group as a feeling type on the Myers-Briggs. The score distributions of subjects who typed themselves as thinking and of those who typed themselves as feeling, and were classified as feeling on the Myers-Briggs scale, were not significantly different. There was somewhat less overlap on the Gray-Wheelwright test.

SUMMARY AND CONCLUSIONS

A group of 28 Jungian analysts practising in California were asked to classify themselves according to Jung's psychological types, and to take the Myers-Briggs Type Indicator and the Gray-Wheelwright Questionnaire. The most significant findings follow:

1. Jungian analysts as a group are markedly differentiated from the general population in the higher incidence of introvert-intuitive types and the low incidence of sensation types.
2. Both tests showed an almost perfect concordance with analysts' self-typing in the introvert/extravert classification.
3. Both tests showed a greater than chance concordance with self-typing in the sensation/intuition classification.
4. The Gray-Wheelwright test showed a greater than chance concordance with self-typing in the thinking/feeling classification and in the perception/judgement classification.

REFERENCES

Gray, H. (1945). "Intuition and psychotherapists," *Stanford medical Bulletin 3*.
Gray, H. (1946). "Jung's psychological types in relation to occupation, race, body-build," *Stanford medical Bulletin 4*.
Gray, H. (1947). "Jung's psychological types: meaning and consistency of the questionnaire," *J. gen. Psychol. 37*.
Gray, H. (1948). "Jung's psychological types in men and women," *Stanford medical Bulletin 6*.
Gray, H. (1949). "Jung's psychological types: ambiguous scores and their interpretation." *J. gen. Psychol. 40.* (a)
Gray, H. (1949). "Psychological types in married people," *J. soc. Psychol. 29.* (b)

Gray, H. (1949). "Freud and Jung; their contrasting psychological types," *Psychoanal. Rev.* 36. (c)

Gray, H. & Wheelwright, J. (1944). "Jung's psychological types and marriage," *Stanford medical Bulletin 2.*

Gray, H. & Wheelwright, J. (1945). "Jung's psychological types, including the four functions," *J. gen. Psychol. 33.*

Gray, H. & Wheelwright, J. (1946). "Jung's psychological types, their frequency of occurrence," *J. gen. Psychol. 34.*

Gray, H. & Wheelwright, J. (1947). "Psychological types and changes with age," *J. clin. Psychol. 3.*

Jung, C. G. (1921). *Psychologische Typen.* Zurich, Rascher. Trans. *Psychological Types.* Dondon, Kegan Paul, 1923: New York, Harcourt Brace, 1923.

Myers, I. B. (1945). *Type as the index to personality.* Swarthmore, Penn., privately printed.

* Myers, I. B. (1962). *The Myers-Briggs Type Indicator.* Princeton, Educational Testing Service.

Saunders, D. R. (1958). Preliminary discussion of the Myers-Briggs Type Indicator. *Research Memorandum* 58-I. Princeton, Educational Testing Service.

* Stricker, L. J. & Ross, J. (1962). A description and evaluation of the Myers-Briggs Type Indicator. *Research Bulletin* 62-6. Princeton, Educational Testing Service.

* These works were published subsequent to the writing and acceptance for publication of this paper.

9

Some Correlates of a
Jungian Personality Inventory

LAWRENCE J. STRICKER
& JOHN ROSS

While Jung's personality typology (Jung, 1923, 1933, 1953) has been widely influential, its main impact on personality measurements has been to promote an abiding interest in just one facet of the typology—extraversion-introversion. The many scales which have been developed through the years to measure this variable attest to the intensity of this interest.

The measurement of the other variables in Jung's typology, however, has not been entirely neglected. Some time ago, the Gray-Wheelwright Psychological Type Questionnaire (Gray, 1947a, 1948, 1949a; Gray & Wheelwright, 1946) was developed to measure all the variables in Jung's typology—the attitudes (extraversion and introversion) as well as the functions (sensation, intuition, thinking, and feeling). More recently, there has been growing interest in a similar inventory, the Myers-Briggs Type Indicator (Myers, 1962b).

In view of the potential value of these inventories in operationally defining Jung's typology, an assessment of their construct validity seems appropriate. Studies concerned with one facet of the Indicator's construct validity—the existence of the underlying typological framework—have already been reported elsewhere (Lord, 1958; Myers, 1962a, 1962b; Stricker & Ross, 1964). The studies in the present article, like some others (Howarth, 1962; Myers, 1962b; Ross, 1961, 1963; Saunders, 1960), primarily bear on another facet of the Indicator's construct validity—the correspondence between the scales and the underlying constructs which are integrated by the typological framework. The series of studies reported in this article were

From L. J. Stricker and J. Ross. Some Correlates of a Jungian Personality Inventory. *Psychological Reports*, 1964, 14, 623–643. Reprinted with permission of author and publisher.

The following people graciously furnished the raw data which are the basis of the studies reported in this article: Dr. William C. Craig of Stanford University, Mr. David W. Galloway of Golden Gate College, Dr. C. Hess Haagen of Wesleyan University, Dr. Harold A. Korn of Stanford University, and Mrs. Kathryn Pruden of Long Island University.

118

undertaken by the present authors to appraise two related issues: (a) whether the Indicator scales appropriately reflect the distinctions embodied in the typology and explicitly described in the conceptual definition of each of the typological variables; and, alternatively, (b) whether the Indicator scales reflect, to a greater or lesser extent, other variables which are not a part of the typology. These studies investigated (a) the scales' correlations with ability, interest, and personality scales and (b) differences on the scales between the sexes, and between high school students in college preparatory and general-vocational programs.

MYERS-BRIGGS TYPE INDICATOR

The Indicator is a self-report inventory which consists of four scales: Extraversion-Introversion (E-I), Sensation-Intuition (S-N),[1] Thinking-Feeling (T-F), and Judging-Perceiving (J-P).

These scales were expressly developed to classify people into type categories (e.g., classification as an extravert, an introvert, or, in those cases where the two tendencies are equal, "indeterminate") which would have real meaning. The cutting (or "zero") points used in making these classifications were so chosen that those people who are on one side of a scale's cutting point, and, hence, in one type category, are presumed to be qualitatively different from those who are on the other side of it, and hence, in the opposite type category. In addition to these categorical classifications, continuous scores for each scale can be derived by arbitrarily considering one end of the scale high (Stricker & Ross, 1963, p. 287).[2]

In the studies described in this article, results are reported for continuous scores, and, in some cases, type categories as well.

[1] Note that the abbreviation of Intuition is N; I is used as the abbreviation of Introversion.

[2] After the studies reported in this article were completed, the Indicator's manual appeared, changing the scoring system so as to eliminate indeterminate type categories. This goal was accomplished by combining a scale's indeterminate type category with one of the two other type categories on that scale. The original continuous scores were also linearly transformed. The use of the new scoring would have no appreciable effect on these studies' type category results, in view of the small number of Ss in the indeterminate type categories, and would not alter the *t* tests and correlations reported for the continuous scores in these present studies, although it does affect the means and standard deviations. Note that in reporting the results of the present studies as well as discussing previous studies, the scoring convention described in the Indicator's manual (Myers, 1962b) has been followed: the I, N, F, and P ends of the scales are high and the E, S, T, and J ends are low. Hence, high scores on the E-I, S-N, T-F, and J-P scales signify, respectively, tendencies toward introversion, intuition, feeling, and perceiving, and low scores on these scales signify, respectively, tendencies toward extraversion, sensation, thinking, and judging. In two previous articles by the present authors (Sticker & Ross, 1963, 1964) the opposite scoring convention was followed: the E, S, T, and J ends of the scales were high.

The conceptual definitions of the four dimensions that the Indicator's scales are presumed to represent (Myers, 1962b) appear below. These definitions seem to differ somewhat from Jung's (Stricker & Ross, 1962).

Extraversion-Introversion

This attitude is defined in the following way.

The introvert's main interests are in the inner world of concepts and ideas, while the extravert's main interests are in the outer world of people and things. Therefore, when circumstances permit, the introvert directs both perception and judgment upon ideas, while the extravert likes to direct both upon his outside environment . . . (Myers, 1962b, p. 57).

Judging-Perceiving

It is argued (a) that a great part of *overt* cognitive activity can be regarded as either judging (coming to a conclusion about something) or perceiving (becoming aware of something),[3] and (b) that there are two ways of judging—thinking and feeling—and two ways of perceiving—sensation and intuition.

There is a fundamental difference between the two attitudes. In the judging attitude, in order to come to a conclusion, perception must be shut off for the time being. The evidence is all in. Anything more is incompetent, irrelevant and immaterial. One now arrives at a verdict and gets things settled. Conversely, in the perceptive attitude one shuts off judgment for the time being. The evidence is not all in. There is much more to it than this. New developments will occur. It is much too soon to do anything irrevocable (Myers, 1962b, p. 58).

Thinking-Feeling

The two modes of judgment—thinking and feeling—are described in the following way.

. . . *thinking* . . . is a logical process, aimed at an impersonal finding. . . . *feeling* . . . is a process of appreciation . . . bestowing on things a personal, subjective value.
        . . . If, when one judges these ideas, he concentrates on whether or not they are true, that is thinking-judgment. If one is conscious first of like or dislike, of whether these concepts are sympathetic or antagonistic to other ideas he prizes, that is feeling-judgment (Myers, 1962b, p. 52).

        [3] No separate and explicit variable reflecting individual differences of this kind is found in Jung's typology, but Jung does classify each of the four functions as either rational and judging or irrational and perceiving.

Sensation-Intuition

The two modes of perception—sensation and intuition—are described in the following way.

There is not only the familiar process of *sensing*, by which we become aware of things directly through our five senses. There is also the process of *intuition*, which is indirect perception by way of the unconscious, accompanied by ideas or associations which the unconscious tacks on to the perceptions coming from outside. These unconscious contributions range from the merest masculine "hunch" or "woman's intuition" to the crowning examples of creative art or scientific discovery.

. . . When people prefer sensing, they find too much of interest in the actuality around them to spend much energy listening for ideas out of nowhere. When people prefer intuition, they are too much interested in all the possibilities that occur to them to give a whole lot of notice to the actualities (Myers, 1962b, pp. 51–52).

STUDY I. Correlations with Scholastic Aptitude Test, Concept Mastery Test, Ship Destination Test, Survey of Study Habits and Attitudes, and Minnesota Multiphasic Personality Inventory

Method

A large battery of tests, including the Concept Mastery Test (Terman, 1956), the Ship Destination Test (Christensen & Guilford, 1956), the Survey of Study Habits and Attitudes (SSHA) (Brown & Holtzman, 1956), and the Minnesota Multiphasic Personality Inventory (MMPI) (Hathaway & McKinley, 1951), was administered to an entering freshman class of 254 male students at Wesleyan University. The Scholastic Aptitude Test's (College Entrance Examination Board, 1962; Dyer & King, 1955) verbal (SAT-V) and mathematical (SAT-M) subtest scores were also obtained from school records. The MMPI was scored for the standard clinical and validity scales and three response style scales: Edwards' (1957b) Social Desirability (SD) scale, a balanced SD scale designed to reduce content and acquiescence effects (Stricker, 1963), and an acquiescence scale based on the same items as the balanced SD scale. The results were analyzed for the 225 students for whom complete data were available.

Results

The product-moment correlations between the Indicator's continuous scores and the other scales appear in Table 9-1.

TABLE 9-1.   Correlations Between Indicator and Scholastic Aptitude
              Test, Concept Mastery Test, Ship Destination Test, Survey
              of Study Habits and Attitudes, and Minnesota Multiphasic
              Personality Inventory for Male Freshmen at Wesleyan
              University (N = 225)

| | Indicator Scale | | | |
Scale	E-I	S-N	T-F	J-P
SAT-V	.27**	.34**	—.10	.08
SAT-M	.20**	.22**	—.15*	—.03
Concept Mastery Test	.29**	.28**	—.09	—.04
Ship Destination Test	—.04	—.01	—.04	—.06
Survey of Study Habits and				
Attitudes	—.07	.12	—.20**	—.31**
MMPI				
?	—.04	.11	.08	—.03
L	—.12	.06	—.17*	—.11
F	.22**	—.05	—.03	.24**
K	—.23**	.06	—.13*	—.18**
Hs	.10	—.05	—.01	.03
D	.39**	—.06	.05	.10
Hy	—.05	.05	.01	.06
Pd	—.08	.11	.12	.23**
Mf	.22**	.33**	.22**	.17*
Pa	.12	.04	.12	.03
Pt	.30**	—.07	.19**	.13*
Sc	.23**	.03	.07	.17*
Ma	—.29**	.09	—.06	.16*
Si	.63**	—.06	.02	.10
Edwards' SD	—.38**	.08	—.19**	—.19**
Balanced SD	—.28**	.03	—.11	—.19**
Balanced Acquiescence	—.19**	.06	.06	.06

     * $p = .05$
     ** $p = .01$

The E-I and S-N scales had a similar pattern of significant ($p < .01$)
correlations with three ability tests: SAT-V, SAT-M, and the Concept Mastery Test. The E-I scale's correlations ranged from .20 to .29, and the S-N
scale's correlations ranged from .22 to .34. However, neither of these Indicator scales correlated significantly ($p > .05$) with a fourth ability test, the
Ship Destination Test, and none of the other Indicator scales correlated
significantly ($p > .05$) with any of the ability tests.

The T-F and J-P scales correlated significantly ($p < .01$) with the
SSHA ($r = -.20$ for the T-F scale and $r = -.31$ for the J-P scale).

The Indicator, had generally low but significant ($p < .05$) correlations with the MMPI clinical scales (corrected for K where appropriate).
One important exception was the E-I scale's correlation of .63 with an ex-

traversion-introversion scale—*Si*. The E-I scale also correlated with a neurotic scale—*D* (*r* = .39) three of the four psychotic scales—*Pt* (*r* = .30), *Ma* (*r* = −.29), and *Sc* (*r* = .23), and a masculinity-femininity scale—*Mf* (*r* = .22). The S-N scale's only significant correlation was one of .33 with a masculinity-femininity scale—*Mf*. The T-F scale had two significant correlations—one of .22 with a masculinity-femininity scale—*Mf*, and the other of .19 with a psychotic scale—*Pt*. The J-P scale's highest correlation was one of .23 with a psychopathic deviate scale—*Pd*.

There were also some low but significant (*p* < .05) correlations with the MMPI validity scales. The highest were the E-I scale's correlations of −.23 with *K* and .22 with *F*, and the J-P scale's correlations of .24 with *F* and −.18 with *K*.

There were also some significant (*p* < .01) correlations with the MMPI response style scales. The E-I scale correlated −.38 with the Edwards SD scale, −.28 with the balanced SD scale, and −.19 with the acquiescence scale. The T-F scale correlated −.19 with the Edwards SD scale, and the J-P scale correlated −.19 with each of the SD scales.

STUDY II. Correlations with Gray-Wheelwright Psychological Type Questionnaire

Method

The Indicator and the 14th edition of the Gray-Wheelwright Psychological Type Questionnaire [4] were administered in counterbalanced order to the 51 students in two undergraduate classes at Golden Gate College. The results for the 47 men were analyzed. They were about evenly distributed between day and evening sessions, and their age range was 19 to 55.

Results

As Table 9-2 indicates, all the product-moment correlations between the continuous scores for the corresponding scales on the two inventories were significant (*p* < .01). The E-I scales correlated .79, the S-N scales cor-

---

[4] A copy of this version of the inventory may be obtained by writing to Dr. Joseph B. Wheelwright, 2206 Steiner Street, San Francisco, California. Gray and Wheelwright report continuous scores based on the percentage of extravert responses to answered E-I items, the percentage of intuitive responses to answered S-N items, and the percentage of feeling responses to answered T-F items (Gray, 1947b, 1949b; Gray, Personal communication, August 14, 1961; Gray & Wheelwright, 1944). In the present study, so as to be consistent with the direction of the scoring used with the continuous Indicator scores, continuous scores for the Gray-Wheelwright inventory were based on the percentage of introvert responses, the percentage of intuitive responses, and the percentage of feeling responses.

TABLE 9-2.   Correlations Between Indicator and Gray-Wheelwright
              Psychological Type Questionnaire for Male Students
              at Golden Gate College (N = 47)

Gray-Wheelwright Scale	Indicator Scale			
	E-I	S-N	T-F	J-P
E-I	.79**	.00	−.37**	−.16
S-N	−.24	.58**	.15	.41**
T-F	−.20	.17	.60**	.33*

* $p = .05$
** $p = .01$

related .58, and the T-F scales correlated .60. In addition, the Indicator T-F
scale correlated −.37 ($p < .01$) with the Gray-Wheelwright E-I scale, and
the Indicator J-P scale correlated .41 ($p < .01$) with the Gray-Wheelwright
S-N scale and .33 ($p < .05$) with the Gray-Wheelwright T-F scale.

STUDY III. Correlations With California Psychological Inventory and Strong Vocational Interest Blank

Method

A battery of tests, including the Indicator, the California Psychological Inventory (CPI) (Gough, 1957), and the Strong Vocational Interest
Blank (SVIB) (Strong, 1959), was administered to an entering male freshman class at Stanford University, which totaled 889 students. Scores were
available for both the Indicator and the CPI for 713 students, and both the
Indicator and the SVIB for 727 students.[5]

Results

The product-moment correlations between the Indicator's continuous
scores and the CPI scales appear in Table 9-3. Many significant ($p < .05$)
correlations were obtained.

The E-I scale's highest correlations, all of which were negative, were
with ascendance and self-assurance scales—*Sy* ($r = -.67$), *Do* ($r = -.53$),
Sa ($r = -.53$), and *Sp* ($r = -.47$). It had somewhat lower negative correlations with a social status scale—*Cs* ($r = -.35$), two achievement and
intellectual potential scales—*Ie* ($r = -.21$) and *Ac* ($r = -.16$), and two

---

[5] In computing the correlations with the SVIB scales, the SVIB standard scores
were grouped into 10 intervals, which were derived from the intervals on which the
SVIB letter ratings are based.

TABLE 9-3. Correlations Between Indicator and California
Psychological Inventory for Male Freshmen at Stanford
University (N = 713)

CPI	Indicator Scale			
Scale	E-I	S-N	T-F	J-P
Do	−.53**	.07	.00	−.06
Cs	−.35**	.29**	.02	.03
Sy	−.67**	.05	.06	−.01
Sp	−.47**	.15**	.00	.22**
Sa	−.53**	.08*	.04	.09*
Wb	−.23**	.02	−.06	−.17**
Re	−.06	.03	−.01	−.30**
So	−.03	−.12**	−.03	−.32**
Sc	.09*	−.10**	−.06	−.34**
To	−.16**	.16**	.03	−.08*
Gi	−.16**	.02	−.01	−.27**
Cm	−.06	−.17**	−.02	−.24**
Ac	−.16**	−.01	−.05	−.37**
Ai	.10**	.27**	.06	.00
Ie	−.21**	.24**	−.06	−.03
Py	.01	.25**	−.07	.02
Fx	.04	.29**	.09*	.45**
Fe	.13**	−.05	.17**	−.19**

* $p = .05$
** $p = .01$

of the three response bias scales—Wb ($r = -.23$) and Gi ($r = -.16$). The
S-N scale's highest correlations, all of which were positive, were with a social
status scale—Cs ($r = .29$), a flexibility scale—Fx ($r = .29$), two achievement and intellectual potential scales—Ai ($r = .27$) and Ie ($r = .24$), and
a "psychological mindedness" scale—Py ($r = .25$). The T-F scale's highest
correlation was one of .17 with a masculinity-femininity scale—Fe. The J-P
scale's highest positive correlations were with a flexibility scale—Fx ($r = .45$),
and a social presence scale—Sp ($r = .22$). Its highest negative correlations
were with an achievement potential scale—Ac ($r = -.37$), and maturity,
socialization, and responsibility scales—Sc ($r = -.34$), So ($r = -.32$), and
Re ($r = -.30$). It also correlated negatively with the three response bias
scales—Gi ($r = -.27$), Cm ($r = -.24$), and Wb ($r = -.17$).

The product-moment correlations between the Indicator's continuous
scores and the SVIB scales appear in Table 9-4.

There were many significant ($p < .05$) correlations with the SVIB
occupational scales. The E-I scale's highest positive correlations were with
the professional (Group I) and technical-scientific (Group II) scales; its
highest negative correlations were with the social service (Group V) and
business contact (Group IX) scales. The S-N scale's highest positive cor-

TABLE 9-4.   Correlations Between Indicator and Strong Vocational Interest Blank for Male Freshmen at Stanford University (N = 727)

SVIB Scale	Indicator Scale			
	E-I	S-N	T-F	J-P
Group I				
Artist	.26**	.37**	.03	.20**
Psychologist	.10**	.55**	.06	.15**
Architect	.29**	.39**	—.01	.13**
Physician	.14**	.44**	.07	.13**
Osteopath	—.01	.22**	.13**	.08*
Dentist	.24**	.19**	—.00	.01
Veterinarian	—.08*	—.18**	.07	—.01
Group II				
Mathematician	.37**	.25**	—.12**	.00
Physicist	.35**	.25**	—.09*	.01
Engineer	.24**	.12**	—.18**	—.05
Chemist	.31**	.28**	—.09*	—.01
Group III				
Production Manager	—.11**	—.15**	—.20**	—.14**
Group IV				
Farmer	.17**	—.15**	—.02	.02
Aviator	.06	.04	—.06	.11**
Carpenter	.11**	—.10**	—.04	—.08*
Printer	.17**	.12**	.04	.03
Math. Phys. Sci. Teacher	.04	.10**	.03	—.07
Ind. Arts Teacher	.03	—.03	—.02	—.06
Voc. Agricul. Teacher	—.10**	—.15**	.09*	—.02
Policeman	—.17**	—.13**	.05	—.07
Forest Service Man	—.05	—.02	.02	.02
Group V				
Y.M.C.A. Phys. Director	—.35**	.12**	.20**	.01
Personnel Director	—.31**	.14**	.07	.01
Public Administrator	—.28**	.21**	.07	.01
Y.M.C.A. Secretary	—.32**	.09*	.19**	—.02
Soc. Sci. H.S. Teacher	—.24**	.03	.17**	—.02
City School Sup't.	—.26**	.19**	.18**	—.03
Social Worker	—.25**	.29**	.18**	.07
Minister	—.17**	.31**	.21**	.04
Group VI				
Musician (Performer)	.05	.37**	.16**	.17**
Group VII				
C.P.A.	.03	.05	—.13**	—.06
Group VIII				
Senior C.P.A.	—.04	—.06	—.10*	—.09*

TABLE 9-4.   Correlations Between Indicator and Strong Vocational
Interest Blank for Male Freshmen at Stanford University
(N = 727) (continued)

SVIB Scale	Indicator Scale			
	E-I	S-N	T-F	J-P
Accountant	—.04	—.29**	—.15**	—.24**
Office Man	—.13**	—.30**	.02	—.18**
Purchasing Agent	—.11**	—.49**	—.22**	—.22**
Banker	—.09*	—.51**	—.09*	—.23**
Mortician	—.33**	—.37**	.09*	—.10**
Pharmacist	—.17**	—.18**	—.01	—.09*
Group IX				
Sales Manager	—.37**	—.22**	—.04	—.03
Real Estate Salesman	—.26**	—.22**	.02	.08*
Life Insurance Salesman	—.35**	—.13**	.14**	.02
Group X				
Advertising Man	—.10**	.25**	.11**	.19**
Lawyer	—.03	.15**	.06	.12**
Author-Journalist	.14**	.29**	.05	.19**
Group XI				
President Mfg. Concern	—.06	—.16**	—.17**	—.09*
Interest Maturity	—.20**	.06	.03	—.09*
Occupational Level	.01	.06	—.06	—.04
Masculinity-Femininity	.05	—.17**	—.22**	—.03

* $p = .05$
** $p = .01$

relations were with the professional (Group I), technical-scientific (Group II), social service (Group V), and verbal (Group X) scales; its highest negative correlations were with the business detail (Group VIII) and business contact (Group IX) scales. The T-F scale's highest positive correlations were with the social service (Group V) scales; it had significant but not appreciable negative correlations with several groups of scales. The J-P scales highest positive correlations were with the verbal (Group X) scales; its highest negative correlations were with the business detail (Group VIII) scales.

There were some scattered significant ($p < .05$) but moderate correlations with the non-occupational scales. The E-I and J-P scales were negatively correlated with the Interest Maturity scale ($r = -.20$ for the former, and $r = -.09$ for the latter), and the S-N and T-F scales were negatively correlated with the Masculinity-Femininity scale ($r = -.17$ for the former and $r = -.22$ for the latter). None of the Indicator scales were significantly ($p > .05$) correlated with the Occupational Level Scale.

STUDY IV. Differences Between Sexes and Between High School Programs

Method

The Indicator was administered to (a) the 12th grade classes of eight Massachusetts high schools, consisting of 397 male and 614 female students; and (b) an entering freshman class at Long Island University (LIU), consisting of 300 male and 184 female students. All but a few of the high school students were classifiable, on the basis of the program that they reported on their Indicator answer sheets, into those in the college preparatory program and those in the general-vocational program.

Differences between the sexes and between high school programs were assessed by χ^2 tests of differences in the distributions of Indicator type categories and t tests of mean scores on Indicator scales.

Results

The distributions of type categories appear in Table 9-5, and the means and standard deviations of the continuous scores appear in Table 9-6. The χ^2 tests appear in Table 9-7 and the t tests in Table 9-8.

There were significant ($p < .05$) differences between the boys and girls within (a) the college preparatory high school group; (b) the general-vocational high school group; and (c) the LIU class. (a) Within the college preparatory group, a greater proportion of girls than boys were classified as sensing and feeling. These findings are supported by the mean differences of the S-N and T-F scales. (b) Within the general-vocational group, a greater proportion of girls than boys were classified as judging. This finding is supported by the mean difference on the J-P scale. The mean difference on the T-F scale indicated that the girls also tended to more feeling. (c) Among the LIU students, a greater proportion of girls than boys were classified as sensing and feeling. These findings are supported by the mean differences on the S-N and T-F scales. The mean differences on the E-I and J-P scales indicated that the girls also tended to be more extraverted and judging.

There also were significant ($p < .05$) differences between students in the college preparatory and general-vocational high school programs. (a) Among the boys, a greater proportion of those in the college preparatory program than those in the other program were classified as extraverts, intuitive, and thinking. These findings are supported by the mean differences on the E-I, S-N, and T-F scales. (b) Among the girls, a greater proportion of

TABLE 9-5. Percentage of Ss in Each Type Category

Group	N	E	X	I	X	S	X	N	T	X	F	J	X	P
High School Students														
Male Coll. Prep.	146	64.4	6.2	29.5		54.8	3.4	41.8	56.2	.7	43.2	55.5	2.1	42.5
Male Gen'l-Vocat.	230	58.3	1.7	40.0		85.2	4.8	10.0	43.5	4.3	52.2	52.6	1.7	45.7
Female Coll. Prep.	148	67.6	2.7	29.7		68.9	2.7	28.4	31.1	2.0	66.9	49.3	2.7	48.0
Female Gen'l-Vocat.	433	61.0	3.5	35.6		87.3	1.8	10.9	37.6	2.3	60.0	62.1	3.0	34.9
LIU Students														
Male	300	68.0	2.7	29.3		64.3	1.7	34.0	58.0	3.7	38.3	60.7	.7	38.7
Female	184	73.4	1.6	25.0		66.8	5.4	27.7	32.1	2.2	65.8	69.0	.5	30.4

TABLE 9-6. Means and Standard Deviations of Indicator Scores

Group	E-I M	E-I SD	S-N M	S-N SD	T-F M	T-F SD	J-P M	J-P SD
High School Students								
Male Coll. Prep.	5.25(E)	11.46	2.04(S)	12.54	1.34(T)	9.24	1.20(J)	12.82
Male Gen'l-Vocat.	2.46(E)	11.77	11.13(S)	9.28	1.12(F)	8.17	1.15(J)	12.05
Female Coll. Prep.	5.20(E)	12.82	4.92(S)	10.95	4.16(F)	9.88	1.64(J)	13.84
Female Gen'l-Vocat.	3.69(E)	12.51	12.02(S)	9.36	3.00(F)	9.65	4.28(J)	12.37
LIU Students								
Male	4.88(E)	11.15	3.80(S)	11.25	2.40(T)	9.84	3.40(J)	14.26
Female	7.10(E)	11.32	6.27(S)	12.17	4.77(F)	9.76	7.15(J)	12.53

Note: The number of Ss in each group is reported in Table 9-5.

TABLE 9-7. χ^2 Tests of Differences in Type Categories for High School and LIU Student Groups

| | Difference Between Sexes | | | Difference Between HS Programs | |
Scale	College Prep. Program	Gen'l-Vocat. Program	LIU	Males	Females
E-I	2.11	2.54	1.78	8.38*	2.06
S-N	6.26*	4.69	6.76*	52.02**	27.01**
T-F	19.11**	4.98	34.35**	8.56*	2.20
J-P	1.15	7.77*	3.45	.39	8.06*

Note: Each χ^2 is based on 2 df.
* $p = .05$
** $p = .01$

TABLE 9-8. t Tests of Differences in Mean Indicator Scores for High School and LIU Student Groups

| | Difference Between Sexes | | | Difference Between HS Programs | |
Scale	College Prep. Program	Gen'l-Vocat. Program	LIU	Males	Females
E-I	.04	1.24	2.11*	2.26*	1.25
S-N	2.10*	1.16	2.27*	7.55†**	7.06†**
T-F	4.93**	2.64†**	2.58**	2.72**	1.25
J-P	.28	3.13**	3.03†**	.04	2.18*

* $p = .05$
** $p = .01$
† t test based on separate rather than pooled variances because variances were significantly ($p < .05$) different.

those in the college preparatory program than those in the other program were classified as intuitive and perceptive. These findings are supported by the mean differences on the S-N and J-P scales.

DISCUSSION

Extraversion-Introversion Scale

The E-I scale is intended to measure a dimension that is conceptually defined as an interest in things and people versus concepts and ideas. Its items, which resemble those on many extraversion-introversion scales, however, seem to describe interest and facility in social relations, frequently involving talkativeness.[6] An interpretation of this scale's meaning on the basis of this item content may be contrasted with the scale's conceptual definition. The emphasis on social relations found in such an item-content interpretation may be a surface reflection of the underlying interest in things and people that the conceptual definition associates with extraversion, but it seems unrelated to the interest in concepts and ideas that the conceptual definition ascribes to introversion.

The E-I scale's high correlations in the present studies with the extraversion-introversion scales on the Gray-Wheelwright Psychological Type Questionnaire and the MMPI, as well as its previously reported high correlation with the Maudsley Personality Inventory (Eysenck, 1959) (MPI) Extraversion scale (Howarth, 1962) and its loading on a factor identified as extraversion-introversion (Ross, 1963) make it appear that this scale is, to a large extent, measuring extraversion-introversion as it commonly defined. None of these relationships necessarily imply, however, that the scale is measuring this variable precisely as it is described by the conceptual definition.

The scale's conceptual definition and the item-content interpretation are both consistent with the scale's positive correlations with the SVIB technical-scientific scales, which involve an interest in concepts and ideas, and a dislike of social relations, and its negative correlations with the CPI *Sy* scale and the SVIB social service and business contact scales, which involve both an interest in things and people and an interest in social relations. These negative correlations with scales which reflect both an interest in things and people as well as an interest in social relations are consistent with the E-I scale's previously reported positive correlation with a rating of Solitary (Myers, 1962b; Ross, 1961), and its negative correlation with the Personality Research Inventory (PRI) Gregariousness scale (Myers, 1962b).

The conceptual definition, but not the item-content interpretation, seems consistent with the scale's positive correlations with three of the four ability tests, which should, at least, reflect a facility with concepts and ideas, if not an interest in them. In previous studies, the E-I scale was also consistently and positively correlated with ability tests (Myers, 1962b), but it did not load a factor identified as general ability (Ross, 1963).

The conceptual definition, however, is not consistent with the scale's negative correlations with two other scales—the CPI *Ac* and *Ie* scales—

---

[6] This interpretation of the item content of the E-I scale, as well as the item-content interpretations for the other scales, is based on an inspection of the items on each of the scales, as they appear on the standard scoring keys, and the results of unpublished item analyses by the present authors. Reproduction of any of the Indicator items in this article is precluded by the refusal of the Indicator's authors, who hold its copyright, to grant such permission.

which should also reflect either an interest in or a facility with concepts and ideas. Moreover, in previous studies, the scale was not significantly correlated with measures that are similar to these two CPI scales—the PRI Liking to Think scale (Myers, 1962b) and ratings of Poor at Analyzing, and Good Grasp of Abstract and Fundamental (Myers, 1962b; Ross, 1961).

The item-content interpretation is more directly supported than the conceptual definition by the finding that the E-I scale was negatively correlated with the CPI *Do* and *Sp* scales, both of which involve a facility in social relations, but not necessarily an interest in things and people. These results are consistent with the scale's previously reported correlations with other measures which should also involve a facility in social relations but not necessarily an interest in people—a positive correlation with a rating of Not a Potential Leader (Myers, 1962b; Ross, 1961), and negative correlations with the PRI Talkativeness and Social Know-How scales (Myers, 1962b). However, the last correlation, though significant, was slight.

Most of the other relevant findings, however, seem inconsistent with the scale's conceptual definition, but neither confirm nor refute the item-content interpretation. One such finding involves the correlations with five SVIB skilled trades scales—Aviator, Farmer, Carpenter, Printer, and Forest Service Man. All these scales primarily reflect an interest in things, though not an interest in people. Hence, on the basis of the conceptual definition, the E-I scale should be expected to correlate negatively with them. In fact, four of its five correlations with these scales were positive, three of them significantly so.

A second inconsistent finding is that the boys in the college preparatory program (the program that should most reflect an interest in concepts and ideas) tended to be more extraverted than those in the general-vocational program. The meaning of this finding may be limited, however, because no corresponding differences were obtained for the girls.

The additional possibility that the scale may also be measuring adjustment is suggested by its positive correlations with several MMPI scales —*D*, *Pt*, and *Sc*. This finding may be limited, however, since the E-I scale correlated negatively with the CPI *Sa* scale, and was not consistently correlated with other relevant MPI scales. Still, this scale was consistently correlated with measures of adjustment in previous studies. It correlated positively with the MPI Neuroticism scale (Howarth, 1962), the PRI Free-Floating Anxiety scale (Myers, 1962b), and such ratings as Needs Psychologist's Attention and Low Stamina (Ross, 1961), and it correlated negatively with such ratings as Carefree (Myers, 1962b; Ross, 1961).

This scale's consistent but typically moderate correlations with the CPI response bias scales and the MMPI validity and SD scales also suggest that this scale may be somewhat susceptible to test-taking distortion.

Sensation-Intuition Scale

The S-N scale's items seem to describe an interest in tangible, realistic things versus an interest in abstract ideas. Interest in tangible, realistic things seems congruent with the conceptual definition of sensation, which stresses the focus of sensation on actualities. Interest in abstract ideas, however, seems to be, at best, only one facet of intuition. The latter is described in the conceptual definition as sensory perception modified and combined with unconscious components, and, in effect, characterized by an interest in "possibilities."

Some of the scale's items seem to resemble those on the Thinking Extraversion scale of the Minnesota T-S-E Inventory (Evans & McConnell, 1957) and the Q_1 scale of the 16 P. F. Test (Cattell, Saunders, & Stice, 1957).

Both the conceptual definition and the item-content interpretation are supported by the scale's positive correlations with the SVIB verbal scales, which presumably reflect either intuition or an interest in abstract ideas, and its negative correlations with the SVIB business detail and business contact scales, all of which involve a focus on tangible things or actualities. In addition, a previous study (Myers, 1962b) found that the scale correlated positively with two other scales which also reflect intuition or an interest in abstract ideas—the PRI Tolerance of Complexity and Artistic vs Practical scales—but did not correlate significantly with the PRI Spiritual vs Material scale.

Two previous findings, involving measures concerned with the focus on possibilities inherent in the notion of intuition, are relevant to the conceptual definition, but not the item-content interpretation. The conceptual definition is supported by the scale's positive correlation with a rating of Shows Originality (Myers, 1962b; Ross, 1961), but it is not supported by the scale's nonsignificant correlation with the scores on the PRI Foresight scale (see, e.g., Myers, 1962b).

The item-content interpretation is also supported by several findings which are consistent with it but are not easily explained in terms of the conceptual definition. These findings involve relationships with variables that cannot be readily characterized as reflecting either sensation or intuition, but seem to reflect either an interest in abstract thinking (i.e., the positive correlations with the SVIB professional and technical-scientific scales), or at least, a facility with it (i.e., the positive correlations with most of the ability scales, the CPI *Ie* scale, and the SVIB social service scales, and the finding that the high school students of each sex in the college preparatory program tended to be more intuitive than those in the general-vocational program). These findings are consistent with previous ones. The scale's positive correlations with measures that reflect an interest in abstract thinking are paralleled by its positive correlation with the PRI Liking to Think Scale (Myers, 1962b) and its positive loading on an intellectuality factor (Ross, 1963); the scale's positive correlations with ability measures are paralleled by its positive correlations with a number of ability tests (Myers, 1962b) and its positive loading on an ability factor (Ross, 1963).

Some findings are inconsistent with both the conceptual definition and the item-content interpretation. One such finding is that the S-N scale only had significant negative correlations with three of the six SVIB skilled trades scales Farmer, Aviator, Carpenter, Printer, Policeman, and Forest Service Man—which should primarily involve an interest in either actualities or tangible things.

Other findings are simply inexplicable in terms of either the scale's conceptual definition or the item-content interpretation. One such finding is that girls tended to be more sensing than boys. Paradoxically, this finding, which is inconsistent with the popular notion that intuition is typically a female trait, is not supported by the S-N scale's correlations with the MMPI and SVIB masculinity-femininity scales. Both of these correlations indicate that femininity is associated with intuition rather than sensation. In previous studies (Myers, 1962b), a sex difference was not apparent on the S-N scale in a junior high school sample, but this scale did correlate with the PRI masculinity-femininity scale in the same direction as the masculinity-femininity scales in the present studies.

A second set of inexplicable findings include the scale's positive correlations with the CPI Cs, Ai, and Fx scales. This pattern, when considered with the S-N scale's previously reported negative correlations with the PRI Gregariousness scale (Myers, 1962b) and such ratings as Willing to Take Direction and Cooperative (Myers, 1962b; Ross, 1961), suggests, in part, independence or nonconformity.

Thinking-Feeling Scale

The content of the T-F scale seems to describe a rational versus a sentimental approach to life. A rational approach to life may correspond to thinking, which is described by the conceptual definition as a "logical process" that relies on objective criteria (e.g., true or false) in evaluating phenomena. A sentimental approach to life, however, seems quite unlike feeling, which is conceptually defined as a relatively personal process that uses subjective criteria (e.g., like or dislike) in evaluating phenomena.

Very few of the variables investigated in the present studies or previous ones are relevant to an assessment of either the conceptual definition or the item-content interpretation. It may be partly as a consequence that the results for his variable are not at all clear-cut.

Slight support for both the conceptual definition and the item-content interpretation comes from the finding that the high school boys in the college preparatory program tended to be more thinking than those in the general-vocational program. No corresponding differences, however, were found for the girls.

Neither the conceptual definition nor the item-content interpretation is particularly supported by the scale's scattered and quite moderate negative correlations with the SVIB technical-scientific and business detail scales, which should reflect either thinking or a rational approach. Previous findings involving other measures which should also reflect either thinking or a rational approach offer even less support. The T-F scale had only a slight, though significant, negative correlation with the PRI Liking to Think scale (Myers, 1962b); it did not correlate significantly with a rating of Poor at Analyzing (Myers, 1962b; Ross, 1961); and it did not load an intellectuality factor (Ross, 1963).

The item-content interpretation is supported by (a) the scale's positive correlations with the SVIB social service scales, which should reflect a sentimental approach; and (b) the finding that, in general, the boys in each of the three student groups tended to be more thinking than the girls, which is paralleled by the T-F scale's correlations with MMPI, CPI, and SVIB masculinity-femininity scales. These two findings agree with previously reported results (Myers, 1962b). The T-F scale's positive correlations with measures which reflect sentimentality are consistent with its positive correlation with the PRI Spiritual vs Material scale, but inconsistent with the T-F scale's nonsignificant correlations with the PRI Altruism and Social Conscience scales. The sex differences on the T-F scale and the scale's correlations with masculinity-femininity scales are consistent with the observed tendency for the boys in a junior high school sample to be more thinking than the girls and the scale's correlation with the PRI masculinity-femininity scale.

Several correlations are inexplicable in terms of the conceptual definition and the item-content interpretation, including the scale's negative correlation with the SSHA. This finding resembles the T-F scale's previously reported negative correlation with the PRI Attitude to Work scale (Myers, 1962b). Other previous findings which are inexplicable include the Indicator scale's positive correlations with the PRI Free-Floating Anxiety scale (Myers, 1962b) and the MPI Neuroticism scale (Howarth, 1962).

Judging-Perceiving Scale

Although judging-perceiving is defined as reaching a conclusion about something versus becoming aware of it, the items on this scale seem to describe planned and organized versus spontaneous activity, time-binding, or even compulsivity. These items appear to be very similar to those on the Orderliness scale of the Edwards Personal Preference Schedule (Edwards, 1957a).

The scale's conceptual definition and the item-content interpretation are both consistent with the scale's positive correlations with the CPI *Fx* scale, which should reflect either an openness to the environment or a tendency toward spontaneity, and its negative correlations with the SVIB business detail scales, which should reflect either a tendency to reach conclusions or engage in planned and organized activity, etc. These findings, however, are not entirely supported by other studies. The J-P scale's correlation with the CPI *Fx* scale is supported by the previously reported positive correlation between the Indicator scale and the PRI Tolerance of Complexity scale (Myers, 1962b), but it receives almost no support from the modest, though significant, positive correlation of the Indicator scale with the PRI Artistic vs Practical scale (Myers, 1962b). The Indicator scale's correlations with the business detail scales are lent little support by its previously reported slight and not always significant positive correlation with a rating of Poor on Details (Myers, 1962b; Ross, 1961).

The conceptual definition, but not the item-content interpretation, is supported by two previous findings, involving measures which should reflect awareness of phenomena—the scale's positive correlation with a rating of Has no Self-Understanding (Ross, 1961), and its slight but significant positive correlation with the PRI Self-Insight scale (Myers, 1962b).

The item-content interpretation is supported by the scale's negative correlations with the CPI *Sc* scale and the SSHA, both of which seem to reflect something like time-binding or compulsivity, rather than readiness to reach conclusions. These results are consistent with the scale's previously reported positive correlations with the PRI Impulsiveness scale (Myers, 1962b) and a rating of Performs Below Capacity (Myers, 1962b; Ross, 1961), and its negative correlations with ratings of Industrious, and Works Steadily and on an Even Keel (Myers, 1962b; Ross, 1961). However, the J-P scale's correlation with the PRI Compulsiveness scale, although significantly negative, was slight (Myers, 1962b).

Several findings seem inexplicable in terms of both the conceptual definition and the item-content interpretation. Some of these findings, including the scale's negative correlations with the CPI *Re*, *So*, and *Ac* scales, when considered together with the scale's negative correlations with the CPI *Sc* scale and the SSHA, suggest still another interpretation of the J-P scale, namely, that it is measuring something akin to prudence. Such an interpretation is further supported by such previous results as the J-P scale's negative loading on a factor identified as prudence for boys, though not for girls (Ross, 1963); and its negative correlations with the PRI Attitude to Work scale (Myers, 1962b) and such ratings as Responsible (Myers, 1962b; Ross, 1961), Mature (Ross, 1961), and Acts Ethically

(Ross, 1961). This interpretation is not consistent, however, with the J-P scale's nonsignificant correlation with a rating of Not Self-disciplined (Ross, 1961).

Other findings point to a sex difference on this scale. With some exceptions, the girls in the various student groups tended to be more judging than the boys. This finding is supported by the scale's correlation with the CPI masculinity-femininity scale but it conflicts with the scale's correlation with the MMPI masculinity-femininity scale. The latter correlation indicates that femininity is associated with perception rather than judgment. Moreover, in other studies (Myers, 1962b) no sex difference was apparent on the J-P scale in a junior high school sample, and the scale was not significantly correlated with the PRI Masculinity-Femininity scale. However, another study (Ross, 1963) did find a sex difference in the factor structure of the scale—it loaded prudence and extraversion-introversion factors for boys, but a general ability factor and an unidentified one for girls.

The interpretation of this scale is further complicated by its consistent but moderate correlations with CPI response bias scales and MMPI validity and SD scales.

Overview

This research bears on the perennial problem that indirect measurement inevitably introduces extraneous sources of variance. The issue is the extent to which the measuring instruments reflect variance attributable to the underlying variables—in the present case, the typological distinctions of the Jungian system—and the extent to which they reflect variance from other, perhaps more superficial, sources. This issue is complicated by the existence of a sequence of questions. First in the sequence is the question of truth or falsity: *Do the underlying variables really exist?* (In the present case, the question takes the form: *Is the Jungian system a set of true assertions about individuals, and, hence, are there basic typological distinctions among human beings?*) If the answer to this first question is negative, the second question becomes unreal, because it is: *Do the measuring instruments validly reflect the underlying variables?* In the present case, for example, since extraversion-introversion is measured by reported talkativeness and other such characteristics, it may be that the E-I scale is more responsive to other determinants of talkativeness than extraversion-introversion, *per se*.

The position advanced in interpreting the results reported in this article was that, in addition to the conceptual definition for each scale, there are one or more equally plausible interpretations of the scale's meaning. These alternative interpretations, which are outside of the Jungian typology, satisfactorily account for many of the properties and correlates of the scale. While many of the findings are also consistent with the conceptual definitions, the empirical support for the alternative interpretations does suggest that the Indicator's scales are strongly subject to influences other than the typological variables. In particular, the E-I and J-P scales seem to reflect something quite different from their postulated dimensions, and the S-N and T-F scales, at best, seem to reflect restricted aspects of them.

Discrepancies of this kind between the empirical meaning of the scales and their conceptual definitions may explain the failure of a series of related studies with the Indicator to find support for the structural properties attributed to the Jungian typology (Stricker & Ross, 1964).

In any event, even if the typology that the Indicator is intended to reflect does exist, it would be premature to assume that the Indicator operationally defines it until (a) on the one hand, the alternative hypotheses about the scales' meaning which are suggested by the findings reported in this article are tested and rejected; and (b) on the other, a body of findings accumulate which explicitly link each scale to its conceptual definition.

REFERENCES

Brown, W. F., & Holtzman, W. H. *Manual, Brown-Holzman Survey of Study Habits and Attitudes.* (Rev. ed.) New York: Psychological Corp., 1956.

Cattell, R. B., Saunders, D. R., & Stice, G. *Handbook for the Sixteen Personality Factor Questionnaire, "The 16 P. F. Test"; Forms A, B, and C.* Champaign, Ill.: Institute for Personality and Ability Testing, 1957.

Christensen, P. R., & Guilford, J. P. *Manual of instructions and interpretations, Ship Destination Test.* Beverly Hills, Calif.: Sheridan Supply Co., 1956.

College Entrance Examination Board. *A description of the College Board Scholastic Aptitude Test.* Princeton, N.J.: Author, 1962.

Dyer, H. S., & King, R. G. *College Board scores: their use and interpretation.* Princeton, N.J.: College Entrance Examination Board, 1955.

Edwards, A. L. *Manual, Edwards Personal Preference Schedule.* (Rev. ed.) New York: Psychological Corp., 1957. (a)

Edwards, A. L. *The social desirability variable in personality assessment and research.* New York: Dryden, 1957. (b)

Evans, C., & McConnell, T. R. *Manual, Minnesota T-S-E Inventory.* (Rev. ed.) Princeton, N.J.: Educational Testing Service, 1957.

Eysenck, H. J. *Manual of the Maudsley Personality Inventory.* London: University of London Press, 1959.

Gough, H. G. *Manual for the California Psychological Inventory.* Palo Alto, Calif.: Consulting Psychologists Press, 1957.

Gray, H. Jung's psychological types: meaning and consistency of the questionnaire. *J. gen. Psychol.*, 1947, 37, 177–186. (a)

Gray, H. Psychological types and changes with age. *J. clin. Psychol.*, 1947, 3, 273–277. (b)

Gray, H. Jung's psychological types in men and women. *Stanford med. Bull.*, 1948, 6, 29–36.

Gray, H. Jung's psychological types: ambiguous scores and their interpretation. *J. gen. Psychol.*, 1949, *40*, 63–88. (a)

Gray, H. Psychological types in married people. *J. soc. Psychol.*, 1949, *29*, 189–200. (b)

Gray, H., & Wheelwright, J. B. Jung's psychological types and marriage. *Stanford med. Bull.*, 1944, *2*, 37–39.

Gray, H., & Wheelwright, J. B. Jung's psychological types, their frequency of occurrence. *J. gen. Psychol.*, 1946, *34*, 3–17.

Hathaway, S. R., & McKinley, J. C. *Manual, Minnesota Multiphasic Personality Inventory.* (Rev. ed.) New York: Psychological Corp., 1951.

Howarth, E. Extroversion and dream symbolism: an empirical study. *Psychol. Rep.*, 1962, *10*, 211–214.

Jung, C. G. *Psychological types.* London: Routledge & Kegan Paul, 1923.

Jung, C. G. *Modern man in search of a soul.* New York: Harcourt, Brace, 1933.

Jung, C. G. *Collected works of . . .* Vol. 7. *Two essays on analytical psychology.* New York: Pantheon, 1953.

Lord, F. M. *Multimodal score distributions on the Myers-Briggs Type Indicator: I.* Princeton, N.J.: Educational Testing Service, 1958. (Res. Memo. 58-8)

Myers, I. B. Inferences as to the dichotomous nature of Jung's types, from the shape of regressions of dependent variables upon Myers-Briggs Type Indicator scores. *Amer. Psychologist*, 1962, *17*, 364. (Abstract) (a)

Myers, I. B. *Manual (1962), the Myers-Briggs Type Indicator.* Princeton, N.J.: Educational Testing Service, 1962. (b)

Ross, J. *Progress report on the College Student Characteristics Study: June, 1961.* Princeton, N.J.: Educational Testing Service, 1961. (Res. Memo. 61-11)

Ross, J. *The relationship between the Myers-Briggs Type Indicator and ability, personality and information tests.* Princeton, N.J.: Educational Testing Service, 1963. (Res. Bull. 63-8)

Saunders, D. R. Evidence for a rational correspondence between the personality typologies of Spranger and of Jung. *Amer. Psychologist*, 1960, *15*, 459. (Abstract)

Stricker, L. J. Acquiescence and social desirability response styles, item characteristics, and conformity. *Psychol. Rep.*, 1963, *12*, 319–341. (Monogr. Suppl. 2-V12)

Stricker, L. J., & Ross, J. *A description and evaluation of the Myers-Briggs Type Indicator.* Princeton, N.J.: Educational Testing Service, 1962. (Res. Bull. 62-6)

Stricker, L. J., & Ross, J. Intercorrelations and reliability of the Myers-Briggs Type Indicator scales. *Psychol. Rep.*, 1963, *12*, 287–293.

Stricker, L. J., & Ross, J. An assessment of some structural properties of the Jungian personality typology. *J. abnorm. soc. Psychol.*, 1964, *68*, 62–71.

Strong, E. K., Jr. *Manual for Strong Vocational Interest Blanks for Men and Women.* Palo Alto, Calif.: Consulting Psychologists Press, 1959.

Terman, L. M. *Manual, Concept Mastery Test, Form T.* New York: Psychological Corp., 1956.

NEOANALYTIC THEORIES: ADLER, HORNEY, AND FROMM

III

ALFRED ADLER and Karen Horney were both trained in the theory and practice of psychoanalysis, and both originally accepted Freud's premises with respect to the biological substratum of motivation in personality functioning. But both changed their minds—or to put it more accurately, their opinions underwent a process of development which carried them away from Freudian conceptions. They repudiated the notion that the individual was an organic mechanism, governed only by drive-reduction controls. Rather than being a mere product of hereditary influences and biological determinants, personality was shaped by, and in turn reacted to, significant influences from the social environment.

Adler broke with Freud more specifically on the matter of the sexual etiology of neurosis. Adler's view was that emotional disturbances reflect exaggerated inferiority feelings which stem from either real or imagined failures to cope with the social environment.

Horney, unlike Adler, who completely renounced his association with psychoanalysis, accepted many Freudian formulations, such as unconscious motivation and the therapeutic uses of free association. However, she opposed Freud on the issue of the biological determinism of both personality and adjustment. Initially, she rejected Freud's description of penis envy in women, postulating instead that the alleged desire for a penis is a symbolic gesture reflecting a desire to obtain the status characteristics of the male. Feminine psychology, she insisted, was not primarily the result of determinants originating in the reproductive organs, but of significant influences which could be identified within the social context.

Erich Fromm rejects outright the libido theory of Freud. It is his belief that Freud's philosophical orientation was molded by nineteenth-century materialist doctrines which assume that all important psychological phenomena must be rooted in corresponding somatic and physiological processes. Fromm denies the importance of innately determined biological motivational patterns, emphasizing, instead, the adaptive nature of the human organism. Where Freud considers biological factors as primary determinants of personality development, Fromm considers them incidental to the problems of adaptation to a social or interpersonal milieu. As an alternative to Freud's evolutionary schema of libido, Fromm postulates a dialectical schema based upon the notion of fundamental contradictions and the unending necessity for new solutions.

The ideas of these three theorists are incorporated in the primary sources which follow. Included are papers of a theoretical nature by each of the three theorists, Adler writing on power, Fromm on neurosis, and Horney on aggression. It should be noted that despite the diversity of the topic areas and, indeed, of the theorists themselves, each paper carries the theme which so clearly differentiates the neoanalysts from the Freudians: social and cultural factors are of prime importance in all aspects of the developing and functioning personality. Also included are papers demonstrating recent applications of the work of Adler and Horney to, respectively, civil rights and marital conflict. Finally, the relative paucity of research generated by the neoanalytic school is reflected in the inclusion here of only a single empirical paper, that of Oberlander and Jenkin on birth order effects. Even here, although the authors credit Adler's contribution, the study is less directly related to Adlerian conceptualizations than to the work of other investigators, such as Harris and Lasko.

10

The Psychology of Power

ALFRED ADLER

To be big! To be powerful! This is and has always been the longing of those who are little or feel they are little. Every child longs for higher goals; everyone who is weak, for superiority; everyone of faint hope, for pinnacles of perfection. This goes for the individual as well as for groups, peoples, states, nations. Whatever men are striving for originates from their urgent attempts to overcome the impression of deficiency, insecurity, weakness.

But in order to go anywhere, men need a guiding image in the future. The fictitious guiding ideal of perfection is not tangible enough to fulfill its purpose. The groping spirit shapes the guiding image concretely in order to walk securely. Whether one sees his perfection in being a coachman, a physician, a Don Juan, a fellowman or a tyrant, he always sees in it the highest fulfillment and confirmation of his nature. Whether his guiding ideal will bring him this fulfillment under given circumstances, depends on his preparation, his training, his choice of method, his optimistic activity on the one hand, and its congruence with the external possibilities, on the other hand. The former factors we can advance through education, the latter we must recognize and see for what they are. All these factors penetrate each other and interact.

We can contribute much toward the attainment of an approximately correct way of life when we have at our disposal an accurate exploration of the external circumstances. Many of the evils which distress man could be more easily borne and fought against if we did not only deplore them, but regarded them as the expression of a movement toward development and progress. We all suffer from the fact that we stand at a crossroad of development which must be overcome through the creative power of mankind.

From A. Adler, The Psychology of Power. *Journal of Individual Psychology*, 1966, 22, 166–172. Reprinted by permission of the publisher.

Translated from the German by permission of Rotapfel-Verlag, Zurich. The order of some of the paragraphs has been changed, and all comments, footnotes and references have been provided by the editors, H. L. & Rowena R. Ansbacher.

THE FALSE IDEAL OF PERSONAL POWER

The Individual Psychologist can maintain with certainty that general and personal suffering are always connected with the fact that today we have constructed our guiding ideal still too little in accordance with social interest and too much in accordance with personal power. The large army of problem children, neurotics, insane, alcoholics, drug addicts, criminals, and suicides in the last analysis all present the same picture: struggle for personal power, or despair of being able to attain it on the generally useful side. Today superiority over others is still being aspired to as the perfect form. Our guiding ideal is concretized as power over others, and this problem is too much in the foreground for everybody, overshadows all other problems, and directs all movements of our psychological life into its path.

The poison of the craving for power creeps into parental love and seeks in the name of authority and filial duty to cling to the semblance of superiority and infallibility. Then it becomes the task of the children to grow beyond their parental educators, to cope with them. It is the same with the teacher. Even love is full of these tricks, and demands of the partner too much devotion. The husband's desire for power, appealing to "natural destiny," demands the submission of the wife. The result is, unhappily, the destruction of all spontaneous relationships and the paralyzing of valuable forces.[1] The dominance of man over woman deprived him of the highest sexual pleasures and must in a more highly developed civilization lead women to rebellion against their feminine role. This would at the same time bring the existence of the human race in question because uncivilized peoples would gain an advantage.

The waves of the power striving of society break into the confines of the nursery. The parents' desires to dominate, servant arrangements in the house, privileges accorded the infant, irresistibly direct the mind of the child toward the achievement of power and predominance, and allow only this position to appear tempting. Not until somewhat later do social feelings enter his soul, usually to fall under the domination of the already developed desire for power. The pleasant games of children disclose to the judge of human nature a self-consistent system of satisfying the craving for power. One finds then during more careful analysis that all character traits are elaborated through the striving for one's own superiority.

When the child enters school or life, he brings with him, from his family, this mechanism which is so harmful to the social sense (*Gemeinsinn*). The ideal of one's own superiority counts upon the social sense of the others.

[1] This paragraph or passage is also found in a paper dated 1918 (Adler, 1918).

The result of individual and social psychological inquiry is therefore: The striving for personal power is a disastrous delusion and poisons man's living together. Whoever desires the human community must renounce the striving for power over others.[2]

To prevail through violence appears to many as an obvious thought. And we admit: the simplest way to attain everything that is good and promises happiness, or even only what is in the line of a continuous evolution seems to be by means of power. But where in the life of men or in the history of mankind has such an attempt ever succeeded? As far as we can see, even the use of mild violence awakens opposition everywhere, even where the welfare of the subjugated is obviously intended. The patriarchal system and enlightened absolutism are such deterring traces. No people could tolerate even their God without contradiction. Lead an individual or a people into the power sphere of another, and immediately a resistance will arise, openly and secretly, and it will not disappear until all shackles have fallen.[1,2]

The victorious struggle of the proletariat against the coercion of capitalism shows clearly this course of development. But the growing power of the organization of labor may, if used carelessly, release a lesser or greater resistance in insecure persons. Wherever it is a question of power, no matter how excellent its intentions and goals, it will come up against the will to power of the individual and arouse opposition.[1]

It would be a gross deception to admit power intoxication only for the individual psyche. The mass also is guided by this goal and the effect of this is the more devastating as in the mass psyche the feeling of personal responsibility is essentially reduced.

How did this harm come into the world? *The striving for personal power is one of the concretizations of the striving for perfection!* And it is one of the most tempting, especially in a civilization which is pressed from all sides. It is an understandable error, borrowed from unbridled events of nature where the perfection of the individual is gained by brutal victory over the weaker.

THE IDEAL OF SOCIAL INTEREST

Modern psychology has shown us that the traits of craving for power, ambition, and striving for power over others, with their numerous ugly concomitants, are not innate and unalterable. Rather they are inoculated into the child at an early age; the child receives them involuntarily from an atmosphere saturated by the titillation of power. In our blood is still the

[2] Used as preamble of a book by Rattner (1963).

desire for the intoxication with power, and our souls are playthings of the craving for power.[1]

One thing can save us: the mistrust of any form of predominance. Our strength lies in conviction, in organizing strength, in a world view, not in the violence of armament and not in emergency laws. With such means other strong forces before us have fought in vain for their existence.[1]

For us the way and tactics emerge from our highest goal: the nursing and strengthening of social feelings.[1]

Even among the animals there are enough tendencies which ameliorate this wild struggle—social instincts, gregarious drives—obviously for the protection of the species, to prevent its extermination. For man, the coercion toward development points much more strongly to the path of social interest, because in the face of nature and the facts of life he, much more than all other living creatures, is forced toward mutual obligation. Without the most highly developed division of labor he is doomed to go under or to lose the fruits of evolution.

We may fight against the working of social feelings in us, but we cannot smother it.[3] Thus the human soul may madly dismiss logic that has been pronounced holy; in suicide vital force defiantly annuls the vital instinct. But logic and vital instinct are realities like the community. Thus such failures are sins against nature, against the holy spirit of the community.[4] It is not at all easy to suppress one's social sense. The criminal needs the intoxication of the senses, before or after the deed, to quiet his social interest. Wayward youths form gangs so that they may share the feeling of responsibility with others and thus mitigate it. Raskolnikov must first lie in bed a month and meditate whether he is a Napoleon or a louse. And then when he ascends the stairs to murder an old worthless usurer he feels his heart palpitating. Through this excitement of his blood, social interest speaks. War is not the continuation of politics with other means, but the greatest mass crime against man's belonging together.[5] What sum of lies and artificial arousal of low passions, what thousandfold violence was necessary to suppress the indignant outcry of the voice of humanity!

[3] Here Adler refers to social interest no longer as an ideal but as the minimum of social identification and integration, of cooperation, that has developed in every one out of the natural "coercion toward . . . social interest" and cooperation.

[4] Phyllis Bottome in her biography of Adler quotes him as having exclaimed at one time, "Anxiety? But is that not high treason against the Holy Ghost?" (Bottome, 1957, p. 219). Those of us who have been puzzled by this statement find that Adler in the above did indeed use the phrase, *der heilige Geist.* But this would be translated as the "Holy Ghost" only if the adjective, *heilige,* were capitalized. However, this is not the case and thus the phrase must be read as the "holy spirit"; furthermore, "of the community" is added. In this way the usage of this phrase by Adler becomes understandable.

[5] According to Dr. Kurt Adler (personal communication, March 10, 1966) this sentence should probably be modified by the material in brackets, to read: "War is not [merely] the continuation of politics with other means, [politics also being usually used as a means to power,] but the greatest mass crime against man's belonging together."

The typical ideal of our time is still the isolated hero for whom fellow men are objects. It is this psychological structure which has made the World War palatable to people, lets them shudder in admiration before the unstable greatness of a victorious military leader.

Social feelings require a different ideal, namely that of the saint, purified, to be sure, from fantastic clinkers originating from superstition. Neither school nor life are later capable of removing the firmly rooted, exaggerated striving for one's own significance at the expense of others.

We need the conscious preparation and advancement of a mighty social interest and the complete demolition of greed and power in the individual and in peoples. What we all lack and for which we struggle relentlessly are new methods to raise the social sense, the new word. In the meantime this progress appears to make its way predominantly through the extermination of the socially unfit. We [humans] are much milder than the facts of life in nature, than this cosmos which calls to him who has a longing for power and violence in the greatest variations: I don't like him, he must be removed! He who like the psychologist witnesses this hard logic of human living together, longs to make this infinitely dark voice audible to all, to warn them of the abyss into which individuals, whole families, and peoples fall, to disappear forever. But—we need the new method, the new word, to make this dreadful voice audible.

REFERENCES

Adler, A. Bolschewismus und Seelenkunde. *Int. Rundsch.*, Zurich, 1918, *4*, 597–600.

Adler, A. *Die andere Seite: eine massenpsychologische Studie über die Schuld des Volkes.* Vienna: Leopold Heidrich, 1919.

Adler, A. Vorrede. In E. Wexberg (Ed.), *Handbuch der Individualpsychologie.* Vol. 1 (1926). Amsterdam: Bonset, 1966. Pp. v–vi.

Adler, A. Psychologie der Macht. In F. Kobler (Ed.), *Gewalt und Gewaltlosigkeit: Handbuch des aktiven Pazifismus.* Zurich: Rotapfel-Verlag, 1928. Pp. 41–46.

Adler, A. *The Individual Psychology of Alfred Adler.* Edited by H. L. & Rowena R. Ansbacher. New York: Basic Books, 1956.

Adler, A. *Superiority and social interest.* Edited by H. L. & Rowena R. Ansbacher. Evanston, Ill.: Northwestern Univer. Press, 1964. Pp. 395–417.

Bottome, Phyllis. *Alfred Adler: a portrait from life.* New York: Vanguard Press, 1957.

Kobler, F. (Ed.) *Gewalt und Gewaltlosigkeit: Handbuch des aktiven Pazifismus.* Zurich: Rotapfel-Verlag, 1928.

Rattner, J. *Individualpsychologie: eine Einführung in die tiefenpsychologische Lehre von Alfred Adler.* Munich: Reinhardt, 1963.

11

Birth Order and Academic Achievement

MARK OBERLANDER
& NOEL JENKIN

Regardless of orientation, most personality theorists are in agreement that early familial relationships and experiences exert a crucial influence on both childhood and adult behavior patterns.

The theoretical framework of the present study is primarily that of Harris (1961; 1964; 1965). He proposes that the divergent tendencies of first and later born children have systematic intellectual repercussions, with first borns, specifically, developing a proclivity for abstract verbal functioning, due to intense interaction with their parents. This proposition was given some confirmation in Harris' work with learning problems (1961) and by his review of empirical studies (1964). The latter included reports on adult first borns who scored higher on the Miller Analogies Test, and on first born children who scored higher than later born children of equivalent ages on the verbal portion of IQ tests. This evidence has led the present authors to propose that the first borns' proclivity for abstract verbal functioning will, in turn, increase their probability of relatively high academic achievement.

Such a conceptualization is consonant with the view of birth order effects as presented by Adler (1927, pp. 321–323) and further elaborated by Dreikurs (1950). In general, the Adlerian contention is that differential parent-child-sibling interactions are in part determined by the ordinal position of a given child, and that specific personality organizations are reflections of goals toward which the individual had striven within the family constellation during the early years of his life.

Several studies found differences in parents' interactions with their offspring of different ordinal positions. Lasko (1954) reports less consistent and less spontaneous expression of warmth by mothers toward their first

From M. Oberlander, and N. Jenkin, Birth Order and Academic Achievement. *Journal of Individual Psychology*, 1967, 23, 103–110. Reprinted by permission of authors and publisher.

The authors wish to acknowledge the very valuable stimulus given by Dr. Irving D. Harris at the inception of this research project.

child than toward later children and more friction between the mother and the first born. He also reports less anxiety, protectiveness, and interference by parents in the case of later children, and more permissiveness.

Sears (Sears, Maccoby, & Levin, 1957) reports decreased parental delight at the prospect of having a child as the number of children in the family increases. Furthermore, the later the child, the less the probability that he will be breast fed. Rosen (1964) claims that, in light of the intensity of the interaction of the first born with his parents, he tends to become very sensitive to parental expectations and sanctions. McArthur (1956), similarly demonstrated that the first born is more likely to be adult-oriented, the second child, to be peer-oriented.

Such evidence has led Harris (1965) to propose that the effects on the child of differential parent-child interactions are related to the question of how soon the child adopts the adult viewpoint, and that first borns tend to adopt the adult viewpoint earlier than later borns.

Based on the work reviewed, we propose that differing strategies are available to children in search of a satisfying family role. Choice of strategy in the case of the first born child is influenced by his reaction to a conflict generally experienced by him. Dethroned by the birth of a sibling, and removed from his position as exclusive recipient of parental care and attention, he has two alternatives: (a) to continue the old, infantile patterns of behavior which previously brought satisfaction; (b) to develop new techniques for obtaining gratification through parental reward, realizing that the sibling is now exploiting the infantile techniques. One strategy as yet unavailable to the younger sibling which the older rapidly finds successful, is linguistic development, intellectual exploration, and school achievement.

Of course, these considerations do not pertain to only children. However, they are nevertheless treated by, and interact with, their parents in a way which is very similar to that of first borns with siblings. For this reason most investigators have included only children in their samples of first borns, as is the case in the present study.

The present study is an attempt to test the hypothesis that the postulated verbal and intellectual advantage given the youthful first born persists throughout the school years, manifesting itself in better grades and higher scores on achievement and intelligence tests.

METHOD

The data for this study were obtained from two school systems in the Chicago area. Sample 1 consisted of available 7th and 8th grade students in a northern suburb of Chicago, characterized by relatively high and homogeneous socio-economic status. The following information was obtained from the school records: (*a*) 7th grade (N = 302, 155 males and 147 females)—IQ scores, scores on the California Achievement Test (reading, language, and total test), and birth order data; (*b*) 8th grade (N = 313, 163 males and 150 females)—IQ scores, scores on the SRA HS Placement Test (all subtests), grade point average in the first semester of high school, and birth order data.

Data for Sample 2 were obtained within the context of a larger study at the Institute for Juvenile Research, and gathered from a school system in a southern suburb of Chicago.[1] Socio-economic status was lower than that of the first sample, and also varied more widely. From the school records, information was obtained for three age groups: (*a*) 5th grade (N = 80, 54 males and 26 females), (*b*) 8th grade (N = 104, 58 males and 46 females), (*c*) 11th grade (N =173, 94 males and 79 females). IQ scores, grades per subject matter from the previous school year, and birth order data were available.

In addition to using the available achievement measures in Sample 1, we also derived a corrected achievement score defined as the algebraic difference between grade placement as determined by total achievement test score and grade placement based on age. In Sample 2, the overall grade point average was used as a general index of academic achievement.

Only children, who accounted for 10 percent of the two samples, were included with the first borns with siblings, as mentioned above. There was no control for family size. Sex was included as a variable. All the measures that were obtained were converted into standard scores to enable us to pool all the subjects within the two samples.

RESULTS

Two analyses were performed for each sample: (*a*) an analysis of variance (either three or two way, depending on the information available) in which an entire sample was used; (*b*) a one-way analysis of covariance for each sex by grade group, where IQ scores were held constant while we tested for differences in achievement measures between the birth order groups. The analyses followed the procedures outlined by Winer (1962) for dealing with unequal cell frequencies.

Tables 11-2 and 11-4 present a summary of F ratios from the analyses of variance, and also the proportions of total variance accounted for by the various significant effects. These tables show that there are indeed meaning-

[1] The authors wish to thank Dr. Elise E. Lessing for making the data available.

ful differences between birth order groups among the variables used for comparison. No statistics from the analyses of covariance are presented, since none of the F ratios reached the required level of significance.

For Sample 1 (see Tables 11-1 and 11-2), the birth order groups differ significantly in their IQ scores, reading achievement scores, and school performance as indicated by grade point average. First born children are found to be superior to later borns. The interaction effect of grade x birth order on IQ (see Table 11-2) occurs because birth order differences are stronger in the 8th grade than in the 7th grade of this sample.

TABLE 11-1.   Means and Standard Deviations of Raw IQ, Achievement Test,[a] and Grade Point Average (GPA) [b] Measures for Sample 1 (Northern Chicago Suburb)

	Males				Females			
	First born		Later born		First born		Later born	
	$\overline{X}$	SD	$\overline{X}$	SD	$\overline{X}$	SD	$\overline{X}$	SD
Grade 7	N = 69		N = 86		N = 69		N = 78	
IQ	113.71	8.43	112.55	11.16	114.30	10.88	115.59	9.75
Achievement[c]	1.25	1.27	1.37	1.35	2.08	1.24	1.96	1.21
Reading	82.51	18.93	78.44	21.53	83.03	20.26	79.99	23.71
Language	59.53	26.36	56.74	25.52	73.09	23.89	71.67	25.01
Total	70.94	23.25	65.93	24.26	76.36	23.82	74.39	24.50
Grade 8	N = 74		N = 89		N = 60		N = 90	
IQ	116.03	11.12	110.63	10.32	114.35	10.57	112.38	10.63
Achievement	1.91	1.31	1.39	1.19	2.22	1.19	2.13	1.04
Reading	77.09	21.78	66.00	26.84	70.17	25.55	67.80	24.31
Language	61.30	27.51	52.77	26.60	77.05	22.39	76.65	22.45
Arithmetic	67.85	27.27	66.61	25.35	71.95	22.71	74.19	22.91
Total	74.03	21.03	67.12	21.60	78.27	20.01	78.22	19.77
GPA	3.33	.65	3.02	.70	3.54	.74	3.51	.65

[a] All achievement test scores expressed in terms of percentile scores.
[b] GPA measures based on a 5-point scale.
[c] Based on grade placement and corrected for age.

The data from Sample 2 (see Tables 11-3 and 11-4) agree with those from Sample 1. Table 11-4 shows that birth order differences are to be found in IQ scores and actual school performance.

In all but three of the birth order-sex-grade group comparisons, the means were in the predicted direction. First borns, including only children, consistently had higher mean scores than did later borns.

TABLE 11-2. Analysis of Variance F Ratios of Standard IQ and Achievement Scores for Sample 1

Source	df	IQ	Achiev.a	Reading	Language	Arith.b	Total	GPAb
Grade (G)	1/604	.654	6.259** (11.62%)	30.877*** (71.20%)	.769		1.578	
Sex (S)	1/604	1.097	38.126*** (70.75%)	.181	69.609*** (89.29%)	4.432* (75.90%)	15.574*** (65.98%)	19.263*** (68.93%)
Birth order (BO)	1/604	4.597* (28.04%)c	2.151	7.148*** (16.48%)	2.611	.031	3.469	4.156* (16.16%)
G × S	1/604	1.092	.888	.924	1.634		.062	
G × BO	1/604	4.865 (29.67%)	2.422	.711	.389		.000	
S × BO	1/604	2.995	.208	1.563	1.325	.377	1.707	3.167
G × S × BO	1/604	.095	2.859	.958	.621		.213	

a Based on grade placement and corrected for age.
b Arithmetic and GPA measures available only for Grade 8. Consequently, F ratios are from a two-way analysis of variance. df = 1/309.
c Proportion of the total variance accounted for.
* $p < .05$
** $p < .025$
*** $p < .01$

TABLE 11-3.   Means and Standard Deviations of Raw IQ and Grade Point Average (GPA) [a] Measures for Sample 2 (Southern Chicago Suburb)

	Males				Females			
	First born		Later born		First born		Later born	
	$\overline{X}$	SD	$\overline{X}$	SD	$\overline{X}$	SD	$\overline{X}$	SD
Grade 5	N = 18		N = 36		N = 11		N = 15	
IQ	111.20	11.31	108.49	14.26	112.54	15.04	102.65	12.17
GPA	10.72	2.30	9.91	2.62	11.88	2.18	10.52	2.21
Grade 8	N = 28		N = 30		N = 23		N = 23	
IQ	103.55	12.86	98.47	11.20	106.30	12.67	100.48	12.89
GPA	9.27	2.61	8.95	2.38	11.62	2.34	10.47	2.60
Grade 11	N = 51		N = 43		N = 42		N = 37	
IQ	92.70	33.89	81.86	34.69	100.31	33.42	90.22	35.13
GPA	9.43	2.81	8.50	2.98	9.78	3.01	8.80	3.05

[a] GPA measures based on a 15-point scale.

TABLE 11-4.   Analysis of Variance F Ratios of Standard IQ and Achievement Scores for Sample 2

Source	df	IQ	GPA
Grade (G)	2/345	4.321*** (19.20%)[a]	9.558*** (29.35%)
Sex (S)	1/345	.287	9.237*** (28.36%)
Birth order (BO)	1/345	12.313*** (56.98%)	10.083*** (30.96%)
G × S	2/345	.698	2.006
G × BO	2/345	.185	.107
S × BO	1/345	2.487	.474
G × S × BO	2/345	.315	.099

[a] Proportion of the total variance accounted for.
*** $p < .01$

DISCUSSION

The results support the hypothesis that first borns surpass later borns in intellectual ability and academic achievement. In light of the fact that the achievement measures correlate highly with IQ scores, and in light of the non-significant results obtained from the analysis of covariance, we must conclude that whatever differences were found between birth order groups are mainly due to differences in skills which the IQ tests measure.

The evidence is consistent with our theoretical formulation and confirms the prediction based upon that formulation. We theorized that first borns might be likely to cope with their dethronement at the birth of a sibling by capitalizing on their superiority over the younger child in intellectual, and especially language, attainments. Our evidence indicates that children in the preschool years should be studied, specifically with respect to possible differences in language ability between first and later borns, together with observations of parental techniques which are differential with respect to first and later borns.

SUMMARY

The hypothesis was tested that first borns, including only children, are superior to later born children in school achievement. Among 972 children in grades 5, 7, 8, and 11, from two differing socio-economic levels, the hypothesis was confirmed in that first borns significantly excelled later borns in IQ and achievement. It is concluded that birth order is a sufficiently important variable to merit consideration when investigating school performance.

REFERENCES

Adler, A. *The practice and theory of Individual Psychology.* New York: Harcourt, Brace, 1927.

Dreikurs, R. *Fundamentals of Adlerian psychology.* New York: Greenberg, 1950.

Harris, I. D. *Emotional blocks to learning.* New York: Free Press of Glencoe, 1961.

Harris, I. D. *The promised seed.* New York: Free Press of Glencoe, 1964.

Harris, I. D. Birth order and creative styles. In J. H. Masserman (Ed.), *Science and psychoanalysis.* Vol. 8. New York: Grune & Stratton, 1965. Pp. 74–90.

Lasko, J. K. Parental behavior toward first and second children. *Genet. Psychol. Monogr.*, 1954, *49*, 97–137.

McArthur, C. Personalities of first and second children. *Psychiatry*, 1956, *19*, 47–54.

Rosen, B. Family structure and value transmission. *Merrill-Palmer Quart.*, 1964, *10* (1), 59–75.

Sears, R. R., Maccoby, E., & Levin, H. *Patterns of child rearing*. Evanston, Ill.: Row Peterson, 1957.

Winer, B. J. *Statistical principles in experimental design*. New York: McGraw-Hill, 1962.

EDITORIAL NOTE

In 1936 N. E. Shoobs (Shoobs & Goldberg, 1942) did a questionnaire study with Brooklyn high school boys from whom he obtained information regarding birth order position and school achievement. From the latter he classified the subjects as to whether they were *advanced*, through skipping one or more terms; *retarded*, through having been left behind at least once; or *normal*. The relationship of this achievement record to birth order is shown in Table 11-5.

TABLE 11-5.   Shoobs' Percentages of Boys With Advanced, Normal and Retarded High School Progress in Relation to Birth Order

High school progress	Birth order position						
	Only	1st	2nd	3rd	4th	Youngest	Total
Advanced	10.7	12.8	15.4	14.0	13.0	16.6	13.1
Normal	50.0	57.3	57.8	58.8	60.0	58.1	56.8
Retarded	39.3	29.9	26.8	27.2	27.0	25.3	30.1
Number	252	737	552	350	191	645	2301*

* The total is obtained by omitting the 645 youngest children as duplications of other positions, and adding 219 children from the 5th position upward, who are not included in the table.

Shoobs' data show among other things that in the case of only children the number retarded was by far greater than in any other category. While various interpretations are possible, the data certainly point to the desirability of treating first children and only children separately, especially in studies of school achievement. Incidentally, Shoobs' study included 11% only children, coming very close to the 10% reported by Oberlander and Jenkin above.

The second major result from Shoobs' study is that even with the only children parceled out, first borns are less successful in school than any other birth order position. With the exception of only children, they show the smallest percentage of advanced and the largest percentage of retarded students. These results are in contradiction to those of Oberlander and Jenkin. While there is at present no ready explanation for this striking discrepancy, we thought these results of 30 years ago should be brought to the attention of the present-day reader for potential further consideration at some future time.

REFERENCE

Shoobs, N. E., & Goldberg, G. *Corrective treatment for unadjusted children.* New York: Harper & Bros., 1942.

12

Implications of Adlerian Theory
for an Understanding
of Civil Rights
Problems and Action

KENNETH B. CLARK

Without question, the most significant and persistent influence on my own thoughts and activities as a social psychologist has been the social dynamic theories of Alfred Adler. I was introduced to the writings of Adler by Professor Francis Cecil Sumner (1895–1954) who initiated me into the field of psychology when I was an undergraduate at Howard University during the early 1930's. The late Professor Sumner was one of the wisest, most scholarly students of psychology I have ever known. He shared with Alfred Adler the fact of being woefully underestimated and unsung, while more flamboyant, fashionable or deliberately obscure or detached social and psychological theorists were being lionized by intellectual faddists and cults. He also shared with him the view that a relevant psychology must be concerned with the destiny and fulfillment of man and society, and the profound hope that man had the capacity to use his rational powers to develop a just and viable society.[1]

While I was still an undergraduate, Sumner's interpretation of psychodynamic theories—and particularly the clarity with which he presented and interpreted Adlerian theory—struck a response within me which caused me to decide to become a psychologist instead of a physician. In looking

From K. B. Clark, Implications of Adlerian Theory for an Understanding of Civil Rights Problems and Action. *Journal of Individual Psychology*, 1967, 23, 181–190. Reprinted by permission of author and publisher.

Address to the American Society of Adlerian Psychology, 15th Annual Meeting, New York, Academy of Medicine, May 26, 1967, commemorating the 30th anniversary of Alfred Adler's death, May 28, 1937.

[1] An idea of Professor Sumner's thinking can be gained from his survey of European psychology on the topic of "Religion and Psychiatry." He found secular and ecclesiastical psychotherapy to agree on the notion of "the losing of one's soul in order to save it" (Sumner, 1946, p. 817), and he quotes among others an Adlerian version of this insight, namely, the recognition of "the healing power of a courageous subdoing of egotism in service to society" (Sumner, 1946, p. 816).

back on the basis of this decision of a college junior, the following factors seem salient:

Adlerian theory provided me with the unifying approach to the problems of the nature of the human predicament and its personal and social paradoxes which I was desperately seeking.

Adlerian theory made it possible for me to see the unity among the various ways in which man sought understanding and mastery of his physical and social environment through religion, philosophy and science.

Adlerian theory made it possible for me to see and believe in the social, moral and technological relevance of the field of psychology.

My introduction to the theories of Alfred Adler was a turning point in my personal and intellectual life. Adlerian ideas have dominated my professional writings and my actions as a person and as a psychologist from my undergraduate days up to the present.

It seems necessary to introduce this discussion of the role of the theories of Alfred Adler in the American civil rights movement with these personal observations because my own involvement in the civil rights movement has been primarily as a psychologist who has sought to bridge the gap between psychological theory, insights and findings on the one hand, and civil rights policy and action on the other hand. To the extent that I have been able to make any contribution to the theoretical and moral assumptions upon which the struggle for racial justice in America has been based, it has been primarily through the appropriate modification and use of the Adlerian perspective and conceptual framework. To the extent that Adlerian theory influenced my own thinking and research, and to the extent that my thought and writings have influenced in any way the civil rights movement, determine, at least in part, the extent to which ideas of Alfred Adler have contributed to the accelerated quest for racial justice in America.

UNDERSTANDING AND COPING WITH
RACIAL HOSTILITY

Basic Adlerian ideas concerning the deep feelings of inferiority which plague man and the various devices by which he seeks to compensate for the gnawing sense of self-doubt have general implications for an understanding of the general problems of race relations in America and the various ways in which man's inhumanity to man manifests itself throughout the world. In addition, Adler at times spoke rather directly on these issues. For example:

Those who have travelled have found that people everywhere are approximately the same in that they are always inclined to find something by which to degrade others. Everyone seeks a means which permits him to elevate himself at little cost. The Frenchman considers the German inferior, whereas the German, in turn, considers himself as belonging to a chosen nation; the Chinaman disdains the Japanese . . . Until mankind consents to take a step forward in its degree of civilization, these hostile trends [prejudices] must be considered not as specific manifestations, but as the expression of a general and erroneous human attitude (Adler, 1956, p. 452; original source, differently translated, Adler, 1963, pp. 111–112).

Adler specified the conditions which increased the chances of hostility in man toward his fellow man and provided the basis for understanding some of the dynamics of racial hostility among whites in America. The depth of his insights can be seen by the following:

Difficulties in earning a livelihood, bad working conditions, inadequate educational and cultural facilities, a joyless existence, and continuous irritation, all these factors increase the feeling of inferiority, produce oversensitivity, and drive the individual to seek "solutions." . . . The class struggle is carried on by groups made up of individuals whose quest for an inwardly and outwardly balanced mode of life is thwarted. Such mass movements, in turn producing further disturbing motives in the individuals, proceed with a firm and resolute step toward destructive aims. Destruction means to the masses a release from situations felt intolerable and thus appears to them as a preliminary condition of improvement (Adler, 1956, pp. 452–453).

There was early evidence that Adler was never content with abstract theorizing and never permitted himself the luxury of either clinical isolation from the very real problems of man or acceptance of the most profound insights as ends in themselves. Adler insisted upon seeking to understand the dynamics of man, as a means toward helping man to move toward justice and dignity in his relations with his fellow man. His concern with and compassion for the victims of social injustice can best be illustrated by the following:

When I have had occasion to talk with individuals of oppressed races, as with Jews and Negroes, I have called their attention to the very great tendency to oppress one's neighbor. . . . We know that children with red hair are exposed to teasing from which they then suffer. This is one of many ancient superstitions which represent gross errors. One must explain to such children that there is a whole series of injustices in mankind, that people often find a means of oppressing others, and that this always takes the same form. If one people wants to depreciate another, if one family considers itself superior to another, then they stress particular traits to use as a point of attack. . . . The redhaired boy must understand that he is not there to serve as a target for the others in letting them irritate him. It is the same all through life; if someone shows irritation, the attack persists. The red-haired boy must consider the attack on account of his hair as a sign of stupidity on the part of the one who launches it (Adler, 1956, pp. 454–455; original source, differently translated, Adler, 1963, pp. 104 & 111).

I have used the above insight as a basis for guiding and protecting my own children against the venom of racial prejudice in America. I have tried to explain to them not without some success, I believe, that attacks and insults directed against them on the basis of their color do not indicate any lack on their part, but rather reflect a profound pathos and inferiority on the part of those who must seek to bolster a sagging self-esteem by attempting to humiliate others.

RESEARCH AND SUPREME COURT DECISION

There are many specific examples of the profound effect of Adlerian thought on my own work as a psychologist. I was first aware of the extent to which Adler had influenced my perspective of man and society, and specifically my thinking on the American race problem, when I wrote a paper as an undergraduate on the manifestations of feelings of inferiority among Negroes. I developed these ideas further for a paper which I wrote when I was a graduate student in the department of psychology at Columbia University. I submitted this later paper to Otto Klineberg, who was my major professor at Columbia. This paper became the basis of a series of discussions with Professor Klineberg. Out of these discussions developed a friendship which persists to this day and which strengthened my commitment to use my training and skills as a psychologist in the attempt to bring about observable changes in the predicament of the Negroes in America and to contribute whatever I could in improving the general moral climate within which American children of all races and religions are required to grow.

In the 1940's soon after I received my doctorate from Columbia University, my wife, Dr. Mamie P. Clark, and I conducted research on racial identification and preference in Negro children (Clark & Clark, 1939a; 1939b; 1940; 1947; 1950). This research was designed to test empirically some hypotheses which were essentially Adlerian. For example, we sought to determine the extent to which the inferior status to which Negro children were relegated in American society became incorporated into their developing self-image and influenced their motivation and personal effectiveness. The findings of this series of studies clearly supported the basic ideas of Adler, namely, that human beings who are treated as inferior develop intensified feelings of inferiority and are likely to engage in a variety of compensatory devices in the attempt to salvage some semblance of dignity and self-esteem.

In 1950, I prepared a report for the Midcentury White House Conference on Children and Youth on the effects of prejudice, discrimination and segregation on personality development of American children, Negro and white (Clark, 1950). This report brought together the then available research findings and speculations on the personality problems and pressures which a society of institutionalized social injustices imposed upon their children. A revised version of this report has appeared in book form in *Prejudice and Your Child* (Clark, 1963). The unifying theoretical theme which made the findings from the various studies cited in this report coherent and eventually useful was that of Adlerian psychodynamic theory.

This report was used as the basis for a social science appendix to the brief submitted by the lawyers of the National Association for the Advancement of Colored People (NAACP) to the United States Supreme Court in the school desegregation case, *Brown* v. *Board of Education of Topeka* (Appendix to appellant's brief, 1963). This appendix was prepared by Stuart Cook, Isidor Chein, and myself and reviewed and endorsed by 32 American social scientists.[2] It might be of value in demonstrating the direct impact of Adlerian theory on this issue to quote at length from this social science brief which summarizes the report:

The report indicates that as minority group children learn the inferior status to which they are assigned—as they observe the fact that they are almost always segregated and kept apart from others who are treated with more respect by the society as a whole—they often react with feelings of inferiority and a sense of personal humiliation. Many of them become confused about their own personal worth. On the one hand, like all other human beings they require a sense of personal dignity; on the other hand, almost nowhere in the larger society do they find their own dignity as human beings respected by others. Under these conditions, the minority group child is thrown into a conflict with regard to his feelings about himself and his group. He wonders whether his group and he himself are worthy of no more respect than they receive. This conflict and confusion leads to self-hatred and rejection of his own group.

The report goes on to point out that these children must find ways with which to cope with this conflict. Not every child, of course, reacts with the same patterns of behavior. The particular pattern depends upon many interrelated factors, among which are: the stability and quality of his family relations; the social and economic class to which he belongs; the cultural and educational background of his parents; the particular minority group to which he belongs; his personal characteristics, intelligence, special talents, and personality pattern.

Some children, usually of the lower socio-economic classes, may react by overt aggressions and hostility directed toward their own group or members of the dominant group. Anti-social and delinquent behavior may often

2 These 32 endorsers were: F. H. Allport, G. W. Allport, Charlotte Babcock, Viola W. Bernard, J. S. Bruner, Hadley Cantril, Mamie B. Clark, Bingham Dai, Allison Davis, Else Frenkel-Brunswik, N. P. Gist, C. S. Johnson, Daniel Katz, Otto Klineberg, David Krech, A. M. Lee, R. N. MacIver, P. F. Lazarsfeld, R. K. Merton, Gardner Murphy, T. M. Newcomb, Robert Redfield, I. D. Reid, A. M. Rose, Gerhart Saenger, R. N. Sanford, S. S. Sargent, M. B. Smith, S. A. Stouffer, Wellman Warner, Goodwin Watson, R. M. Williams.

be interpreted as reactions to these racial frustrations. These reactions are self-destructive in that the larger society not only punishes those who commit them, but often interprets such aggressive and anti-social behavior as justification for continuing prejudice and segregation.

Middle class and upper class minority group children are likely to react to their racial frustrations and conflicts by withdrawal and submissive behavior. Or, they may react with compensatory and rigid conformity to the prevailing middle class values and standards and an aggressive determination to succeed in these terms in spite of the handicap of their minority status.

The report indicates that minority group children of all social and economic classes often react with a generally defeatist attitude and a lowering of personal ambitions. This, for example, is reflected in a lowering of pupil morale and a depression of the educational aspiration level among minority group children in segregated schools. In producing such effects, segregated schools impair the ability of the child to profit from the educational opportunities provided him.

Many minority group children of all classes also tend to be hypersensitive and anxious about their relations with the larger society. They tend to see hostility and rejection even in those areas where these might not actually exist.

The report concludes that while the range of individual differences among members of a rejected minority group is as wide as among other peoples, the evidence suggests that all of these children are unnecessarily encumbered in some ways by segregation and its concomitants.

With reference to the impact of segregation and its concomitants on children of the majority group, the report indicates that the effects are somewhat more obscure. Those children who learn the prejudices of our society are also being taught to gain personal status in an unrealistic and non-adaptive way. When comparing themselves to members of the minority group, they are not required to evaluate themselves in terms of the more basic standards of actual personal ability and achievement. The culture permits and at times encourages them to direct their feelings of hostility and aggression against whole groups of people the members of which are perceived as weaker than themselves. They often develop patterns of guilt feelings, rationalizations and other mechanisms which they must use in an attempt to protect themselves from recognizing the essential injustice of their unrealistic fears and hatreds of minority groups.

The report indicates further that confusion, conflict, moral cynicism, and disrespect for authority may arise in majority group children as a consequence of being taught the moral, religious and democratic principles of the brotherhood of man and the importance of justice and fair play by the same persons and institutions who, in their support of racial segregation and related practices, seem to be acting in a prejudiced and discriminatory manner. Some individuals may attempt to resolve this conflict by intensifying their hostility toward the minority group. Others may react by guilt feelings which are not necessarily reflected in more humane attitudes toward the minority group. Still others react by developing an unwholesome, rigid, and uncritical idealization of all authority figures—their parents, strong political and economic leaders. As described in *The Authoritarian Personality* (Adorno, Frenkel-Brunswick, Levinson, & Sanford, 1950), they despise the weak, while they obsequiously and unquestioningly conform to the demands of the strong whom they also, paradoxically, subconsciously hate.

With respect to the setting in which these difficulties develop, the report emphasized the role of the home, the school, and other social institutions. Studies have shown that from the earliest school years children are not only aware of the status differences among different groups in the society but begin to react with the patterns described above (Appendix to appellant's brief, 1963, pp. 168–171).

The impact of Adlerian thought in this historic quest for racial justice and equality can best be indicated by citing the words of the unanimous decision of the United States Supreme Court which ruled that all laws which required or permitted racial segregation in public education violated the equal protection clause of the 14th Amendment of the United States Constitution. In the historic Brown decision of May 17, 1954, reached in the Kansas case, *Brown* v. *Board of Education*, 347 U.S. 483, in which the plaintiffs were Negro children of elementary school age residing in Topeka, the Supreme Court stated:

To separate them [meaning the Negro children] from others of similar age and qualifications solely because of their race generates a feeling of inferiority as to their status in the community that may affect their hearts and minds in a way unlikely ever to be undone. The effect of this separation on their educational opportunities was well stated by a finding in the Kansas case by a court which nevertheless felt compelled to rule against the Negro plaintiffs:

"Segregation of white and colored children in public schools has a detrimental effect upon the colored children. The impact is greater when it has the sanction of the law; for the policy of separating the races is usually interpreted as denoting the inferiority of the Negro group. A sense of inferiority affects the motivation of a child to learn. Segregation with the sanction of the law, therefore, has a tendency to retard the educational and mental development of Negro children and to deprive them of some of the benefits they would receive in a racially integrated school system."

Whatever may have been the extent of psychological knowledge at the time of *Plessy* v. *Ferguson*, this finding is amply supported by modern authority.[3] Any language in *Plessy* v. *Ferguson* contrary to this finding is rejected (Text of the Supreme Court opinions, 1963, p. 159).

I do not believe that it is an unpardonable exaggeration to assert that this finding reflects a major contribution of Alfred Adler to man's endless struggle for justice and dignity.

[3] Footnote 11 which is appended in the original at this point lists seven social science documents, beginning with K. B. Clark, *Effect of Prejudice and Discrimination on Personality Development* (1950).—Ed. note.

The permeating influence of Adler on the thoughts of American social scientists and social psychologists was to be found throughout many of the studies which I reviewed and included in the report which was cited by the United States Supreme Court in the Brown decision. The work of the group of social psychologists at the University of California on *The Authoritarian Personality* (Adorno, Frenkel-Brunswik, Levinson, & Sanford, 1950) owes much of the theoretical basis for its empirical findings to the ideas of Adler.

TOWARD A RELEVANT SOCIAL SCIENCE

My own recent concerns with the problems of social power and social change bear the direct stamp of Adlerian psychodynamic theory. As I have stated:

Adler's insistence upon the universality of various forms of compensation and "styles of life" which dominate the struggle for a tolerable sense of worth and dignity, may be seen as the intra- and interpersonal level of social power. The implications of Adlerian theory for understanding personality development could provide the bridge for understanding and testing the relationship between a personal and familial level of power struggle on the one hand and the social and intergroup level of power conflict and accommodation on the other.

But such a leap poses a real risk of psychological oversimplification of complex social problems. It is all to easy to assume that one understands social conflict through understanding the child's struggle to achieve a sense of worth in his conflict with punitive or overindulgent parents who equally constrict his ability to develop. Adult conpensatory, self-protective, evasive and escapist behavior *may* be so explained. But despite the evidence from such studies as *The Authoritarian Personality*, and the immense amount of evidence and speculation from clinical experience, such explanations have not yet been verified. The promise of a unification of clinical and social psychology inherent in Adler's social dynamic theory and its influence on theorists and practitioners such as Karen Horney, Harry Stack Sullivan and Erich Fromm, can be fulfilled only with further research. So, too, must future research make more precise the relationship between Adler's insights of the struggle for power and the organismic motivational theory of Kurt Goldstein, who succeeded in incorporating the concepts of a neurophysiological psychology into a psychodynamic theoretical system of striving for self-fulfillment (Clark, 1965, pp. 13–14).

Adler's contribution to the present status of the American civil rights movement can be understood not only in terms of the relevance of his theories to the problems of racial justice, not only in terms of his influence on a group of social psychologists who have been in the forefront of the struggle for justice in America, but must also be understood in terms of the fact that Adler as a social analyst and social critic dared to assert and insist that social values and the quest for social morality were legitimate and inescapable ingredients of a relevant social science. Adler the man and the social philosopher insisted upon viewing man not only in terms of his predicament, but also in terms of his potential.

Adler's emphasis upon the potential social sensitivity and empathy in man provided the important motivational base for an affirmative social technology. The contemporary social science, concerned with problems of social action and social change, cannot afford to be encumbered with fatalistic or misanthropic psychodynamic theories. Adlerian theory aside from the empirical base and in addition to the stimulation which it offers for future research and action, also offers that hope which is essential if man is to continue to seek ways of using his intelligence to assure human survival and progress. Adler provides the contemporary challenge to concerned social psychologists in insisting:

The honest psychologist cannot shut his eyes to social conditions which prevent the child from becoming a part of the community and from feeling at home in the world, and which allow him to grow up as though he lived in enemy country. Thus the psychologist must work against nationalism when it is so poorly understood that it harms mankind as a whole; against wars of conquest, revenge, and prestige; against unemployment which plunges peoples into hopelessness; and against all other obstacles which interfere with the spreading of social interest in the family, the school, and society at large.

We should be concerned to create and foster those environmental influences which make it difficult for a child to get a mistaken notion of the meaning of life and to form a faulty style of life. . . . Hence, anyone who hopes to put a stop to misdirected social movements must be able to prove cogently that the feeling of insignificance of the group can be securely relieved only by some other and better means, one which is more in tune with the spirit and the idea of the community of mankind (Adler, 1956, p. 454).

REFERENCES

Adler, A. *The problem child* (1930). New York: Capricorn Books, 1963.

Adler, A. *The Individual Psychology of Alfred Adler*. Edited by H. L. & Rowena R. Ansbacher. New York: Basic Books, 1956.

Adorno, T. W., Frenkel-Brunswik, Else, Levinson, D. J., & Sanford, R. N. *The authoritarian personality*. New York: Harper, 1950.

Appendix to appellant's brief. The effects of segregation and the consequences of desegregation: A social science statement (1952). In K. B. Clark, *Prejudice and your child*. (2nd. ed.) Boston: Beacon Press, 1963. Pp. 166–184.

Clark, K. B. *Effect of prejudice and discrimination on personality development. Fact finding report Midcentury White House Conference on Children and Youth.* Washington, D.C.: Children's Bureau, Federal Security Agency, 1950. Mimeographed.

Clark, K. B. *Prejudice and your child.* (2nd ed., enlarged.) Boston: Beacon Press, 1963.

Clark, K. B. Problems of power and social change: toward a relevant social psychology. *J. soc. Issues,* 1965, *21*(3), 4–20.[4]

Clark, K. B., & Clark, Mamie, P. The development of consciousness of self and the emergence of racial identification in Negro pre-school children. *J. soc. Psychol.,* 1939, *10,* 591–599. (a)

Clark, K. B., & Clark, Mamie K. Segregation as a factor in the racial identification of Negro pre-school children. *J. exper. Educ.,* 1939, *8,* 161–163. (b)

Clark, K. B., & Clark, Mamie K. Skin color as a factor in racial identification of Negro pre-school children. *J. soc. Psychol.,* 1940, *11,* 159–169.

Clark, K. B., & Clark, Mamie K. Racial identification and preference in Negro children. In T. M. Newcomb & E. L. Hartley (Eds.), *Readings in social psychology.* New York: Holt, 1947. Pp. 169–178.

Clark, K. B., & Clark, Mamie K. Emotional factors in racial identification and preference in Negro children. *J. Negro Educ.,* 1950, *19,* 341–350.

Sumner, F. C. Religion and psychiatry: an approach to European psychology of religion. In P. L. Harriman (Ed.), *Encyclopedia of psychology.* New York: Phil. Libr., 1946. Pp. 814–831.

Text of the Supreme Court opinions, May 17, 1954. In K. B. Clark, *Prejudice and your child.* (2nd ed.) Boston: Beacon Press, 1963. Pp. 156–165.

---

[4] This paper was Professor Clark's address to the Society for the Psychological Study of Social Issues upon receiving the Society's Kurt Lewin Memorial Award, 1965. —Ed. note.

13

Der Kampf in der Kultur (Culture and Aggression): Einige Gedanken und Bedenken zu Freud's Todestrieb und Destruktionstrieb

KAREN HORNEY

For a psychoanalyst, the problem of describing the part played by aggressive tendencies of mankind in the construction and destruction of culture is bound to be stimulating, since it leads into an almost wholly unexplored area. However, this problem is of such tremendous scope that it would require no less than a lifetime of work in the field of social psychology. I must, therefore, content myself with showing you a few aspects of the problem which resulted from psychoanalytic thinking.

Even the simpler task of working up a brief sketch of Freud's views based on his psychoanalytical thinking, as expressed in *Civilization and Its Discontents* is not quite so easy, since precisely in this area almost everything is problematic. Precisely those ideas, recently advocated by Freud, on the innate aggressive tendencies in mankind, in contrast to other psychoanalytic concepts, have not developed from empirical observations, but are the product of speculative thinking. As such, they are open to criticism and to attack in psychoanalytic circles.

Those who have carefully followed the development of analysis in recent years realize that this statement about the purely speculative origin can be only partially correct. For out of clinical experience there has been effected a very gradual change based on increasing evidence of destructive tendencies as pathogenic factors. We could also say that *Civilization and Its Discontents* is the ultimate expression of such empirical observation.

At this point we are faced with two divergent impressions. Are Freud's ideas the product of his ingenious, although totally subjective, speculative imagination, or are they a reflection of a first, courageous

From K. Horney, Culture and Aggression. (Some Considerations and Objections to Freud's Theory of Instinctual Drives Toward Death and Destruction.) Reprinted by permission of *The American Journal of Psychoanalysis*, 1960, 20(2), 130–138, Harold Kelman, M.D., Editor.

affirmation of what was experienced and observed in the other? Perhaps we should not waste time on either, or on questioning, but should keep our eyes open to the boundary line separating one from the other.

Now let us see what we find on closer examination of the empirical observations. What is the nature of the change in focus to which I have previously referred? First and foremost, we must consider the changes in the concept of anxiety. Originally, anxiety was regarded as an expression of dammed-up libidinal energies, attributed to inappropriate use of sexual energies. Later, the concept of anxiety was freed from this restricting context in which anxiety was connected only with sexual factors. Then the concept was extended in the direction of regarding anxiety as an expression of the perception of all the dangers threatening us from the still-lively volcanic forces operative within. These may be strong, uncontrolled sexual forces, but much more frequently anxiety is provoked by destructive forces fused with sexual energies. Even more anxiety-provoking is the perception of destructive forces in pure culture. Even in anxiety of apparently sexual origin, as, for example, anxiety over the perception of unconscious prostitution fantasies, or over the horrible consequences of masturbation, we can at least see that the content of such anxiety is conditioned by the admixture of repressed destructive drives. The fruitfulness of such a broadened view is reflected in our understanding of the universality of masturbation anxiety.

To Freud we owe this broader perspective on the sexual problems confronting us, a perspective which has made it possible for us to start wondering about the ubiquity of masturbation-anxiety. We are not especially surprised that religious people, who turn aside from all sexual matters, would consider masturbation a heinous sin. What is even more significant is that we find anxieties not only among those who have read articles depicting every kind of terrifying consequence of masturbation, but that we also find secret anxieties in countless people who are mostly ignorant of any connection between anxiety and masturbation. The same anxieties are found, in this or that guise, in those who are not especially bothered by ethical concerns over sexual matters. Furthermore, these anxieties are not restricted to any age or cultural class. Such findings should make us thoughtful.

At first, psychoanalytic experience indicated that anxiety could be traced to threats about masturbation in childhood and that, although deeply repressed, these threats continued to operate as a residual source of anxiety. However, such threats were not elicited to any noteworthy degree in all patients. And even if they had been uncovered, it would mean only that the problem had to be shifted to the previous generation. We would then have to raise this question: What accounts for such a general parental prohibition of masturbation? Medically speaking, there is no known or rational basis for connecting masturbation with every possible illness. The tendency to make such a correlation is in itself an expression of anxiety. Educators have objected to masturbation on the ground that fostering such an easily attainable pleasure undermines character development and contributes to antisocial and egocentric behavior. They have a point, but their argument does not in the least clarify the roots of the anxiety in which masturbation is imbedded.

Actually, masturbation-anxiety cannot be comprehended from those aspects which are accessible to consciousness, but can only be inferred from the guilt feelings generated by the unconscious fantasies accompanying or leading to masturbation. The content of the sexual fantasies in themselves, no matter how infantile or prohibited, cannot make understandable those specific anxieties which are found in those who unconsciously fear or consider every deprivation in life, every conceivable illness, every failure a consequence of masturbation. If there is one principle which is inviolable and operative in the unconscious, it is the ancient principle of Talion (Vengeance): an eye for an eye, a tooth for a tooth. If with your heart and soul you wish illness to another person, desire to eliminate him from the competitive struggle, desire his ruin or his death, you must unconsciously fear retaliation with a similar fate for yourself. In other words, only the more potent mixture of unconscious destructive elements with masturbation can make understandable the extreme ease with which anxiety is provoked.

An example may illustrate this point. An exact, detailed, psychological history of a compulsion neurosis may often show the following onset: In reaction to certain anxieties, a man has suddenly suppressed masturbation. At precisely this point, compulsive phenomena appear for the first time. What has occurred? Prior to this point, the individual has succeeded in fusing unusually large components of hostile impulses with libidinal impulses. Of course, he has had anxieties, but they have not, so to speak, threatened his very existence. As soon as the libidinal fusion is dissolved, and the hostile impulses break through and, as such, lurked naked and undisguised within the depths of the individual, he must protect himself in very different ways from the threatening danger. At this point, the compulsive phenomena arise as security measures against the unmixed destructive drives.

Now let us consider an even more common problem. We all know people who are not actually considered ill and, yet in characteristic ways seem fated to fail in the areas of work, love, and friendship. Here, as well, we find that the particular restricting hand which appears to be fate is actually an expression of repressed aggressions. Perhaps it goes like this: for such people every competitive situation at work or in love becomes impossible and resembles life-and-death matters unconsciously. They therefore prefer to condemn themselves to failure.

Now let us take an example from an area nearer to general experience in a normal life. We might inquire as to why there are so few successful marriages. Why do we find in the most ordinary exchange between husband and wife such easily provoked undercurrents of defensiveness, anxiety, and distrust? Why must the husband belittle his wife in one way or another? The source of these reactions does not involve the sexual area, for in actuality Eros binds husband and wife. What is really involved here is this: precisely the strongest and least controllable affects grow in the same soil as the most potent hostility; and these have been developing since childhood and are carried over to the adult in the form of a readiness to distrust.

This is not a particularly new premise. We have always realized that hostility and retaliatory drives contribute not only to the genesis of neurosis, but also to ordinary human conflicts. What has really taken place in psychoanalytic thinking is a shift from considering only the sexual factors to emphasis on the destructive forces as the true operative pathogenic factor.

And yet this shift seems to encompass more than a mere change in emphasis, at least insofar as theoretical constructs are concerned. We cannot reproach Freud for underestimating the importance of the contribution of hostile-aggressive drives in the factors affecting both the individual and society. How have we previously classified these drives directed toward destruction of the object? By and large, they were included under sadism. Sadism was commonly described as a partial drive of sexuality appearing during a particular phase in the development of infantile sexuality. Infantile cruelty appeared as its direct expression; the picture of compassion and consideration was regarded as reaction-formations against sadism. Sadism was seen as a perversion, as a regression to this phase, and residual aggressions as more or less ego-shaping transformations. Specific occupations, such as soldier and surgeon, were considered as sublimations. This mode of classification has not been satisfactory inasmuch as there are many pathological and normal phenomena which do not in the slightest degree show any connection between the destructive drives and sexuality. We could have seen the untenability of this argument earlier when Abraham, by way of a theoretically consistent extension of this concept, raised objections to this correlation and postulated a "post-ambivalent" phase. This would mean that we could expect the following: If all the streams of sexuality were unified in the phase of genital primacy, and thus an individual had fully developed his capacity for love, then every shred of sadism, as such, would have disappeared and, therefore, the individual would no longer harbor any ambivalent emotions of love and hate towards the love-object.

In context with earlier theory, this postulate would be indisputable, but reality upsets the argument. Freud, himself, has often enough stressed that even under normal conditions a person does not reach this ideal state. The sharpening of our theoretical understanding of sadism has been hampered by an unsuitable broadening of the term, which grew out of a tendency to create a maximally unified concept from phenomena, in this instance from sexuality.

The newer concept of a duality of instincts seems to fit in better with the facts. I, therefore, believe that the great psychoanalytic significance of *Civilization and Its Discontents* stems from the fact that here, for the first time, the important role of non-erotic aggressive tendencies is fully appreciated. This is expressed by Freud as follows: "I can no longer understand how we could have overlooked the universality of non-erotic aggression and destructiveness and how we could have failed to give it its due significance in the interpretation of life." Up to this point there is hardly anything that is problematic, and this is as far as empirical observation takes us.

What I find questionable is Freud's derivation of these destructive drives from the death instinct. The assertion of a death instinct would, grossly simplified, mean that as we find in all organic matter the biological rhythm of creation and destruction, anabolism and catabolism, and a cycle of life, growth, and death, so also we could find corresponding processes in drives which could be designated as life-and-death instincts, or as Eros and Destruction. Freud himself concedes that the arguments for such a state of affairs were not convincing. No matter how ingeniously the material derived from biology is used, it does not lend itself very well to analogies. Even the psychological arguments are not convincing as supportive evidence for the phenomena of "repetition compulsion" and "primary masochism," which could be interpreted differently and are in themselves problematic. Furthermore, the death instinct can neither be experienced, as Freud himself states, nor can it in any way be discovered in isolation, but "works silently within the organism toward its disintegration." Freud thinks that "the more productive idea is this one, that a component of the instinct is directed outward and then manifests itself as the drive to aggression and destruction." We must carefully examine the meaning of this sentence. Although the claim of a death instinct in itself may belong in the realm of speculation, nevertheless his idea may furnish us with a useful working hypothesis. The meaning of this statement is no more and no less than this, that "man possesses an innate tendency to evil, aggression, destruction and ultimately to inhumanity." Freud is correct in adding that none of us cares to hear things of this nature. However, our aversion does not constitute evidence to the contrary. What should really concern us is whether this statement can or cannot be corroborated by the available psychological data. One fact stands out in the foreground: the widespread occurrences throughout history of ruthless attitudes and behavior have no bearing at all on this assertion, since the question of the innate nature of such tendencies is left open, or at least the value of such observations cannot be gauged without a careful investigation into the nature of the psychological and social pressures which might perhaps have produced them.

I believe rather that this is the more cardinal question: Can every action which appears to be directed toward destruction be considered as a derivative of a drive to destruction? Our first task is to clarify the difference between the concepts of aggression and destruction. Freud's tendency to string these two concepts together and to equate one with the other did not occur by chance or through carelessness of expression. He intentionally related them very closely and this becomes much clearer when we realize that he wants us to regard the drives to rule, to exert power, to master nature as "modified and controlled, quasi aim-inhibited expressions of this drive to destruction."

I ask you, can the constructive in man be regarded as an aim-inhibited expression of the destructive? Isn't this a rather debatable generalization of that extraordinary, otherwise fruitful, analytical thinking which assumes that the factual results of an action indicate often enough the direction in which we must search for the appropriate instinctual drive behind it? Of course, we need not be fearful of turning antiquated truths upside down— to change "man destroys in order to live" into "man lives in order to destroy"; but if we do this we must have a more cogent basis than the merely scientific urge to embrace all living processes in one powerful, but perhaps rather overwhelmingly stretched synthesis, the synthesis of Eros and Destruction.

To be sure, every step forward in our conquest of nature also gratifies our sense of mastery. But apart from the fact that mastery gives us a heightened sense of aliveness, hunger would have driven man to conquer nature anyhow, or, to say it more succinctly, the drives to preserve life and improve the necessary conditions for life would push us in that direction. The aggressive tendencies definitely play a significant part in the drives for self-preservation. With equal certainty, we can speak of the aggressive drives as innate if we understand them in their fundamental sense as referrable to impulses to touch, grasp, seize, take hold of, and possess. We can see expressions of the *anlage* for this drive even in the infant, and it is clear enough when we see the infant reaching for and attempting to take hold of everything. From this point onward, we can easily extend the line of development to later manifestations of making demands, making claims, wanting to win out, wanting to conquer people and things, and wield power over them.

But where in all this can we identify the destructive force? Is it not possible to consider all tendencies of this order as varied expressions of a vital urge for expansion? Are not all these impulses exquisitely life-affirming? Are they not clearly residuals of phylogenetically acquired tendencies necessary to man in his efforts to acquire and defend his foodstuffs, his love-objects, and his family? The well-known lioness protecting her cubs becomes ferocious when anyone comes too close to them. However, are we dealing here with hostility, destructiveness, or desires to annihilate? Or are we actually dealing with impulses to defend and preserve life? What here leads to actual destruction of another life is unequivocally determined by a drive to life. Furthermore, under what conditions does an animal generally attack? A hungry animal attacks, as does an animal anticipating attack—again always in the service of self-preservation.

Furthermore, I see no different picture in deep analyses. Of course, we find inordinate fury and destructive impulses in the course of analysis of even the most placid and decent people. Why do we not then recoil in horror? Why is it that the better we understand the patient, the easier it becomes for us to feel with him? Probably this happens because we realize that all this fury has, or has had, a real basis in the patient's experiences with insults, frustrations, and above all with anxiety. Clinical experience shows that when these grounds cease to operate and the intensity of unconscious anxiety has been reduced through analysis, these patients lose their tendencies to hostility. Not that these patients become particularly good, but their unconscious strivings are no longer directed toward destruction, and they become active in their own behalf, assume responsibility for their lives, are able to make requests, assert themselves, work, acquire possessions, and defend themselves. We know that we cannot be magicians, a fact which Freud was the first to emphasize. We would not be able to mobilize life-affirming forces if they were not there in the patient from the beginning; only under the stress of anxiety and dammed-up libidinal drives have they turned into destructive impulses, sadism, and cruelty.

It would be ridiculous to suppose that Freud had not seen these connections, since he was the one who first taught us to use them. The inference to be drawn from his thesis is, however, that destructive drives, which are of necessity directed to the outer world, are triggered off by insults, frustrations, and anxiety which bring to light an unalterable, innate, constitutional, instinctual drive to destruction. He postulates a given human tendency to be provoked to animosity, hostility, and destruction, which seizes every opportunity to discharge itself in thoughts and actions. It cannot be denied that many events in the history of nations, as well as in the history of individuals, may, at first, give this impression. However, on analytic examination, amenable to verification, we find thoroughly adequate grounds for overt and covert hostility. This hostility disappears when these grounds are removed. It was Freud who also opened the way for understanding the frequency of man's innate predisposition to hostility. He showed us unalterable factors contributing to this state. The long period of the child's dependency and helplessness presents many opportunities for clashes between the child's powerful, continuous instinctual demands and the necessary, culturally imposed demands to inhibit these drives, and accounts for a residue of anxiety and defensiveness.

It is on analytic grounds, therefore, that I feel obliged to reject the thesis of the death instinct and an innate destructive instinct, as well as the thesis of innate evil in man. I do not in the slightest wish to replace this thesis with the claim that man is basically "good." As I see it, man is born with a vital necessity for self-expanding—a necessity which drives him to grasp as much as he possibly can of life and its possibilities. Even our most frantic death wishes and our strongest drives for vengeance are dictated by this will to live and this desire to obtain as much love, success, strength, and satisfaction in living as possible. In this framework, we would regard anyone as our enemy who stands in our way or who prevents us from achieving these ends. It is not the will to destroy that drives us, but the will-to-life that forces us to destroy.

And ' now to a consideration of the will-to-life and the inseparable anxiety about death which leads me to another unsolved problem in psychoanalysis. What, in Freud's thesis, becomes of the anxiety about death? Freud supposes that the unconscious has no concept of death or non-being and, therefore, he tends to deny the fear of death as a powerful force in our mental life. This thesis has always been unacceptable to me, as well as to many others. I would venture a conjecture that the denial of anxiety about death is accounted for by the death instinct in this way: we have no fear of death—on the contrary, something in the core of our being drives us toward death.

So much for criticism. From my remarks you will no doubt see that psychoanalysis is not a cult requiring that its adherents display blind allegiance to Freud's every word, although we have often been accused of this. To be sure, we are dealing here less with variations in the method of true scientific inquiry into facts than with differences of opinion over our emotional or, shall we say, philosophic backgrounds regarding the nature of man.

It is obvious, furthermore, that these differences extend beyond the field of theoretical problems in psychoanalysis and into the field of cultural problems. If we share Freud's viewpoint of innate destructive tendencies in man, then we must be absolutely pessimistic about the inevitability of the explosions of these instincts in crime, war, and its atrocities, as well as in vicious interclass and international struggles for power. If we do not share Freud's point of view, there is left for us a primary—and maybe the strongest—impression that man is tragically and inextricably trapped in his relationship to culture, that man, more helpless than the beast, requires certain patterns of living which bind him to the culture so that he can exist at all. This would entail a variety of restrictions, changing in quality and quantity, on the sexual and aggressive drives. Man does not respond favorably to these restrictions especially in childhood; he perceives them as a threat and reacts with anxiety and a hidden capacity for hostility. So from this standpoint as well there is no rosy, happy-ending optimism, yet this represents a basically different point of view from that of Freud's because it contains some factors amenable to change.

Of course, cultural demands for curbs on instinctual drives are unavoidable. In this process, the individual becomes subdued and to some extent forfeits happiness and possibilities for happiness. To a certain degree it becomes unavoidable in the course of this curbing process that our sexual and aggressive drives may also be transformed into destructive tendencies.

In every observation of individual fates we find that the vital point in this inhibiting process revolves around this crucial question: Is the child being exposed to realistic discipline and are the necessary limitations conveyed to him without his being intimidated or spoiled? Or, is he growing up in an atmosphere rife with orders, prohibitions, threats and anxiety? *The basic emotional attitude of the parents is more significant than any specific method of child-rearing.* If the parents live under excessive pressures, they will in turn be forced to pressure their children. These pressures, if rooted in sexual frustration, may be manifested in excessive tenderness toward the child. Other forms of parental discontent may lead to overt or covert hostility toward the child. The less a child is burdened by superimposed pressures connected with the emotional problems of the parents, the less likelihood there is that he will suffer from destructiveness.

The next problem to be considered would be how to provide the child with more contented and less pressured parents. However, this takes us far beyond the field of psychology, and cannot be answered by focusing on a partial aspect of the problem—the institution of marriage. The problem leads us into two areas. The first is economic and political. Here we would have to investigate all the factors in the culture that could produce more favorable social conditions for the masses of humanity and would give them a greater measure of economic security. Establishing such conditions might mitigate the tragic struggle for existence to which the masses are exposed. If these goals could be achieved, psychologically speaking, we might then have conditions of decreased external pressures. Thus the masses would have a better opportunity for uninterrupted development of their vital forces. And the coming generation might grow up under less pressure.

In the second area we are concerned with woman and her specific pressures. As a mother, woman exerts such a decisive influence on the development of future generations that it is difficult to understand why there exists so little appreciation of the obvious fact that it is woman who has been, and is, living under special pressures. Here, again, we have to consider that suppression or repression of the vital life-affirming forces in general, and the sexual drives in particular, must contribute to an increase in unconscious destructive elements. Hence, if the woman possesses greater inner security and is more self-fulfilled, she can become the strongest force in promoting the healthy growth of the younger generation.

This hope for the future may be an illusion. Nevertheless, the insights we have obtained from psychoanalysis into unconscious psychological processes are of such a nature that the realization of such a hope may be very logically anticipated.

Now, to summarize the most general conclusions of these observations. Struggle, in the sense of aggression has and will always exist. We accept that kind of aggression which is an expression of the will to live. According to Freud, aggression in the sense of various forms of mild to extreme destructiveness occurs inevitably in mankind and is as powerful as he asserts. At times this destructiveness is not overtly expressed, since the destructive drive is inhibited by civilization. However, if we adopt the view that destructive drives in man are not innate, but that they have been acquired under specific conditions, we then have to concede the existence of possibilities for reducing their intensity and extensiveness. These possibilities would have to be derived from the psychological insights which would delineate the exact influences fostering or preventing the growth of destructiveness. Such a project would be invaluable since the future of civilization, as well as that of man as an individual, might depend on how effectively we can deal with the threat that arises from this destructiveness.

14

The Diagnosis
of Marital Conflicts

PAUL LUSSHEIMER

In a panel discussion on "The Diagnosis and Treatment of Marital Conflicts," one has to decide how to utilize the relatively short time allotted to each discussant. There is agreement among my colleagues to limit ourselves, more or less, to a special area, and I am privileged to discuss the Diagnosis of Marital Conflicts. Much has been said and written on this subject by psychiatrists and nonpsychiatrists (Laidlaw, 1955). Nevertheless, when we, the panelists, decided to take up the topic, we did so hoping to add something new that will be valuable to those who are professionally involved in marriage counseling, but also to those who personally, directly or indirectly, may benefit from our discussions.

My own contribution will be devoted to Karen Horney's theories; I shall try to show how Horney's concepts can be fruitfully applied to the understanding of marital conflicts. With the title of her book, *Our Inner Conflicts* (Horney, 1950), she has already expressed by implication that one has to differentiate between outer and inner conflicts. While outer conflicts do not necessarily belong to the realm of the psychiatrist, inner conflicts do. There are inner, but normal conflicts where there is an awareness of wishes and feelings and willingness and ability to make a choice. Most of the inner conflicts one observes in marital counseling are, however, not normal but neurotic conflicts. They do not exist in one of the marital partners only, but more frequently than not, to some lesser or greater degree, in both.

Experience shows that usually the inner conflicts which interfere with a healthy mutuality in a marriage are hidden behind one or many façade

From P. Lussheimer, The Diagnosis of Marital Conflicts. Reprinted by permission of *The American Journal of Psychoanalysis*, 1967, 27, 127–131, Harold Kelman, M.D., Editor, and the author.

The papers in this Panel Discussion were presented to the Association for the Advancement of Psychoanalysis at the New York Academy of Medicine, October 20, 1965.

conflicts (Mudd, 1951), which are sufficiently strong to prevent the marital partners from awareness of the existence of anything deeper that might be wrong; at best one or the other sees or senses the splinter in the other's eyes without realizing the beams in his own. I leave it to the imagination of the listener to ponder over what the façade conflicts may be; many things may come to mind, and I mention only two examples from my recent experience to stimulate your fantasy. In one instance it was a continuous haggling about whether the new automobile should be black or some other color; in another case it was the choice of the daily newspaper— should it be *The New York Times* or the *Herald Tribune*. Hours were wasted and vile words were exchanged between the respective couples and bad feelings continued on and on over these issues.

Conflicts like those just mentioned can be easily solved in cases where no strong neurotic factor prevails in one or both partners. Any outsider may then be of help; no psychiatrist is needed in such cases. In situations where the fighting about problems goes on with stubbornness and one such difference of opinion is followed by another, psychiatric help is needed without doubt.

There are large numbers of marital situations which are serious enough to need trained but not necessarily psychiatric counselors; these are the situations which are of an external nature, important enough to call for expert outside help. But the danger exists that couples may present to the counselor a serious conflict which is a surface conflict and leave the deeper conflicts untouched. One could say: Why touch on the existing deeper conflicts in a couple and activate unnecessary anxieties if the acute problem has been taken care of? This would be acceptable in cases where, after the counseling, one could say that they "lived happily ever after." So far I have not seen any statistics which could definitely prove the fact of a permanent success, and Dean Johnson's admonition to marriage counselors consistently to utilize psychiatric consultation deserves serious consideration (Johnson, 1961). The steadily increasing number of couples sent by marriage counselors to psychiatrists or who ask spontaneously for psychiatric consultation indicates the growing acceptance of the fact that something below the façade may be wrong and deserves thorough study.

During the past quarter of a century during which I have become more and more involved with consultations in connection with marriage problems, I have learned two facts of great significance: (1) People coming for marriage consultation are not affected by their marriages but have deep-seated neurotic difficulties. (In most cases both marital partners have such difficulties and very occasionally is it only one, but then all the worse.) Also, not only are they not aware of the neurotic pattern that pervades their life orientation, but it is, in many instances, difficult to convince them of the existing trouble. (2) There is practically no married person in psychoanalytic treatment whose neurosis does not affect the marriage in one way or another.

Ever since the beginning of history, marital conflicts have existed. The biblical story of Adam and Eve, their temptation by the serpent and their expulsion from the paradise is the earliest evidence of a marital conflict. Without trying to analyze the mechanisms of that conflict, we have to remind ourselves that our psychoanalytic thinking is strongly directed by cultural considerations, and that, as Horney pointed out in the title of her first book, one has to pay attention to *The Neurotic Personality of our Time* (Horney, 1937). Studying the contradictions in our culture, we learn that the neurotic is unable to cope with the conflicting tendencies everyone is confronted with day in and day out. In marital life the neurotic partner tries in his inner struggle and in the relationship with the partner to reconcile tendencies toward aggressiveness and those toward yielding, fears of making excessive demands and not getting anything, needs for self-aggrandizement and feelings of personal helplessness. In all these instances the neurotic fights a battle on two fronts: he is at war within himself and with the partner.

In view of the above remarks, one sees that in marital life, more than in any other form of interpersonal relationship, there is a great need to see the difference between normal and neurotic conflict. Marital conflicts are unavoidable, but while the normal conflict can be resolved through a spirit of mutuality and flexibility, the compulsive character of the neurotic conflict stands between the partners and in the way of a solution.

The starting point for a mismatched marriage can be frequently discovered as being the moment when the two partners met each other. Most outstanding is the factor that the mates know each other very little but are in a hurry to get married. One of my patients expressed it this way: "The first time I had an inkling of what kind of a person my husband is and how he and I never would find the common denominator, was during our honeymoon." All that one has to add to this is that the patient realized the mistake earlier in her marriage than many, many others. But she added something that reveals self-insight: "I might have hesitated to marry him but there was an overly strong urge in me to get away from home." Now she sees that many of her dissatisfactions directed at her parents were in reality feelings in and towards herself which she externalized. We are indebted to Horney for describing the concept of externalization which she defines as "the tendency to experience internal processes as if they occurred outside oneself and, as a rule, to hold these external factors responsible for one's difficulties. . . . Externalization is . . . essentially an active process of self-elimination" (Horney, 1950a).

What happened to the patient whose statements I briefly quoted is a phenomenon that is carried over from premarital into marital life or, if not previously evident, develops during marriage, with the marital partner as a convenient object for externalization.

In diagnostic work, establishment of the existence and the degree of externalization is of greatest help; it is the portal of entry to the neurosis and is usually easily discovered in marriage consultations. The unusual situation of the couple interviewed together and then each of the partners separately is conducive to revelations which give the consulting psychiatrist an opportunity to find what he is looking for. The image which each partner has of himself and the spouse reveals which one is the morbid personality and the degree of alienation, as seen through the partner's eyes, but without proper awareness in the affected individual. The diagnosis of elements of a marriage disturbance is like the result in a picture clear enough to lend itself to the understanding required for the initiation of a proper therapy.

In the beginning of my presentation I pointed out how much has been published on the problem of marital conflicts. Bergler (1949) has given a "Catalogue of twelve marital difficulties . . . that covers most of the common causes of disaster." In studying this well-selected list, one comes to the conclusion that anything and everything may result in marital difficulties; in all instances, a certain degree of neurosis of one or both partners manifests itself in the marital difficulties leading to disaster. The diagnosis of marital conflicts requires, however, another and more profound study dealing with the character structure of the partners.

Horney has described most precisely in her later works (*Our Inner Conflicts, Neurosis and Human Growth* [Horney, 1950a; b]) how the neurotic individual in need of coping with his problems eventually acquires a neurotic solution which becomes the predominating feature in his behavior pattern. She coined three main categories of character patterns of the neurotic: the compliant, the aggressive, and the detached. Ever since Horney created this concept it has become essential to me and no doubt to all my colleagues who follow Horney's teachings. I have found that Horney's way of thinking proved helpful, not only in my psychoanalytic practice but even more so in my study of marital problems in my private practice and in the consultation work at the Karen Horney Clinic. The application of Horney's categorization in the study of married couples comes close to Bela Mittelman's (1956) study of complementary patterns. Horney's detailed description of the various categories lends itself extremely well to diagnostic and prognostic work in marriage consultations. In evaluating the prognosis and the question of therapy, not only the kind of neurotic solution is essential but just as important is the degree of neurotic manifestations in each partner.

In studying the various combinations of marital partners I have found that two aggressive, highly neurotic individuals have the most difficult time in getting along, and it takes more of the therapist's time and energy to help them to make the proper adjustments. A similar situation exists when two compliant individuals are married; in this particular case it usually takes longer before clashes occur but when one or both discover the over-solicitous patterns as a mirror image of their own behavior, trouble ensues. The behavior pattern of one or both may suddenly change, and hidden aggressive traits may come to the fore and replace the previous neurotic picture. It may be of interest to you that in all the time I have been concerned with marriage consultation work, I have not yet seen one case in which both partners belonged to the category which Horney originally named the detached personality. It is known how many detached neurotics exist in our culture, and one cannot assume that detached individuals have no affinity to each other. It is merely conjecturing if one states that marriage between detached individuals has to be likened to the two rails of a railroad: they run parallel without disturbing each other.

A marriage of two people with different kinds of neurotic solution may, at least for some time, function well. An impressive example is the marriage of an aggressive partner to a compliant self-effacing individual. There are two possibilities as to how such a marriage may develop. If the aggressive domineering partner exerts sufficient pressure on the compliant spouse, the latter mobilizes hidden aggressive trends, perhaps begins to counter the partner's sadistic behavior with his own heretofore hidden sadism and may imperil the marriage by walking out on the spouse. The other possibility of a match between an aggressive and a compliant individual corresponds to Robert F. Winch's theory of "complementary need systems" (Dicks, 1964; Winch, 1958). The marital partners make a morbid but lasting adjustment because they cannot do without each other. They do not see the marriage counselor and, if they ever do, they ignore what the counselor might say and carry on as before.

There is no time nor, do I think, any need to elaborate further on the outcome of marriages of neurotic partners with dissimilar neurotic solutions. In marriages where one of the partners is neurotic and the other what we may call relatively normal, much depends on the latter's capacity, to make the proper adjustments and influence intellectually and emotionally the neurotic partner. If this latter partner realizes that in our time neurotics can be helped by proper therapy, the prognosis for the marriage becomes more favorable.

Many questions pertaining to the subject have by necessity remained unanswered so far; maybe they can be taken up during the discussion. In review, I want to emphasize that in Horney's concept a great instrument has been created that can be successfully applied in the understanding of marital conflicts and their underlying forces.

Much work is being done to further matters, both in psychiatry, psychology (Harrower, 1956; 1965) and other disciplines. This has gone so far that the computer has been tried as a means of diagnosis. In our complicated modern society, the difficulties in marriage have become so widespread that some authors even speak of the marriage as the "patient." But this is an abstraction. Marriage still consists of the most intimate give and take between two individuals, and all our efforts must be directed toward the diagnosis and therapy of the individual's conflict so that the marriage may be saved.

Whatever the approach may be that supports the Horney-oriented way of diagnosing, the fact remains that help in marital conflicts has to be provided, and this supports the attempt to give the institution of marriage, as the most intimate of inter-human relationships, the unprejudiced attention it deserves.

REFERENCES

Bergler, E. *Conflicts in Marriage*. New York: Harper, 1949.

Dicks, H. V. Concepts of Marital Diagnosis and Therapy as Developed at the Tavistock Family Psychiatric Units, London, England, in *Marriage Counseling in Medical Practice*, E. Nash, and others (eds)., Chapel Hill, N.C.: The University of North Carolina Press, 1964.

Harrower, M. The Measurement of Psychological Factors in Marital Maladjustment, in Neurotic *Interaction in Marriage*, V. W. Eisenstein (ed.), New York: Basic Books, 1956.

Harrower, M. Influence of Neurotic Trends in Marriage, in *Marriage, a Psychological and Moral Approach*, W. C. Bier (ed.), New York: Fordham University Press, 1965.

Horney, K. *The Neurotic Personality of Our Time*. New York: Norton, 1937.

Horney, K. *Our Inner Conflicts*. New York: Norton, 1950. (a)

Horney, K. *Neurosis and Human Growth*. New York: Norton, 1950. (b)

Johnson, D. *Marriage Counselling, Theory and Practice*. Englewood Cliffs, N.J.: Prentice-Hall, 1961.

Laidlaw, R. W. Introduction, in *Successful Marriage*, M. Fishbein and E. W. Burgess (eds.), Garden City, N.Y.: Doubleday, 1955.

Mittelmann, B. Analysis of Reciprocal Neurotic Patterns in Family Relationships, in *Neurotic Interaction in Marriage*, V. W. Eisenstein (ed.), New York: Basic Books, 1956.

Mudd, E. H. *The Practice of Marriage Counseling*. New York: Association Press, 1951.

Winch, R. F. *Mate Selection*. New York: Harper, 1958.

15

Individual and Social Origins of Neurosis

ERICH FROMM

The history of science is a history of erroneous statements. Yet these erroneous statements which mark the progress of thought have a particular quality: they are productive. And they are not just *errors* either; they are statements, the truth of which is veiled by misconceptions, is clothed in erroneous and inadequate concepts. They are rational visions which contain the seed of truth, which matures and blossoms in the continuous effort of mankind to arrive at objectively valid knowledge about man and nature. Many profound insights about man and society have first found expression in myths and fairy tales, others in metaphysical speculations, others in scientific assumptions which have proven to be incorrect after one or two generations.

It is not difficult to see why the evolution of human thought proceeds in this way. The aim of any thinking human being is to arrive at the *whole* truth, to understand the *totality* of phenomena which puzzle him. He has only *one* short life and must want to have a vision of the truth about the world in this short span of time. But he could only understand this totality if his life span were identical with that of the human race. It is only in the process of historical evolution that man develops techniques of observation, gains greater objectivity as an observer, collects new data which are necessary to know if one is to understand the *whole*. There is a gap, then, between what even the greatest genius can visualize as the truth, and the limitations of knowledge which depend on the accident of the historical phase he happens to live in. Since we cannot live in suspense, we try to fill out this gap with the material of knowledge at hand, even if this material is lacking in the validity which the essence of the vision may have.

Every discovery which has been made and will be made has a long history in which the truth contained in it finds a less and less veiled and

From E. Fromm, Individual and Social Origins of Neurosis. *The American Sociological Review*, 1944, 9, 380–384. Reprinted by permission of the author and the American Sociological Association.

Presented to the annual meeting of the Eastern Sociological Society, Columbia University, April 22–23, 1944.

distorted expression and approaches more and more adequate formulations. The development of scientific thought is not one in which old statements are discarded as false and replaced by new and correct ones; it is rather a process of continuous *reinterpretation* of older statements, by which their true kernel is freed from distorting elements. The great pioneers of thought, of whom Freud is one, express ideas which determine the progress of scientific thinking for centuries. Often the workers in the field orient themselves in one of two ways: they fail to differentiate between the essential and the accidental, and defend rigidly the whole system of the master, thus blocking the process of reinterpretation and clarification; or they make the same mistake of failing to differentiate between the essential and the accidental, and equally rigidly fight against the old theories and try to replace them by new ones of their own. In both the orthodox and the rebellious rigidity, the constructive evolution of the vision of the master is blocked. The real task, however, is to reinterpret, to sift out, to recognize that certain insights had to be phrased and understood in erroneous concepts because of the limitations of thought peculiar to the historical phase in which they were first formulated. We may feel then that we sometimes understand the author better than he understood himself, but that we are only capable of doing so by the guiding light of his original vision.

This general principle, that the way of scientific progress is *constructive reinterpretation of basic visions* rather than repeating or discarding them, certainly holds true of Freud's theoretical formulations. There is scarcely a discovery of Freud which does not contain fundamental truths and yet which does not lend itself to an organic development beyond the concepts in which it has been clothed.

A case in point is Freud's theory on the origin of neurosis. I think we still know little of what constitutes a neurosis and less what its origins are. Many physiological, anthropological and sociological data will have to be collected before we can hope to arrive at any conclusive answer. What I shall do is to use Freud's view on the origin of neurosis as an illustration of the general principle which I have discussed, that reinterpretation is the constructive method of scientific progress.

Freud states that the *Oedipus complex* is justifiably regarded as the kernel of neurosis. I believe that this statement is the most fundamental one which can be made about the origin of neurosis, but I think it needs to be qualified and reinterpreted in a frame of reference different from the one Freud had in mind. What Freud meant in his statement was this: because of the sexual desire the little boy, let us say, has for his mother, he becomes the rival of his father, and the neurotic development consists in the failure to cope with the anxiety rooted in this rivalry in a satisfactory way. I believe that Freud touched upon the most elementary root of neurosis in pointing to the conflict between the child and parental authority and the failure of the child to solve this conflict satisfactorily. But I do not think that this conflict is brought about essentially by the sexual rivalry, but that it results from the child's reaction to the pressure of parental authority, the child's fear of it and submission to it. Before I go on elaborating this point, I should like to differentiate between two kinds of authority. One is *objective*, based on the competency of the person in authority to function properly with respect to the task of guidance he has to perform. This kind of authority may be called *rational* authority. In contrast to it is what may be called *irrational* authority, which is based on the power which the authority has over those subjected to it and on the fear and awe with which the latter reciprocate.

It happens that in most cultures human relationships are greatly determined by irrational authority. People function in our society as in most societies, on the record of history, by becoming adjusted to their social role at the price of giving up part of their own will, their originality and spontaneity. While every human being represents the whole of mankind with all its potentialities, any functioning society is and has to be primarily interested in its self-preservation. The particular ways in which a society functions are determined by a number of *objective* economic and political factors, which are given at any point of historical development. Societies have to operate within the possibilities and limitations of their particular historical situation. In order that any society may function well, its members must acquire the kind of character which makes them *want* to act in the way they *have* to act as members of the society or of a special class within it. They have to *desire* what objectively is *necessary* for them to do. *Outer force* is to be replaced by *inner compulsion*, and by the particular kind of human energy which is channeled into character traits. As long as mankind has not attained a state of organization in which the interest of the individual and that of society are identical, the aims of society have to be attained at a greater or lesser expense of the freedom and spontaneity of the individual. This aim is performed by the process of child training and education. While education aims at the development of a child's potentialities, it has also the function of reducing his independence and freedom to the level necessary for the existence of that particular society. Although societies differ with regard to the extent to which the child must be impressed by irrational authority, it is always part of the function of child training to have this happen.

The child does not meet society directly at first; it meets it through the medium of his parents, who in their character structure and methods of education represent the social structure, who are the psychological agency of society, as it were. What, then, happens to the child in relationship to his parents? It meets through them the kind of authority which is prevailing in the particular society in which it lives, and this kind of authority tends to break his will, his spontaneity, his independence. But man is not born to be broken, so the child fights against the authority represented by his parents; he fights for his freedom not only *from* pressure but also for his freedom to be himself, a full-fledged human being, not an automaton. Some children are more successful than others; most of them are defeated to some extent in their fight for freedom. The ways in which this defeat is brought about are manifold, but whatever they are, the scars left from this defeat in the child's fight against irrational authority are to be found at the bottom of every neurosis. This scar is represented in a syndrome the most important features of which are: the weakening or paralysis of the person's originality and spontaneity; the weakening of the self and the substitution of a pseudo-self, in which the feeling of "I am" is dulled and replaced by the experience of self as the sum total of expectations others have about me; the substitution of autonomy by heteronomy; the fogginess, or, to use Dr. Sullivan's term, the parataxic quality of all interpersonal experiences.

My suggestion that the Oedipus complex be interpreted not as a result of the child's sexual rivalry with the parent of the same sex but as the child's fight with irrational authority represented by the parents does not imply, however, that the sexual factor does not play a significant role, but the emphasis is not on the incestuous wishes of the child and their necessarily tragic outcome, its original sin, but on the parents' prohibitive influence on the normal sexual activity of the child. The child's physical functions—first those of defecation, then his sexual desires and activities—are weighed down by moral considerations. The child is made to feel guilty with regard to these functions, and since the sexual urge is present in every person from childhood on, it becomes a constant source of the feeling of guilt. What is the function of this feeling of guilt? It serves to break the child's will and to drive it into submission. The parents use it, although unintentionally, as a means to make the child submit. There is nothing more effective in breaking any person than to give him the conviction of wickedness. The more guilty one feels, the more easily one submits because the authority has proven its own power by its right to accuse. What appears as a feeling of guilt, then, is actually the fear of displeasing those of whom one is afraid. This feeling of guilt is the only one which most people experience as a moral problem, while the genuine moral problem, that of realizing one's potentialities, is lost from sight. Guilt is reduced to disobedience and is not felt as that which it is in a genuine moral sense, self-mutilation.

To sum up this point, it may be said that it is the defeat in the fight against authority which constitutes the kernel of the neurosis, and that not the incestuous wish of the child but the stigma connected with sex is one among the factors in breaking down his will. Freud painted a picture of the necessarily *tragic* outcome of a child's most fundamental wishes: his incestuous wishes are bound to fail and force the child into some sort of submission. Have we not reason to assume that this hypothesis expresses in a veiled way Freud's profound pessimism with regard to any basic improvement in man's fate and his belief in the indispensable nature of irrational authority? Yet this attitude is only one part of Freud. He is at the same time the man who said that "from the time of puberty onward the human individual must devote himself to the great task of freeing himself from the parents"; he is the man who devised a therapeutic method the aim of which is the independence and freedom of the individual.

However, defeat in the fight for freedom does not always lead to neurosis. As a matter of fact, if this were the case, we would have to consider the vast majority of people as neurotics. What then are the specific conditions which make for the neurotic outcome of this defeat? There are some conditions which I can only mention: for example, one child may be broken more thoroughly than others, and the conflict between his anxiety and his basic human desires may, therefore, be sharper and more unbearable; or the child may have developed a sense of freedom and originality which is greater than that of the average person, and the defeat may thus be more unacceptable. But instead of enumerating other conditions which make for neurosis, I prefer to reverse the question and ask what the conditions are which are responsible for the fact that so many people do *not* become neurotic in spite of the failure in their personal fight for freedom. It seems to be useful at this point to differentiate between two concepts: that of defect and that of neurosis. If a person fails to attain freedom, spontaneity, a genuine experience of self, he may be considered to have a severe defect, provided we assume that freedom and spontaneity are the objective goals to be attained by every human being. If such a goal is not attained by the majority of members of any given society, we deal with the phenomenon of *socially patterned defect*. The individual shares it with many others; he is not aware of it as a defect, and his security is not threatened by the experience of being different, of being an outcast, as it were. What he may have lost in richness and in a genuine feeling of happiness is made up by the security of fitting in with the rest of mankind—*as he knows them*. As a matter of fact, his very defect may have been raised to a virtue by his culture and thus give him an enhanced feeling of achievement. An illustration is the feeling of guilt and anxiety which Calvin's doctrines aroused in men. It may be said that the person who is overwhelmed by a feeling of his own powerlessness and unworthiness, by the unceasing doubt of whether he is saved or condemned to eternal punishment, who is hardly capable of any genuine joy and has made himself into the cog of a machine which he has to serve, has a severe defect. Yet this very defect was culturally patterned; it was looked upon as particularly valuable, and the individual was thus protected from the neurosis which he would have acquired in a culture where the defect would give him a feeling of profound inadequacy and isolation.

Spinoza has formulated the problem of the socially patterned defect very clearly. He says: "Many people are seized by one and the same affect with great consistency. All his senses are so strongly affected by one object that he believes this object to be present even if it is not. If this happens while the person is awake, the person is believed to be insane. . . . But if the *greedy* person thinks only of money and possessions, the *ambitious* one only of fame, one does not think of them as being insane, but only as annoying; generally one has contempt for them. But *factually* greediness, ambition, and so forth are forms of insanity, although usually one does not think of them as 'illness.' " These words were written a few hundred years ago; they still hold true, although the defect has been culturally patterned to *such* an extent now that it is not generally thought any more to be annoying or contemptuous. Today we come across a person and find that he acts and feels like an automaton; that he never experiences anything which is really his; that he experiences himself entirely as the person he thinks he is supposed to be; that smiles have replaced laughter, meaningless chatter replaced communicative speech; dulled despair has taken the place of genuine pain. Two statements can be made about this person. One is that he suffers from a defect of spontaneity and individuality which may seem incurable. At the same time it may be said that he does not differ essentially from thousands of others who are in the same position. With *most* of them the cultural pattern provided for the defect saves them from the outbreak of neurosis. With *some* the cultural pattern does not function, and the defect appears as a severe neurosis. The fact that in these cases the cultural pattern does not suffice to prevent the outbreak of a manifest neurosis is in most cases to be explained by the particular severity and structure of the individual conflicts. I shall not go into this any further. The point I want to stress is the necessity to proceed from the problem of the *origins of neurosis* to the problem of the *origins of the culturally patterned* defect; to the problem of the *pathology of normalcy*.

This aim implies that the psychoanalyst is not only concerned with the readjustment of the neurotic individual to his given society. His task must be also to recognize that the individual's ideal of normalcy may contradict the aim of the full realization of himself as a human being. It is the belief of the progressive forces in society that such a realization is possible, that the interest of society and of the individual need not be antagonistic forever. Psychoanalysis, if it does not lose sight of the human problem, has an important contribution to make in this direction. This contribution by which it transcends the field of a medical specialty was part of the vision which Freud had.

EGO PSYCHOLOGY | IV

Classical freudian theory postulates a psychic structure comprised of three major agencies, the id, the ego, and the superego. The id is a primitive, instinctual, pleasure-seeking energy reservoir. The ego is the organizer and executive of the personality and the principal means of contact between the individual and outer reality. And the superego is essentially (though not entirely) a conscience, an internalized representation of moral values, which strives for perfection. While there were, in Freud's writings, many complex aspects of the interrelationships among the psychic structures, one of the most significant is the nature of ego development. Freud held, particularly in his earlier work, that the ego is, at birth, without energy. All psychic energy is initially found in the id, and the ego must therefore gain its energy from the id and is, in that sense, dependent upon the more primitive structure. Unfortunately, the process by which the ego obtains energy was never made entirely clear in Freudian theory.

While the ego energy question remained unresolved, there was an ongoing development and modification of the ego concept in Freud's writings. Although he never completed, to his own satisfaction or that of certain other analysts, a systematic theory of the ego, there were indications in some of Freud's last papers, such as "Analysis Terminable and Interminable" (1937), of the directions in which he was moving. In particular, it seemed clear to some that he was attributing to the ego much greater significance and independence from the id than had earlier been the case.

The further development of ego theory was taken up along these and certain other lines shortly before and after Freud's death by two leaders in the continuing psychoanalytic movement, Freud's daughter, Anna, and Heinz Hartmann. Anna Freud concentrated primarily on the ego mechanisms of defense and has continued her work principally in the area of child analysis, where she is a major figure. Heinz Hartmann, our primary focus here, took as a major point of departure the position that the ego is not dependent upon the id for its energy, but is autonomous from birth. He argued further that the ego does not develop, as Freud held, entirely through conflictual processes, but partially in a positive, conflict-free sphere.

Of all the various post-Freudian analytic approaches, ego psychology represents the principal avenue of continuing progress in Freudian psychoanalysis. Major figures in addition to Hartmann associated with the ego school have included Ernst Kris, Rudolph Loewenstein, David Rappaport, and Erik Erikson. These individuals, and others associated with the ego movement, have pushed the ego into a place of major prominence in current psychoanalytic theory and have brought psychoanalysis and other lines of psychological thought much closer together.

The two articles selected for inclusion here are representative of the ego psychology movement. In the first, Hartmann and his collaborators of many years, Kris and Loewenstein, deal with the ego analytic view of the development of psychic structure. Of particular significance are the discussions of ego development and of the observational sources upon which the data base of psychoanalysis is built.

Erik Erikson, author of the second article, has, like Hartmann, been a major contributor to ego psychology. His widely acclaimed work, *Childhood and Society* (1950), presents a theory of ego development, in defined stages, throughout the life cycle. His major construct, *identity*, is defined as the individual's ". . . awareness that his individual way of mastering experience (his Ego synthesis) is a successful variant of a group identity and is in accord with its space-time and life plan . . ." (Erikson, 1950, p. 208). The child's sense of identity can develop only through culturally meaningful achievement. The Erikson article presented here is of particular current interest in its treatment of ego identity in Negro youth.

REFERENCES

Erikson, E. *Childhood and society*. New York: Norton, 1950.
Freud, S. "Analysis terminable and interminable." *International Journal of Psycho-Analysis*, 1937, 18.

16

Comments on the Formation of Psychic Structure

HEINZ HARTMANN, ERNST KRIS, & RUDOLPH M. LOEWENSTEIN

I. INTRODUCTION

Concern with clarification of terms is unpopular amongst psycho-analysts and rare in psychoanalytic writing. This is partly due to Freud's example. Semantics could hardly be the concern of the great explorer and some inconsistency in the usage of words may well be considered the pre-rogative of genius.[1] It is a different matter when a generation or two of scientists assume a similar prerogative; then scientific communication may tend to suffer and controversy to dissolve into soliloquies of individuals or groups. The latter conditions seem to prevail in recent psychoanalytic writing and clarification of terminology may well be one of the means to counteract it.

Psychoanalysis has developed under social conditions rare in science. Small teams of private practitioners everywhere formed the nuclei of larger professional groups. During the early stages of team work, written communication was supplemented to such an extent by personal contact on an international scale—mainly by training analyses with the few instructors—that mutual understanding was not endangered by uncertainties of terminology. With the increase of the number of psychoanalysts, that condition was bound to change. The situation of the 1940's is hardly reminiscent of the period of early team work; large groups of psychoanalysts work in ever looser contact with each other and the diffusion of psychoanalytic concepts in psychiatry, their extension into psychosomatic medicine, social work and various educational and psychological techniques opens up new vistas of development. Every step in this development, every new context in which psychoanalytic propositions are being tested or used raises anew the prob-

From H. Hartmann, E. Kris, and R. M. Loewenstein, Comments on the Forma-tion of Psychic Structure. *Psychoanalytic Study of the Child*, 1946, 2, 11–38. Reprinted by permission of author and publisher.

[1] See also E. Kris (1947), a contribution written at the same time as this paper.

lem of adequate communication. Since scientific communication is impaired by ambiguity of meaning, the need for clarification has become urgent.

Psychoanalytic hypotheses have undergone far-reaching modifications in Freud's own work and in that of his earlier collaborators. The importance of some of these reformulations was in many instances underrated at the time of their publication; and we believe that the importance of the most radical and farsighted ones, suggested in Freud's *Inhibitions, Symptoms and Anxiety*, has not yet been fully appreciated. Briefly, since a structural viewpoint was introduced into psychoanalytic thinking, hypotheses established previously must be reintegrated. The task of synchronization is larger than it might seem at first. For the newcomer the study of psychoanalysis will remain cumbersome until this is accomplished: he can hardly turn to any one book or any one presentation. While psychoanalysis has reached the "handbook stage," no handbook exists.[2] In order to grasp the systematic cohesion of psychoanalysis as a theory, the student has to study its development. This detour alone seems to guarantee full understanding; it is a detour which only a few devoted workers choose. Yet without it, there is some danger that part of what has been presented in many years of psychoanalytic writings is lost to the student, that rediscoveries of what once was discarded for valid reasons may occur ever more frequently, but also that the degree of relevance of various hypotheses may not always clearly be established and a systematic understanding of hypotheses seems to indicate that shifts in emphasis are unavoidable. Without these shifts, progress in insight tends to be retarded at a moment which otherwise lends itself uniquely to concentrated efforts of research. In restating some of the most general propositions of psychoanalysis, we have such concentrated efforts of research in mind.

In the writings of Freud and of other psychoanalysts, a large number of assumptions are tacitly implied, partly because the atmosphere of team work made full explicitness seem unnecessary; partly because the novelty of the clinical phenomena suggested global rather than detailed explanation. Thus, in turning to any one statement in the literature on a given subject, the student is likely to find incompletely stated hypotheses, and those who rely on random quotations from Freud's work have an easy time obscuring his meaning. When verification of hypotheses is at stake, incomplete statements are bound to encumber the way. Yet verification is essential in many areas; in none so much as in genetic questions (Hartmann & Kris, 1945). In the present paper we attempt to formulate just those propositions that are concerned with the formation of psychic structure; and within this group we select some that may be considered as models; i.e., many parallel hypotheses are being used in other areas of psychoanalytic theory. Our selection of propositions is also guided by consideration of actual or potential

[2] This point was made by H. Hartmann at the Symposium on Present Trends in Psychoanalytic Theory and Practice, at the Psychoanalytic Congress in Detroit, 1943.

misunderstandings. We are therefore less concerned with problems of libidinal development, its stages and its manifestations, and more with some problems of ego development and superego formation, and with the part played by maturation in these developments.

II. THE STRUCTURAL CONCEPTS

Precursors of structural concepts appeared in Freud's work when, at the end of the nineteenth century, he implemented his first startling discoveries by explanatory concepts which his subject matter had forced upon him. That subject matter was the study of psychic conflict.

The concept of a psychic conflict is integral to many religious systems and many philosophical doctrines. Ever more frequently since the days of enlightenment had the great masters of intuitive psychology, had writers, poets, and philosophers described the life of man as torn between conflicting forces. Freud's contribution conquered this area for the rule of science. The study of psychic conflict in general, and more specifically that of the pathognomic nature of certain conflicts, suggested that the forces opposing each other in typical conflict situations were not grouped at random; rather that the groups of opposing forces possessed an inner cohesion or organization. These impressions were undoubtedly stimulated by a topic that in the 1880's and 1890's played a considerable part in French psychiatry: that of multiple personality.[3] The intermittent eruptions observed in these cases supported the idea that other less dramatic manifestations of mental illness could be understood in terms of "man divided against himself."

Freud's first approach to this division and his first understanding of its implications was guided by the physicalist school in the German physiology of his time (Bernfeld, 1944), and by the evolutionist thinking of Darwinism. Under these influences he tentatively suggested his first formulations on the nature of "the psychic apparatus" whose complex functions would account for the kind of bewildering phenomena that had emerged: disturbances of memory, indirect expression of impulses in symptoms or symbols, the nature of dreams, fantasy and delusion; all these appeared in a new context, once the limitation of psychology to consciousness had been abandoned; all had to be explained in the light of the clinical study of conflict situations.

We shall not describe in detail here how, in a set of reformulations, the first hypotheses concerning the psychic apparatus were gradually modified; how step by step the concepts emerged which in the early 1920's Freud introduced under the names of "id," "ego," and "superego." These

---

[3] See in this connection Azam, Binet, Bourru and Burot, Camuset, Dufay, Paul Janet, Pierre Janet.

three psychic substructures or systems are not conceived of as independent parts of personality that invariably oppose each other, but as three centers of psychic functioning that can be characterized according to their developmental level, to the amount of energy vested in them, and to their demarcation and interdependence at a given time. Under specific conditions one of the centers may expand its area, and another or the two others may recede; more correctly, we should say that functions exercised by one of the systems may temporarily be more or less influenced by one of the others.

Thus, three of the foremost functions of the ego, *thinking, perception* and *action*, are frequently put into the service of either the id or the superego.

Thinking may be used for the gratification of instinctual as well as self-critical tendencies. In pathological cases, e.g. in compulsive thinking, it can become a substitute for masturbation. In psychoses, e.g. in paranoic delusions, it is overwhelmed by id and superego functions.

Perception may be used for the gratification of instinctual wishes in scoptophilic activity. In pathological cases, it might lead to hysterical disturbances of vision. In dreams and in psychoses perception is modified in a different sense; hallucinatory phenomena are perceptions without objects in the outside world. The perceptual function in these cases can be used by both the id and the superego.

Normal actions may serve instinctual gratification or superego demands, completely disregarding the interests of the ego. In pathological cases, interference of these systems may lead to hysterical symptoms, e.g. paralyses. In extreme cases, in catatonic states, for instance, motor activity loses even residues of ego functions, its coordination into deliberate acts.

In using more precise formulations, we have indicated the criteria used in defining the three substructures: the psychic systems are defined by the functions attributed to them.

A word need be said here as to how these definitions were arrived at. Definitions are matters of "convenience," and convenience in science consists of an adequate relation to the observed facts. Freud established his definitions of the psychic systems after careful and repeated scrutiny of his clinical material. That material suggested that in a typical psychic conflict one set of functions is more frequently on "the one side" than on "the other side" of the conflict. Functions that we find "together on one side" have common characteristics or properties. The relatedness is one of frequency.

Functions of the id center around the basic needs of man and their striving for gratification. These needs are rooted in instinctual drives and their vicissitudes (we do not here deal with these drives themselves and the theory of instincts as developed by Freud). Functions of the id are characterized by the great mobility of cathexes of the instinctual tendencies and their mental representatives, i.e., by the operation of the primary process. Its manifestations are condensation, displacement, and the use of special symbols.

Functions of the ego center around the relation to reality. In this sense, we speak of the ego as of a specific organ of adjustment. It controls the apparatus of motility and perception; it tests the properties of the present situation at hand, i.e., of "present reality," and anticipates properties of future situations. The ego mediates between these properties and requirements, and the demands of the other psychic organizations.

Functions of the superego center around moral demands. Self-criticism, sometimes heightened to incentives to self-punishment, and the formation of ideals, are essential manifestations of the superego.

In adopting the *functions* exercised in mental processes as the decisive criterium for defining the psychic systems Freud used physiology as his model in concept formation. However, this does not imply any correlation of any one of the systems to any specific physiological organization or group of organs, though Freud considered such a correlation as the ultimate goal of psychological research. Psychological terminology, he assumed, has to be maintained as long as it cannot be adequately substituted by physiological terminology.[4] It seems that the time for such substitution has not yet come. We therefore do not dwell, in the following, on parallels between the psychic systems in Freud's definition and certain organizations of the central nervous system.

The structural concepts of psychoanalysis have met with much criticism. It has been said that through their use clinical description has been obscured, since the terms were dramatic in an anthropomorphic sense (Glover, 1930; Masserman, 1946). Clearly, whenever dramatization is encountered, metaphorical language has crept into scientific discourse and that there is danger in the use of metaphor in science hardly needs to be demonstrated; danger, it should be added, to which Freud (1933) himself drew our attention. However, it remains a problem worth some further discussion, under what conditions the danger outweighs the advantage. The danger obviously begins if and when metaphor infringes upon meaning: in the case in point, when the structural concepts are anthropomorphized. Then the functional connotation may be lost and one of the psychic systems may be substituted for the total personality. There are cases in psychoanalytic literature where dramatizations have led to anthropomorphisms of this kind. To quote one conspicuous example: in Alexander's *Psychology of the Total Personality* (1927), the id, ego and superego have indeed become exalted actors on the psychic stage.

In order to illustrate the vicissitudes of meaning in this area, we select

---

[4] *Jenseits des Lustprinzips*, Gesammelte Werke, XIII, p. 65. The English translation (*Beyond the Pleasure Principle*) by omitting one word, fails to render Freud's meaning.

as an example the Freudian sentence: "The Ego presents itself to the Superego as love object." The metaphor expresses the relations of two psychic organizations by comparing it to a love relation between individuals, in which the one is the lover and the other the beloved. However, the sentence expresses an important clinical finding: self-love can easily and does, under certain conditions, substitute for love of another person. Self-love in this formulation indicates that approval of the self by the superego concerns the self in lieu of another person.

We replace the word "ego" in Freud's text by the word "self." We do so since the ego is defined as part of the personality, and since Freud's use of the word is ambiguous. He uses "ego" in reference to a psychic organization and to the whole person. Before we can attempt to reformulate Freud's proposition, it is essential to go one step further. In a more rigorous sense, we find it advisable not to speak of "approval" or "disapproval" by the superego, but simply to speak of different kinds and degrees of tension between the two psychic organizations, according to the presence or absence of conflict between their functions. Approval would be characterized by a diminution of tension; disapproval by its increase.

There can be little doubt that a reformulation of this kind that tries to restrict the use of metaphors, considerably impoverishes the plasticity of language, as compared to Freud's mode of expression. Man frequently experiences self-satisfaction as if an inner voice expressed approval, and self-reproaches as if the inner voice expressed reprobation (Loewenstein, 1938). Thus the metaphorical expression comes closer to our immediate understanding, since the anthropomorphism it introduces corresponds to human experience. Our reformulation shows that not the concepts which Freud introduced are anthropomorphic, but that the clinical facts he studied and described led us to understand what part anthropomorphism plays in introspective thinking.

When the French psychiatrists of the nineteenth century turned to the clinical study of human conflict, they used a metaphorical language of their own. Their descriptive skill lives in the papers of Pierre Janet and others; it has rarely been emulated in the descriptive psychiatry of other schools. But the metaphorical language of descriptive psychiatry did not permit in the nineteenth century, and no reformulation in terms of existential psychology will permit in the twentieth century, the step from empathy to causal explanation. This step became possible only after conceptual tools had been adopted which permitted a more generalized penetration of the phenomena; a penetration that becomes possible only at some distance from immediate experience. This was the function of Freud's structural concepts. If we use these concepts in a strict sense, the distance from experience grows. Freud's metaphorical usage of his own terms was clearly intended to bridge this gap. It might thus be said that Freud's usage bears the imprint of the clinical source from which the concepts were originally derived, the imprint of the communication with the patients. Requirements of communication may ever again suggest richness of metaphor, but metaphors should not obscure the nature of the concepts and their function in psychoanalysis as a science. That function is to facilitate explanatory constructs. Briefly, the structural concepts are amongst our most valuable tools, since they stand in a genetic context.

III. THE FORMATION OF PSYCHIC STRUCTURE

Whenever in psychoanalysis we use biological concepts, we are faced with one of three cases. First, the case of immediate borrowing: we refer to a biological or physiological phenomenon and use the terms current in these sciences; for instance, when we refer to the physiological changes within the personality at the age of puberty as distinguished from the concomitant psychological processes of adolescence. Second, a term may be borrowed, but its meaning may be changed by the context in which it is used and new properties may accrue. A case in point is the term "regression." Through its use in psychoanalysis, it has acquired meanings far transcending those in its original neurological setting. Third, biological terms may be used in a different context. Their definition is taken over from the old context, since the requirements of the new are similar to those in which they have originated.

In describing developmental functions, child psychology and psychoanalysis use the concept of differentiation and integration.[5] Differentiation indicates the specialization of a function; integration, the emergence of a new function out of previously not coherent sets of functions or reactions. The terms maturation and development are not always so clearly distinguished. We use both terms here in the sense that maturation indicates the processes of growth that occur relatively independent of environmental influences; development indicates the processes of growth in which environment and maturation interact more closely.

The relation between stimulus and response becomes, during growth, ever more specific. One might say that a specific structure of stimulus-response correlations is characteristic of a specific phase through which the child goes. Thus a stimulus that was of little relevance in one phase of its development may be of decisive relevance in another. The best known examples of this correlation can be found in the way children react to sexual experiences. Their reactions depend upon both the nature of the experience and the stage of the child's development. The "Wolfsman's" observation of the primal scene at the age of one-and-a-half became of pathogenic

[5] For closer definitions see Allport (1937).

importance only at the age of three when specific conflicts reactivated this memory (Freud, 1918).

Differentiation and integration in the child's early phases of development are partly regulated by maturational sequence, but even where they are influenced by environmental conditions, we are compelled to assume a principle regulating their interaction (Hartmann, 1939). Thus acceleration of certain integrative processes may become pathological. Premature ego development, for example, may in this sense be considered as one of the factors predisposing to obsessional neurosis. The regulation of this interaction can be attributed to a principle of balance, one that does not work in the cross-section only, but that regulates balance of development.

a) The Undifferentiated Phase [6]

We assume that the essential elements in the structure of personality exist in children of our civilization at the age of five or six. Developmental processes occurring after that age can be described as modifications, as enrichment, or, in pathological cases, as restriction of the then existing structure. Developmental processes before that age can be described in terms of formation of this structure. In introducing his concepts of psychic structure, Freud speaks of a gradual differentiation of the ego from the id; as an end result of this process of differentiation the ego, as a highly structured organization, is opposed to the id. Freud's formulation has obvious disadvantages. It implies that the infant's equipment existing at birth is part of the id. It seems however that the innate apparatus and reflexes cannot all be part of the id, in the sense generally accepted in psychoanalysis. We suggest a different assumption, namely that of an undifferentiated phase during which both the id and the ego gradually are formed. The difference is not merely one of words. The new formulation permits a better explanation of some of the basic properties of both id and ego. During the undifferentiated phase there is maturation of apparatuses that later will come under the control of the ego, and that serve motility, perception, and certain thought processes.[7] Maturation in these areas proceeds without the total organization we call ego; only after ego formation will these functions be fully integrated. To the degree to which differentiation takes place man is equipped with a specialized organ of adaptation, i.e., with the ego. This does not mean that there do not remain in the id certain elements that further the "maintenance" or preservation of the individual (Loewenstein, 1940). However, the differentiation accounts for the nature of the instinctual drives of man, sharply distinguished as they are from animal

---

[6] This section follows Hartmann (1939).

[7] For a somewhat divergent discussion of these problems see Hendrik (1942).

instincts. One gains the impression that many manifestations of the id are further removed from reality than any comparable behavior of animals. The instincts of the animal (Lashley, 1938) mediate its adjustment to the reality in which it lives and their properties determine the extent of the possible adaptation. With man, adjustment is mainly entrusted to an independent organization. One may raise the question whether, early in the infant's life, a residual equipment of "instincts" exists, that later loses its function of adjusting to the environment.

b) The Self and the Environment

We have refrained from indicating at what time during early infancy the successive steps leading to structural differentiation take place, and from what time the psychic systems of id and ego oppose and supplement each other. While we do not wish to draw rigid chronological lines, we shall summarize some of the steps in the child's growth, which lead to the formation of the ego and partly represent its earliest functions. The first and most fundamental of these steps concerns the ability of the infant to distinguish between his self and the world around him. At birth, environmental circumstances have suddenly changed; the organism grows no longer under conditions of total shelter from all disturbances from outside, and no longer, comparatively speaking, under conditions of total gratification of all basic needs. The most essential part of the new environment is the infant's mother; she controls the physical properties of the environment, providing shelter, care and food.

The nature of the biological equipment of the infant, and the nature of its environment account for the fact that the infant's first reactions are related to indulgence and deprivation experienced at the hands of its mother. Freud assumes that as long as all needs are gratified, i.e., under "total" indulgence, the infant tends to experience the source of satisfaction as part of the self; partial deprivation thus is probably an essential condition for the infant's ability to distinguish between the self and the object. The classical example concerns the child's relation to the feeding breast or its substitutes. To the extent to which indulgence prevails, comprehension of the breast as part of the self is dominant; to the extent to which deprivation is experienced, or indulgence delayed, the distinction becomes possible. That distinction, however, seems to become impossible unless a certain amount of gratification is allowed for. There is some reason to believe that the neutral term "distinction" may be preceded by or cover a number of highly significant experiences: they may range from expectation of or longing for gratification, to feelings of disappointment, and even rage against the source of frustration.

Deprivation, we have said, is a necessary, but clearly not a sufficient condition for the establishment of the distinction between the self and the object. The process of distinguishing has a cognitive or perceptual side; it is thus dependent on the maturation of the child's perceptual equipment. Moreover, psychoanalysis works with the hypothesis of another necessary condition, which concerns the distribution of psychic energy. Freud assumed that with the newborn, psychic energy is concentrated upon the self (primary narcissism). When we state that an object in the external world is experienced as part of the self, we imply that the object partakes in its narcissistic cathexis. When we speak of a distinction between the self and the external object, we assume that the object which is experienced as independent from the self has retained cathexis in spite of the separation; we infer that primary narcissistic cathexis has been transformed into object cathexis.

These processes we here describe are not accomplished in one step; they proceed in ever repeated trial experiences. Some of these trials follow a pattern established by the physiological organization of man; predominant modes of this pattern are incorporation and ejection; its psychological counterparts are introjection and projection.

These processes seem to accompany the earliest sequences of indulgence and deprivation in the child's life.

". . . the course of gratification of instinctual needs during the period immediately following birth can be presented as follows: the instinctual need —crying—gratification. The next possible step in the course of the process would be: instinctual need—hallucinated gratification which does not suffice— crying which brings on the real gratification; the child can then sleep again." (Benedek, 1938)

We have no means to assess what might happen if even under such early conditions indulgence were maximized; no conditions of infancy have been observed in which nursing procedures occur that could be described in these terms; they do not exist in human society, and would have to be created for the purpose of an experiment. We are better informed on consequences of intensive deprivation, and have learned recently that the prolonged absence of maternal care, or the lack of adequate stimulation (from the first quarter of the first year of life) tends to produce irreversible retardations that even affect maturation (Durfee and Wolf, 1933; Spitz, 1945). It seems reasonable to assume that the infant's apparatus of control and adjustment are given their best training chances at a distance considerably closer to the maximum of indulgence than to that of deprivation. As the maturation of the apparatus proceeds, the child shows signs of expectation and recognition; he turns his head towards the mother's breast, searches for the breast when put in a feeding position, and between the third and fifth month of his life, he learns to anticipate the feeding situation without crying. He recognizes his mother while she prepares his food. (For a good summary, see Benedek p. 207.)

As the child learns to distinguish between himself and the mother, he develops understanding for her communications. Little is known about the detailed processes by which this understanding is established; reactions to the actual handling of the child by the mother, to touch and bodily pressure, certainly play a part; gradually, the understanding of the child for the mother's facial expression grows. It seems probable that experiences concerning emotive processes and expressive movements in the infant itself form the basis or are a necessary condition for the infant's understanding of the mother's expression (Freud, 1905; Schilder, 1935). But the cognitive side of the process, the understanding of signs of communication, is part of the libidinal tie existing between the two. The identification of the child with the mother that we assume to exist at an early stage, gradually develops into an object relation.[8] The mother, as the first love object, is the object most highly cathected in the child's world, and the child's earliest learning proceeds partly by identifying with this object.

In this connection we mention Freud's latest suggestion on the subject, communicated in 1940 in a paper by Ruth M. Brunswick: Freud indicates the possibility that the development of the child's activity is decisively influenced by the identification with the nursing mother.

Maturational changes proceeding during the second half of the first year give the child further control of his own body and enable him partly to master the inanimate objects in his life space.[9] Some kind of anticipation of future events plays its part in each of these operations. They represent a central function of the ego; that which makes the transfer from the pleasure principle to the reality principle possible. The two regulatory principles of mental functioning express two tendencies of man. The one strives toward the immediate and unconditional gratification of demands; the other accepts the limitations of reality, postponing gratification in order to make it more secure (Freud, 1911).

Various theories have attempted to explain the relation of the two principles (Ferenczi, 1926; French, 1936). No explanation is satisfactory unless we assume that the transition from one principle to the other is rendered possible by the formation of the ego, which enters the process as an independent variable (Hartmann, 1939; see also Mahler, 1945).

---

[8] Balint (1937) and others assume, in addition, the existence of an early object relation in the newly born infant. We do not decide how far this assumption is warranted. Freud's theory of "primary narcissism" seems still best to account for facts observable immediately after birth.

[9] We do not however follow Hendrick (1942) in assuming the existence of an "instinct to master."

c) Some Influences on Ego Formation

The development of the ego proceeds along with that of the child's object relations. Amongst the factors that threaten object relations and thereby endanger the stability of the child's ego functions, we here discuss ambivalence. Theories on the origin of ambivalence are in part identical with those concerning the origin of aggression. Thus Freud (1930) considers the possibility that ambivalence arises as a necessary protection of the individual against destructive impulses bound within the self; their externalization would then be a prerequisite of survival. Some of the characteristics of ambivalence, the rapid oscillation from manifestations of positive to manifestations of negative attitudes in infant and child suggests another possibility: one might assume that the intermittent changes between projection and introjection, which were necessary concomitants of the infant's trials to establish a distinction between the self and the environment survive as a tendency towards and away from the human object. Better founded in observable fact, and not necessarily in contradiction with these assumptions, is another explanation: without discussing the problem whether or not instinctual drives tending towards destructive aims are part of the original equipment of man, one may be satisfied to assume that in the earliest phases of the infant's life any transition from indulgence to deprivation tends to elicit aggressive responses. The child's ambivalence towards his first love objects, one might say, corresponds to their position within the continuum leading from indulgence to deprivation (Ferenczi, 1926). All human relations would, according to this suggestion, be permanently colored by the fact that the earliest love relations in the child's life were formed at a time when those whom the child loves are those to whom it owes both indulgence and deprivation.

However tempting it might be to assume a correlation between the frequency and intensity of the infant's deprivational experiences, and the frequency and intensity of the child's aggressive impulses as manifested in his ambivalence, evidence does not support such simple conclusions. Too many variables exist that tend to obscure the issue, except possibly in extreme cases such as described by Bender, Schilder and Kaiser (1936), who were exposed to neglect and hostility, in an environment hardly interested in their survival. In less extreme cases, the complexity of the emotional processes can hardly be overestimated. Deprivations in earliest infancy are unavoidable in that the rising intensity of demand of the crying child waiting for the mother is experienced as deprivation; deprivations on this level are, as we have said, essential incentives for the distinction of the world from the self. At a later stage, when the child learns to exchange immediate for future indulgence, he is again exposed to a deprivational experience, one that, as we shall see, is a prerequisite for the formation of the world of thought and the further development of his ego. The child delays his demands in order to comply with the mother's request. There can be little doubt that the better assured the child is that indulgence will follow the postponement of demands, the more easily will the deprivation be tolerated. (Benedek, in this connection, stresses the importance of the element of confidence.) And yet one cannot overlook the fact that each of the basic demands of the child, the fulfillment of which is postponed, contain both libidinal and aggressive impulses. They are linked to every one of the dominant biological functions, to the nutritive as well as the eliminative, and both libidinal and aggressive tendencies find their expression on the oral and anal level of libidinal development. Any attempt to study the child's reaction to deprivation should therefore take at least three aspects into account: the nature of deprivation, its timing, and the modes of its administration.

The situation seems clearest where the third point is concerned. The mother's role is a double one. She sets the premium on learning: in order to retain her love, the child has to comply. Secondly, once the ego organization is established, by the consistency of her requests the mother supports the child's ego in his struggle against his impulses. Both roles are best fulfilled if education is conducted in an atmosphere of loving attention, i.e., if no conscious or unconscious manifestations of aggression on the part of the adult elicit counter-aggression of the child. We do not discuss here the problem of how the child senses the adult's hostility—even when it is carefully controlled—but we assume that the child's capacity to perceive it is greater than has been assumed until recently, and that this capacity develops at an extremely early age.[10]

The effect of the adult's attitude upon the child when administering deprivation has been studied in the set-up of restraint situations. The child does not only experience deprivation when one of his demands is denied— the demand for food, care or attention—but also when the adult interferes with one of his spontaneous activities, whether they serve the gratification of a drive or the solution of a problem. In the child's life, various types of activities tend to be not as sharply delimited from each other as they normally are with the adult. All action is closer to instinctual drives; problem-solving and fantasy play tend to interact; even the older child eats while it plays, and may at any moment shift from one type of gratification to the other. Many attempts to "stop the child from doing something" restrict, therefore, processes that are highly cathected. In order to characterize these manifold occurrences, we speak of restraint situations.

By and large, the child tends to react to restraint by some manifestation of aggression. However, that response is not regular. Infants swaddled during long periods of the first year of life are said not to show any more pronounced proclivity to aggression than infants who could move their

[10] For problems later in the child's life, see Burlingham (1935).

bodies freely (Greenacre, 1944). This finding seems to suggest that early swaddling, especially if it is a part of a cultural tradition, and not the expression of an individual preference of the mother, does not stimulate aggressive response, since it does not interrupt an activity but prevents one (Buxbaum, 1947).

The assumption that early in childhood the interruption of activity rather than the prevention, may be a crucial experience—though the point should be generalized only with care—leads us to the hypothesis that many kinds of "practising" activities are highly cathected, and thus indirectly to the proposition that interruption of practice, prevention of what one calls "completion of the act" is likely to upset the balance in psychic energy. This proposition is generally true of man's life; a host of experiments on act completion with normal adults and one set of experiments with obsessional patients has given ample evidence in this area (Zeigarnik, 1927; Hartmann, 1933; Gerö, 1933). The similarity in the behavior of child and adult extends even to those cases where the completion is prevented by failure: a child who fails in handling a toy properly, or who fails to solve a problem he has set himself, may turn from activity to rage-like reactions. Frustrations imposed upon adults by unsolvable problems elicit a similar response—except that their frustration tolerance is greater.

However, the relevant point in our context is that the child's tendency to aggressive outbursts when he experiences restraint can easily be modified by the behavior of the restraining adult: friendly restraint tends to reduce aggressive response. One distracts a child best by loving attention. Cathexis directed towards action is thus transformed into object cathexis. The importance of this area of problems is considerable, since the sequence of restraint of the child's spontaneous activities and decrease of aggressive impulses in the child affects many learning situations.

We do not here attempt to enter into the question of what contributions psychoanalysis might make to a general theory of learning, or how the presentation of certain psychoanalytic hypotheses could profit in general, if formulated in terms of learning. We briefly note that learning processes may lead to the gratification of instinctual impulses, since they make the mastery of reality possible, but that, at the same time, they represent an essential requisite for the development of the child's defenses against danger. As far as the child's early experiences in learning are concerned, psychoanalytic hypotheses tend to take mainly four factors into account: first, the stage of maturation of the apparatuses; second, the reaction of the environment; third, the tolerance for deprivation; and fourth, the various types of gratification afforded by the processes of learning and the satisfactions that can be obtained as consequences of mastery. Among the specific learning situations that tend to become crucial for the child's life, as a sort of model in which ego control is developed, we wish to discuss habit training.

There are plausible reasons of a physiological and psychological order to which we may refer in an attempt to account for the extreme importance of this specific situation in the child's life. The demand for control of habits has two phases; it involves the demand for retention and for elimination. Compliance therefore involves two opposite innervations of both the voluntary urethral and anal sphincters. On the other hand, the same innervation may at various times express opposite things—compliance at one time; defiance at the other.[11]

Compliance is facilitated when the child understands the adult's request, and when the muscular apparatus itself is fully developed. The recent tendency to postpone habit training to the second year of life takes these factors into account. But not only the intellectual capacity and the muscular apparatus have matured: another maturational process, that of the libidinal cathexis of the anal zone, takes place approximately at the same time. Learning takes place at a time when the stimulation of the anal passage is likely to create intense sexual experiences.[12] The situation of the child during the period of toilet training represents in a nutshell the nature of its conflict situation at that age. That conflict situation is threefold: first, there is the conflict between two instinctual tendencies, that of elimination and retention (instinctual conflict); second, there is the conflict between either one of these tendencies, and the child's attempt to control them and to time his function: it is a conflict between the id and the ego (structural conflict); and third, there is the conflict with the external world that has made the structural conflict necessary: the mother's request for timing of elimination.

The power of this request rests in the premium which the mother offers: approval or disapproval in all their manifold intensities. Approval may range from the mother's smile to caresses or gifts, disapproval from the disappearance of the smile to spanking. But again, it is not the intensity, or not only the intensity of approval or disapproval that is relevant; not the tangible manifestations of indulgences and deprivation, since whatever the intensity of manifestation, the threat of disapproval embodies the greatest danger in the child's life.

At the end of the first year, in the early phases of ego development, the child has formed lasting object relations; his attachment can outlast deprivation, and libidinal energy directed toward the love object has been partly transformed into aim-inhibited libidinal energy, transient into permanent cathexis.

As long as the demand for immediate indulgence prevails, any absence of those on whose care the child depends is experienced as a threat; gradually, as ego development proceeds, abstraction from the concrete situ-

---

[11] A somewhat similar viewpoint has been suggested by Erikson (1940).

[12] It is possible that "premature" toilet training could accelerate the libidinal cathexis of the zone.

ation becomes possible. The threat becomes, to some extent, independent of the presence or absence of the mother. These two stages coexist in the child's life for a long time and are embodied in a variety of highly complex situations. Freud (1926) comprehended these situations in the formulation that the fear of losing the love object is supplemented by the fear of losing love. Thus, one might say that the child in acquiring this new security acquires also a new kind of vulnerability; anxiety may now invade its life under new conditions.

The meaning of fear itself undergoes parallel transformations: it has been integrated into the child's structural equipment. Originally, fear is a reflex-like response to danger, i.e., to changes that tend to evoke feelings of helplessness; later, it acts as a signal that warns of changes to come. It is only when the ego cannot act upon the warning of the signal, that the intensity of anxiety grows and the state of anxiety may develop. That change in the function of anxiety is another instance of what we shall call later the extension of the inner world: anxiety as a signal can operate only when the child has learned to anticipate the future.

Only since in 1926 Freud introduced the concept of the danger situation, has the full impact of the problem of the child's defense against danger been studied in some detail. In the present context, two aspects of the problem of defense deserve our particular attention: we have said that in order to retain the love of his environments, the child learns to control his instinctual drives: this means that the differentiation between id and ego becomes ever more complete as the child grows, and that those of the child's defenses that are directed against the power of his drives serve to maintain that differentiation. The vicissitudes of these conflicting forces can be studied in the instances of regressive behavior, and of sudden eruptions of instinctual impulses in the child's early life: we do not here enter into this area of problems, since they require a discussion of the functions and the strength of the ego.

The term "defense" should not suggest the misapprehension that the process here referred to is either pathological or only of a negative importance. Rather is it correct to say that the human personality is formed by psychic mechanisms which serve, also, the purpose of defense. Some of these mechanisms first operate in other areas; thus projection and introjection are used in order to establish the distinction between the self and the non-self; regression, as a regular and temporary transformation of psychic functioning, accompanies the daily cycle from awakeness to sleep; and denial of the unpleasant represents probably an initial phase in the elimination of all disturbing stimuli. These and other mechanisms, which in the infant's life serve the function of adjustment and may be rooted in the reflex equipment of the newborn, may later function as mechanism of defense and thus produce changes in the child's personality (Hartmann, 1939). Some of these changes are only temporary, others may become permanent. The ego may develop a preference for one or the other kind of defense, use it in coping with both the id and the outer world, and later the superego; thus in all, or many, of its functions, the ego may bear the imprint of the reaction to early danger situations (Anna Freud, 1936). Certain mechanisms of defense regularly leave their traces in a permanent modification of the structure of personality: repression and identification are cases in point.

There is no reason here to state anew Freud's hypotheses concerning repression (1915) and its consequences for the dynamics, the economy and the structuralization of the personality. Suffice it to say that with the existence of repression the demarcation between id and ego is drawn more sharply and maintained by counter-cathexes.

It is different with identification. Whereas repression is a specific mechanism, not previously operating—unless we assume the tendency to denial to be its precursor, as we well may—identification has been one of the major, if not the major mechanism contributing to the child's early formation of personality; secondly, and under the pressure of danger, it can also be used for purposes of defense. But the two functions, the primary function of identification, its part in growing, and its secondary function, as a defense against danger, can hardly ever be sharply distinguished. The roots of identification can be traced to those impulses of the id, which strive towards incorporation; the psychological mechanism of identification is a correlate of and is built upon the model of this striving. In the earliest phases of the child's ego development, the child relies upon the adult in his dealing with the external world; he participates in their reactions and thus acquires their methods of solving problems and coping with emergencies. The impact of identification on the child's ego development is not known in detail. Our impressions are clearest in regard to moral behavior.

In taking over the parent's attitudes, the child strengthens his resistance against the onslaught of instinctual demands that he has learned to consider as undesirable. He pays for this greater security with the sense of guilt in case of failure, and acquires the precarious faculty of using the archaic mechanism of turning the drive against the self for auto-punitive purposes. The siding with the parents' requests, the acceptance of their demands as part of what the child wishes himself strengthens his ego against id impulses. This security also plays its part in the organization of the child's intellectual world.

The maturational sequence of the child's growing intellectual capacities is known in great detail. There is an interrelation of this maturation with the formation of psychic structure; the maturational factors in this connection concern the apparatuses that the ego controls. The relationship of the child to the world around him changes in character when the reality principle, at least in part, replaces the pleasure principle. That "replacement" may be described as a process of learning. The child gradually becomes aware of probable changes in his environment; the anticipation of the future centers on considerations such as these: "When I behave in a certain way, my environment will react in a certain way"—and thus behavior can be regulated in order to meet expectations.

This step becomes possible only if and when the urgency of demands can be reduced, when, as we said, future gratification can be substituted for immediate gratification. As a consequence, experience with those whom the child loves is no longer exclusively in terms of indulgence or deprivation. The child's attachment to them can outlast deprivation and they gain characteristics of their own that the child tries to understand. In studying this process with respect to the distribution of psychic energy, we have said that libidinal energy has been transformed into aim-inhibited libidinal energy; with respect to the child's ego functions, we may say that the child has learned to establish objective criteria and to use them in action and thought.

The child's thoughts are not only concerned with the problem of finding new ways in order to gain formerly valued gratifications. This clearly plays a part; the child "learns" in order to obtain the candy and in order to elicit the parents' caresses. But there are new pleasures corresponding to each level of development. Moreover, the mastery of difficulties, the solving of problems, becomes a novel source of delight. And thinking itself yields gratification. Thought processes can operate on various levels; thought and fantasy interact. The child can imagine and pretend; he can, in his fantasies, reenact his relationship with his environment; he can play at being an adult—briefly, the child has created a world of his own.

His independence from the outer world, his resistance to immediate reactions to stimuli, has led to an enlargement of his inner, his intellectual world.

d) Superego Formation

The processes of differentiation and integration in early childhood show the constant interaction between maturational and developmental factors. The processes leading to the formation of the third psychic organization, the superego, are to a higher degree independent of maturation. There is no specific apparatus whose maturation is essential for the growth of conscience; only a certain stage of development of intellectual life forms an essential precondition. But though the formation of the superego is the result of social influences and of processes of identification, these processes take place under the pressure of a specific situation in the child's life that is brought about by maturation.

The child reaches the phallic phase of its sexual development usually in the third or fourth year. (We here discuss these problems only as they concern the male child.) The manifestations in behavior of the cathexis of and the interest in the genital zone are manifold; the higher frequency of genital masturbation, the greater desire for physical contact with others, particularly with members of the opposite sex, and the predominance of tendencies towards phallic exhibitionism are outstanding examples. Other manifestations frequently interacting with those of behavior pertain to fantasy life. That interaction has best been studied where masturbatory activity is concerned. The link between fantasies of sexual activities with incestuous objects, and of fantasies of being prevented from or punished for such activities (by castration or its equivalent) account for the fact that masturbation during the phallic phase frequently acquires a crucial significance for symptom- and character-formation.

The reaction of the environment to the manifestation of the boy's demand during the phallic phase is no less decisive than the reaction to his earlier strivings. As far as incestuous demands are concerned, deprivation at this stage is regular. The boy's reaction to the new deprivational experience, however, can as a rule not be sharply isolated from his previous experiences in indulgence and deprivation. The intensity of his reaction to deprivation is at this stage partly under the shadows of the past. This relation is in many cases, if not regularly, sharpened by the phenomena of regression: under the pressure of the oedipal conflict, the boy tends temporarily to return to earlier phases of his libidinal development.

The oedipus constellation itself, best studied under conditions of western civilization, is replete with a series of unavoidable conflicts: the phallic demands of the boy directed against the mother are not only doomed to meet with partial rejection or restraint on her part, but they involve the boy in inescapable conflict with his father. That conflict represents a complete structure: there is the boy's hostility against the rival and his fear of the father's retaliation; the climax of this fear is the fear of castration. There also is the fear that the boy's hostility may actually endanger the father, who outside the area of conflict is a love object of paramount importance.

Freud originally stressed the idea of a phylogenetic factor, predisposing the individual to castration fear. Hartmann and Kris (1945) have formulated alternative views, as follows:

". . . Freud argues that the intensity of the fear of castration experienced by the male child in our civilization is unaccountable if we consider it as a reaction to the actual threats to which the boy is being exposed in the phallic phase; only the memory of the race will explain it. To this, we are inclined to reply with Freud's own arguments. While in many cases the child in our civilization is no longer being threatened with castration, the intensity of the veiled aggression of the adult against the child may still produce the same effect. One might say that there always is 'castration' in the air. Adults who restrict the little boy act according to patterns rooted in their own upbringing. However symbolic or distant from actual castration their threats might be, they are likely to be interpreted by the little boy in terms of his own experiences. The tumescent penis with which he responds in erotic excitement, that strange phenomenon of a change in a part of his body that proves to be largely independent of his control, leads him to react not to the manifest content but rather to the latent meaning of the restriction with which his strivings for mother, sister, or girl-playmate meet. And then, what he may have seen frequently before, the genitals of the little girl, acquire a new meaning as evidence and corroboration of that fear. However, the intensity of fear is not only linked to his present experience, but also to similar experiences in his past. The dreaded retaliation of the environment revives memories of similar anxieties when desires for other gratifications were predominant and when the supreme fear was not that of being castrated but that of not being loved . . .''

The importance of castration fear in the economy of man's anxiety is best illustrated by the fact that it even affects man's attitude to death. Like all higher organisms, man fears death, but this fear is colored by all previous conditions that have evoked anxiety; particularly by the fear of castration and by the "fear of the superego." The formation of the superego and its specific relation to the situation of the child during the phallic phase has been frequently discussed. We approach the problem from one point of view: we ask ourselves to what degree earlier experience in the same area, i.e., that of moral conduct, can be related to the formation of the superego. The identification with the parents and the compliance with their demands exists, as we have said, at an earlier stage of the boy's development. So does the feeling of guilt in case of failure to comply with the parents' requests; and even actions as a result of hostility turned towards the self occur in the younger child. In order to differentiate the functions of the superego from their precursors, we sharply distinguish two aspects of the process of superego formation.

First, the child identifies with the parents in a new way in order to escape the conflict between love, hate and guilt and the torments of anxiety. He does not identify with the parents as they are, but with the idealized parent, i.e., the child purifies their conduct in his mind and the identification proceeds as if they were consistently true to the principles they explicitly profess or aspire to observe. Hence Freud's formulation, the child identifies with the superego of the parents.

It would be erroneous to assume that idealization of the parents starts at this age; it rather reflects the concomitant stage of the child's mentation and is possibly linked to its original ambivalence. All primitive mental operations tend to sharpen contrasts and to "agglutinate values" (Hartmann, 1947). The child's proclivity in this area has been repeatedly studied.

However, it seems that at the pre-phallic stage, idealization is predominantly concerned with the area of puissance: the child aggrandizes the parents in order magically to partake in their protection and power. At the end of the phallic phase, under the pressure of the fear of castration, idealization concerns moral behavior.

Second: the process of identification that takes place is different from previous processes of identification, through the concomitant change in the economy of psychic energy. The newly acquired identifications of the child retain permanently part of the cathexis previously attached to the objects. The relative independence from the objects on the one hand and from the ego on the other constitutes the superego as an organization, distinct from either the id or the ego.

In the course of this process, libidinal energy is desexualized: the dangerous, or sexual part of the boy's attachment to the mother is sublimated and partly used in idealization. The aggressive attitudes towards the father are internalized; they become the force with which the demands of the superego are equipped.

The clearest manifestation of the existence of the newly formed organization is that as a consequence a new anxiety situation is introduced in the child's life. The fear of loss of the love object or of loss of love, in the pre-phallic phase, the fear of castration in the phallic phase, are supplemented, but naturally not supplanted by a new fear; the new factor, that of superego anxiety, creates the possibility for the child's moral independence of his environment. Man has acquired an inner voice.

The development of personality is not concluded at this point, and we feel that the potentialities of its transformation throughout latency and adolescence have for some time been underrated in psychoanalytic writings: But it seems that the basic structure of the personality and the basic functional interrelation of the systems have been fixed to some extent. The child does not stop growing and developing, but after that age both growth and development modify an existing structure. The newly formed superego organization is exposed to many conflicting demands. At first, it tends to be over-rigid. It does not compromise—it rather yields. The over-rigidity expresses itself in its "moral absolutism" (Piaget, 1932). Psychoanalytic observation adds that at this stage, early in latency, obsessional symptoms are highly frequent amongst children.

Throughout latency, one can watch a gradual adjustment of superego functions. That adjustment is partly due to the growth of intellectual comprehension, and educational or religious indoctrination, but partly also to the fact that the function of the superego is less endangered; therefore it needs less protection. The pubertal change creates new dangers; they reactivate the situation that once led to superego formations. The ensuing polarization of behavior between asceticism and indulgence has repeatedly been described (Anna Freud, 1936). Less clearly has it been realized that at this stage a new set of ideals is frequently chosen. They become part of the adolescent's conscious moral equipment (ego ideal). Again, that choice is not sudden. Throughout latency, the child has identified with many models —teachers; friends; policemen; leaders in battle, state or community; and the whole set of images that his culture makes available. But during adolescence, identifications gain a new impact; they become more compelling, and the need for support from outside is greater.

Hence the obvious importance of cultural conditions for the function of the superego. We do not enter into the area of problems that exist here; we do not discuss under what conditions idealism and cynicism tend to develop as transitory phases of development, and how gradually balance is reestablished. We only point to one alternative: if social values rapidly change, if new values do not fully substitute for old ones, if no new conduct ideals supplement the older structure of the superego, then we may be faced with behavior in the adult that maximizes compliance with what "the neighbors" do. The intensity with which ideals are invested in a society assured of its social values may manifest itself then in a compulsory drive to be exactly like "the others are." Conformity then has become the supreme good.

IV. THE DATA OF OBSERVATION

The genetic hypotheses here discussed represent a selection from those formulated by psychoanalysts in order to explain the formation of psychic structure. Without saying so explicitly, we have also frequently implied dynamic propositions; in the context of the system of psychoanalytic psychology, as in any other scientific system, hypotheses support each other, and where support is at default, there is room for doubt. Whether in science one retains any one hypothesis, a set of hypotheses, or even the assumptions and concepts that hold the system together, depends on their usefulness as tools in the causal explanation of the phenomena studied.

Freud, and those with him, who based upon the assumptions and concepts of psychoanalysis definite genetic propositions, were, on the whole, faced with four sets of specific data that they attempted to integrate. We enumerate these data according to their probable importance at the time:

1. The reconstruction of life histories in psychoanalytic observation.
2. The study of regressive phenomena in normal, but mainly in pathological behavior, largely in the study of neuroses and psychoses.
3. Observations on child development.
4. Data from history and anthropology mainly interpreted in the light of evolutionism and used for the formulation of "prehistoric" constructs. These constructs were then linked to ontogenetic observations.

In partially reformulating some of these hypotheses, we have not only tried to eliminate terminological impasses and certain contradictions within the systematic cohesion of hypotheses. We have also attempted implicitly to reevaluate, to some extent, the contributions of the data. The difference can be stated as follows:

We have avoided all connection between ontogenetic hypotheses and prehistoric constructs; we did so not because we doubt the importance of such constructs as sources of valuable clues, but because we doubt their value within the more rigorous set of hypotheses that aim at verification by empirical procedures. On the other hand, we tried to allow for a better integration between the three other types of data, those gained from the study of regressive phenomena in general, from psychoanalytic reconstructions and from direct observation of the growing child. All three are essential and their interrelation in the formulation of psychoanalytic hypotheses deserves some more detailed discussion.

In order to explain the earliest processes of differentiation and integration, we turn to the study of phenomena that we attribute to regression to these stages. Thus, the loss of the distinction between the self and the non-self is familiar from many psychotic processes. The schizophrenic experience of the emptiness of the external world, and many other hallucinatory and delusionary processes, as well as the psychological aspect of sleep, are explained according to Freud's hypothesis as a withdrawal of cathexis from the world to the self. These phenomena and their opposites supply the models for the hypothesis of transformations of object cathexis into narcissistic cathexis, and vice versa.

On the other hand, the fact that the distinction between the self and the outer world gradually develops, and the ways and time intervals in which it develops, belong to a series of data which can be ascertained by the study of infant and child behavior. The importance of these latter data is, we believe, indicated by some of our reformulations, for instance, by those that stress the importance of maturational processes.

Only in exceptional cases have we directly referred to the data themselves; their systematic integration with psychoanalytic observations and hypotheses represents a task for monographic studies in many areas. The data now available will not suffice. Only studies in child development, guided by these psychoanalytic hypotheses, can supply a better empirical foundation. As far as studies in this area proceed, they prove to be of great value. That value will increase when they fully deal with the communication between the child and the mother in the pre-verbal stage, or in the earliest verbal stages. What we need is an observational check on our hypotheses concerning object formation. Similarly, hypotheses concerning the reactions of mother and child to toilet training, and many other hypotheses concerning early childhood, could be formulated more concretely and probably more correctly if observational data were more ample.

Observations of this kind will still not replace the findings of psycho-analytic reconstruction. In the observation of the behavior detail, the potential importance of one experience cannot always be seen. Retrospective investigation alone can elucidate that importance.

Thus we repeat what has been said elsewhere, that the systematic study of large numbers of life histories from birth on, based on an integration of many skills of observation, permits the greatest chance for verification or falsification of hypotheses. There are areas in which objective observations cannot, as yet, contribute to the formulation of hypotheses; but they are often eminently useful in excluding hypotheses that are in contradiction to observation.

BIBLIOGRAPHY

Alexander, F. 1930. *Psychoanalysis of the Total Personality*.

Allport, G. 1937. *Personality, a Psychological Interpretation*.

Azam. 1876. "Histoire de Félida," *Comptes Rendus de l'Académie des Sciences Morales et Revue Scientifique*.

Balint, M. 1937. "Fruehe Entwicklungsstadien des Ichs. Primaere Objektliebe," *Imago*, XXIII.

Bender, L., Schilder, P. and Kaiser, S. 1936. "Studies in Aggressiveness," *Gen. Psychol. Mon.*, XVIII, 5, 6.

Benedek, T. 1938. "Adaptation to Reality in Early Infancy," *Psa. Quarterly*, VII.

Bernfeld, S. 1944. "Freud's Earliest Theories and the School of Helmholtz," *ibid*. XIII.

Binet, A. 1892. *Alteration de la Personnalité*.

Bourru and Burot. 1888. *Variations de la Personnalité*.

Burlingham, D. T. 1935. "Child Analysis and the Mother," *Psa. Quarterly*, IV.

Buxbaum, E. 1947. "Activity and Aggression in Children," *Amer. J. Orthopsychiatry*, XI (in print).

Camuset. 1882. "Un cas de Dédoublement de la Personnalité," *Ann. Med. Psychologiques*.

Dufay. 1876. "Lettre sur la Notion de Personnalité," *Rev. Scientifique*.

Durfee, H. and Wolf, K. M. 1933. "Anstaltspflege und Entwicklung im ersten Lebensjahr," *Zeit. f. Kinderforschung*, 42/3.

Erikson, E. H. 1940. "Studies in the Interpretation of Play," *Gen. Psychol. Mon.*, XXII.

Ferenczi, S. 1926. "The Problem of Acceptance of Unpleasant Ideas—Advances in Knowledge of the Sense of Reality," *Further Contributions*.

French, T. 1936. "A Clinical Study in the Course of a Psychoanalytic Treatment," *Psa. Quarterly*, V.

Freud, A. 1937. *The Ego and the Mechanisms of Defence*.

Freud, S. 1905. *Wit and Its Relation to the Unconscious*.

Freud, S. 1911. "Formulations Regarding the Two Principles in Mental Functioning," *Coll. Papers*, IV.

Freud, S. 1915. "Repression," *ibid*.

Freud, S. 1918. "From the History of an Infantile Neurosis," *ibid*.

Freud, S. 1923. *The Ego and the Id*.

Freud, S. 1926. *Inhibitions, Symptoms and Anxiety* (American transl. 1936 as *The Problem of Anxiety*).

Freud, S. 1930. *Civilization and its Discontents*.

Freud, S. 1933. *New Introductory Lectures*.

Gerö, G. 1933. Review of Dembo, T. "Der Aerger als dynamisches Problem" in Psychol. Forschung, XV; *Imago*, XIX.

Glover, E. 1930. "Introduction to the Study of Psychoanalytical Theory," *Int. J. Psa.*, XI.

Greenacre, P. 1944. "Infants' Reactions to Restraint. Problems in the Fate of Infantile Aggression," *Amer. J. Orthopsychiatry*, XIV.

Hartmann, H. 1933. "Ein experimenteller Beitrag zur Psychologie der Zwangsneurose," *Jahr. f. Psychiatrie u. Neur.*, 50.

Hartmann, H. 1939. "Ichpsychologie und Anpassungsproblem," *Int. Zeit. f. Psa. u. Imago*, XXIV.

Hartmann, H. 1947. "On Rational and Irrational Action," *Psa. and Social Science*, ed. G. Róheim (in print).

Hartmann, H., and Kris, E. 1945. "The Genetic Approach in Psychoanalysis," *this Annual*, I.

Hendrick, I. 1942. "Instinct and the Ego during Infancy," *Psa. Quarterly*, IX.

Janet, P. 1876. "La Notion de Personnalité," *Rev. Scientifique*.

Kaiser, S. See Bender.

Kris, E. 1947. "Methodology of Clinical Research," Contrib. Round Table Discussion, *Amer. J. Orthopsychiatry*, XI (in print).

Kris, E. See Hartmann.

Lashley, K. S. 1938. "Experimental Analysis of Instinctual Behavior," *Psychol. Rev.*, 45.

Loewenstein, R. 1938. "Les Origines du Masochisme et la Théorie des Pulsions," *Rev. Franc. de Psa.*, X.

Loewenstein, R. 1940. "On Vital and Somatic Drives," *Int. J. Psa.*, X.

Mack-Brunswick, R. 1940. "The Pre-Oedipal Phase of Libido Development," *Psa. Quarterly*, IX.

Mahler, M. S. 1945. "Ego Psychology Applied to Behavior Problems," *Modern Trends in Child Psychiatry*, ed. Lewis and Pacella.

Masserman, J. H. 1946. *Principles of Dynamic Psychiatry*.

Piaget, J. 1932. *The Moral Judgment of the Child*.

Schilder, P. 1935. "The Image and Appearance of the Human Body," *Psych. Mon.*, 4.

Spitz, R. A. 1945. "Hospitalism: an Inquiry into the Genesis of Psychiatric Conditions of Early Childhood," *this Annual*, I, II.

Wolf, K. M. See Durfee.

Zeigarnik, B. 1927. "Das Bahalten erledigter und unerledigter Handlungen," *Psychol. Forschung*, IX.

17

A Memorandum on Identity
and Negro Youth

ERIK H. ERIKSON

INTRODUCTION

A lack of familiarity with the problem of Negro youth and with the actions by which Negro youth hopes to solve these problems is a marked deficiency in my life and work which cannot be compensated for with theoretical speculation; and this least of all at a time when Negro writers are finding superb new ways of stating their and our predicament and when Negro youth finds itself involved in action which would have seemed unimaginable only a very few years ago. But since it is felt that some of my concepts might be helpful in further discussion, I will in the following recapitulate the pertinent ideas on identity contained in my writings.[1] This I do only in the hope that what is clear may prove helpful and what is not will become clearer in joint studies.

The fact that problems of Negro youth span the whole phenomenology of aggravated identity confusion and rapid new identity formation —cutting across phenomena judged antisocial and prosocial, violent and heroic, fanatic and ethically advanced—makes it advisable to include remarks concerning the origin of the concept of ego-identity in clinical observation in this review. However, the concept has come a long way since we first used it to define a syndrome in war—neurotics in World War II: I recently heard in India that Nehru had used the term "identity" to describe a new quality which, he felt, Gandhi had given India after offering her the equivalent of a "psychoanalysis of her past."

From E. Erikson, A Memorandum on Identity and Negro Youth. *Journal of Social Issues*, 1964, 20, 4, 29–42. Reprinted by permission of author and publisher.

[1] See: *"Childhood and Society,"* W. W. Norton and Co., Inc., New York, 1950; *"Wholeness and Totality,"* in *Totalitarianism,* Proceedings of a Conference held at the Am. Academy of Arts and Sciences, C. J. Friedrich (ed.), Cambridge: Harvard University Press, 1954; "Identity and the Life Cycle," Monograph, *Psychological Issues,* Vol. I, No. 1, New York: Int'l Universities Press, 1959 with an intro. by D. Rapaport; *"Youth: Fidelity and Diversity"* *Daedalus,* 91:5–27, 1962.

1. CHILDHOOD AND IDENTITY

a. The growing child must derive a vitalizing sense of reality from the awareness that his individual way of mastering experience is a successful variant of a group identity and is in accord with its space-time and life plan. Minute displays of emotion such as affection, pride, anger, guilt, anxiety, sexual arousal (rather than the words used, the meanings intended, or the philosophy implied), transmit to the human child the outlines of what really counts in his world, i.e., the variables of his group's space-time and the perspectives of its life plan.

Here is the first observation I made (a decade and a half ago) on Negro children. I will quote it to characterize the point-of-view with which I started. The babies of our colored countrymen, I said, often receive sensual satisfactions which provide them with enough oral and sensory surplus for a lifetime, as clearly betrayed in the way they move, talk, sing. Their forced symbiosis with the feudal South capitalized on this oral sensory treasure and helped to build a slave's identity: mild, submissive, dependent, somewhat querulous, but always ready to serve, with occasional empathy and childlike wisdom. But underneath a dangerous split occurred. The Negro's unavoidable identification with the dominant race, and the need of the master race to protect its own identity against the very sensual and oral temptations emanating from the race held to be inferior (whence came their mammies), established in both groups an association: light—clean—clever—white, and dark—dirty—dumb—nigger. The result, especially in those Negroes who left the poor haven of their Southern homes, was often a violently sudden and cruel cleanliness training, as attested to in the autobiographies of Negro writers. It is as if by cleansing, a whiter identity could be achieved. The attending disillusionment transmits itself to the phallic-locomotor stage, when restrictions as to what shade of girl one may dream of interfere with the free transfer of the original narcissistic sensuality to the genital sphere. Three identities are formed: (1) mammy's oral-sensual "honey-child"—tender, expressive, rhythmical; (2) the evil identity of the dirty, anal-sadistic, phallic-rapist "nigger"; and (3) the clean, anal-compulsive, restrained, friendly, but always sad "white man's Negro."

So-called opportunities offered the migrating Negro often only turn out to be a more subtly restricted prison which endangers his only historically "successful" identity (that of the slave) and fails to provide a reintegration of the other identity fragments mentioned. These fragments, then, become dominant in the form of racial caricatures which are underscored and stereotyped by the entertainment industry. Tired of his own caricature, the colored individual often retires into hypochondriac invalidism as a condition which represents an analogy to the dependence and the relative safety of defined restriction in the South: a neurotic regression to the ego identity of the slave.

Mixed-blood Sioux Indians in areas where they hardly ever see Negroes refer to their full-blood brothers as "niggers," thus indicating the power of the dominant national imagery which serves to counterpoint the ideal and the evil images in the inventory of available prototypes. No individual can escape this opposition of images, which is all-pervasive in the men and in the women, in the majorities and in the minorities, and in all the classes of a given national or cultural unit. Psychoanalysis shows that the unconscious evil identity (the composite of everything which arouses negative identification—i.e., the wish not to resemble it) consists of the images of the violated (castrated) body, the "marked" outgroup, and the exploited minority. Thus a pronounced he-man may, in his dreams and prejudices, prove to be mortally afraid of ever displaying a woman's sentiments, a Negro's submissiveness, or a Jew's intellectuality. For the ego, in the course of its synthesizing efforts, attempts to subsume the most powerful evil and ideal prototypes (the final contestants, as it were) and with them the whole existing imagery of superior and inferior, good and bad, masculine and feminine, free and slave, potent and impotent, beautiful and ugly, fast and slow, tall and small, in a simple alternative, in order to make one battle and one strategy out of a bewildering number of skirmishes.

I knew a colored boy who, like our boys, listened every night to Red Rider. Then he sat up in bed, imagining that he was Red Rider. But the moment came when he saw himself galloping after some masked offender and suddenly noticed that in his fancy Red Rider was a colored man. He stopped his fantasy. While a small child, this boy was extremely expressive, both in his pleasures and in his sorrows. Today he is calm and always smiles; his language is soft and blurred; nobody can hurry him or worry him —or please him. White people like him.

As such boys and girls look around now, what other ideal (and evil) images are at their disposal? And how do they connect with the past? (Does non-violence connect totalistically or holistically with traditional patience and tolerance of pain?)

b. When children enter the stage of the adolescent Identity Crisis, a factor enters which characterizes the real kind of *crisis*, namely, a moment of decision between strong contending forces. "A moment" means that here something can happen very rapidly; "decision," that divergence becomes permanent; "strong and contending," that these are intense matters.

Developmentally speaking the sense of ego identity is the accrued confidence that one's ability to maintain inner sameness and continuity (one's ego in the psychoanalytic sense) is matched by the sameness and continuity of one's meaning for others. The growing child must, at every step, derive a vitalizing sense of reality from the awareness that his individual way of mastering experience is a successful variant of the way other people around him master experience and recognize such mastery.

In this, children cannot be fooled by empty praise and condescending encouragement. They may have to accept artificial bolstering of their self-esteem in lieu of something better, but what I call their accruing ego identity gains real strength only from wholehearted and consistent recognition of real accomplishment, that is, achievement that has meaning in their culture. On the other hand, should a child feel that the environment tries to deprive him too radically of all the forms of expression which permit him to develop and to integrate the next step in his ego identity, he will resist with the astonishing strength encountered in animals who are suddenly forced to defend their lives. Indeed, in the social jungle of human existence, there is no feeling of being alive without a sense of ego identity. Or else, there may be total self-abnegation (in more or less malignant forms) as illustrated in this observation. And here is an example of total denial of identity:

A four-year-old Negro girl in the Arsenal Nursery School in Pittsburgh used to stand in front of a mirror and scrub her skin with soap. When gently diverted from this she began to scrub the mirror. Finally, when induced to paint instead, she first angrily filled sheets of paper with the colors brown and black. But then she brought to the teacher what she called "a really *good* picture." The teacher first could see only a white sheet, until she looked closer and saw that the little girl had covered every inch of the white sheet with white paint. This playful episode of total self-eradication occurred and could only occur in a "desegregated" school: it illustrates the extent to which infantile drive control (cleanliness) and social self-esteem (color) are associated in childhood. But it also points to the extent of the crime which is perpetrated wherever, in the service of seemingly civilized values, groups of people are made to feel so inexorably "different" that legal desegregation can only be the beginning of a long and painful inner reidentification.

Such crises come when their parents and teachers, losing trust in themselves and using sudden correctives in order to approach the vague but pervasive Anglo-Saxon ideal, create violent discontinuities; or where, indeed, the children themselves learn to disavow their sensual and overprotective mothers as temptations and a hindrance to the formation of a more "American" personality.

If we, then, speak of the community's response to the young individual's need to be "recognized" by those around him, we mean something beyond a mere recognition of achievement; for it is of great relevance to the young individual's identity formation that he be responded to, and be given function and status as a person whose gradual growth and transformation make sense to those who begin to make sense to him. Identity formation goes beyond the process of *identifying oneself* with ideal others in a one-way fashion; it is a process based on a heightened cognitive and emotional capacity to *let oneself be identified* by concrete persons as a circumscribed individual in relation to a predictable universe which transcends the family. Identity thus is not the sum of childhood identifications, but rather a new combination of old and new identification fragments. For this very reason societies *confirm* an individual at this time in all kinds of ideological frameworks and assign roles and tasks to him in which he can *recognize himself* and *feel recognized*. Ritual confirmations, initiations, and indoctrinations only sharpen an indispensable process of self-verification by which healthy societies bestow and receive the distilled strength of generations. By this process, societies, in turn, are themselves historically verified.

The danger of this stage is *identity diffusion*; as Biff puts it in Arthur Miller's *Death of a Salesman*, "I just can't take hold, Mom, I can't take hold of some kind of a life." Where such a dilemma is based on a strong previous doubt of one's ethnic and sexual identity, delinquent and outright psychotic incidents are not uncommon. Youth after youth, bewildered by some assumed role, a role forced on him by the inexorable standardization of American adolescence, runs away in one form or another; leaving schools and jobs, staying out all night, or withdrawing into bizarre and inaccessible moods. Once "delinquent," his greatest need and often his only salvation, is the refusal on the part of older friends, advisers, and judiciary personnel to type him further by pat diagnoses and social judgments which ignore the special dynamic conditions of adolescence. For if diagnosed and treated correctly, seemingly psychotic and criminal incidents do not in adolescence have the same fatal significance which they have at other ages. Yet many a youth, finding the authorities expect him to be "a nigger," "a bum," or "a queer," perversely obliges by becoming just that.

To keep themselves together, individuals and groups treated in this fashion temporarily overidentify, to the point of apparent complete loss of individual identity, with the heroes of cliques and crowds. On the other hand, they become remarkably clannish, intolerant, and cruel in their exclusion of others who are "different," in skin color or cultural background, in tastes and gifts, and often in entirely petty aspects of dress and gesture arbitrarily selected as *the* signs of an in-grouper or out-grouper. It is important to understand (which does not mean condone or participate in) such intolerance as the necessary *defense against a sense of identity diffusion*, which is unavoidable at a time of life when the body changes its proportions radically, when genital maturity floods body and imagination with all manners of drives, when intimacy with the other sex offers intense complications, and when life lies before one with a variety of conflicting possibilities and choices. Adolescents help one another temporarily through such discomfort by forming cliques and by stereotyping themselves, their ideals, and their enemies.

In general, one may say that we are apt to view the social play of adolescents as we once judged the play of children. We alternately consider such behavior irrelevant, unnecessary, or irrational, and ascribe to it purely delinquent or neurotic meanings. As in the past the study of children's spontaneous games were neglected in favor of that of solitary play, so now the mutual "joinedness" of adolescent clique behavior fails to be properly assessed in our concern for the individual adolescent. Children and adolescents in their presocieties provide for one another a sanctioned moratorium and joint support for free experimentation with inner and outer dangers (including those emanating from the adult world). Whether or not a given adolescent's newly acquired capacities are drawn back into infantile conflict depends to a significant extent on the quality of the opportunities and rewards available to him in his peer clique, as well as on the more formal ways in which society at large invites a transition from social play to work experimentation, and from rituals of transit to final commitments: all of which must be based on an implicit mutual contract between the individual and society.

2. TOTALISM AND NEGATIVE IDENTITY

If such contact is deficient, youth may seek perverse restoration in a negative identity, "totalistically" enforced. Here we must reconsider the proposition that the need for identity is experienced as a need for a certain wholeness in the experience of oneself within the community (and community here is as wide as one's social vision); and that, where such wholeness is impossible, such need turns to "totalism."

To be a bit didactic: *Wholeness* connotes an assembly of parts, even quite diversified parts, that enter into fruitful association and organization. This concept is most strikingly expressed in such terms as wholeheartedness, wholemindedness, and wholesomeness. In human development as well as in history, then, wholeness emphasizes a progressive coherence of diversified functions and parts. *Totality*, on the contrary, evokes a Gestalt in which an absolute boundary is emphasized: given a certain arbitrary delineation, nothing that belongs inside must be left outside; nothing that must be outside should be tolerated inside. A totality must be as absolutely inclusive as it is absolutely exclusive. The word "utter" conveys the element of force, which overrides the question whether the category-to-be-made-absolute is an organic and a logical one, and whether the parts, so to speak, really have a natural affinity to one another.

To say it in one sentence: Where the human being despairs of an essential wholeness of experience, he restructures himself and the world by taking refuge in a totalistic world view. Thus there appears both in individuals and in groups a periodical need for a totality without further choice or alternation, even if it implies the abandonment of a much-needed wholeness. This can consist of a lone-wolf's negativism; of a delinquent group's seeming nihilism; or in the case of national or racial groups, in a defiant glorification of one's own caricature.

Thus, patients (and I think it is in this respect that patients can help us understand analogous group processes) choose a *negative identity*, i.e., an identity perversely based on all those identifications and roles which, at critical stages of development, had been presented to them as most undesirable or dangerous, and yet also as most real. For example, a mother having lost her first-born son may (because of complicated guilt feelings) be unable to attach to her later surviving children the same amount of religious devotion that she bestows on the memory of her dead child and may well arouse in one of her sons the conviction that to be sick or dead is a better assurance of being "recognized" than to be healthy and about. A mother who is filled with unconscious ambivalence toward a brother who disintegrated into alcoholism may again and again respond selectively only to those traits in her son which seem to point to a repetition of her brother's fate, in which case this "negative" identity may take on more reality for the son than all his natural attempts at being good: he may work hard on becoming a drunkard and, lacking the necessary ingredients, may end up in a state of stubborn paralysis of choice. The daughter of a man of brilliant showmanship may run away from college and be arrested as a prostitute in the Negro quarter of a Southern city; while the daughter of an influential Southern Negro preacher may be found among narcotic addicts in Chicago. In such cases it is of utmost importance to recognize the mockery and the vindictive pretense in such role playing; for the white girl may not have really prostituted herself, and the colored girl may not really become an addict—yet. Needless to say, however, each of them could have placed herself in a marginal social area, leaving it to law-enforcement officers and to psychiatric agencies to decide what stamp to put on such behavior. A corresponding case is that of a boy presented to a psychiatric clinic as "the village homosexual" of a small town. On investigation, it appeared that the boy had succeeded in assuming this fame without any actual acts of homosexuality, except that much earlier in his life he had been raped by some older boys.

Such vindictive choices of a negative identity represent, of course, a desperate attempt to regain some mastery in a situation in which the available positive identity elements cancel each other out. The history of such choice reveals a set of conditions in which it is easier to derive a sense of identity out of a *total* identification with that which one is *least* supposed to be than to struggle for a feeling of reality in acceptable roles which are unattainable with the patient's inner means.

There is a "lower lower" snobbism too, which is based on the pride of having achieved a semblance of nothingness. At any rate, many a late adolescent, if faced with continuing diffusion, would rather *be a total nobody, somebody totally bad, or indeed, dead—and all of this by free choice —than be not-quite-somebody.*

Thus, individuals, when caught up in the necessity to regroup an old identity or to gain a new and inescapable one, are subject to influences which offer them a way to wholeness. Obviously, revolutions do the first to gain the second. At any rate, the problem of totalism vs. wholeness seems to be represented in its organized form in the Black Muslims who insist on a totally "black" solution reinforced by historical and religious mysticism on the one hand; and the movement of non-violent and legal insistence on civil rights, on the other. Once such a polarization is established, it seems imperative to investigate what powerful self-images (traditional, revolutionary and, as it were, evolutionary) have entered the picture, in mutually exclusive or mutually inclusive form, and what the corresponding symptoms are, in individuals and in the masses.

3. "CONVERSION" AND MORE INCLUSIVE IDENTITY

In a little-known passage, Bernard Shaw relates the story of his "conversion": "I was *drawn into* the Socialist *revival* of the early eighties, among Englishmen *intensely serious* and *burning with indignation* at very *real* and *very fundamental evils* that affected *all the world.*" The words here italicized convey to me the following implications. "Drawn into": an ideology has a compelling power. "Revival": it consists of a traditional force in a state of rejuvenation. "Intensely serious": it permits even the cynical to make an investment of sincerity. "Burning with indignation": it gives to the need for repudiation the sanction of righteousness. "Real": it projects a vague inner evil onto a circumscribed horror in reality. "Fundamental": it promises participation in an effort at basic reconstruction of society. "All the world": it gives structure to a totally defined world image. Here, then, are the elements by which a group identity harnesses the young individual's aggressive and discriminative energies, and encompasses, as it completes it, the individual's identity in the service of its ideology. Thus, identity and ideology are two aspects of the same process. Both provide the necessary condition for further individual maturation and, with it, for the next higher form of identification, namely, the *solidarity linking common identities.* For the need to bind irrational self-hate and irrational repudiation makes young people, on occasion, mortally compulsive and conservative even where and when they seem most anarchic and radical; the same need makes them potentially "ideological," i.e., more or less explicitly in search of a world image held together by what Shaw called "a clear comprehension of life in the light of an intelligible theory."

What are, then, the available ideological ingredients of the new Negro and the new American identity? For (such is the nature of a revolutionary movement) the new Negro cannot afford any longer just to become "equal" to the old White. As he becomes something new, he also forces the white man as well as the advanced Negro to become newer than they are.

4. WEAKNESS AND STRENGTH

a. In my clinical writings I have suggested that delinquent joining stands in the same dynamic relationship to schizoid isolation, as (according to Freud) perversion does to neurosis: negative *group* identities (gangs, cliques, rings, mobs) "save" the individual from the symptoms of a negative identity neurosis, to wit: a disintegration of the sense of time; morbid identity consciousness; work paralysis; bisexual confusion; and authority diffusion.

Unnecessary to say, however, a *transitory* "negative identity" is often the necessary pre-condition for a truly positive and truly new one. In this respect, I would think that American Negro writers may turn out to be as important for American literature as Irish expatriates were in the Europe of an earlier period.

On the other hand, there are certain strengths in the Negro which have evolved out of or at least along with his very submission. Such a statement will, I trust, not be misunderstood as an argument for continued submission. What I have in mind are strengths which one would hope for the sake of all of us, could remain part of a future Negro identity. Here I have in mind such a traditional phenomenon as the power of the Negro mother. As pointed out, I must glean examples from experiences accessible to me; the following observation on Caribbean motherhood will, I hope, be put into its proper perspective by experts on the whole life-space of the Negro on the American continent.

b. Churchmen have had reason to deplore, and anthropologists to explore, the pattern of Caribbean family life, obviously an outgrowth of the slavery days of Plantation America, which extended from the Northeast Coast of Brazil in a half-circle into the Southeast of the United States. Plantations, of course, were agricultural factories, owned and operated by gentlemen, whose cultural and economic identity had its roots in a supra-regional upper class. They were worked by slaves, that is, men who, being mere equipment put to use when and where necessary, had to relinquish all chance of being the masters of their families and communities. Thus, the women were left with the offspring of a variety of men who could give no protection as they could provide no identity, except that of a subordinate species. The family system which ensued can be described in scientific terms only by circumscriptions dignifying what is not there: the rendering of "sexual services" between persons who cannot be called anything more definite than "lovers"; "maximum instability" in the sexual lives of young girls, whose pattern it is to relinquish the care of their offspring to their mothers; and mothers and grandmothers who determine that "standardized mode of co-activity" which is the minimum requirement for calling a group of individuals a family. They are, then, mostly called "household groups"— single dwellings, occupied by people sharing a common food supply. These households are "matrifocal," a word understating the grandiose role of the all powerful mother-figure who will encourage her daughters to leave their infants with her, or, at any rate, to stay with her as long as they continue to bear children. Motherhood thus becomes community life; and where churchmen could find little or no morality, and casual observers, little or no order at all, the mothers and grandmothers in fact also became father and grandfathers,[2] in the sense that they exerted that authoritative influence which resulted in an ever newly improvised set of rules for the economic obligations of the men who had fathered the children, and upheld the rules of incestuous avoidance. Above all, they provided the only super-identity which was left open after the enslavement of the men, namely, that of the mother who will nurture a human infant irrespective of his parentage. It is well known how many poor little rich and white gentlemen benefited from the extended fervor of the Negro women who nursed them as Southern mammies, as creole das, or as Brazilian babas. This cultural fact is, of course, being played down by the racists as mere servitude while the predominance of maternal warmth in Caribbean women is characterized as African sensualism, and vicariously enjoyed by refugees from "Continental" womanhood. One may, however, see at the root of this maternalism a grandiose gesture of human adaptation which has given the area of the Caribbean (new searching for a political and economic pattern to do justice to its cultural unity) both the promise of a positive (female) identity and the threat of a negative (male) one: for here, the fact that identity depended on the procreative worth of being born, has undoubtedly weakened the striving for becoming somebody by individual effort.

(This is an ancient pattern taking many forms in the modern Negro world. But—parenthetically speaking—it may give us one more access to a better understanding of the magnificently bearded group of men and boys who have taken over one of the islands and insist on proving that the Caribbean male can earn his worth in production as well as in procreation.)

My question is whether such maternal strength has survived not only in parts of our South but also in family patterns of Negro migrants;

[2] See the title "My Mother Who Fathered Me."

whether it is viewed as undesirable and treated as delinquent by Negroes as well as whites; and whether America can afford to lose it all at a time when women must help men more planfully not only to preserve the naked life of the human race but also some "inalienable" values.

c. This brings me, finally, to the issue of Fidelity, that virtue and quality of adolescent ego strength which belongs to man's evolutionary heritage, but which—like all the basic virtues—can arise only in the interplay of a stage of life with the social forces of a true community.

To be a *special kind*, has been an important element in the human need for personal and collective identities. They have found a transitory fulfillment in man's greatest moments of cultural identity and civilized perfection, and each such tradition of identity and perfection has highlighted what man could be, could he fulfill all his potentials at one time. The utopia of our own era predicts that man will be one species in one world, with a universal identity to replace the illusory super-identities which have divided him, and with an international ethic replacing all moral systems of superstition, repression, and suppression. Whatever the political arrangement that will further this utopia, we can only point to the human strengths which potentially emerge with the stages of life and indicate their dependence on communal life. In youth, ego strength emerges from the mutual confirmation of individual and community, in the sense that society recognizes the young individual as a bearer of fresh energy and that the individual so confirmed recognizes society as a living process which inspires loyalty as it receives it, maintains allegiance as it attracts it, honors confidence as it demands it. All this I subsume under the term Fidelity.

Diversity and fidelity are polarized: they make each other significant and keep each other alive. Fidelity without a sense of diversity can become an obsession and a bore; diversity without a sense of fidelity, an empty relativism.

But Fidelity also stands in a certain polarity to adolescent sexuality: both sexual fulfillment and "sublimation" depend on this polarity.

The various hindrances to a full consummation of adolescent genital maturation have many deep consequences for man which pose an important problem for future planning. Best studied is the regressive revival of that earlier stage of psychosexuality which preceded even the emotionally quiet first school years, that is, the infantile genital and locomotor stage, with its tendency toward auto-erotic manipulation, grandiose phantasy, and vigorous play. But in youth, auto-erotism, grandiosity, and playfulness are all immensely amplified by genital potency and locomotor maturation, and are vastly complicated by what we will presently describe as the youthful mind's historical perspective.

The most widespread expression of the discontented search of youth is the craving for locomotion, whether expressed in a general "being on the go," "tearing after something," or "running around"; or in locomotion proper, as in vigorous work, in absorbing sports, in rapt dancing, in shiftless *Wanderschaft*, and in the employment and misuse of speedy animals and machines. But it also finds expression through participation in the movements of the day (whether the riots of a local commotion or the parades and campaigns of major ideological forces); if they only appeal to the need for feeling "moved" and for feeling essential in moving something along toward an open future. It is clear that societies offer any number of ritual combinations of ideological perspective and vigorous movement (dance, sports, parades, demonstrations, riots) to harness youth in the service of their historical aims; that where societies fail to do so, these patterns will seek their own combinations, in small groups occupied with serious games, good-natured foolishness, cruel prankishness, and delinquent warfare. In no other stage of the life cycle, then, are the promise of finding oneself and the threat of losing oneself so closely allied.

To summarize: Fidelity, when fully matured, is the strength of disciplined devotion. It is gained in the involvement of youth in such experiences as reveal the essence of the era they are to join—as the beneficiaries of its tradition, as the practitioners and innovators of its technology, as renewers of its ethical strength, as rebels bent on the destruction of the outlived, and as deviants with deviant commitments. This, at least, is the potential of youth in psychosocial evolution; and while this may sound like a rationalization endorsing any high sounding self-delusion in youth, any self-indulgence masquerading as devotion, or any righteous excuse for blind destruction, it makes intelligible the tremendous waste attending this as any other mechanism of human adaptation, especially if its excesses meet with more moral condemnation than ethical guidance. On the other hand, our understanding of these processes is not furthered by the "clinical" reduction of adolescent phenomena to their infantile antecedents and to an underlying dichotomy of drive and conscience. Adolescent development comprises a new set of identification processes, both with significant persons and with ideological forces, which give importance to individual life by relating it to a living community and to ongoing history, and by counterpointing the newly won individual identity with some communal solidarity.

In youth, then, the life history intersects with history: here individuals are confirmed in their identities, societies regenerated in their life style. This process also implies a fateful survival of adolescent modes of thinking in man's historical and ideological perspectives.

Historical processes, of course, have already entered the individual's core in childhood. Both ideal and evil images and the moral prototypes guiding parental administrations originate in the past struggles of contending cultural and national "species," which also color fairytale and family lore, superstition and gossip, and the simple lessons of early verbal training. Historians on the whole make little of this; they describe the visible emergence and the contest of autonomous historical ideas, unconcerned with the fact that these ideas reach down into the everyday lives of generations and re-emerge through the daily awakening and training of historical consciousness in young individuals.

It is youth which begins to develop that sense of historical irreversibility which can lead to what we may call acute historical estrangement. This lies behind the fervent quest for a sure meaning in individual life history and in collective history, and behind the questioning of the laws of relevancy which bind datum and principles, event and movement. But it is also, alas, behind the bland carelessness of that youth which denies its own vital need to develop and cultivate a historical consciousness—and conscience.

To enter history, each generation of young persons must find an identity consonant with its own childhood and consonant with an ideological promise in the perceptible historical process. But in youth the tables of childhood dependence begin slowly to turn: it is no longer exclusively for the old to teach the young the meaning of life, whether individual or collective. It is the young who, by their responses and actions, tell the old whether life as represented by their elders and as presented to the young has meaning; and it is the young who carry in them the power to confirm those who confirm them and, joining the issues, to renew and to regenerate, or to reform and to rebel.

I will not at this point review the institutions which participate in creating the retrospective and the prospective mythology offering historical orientation to youth. Obviously, the mythmakers of religion and politics, the arts and the sciences, the stage and fiction—all contribute to the historical logic presented to youth more or less consciously, more or less responsibly. And today we must add, at least in the United States, psychiatry; and all over the world, the press, which forces leaders to make history in the open and to accept reportorial distortion as a major historical factor.

Moralities sooner or later outlive themselves, ethics never: this is what the need for identity and for fidelity, reborn with each generation, seems to point to. Morality in the moralistic sense can be shown by modern means of inquiry to be predicated on superstitions and irrational inner mechanisms which ever again undermine the ethical fiber of generations; but morality is expendable only where ethics prevail. This is the wisdom that the words of many languages have tried to tell man. He has tenaciously clung to the words, even though he has understood them only vaguely, and in his actions has disregarded or perverted them completely. But there is much in ancient wisdom which can now become knowledge.

What then, are the sources of a new ethical orientation which may have roots in Negro tradition and yet also reach into the heroic striving for a new identity within the universal ethics emanating from world-wide technology and communication? This question may sound strenuously inspirational or academic; yet, I have in mind the study of concrete sources of morale and strength, lying within the vitality of bodily experience, the identity of individual experience, and the fidelity developed in methods of work and cooperation, methods of solidarity and political action, and methods permitting a simple and direct manifestation of human values such as have survived centuries of suppression. As a clinician, I am probably more competent to judge the conditions which continue to *suppress* and attempt to *crush* such strengths; and yet I have also found that diagnosis and anamnesis can turn out to be of little help where one ignores sources of recovery often found in surprising and surprisingly powerful constellations.

INTERACTION CONCEPTS OF PERSONALITY | V

Working within the general theoretical umbrella of the psychoanalytic orientation, the ego psychologists and the neoanalysts noted the importance of the individual's interactions with the external environment in the shaping of his personality. Some theorists, particularly those of more recent years, have gone beyond this early emphasis to hold that sociocultural influences—and the interpersonal communications which transmit these influences—are *the* central factors determining personality development and functioning.

Sometimes counted among the neoanalysts, Harry Stack Sullivan is viewed here as the first of the major interactionists. Where Adler, Horney, and Fromm stressed a variety of factors in the society and culture, Sullivan emphasized the importance of interpersonal interaction—the day-to-day, ongoing transactions between the individual and his immediate social environment. Where the other theorists continued to utilize many of Freud's constructs, even after breaking with him, Sullivan was more innovative, making little use of Freudian concepts in his later writings.

While no papers by Sullivan, himself, are included here, we have provided an interesting paper in which Goldman discusses Sullivanian concepts and seeks to apply them to group psychotherapy. He discusses such Sullivanian concepts as *need system* and *self system* in relation to group therapy and provides an example from one of his groups of how certain problems were dealt with in terms of the conceptual framework supplied by Sullivan. His main contention is that "in a group situation the patient can become aware of unsatisfied strivings that are typical of some early developmental stage" (1957, p. 390), with the implication that such awareness brings about the capacity for therapeutic change.

While Goldman's article represents an interesting attempt to apply Sullivan's concepts in the challenging context of group psychotherapy, other investigators have been more interested in seeking to explore some of the complex methodological and theoretical issues introduced by the conceptualization of personality in interactional terms. Leary and his colleagues at the Kaiser Foundation are credited with introducing the idea that interpersonal behavior can be ordered *circumplicially*. A circumplex model of interpersonal behavior conceives of interactions in complementary terms, i.e., dominance vs. submission, hate vs. love, etc., within a framework that has no definite beginning or end. The advantages of such a model for both research and potential therapeutic application are substantial and fairly obvious.

Lorr and McNair, whose work is presented in the article entitled "Expansion of the Interpersonal Behavior Circle," have conducted an extensive series of studies in the development of a circumplex interactional model of their own. The rating instrument on which their investigations are based is the Interpersonal Behavior Inventory (IBI), which has changed considerably during the course of their research on a wide variety of subjects. The latest form of the IBI includes 140 statements of manifest interpersonal behaviors that yield category scores on 15 circumplicially arranged variables. There might have been some merit in including a later article, which reviews and summarizes the entire program of research conducted by Lorr and his associates. However, it was felt that inclusion of the earlier article would provide the reader with a glimpse of the IBI and its employment at a state in development when the investigators were still fairly close to the original Leary model.

The paper by Ringuette and Kennedy introduces still another area of inquiry which has evolved from the work of a group of investigators at Palo Alto, whose contributions are among the most original and potentially exciting intellectual developments of the past decade and a half. The "double bind" hypothesis was first advanced by Bateson and his colleagues. Essentially it is a theory which emphasizes the communication which takes place between parents and child. According to the theory, the parents (usually the mother) continually communicate conflicting or incongruent messages to the child. This occurs because for some reason the mother has an aversion toward intimate contact with the child but cannot accept this aversion and denies it by overtly expressing "loving" behavior. The presentation of these incongruent messages poses a grave problem for the child. Since the mother is the primary love object, the child would like to be able to discriminate accurately between the messages he receives from her. However, if he does this, he will be punished by the realization that his mother does not really love him. On the other hand, if he does not discriminate accurately between the messages and accepts his mother's simulated loving behavior as real, he will then approach his mother. When he does this, she will become hostile toward him, causing him to withdraw. After he withdraws, she will punish him verbally for withdrawing from her because such an action indicated to her that she was not a loving mother. The child is thus punished for either accurately or inaccurately discriminating between the messages and hence finds himself in a double bind.

The only real escape for the child from this situation is to communicate with his mother about the position in which she has put him. However, if he does this, she will probably take his comment as an accusation that she is not a loving mother and will punish him for saying it. In other words, the child is not allowed to talk about the situation in an effort to resolve it. Because this sequence of events occurs over and over again in the child's home life, his ability to communicate with others about their communication to him is greatly impaired. As a result, he is incompetent in determining what other people really mean when they communicate with him and also incompetent in expressing what he really means when he communicates with others. Due to this impairment of his ability to relate to others effectively, the child may begin to respond defensively to others with incongruent responses when presented with this double-bind situation. In addition, he may manifest withdrawal or other mechanisms of defense which are part of the symptomatology of schizophrenia.

The double-bind concept was first introduced by Bateson and others and has since been dealt with both discursively and empirically by a number of workers, including Haley, Jackson, Weakland, Ruesch, and others. In the paper reprinted here, Ringuette and Kennedy followed up the suggestion that double-bind communication is apparent in the letters of mothers to their schizophrenic offspring. Using expert judges to ascertain the presence of double-bind communication, they did not find support for the double-bind hypothesis.

The final selection, that by Eric Berne, presents the application of still another interactional approach to group psychotherapy. In this paper, Berne presents some of the major constructs of his game-theory approach, exemplifying their application to group therapy through the inclusion of case materials.

18

Some Applications
of Harry Stack Sullivan's Theories
to Group Psychotherapy

GEORGE D. GOLDMAN

A brief summary of how I view psychoanalytic theory and Sullivan's place in it [1] seems to be in order before I proceed to his specific formulations. Psychoanalysis originated in a nineteenth-century Vienna to help the people of that day and place with their specific problems in living. In these earliest days it dealt primarily with problems of sexual and love frustrations that were experienced in growing up in this particular, rather restricting, setting. These conflicts seemed to be handled by the patients in fairly specific common ways—mainly through the development of hysterical symptoms. The therapy was therefore geared to peel back the layers protecting the patient's disrupting sexual memory and allow for a more effective solution to this experience. After Freud discovered that these "memories" were oft more fancied than real, a different theory to account for the patient's problems in living had to be formed. The advent of libido theory and renunciation of the recall method necessitated interpreting the patient's experiences in terms of this new theory. Soon one was not said to be doing psychoanalysis unless one was making the patient's unconscious conscious, and accomplishing it through "analysis of the transference." It appears to me as though the patient's memory of events had been replaced by his being educated to use a new and exclusive system of words and ideas to explain himself to himself.

This brief, not too complete, characterization of Freudian theory is not meant to minimize Freud's monumental contributions to the field but to point out factors that underlie the limitations of using any one frame of reference. This theory is in many ways outmoded, specifically to name a few

From G. D. Goldman, Some Applications of Harry Stack Sullivan's Theories to Group Psychotherapy. *International Journal of Group Psychotherapy*, 1957, 7: 385–391. Reprinted by permission of author and publisher.

[1] For their invaluable teachings in this area, I thank Drs. Mary White Hinckley, Meyer Maskin, and Clara Thompson.

240

of these ways, in the areas of infantile sexuality, libido theory, and structure of the personality.

In the years since Freud formulated his theories of personality our economic, political and social worlds have changed greatly and with these changes have come concomitant changes in the people in it. Vienna of the nineteenth century is not New York of 1956. Perhaps this can in some way help us to understand that our present-day patients are different and have different ways of handling their problems. This theme is amplified in a previous paper [2] so I will not discuss it further at this time.

Sullivan was a product of our present-day American culture, he was exposed to and influenced by the scientists and social scientists of our time. Meyer's influence was most strongly felt in his early ideas of psychiatry.[3] Cooley's work was seen in Sullivan's formulations of the self-system.[4] Lewin's field theory and Moreno's situational approach parallel his work.[5] I have tried to apply these theories of group dynamics to group psychotherapy in an approach utilizing Sullivanian principles in a study previously reported.[6]

As a man, he appears to have used "the obsessional dynamism" more than most and his theories with their intricacies of language and thought reflect this as well. The various major theoreticians had to, by the very nature of their being human beings, focus on specific core problems in a specific way which not only characterized the patients they met in their practice but characterized their own individuality and personal view of life and the major problems human beings face. This paper presents an approach that I have found consistent with my view of life and one which I can use effectively with the patients in my practice.

I see Sullivan as having been quite concerned with what are psychiatric problems and what are not.[7] While it surely is one's task to help people and, more specifically, to help people understand their behavior, there are many ways in which this can be done. One could give direct advice, or even be the warm, loving, giving parental substitute who would make up for all the deprivation the patient had suffered. Sullivan, however, felt that the most respectful role, as well as the most scientifically and

[2] G. D. Goldman. Group Psychotherapy and the Lonely Person in Our Changing Times. *Group Psychother.*, 8:247–253, 1955.

[3] *The Common Sense Psychiatry of Adolf Meyer.* Edited with Biographical Narrative by Alfred Lief. New York: McGraw Hill, 1948.

[4] C. H. Cooley. *Human Nature and Social Order.* 1902.

[5] K. Lewin. *A Dynamic Theory of Personality.* New York: McGraw Hill, 1935; J. L. Moreno, *Who Shall Survive.* Washington, D.C.: Nervous and Mental Disease Publishing Co., 1934.

[6] J. L. Singer, and G. D. Goldman. An Experimental Investigation of Contrasting Social Atmospheres in Group Psychotherapy with Chronic Schizophrenics. *J. Soc. Psychol.*, 40:23–37, 1954.

[7] H. S. Sullivan. *The Psychiatric Interview.* New York: Norton, 1954.

empirically correct role, was that of an expert at understanding those events which would clarify for patients the processes that involve or go on between people. The patient, of course, was the expert on his specific history of significant interrelationships. Sullivan felt that the analyst could function most effectively by *sampling* those events that are characteristic of the patient's interactions with other people. What better laboratory to observe and document these dynamic events than in the therapy group, where the analyst is, in the fullest sense of Sullivan's usage, participant observer of human interaction?

Interaction, characteristic of the patient's interpersonal operations, is thus constantly under observation for its anxiety-laden overtones and for awareness of what else might have been going on other than what the patient assumed was happening.

Having mentioned the patient and his anxiety I feel I can not go any further without briefly outlining both how the patient got to be first a person and then a patient, and how and why his anxiety appears. Sullivan did not see patients as being different in kind from other human beings; it was rather a matter of degree.[8] The human animal with its biologically determined substratum becomes a distinct person through an infinitely complex series of interactions throughout its developing years with a multitude of significant persons ranging from parents to chums. To be a bit more specific: the "self-system" comes into being very early in the child's education and socialization as the developing human copes with the complex demands, expectations, limitations, appraisals, and security operations of the parents. The self-system controls the patient's awarenesses to his environmental pressures, to the specific demands and attitudes of significant others that are intolerable, by specific dynamisms. The overuse of a specific dynamism, whether it be selective inattention or obsessionalism, differentiates *the patient* from other persons. The self-system develops through the various eras from infancy through late adolescence, learning from the social heritage passed on by the developing human's parents, teachers and friends. This learning has to take place since humans in their humanness have characteristically certain tendencies to interact and integrate interpersonally. These interactions are governed by the nature of the "need systems," the goals, or integrating tendencies of human beings. These can be classified under two main headings: those having to do with the individual in his culture, his comfort, belongingness, apartness, his security or insecurity with others are called the "pursuit of security"; those that have to do with his more biologically derived needs are grouped under the "pursuit of satisfactions." The person, in his living with other people, is thus constantly striving to avoid anxiety in the pursuit of these two universal needs.

[8] H. S. Sullivan. *The Interpersonal Theory of Psychiatry*. New York: Norton, 1953.

Sullivan saw the vast majority of the work we do in therapy as having to do with acquainting the patient with the various processes and techniques which are his maneuvers for minimizing or avoiding anxiety. Anxiety responses are derived from antecedent historical events involving earlier human situations. These earlier human situations occurred as interaction with *all* significant persons as the developing person with his biologically given substrata progressed (through the stages of development) from infancy to adulthood. Mental illness can be defined as interference with this progression and in the attainment of satisfactions and security.

As an example of what I have been saying, let me illustrate by telling an event that recently took place in one of my groups, showing how it was handled and relating it to the above theoretical framework.

About twenty minutes after one of my group sessions had started, Ann timidly poked her head in the doorway of my office, looked around and scurried to a seat. Within the next five minutes she had verbally lashed out at three different group members, especially the analyst. Joe, who had been in the group with Ann for some time, observed that this was a fairly typical way of behaving for Ann when she felt she had done something wrong. Focusing on Ann in this event, let us examine her behavior as the group interaction highlighted it. As the group members confronted Ann with their reactions to her conduct, she became vividly aware of her anxiety. Our initial task was to understand what her behavior was geared to do for her in relation to minimizing anxiety and later to understand the historical perspective of her behavior in the safety of the analytic relationship. This, parenthetically, is my therapeutic method in individual treatment as well. The interpersonal operation involved was delineated as follows: when Ann felt she had done something that would be thought of as bad, wrong or incorrect by those around her she anticipated a rebuke of such severe intensity that it would destroy her self-esteem. To block the expected attack Ann attacked first at what she felt were the weak spots in those around her. In her framework she was neutralizing those in the group who might hurt her. If they were shown to be weak they were not to be feared. In reality she was acting in direct opposition to her wish to be accepted and was provoking the very behavior she feared most.

Our next task was to explore the historical perspective of this interpersonal operation in order to understand the parataxes involved and advance toward a more mature integration. By parataxes I mean the carryovers into the present of her personalized childhood fantasies about a situation. Thus, as a child to be yelled at disapprovingly, was seen by her as being destroyed, and to err ever so slightly was the invitation to be yelled at. The developing self-system could not tolerate the destructive criticism of Ann's mother (in this case). The dynamism used in adjusting could keep the disruptive appraisal of her mother out of her awareness and thus avoid the anxiety. This approach is both Sullivanian and a distinct contribution in its awareness of personality being studied only in an interaction with another human being; in its realization that it is the adult Ann that gets into difficulty as an adult from using an adaptation of a childhood pattern (rather than exact repetition); in its understanding of dynamisms to keep unfavorable appraisals by others out of our awareness, and finally that these appraisals historically could have come from any significant person. I am going to omit the specific details of Ann's history since my emphasis is only on presenting an example of Sullivan's method.

To apply this method specifically to further our understanding of group therapy theory, I want to mention that this same behavior had been previously brought to Ann's attention in our individual session with little apparent effect. I feel it was the *immediacy* and *vividness* of her being confronted with behavior that had been acted out in a life situation, analogous to the original childhood situation, helped her accept the present interpretation. For this lonely and isolated girl, the security that came from belonging to a group and the knowledge some part of her had that she was really accepted by the group gave her the strength to "look at herself" in the group. Also operating for Ann as a support to go on to explore her problem was the experience she had had in the group of how similar exploration had helped others. The group in this case was a valuable adjunct to Ann's individual treatment.

More generally speaking, the group is an ideal place vividly to act out patterns of interaction that are characteristic of the patient's particular relatedness; in turn, the relatedness of specific group members often stirs up unique reactions in fellow patients. Consensual validation can indicate the parataxic elements in the various reactions. To clarify this, let me illustrate more of the various forces and pulls going on interpersonally during "an event" and how this is characteristicly handled in my groups. The patients in the group all have concomitant individual treatment. The group interaction therefore can center around the various group members interrelating with each other. These interactions are seen as representative of their relations in general, and are used to spark further exploration of patterns of operation. A specific event, then, could potentially affect each of the ten patients in the group and enable them to learn something about their feelings, reactions, attitudes, etc. Turning once more to the event previously used as an illustration, we could have focused on Joe and tried to understand what was behind his sensitivity to Ann. What was there in him that was awakened by this angry woman? Was he defending the analyst? If so, what did this mean? Why did he remember that Ann attacked when she felt she was wrong? To clarify Ann's behavior, four members of the group gave identical reactions to her being destructively belittling. It is this consensual validation by a group of significant peers that made her realize her behavior. The importance of the people and strength of their reactions was too great to have been kept out of awareness by the dynamism of selective inattention. Once vividly aware of what she was doing, Ann could and did analyze her behavior. As Ann talked of her feelings in anticipation of being criticized, a strong reaction was stirred up in Art, another group member, who spoke of his perfectionistic music teacher and his demands. In this way the group members' characteristic interpersonal operations are highlighted, thus giving each the opportunity to feel the anxiety concomitant with the reaction and to become aware of acts and feelings that he has been perhaps totally unaware of.

In the group situation the patient can become aware of unsatisfied strivings that are typical of some early developmental stage. He can re-experience the pain of the frustration of his desires in as close to the original situation as his chronological age allows with a minimum loss of self-esteem, for the group is a place where his imaginary or fantasied people come to life and are most vividly felt. This re-experiencing with its concomitant bringing to awareness the feelings that have been dissociated makes for growth. The patient in his group treatment can relive, in a symbolic way, all his life experience, and can experience the unique opportunity to live his psychic life over again.

Let me amplify this point. The groups that I have are heterogeneous in composition, with all age ranges represented. It is possible in the group situation to relive and work through feelings and attitudes that are typical of infancy, childhood, the juvenile era, preadolescence, early or late adolescence. At one time for one or more patients the group is a peer group and we would find cooperation, banding together of peers against authority, competition and conformity. Another patient may see the group as the family and he may be experiencing some of the somatic feelings of anxiety that had their origins at a preverbal level in infancy. If the patient had never had the experience of finding one person who was particularly important to him, a chum, he might start this type of relationship in the group. It is through the development of this relationship that Sullivan felt that one's capacity to love matures. From the above it is clear that I believe the group is not necessarily either a family or a peer group, but will become for the patient what his and his therapist's parataxes demand and allow respectively.

In terms of directly handling a patient's needs for satisfactions and security, group membership gives one the feeling of being part of something and belonging that is often so hard to find in our present-day urban society. His emptiness and loneliness are more directly alleviated in his contact with other people, who are, after all his fears and expectations, human and therefore more similar than different from himself.

I do not feel that I can conclude this paper without a brief word on this last point—humanness and the respect of it that characterized Sullivan, the man, and his technique. For it is not only the expertness of the analyst that helps the patient to grow and change. Rather it is his personality and the respect for other human beings and feelings for their suffering that he communicates. In the group situation by his gestures, facial expression, or nonverbal acceptance, as well as his verbalizations, the therapist communicates his respect for others. This is sensed by all and helps in the formulation of the group atmosphere, an atmosphere where each can without humiliation and with dignity expose his specific patterns of interpersonal relations. It is in such an atmosphere that parataxes can be pointed out without overwhelming anxiety and their resolution can take place.

In summary, we have attempted to show the relevance of Sullivanian principles to meet the challenge of working with patients in our present-day practice. These principles were shown to be based on the concept of an ever interacting, constantly changing human being evolving from the human animal through absorbing the social and cultural perspective of those around him. The developing self-system was shown to have used certain dynamisms to protect itself. Through the example of an event in the group used to make the patients vividly and dramatically aware of their interpersonal operations, Sullivan's theory was applied to group practice. Group treatment was thus seen as an effective laboratory to explore and vividly verify one's patterns of interpersonal reaction as a prelude to learning their historical perspective and eventually changing one's behavior.

19

Expansion of the
Interpersonal Behavior Circle

MAURICE LORR
& DOUGLAS M. McNAIR

A recent report (Lorr & McNair, 1963) presented evidence for a circular rank ordering of nine categories of interpersonal interaction. In addition, the authors postulated an expanded set of 16 modes of relating interpersonally which they deduced from available data. The concern of the present report is with experimental data in support of the extended circular order. The specific aims of the study were to: test by multiple factor analysis for the existence of 16 hypothesized interpersonal behavior categories; examine the evidence for an expanded circular ordering of the interpersonal categories established.

Three conceptualizations of interpersonal behavior have been reported in the literature. One scheme proposed by LaForge and Suczek (1955) involves a circular arrangement of eight interpersonal categories derived from a 134-item check list of adjectives and short phrases. The categories are labeled: Managerial-Autocratic, Competitive-Exploitative, Blunt-Aggressive, Skeptical-Distrustful, Modest–Self-Effacing, Docile-Dependent, Cooperative-Conventional, and Responsible-Overgenerous. Schutz (1958) has developed a system based on three basic interpersonal needs regarded as sufficient to account for interpersonal behavior. The three needs of Inclusion, Control, and Affection are evaluated by means of a set of Guttman scales called FIRO-B. Stern (1958) also has developed a taxonomy of personal interaction characteristics although his primary interest is in the measurement of needs. Forty-two needs proposed by Murray (1938) are reflected in 300 activities to which the respondent reacts by indicating his likes and dislikes. Stern found that his nine major clusters could be arranged into a circular order. Only six of the clusters, however, are interpersonal in character.

The investigations reported here and previously grew, in part, out of a

From M. Lorr, and D. M. McNair, Expansion of the Interpersonal Behavior Circle. *Journal of Personality and Social Psychology*, 1965, 2, 823–830. Copyright 1965 by the American Psychological Association, and reproduced by permission of publisher and author.

critical examination of the LaForge-Suczek, the Schutz, and the Stern interpersonal behavior categories. The sufficiency of a tripartite scheme proposed by Schutz for accounting for all interpersonal interactions appears doubtful, even if the three needs are regarded as broad second-order factors. Schutz' own factorial reports are inconsistent with the hypothesis of such a small number of factors. There is also a lack of supporting data for the independence of the LaForge-Suczek categories and little published evidence in support of the postulated circular ordering. Inspection of the adjectives defining the various categories also casts doubt on category homogeneity. Finally adjectives such as those in the Interpersonal Check List (ICL), have quite diverse connotations and thus lack the precision of meaning necessary for the definition of the dimensions of interpersonal behavior. It thus seemed useful and important to establish rigorously a set of overlapping interpersonal categories on the basis of rated manifest behavior statements, and to test for the presence of a circular rank ordering.

METHOD

Two experiments were conducted. The plan of procedure in both studies was to: hypothesize a specific set of interpersonal categories; construct a set of statements descriptive of each of the postulated factors for incorporation into an inventory; collect data on a substantial sample of patients or normals; obtain the product-moment correlations among the inventory variables; factor the table of correlations; obtain factor scores for each individual in the sample; arrange the correlations among factor scores in the expected sequence and test for the presence of a circular order.

The circular order concept applied here derives from Guttman (1954). The basic hypothesis is that qualitatively different traits in a given domain may have a rank order among themselves without beginning or end. Since a circle is a closed sequence, it describes such an order. In a correlation matrix exhibiting a circular order, the highest correlations are next to the principal diagonal which runs from the upper left to the lower right corner. Along any row (or column) the correlations decrease in size as one moves further away from the main diagonal and then increase again. A more rigorous statesment is that the correlations of any specified variable with its neighbors decrease monotonically in size and then increase monotonically as a function of their sequential separation. Contiguous variables correlate positively while more distant variables correlate close to zero. However, if personality variables are represented some of the correlations are likely to be negative, implying the presence of common bipolar elements. The central notion in this conceptualization is order and the idea of dimensionality is extraneous as Guttman is careful to point out. Guttman proposed a certain algebraic structure to explain manifest data that exhibit a circular order and called it a "circumplex." Jones (1960) has also suggested a latent structure to account for the data. Since neither structure was tested here, only the concept of a closed sequence of ordered variables is utilized.

To test the hypothesis of a circular rank order, the variables in the correlation table are arranged in a sequence suggested by knowledge of variable similarity or on the basis of theory. When a circular order exists the correlations will decrease and increase in size as a function of sequential separation and within limits of error variance. The highest positive correlations will be along the principal diagonal. Also the anticipated or predicted sequence will coincide with the actual rank order.

Experiment I

In the study previously reported (Lorr & McNair, 1963), 9 of the 14 factors extracted could be arranged into a circular rank order with one gap. The categories included in the circular ordering were Dominance, Hostility, Mistrust, Inhibition, Abasiveness, Passive-Dependency, Nurturance, Affiliativeness, and Sociability. The gap in the sequence occurred between Passive-Dependency and Nurturance and was manifested by a negative correlation. In addition to the 9 categories found in that analysis it was hypothesized that: Autonomy and Withdrawal would fit between Mistrust and Abasiveness; Approval-Seeking, Conformity, and Responsibility would fit between Passive-Dependency and Nurturance, Attention Seeking would be located between Dominance and Sociability.

The revised inventory (IBI₂) consisted of the statements most clearly defining the nine categories isolated earlier as well as a newly constructed set. All of the 144 statements in the inventory were completed by the rater by circling a Yes or a No. Therapists, numbering 265, at 44 Veterans Administration Clinics rates 523 outpatients who had been in individual psychotherapy at least 3 months. The sample included neurotics, personality disorder cases, psychotics, and a few psychophysiological reactions. The product-moment correlations among the variables were grouped into 15 clusters. However, only 14 factors were extracted by the multiple-group procedure. These were then rotated to oblique simple structure.

The analysis revealed that the hypothesized Autonomy and Withdrawal factors could not be established. The remaining four factors postulated were confirmed. However, the Conformity and Responsibility factors were rejected as being insufficiently interpersonal in nature. In addition the Passive-Dependent cluster split into two distinguishable factors: Submissiveness and Succorance. Thus, 12 categories remained.

A new key was developed on the basis of the factor-analysis findings. Each interpersonal factor was defined by 5 to 11 items. The IBI₂ forms were then scored for each of the 12 interpersonal factors retained. The product-moment correlation among the category scores exclusive of approval-seeking are presented in Table 19-1. Approval-Seeking was dropped because it clearly did not fit into part of the circular sequence. The correlations of each remaining category with all others were plotted and ordinates against the rank-order sequence on the abscissa. The fairly smooth curves obtained resembled open parabolas and provided support for the required monotonic order. The largest deviations from monotonicity are between Succorance and Detachment, between Affection and Dominance, and between Exhibition and ·Affection. Contiguous variables are all correlated positively as required. The major discrepancy in the anticipated sequence is the location of Abasiveness after Succorance instead of after Detachment.

Experiment II

On the basis of findings from Experiment I, 16 interaction categories were postulated: Dominance, Recognition, Hostility, Mistrust, Autonomy, Detachment, Inhibition, Abasement, Submissiveness, Succorance, Deference, Agreeableness, Nurturance, Affection, Sociability, and Exhibition. The added constructs hypothesized were Recognition, Autonomy, Inhibition, Deference, and Agreeableness. The concept of Autonomy was reformulated in light of the previous study. New behavior statements were constructed consistent with a set of definitions of the underlying variables. The new items were added to those already defining the 11 categories in IBI_2. The revised inventory (IBI_3) consisted of 160 statements.[1] Each interpersonal category was defined by 10 manifest behaviors. The rating format was

TABLE 19-1.　Correlations among 11 Category Scores of IBI_2

	1	2	3	4	5	6	7	8	9	10	11
1. Dominance											
2. Hostility	51										
3. Mistrust	31	64									
4. Detachment	−15	21	33								
5. Submissiveness	−25	−02	18	43							
6. Succorance	−06	−10	06	−13	39						
7. Abasement	−10	−20	04	09	34	36					
8. Nurturance	09	−33	−27	−50	−29	−01	21				
9. Affection	−12	−50	−53	−55	−21	07	10	62			
10. Sociability	26	−04	−12	−54	−23	06	03	41	35		
11. Exhibition	55	19	13	−33	−22	07	04	21	04	45	

Note: Decimal points are omitted.

[1] Copies of the inventories may be obtained from the first author.

also altered to permit the rater to indicate how often the person rated exhibited the behavior in question: not at all, occasionally, fairly often, quite often.

A nationwide sample of psychotherapists in private practice, in universities, and in other public clinics provided the ratings. Each of the 115 therapists was asked to describe several nonpsychotic patients he had been seeing in treatment for at least 4 months. Ratings were thus obtained on 525 men and women in treatment. The product-moment correlations among the 160 variables were factored by the multiple-group method with use of an a priori hypothesis matrix (Horst, 1956) and then rotated to simple structure. The fit to the hypothesized structure was strongly supported. Since it was predicted that each variable would correlate highest with the factor to which it was allocated an objective check was available. In no instance were fewer than 7 confirmations secured on the predicted correlations. The percentage of correct predictions for the 160 items was 84.

To test the hypothesis of a circular order, a key for scoring was prepared on the basis of the factor analysis. A score was simply the sum of the unit-weighted items defining the factor. All patients were rescored on 15 categories, each defined by 7–11 items. Since the Autonomy factor was still not sufficiently well defined it was excluded. The product-moment correlations among the total scores are given in Table 19-2. The category labeled Succorance failed to fit the circular order satisfactorily and was excluded. To check the degree of fit to the circular ordering the correlations of each category with all other categories were plotted as ordinates against the anticipated circular sequence. By and large a smooth curve resembling an

TABLE 19-2. Correlations among 14 Category Scores of IBI_3 for Patients

	1	2	3	4	5	6	7	8	9	10	11	12	13
1. Dominance													
2. Recognition	75												
3. Hostility	53	59											
4. Mistrust	21	38	69										
5. Detachment	−40	−21	07	27									
6. Inhibition	−53	−32	−06	26	66								
7. Abasement	−38	−28	−29	03	17	48							
8. Submissiveness	−52	−39	−51	−18	20	46	66						
9. Deference	00	06	−37	−22	−16	04	41	49					
10. Agreeableness	−01	−09	−53	−44	−31	−24	17	28	54				
11. Nurturance	10	−06	−40	−34	−35	−21	25	26	44	70			
12. Affection	19	−01	−36	−48	−57	−42	09	13	43	61	69		
13. Sociability	55	39	00	−17	−75	−57	−10	−10	31	45	49	64	
14. Exhibition	74	65	50	25	−43	−44	−16	−33	05	−12	05	22	54

Note: Decimal points are omitted.

open parabola could be fitted to each plot. It should also be noted that: contiguous variables are all correlated positively; the increases and decreases in correlations are by and large monotonic; the obtained order agrees completely with that expected. As was noted earlier Succorance does not fit into the sequence. A few small deviations from monotonicity occur between Abasiveness and Submissiveness. At several points Deference exhibits correlations not consistent with its position.

RESULTS

A Cross-Validation Study

In the initial published report, data from normals and neurotics were pooled. An important question is whether ratings of a group of normals by relatively untrained raters would yield the same interpersonal categories and the same circular order. The use of clinically untrained raters would provide a severe test of the factors emerging from therapist judgments. Ratings were secured on IBI$_3$ from a group of 254 seniors and graduates in psychology on "normal" men and women with whom they were well acquainted for at least a year. Excluded from rating were immediate family members, spouses, and close friends of the opposite sex. Included were 290 individuals, both male and female, representing a diversity of occupations and socioeconomic classes.

Intercorrelations were obtained among the first 80 and the second 80 variables of IBI$_3$. Each set included 5 variables representing each of the 16 hypothesized factors. The correlations in each set were factored by the method of principal components with unity in the diagonals. The 16 factors with associated latent roots of 1.0 or higher were then rotated directly to the hypothesized simple structure (Horst, 1956). In Set 1, Autonomy could not be confirmed; in Set 2, Agreeableness was not substantiated. The number of confirmations of predicted highest correlations of each variable ranged from 6 to 10 except for Autonomy and Agreeableness which were defined, as predicted, by 3 variables each. The major factors postulated were thus confirmed within the normal sample.

The same key applied in scoring the patients was used to score the normal sample. The correlations among the category scores are shown in Table 19-3. The same circular order of categories obtained with patient subjects was found for the normal sample. Succorance again was excluded as it failed to fit into the expected sequence. Small discrepancies from monotonicity occur with other scores. Abasiveness should correlate negatively with Recognition but does not. Deference should correlate negatively with Dominance and Recognition instead of positively. However, the degree of agreement with the circular order found for patients is clearly high.

TABLE 19-3. Correlations among 14 Category Scores of IBI₃ for 290 Normals

	1	2	3	4	5	6	7	8	9	10	11	12	13	14
1. Dominance														
2. Recognition	74													
3. Hostility	50	57												
4. Mistrust	31	52	67											
5. Detachment	−24	−06	35	36										
6. Inhibition	−33	−17	14	33	56									
7. Abasement	−15	00	−05	24	16	50								
8. Submissiveness	−38	−27	−29	−02	11	47	52							
9. Deference	10	16	−14	−02	−18	10	39	32						
10. Agreeableness	−11	−27	−54	−42	−40	−21	14	19	39					
11. Nurturance	−10	−32	−46	−34	−33	−13	22	19	26	69				
12. Affection	−05	−27	−54	−45	−53	−28	15	19	33	71	72			
13. Sociability	38	25	−15	−14	−74	−44	00	00	33	44	34	51		
14. Exhibition	65	68	47	41	−21	−24	−02	−20	09	−22	−21	−10	37	

Note: Decimal points are omitted.

A final set of data was obtained on 60 neurotics who were rated by their therapists 10 weeks after initiating once-a-week treatment. The correlations among the total scores based on the IBI₃ patient key are shown in Table 19-4. The sequence of Abasiveness and Submissiveness appears to be somewhat in doubt as their correlations deviate slightly from monotonicity. Nevertheless, the hypothesized circular sequence of interpersonal categories is supported.

TABLE 19-4. Correlations among 14 Category Scores of IBI₃ for 60 Patients

	1	2	3	4	5	6	7	8	9	10	11	12	13	14
1. Dominance														
2. Recognition	74													
3. Hostility	37	39												
4. Mistrust	12	25	68											
5. Detachment	−28	−20	16	36										
6. Inhibition	−47	−34	−02	22	69									
7. Abasement	−21	−12	−37	−15	27	48								
8. Submissiveness	−36	−39	−46	−18	22	48	75							
9. Deference	24	33	−33	−19	−10	00	59	51						
10. Agreeableness	30	13	−38	−33	−28	−13	35	30	61					
11. Nurturance	30	27	−37	−24	−25	−21	34	23	69	78				
12. Affection	31	22	−40	−35	−55	−32	37	27	66	70	74			
13. Sociability	60	52	−05	−16	−65	−51	04	−07	49	56	55	77		
14. Exhibition	67	56	24	02	−39	−53	−17	−22	22	20	22	40	60	

Note: Decimal points are omitted.

Interpersonal Behavior Categories

Statements illustrating each of the 14 interpersonal behavior categories are given in Table 19-5. Figure 19-1 illustrates the circular order. The term interpersonal is used here to refer to a relation between people. An interpersonal situation is one involving two or more persons in which the individuals interact for some purpose (Schutz, 1958). It need not involve the physical presence of both members since the behavior may be determined by expectations of the behavior of others not physically present. As may be seen, the statements are descriptive of overt actions rather than inferred feelings.

Dominance involves the tendency to lead, direct, influence, and control others. It is related to Recognition which represents the tendency to seek and to compete for recognition and status. The Hostility category is

TABLE 19-5. **Statements Exemplifying the 14 Interpersonal Categories of IBI$_3$**

Category	Statements
Dominance	Bosses his friends and associates around.
	Takes charge of things when he's with people.
Recognition	Seizes opportunities to rival and surpass others.
	Strives for symbols of status and superiority to others.
Hostility	Ridicules, belittles, or depreciates others.
	Uses a sarcastic or biting type of humor.
Mistrust	Mistrusts the intentions of others toward him.
	Expresses suspicion when someone is especially nice to him.
Detachment	Acts businesslike and impersonal with co-workers.
	Keeps aloof from his neighbors.
Inhibition	Shows discomfort and nervousness when people watch him at work or at play.
	Shows signs of self-consciousness with strangers.
Abasement	Blames himself when interpersonal friction with others occurs.
	Apologizes for not having done better when he completes a task.
Submissiveness	Gives in rather than fight for his rights in a conflict.
	Lets his friends or spouse push him around.
Deference	Carries out orders of his superiors with zest.
	Takes the role of helper or supporter of authority figures.
Agreeableness	Contributes positively as a member of some group or team.
	Relates to and treats people as equals.
Nurturance	Listens sympathetically to others talk about their troubles.
	Puts aside his own work or pleasure if someone asks for help.
Affection	Shows a real liking and affection for people.
	Acts close and personal with people.
Sociability	Invites friends and acquaintances to his home.
	Drops in to visit friends just to socialize.
Exhibition	Draws attention to himself in a group by telling jokes and anecdotes.
	Acts the clown or amuses others at a party.

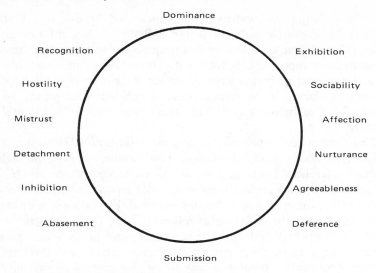

Figure 19-1. **The interpersonal circle.**

tied to Recognition and represents the tendency to criticize, ridicule, punish, or aggress against others. Hostility leads to mistrust, the tendency to doubt or suspect the attitudes, feelings, and intentions of others. Mistrust is related to Detachment which describes aloof, withdrawn, and seclusive tendencies. Associated with Detached behavior is Inhibition, or activities involving withdrawal from attention and shyness with others. The tendency towards Inhibition is related to Abasement, a proneness to accept blame, to belittle the self, and to apologize. Following Abasement is Submission which is characterized by passivity, docility, and appeasement. Abasive tendencies are related to Deference, or actions involving support and service to a superior or leader. Agreeableness or the tendency to be cooperative, helpful, considerate, and equalitarian follows Deference. In Nurturance the cooperativeness found in Agreeableness moves towards more active support, sympathy, and counsel. Related to Nurturance is Affection, the tendency to express liking, warmth, and friendliness towards others. Sociability, next in the sequence, involves a more active tendency to join groups, to be with people, to be gregarious. Finally, locking into Dominance is Exhibition which is characterized by attention-seeking activities involving another type of control evidenced in Dominance.

DISCUSSION

Foa (1961) has reviewed a wide range of reports regarding the structure of interpersonal behavior. He interpreted these to suggest that a similar circular ordering was evident in data presented by Borgatta, Cottrell, and Mann (1958), by Schaefer, Bell, and Bailey (1959), and La Forge and Suczek (1955). In the same review Foa proposed a facet structure based on four principal components. Subsequently Foa (1964) modified his proposed structure and suggested a circular order of eight types of relationships based on three facets. These were content of behavior (acceptance and rejection), object of behavior (self and other), and mode of behavior (love and status).

The facet model represents an ingenious beginning. However, it has certain defects which require discussion. The "profiles" of types are defined in abstract inferential language such as "Social acceptance of other." The actual rated statements are overlapping and not especially helpful in identifying the actual interpersonal behaviors involved. For example a husband's social acceptance of the wife runs as follows: "Isaac thinks his wife is very successful and especially esteems her personality and her actions." In addition the facets, such as acceptance and rejection, status and love, are left undefined. Apparently acceptance may mean giving or receiving; rejection may mean denying, withholding, or a hostile act. Status appears to mean prestige, control, and possibly inclusion. Also the circular sequence is attained by unusual scoring. A low score means weak acceptance or strong rejection. Consequently a positive correlation between acceptance and rejection indicates that the higher the acceptance the lower the rejection. With conventional scoring the correlations between accepting and rejecting behaviors are negative. Foa has thus established only a half circle and not a complete circle. For instance, acceptance of other and social rejection of other (bipolar opposites) are located next to each other in Foa's model. Finally it would appear that the number of facets required to explain known interpersonal interactions established in the present study should be greater than three. The Foa facets cannot account for the 14 categories found.

Schaefer's (1959) hypothetical ordering of maternal behavior has some similarity to the sequence presented here. The categories are concerned with the role of a parent towards a child and thus do not include peer-peer behaviors such as Deference or Abasement. Later Schaefer (1961) offered evidence from a variety of studies including Kassebaum, Couch, and Slater (1959) for a circular order among a broader range of social and emotional traits. His hypothetical circular ordering was defined by Extraversion, Friendliness, Love, Conformity, Introversion, Withdrawal, Hostility, and Aggressiveness. These categories are quite similar to those described in the present report.

The LaForge-Suczek (1955) categories are most similar to those presented here and conform to much the same sequence. However, these 16 interpersonal categories have never been demonstrated to be independent. Instead these authors postulate a correlational structure defined by three orthogonal factors: Dominance versus Submission, Love versus Hate, and Intensity. The intensity or vertical axis of the cone represented is based on the numbers of items checked. The categories not represented appear to be Detachment, Deference, Affection, Sociability, and Exhibition.

To what extent are the Cattell (1957) primary personality factors represented among the interpersonal categories? A major obstacle to comparison is the bipolar nature of most of the original Cattell rating scales. The factors obtained are as a consequence also predominantly bipolar. The approach taken here has been to let the data determine the unipolar or bipolar nature of the factor. Evidence in the current study strongly supports the existence of a set of unipolar first-order factors. Logical and verbal opposites are not necessarily psychological or behavioral alternatives. For instance, Submission is not necessarily the alternative for Dominance. An individual may not exhibit dominant behavior, or he may be rebellious or an autonomous lone wolf. Table 19-6 presents a rough matching of Cattell factors and the IBI$_3$ interpersonal categories.

As may be seen from Table 19-6, although the labels may differ, there is fairly good congruence among the various theoretical and empirical approaches. Both Foa and Schaefer have presented evidence in support of such convergences in the nature of interpersonal categories and in their circular rank ordering.

There is much to be said in favor of the circular ordering of interpersonal constructs as opposed to a conventional factorial interpretation. The proposed circular ordering provides a useful conceptual organization of a set of otherwise unrelated constructs. The scheme has heuristic power insofar as it enables the experimenter to infer missing categories. Moreover the arrangement is fruitful in clinical diagnosis and in understanding how vari-

TABLE 19-6. Interpersonal Categories Isolated or Hypothesized

Lorr and McNair	LaForge and Suczek	Stern	Schaefer	Cattell
Dominance	Managerial	Dominance	Aggressiveness	Dominance E+
Recognition	Competitive			
Hostility	Blunt-Aggressive	Aggression	Hostility	Schizothymia A−
Mistrust	Skeptical-Distrust			Protension L+
Detachment		Rejectance	Withdrawal	
Inhibition	Modest			Threctia H−
Abasement	Self-Effacing	Abasiveness	Introversion (?)	Guilt-Proneness O+
Submission	Docile			Submission E−
Deference		Deference	Conformity (?)	
Agreeableness	Cooperative			Zeppia J− (?)
Nurturance	Response-Generous	Nurturance	Love (?)	
Affection	Conventional		Friendliness	
Sociability		Exhibition	Extroversion (?)	Cyclothymia A+ (?)
Exhibition		Affilativeness		

ous psychological defenses operate. Finally the ordering of behaviors should have developmental implications. It should provide a useful base for studying the parental patterns which elicited and reinforced the behaviors manifest in interpersonal acts long after the parent figures are gone.

REFERENCES

Borgatta, E. F., Cottrell, L. S., Jr., & Mann, J. M. The spectrum of individual interaction characteristics: An interdimensional analysis. *Psychological Reports*, 1958, *4*, 279–319.

Cattell, R. B. *Personality and motivation structure and measurement*. Yonkers-on-Hudson, N.Y.: World Book, 1957.

Foa, U. G. Convergences in the analysis of the structure of interpersonal behavior. *Psychological Review*, 1961, *68*, 341–353.

Foa, U. G. Cross-cultural similarity and difference in interpersonal behavior. *Journal of Abnormal and Social Psychology*, 1964, *68*, 517–522.

Guttman, L. A new approach to factor analysis: The radex. In P. F. Lazarsfeld (Ed.), *Mathematical thinking in the social sciences*. Glencoe, Ill.: Free Press, 1954. Pp. 248–348.

Horst, P. A simple method for rotating a centroid factor matrix to a simple structure hypothesis, *Journal of Experimental Education*, 1956, *24*, 251–258.

Jones, M. B. Molar correlational analysis. *USN Sch. Aviat. Med. res. Rep.*, 1960, Monogr. No. 4.

Kassebaum, G. G., Couch, A. S., & Slater, P. E. The factorial dimensions of the MMPI. *Journal of Consulting Psychology*, 1959, *23*, 226–235.

LaForge, R., & Suczek, R. The interpersonal dimension of personality: III. An interpersonal checklist. *Journal of Personality*, 1955, *24*, 94–112.

Lorr, M., & McNair, D. M. An interpersonal behavior circle. *Journal of Abnormal and Social Psychology*, 1963, *67*, 68–75.

Murray, H. A. *Explorations in personality*. New York: Oxford University Press, 1938.

Schaefer, E. S. A circumplex model for maternal behavior. *Journal of Abnormal and Social Psychology*, 1959, *59*, 226–235.

Schaefer, E. S. Converging conceptual models for maternal behavior and for child behavior. In J. C. Glidewell (Ed.), *Parental attitudes and child behavior*. Springfield, Ill.: Charles C Thomas, 1961. Pp. 124–146.

Schaefer, E. S., Bell, R. O., & Bayley, Nancy. Development of a maternal behavior research instrument. *Journal of Genetic Psychology*, 1959, *95*, 83–104.

Schutz, W. C. *FIRO: A three-dimensional theory of interpersonal behavior*. New York: Rinehart, 1958.

Stern, G. G. *Preliminary manual: Activities index*. Syracuse: Syracuse University Psychological Research Center, 1958.

20

An Experimental Study
of the Double Bind Hypothesis

EUGENE L. RINGUETTE
& TRUDY KENNEDY

The double bind hypothesis states, in brief, that schizophrenic symptoms are reactions to an inability to judge exactly the meaning of communications which are received from others. It is postulated that this difficulty results from an inability to assess properly the context within which information is received, and, hence, the meaning or interpretation of the information is uncertain. It is further postulated that this inability to understand and discriminate among the abstract aspects of communication is caused by prolonged exposure to an environment in which simultaneous communications at various levels of abstraction are consistently incongruent. Such communication, in which incongruent messages are received at different abstract levels, is termed "double bind" communication (Bateson, Jackson, Haley, & Weakland, 1956).

It is also postulated that double bind communication is a consistent and integral aspect of communication within the families of schizophrenics, as well as in letters from mothers to schizophrenic offspring, and is regarded as a factor in the etiology of the disorder.

Our hope is that these operations will provide a clearly evident record of the continuing, repetitive double binding which we hypothesize goes on steadily from infantile beginnings in the family situation of individuals who become

From E. L. Ringuette, and T. Kennedy, An Experimental Study of the Double Bind Hypothesis. *Journal of Abnormal Psychology*, 1966, 71, 136–141. Copyright 1966 by the American Psychological Association and reproduced by permission of publisher and authors.

This study was aided by a grant from the Medical Staff Association Fund, Department of Psychiatry, Center for the Health Sciences. Appreciation is also expressed to O. L. Gericke, Superintendent, and the staff of Patton State Hospital for their help in securing material for the study.

Special acknowledgment and gratitude is extended to the following persons who participated as judges in the study: Gregory Bateson, James H. Bryan, Alexander B. Caldwell, William F. Fry, Ralph Greenson, Peter B. Gruenberg, John Hanley, Edward J. Kollar, Ronald Sager, Lowell H. Storms, Charles W. Tidd, and Paul Watzlawick.

schizophrenic. This basic family situation, and the overtly communicational characteristics of schizophrenia, have been the major focus of this paper [Bateson et al., 1956, p. 262].

Finally, we may note again that both the major pattern of communication discerned in these letters and its effects on their recipients agree closely with our research group's original and prior concept of the double bind as a communicational pattern and our hypothesis of its relationship to schizophrenia and its etiology [Weakland & Fry, 1962, p. 623]. It is found that: 1) While the letters vary greatly in details of content, style, etc., they exhibit similar pervasive and highly influential patterns of incongruent communication. 2) These letters agree with another schizophrenic's characterization of such letters generally. 3) The observed pattern fits prior general statements of the authors' research group about the "double bind" and incongruent communication in schizophrenia [Weakland & Fry, 1962, p. 604].

It is further stated that letters written by the families of schizophrenics are especially suited to analysis of double bind communication in that they are objective, free of extraneous vocal, facial, and gestural messages, and are condensed and unitary examples of the writer's communicative habits.

It is therefore reasonable to assume that while a letter, in comparison with ordinary speech, is a form easier for analytic study, it remains typical of the sender's communicative habits in major respects, and indeed may highlight these because of the selectivity which the writer has exercised [Weakland & Fry, 1962, p. 605].

A review of the double bind literature, then, indicates that, as a theory, the double bind hypothesis postulates the following: (a) The "double bind" is a definable phenomenon of communication. (b) It involves a major communicational pattern within the families of schizophrenics and is a factor in the etiology of the disorder. (c) The letters of mothers of schizophrenics to their schizophrenic offspring (although the phenomenon may not be restricted to mothers' communication) exhibit discernible pervasive patterns of incongruent communication, that is, evidence of double bind communication. (d) Such letters are particularly suited to analysis of double bind communication.

In view of the above, the purpose of the present study was to assess whether persons highly conversant with the concept of the double bind, in the sense of being significantly associated with its formulation or elaboration, could agree with regard to its presence or absence in communication. Its presence in letters written by parents of schizophrenics is, of course, assumed by the double bind hypothesis.

A second consideration relating to the reliability of the construct was whether or not it could be reliably identified by persons trained to do so, because if this were not possible the applicability of the double bind hypothesis would be restricted to only a few expert persons.

In addition to the above, there were certain secondary considerations which were contingent upon the reliability with which double bind communication could be identified. If the double bind were a reliable phenomenon in letters, the expectation derived from the double bind hypothesis would be that it should occur more frequently in letters written by parents of schizophrenics than in other letters. In an effort to evaluate this eventuality, two comparison groups of letters, one written by parents of nonschizophrenic psychiatric patients and one written by hospital volunteers, were included. Finally, other types of judges, judging the letters on variables other than presence-absence of double bind communication, were included in order to evaluate the power of the double bind hypothesis to discriminate between schizophrenia and nonschizophrenia, relative to other measures such as clinical judgment, which might be applied to the letters. A consideration of the latter, again, depends upon a demonstration that the judged presence-absence of double bind communication is a reliable phenomenon in the letter sample, so the primary aim of the study was specifically to assess the reliability with which double bind communication in letters could be identified.

METHOD

Sixty letters were used; 40 were letters which had been received by patients in a state hospital from their parents, and 20 were letters written by hospital volunteers as if they were writing to offspring hospitalized at the state hospital from which the patient letters were obtained. Half of the patients whose letters were used had a hospital diagnosis of schizophrenia, and half had nonschizophrenic diagnoses. The criteria used for including a patient's letter in the sample were that the patient be between the ages of 18 and 30 years, that this be his first known admission, that he had been hospitalized for less than 6 months, and that he be Caucasian and English-speaking. The volunteers who wrote letters ranged in age from 38 to 62, and had no children who had been hospitalized for psychiatric reasons. They were used as a comparison group because of the fact that letters received by nonpsychiatric patients were found to be easily differentiated from psychiatric patient letters on the basis of content. This group of letters written by volunteers, then, was not presumed to constitute a control group; rather, it is a second comparison group, in addition to the letters received by nonschizophrenic patients, in which double bind communication would not be expected to exist according to the terms of the double bind hypothesis.

In summary, then, there were 60 letters used in the study, of which 20 had been received by schizophrenic patients from their parents, 20 had been received by nonschizophrenic patients from their parents, and 20 had been written by volunteers as if they were writing to hospitalized offspring.

All letters were presented in mimeographed typewritten form to the judges participating in the study, and the letters were presented in a different randomized order to each judge.

Five types of judges were used in the study, with three judges in each type. The "expert double bind" judges were persons closely involved in the formulation of the double bind hypothesis and, hence, highly conversant with the concept. These judges were told that "the attached letters were written *by parents* to their adult or adolescent *offspring*. Some of these offspring are schizophrenic and some are not, but the numbers of schizophrenic and nonschizophrenic offspring are not equal." They were then asked to rate each letter on a 7-point scale with regard to the extent to which it suggested the presence or absence of double bind communication, with one representing presence and seven representing absence. They were not asked to judge whether each letter had been received by a schizophrenic or nonschizophrenic person.

A second group of judges was termed the "trained double bind" type. These were first-year psychiatric residents whose familiarity with the double bind concept was gained in a formal seminar and in a subsequent meeting with the authors of the present study. These judges read selected articles relating to the concept and then were asked to make the same judgments as were made by the expert judges except that they were instructed to use the specific criteria for identifying double bind communication which had been enumerated by Weakland and Fry (1962).

A third category of judges was termed the "uninformed clinicians." These were experienced clinicians who were given the same information regarding the letters as had been given the expert and trained judges. They were asked to judge whether each letter had been written by the parent of a schizophrenic or nonschizophrenic person.

A fourth type of judges was termed the "informed clinicians." This group was comprised of experienced clinicians who were informed regarding the origin of the letters and were instructed to sort the letters into their respective groups, that is, those received by schizophrenic patients, those received by nonschizophrenic patients, and those written by volunteers.

The fifth group of judges was termed the "naive" type. These were persons of comparable educational level to the other judges but not associated with medicine or the social sciences. They were instructed to rate each letter on a 7-point scale, with one representing "like" and seven representing "dislike," with regard to "whether your general reaction to the letter is a positive or negative one; that is, is it a letter you would or would not like to receive."

RESULTS

The frequencies with which each judge in the expert, trained, and naive judge types used each point on their respective 7-point scales are shown in Table 20-1.

TABLE 20-1. Distributions of the Ratings of the Expert, Trained, and Naive Judges

	Rating scale						
Judges	1	2	3	4	5	6	7
Expert 1	5	16	2	12	7	7	11
Expert 2	4	6	1	8	16	18	7
Expert 3	7	11	4	5	4	7	22
Trained 1	18	12	2	5	8	5	10
Trained 2	15	10	4	0	6	8	17
Trained 3	0	15	1	7	6	17	14
Naive 1	3	16	25	5	3	6	2
Naive 2	4	14	14	13	7	7	1
Naive 3	1	9	15	11	6	14	4

The average interjudge correlations for these judge types were: expert = .19, trained = .26 ($p < .05$), and naive = .39 ($p < .01$). In view of the low interjudge correlations of the expert double bind judges, interjudge correlations were calculated separately for their ratings of the 20 letters written by mothers of schizophrenics on the chance that they had achieved some agreement on those letters which was obscured by lack of agreement on the two comparison groups of letters. The three interjudge correlations for the expert judges' ratings of the letters written by mothers of schizophrenics were .14, .27, and .17, none of which is significant, and which again average .19.

Interjudge contingency coefficients and chi-square tests of significance were computed for the uninformed and informed clinician judges. The average coefficient for the uninformed clinicians was .13, while that for the informed clinicians was .44. The chi-squares obtained for the informed clinicians were all significant well beyond the 0.5 level of confidence, and the coefficient for the informed judges seems particularly high in view of the fact that the upper limit of a contingency coefficient for a 3 × 3 table is .82 (Siegel, 1956).

The results indicate, then, that the judgments of the informed clinicians, naive judges, and, to a lesser extent, the trained double bind judges reflect statistically significant interjudge reliability, while those of the expert double bind judges and uninformed clinicians do not.

An analysis of variance was performed with diagnostic groups (D) and judge types (T) as the two factors. The three levels of D were schizophrenic letters, nonschizophrenic letters, and volunteer letters, while the three levels of T were expert, trained, and naive judge types.

A significant effect was obtained due to letters within diagnostic groups which reflects the fact that mean ratings, over all judges, of the letters differed within each diagnostic group. In effect, this suggests that the ratings were not randomly assigned. A significant effect due to judges within judge types also was obtained which indicated that the judges within each judge type differed with respect to the mean ratings which they assigned; that is, within each judge type, the judges differed in terms of the part of the rating scale which they tended to use. This trend may also be seen in the distribution of judges' ratings presented above (see Table 20-2).

TABLE 20-2.   Analysis of Variance Summary of the Ratings of the Expert Double Bind, Trained Double Bind, and Naive Judges

| | | | Comparison || |
Source	df	MS	df	MS	F
D	2	12.20	57	7.15	1.71
T	2	41.11	7.26[a]	20.00	2.05
L(D)	57	7.15	342	2.84	2.52**
J(T)	6	18.15	342	2.84	6.39**
DT	4	11.78	114	4.96	2.51*

[a] Equivalent degrees of freedom for the judge types comparison mean square calculated according to Bennett and Franklin (1954), p. 368.

$* p < .05$
$** p < .01$

The diagnostic groups did not differ significantly with regard to mean ratings received, nor did the judge types differ significantly with regard to mean ratings assigned. There was, however, a significant interaction effect between diagnostic groups and judge types which indicated that there were significant differences between the mean ratings assigned to the diagnostic groups as a function of judge type. The mean ratings of diagnostic groups by judge types are given in Table 20-3.

Table 20-3 illustrates the failure of any of the judge types to differentiate between the schizophrenic and nonschizophrenic letter groups. The only significant difference found was for the naive judges who assigned a lower mean rating to the volunteer letters than to the schizophrenic or nonschizophrenic letters ($t = 2.68$, $df = 19$, $p < .02$).

TABLE 20-3. Mean Ratings Assigned to the Volunteer, Nonschizophrenic, and Schizophrenic Letters by the Expert Double Bind, Trained Double Bind, and Naive Judge Types

	Type			
Letters	Expert	Trained	Naive	
Diagnosis				
Volunteer	4.78	3.83	2.83*	3.82
Nonschizophrenic	4.37	4.27	4.12	4.25
Schizophrenic	4.62	4.28	3.95	4.28
Total	4.59	4.13	3.63	4.11

The judgments of the uninformed and informed clinicians, who were treated separately, were cross-tabulated with the diagnostic groups to which the letters belonged. These cross-tabulations, pooled for illustrative purposes, are presented in Tables 20-4 and 20-5.

TABLE 20-4. Cross-Tabulation of the Pooled Judgments of the Uninformed Clinicians and the Diagnostic Groups of the Letters

	Judgments		
Letters	Nonschizophrenic	Schizophrenic	
Diagnosis			
Volunteer	38	22	60
Nonschizophrenic	9	51	60
Schizophrenic	12	48	60
Total	59	121	180

TABLE 20-5. Cross-Tabulation of the Pooled Judgments of the Informed Clinicians and the Diagnostic Groups of the Letters

	Judgments			
Letter	Volunteer	Nonschizophrenic	Schizophrenic	
Diagnosis				
Volunteer	34	18	8	60
Nonschizophrenic	12	20	28	60
Schizophrenic	9	24	27	60
Total	55	62	63	180

Inspection of these cross-tabulations clearly illustrates that the clinician judges were unable to differentiate between the schizophrenic and nonschizophrenic letters. It is equally clear, however, that the clinicians' judgments with regard to the volunteer letters appear to be considerably more valid. Two-by-two tables comparing each uninformed clinician's judgment of schizophrenic or nonschizophrenic with whether the letters belonged to the volunteer or patient groups were formed. Similar tabulations were done for the informed clinicians in which their judgments of volunteer and patient were compared with whether the letters belonged to the volunteer or patient groups. The chi-square test was performed for each clinician judge, and each obtained chi-square value was significant at the .01 level of confidence.

In summary, it appears that none of the judge types was able to differentiate between the letters received by schizophrenic patients and those received by nonschizophrenic patients. With the exception of the expert and trained double bind judges, however, the ratings of all of the other judges significantly differentiated the volunteer from the patient letters.

Because of the fact that none of the judge types successfully differentiated between the letters received by schizophrenics and those received by nonschizophrenics, the authors were prompted to pursue some a posteriori investigation. Using the Thorndike-Lorge word frequency dictionary (1944), the percentage of infrequent verbs was calculated for each letter. The median percentages of infrequent verbs for the volunteer, schizophrenic, and nonschizophrenic letters were 7.5%, 6.5%, and 4.0%, respectively. Application of the Extension of the Median Test (Siegel, 1956) produced a χ^2 value of 6.61 ($p < .05$).

The mean number of words of the letters in each group was also calculated and found to be 140.95 for the volunteer letters, 151.20 for the nonschizophrenic letters, and 195.30 for the schizophrenic letters. Although the greater mean length of the schizophrenic letters is notable, the F ratio obtained from a one-way analysis of variance was 2.21, which falls short of the value of 3.15 representing significance at the .05 level of confidence. Thus, length in itself does not appear to constitute a cue for differentiating the letter groups.

DISCUSSION

According to the terms of the double bind hypothesis, the "double bind" is a definable and identifiable phenomenon in communication and has a causal, though complex, relationship to schizophrenia. In addition, the theory postulates that it is a consistent aspect of communication within schizophrenic families and is present and discernible in letters written by mothers of schizophrenics. To paraphrase Weakland and Fry's (1962) statement regarding "specific connections between data and theory" [p. 623], letters are a ground upon which data and the double bind hypothesis meet.

Accepting the propositions of the theory, the aim of the present study was to ascertain whether persons truly knowledgeable with regard to the double bind formulation could reliably identify this phenomenon in a form of communication which had been proposed as being especially suited for this by proponents of the double bind hypothesis. The results clearly indicate that they were not able to do this. It is axiomatic, of course, that the validity of a phenomenon can be neither verified nor refuted if reliable measurement is lacking. In short, unless a phenomenon can be reliably identified, it cannot be considered to be a meaningful or valid phenomenon.

The failure of the expert double bind judges to achieve reliability in the present study seems especially compelling in view of the fact that they represented a select and relatively large sample. As "expert" was defined in the study, a perusal of the literature on the double bind hypothesis indicates that perhaps six to eight persons could claim such expertness. Thus, the sample of expert judges constituted one-third to one-half of the population of such persons.

In view of the present results obtained using a sample of letters, one might propose the use of films, tape recordings, or a series of such communications as alternative media especially suited to such analysis. Such a proposal, however, is a question for empirical verification rather than debate.

In spite of the negative results with regard to the double bind, other variables showed promise of reliability. The task of the informed clinician judges was such that significant reliability was not surprising. Their task was essentially less difficult and more restricted. Of more interest, perhaps, is the fact that the like-dislike dimension was a meaningful one.

The results of the study prompt the general conclusion that the double bind hypothesis requires more critical appraisal than it has had. It is a theoretical formulation which has not been anchored in data, and, taken on its stated ground in the present instance, the double bind appears to be an unreliable phenomenon or a nonexistent one. The theory postulates that double bind communication is present and discernible in letters; yet, persons most knowledgeable regarding the "double bind" cannot reliably identify it in letters. The possible reasons for this are: (*a*) double bind communication is not present in letters, in which case a postulate of the theory is clearly invalid; (*b*) it is not presently a measurable phenomenon; (*c*) it actually does not exist.

REFERENCES

Bateson, G., Jackson, D., Haley, J., & Weakland, J. Towards a theory of schizophrenia. *Behavioral Science*, 1956, *1*, 251–264.

Bennett, C., & Franklin, N. *Statistical analysis in chemistry & the chemical industry*. London: Wiley, 1954.

Siegel, S. *Nonparametric statistics for the behavioral sciences*. New York: McGraw-Hill, 1956.

Thorndike, E., & Lorge, I. *The teacher's word book of 30,000 words*. New York: Teachers College, Columbia University, Bureau of Publications, 1944.

Weakland, J., & Fry, W. Letters of mothers of schizophrenics. *American Journal of Orthopsychiatry*, 1962, *32*(4).

21

Transactional Analysis:
A New and Effective Method
of Group Therapy

ERIC BERNE

There is need for a new approach to psychodynamic group therapy specifically designed for the situation it has to meet. The usual practice is to bring into the group methods borrowed from individual therapy, hoping, as occasionally happens, to elicit a specific therapeutic response. I should like to present a different system, one which has been well-tested and is more adapted to its purpose, where group therapists can stand on their own ground rather than attempting a thinly-spread imitation of the sister discipline.

Generally speaking, individual analytic therapy is characterized by the production of and a search for material, with interpersonal transactions holding a special place, typically in the field of "transference resistance" or "transference reactions." In a group, the systematic search for material is hampered because from the beginning the multitude of transactions takes the center of the stage. Therefore it seems appropriate to concentrate deliberately and specifically on analyzing such transactions. Structural analysis, and its later development into transactional analysis, in my experience, offers the most productive framework for this undertaking. Experiments with both approaches demonstrate certain advantages of structural and transactional analysis over attempts at psychoanalysis in the group. Among them are increased patient interest as shown by attendance records; increased degree of therapeutic success as shown by reduction of gross failures; increased stability of results as shown by long-term adjustment; and wider applicability in difficult patients such as psychopaths, the mentally retarded and pre- and post-psychotics. In addition, the intelligi-

From E. Berne, Transactional Analysis: A New and Effective Method of Group Therapy. Originally published in the *American Journal of Psychotherapy*, 1958, 12, 735–743. Reprinted by permission of author and publisher.

Read at the Western Regional Meeting of the American Group Psychotherapy Associations, Los Angeles, November, 1957. (By invitation.)

bility, precision, and goals of the therapeutic technique are more readily appreciated by the properly prepared therapist and patient alike.

This approach is based on the separation and investigation of exteropsychic, neopsychic, and archaeopsychic ego states. Structural analysis refers to the intrapsychic relationships of these three types of ego states: their mutual isolation, conflict, contamination, invasion, predominance, or cooperation within the personality. Transactional analysis refers to the diagnosis of which particular ego state is active in each individual during a given transaction or series of transactions, and of the understandings or misunderstandings which arise due to the perception or misperception of this factor by the individuals involved.

I have discussed in a previous publication (Berne, 1957) the nature of ego states in general, and of their classification according to whether they are exteropsychic, that is, borrowed from external sources; neopsychic, that is, oriented in accordance with current reality; or archaeopsychic, that is, relics fixated in childhood. These distinctions are easily understood by patients when they are demonstrated by clinical material, and when the three types are subsumed under the more personal terms Parent, Adult, and Child, respectively.

As this is a condensation in a very small space of a whole psychotherapeutic system, I can only offer a few illustrative situations, choosing them for their relative clarity and dramatic quality in the hope that they will draw attention to some of the basic principles of structural and transactional analysis.

STRUCTURAL ANALYSIS

The first concerns a patient named Matthew, whose manner, posture, gestures, tone of voice, purpose, and field of interest varied in a fashion which at first seemed erratic. Careful and sustained observation, however, revealed that these variables were organized into a limited number of coherent patterns. When he was discussing his wife, he spoke in loud, deep, dogmatic tones, leaning back in his chair with a stern gaze and counting off the accusations against her on his upraised fingers. At other times he talked with another patient about carpentry problems in a matter of fact tone, leaning forward in a companionable way. On still other occasions, he taunted the other group members with a scornful smile about their apparent loyalty to the therapist, his head slightly bowed and his back ostentatiously turned to the leader. The other patients soon became aware of these shifts in his ego state, correctly diagnosed them as Parent, Adult, and Child, respectively, and began to look for appropriate clues concerning Matthew's actual parents and his childhood experiences. Soon everyone in the group, including the patient, was able to accept the simple diagram shown in Figure 21-1 as a workable representation of Matthew's personality structure.

In the course of Matthew's therapy, he asked the physician to examine his father, who was on the verge of a paranoid psychosis. The therapist was astonished, in spite of his anticipations, to see how exactly Matthew's Parent reproduced the father's fixated paranoid ego state. During his interview, Matthew's father spoke in loud, deep, dogmatic tones, leaning back in his chair with a stern gaze, and counting off on his upraised fingers his accusations against the people around him.

It should be emphasized that Parent, Adult, and Child, are not synonymous with superego, ego, and id. The latter are "psychic agencies"

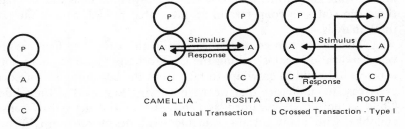

P
A
C
MATTHEW

Figure 21—1.
STRUCTURAL ANALYSIS

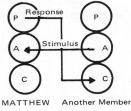

P
A
C
Stimulus
Response
CAMELLIA
ROSITA
a Mutual Transaction
Response
CAMELLIA
ROSITA
b Crossed Transaction - Type I

Figure 21—2. SIMPLE TRANSACTIONAL ANALYSIS

Response
Stimulus
P
A
C
MATTHEW
Another Member

Figure 21—3.
CROSSED TRANSACTION TYPE II

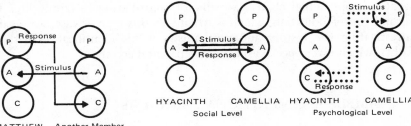

P
A
C
Stimulus
Response
HYACINTH
CAMELLIA
Social Level
HYACINTH
CAMELLIA
Psychological Level

Figure 21—4. A GAME

P — Parent
A — Adult
C — Child

P
A
C
a BEFORE
b AFTER

Figure 21—5. THERAPEUTIC EFFECT

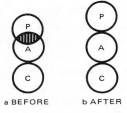

(Freud, 1949), while the former are complete ego states, each in itself including influences from superego, ego, and id. For example, when Matthew reproduced the Parental ego state, he not only behaved like a stern father, but also distorted reality the way his father did, and vented his sadistic impulses. And as cathexis was transferred from the Parental ego state into that of the scornful Child, the planning of his attacks and the accompanying guilt feelings had a childlike quality.

In therapy, the first task was to clarify in Matthew's mind what was Parent, what was Adult, and what was Child in his feelings and behavior. The next phase was directed toward maintaining control through the Adult. The third phase was to analyze the current conflicts between the three ego states. Each of these phases brought its own kind of improvement, while the ultimate aim in this pre-psychotic case was to enable all three ego states to cooperate in an integrated fashion as a result of structural analysis.

There were two contra-indications in this case. The first was the universal indication against telling the Child to grow up. One does not tell a two-year-old child to grow up. In fact, from the beginning it is necessary in every case to emphasize that we are not trying to get rid of the Child. The Child is not to be regarded as "childish" in the derogatory sense, but childlike, with many socially valuable attributes which must be freed so that they can make their contribution to the total personality when the confusion in this archaic area has been straightened out. The child in the individual is potentially capable of contributing to his personality exactly what a happy actual child is capable of contributing to family life. The second contra-indication, which is specific to this type of case, was against investigating the history and mechanism of his identification with his father, which was a special aspect of his parental ego state.

SIMPLE TRANSACTIONAL ANALYSIS

A patient named Camellia, following a previous train of thought said that she had told her husband she wasn't going to have intercourse with him anymore and that he could go and find himself some other woman. Another patient named Rosita asked curiously: "Why did you do that?" Whereupon Camellia, much to Rosita's discomfort, burst into tears and replied: "I try so hard, and then you criticize me."

This transaction may be analyzed according to the diagram in Figure 21-2. This figure was drawn and analyzed for the group as follows. The personalities of the two women are represented structurally as comprising Parent, Adult, and Child. The original transactional stimulus is Camellia's statement about what she told her husband. She related this in her Adult ego state, with which the group was familiar. It was received in turn by an Adult Rosita, who in her response exhibited a mature, reasonable interest in the story. As shown in Figure 21-2a, the transactional stimulus was Adult to Adult, and so was the transactional response. If things had continued at this level, the conversation might have proceeded smoothly.

Rosita's question ("Why did you do that?") now constituted a new transactional stimulus, and was intended as one adult speaking to another. Camellia's weeping response, however, was not that of one adult to another, but that of a child to a critical parent. Camellia's misperception of Rosita's ego state, and the shift in her own ego state, resulted in a crossed transaction and broke up the conversation, which now had to take another turn. This is represented in Figure 21-2b.

This particular type of crossed transaction, in which the stimulus is Adult to Adult, and the response is Child to Parent, is probably the most frequent cause of misunderstandings in marriage and work situations, as well as in social life. Clinically, it is typified by the classical transference reaction, which is a special case of the crossed transaction. In fact this particular species of crossed transaction may be said to be the chief problem of psychoanalytic technique.

In Matthew's case, when he was talking about his wife, the crossing was reversed. If one of the other members, as an Adult, asked him a question, expecting an Adult response, Matthew instead usually answered like a supercilious parent talking to a backward child, as represented in Figure 21-3.

Therapeutically, this simple type of transactional analysis helped Camellia to become more objective about her Child. As the Adult gained control, and the Child's responses at home were suppressed for later discussion in the group, her marital and social life improved even before any of the Child's confusion was resolved.

THE ANALYSIS OF GAMES

Short sets of ongoing transactions may be called operations. These constitute tactical maneuvers, in which it is the other members of the group who are maneuvered. Thus the conversation has to be analyzed again at a deeper level, when it soon appears that the need of Camellia's Child to feel criticized was one of the motives for telling this particular story to the group.

A series of operations constitutes a "game." A game may be defined as a recurring series of transactions, often repetitive, superficially rational, with a concealed motivation; or more colloquially, a series of operations with a "gimmick."

Hyacinth recounted her disappointment and resentment because a friend of hers had given a birthday party which she herself had planned to give. Camellia asked: "Why don't you give another party later?" To which Hyacinth responded: "Yes, but then it wouldn't be a birthday party." The other members of the group then began to give wise suggestions, each beginning with: "Why don't you . . ." and to each of these Hyacinth gave a response which began: "Yes, but . . . ."

Hyacinth had told her story for the purpose of setting in motion the commonest of all the games which can be observed in groups the game of "Why don't you . . . Yes but . . ." This is a game which can be played by any number. One player, who is "it," presents a problem. The others start to present solutions, to each of which the one who is it objects. A good player can stand off the rest of the group for a long period, until they all give up, whereupon "it" wins. Hyacinth, for example, successfully objected to more than a dozen solutions before the therapist broke up the game. The gimmick in "Why don't you . . . Yes but . . ." is that it is played not for its ostensible purpose (a quest for information or solutions), but for the sake of the fencing; and as a group phenomenon it corresponds to Bion's basic assumption "F" (Bion, 1952).

Other common games are "How Am I Doing?" "Uproar," "Alcoholic," "P.T.A.," "Ain't it Awful?" and "Schlemiel." In "Schlemiel," the one who is "it" breaks things, spills things, and makes messes of various kinds, and each time says: "I'm sorry!" This leaves the inexperienced player in a helpless position. The skillful opponent, however, says: "You can break things and spill things all you like; but please don't say 'I'm sorry!'" This response usually causes the Schlemiel to collapse or explode, since it knocks out his gimmick, and the opponent wins. I imagine that at this point many of you are thinking of Stephen Potter, but I think the games I have in mind are more serious; and some of them, like "Alcoholic," with all its complex rules published by various rescue organizations, are played for keeps. "Alcoholic" is complicated because the official form requires at least four players: a persecutor, a rescuer, a dummy, and the one who is "it."

The transactional analysis of Hyacinth's game of "Why don't you . . . Yes but . . ." is represented in Figure 21-4. This figure was drawn and analyzed for the group. In the guise of an Adult seeking information, Hyacinth "cons" the other members into responding like sage parents advising a helpless child. The object of the game can proceed because at the superficial level, both stimulus and response are Adult to Adult, and at a deeper level they are also complementary, Parent to Child stimulus ("Why don't you . . . ?") eliciting Child to Parent response ("Yes, but . . ."). The second level is unconscious on both sides.

The therapeutic effect of this analysis was to make Hyacinth aware of her defensive need to confound, and to make the others aware of how easily they could be conned into taking a parental role unawares. When a new patient tried to start a game of "Why don't you . . . Yes but . . ." in this group, they all played along with her in order not to make her too anxious, but after a few weeks they gently demonstrated to her what was happening. In other words, they now had the option of playing or not playing this game, as they saw fit, where formerly they had no choice but to be drawn in. This option was the net therapeutic gain, which they were able to apply profitably in their more intimate relationships. In structural terms, this improvement is represented in Figure 21-5. Figure 21-5a shows the original contamination of the Adult by the Parent, and Figure 21-5b shows the decontaminated Adult which can now rationally control their behavior in this particular situation.

THE ANALYSIS OF SCRIPTS

A script is an attempt to repeat in derivative form not a transference reaction or a transference situation, but a transference drama, often split up into acts, exactly like the theatrical scripts which are intuitive artistic derivatives of these primal dramas of childhood. Operationally, a script is a complex set of transactions, by nature recurrent, but not necessarily recurring, since a complete performance may require a whole lifetime. A common tragic script is that based on the rescue fantasy of a woman who marries one alcoholic after another. The disruption of such a script leads to despair. Since the magical cure of the alcoholic husband which the script calls for is not forthcoming, a divorce results and the woman tries again. A practical and constructive script, on the other hand, may lead to great happiness if the others in the cast are well chosen and play their parts satisfactorily. A game usually represents a segment of a script.

The ultimate goal of transactional analysis is the analysis of scripts, since the script determines the destiny and identity of the individual. Space, however, does not permit a discussion of the technique, aim, and therapeutic effect of script analysis, and this topic will have to be reserved for another communication.

SELF-ANALYSIS

Structural and transactional analysis lend themselves to self-examination more rapidly than orthodox psychoanalysis does, since they effectively bypass many of the difficulties inherent in self-psychoanalysis. The therapist who has some knowledge of his own personality structure has a distinct advantage in dealing with his countertransference problems: that is, the activity of his own Child or Parent with its own favorite games, its own script, and its own motives for becoming a group therapist. If he has a clear insight, without self-delusion, as to what is exteropsychic, what is neopsychic, and what is archaeopsychic in himself, then he can choose his responses so as to bring the maximum therapeutic benefit to his patients.

I have condensed into this brief communication material which would easily fill a book, and which is best made clear by six months or a year of clinical supervision. In its present form, however, it might stimulate some people to more careful observation of ego states in their patients, and to some serious and sustained experiments in structural interpretation.

SUMMARY

(1) A new approach to group therapy is outlined, based on the distinction between exteropsychic, neopsychic, and archaeopsychic ego states. The study of the relationships within the individual of these three types of ego states, colloquially called Parent, Adult, and Child, respectively, is termed structural analysis, and has been discussed in a previous publication.

(2) Once each individual in the group has some understanding of his own personality in these terms, the group can proceed to simple transactional analysis, in which the ego state of the individual who gives the transactional stimulus is compared with the ego state of the one who gives the transactional response.

(3) In the next phase, short series of transactions, called operations, are studied in the group. More complex series may constitute a "game," in which some element of double-dealing or insincerity is present. In the final phase, it is demonstrated that all transactions are influenced by complex attempts on the part of each member to manipulate the group in accordance with certain basic fantasies derived from early experiences. This unconscious plan, which is a strong determinant of the individual's destiny, is called a script.

(4) Clinical examples are given, and the therapeutic gain expected from each phase of structural and transactional analysis is indicated.

BIBLIOGRAPHY

Berne, E. Ego states in psychotherapy. A. J. Psychother., 11, 293–309, 1957.
Freud, S. An outline of psychoanalysis. New York: Norton, 1949.
Bion, W. R. Group dynamics: A re-view. Internat. J. Psycho-Anal., 33, 235–247, 1952.

PERSONOLOGY: GORDON W. ALLPORT AND HENRY A. MURRAY

VI

AT THE TIME of his death in 1967, Gordon Allport had a host of respectful admirers but no band of devoted followers. His influence, although widespread and pervasive, was indirect, and he was more praised than carefully read by a generation of research-oriented personologists for whom Allport's benign eclecticism and catholic interests held little that was appealing or "relevant," to use a much-abused contemporary term. There is not much in Allport's latest writings to indicate that he was much concerned with this state of affairs. His entire career was an eloquent testimonial to the conviction, which never deserted him, that it is often the most unpopular subjects of scientific inquiry which are the most important. A lengthy list of topics that Allport has championed at one time or another could be compiled in support of this contention: his emphasis upon conscious determinants of behavior at a time when these had suffered interdiction in psychology; his work in revising and clarifying the ego concept; his emphasis upon the unique, the idiographic, and the organismic at a time when most of his colleagues were emphasizing the general, the nomothetic, and the environmental; and his persistent attempts to forge links between scientific, brass-instrument approaches and the phenomena which interest and concern the social psychologist and the clinician.

The two Allport articles selected for this section were published 12 years apart and reflect two major themes in Allport's thinking: the study of the individual and the study of normality. The first, entitled "Personalistic Psychology as Science: A Reply," was written in rebuttal to an earlier critique of Allport's work in which Skaggs expresses the view that idiographic knowledge (information gained from the study of a single individual) can hardly be called scientific. It is rather characteristic of Allport that his answer to Skaggs covers a range of references from Windelband to Stern and that his definition of science ("a form of knowledge that enhances our understanding, prediction, and control of phenomena above the level achieved by unaided common sense") is probably much closer to the view endorsed by contemporary psychologists than is the more rigid definition proposed by Skaggs.

The second article, "Personality: Normal and Abnormal," contains a thoughtful discussion and review of the moral and ethical issues involved in defining deviance and normality. The concerns he expresses are extremely similar to those voiced by existentialist and humanistic psychologists in recent years; and once again it is characteristic of Allport that he should address himself to these issues.

Allport's concern for the study of the normal, functioning, individual personality is reflected by a second major personologist, Henry Murray. In terms of educational background and expressed interest, Murray is perhaps the most diversified of all major personality theorists, a fact which helps to account for the broad scope of his personality theory. Some indications of this diversity can be seen in his early professional background: In 1915, Murray received an AB in history from Harvard University, in 1919, an MD degree and, thereafter, an MA in biology from Columbia University. After serving as an instructor in physiology at Harvard and carrying out studies in embryology and psychology, he received, in 1927, a Ph.D. in biochemistry, taking immediately thereafter (in 1928) a position as director of the Psychological Clinic at Harvard. Despite this rapid early fluctuation of his interests, Murray has since 1928 been almost exclusively associated with psychology.

Murray is best known on the one hand for the broad outline of his integrative theoretical orientation to personality (though many of the detailed constructs have never become popular) and on the other for his approach to personality assessment and research, particularly for his development of a projective technique, the Thematic Apperception Test (TAT). Murray's orientations to both theory and research in personality can be characterized, as can those of many major theorists, as, in part, reactions against extant orientations in the field. Murray, like All-port, observed that in the world of psychological research, most psychologists have tended to neglect the intensive study of individual personalities. Most seem to prefer, in-stead, the study of groups of individuals (the larger the better), applying correlational techniques, collecting norma-tive data, or utilizing highly controlled experimental de-signs in the study of behavior. Reacting against this ori-entation, Murray became one of the pioneers among the relatively small group of psychologists interested primarily in the intensive, holistic study of the individual person-ality. In the works selected for inclusion here, we have at-tempted to provide a feeling for this orientation, as well as examples of the application of Murray's work by other researchers.

While Murray's theoretical orientation has undergone modification over the years, his early article, "Basic Con-cepts for a Psychology of Personality," remains a classic and is still one of the best available overviews of the major constructs in his theory. A second Murray article details his recent concern about the present and future of psy-chology, outlines a set of methodological principles which Murray has long advocated, and provides an example of research conducted in the model most consonant with this theorist's orientation.

The remaining articles deal with applications of Murray's work by others. The first concerns the TAT. In this major test, currently second in usage only to the Rorschach among projective techniques, the research sub-ject or clinical patient is shown a series of vague, ambigu-ous pictures and asked to write stories concerning scenes portrayed. The stories are interpreted on the basis of vari-ous scoring systems, including Murray's own, either to achieve a specific research objective or to provide one as-pect of the clinical assessment of the patient. The article included here, by Little and Shneidman, represents an at-tempt to establish an index of the validity of thematic projectives. It should be added that judgment of the TAT cannot be based entirely on any one article, as literally hundreds of articles and several books dealing with the va-lidities of various applications of this technique have ap-peared.

Another (closely related) aspect of Murray's work is his development of a system of human needs. This need system, a part of the overall theory, has been applied in a variety of settings, including the interpretation of the TAT and the differentiation of groups on a dimension of need–attitudes. The final article in this section provides an example of the latter application.

22

Personalistic Psychology
as Science: A Reply

GORDON W. ALLPORT

In a recent number of this Journal Dr. E. B. Skaggs expresses his conviction that "idiographic" knowledge does not deserve to be called "scientific" (Skaggs, 1945). It would not be profitable to dispute this statement of semantic taste, for *science*—a "purr word," highly charged with positive affect—is at the present time peculiarly resistant to a dispassionate search for its most appropriate referent. And yet I cannot let Dr. Skaggs' confession of taste pass unnoticed because in stating his preferences he has unintentionally misrepresented some of my own views regarding the methods and theories suited to the study of personality.

He writes, "Now any system of personalistic psychology, such as that presented by Allport, where the effects of learning are stressed so heavily and where individual uniqueness constitutes the data of study, cannot meet the . . . criteria of scientific data or content" (Skaggs, 1945, p. 237). The criteria for scientific subject-matter, he proposes, are (*a*) durability in the phenomenon that is the object of the scientists' interest, and (*b*) the universality of this phenomenon.

My first criticism arises from his inaccurate understanding of personalistic psychology. It so happens that there is only one self-styled system of personalistic psychology, namely that set forth by William Stern. A reading of his *General Psychology from a Personalistic Standpoint* (Stern, 1938) shows that Stern's dimensions (or variables) almost without exception fulfill the criteria of durability and universality. In fact, Stern's writing is as nomothetic as one's heart could possibly desire. Hence, to identify personalistic psychology and the idiographic outlook is Dr. Skaggs' first serious error.

If he wishes to label my own views "personalistic" I cannot prevent him, but because of the many differences between Stern's "system" and my own, I myself would hesitate to accept the label. Stern has prior rights

From G. W. Allport, Personalistic Psychology as Science: A Reply. *Psychological Review*, 1946, 53, 132–135. Copyright 1946 by the American Psychological Association, and reproduced by permission of the publisher.

to it. In Chapter 20 of the book that Dr. Skaggs criticizes I have explained in some detail the differences between personalistic psychology and the psychology of personality as I see it (Allport, 1937a). Elsewhere I have summarized Stern's views at still greater length and again recorded my criticisms of them (Allport, 1937b). Dr. Skaggs seems far more certain than I that I am a "personalistic" psychologist.

In attacking the idiographic point of view (which, as I say, is not the same as the personalistic point of view), Dr. Skaggs writes, "Literally there would be as many separate psychologies as there are individuals, if we carried Allport's doctrine to the extreme!" (Skaggs, 1945, p. 237). Such a statement is like saying, "Penicillin is good for everything, including nearsightedness and ingrowing toenails, if we carry the penicillin-enthusiast's view to the extreme." Who wants to carry it to the extreme? Not I. In discussing the proposed distinction made by Windelband and others between the nomothetic and idiographic approaches to mental life, I state explicitly, "The dichotomy, however, is too sharp; it requires a psychology divided against itself. As in the case of the two psychologies (the analytical and the descriptive) advocated by Dilthey and Spranger, the division is too drastic. It is more helpful to regard the two methods as overlapping and as contributing to one another. . . . A complete study of the individual will embrace both approaches" (Allport, 1937a, p. 22). The psychology of personality, I have therefore explicitly maintained, should be *both* nomothetic and idiographic.

Again, Skaggs writes, "Allport, who so severely criticizes the older scientific psychology which dealt with facts common to all mankind, ends up by *abstracting certain general laws and methodologies!*" (p. 236). Why, may I ask, is this so scandalous? Why should not a discipline that is *both* nomothetic and idiographic deal with common laws and methods? For that matter, why should not a discipline almost entirely idiographic in nature, such as history, fine arts, or medical diagnosis, employ as background laws and common methods in so far as these are helpful in comprehending uniqueness?

Dr. Skaggs goes on to state correctly my aspiration when he says that the difference between "his laws and methodologies and those of a Wundt or a Titchener lies in the fact that his are (presumably) more serviceable in giving self-understanding and understanding of other people" (p. 236). Dr. Skaggs is right. I try in my book to offer nomothetic constructs that *improve* upon those traditionally employed. While they are nomothetic in nature, many of them have an idiographic *intent*. To illustrate: such constructs as the theory of individual traits, of the ego, of functional autonomy, of congruence, of the empirical-intuitive nature of understanding, all are generalizations which if adopted would give psychologists greater predictive ability in dealing with single individuals. Similarly, among the *methods* having idiographic intent, and emphasized by me, are the case study, the personal document, interviewing methods, matching, personal structure analysis, and other procedures that contrive to keep together what nature itself has fashioned as an integrated unit—the single personality. My whole purpose is to show how the psychology of personality can do a better job than it has traditionally done in handling the phenomenon of individuality.

But Dr. Skaggs is not pleased. To him it seems mildly treasonable to suppose that science can extend itself to the phenomenon of individuality. He writes, "If we define personalistic psychology as does Allport [the error here I have already explained] each person is a 'unique individual' " (p. 236). My reply to Dr. Skaggs is that each person *is* a unique individual regardless of who defines what how.

Although I am apparently more impressed than he by the inescapable uniqueness of personality, and by the psychologist's obligation to deal with it, I think I allow adequately for the contributions of the familiar actuarial methods of our discipline. For example, there is merit in the postulation of universal needs and capacities, and in their measurement in the customary language of individual differences. All testing (of the standardized order) must, I fully grant, proceed from the assumption of "common traits." Uniqueness in respect to any single variable is known only in terms of its *deviation* from the mean of the standardization group with which the individual is being compared. Where my view is 'unorthodox' is in my contention that psychological science (and I mean here the total course of psychological inquiry) cannot stop with common traits, factors, IQ's, and like nomothetic dimensions, but must admit additional methods and theories to handle the organic inter-relation of the artificialized variables with which nomothetic science deals, and must represent better than it has the personalized coloring of these variables in the individual life. I say in effect: "No doors should be closed in the study of personality. Abstract dimensions have their place. Let us use them even though they merely *approximate* the unique cleavages which close scrutiny shows are characteristic of each separate personality. Then let us add new methods and concepts where they are needed to grasp better than we have the phenomenon of individual pattern."

The most startling feature of Dr. Skagg's position in his contention that the biological aspects of personality are legitimate data for science whereas the acquired aspects are not (p. 237). He rules out "such content as ideas, ideals, attitudes, interests, sentiments, purposes, beliefs, idealogies [sic], 'personality traits' " because these "are definitely not common to all people the world over" (p. 235). He maintains that whatever is learned cannot be the object of scientific interest, because learning results in progressive individuality. I daresay that biologists and geneticists would be glad to call Dr. Skaggs' attention to the *unique* inheritance that results from combinations of genes. An inborn temperament is certainly no less unique than acquired habit-systems, and, I suspect, not nearly so universal.

Yet he insists that "any effects wrought in man through experience or learning would be unscientific content for psychology because they would not meet the criteria of durability and commonness" (p. 237). To draw the line here would exclude from the scope of science such pursuits as market research, opinion study, vital statistics, comparative national psychology, humor, custom, much of psychopathology, and, if I understand him correctly, most of the phenomena of perception, memory, judgment, reasoning, language, and motivation, for these are all variable and socially conditioned.

To the purged hall of science he would, however, admit such constructs as Spearman's g and Thurstone's "basic factors" (p. 235). Yet Tolman has shown clearly that nothing is more culture-bound than precisely these factors. Who, knowing the type of culturally conditioned test-matrix from which factors emerge, can deny Tolman's conclusion that "it is quite obvious that this London (or New York) g would not carry over, as such, to the Trobriand Islands"? (Tolman, 1945, p. 2). And I question whether Dr. Skaggs is on safer ground with his contention that learning theory, or the Weber-Fechner law, is of eternal and universal applicability, for the operation of both, I suspect, is so basically dependent upon culture-bound and personality-bound interests, that the purely biological component is not only impossible to isolate, but worthless when isolated.

The author insists that "science as we know it to-day, thinks in terms of millions of years" (p. 238). If this be so, I doubt that any biological or psychological discipline qualifies unless its subject matter be trilobites or something else equally remote from human concern. The author's insistence upon durability and universality in the phenomena under investigation would, it seems to me, disqualify nearly every psychologist now at work. Oddly enough, Stern, the personalistic psychologist, would qualify as well as anyone, for his dimensions for the study of mental life are highly abstract and in themselves nearly content-less.

It is much more customary to define science as that form of knowledge that enhances our *understanding, prediction,* and *control* of phenomena above the level achieved by unaided common sense. Elsewhere I have argued that in order to attain a higher degree of scientific power thus defined, psychology would do well to adopt the idiographic orientation of its work (Allport, 1942). For in matters of mental life *understanding, prediction,* and *control* are likely to be more complete when the single organism is understood in its own special uniqueness than when exclusively nomothetic (actuarial) probabilities are applied. Although this point reaches beyond the scope of Dr. Skaggs' paper I mention it here because, if

I am correct in my analysis of the situation, then according to this *more usual* definition of science, idiographic knowledge fully qualifies for a place of honor.

True, this claim that understanding, prediction and control of personality are better achieved under an idiographic than under a nomothetic mode of approach, has been disputed. But in principle, at least, the hypothesis can be submitted to experimental testing. I have already cited some evidence in its favor (Allport, 1942, p. 34), Sarbin some against (Sarbin, 1944). The subject is not yet closed. I shall not discuss it more fully here, because it digresses too far from Dr. Skaggs' argument.

In the last analysis his position, I regret to point out, turns on a struggle for status, the motive being revealed in several passages:

> Allport takes a bold stand for the broadening of the concept of science. This may be the proper progressive stand to take but we doubt that our fellow scientists in physics, chemistry, and astronomy will be very receptive to the idea (p. 234).
>
> While the study of attitudes, beliefs, habits and skills may be of immense practical and theoretical importance, such studies are not science in the eyes of our colleagues in physics, chemistry and astronomy (p. 237).
>
> Our colleagues in physics and chemistry might, and probably would resist any such change in the scientific concept (p. 238).
>
> When a colleague in physiology or chemistry tells us that our data are not scientific, we become rather upset (p. 238).
>
> We all want to bask in the light of the great Sun-God Science (p. 238).

In short, psychology, the climber, must not offend those who have arrived. If it does so, it won't make the club.

This logic of appeasement has little attractiveness for me. Prestige for psychology will scarcely be won by aping those who, at this particular moment in the world's history, enjoy exalted status. Rather, when psychology has ripe wisdom to offer concerning the development of human personality, whether it offers it in a nomothetic or idiographic manner (or both), it will then merit the high position which Dr. Skaggs covets for it.

Though I have disagreed with him in his interpretations and outlook, I am grateful to Dr. Skaggs for initiating a discussion of such basic issues in the study of personality, and for the opportunity he has given me to clarify some of my own views on the subject.

REFERENCES

Allport, G. W. *Personality: A psychological interpretation.* New York: Henry Holt & Co., 1937. (a)

Allport, G. W. The personalistic psychology of William Stern. *Char. & Pers.*, 1937, 5, 231–246. (b)

Allport, G. W. *The use of personal documents in psychological science.* New York: Social Science Research Council, Bull, 49, 1942.

Sarbin, T. R. The logic of prediction in psychology. *Psychol. Rev.*, 1944, *51*, 210–228.

Skaggs, E. B. Personalistic psychology as science. *Psychol. Rev.*, 1945, *52*, 234–238.

Stern, W. *General psychology from the personalistic standpoint.* New York: Macmillan (transl.), 1938.

Tolman, E. C. A stimulus-expectancy need-cathexis psychology. *Science*, 1945, *101*, 160–166.

23

Personality: Normal and Abnormal

GORDON W. ALLPORT

The word *norm* means "an authoritative standard," and correspondingly *normal* means abiding by such a standard. It follows that a normal personality is one whose conduct conforms to an authoritative standard, and an abnormal personality is one whose conduct does not do so.

But having said this much we immediately discover that there are two entirely different kinds of standards that may be applied to divide the normal from the abnormal: the one statistical, the other ethical. The one pertains to the average or usual, and the other to the desirable or valuable.

These two standards are not only different, but in many ways they stand in flat contradiction to one another. It is, for example, *usual* for people to have some noxious trends in their natures, some pathology of tissues or organs, some evidences of nervousness and some self-defeating habits; but though usual or average such trends are not healthy. Or again, society's authoritative standard for a wholesome sex life is, if we are to accept the Kinsey Report, achieved by only a minority of American males. Here too the usual is not the desirable; what is normal in one sense is not normal in the other sense. And certainly no system of ethics in the civilized world holds up as a model for its children the ideal of becoming a merely average man. It is not the actualities, but rather the potentialities, of human nature that somehow provide us with a standard for a sound and healthy personality.

Fifty years ago this double meaning of *norm* and *normal* did not trouble psychology so much as it does today. In those days psychology was deeply involved in discovering average norms for every conceivable type of mental function. Means, modes and sigmas were in the saddle, and differential psychology was riding high. Intoxicated with the new-found beauty of the normal distribution curve, psychologists were content to declare its slender tails as the one and only sensible measure of "abnormality." Departures from the mean were abnormal and for this reason slightly unsavory.

From Allport, G. W. Personality: Normal and Abnormal. *Sociological Review*, 1958, 6, 167–180. Reprinted by permission of author and publisher.

Address delivered at the Fifth Interamerican Congress of Psychology, Mexico City, December, 1957; reprinted by permission from the Congress Proceedings.

288

In this era there grew up the concept of "mental adjustment," and this concept held sway well into the decade of the 20's. While not all psychologists equated adjustment with average behaviour this implication was pretty generally present. It was, for example, frequently pointed out that an animal who does not adjust to the norm for his species usually dies. It was not yet pointed out that a human being who does so adjust is a bore and a mediocrity.

Now times have changed. Our concern for the improvement of average human behavior is deep, for we now seriously doubt that the merely mediocre man can survive. As social anomie spreads, as society itself becomes more and more sick, we doubt that the mediocre man will escape mental disease and delinquency, or that he will keep himself out of the clutch of dictators or succeed in preventing atomic warfare. The normal distribution curve, we see, holds out no hope of salvation. We need citizens who are in a more positive sense normal, healthy and sound. And the world needs them more urgently than it ever did before.

It is, for this reason, I think, that psychologists are now seeking a fresh definition of what is normal and what is abnormal. They are asking questions concerning the *valuable*, the *right*, and the *good* as they have never asked them before.

At the same time psychologists know that in seeking for a criterion of normality in this new sense they are trespassing on the traditional domain of normal philosophy. They also know that, by and large, philosophers have failed to establish authoritative standards for what constitutes the sound life—the life that educators, parents, and therapists should seek to mould. And so psychologists for the most part, wish to pursue the search in a fresh way and if they can, avoid the traditional traps of axiology. Let me briefly describe some recent empirical attempts to define normality and afterward attempt to evaluate the state of our efforts to date.

NATURALISTIC DERIVATIONS OF "NORMALITY"

During the past few months two proposals have been published that merit serious attention. Both are by social scientists, one a psychologist in the United States, the other a sociologist in England. Their aim is to derive a concept of normality (in the value sense) from the condition of man (in the naturalistic sense). Both seek their ethical imperatives from biology and psychology, not from value-theory directly. In short, they boldly seek the *ought* (the goal to which teachers, counsellors, therapists should strive) from the *is* of human nature. Many philosophers tell us that this is an impossible undertaking. But before we pass judgment let us see what success they have had.

E. J. Shoben asks, What are the principal psychological differences between man and lower animals? (Shoben, 1957.) While he does not claim that his answer is complete he centres upon two distinctively human qualities. And he makes the extra-psychological assumption that man *should* maximize those attributes that are distinctively human. The first quality is man's capacity for the use of propositional language (symbolization). From this particular superiority over animals Shoben derives several specific guidelines for normality. With the aid of symbolic language, for example, man can delay his gratifications, holding in mind a distant goal, a remote reward, an objective to be reached perhaps only at the end of one's life or perhaps never. With the aid of symbolic language, he can imagine a future for himself that is far better than the present. He can also develop an intricate system of social concepts that leads him to all manner of possible relations with other human beings, far exceeding the rigid symbiotic rituals of, say, the social insects.

A second distinctive human quality is related to the prolonged childhood in the human species. Dependence, basic trust, sympathy and altruism are absolutely essential to human survival, in a sense and to a degree not true for lower animals.

Bringing together these two distinctive qualities Shoben derives his conception of normality. He calls it a model of integrative adjustment. It follows, he says, that a sense of *personal responsibility* marks the normal man for responsibility is a distinctive capacity derived from holding in mind a symbolic image of the future, delaying gratification, and being able to strive in accordance with one's conceptions of the best principles of conduct for oneself. Similarly *social responsibility* is normal; for all these symbolic capacities can interact with the unique factor of trust or altruism. Closely related is the criterion of *democratic social interest* which derives from both symbolization and trust. Similarly the *possession of ideals* and the necessity for *self-control* follow from the same naturalistic analysis. Shoben rightly points out that a *sense of guilt* is an inevitable consequence of man's failure to live according to the distinctive human pattern, and so in our concept of normality we must include both guilt and devices for expiation.

Every psychologist who wishes to make minimum assumptions and who wishes to keep close to empirical evidence, and who inclines toward the naturalism of biological science, will appreciate and admire Shoben's efforts. Yet I imagine our philosopher friends will arise to confound us with some uncomfortable questions. Is it not a distinctively human capacity, they will ask, for a possessive mother to keep her child permanently tied to her apron strings? Does any lower animal engage in this destructive behaviour? Likewise is it not distinctively human to develop fierce in-group loyalties that lead to prejudice, contempt, and war? Is it not possible that the burden of symbolization, social responsibility, and guilt may lead a person to depression and suicide? Suicide, along with all the other destructive patterns I have mentioned, is distinctively human. A philosopher who raises these questions would conclude, "No, you cannot derive the *ought* from the *is* of human nature. What is distinctively human is not necessarily distinctively good."

Let us look at a second attempt to achieve a naturalistic criterion of normality. In a recent book entitled *Towards a Measure of Man*, Paul Halmos prefers to start with the question, "What are the minimum conditions for survival?" (Halmos, 1957.) When we know these minimum conditions we can declare that any situations falling below this level will lead to abnormality, and tend toward death and destruction. He calls this criterion the *abnorm* and believes we can define it, even if we cannot define normality, because people in general agree more readily on what is bad for man than on what is good for him. They agree on the bad because all mortals are subject to the basic imperative of survival.

The need for survival he breaks down into the need for growth and the need for social cohesion. These two principles are the universal conditions of all life, not merely of human life. *Growth* means autonomy and the process of individuation. *Cohesion* is the basic fact of social interdependence, involving, at least for human beings initial trust, heteronomy, mating and the founding of family.

Now Halmos believes that by taking an inventory of conditions deleterious to growth and cohesion we may establish the "abnorm." As a start he mentions first and foremost disorders of child training. He says, "continued or repeated interruption of physical proximity between mother and child," or "emotional rejection" of the child by the mother are conditions that harm survival of the individual and the group. In his own terms this first criterion of abnormality lies in a "rupture in the transmutation of cohesion into love." Most of what is abnormal he traces to failures in the principle of cohesion, so that the child becomes excessively demanding and compulsive. Here we note the similarity to such contemporary thinkers as Bowlby, Erikson and Maslow.

The author continues his inventory of the "abnorm" by accepting syndromes that psychiatrists agree upon. For instance, it is abnormal (inimical to survival) if repetition of conduct occurs irrespective of the situation and unmodified by its consequences; also when one's accomplishments constantly fall short of one's potentialities; likewise when one's psychosexual frustrations prevent both growth and cohesion.

It is well to point out that the basic functions of growth and cohesion postulated by Halmos occur time and time again in psychological writing. Bergson, Jung and Angyal are among the writers who agree that normality requires a balance between individuation and socialization, between autonomy and heteronomy. There seems to be considerable consensus in this matter. Let me quote from one of the founders of this Society whose recent death has brought sorrow to us all. Werner Wolff writes:

"When an individual identifies himself to an extreme degree with a group, the effect is that he loses his value. On the other hand, a complete inability to indentify has the effect that the environment loses its value for the individual. In both extreme cases the dynamic relationship between individual and environment is distorted. An individual behaving in such a way is called "neurotic." In a normal group each member preserves his individuality but accepts his rôle as participator also. (Wolff, 1950.)

While there is much agreement that the normal personality must strike a serviceable balance between growth as an individual and cohesion with society, we do not yet have a clear criterion for determining when these factors are in serviceable balance and when they are not. Philosophers, I fear, would shake their heads at Halmos. They would ask, "How do you know that survival is a good thing?" Further, "Why should all people enjoy equal rights to the benefits of growth and cohesion?" And, "How are we to define the optimum balance between cohesion and growth within the single personality?"

IMBALANCE AND CREATIVITY

Halmos himself worries especially about the relation between abnormality and creativity. It was Nietzsche who declared, "I say unto you: a man must have chaos yet within him to be able to give birth to a dancing star." Have not many meritorious works of music, literature, and even of science drawn their inspiration not from balance but from some kind of psychic chaos? Here, I think, Halmos gives the right answer. He says in effect that creativity and normality are not identical values. On the whole the normal person will be creative, but if valuable creations come likewise from people who are slipping away from the norm of survival, this fact can only be accepted and valued on the scale of creativity, but not properly on the scale of normality.

IMBALANCE AND GROWTH

In this day of existentialism I sense that psychologists are becoming less and less content with the concept of adjustment, and correspondingly with the concepts of "tension reduction," "restoration of equilibrium," and "homeostasis." We wonder if a man who enjoys these beatific conditions is truly human. Growth we know is not due to homeostasis but to a kind of "transistasis." And cohesion is a matter of keeping our human relationships moving and not in mere stationary equilibrium. Stability cannot be a criterion of normality since stability brings evolution to a standstill, negating both growth and cohesion. Freud once wrote to Fliess that he finds "moderate misery necessary for intensive work."

A research inspired by Carl Rogers is interesting in this connection. One series of patients before treatment manifested a zero correlation between their self-image and their ideal self-image. Following treatment the correlation was +.34, not high but approaching the coefficient of +.58 that marked a healthy untreated group. Apparently this magnitude of correlation is a measure of the satisfaction or dissatisfaction that normal people have with their own personalities(Hall & Lindzey, 1957). In other words, a zero correlation between self and ideal-self is too low for normality; it leads to such anguish that the sufferer seeks therapy. At the same time normal people are by no means perfectly adjusted to themselves. There is always a wholesome gap between self and ideal self, between present existence and aspiration. On the other hand, too high a satisfaction indicates pathology. The highest coefficient obtained, +.90, was from an individual clearly pathological. Perfect correlations we might expect only from smug psychotics, particularly paranoid schizophrenics.

And so whatever our definition of normality turns out to be it must allow for serviceable imbalances within personality, and between person and society.

AN EMPIRICAL APPROACH TO SOUNDNESS

The work of Barron illustrates an approach dear to the psychologist's heart. He lets others establish the criterion of normality, or as he calls it, *soundness,* and then proceeds to find out what *"sound"* men are like. Teachers of graduate students in the University of California nominated a large number of men whom they considered sound, and some of the opposite trend. In testing and experimenting with these two groups, whose identities were unknown to the investigators, certain significant differences appeared (Barron, 1954). For one thing the sounder men had more realistic perceptions; they were not thrown off by distortions or by surrounding context in the sensory field. Further, on adjective check-lists they stood high on such traits as *integrated pursuit of goals, persistence, adaptability, good nature.* On the Minnesota Multiphasic Personality Inventory they were high in *equanimity, self-confidence, objectivity,* and *virility.* Their *self-insight* was superior, as was their *physical health.* Finally they came from homes where there was *little or no affective rupture*—a finding that confirms Halmos's predictions.

INVENTORY APPROACHES

Most authors do not have the benefit of professorial consensus on soundness. They simply set forth in a didactic manner the attributes of normality, or health, or soundness, or maturity, or productivity, as they see them. Innumerable descriptive lists result. Perhaps the simplest of these is Freud's. He says the healthy person will be able to "love" and to "work." One of the most elaborate is Maslow's schedule of qualities that include among others: efficient perception of reality, philosophical humour, spontaneity, detachment, and an acceptance of self and others. Such lists are not altogether arbitrary since their authors base them on wide clinical experience, as did Freud, or on a deliberate analysis of case materials, as did Maslow (1954).

There are so many lists of this type now available that a new kind of approach is possible,—namely, the combining of these insightful inventories. From time to time I have assigned this task to my students, and while all manner of groupings and re-groupings result, still there are recurrent themes that appear in nearly all inventories. If I were to attempt the assignment myself I should probably start with my own list of three criteria, published 20 years ago, but I would now expand it (Allport, 1937).

The three criteria I originally listed were:

i. ego-extension—the capacity to take an interest in more than one's body and one's material possessions. The criterion covers, I think, the attributes that Fromm ascribes to the productive man.

ii. self-objectification—which includes the ability to relate the feeling tone of the present experience to that of a past experience provided the latter does in fact determine the quality of the former; self-objectification also includes humour which tells us that our total horizon of life is too wide to be compressed into our present rigidities.

iii. unifying philosophy of life—which may or may not be religious, but in any event has to be a frame of meaning and of responsibility into which life's major activities fit.

To this inventory I now would add:

iv. the capacity for a warm, profound, relating to one's self to others—which may, if one likes, be called "extroversion of the libido" or "Gemeinschaftsgefühl."

v. The possession of realistic skills, abilities, and perceptions with which to cope with the practical problems of life.

vi. a compassionate regard for all living creatures—which includes respect for individual persons and a disposition to participate in common activities that will improve the human lot.

I am aware that psychoanalists are partial to the criterion of "ego strength": a normal person has a strong ego, an abnormal person a weak ego. But I find this phrase ill defined, and would suggest that my six somewhat more detailed criteria succeed in specifying what we mean by the looser term, "ego strength."

The weakness of all inventories, including my own, is that the philosopher's persistent questions are still unanswered. How does the psychologist know that these qualities comprise normality, that they are good, and that all people should have them? Before I attempt to give a partial answer to our irritating philosopher friend, let me call attention to one additional psychological approach.

CONTINUITY OF SYMPTOM AND DISCONTINUITY OF PROCESS

I refer to a fresh analysis of the problem of continuity-discontinuity. Is abnormality merely an exaggerated normal condition? Is there unbroken continuity between health and disease? Certainly Freud thought so. He evolved his system primarily as a theory of neurosis. But he and his followers came to regard his formulations as a universally valid science of psychology. Whether one is normal or abnormal depends on the degree to which one can manage his relationships successfully. Furthermore, the earlier enthusiasm of psychologists for the normal distribution curve helped to entrench the theory of continuity. The strongest empirical evidence in favour of this view is the occurrence of borderline cases. Descriptively there is certainly a continuum. We encounter mild neurotics, borderline schizophrenics, hypomanics, and personalities that are paranoid, cycloid, epileptoid. And if scales and tests are employed there are no gaps; scores are continuously distributed.

But—and let me insist on this point—this continuum pertains only to symptoms, to appearances. The *processes* (or "mechanisms") underlying these appearances are not continuous. There is, for example, a polar difference between confronting the world and its problems (which is an intrinsically wholesome thing to do) and escaping and withdrawing from the world (which is an intrinsically unwholesome thing to do). Extreme withdrawal and escape constitute psychosis. But you may ask, do not we all do some escaping? Yes, we do, and what is more, escapism may provide not only recreation but may sometimes have a certain constructive utility, as it has in mild day-dreaming. But still the process of escape can be harmless only if the *dominant* process is confrontation. Left to itself escapism spells disaster. In the psychotic this process has the upper hand; in the normal person, on the contrary, confrontation has the upper hand.

Following this line of reasoning we can list other processes that intrinsically generate abnormality, and those that generate normality. The first list deals with catabolic functions. I would mention:

Escape or withdrawal (including fantasy)
Repression or dissociation
Other "ego defences" including rationalization, reaction formation, projection, displacement
Impulsivity (uncontrolled)
Restriction of thinking to concrete level
Fixation of personality at a juvenile level
All forms of rigidification

The list is not complete, but the processes in question, I submit, are intrinsically catabolic. They are as much so as are the disease mechanisms responsible for diabetes, tuberculosis, hyperthyroidism, or cancer. A person suffering only a small dose of these mechanisms may appear to be normal, but only if the *anabolic* mechanisms predominate. Among the latter I would list:

Confrontation (or, if you prefer, "reality testing")
Availability of knowledge to consciousness
Self-insight, with its attendant humour
Integrative action of the nervous system
Ability to think abstractly
Continuous individuation (without arrested or fixated development)
Functional autonomy of motives
Frustration tolerance

I realize that what I have called processes, or mechanisms, are not in all cases logically parallel. But they serve to make my point, that normality depends on the dominance of one set of principles, abnormality upon the dominance of another. The fact that all normal people are occasionally afflicted with catabolic processes does not alter the point. The normal life is marked by a preponderance of the anabolic functions; the abnormal by a preponderance of the catabolic.

CONCLUSION

And now is it possible to gather together all these divergent threads, and to reach some position tenable for psychology today? Let us try to do so.

First, I think, we should make a deep obeisance in the direction of moral philosophy and gracefully concede that psychology by itself cannot solve the problem of normality. No psychologist has succeded in telling us why man ought to seek good health rather than ill; nor why normality should be our goal for all men, and not just for some. Nor can psychologists account for the fact that meritorious creativity may be of value even if the creator himself is by all tests an abnormal person. These and a variety of other conundrums lie beyond the competence of psychology to solve. That moral philosophers have not agreed among themselves upon solutions is also true; but we gladly grant them freedom and encouragement to continue their efforts.

At the same time the lines of research and analysis that I have here reviewed are vitally related to the philosopher's quest. After all it is the psychologists who deal directly with personalities in the clinic, in schools, industry, and in laboratories. It is they who gather the facts concerning normality and abnormality and who try to weave them into their own normative speculations. *A fact and a moral imperative are more closely interlocked than traditional writers on ethics may think.* Among the facts that psychology can offer are the following:

i. Investigations have told us much concerning the nature of human needs and motives, both conscious and unconscious. A grouping of these needs into the broad categories of growth and cohesion is helpful. Much is known concerning the pathologies that result from frustration and imbalance of these needs. It would be absurd for moral philosophers to write imperatives in total disregard of this evidence.

ii. We know much about childhood conditions that predispose toward delinquency, prejudice, and mental disorder. A moralist might do well to cast his imperatives in terms of standards for child training. I can suggest, for example, that the abstract imperative "respect for persons" should be tested and formulated from the point of view of child training.

iii. By virtue of comparative work on men and animals we know much about the motives common to both, but also, as Shoben has shown, about the qualities that are distinctively human. Let the philosophers give due weight to this work.

iv. While I have not yet mentioned the matter, psychology in cooperation with cultural anthropology has a fairly clear picture today of the rôle of culture in producing and in defining abnormality. We know the incidence of psychosis and neurosis in various populations; we know what conditions are labelled abnormal in some cultures but are regarded as normal in others. We also know, with some accuracy, those conditions that are considered abnormal in all cultures. Since our president, Professor Klineberg, is addressing the Congress on this subject I shall say no more about it; but shall simply point out that these facts are highly relevant to the deliberations of the moral philosopher.

v. Following the lead of Halmos, we may say that biologists, psychologists and sociologists know much about the conditions of individual and group survival. While these facts in themselves do not tell us why we should survive, still they provide specifications for the philosopher who thinks he can answer this riddle.

vi. Still more important, I think, is the empirical work on consensus that is now available. We have cited Barron's method of determining the attributes of men judged to be "sound" as distinguished from those of men judged to be "unsound." While the philosopher is not likely to accept the vote of university professors as an adequate definition of soundness, still he might do well to heed opinions other than his own.

vii. Another type of consensus is obtained from the inventories prepared by insightful writers. These authors have tried according to their best ability, to summarize as they see them the requirements of normality, health or maturity. They do so on the grounds of extensive experience. As we survey these inventories we are struck both by their verbal differences and by an underlying congruence of meaning that no one has yet succeeded fully in articulating. Here again the philosopher may balk at accepting consensus, and yet he would do well to check his own private reasoning against the conclusions of others no less competent, and probably more clinically experienced, than he.

viii. He would do well, I think, to explore the goals of psychotherapy as stated or implied in leading therapeutic systems. If he were to comb the writings of behaviouristic therapists, for example, he might reasonably conclude that *efficiency* (the ability to cope with problems) is the principal goal; in Zen therapy, by contrast, the stress seems to be on restored *cohesion* with the group. Non-directive therapy clearly prizes the goal of *growth*; the desideratum for Goldstein, Maslow, and Jung is *self-actualization*; for Fromm *productivity*; for Frankl and the logotherapists *meaningfulness* and *responsibility*. Thus each therapist seems to have in mind a preponderant emphasis which, in terms of value theory, constitutes for him a definition of the good way of life and of health for the personality. While the emphasis differs and the labels vary, still there seems to be a confluence of these criteria. Taken together they remind us of the tributaries to a vast river system, none the less unified for all their differences of source and shape. This confluence is a factor that no moralist can afford to overlook.

ix. Finally the distinction between the anabolic and catabolic processes in the formation of personality represents a fact of importance. Instead of judging merely the end-product of action, perhaps the moralist would do well to focus his attention upon the processes by which various ends are achieved. Conceivably the moral law could be written in terms of strengthening anabolic functions in oneself and in others whilst fighting against catabolic functions.

It is true that the preferred method of moral philosophy is to work "from the top down." Apriorism and reason are the legitimate tools of philosophy. Up to now this method has yielded a wide array of moral imperatives, including the following: *so act that the maxim of thy action can become a universal law; be a respecter of persons; seek to reduce your desires; harmonize your interests with the interests of others; thou are nothing, thy folk is everything; thou shalt love the Lord thy God with all thy heart, and with all thy soul, and with all thy mind . . . and thy neighbour as thyself.*

We have no wish to impede this approach from above, for we dare not block the intuitive and rational springs of ethical theory. But I would say—and this is my point of chief insistence—that each of these moral imperatives, and all others that have been or will be devised, can and should be tested and specified with reference to the various forms of psychological analysis that I have here reviewed. By submitting each imperative to psychological scrutiny we can tell whether men are likely to comprehend the principle offered; whether and in what sense it is within their capacity to follow it; what the long-run consequences are likely to be; and whether we find agreement among men in general and among therapists and other meliorists that the imperative is indeed good.

One final word. My discussion of the problem of normality and abnormality has in a sense yielded only a niggardly solution. I have said, in effect, that the criterion we seek has not yet been discovered; nor is it likely to be discovered by psychologists working alone, nor by philosophers working alone. The cooperation of both is needed. Fortunately today psychologists are beginning to ask philosophical questions, and philosophers are beginning to ask psychological questions. Working together they may ultimately formulate the problem aright and conceivably solve it.

In the meantime let me state it as my opinion that the work I have reviewed in this paper represents a high level of sophistication, far higher than that which prevailed a short generation ago. Psychologists who in their teaching and counselling follow the lines now laid down will not go far wrong in guiding personalities toward normality.

REFERENCES

Allport, G. W. *Personality: A Psychological Interpretation*, New York: Henry Holt, 1937, Chap. 8.

Barron, F. *Personal Soundness in University Graduate Students.* (Publications of Personnel Assessment Research, No. 1.) Berkeley: California Univ. Press, 1954.

Cited by C. Hall and G. Lindzey. *Theories of Personality*, New York: John Wiley, 1957, pp. 492–496.

Halmos, P. *Towards a Measure of Man: the Frontiers of Normal Adjustment*, London: Routledge & Kegan Paul. 1957.

Maslow, A. H. *Motivation and Personality*, New York: Harper, 1954, Chap. 12.

Shoben, E. J., Jr. "Toward a concept of the normal personality," *Amer. Psychologist*, 1957, *12*, 183–189.

Wolff, W. *The Threshhold of the Abnormal*, New York: Hermitage House, 1950, pp. 131 f.

24

Basic Concepts for
a Psychology of Personality

HENRY A. MURRAY

At the present time the greatest interference to the well-being of psychology is the separation and opposition of radically different schools of thought, each of them blind to the need for an idealogy which is general enough to include them all. The schoolmen are unwilling to acknowledge that the application of their theories is limited to the particular aspect of things which they have chosen to investigate. We are thinking particularly of the Introspectionists, the Behaviorists, and the Psychoanalysts with their respective intellectual provincialisms. These schools differ not only in their opinions as to the proper subject matter and methodology of psychology, but they are at odds—and this is the most unfortunate feature —in respect to basic theories and hypotheses. The existence of utterly different terminologies based upon different metaphysical assumptions prevents communication and understanding and tends to promote futile antagonisms. It is as with the blind men— in the fable of the blind men and the elephant—each of whom stoutly affirmed that the part of the elephant which he held in his hands—the trunk, the tail, an ear, a tusk, or a leg—was *the elephant*.

If it is true—as it appears to be—that each school has made important contributions to our knowledge of human nature, then what is required is a new scheme which will be comprehensive enough to include, as subsidiary concepts, the best of the existing formulations. The time is ripe for a unifying theory of this sort—one which will provide psychologists with a common final goal, and by so doing allow for the proper orientation of the special fields.

From H. A. Murray, Basic Concepts for a Psychology of Personality. *Journal of General Psychology*, 1936, 15, 241–266. Reprinted by permission of author and publisher.

We have used the expression "psychology of personality" in the title out of deference to custom. It is a clumsy, tautological phrase and we propose that "personology" be substituted for it.

DEFINITIONS OF PSYCHOLOGY

Psychology has been defined by some authors as the science of consciousness, mind, or soul, by others as the science of action or conduct, and, finally, by many modern writers as "the science of both consciousness and behavior" (Bridges, 1930, p. 6). What is the implication? Is psychology, in fact, two sciences, each with its own terminology and conceptual scheme? At first blush it would seem so, since action, as such, is describable only in physical terms—movements in space characterized by a certain velocity and duration—and consciousness, as such, is describable only in physical terms —images, feelings, volitions, and so forth. This impression of the incommensurability of the two kinds of phenomena commonly considered to be within the domain of psychology is reenforced by an examination of the history of methodology and theory. Introspectionism, by confining itself to the detailed analysis of conscious perceptions, has almost completely neglected behavior; whereas Behaviorism, in an attempt to be purely objective, has eliminated consciousness.

Now, to common sense, it seems that conscious processes and behavior must be related, since, to take one example, the conscious intention to make a particular movement is so invariably followed by *just* that movement. Everyday speech, indeed, by assuming causal connections between inner and outer events, is an implicit avowal of this belief. Behavior, an objective phenomenon, is explained by reference to certain desires and intentions; and perception, a subjective phenomenon, is explained by reference to physical objects. Common sense, however, is unable to justify its faith by explaining, in terms which satisfy the sophisticated, just how the two sets of phenomena are related. Thus, the mind-body problem has recurrently arisen.

BEGINNING AT THE BEGINNING

Though it may be some irrational bias which inclines us to agree with the currently expressed opinion that psychology should commence with the objective study of behavior, this decision seems reasonable, since people can most readily agree in their descriptions of objective phenomena and it is always well to begin at a point where agreement is possible. In studying behavior, moreover, and in attempting to construct concepts to explain it, the psychologist aligns himself with other students of nature—physicists, chemists, and physiologists. He comes to take his proper place as a general biologist between the zoologist and the sociologist. Finally, since the enjoyable existence of living organisms is largely determined by their actions, we being interested in the former, must be interested in the latter. This initial orientation is, I believe, so correct that one should be suspicious of any scheme for representing human nature which does not give a thorough account of behavior.

THE NECESSITY FOR THE FORMULATION OF CENTRAL PROCESSES

Some Behaviorists have maintained that a science of human nature can be built upon the familiar stimulus-response formula without reference to central processes within the brain of the subject. By this simplification the investigator can maintain an utterly objective, positivistic attitude. But a man who holds this opinion is disregarding the plain fact that the actual stimulus is something which affects the brain of the subject, not something which affects his own brain; in other words, what the subject perceives is usually different from what the investigator perceives. Furthermore, it becomes clear, when the psychologist attempts to explain the simplest conditioned reflex, that central processes must be included. In the classical experiment of Pavlov, for instance, one cannot explain the dog's salivation when a bell is sounded without referring in some way to the original food stimulus with which the bell was temporally associated. Since the food, as such, is not present, and, since in describing an occurrence one cannot include factors which are not within the field, one is forced to assume the activity of an enduring impression, or *trace*, of the food within the animal's brain, and in so doing to take central processes into account. Another and more important common phenomenon which calls for the conceptualization of dominant central processes is the occurrence of long-continued single trends of activity characterized by motor movements of the most diverse sort. Since a description of the overt movements, as such, will not explain the sustained tendency—which may occur even when specific stimuli are absent—to achieve certain objective effects by one means or another, the psychologist must refer to some central directional process which persists—in most instances, at least—until the goal is attained. The Behaviorists, by limiting themselves to the study of simple reflexes and action patterns, are able—without too gross error—to exclude consciousness and to minimize the importance of integrating or motivating cephalic processes. But, when they limit the field of study in this way, they then exclude what is most typically "psychological." Since this aspect of behavior cannot be neglected, and since it cannot be described in terms of motor movements, *qua* movements, we find ourselves compelled to attempt the formulation of the determining processes in the brain.

The judgment that one should seek an understanding of dominant cephalic processes harmonizes with the current organismic notion that behavior should be defined as the activity carried out by an organism-as-a-whole in making adjustments to its environment (Wheeler, 1929). Such a definition differentiates psychology from physiology—the science of subordinate or component organic processes functioning within an internal environment—and directs attention to the dynamisms of directional dominance. For, if the expression "organism-as-a-whole" means anything, it means that at any one moment numerous separable activities of the organism are harmoniously directed towards the realization of a single result. Such coordinated activity calls for a center of unifying control which, through lower centers, is connected with every part of the body. This center of dominance is certainly in the brain region.

Introspectionists, with the implicit assumption that the human being is a consciously perceptive mechanism, commonly commence their textbooks of psychology with an elaborate analysis of sensory processes and finish with a small, begrudgingly admitted section on action and personality. Men of this persuasion object to the practice of beginning with behavior and by their neglect of this subject dissociate themselves from the tradition of science. They seem to forget that the data which they obtain depend upon the proper motivation of their subjects, that perception is merely the first phase of a total stimulus-response event, and that the variables into which they analyze this phase have little to do with the functioning of the total organism. The Introspectionists, however, would undoubtedly agree that it is the activities which occur in the brain region that must be conceptualized by the psychologist.

The opinion of the extreme Behaviorists, on the other hand, is exactly the opposite. They emphasize action but they are usually disinclined to create hypothetical intra-cranial entities. Although physical scientists—to whom Behaviorists play flunkey—believe it is their business to introduce "fictional" and even unimaginable entities (cf. the ether) into their theories, Behaviorists think it is more scientific not to do so. By this refusal, however, they make a *rapprochement* with Introspectionism impossible, divide psychology into two distinct disciplines, and leave unformulated most of the phenomena of psychopathology as well as other subjective experiences—such as the fact of happiness. A psychology which on principle neglects the problem of happiness can never be more than an eccentric collection of dogmas.

THE REGNANCY

Since muscular contractions are due to the stimulation of efferent (motor) nerves, complex motor acts characterized by contractions in widely separated parts of the organism—contractions which manifest-synchronous and consecutive coordination—must be the outcome of directional processes occurring in some central region of stimulation. And since the only area to and from which all nerves lead is the brain, we must conclude that the behavior of an organism functioning as-a-whole is the result of configurated excitations in the motor areas of the brain—cortical or subcortical. It is generally held, indeed, that the system which allows the organism to act as a unit is a hierarchy of controlling processes at the summit of which is a dominant integrate—here termed the *regnancy*—to which, under the best conditions, lower centers are directly or indirectly subservient. We do not know where the *regnancy* is located, beyond the fact that it is within the brain. There are reasons to suppose that it moves about the brain. It may be something in the nature of an electrical field, or electronic matrix, interpenetrating like a web the entire cephalic region, involving first one area and then another. It traverses, perhaps, the empty spaces of the brain. But, wherever it may be located, the proper aim of the psychologist is the conceptualization of its constitution. The regnancy may, at this point, be defined as the organized aggregate of mutually dependent processes which momentarily determines the functioning of the organism "as a unit." Thus, the regnancy dominates the activity of the organism when this activity has a "total" character. The principles of Gestalt psychology are applicable here, since, when the organism is functioning economically, one cannot conceive of a regnancy except as a temporally configurated whole. The conjunctivity of regnancy, however, should not be overemphasized, since there are many states—conflict, emotional panic, dissociation, schizophrenia—which are undoubtedly accompanied by division and disorganization of the central processes. For the sake of clarity, however, it is best to begin by considering only integrated (conjunctive) regnancies.

So far we have spoken only of the motor phase of the regnancy, but it must be obvious that the sensory phase is an equally important part of it. Furthermore, the regnancy includes integrative (cognitive) and emotive (affective) processes, all of which may be regarded as electrical in nature. Finally, since the processes of the regnancy occur within or through a fluid medium, to explain certain states one must take account of the chemical constitution of the blood and lymph in the cephalic region. The importance of this factor is suggested by what is known about the effect upon cerebral activity of internal secretions, drugs, anaesthetics, and changes in oxygen tension.

Since the regnancy differs from moment to moment, one must conceive of a person's life as a temporal series of regnancies, each of which—though related in various ways to preceding and succeeding regnancies—is unique. This is a conception which stresses dominant functional activity—the most actual *thing* being a single regnancy. As Whitehead puts it:

> In speaking of any actual individual, such as a human being, we must mean that man in one occasion of his experience. Such an occasion, or act, is complex and therefore capable of analysis into phases and other components. It

is the most concrete actual entity, and the life of man from birth to death is a historic route of such occasions. These concrete moments are bound together into one society by a partial identity of form, and by the peculiarly full summation of its predecessors which each moment of the life-history gathers into itself. The man-at-one-moment concentrates in himself the color of his own past, and he is the issue of it. The "man in his whole life history" is an abstraction compared to the "man in one such moment" (Whitehead, 1927, p. 27).

According to our conception the processes which go to make up personality should be "placed" in the brain. Personality is not the constitution of the entire body. Though we know that various physiological activities may modify personality profoundly they are, strictly speaking, "outside" of personality. They belong to its *internal* environment just as war, which may also modify personality, belongs to its *external* environment. This view is in direct contrast to Menninger's notion that personality "means the individual as a whole, his height and weight and loves and hates and blood-pressure and reflexes; his smiles and hopes and bowed legs and enlarged tonsils. It means all that anyone is and all that he is trying to become" (Menninger, 1930).

THE REGNANCY AND CONSCIOUSNESS: THE DOUBLE-ASPECT THEORY

The regnancy is by definition the momentary cephalic process which is initiated by incoming excitations (from within and without the body) and terminated (as a rule) by outgoing activations. Sensory and motor processes are said to be regnant when it can be shown that they influence the course of the total organism.

From this it would seem that there must be a close relationship between the regnancy and a moment of conscious experience. For everyday experience and the experiments of psychophysicists have demonstrated that under ordinary circumstances there is an absolute correlation between the sufficient stimulation of sensory end-organs and the subjective experience of perceiving, as well as between the subjective experience of conation (striving) and the overt movements of the body. It is the verdict of experience, moreover, that in many instances particular bodily movements are the necessary outcome of particular perceptions. Thus, perception seems to be correlated with incoming regnant excitations and conation seems to be correlated with outgoing regnant activations. Anybody can perform this experiment: strive to flex the right thumb and observe the result. Under average conditions there will be an invariable temporal relationship between the awareness of striving and the movement of the thumb. This experiment— which is as valid as any that can be done in science—leads to the conclusion that striving is coexistential with activations at the motor pole of the regnancy.

These and other such facts suggest the conclusion that consciousness is an attribute of at least some regnant processes, and that the determining seat of consciousness is in the brain—a conclusion which is reinforced by a mass of data showing the close relationship between changes in the brain and changes in conscious states. Thus, we arrive at the proposition that subjective realities and objective realities—that is to say, physical processes in the brain which would be objective realities to an experimenter, were he able to observe them—are somehow intimately related.

The best and most widely accepted solution of the mind-body dilemma is the double-aspect hypothesis. This states that a conscious experience and certain physical processes in the brain are simply two aspects of one actual event. The former represents the inner or subjective aspect—how the process appears to itself—and the latter represents the outer or objective aspect—how the process, if it could be observed, would appear to others. All mental activity, according to this notion, is associated with physical activity—let us say of an electronic nature. A change in one signifies a change in the other. This proposition, though it can neither be proved nor disproved, seems to be the most convenient working hypothesis for a psychologist to adopt. It is useful because it establishes a theoretical ground for the construction of a conceptual scheme which both groups—Introspectionists and Behaviorists alike—should be able to accept.

UNCONSCIOUS REGNANT PROCESSES

Now, the double-aspect hypothesis states that every conscious process is the subjective aspect of some regnant process, but it does not state that every regnant process has a conscious correlate. It appears, indeed, that to explain any conscious event as well as to explain any behavioral event one must take account of more variables than those which are at the moment present in consciousness. "Regarded as events," Köhler points out, "the facts and sequences of our direct experience do not, taken by themselves, represent complete wholes. They are merely parts of larger functional contexts" (Köhler, 1930). The following examples, some of which are taken from Köhler, support this opinion:

1. The perception of the "Dipper" is an immediate experience in which the form is given as-a-whole. The stars are not organized into this common shape by a conscious process. It comes to us ready made. Presumably there have been previous impressions of actual dippers which have left traces in the brain, and in the present act of perception some interaction between the memory image of a dipper and the impression from the

heavens has occurred. But this memory image is not in consciousness.

2. In the recognition of a person whom we have met once and not seen for a long time, we are frequently conscious of the interaction between the memory image and the present impression. But later, after frequent encounters, immediate recognition occurs. On such occasions, though the memory image is not in consciousness, to explain the recognition we must suppose that it is still functioning.

3. When of an evening I am conversing with a friend, I am reacting from moment to moment on the basis of a great many recognitions and suppositions which are not in consciousness. For instance, that the floor stretches out behind me—I should be anxious if there were a yawning chasm behind my chair—that I will be free to leave at a certain hour, and so forth. Such assumptions, though not conscious, are providing a time-space frame for conscious events and hence are determining their course.

4. One may pass a man in the street and immediately think: he appears anxious, as if he were about to face some ordeal. The conscious perception of the man's face as a physical schema, however, may have been so indefinite that one is utterly unable to describe the features which contributed to the apperception of his inner state.

5. When one is learning to drive an automobile, one is, at first, aware of every accessory intention and subsequent motor movement, but later, when proficiency has been attained, the details of the activity are seldom in consciousness. We must suppose, nevertheless, that ordered activations are occurring at the motor pole of the regnancy.

6. Absent-minded acts which involve movements of the body as-a-whole are performed without awareness of conations similar to those which usually precede such actions.

7. When a man is building a house, let us say, he is usually conscious from moment to moment of his intention to realize a particular subsidiary effect. Though the idea of the major effect—the image of the completely constructed house—is not in consciousness, it must be active, since each conscious conation and movement is so obviously subservient to the underlying total purpose.

These examples point to the fact that the extent of the regnancy is greater than the extent of consciousness. It is as if consciousness were the illumined region of the regnancy; as if a spotlight of varying dimensions moved about the brain, revealing first one and then another section of successive, functionally-related regnancies. The examples demonstrate, furthermore, that, since a conscious experience depends upon interrelated extra-conscious variables, it can be understood only when it is viewed as part of a larger whole. Thus, to explain a conscious event, as well as to explain a behavioral event, all the major variables of the regnancy must be known. According to this conception, then, the goal of the Introspectionists and the goal of the Behaviorists becomes the same—to determine the constitution of significant regnancies. To agree about this matter, however, the Introspectionists must accept the theory of unconscious regnant processes, and the Behaviorists must attempt, as physicists, chemists, and biologists have attempted, to conceptualize the phenomena which underlie appearances.

VARIABLES OF THE REGNANCY:
THE PROBLEM OF TERMINOLOGY

According to the double-aspect theory, if one group of experimenters tried to arrive at the constitution of the regnancy by studying behavior, and another group by studying the presentations of consciousness, the final outcome—if both attempts were successful—would be two sets of exactly equal equations, one set composed of subjectively derived symbols and the other composed of objectively derived symbols. For convenience, one or the other could be selected, and, thenceforth, it would be understood that each symbol (component, attribute, or dimension) represented *both* the subjective and the objective aspect of a single variable. Since the chances of determining the constitution of the regnancy are greatly enhanced if objective behavioral data are contemporaneously supplemented by adequate subjective reports—that is to say, if the investigator maintains the two points of view at once—and since a single set of variables, descriptive or explanatory of both consciousness and behavior, is the desired result, it might be better to decide ahead of time whether we should attempt to pattern our hypothetical formulae upon the existing objective (physical or physiological) constructs or upon the existing subjective (psychological) constructs.

The student of behavior has for his data the records of the physical movements of organisms and the objective effects which they achieve. He starts, in other words, in the domain of physics; and so, when he attempts to develop explanatory concepts for what he has observed, he turns, quite naturally, to the facts and theories of neurophysiology. Now, it happens that neurophysiologists have discovered that the mechanistic theories handed down to them by the physicists of the nineteenth century are quite adequate to explain the characteristics of the isolated organic processes —such, for instance, as the nerve impulse—which they have made it their business to investigate. Consequently, the psychologist may be inclined to adopt the language of neuroanatomy and of neurophysiology, and, believing himself firmly grounded upon the fundamental sciences, construct a mechanistic scheme to explain what happens between the time the stimulus is received and the response given. Thus, he may come to talk about stable nerve connections, synaptic facilitation, sensitization of nerve paths, chronactic indices, and so forth. Facts of this sort are undoubtedly important, but, by referring to them alone, one is utterly unable to account for the novel, complex, adaptive, motor, and verbal acts of human subjects.

Neurophysiologists have not yet attempted the almost impossible task of studying the physical aspect of regnant processes, though these were suggested as worthy of investigation as long ago as 1879 by St. George Mivart:

> But as each living creature is a highly complex unity—both a unity of body and also a unity of force, or a synthesis of activities—it seems to me that we require a distinct kind of physiology to be devoted to the investigation of such syntheses of activities as exist in each kind of living creature. I mean to say that just as we have a physiology devoted to the several activities of the several organs, so we need a physiology specially directed to the physiology of the living body considered as one whole, that is, to the power which is the function, so to speak, of that whole, and of which the whole body in its totality is the organ. In a word, we need a physiology of the individual (Mivart, 1879, p. 223).

If neurophysiologists turned their attention to the study of regnant processes, they would soon discover what modern physicists have demonstrated when dealing with their own data, namely, that mechanistic theories are not applicable. But, whether this is strictly true or not, the fact remains that no adequate physical concepts to describe the regnancy have been devised by Behaviorists, physiologists, or physicists. And so we must turn to the presentations of consciousness and consider whether the entities identified by introspection are adequate for our purpose.

Though it is usually impossible, as I have pointed out, to explain either a conscious experience or a behavioral event by limiting oneself to the elements which were, at the moment in question, within the field of awareness, it seems to be possible for fully conscious human beings, under favorable conditions, by giving attention now to one, now to another aspect of the total situation, to bring to mind most of the factors necessary for an explanation of the original event. When there is a clear presentation of the stimulus situation and there is time for the perception of the internal sensations, affections, and evoked images, a trained introspectionist may usually recognize the processes which are engendering the inclination towards a certain response. We suppose that what happens under such conditions is that elements come to the focus of attention which were just previously active though unconscious.

At this point, a much debated question presents itself: If at one moment a variable—let us say the image of a piece of food (unconditioned stimulus)—is conscious and therefore regnant, and at the next moment is unconscious though still regnant—because it causes salivation—what term shall we apply to it at the second of these two moments? There are some men who have argued that the word "image"—as well as every other consciously derived variable—applies to an element in consciousness, and that to use the term for something that is unconscious is to commit a logical fallacy. They favor the use of a term which refers to a physical entity in the brain. I find it impossible to agree with this conclusion for the following reasons:

1. By performing the classical conditioning experiment of Pavlov (bell-food-salivation) on a human subject, it may be demonstrated that the impression of the formerly perceived piece of food functions in exactly the same way—that is, it excites salivation—when it has a subjective correlate (conscious image of food), as it does when it has no subjective correlate. It is evidently the same variable in both events, and hence, if it is called an image in one instance, it should be called an image in the other—though in the latter event it should be termed an unconscious image.

2. According to the double-aspect theory, a conscious image is co-existent with a physical process. We can hardly imagine what the nature of such a physical process may be, but, for the moment, let us call it X. The image is the conscious subjective aspect of a process, the objective aspect of which is X. If this is true, it is admissible, when referring to this process, to use either term. Thus, even when X has no subjective correlate one may speak of it as an image—in this case an unconscious image.

3. The psychologists who object to this termiology would use the term "image" when X develops a subjective aspect, and some such term as neurogram when X is unconscious. We object to such a practice, however, on the grounds that one should avoid mixing symbols which refer to the subjective aspect of events with those which refer to the physical aspect. One should speak of either a neurogram throughout or an image throughout.

4. We have no way to describe the interacting trace of a previously perceived object, such as a piece of food, except in terms of organized sense perceptions. These give us objects in settings, or figures on grounds. If the impression left by a former precept is functioning unconsciously, it must still be represented in perceptual terms, for we have no others. Therefore, even if we should prefer to describe this unconscious factor by a term which refers to some hypothetical neurological entity—a neurogram, let us say—we should have to speak of it as a neurogram of a certain object in a certain setting. This would be even more illogical than referring to an unconscious image, since it is hardly conceivable that by examining the brain one could observe there photographic replicas of previously observed objects. We shall probably never wish to substitute for perceived "wholes"—chairs and tables—an account of the physiological processes engendered by them.

5. Since any concepts which can be developed to describe unconscious regnant processes must necessarily be hypothetical (convenient fictions), it is scientifically permissible to imagine such processes as having

the properties of conscious processes, if, by so doing, we provide the most reasonable interpretation of the observed facts. That the theory of unconscious psychic processes has great resolving power becomes apparent when one applies it to the heretofore mysterious phenomena of psychopathology.

The conclusion at which we arrive is this: in formulating regnant phenomena, constructs derived from subjective experience are at present more useful than those derived from physiological investigations. Consequently, we propose that the former be employed, and, for the sake of consistency, be employed throughout. Since it is proper to begin with the study of behavior—the behavior of organisms which cannot verbalize their subjective experiences as well as those that can—one must so define the regnant variables that their occurrence may be inferred on the basis of objective data alone. Thus, such symbols as "perception," "image," "conation" may be used to refer to hypothetical physical processes—the nature of which may or may not be known—and, if there is sufficient objective evidence, they may be used whether or not the processes for which they stand are accompanied by consciousness. MacCurdy, whose excellent book, *Common Principles in Psychology and Physiology*, has not been accorded sufficient attention in this country, uses the term "image," or "imaginal process," in this way. MacCurdy's definition is as follows:

An imaginal process, from the standpoint of an objective observer, is some kind of a reproduction of a specific bit of past sensory experience, which is inferred to exist from the presence of a reaction for which the specific experience would be the appropriate stimulus—this reaction not being completely accounted for by any demonstrable environmental event (MacCurdy, 1928, p. 14).

Adopting a somewhat similar point of view, Tolman (1932) uses "cognition," and other subjectively derived terms, to stand for separable determinants of behavior (regnant processes)—the activity of each of which is manifested by some particular behavior characteristic. Thus, everything that we have said about this problem of terminology is merely confirming MacCurdy and Tolman.

The physical aspects of most variables are extremely hypothetical. For, though there is considerable knowledge of the correlates of sensory experience—knowledge which Boring (1933) has so succinctly summarized —the psychophysics of efferent activations remains a relatively undeveloped field.

EVENT AND THEMA

Psychologists have always agreed that conscious experience should be analyzed into separable variables (components, attributes, or relations).

But, it is only now that some are becoming convinced not only that each of the selected variables must be considered to have an objective aspect, but also that one or more of these variables may at any time be unconscious —that is, it may determine a conscious experience or a course of action without the subject's being aware of it. Gestalt psychologists have taught us, furthermore, that our variables are not dependent entities. They are mutually dependent parts of configurated wholes, which the psychologist abstracts by analysis, and later mentally resynthesizes in order to arrive at an imaginative representation of the original totality. Though one should not exaggerate the unity of regnancies, it is best to begin by assuming that each of them is an ordered whole. We must remember that, if there were no organization, there would be no organism.

To accord with the philosophy of organism as developed by Whitehead (1929), a regnancy, I believe, should be regarded as a single, complex temporal gestalt, a "drop of experience," to use William James's phrase, which consumes, let us say, a small fraction of a second. It is one kind of "actual entity"; for a psychologist the most "real thing." Unfortunately, we are unable to observe, subjectively or objectively, the manifestations of a single regnancy. Just as perception is unable to distinguish what the new cameras reveal—for instance, the separate flashes of a single bolt of lightning—so is introspection, because of its limited span and speed of discrete awareness, unable to grasp a single regnant moment and hold it for analysis. From numberless, successive regnancies one apprehends only fragments and much of this is immediately forgotten. Consequently, one cannot deal directly with the ultimate organic units.

It seems, however, that, since successive acts, as well as successive moments of subjective experience, frequently manifest an obvious degree of functional coordination, successive regnancies must be bound together into larger temporal wholes; and, if this is true, these may be selected as our fundamental psychological units. We have only to decide upon the best criterion for distinguishing separate, single, temporal wholes. But, before attempting to do this, we should ask ourselves: what is it that organizes a single regnancy or a succession of regnancies?

The expression "functional organization" is used when significant effects are economically achieved by the harmonious coordination of a number of different parts. In the simplest case several mutually dependent processes contribute to the achievement of a single result. This is not to be taken as a manifestation of conscious purpose, but as a manifestation of a tendency towards temporary end states. It is similar to the phenomena described by the Second Law of Thermodynamics. Thus, since organization always involves a directional tendency, that is to say, a tendency to achieve certain effects, and, since it is this tendency which unifies diversities of function, a succession of regnancies may be taken as a single temporal gestalt when the same tendency recurs in (or perseverates through) each of them. According to the terminology which we have adopted, the regnant directional tendency is the immediate result of a *need*—a *need* being defined as a regnant tension which is evoked by the perception (conscious or unconscious) of a certain kind of internal state or external situation. The tension tends to persist and to incite effective activity until an internal state or external situation (opposite in kind to the one which stimulated it) has been arrived at. Thus, as long as a single need persists, successive regnancies will be more or less unified. Even when nothing is achieved—due to the organism's ineptitude—there is, at least, a perseveration of directional effort. The exposition of the concept of need must be postponed, but enough has been said about it, I think, to suggest the following proposition: since the organization of successive regnancies into one society is due to the operation of a single need, the two limits of such a society—a distinct, temporal gestalt—are established by the arousing and stilling, respectively, of that need. Thus, other things being equal, degree of regnant integration is a function of the intensity and protensity of an uncontested need. Since, according to our formulation, effective activity is the direct outcome of a need, we may regard the latter as the underlying, motivating force of the organism. A *mode* (action pattern)—a subordinate concept—is the means whereby a need is stilled (equilibrium is restored, the organism is "satisfied"). It is important to distinguish between these two, since approximately similar effects (need-satisfactions) are achieved by different modes, and approximately similar modes may lead to different effects.

A primary (somagenic) need is the direct resultant of the internal perception (conscious or unconscious) of a specific bodily state. This state may be aroused spontaneously, that is, it may be the product of a succession of physiological events, or it may—during its *ready* period—be excited by the (external) perception of appropriate incentives. In most cases we should start with the internally evoked need rather than with the external stimulus, since (1) self-generated activity is the primary "givenness" of all living organisms, (2) a need may be internally generated in the absence of external objects—the organism may search for food, (3) the selective perception of some rather than other external incentives is due to the operation of a particular need, and (4) even an unconditioned external incentive does not evoke specific regnant tension unless the need in question is in a state of readiness—a replete organism does not respond to food. Since we know, however, that the organism usually has many potential needs in readiness, which one of these is stimulated will be decided by what incentives are present in the environment. Furthermore, the characterization of the incentive which arouses or is sought by the need serves as a further characterization of the need itself. Finally, we know that the frequency, the characteristic intensity and protensity, as well as the integration of recurrent needs may be temporarily or permanently modified by manipulating the environment. Consequently, the discovery of possible stimulus-response patterns is a matter of prime importance.

The special task of the student of motivation, then, becomes the discovery of all the separable variables (components, attributes, and dimensions) which may combine to determine the trend of behavior as well as those which may combine to determine the specific modes employed. As Lewin puts it: "The *cause* of the events is the *relationship between the parts of the situation as dynamical facts,* and a complete characterization of these dynamical facts would be a complete analysis" (Lewin, 1933). It may be suggested that this is the major problem of general psychology.

To accord with these considerations the fundamental dynamic unit might be said to consist of a single stimulus-response pattern. Unfortunately this convenient terminology does not suit us, since the term "stimulus" usually stands for a single excitation, and "response" for a single reflexive contraction. In our dynamic unit the stimulus is not to be understood as a single sense-impression, structured or unstructured. For, just as we have argued that the fundamental response is not the immediate specific act, *qua* act, but the trend of activity as manifested by the succession of subsidiary effects achieved by many different acts, so also do we argue that stimuli usually appear objectively as an ordered succession of related impressions, that is, as a stimulus-gestalt which may be taken as-a-whole. The successive single stimuli are organized as a totality either because they "mean" the same thing or because they represent different aspects of the same thing—they may be words, for instance, spoken by an object, words which manifest a single, persisting attitude—or because they represent harbingers, agency objects, or pathways prospective of certain consequences if approached, manipulated, avoided, or otherwise responded to. For such a stimulus-gestalt we shall employ the term press.[1]

Thus, instead of using the phrase "stimulus-response pattern" we shall refer to a "press-need (p-n) pattern." [2] The stimulus-response pattern is adequate for reflexes (fixed relations), but when, as is usually the case, it is a matter of complex behavior, we must use the p-n formula. As a rule, a p-n occurrence may be analyzed into numberless subsidiary stimulus-response connections, but what is important to note is that the latter will usually differ according to the nature of the press-need relations, a fact which proves the subsidiary dependence of the former.

Thus, the limits of a temporal gestalt are usually set by the duration of the press-need combination rather than by the duration of the need alone. A succession of regnancies which forms a temporal gestalt of this

---

[1] As a plural form we select "press" (rather than "presses").

[2] A need may be either exopsychic—directly achieving physical or social effects in the environment—or endopsychic—achieving internal psychical effects (such as creating imaginal or verbal reconstructions of emotional experience, solving intellectual problems, arriving at judgments of value, constructing conceptual schemes, resisting temptation, developing will power, and so forth). In the present discussion, however, I have limited myself to the consideration of exopsychic needs, and I shall continue to do so.

kind—a complex series of processes coordinated and limited by the endurance of the combination of a single press (dynamically related series of perceptions) and a single need (regnant directional tension)—will be called an *event*. Since the perceptions of the subject usually correspond to the perceptions of the investigator, and since the activity of exopsychic needs is usually manifested by a particular trend of overt action, the word *event* may be conveniently, though loosely, used to designate an objective occurrence or episode—for instance a single subject-object interaction. An event, then, is any actual, concrete occurrence which has a simple p-n structure. Since there are many possible presses and many needs, there are an even greater number of press-need combinations (kinds of events). The term which has been selected to designate the particular press-need combination is *thema*—*thema* being defined as the dynamical (p-n) structure of an event. A *thema* also includes a reference to the outcome of the subject-object interaction, expressed in terms of degrees of satisfaction or dissatisfaction (success or failure) for the subject. Thus, a person's life may be dynamically formulated as a succession of more or less interrelated *themas* —some of them recurrent and typical, others occasional and critical.

When nothing is known of the press, or the press is merely the usual environment, the *thema* will consist merely of the subject's initiating need. When, on the other hand, only the press is known or the press is of sole importance—something happens, or an object does something and the subject merely experiences it or adapts himself to it—the *thema* is constituted by the press alone. In representing an event, the symbol "p" is used as a prefix before the word which characterizes the environmental press (incitement or reaction), but no symbol is attached to the word which characterizes the subject's need (initiation or response). In events which involve two human beings the press may be appropriately described in terms of the object's action (manifest need). Thus: Robbery → pPunishment → Atonement th signifies that the subject stole something, was punished by the object, and then, later, atoned for his act. Events which are merely phantasied or dreamt are differentiated by enclosing the *thema* within square brackets and putting the abbreviation "ph" before them: ph [pPursuit (Monster) → Flight → pCapture]. It is a great mistake to suppose that one can arrive at a satisfactory understanding of personality by limiting oneself to the observation of overt behavior. Inner states are facts of experience and as much a part of personality as overt actions. Our own procedure is to make a distinction between *latent* and *manifest* aspects of personality.

The press is named in terms of its common *signification*—its usual, socially-accepted (objective) meaning. In this context "meaning" refers to the "bearing" of the press upon the enjoyable existence of most subjects. The meaning which the subject gives the press is indicated by his response. It may be a special, private (subjective) meaning. If, in any instance, it is necessary to represent the strength of a press or the force of a need, this may be done by the use of a number [from a 0 (zero) to 5 (five) scale] placed after the term, thus: pDanger 2, or Aggression 4, and so forth.

ANALYSIS AND CLASSIFICATION OF EVENTS

If personology is ever to become a systematic discipline, it must begin with an analytical description and classification of its subject matter. If, as we have suggested, psychological events form the subject matter of personology, then it is these which must be analyzed and classified. This is a methodological step which other sciences—chemistry, zoology, and botany —have had to take, and there is no reason to believe that personology can avoid it. If this opinion is correct, we must analytically describe events and then mentally separate those which are dissimilar and aggregate those which are similar. Each aggregate will manifest a uniformity—a uniformity which must then be defined and named. This will form the basis of a classification.

Each event may be analyzed (described) in a variety of ways. It depends upon what kinds of attributes, or variables, are shown to be significant. The mode of analysis which we have suggested—by which an event is differentiated in terms of a particular press-need combination—may be termed *thematical*. What could be called a *structural* analysis would distinguish and measure such general variables as reactivity (speed of response), tempo (rate of functioning), intensity (force of response), protensity (endurance of response), conjunctivity (coordination of response), and so forth. Together with "emotionality" these are considered by some psychologists to be variables of *temperament* [F. H. Allport (Allport & Vernon, 1930), Bloor, and others]. McDougall, on the other hand, calls them variables of *temper*. There are other modes of analysis, some of which will have to be simultaneously employed in order to obtain an adequate representation of a personality, but this a matter which falls outside the compass of present considerations.

THE ORDER OF PERSONOLOGICAL VARIABLES

It will be noted that a dynamical analysis yields variables of a high order—a kind of press and a kind of need, each of which is necessarily a rather ill-defined, complex, abstract entity. For in an actual event the press is the product of innumerable, nameless low-order variables, and the need is objectified by action patterns which may be analyzed into countless contributing modes. A concrete press, for instance, might be the sudden encountering in the wilderness of a grizzly bear facing the subject a few feet away—the subject being on foot and without a gun. This might be designated "pDanger (Wild Animal)." If the encounter were less sudden, if it occurred near a convenient retreat, if the bear were tame or a cub or a black bear or chained or in a cage or a long distance away or looking in the opposite direction, if the man were armed or in an automobile, the press might be different. It might no longer be "pDanger." Likewise, the response to pDanger might be the need for Security, but what one would actually observe would be a man climbing a tree—an action which could be analyzed into a vast number of extensions, flexions, rotations, abductions, and adductions of both limbs.

It is the business of general psychology to study these low-order variables. They are important determining factors, but they do not fall within the domain of personology.[3] If personology stopped to analyze every event into its molecular parts, it would never get on with its proper business— the representation of personality as-a-whole. It is a general principle in science that the subject matter of each discipline demands concepts which are directly applicable to its own level of complexity. The concrete phenomena should be immediately illumined by the variables employed. Any amount of analysis is permissible, but it must be shown how the low-order entities thus disclosed were combined to form the high-order entities originally distinguished. In applying this principle to the matter at hand, we should say that the personologist has to deal with the reception in the regnancy of a pattern of afferent processes originating in a press and the excitation there of a pattern of efferent processes to form a trend, each pattern taken as a single variable. It is the psychophysicist or psychophysiologist who busies himself with the details of sensory and motor processes. The variables of the personologist are complex products of numberless determinants, which is one of the many reasons why they can never be more than inaccurate generalities.

THE REPRESENTATION OF PERSONALITY

If the *thematical* mode of analysis can be made efficient and the most important *themas* are defined and named, it may be feasible abstractly to represent a person's life in terms of successive *themas*. This abstract biography, or *psychograph*, would resemble a musical score. It would show what differentiations and developments occurred with age and also what *themas* were most frequently repeated during any particular period. Presumably

---

[3] General Psychology attempts to discover the changes in the group (or majority) response which occur when the environment is systematically modified, whereas Differential Psychology (McDougall's term), or Personology (our term), takes note of the differences between individual responses to the same environment. It must be obvious that the two points of view are complementary to one another.

such a graph would have a recognizable time-structure. For just as each event is organized within itself, so also are successive events organized in respect to each other—at least to some extent.

These considerations suggest—as Whitehead (1927) has pointed out—that there are three possible meanings for the notion of a particular personality: (1) the configuration of the regnancies during one event in a subject's life—the most concrete meaning, (2) the historic route of such configurations from birth to death, and (3) the most commonly repeated configurations during any period of his existence. These may be named: momentary personality, life-time personality, and common personality, respectively. The latter, which is the most abstract, is the one which psychologists usually have in mind when they use the term "personality."

A psychograph of a life-time personality may be greatly abbreviated by omitting the *themas* which recur in the everyday experience of all people. This procedure would be in accord with definitions of personality based upon idiosyncrasy: Personality "consists in those attributes which differentiate it from other individuals" (Ritter, 1929), is that "combination of behaviour forms in the individual . . . which distinguish that individual from others of a group" (Yoakum, 1924), is "the organized system, the functioning whole or unity, of habits, dispositions and sentiments that mark off any one member of a group as being different from any other member of the same group" (Tolman, 1932).

As important as the recognition of simple and complex *themas* is the recognition of the change of *themas* and the change of thematic relations with age. This involves a *developmental analysis*, which calls for a separate set of variables.

Common experience and research have shown that many of the press in a person's life are not merely thrust upon him. They are searched for or selected. Dominant needs drive him towards certain situations and away from others. There is, in other words, a phantasy, plan, or purpose determining his activity which includes imaginal representations (conscious or unconscious) of the desired or undesired objects. Thus, an inner tension is usually combined with a temporal gestalt of images. Together they constitute what may be called a need-integrate. Since a need-integrate is a phantasied, wished-for event, it may be analyzed thematically. Thus, we may say that a person is motivated (consciously or unconsciously) by one or more need-*themas*. With these considerations in mind, a much briefer formulation of a personality may be arrived at if it is found that certain simple or complex *themas* recur frequently and that these may be explained by assuming the activity of an underlying need-*thema*. A widely and persistently determining need-*thema* of this kind may be called a *unity-thema*. A *unity-thema* is usually found to be the repetition of or a reaction formation to some infantile experience—usually an excessive gratification, frustration, deprivation, or trauma.

It is often illuminating to portray the life of a subject in terms of his interactions with objects of special interest. A single meeting, or a series of recurring associations between a subject and a particular object (a thing, an animal, a human being, or an institution), may be called a *relational*. Since an enduring relational may be represented as a sequence of constituent *themas*, relationals are convenient foci for the organization of thematical material.

This, in brief, is our tentatively adopted procedure for the analysis and representation of the dynamical constitution of a human being. To those who complain that there are hundreds of distinguishable *themas*, and to describe them all would be a Herculean task, our answer would be that until the task is performed the science of personology will be adrift.

SUMMARY

In the present communication I have suggested that the disciplined study of human nature—personology—urgently requires a plan of procedure which is founded upon an adequate conceptual scheme. For research that is unenlightened by basic theory tends to be haphazard, irrelevant, and wasteful. This conviction has led to the proposal of the following tentative hypotheses: (1) The processes which are of final interest to the psychologist are those which organize the experience and control the behavior of living organisms. (2) In higher forms these processes occur in the brain region—at the top of a hierarchical system of dominant nerve centers. (3) It is these organizing and controlling cephalic processes which the psychologist must attempt to conceptualize. (4) The apparently continuous stream of processes is made up of discontinuous, rapidly succeeding occurrences. If this is not strictly correct, it is at least permissible for theoretical purposes to divide the ceaseless flow into very small temporal units—each to be called a *regnancy*. (5) Each regnancy may be regarded as a sensorimotor propagation—a complex integrate of mutually dependent processes which endures for a fraction of a second. (6) According to the double-aspect theory—the most convenient working hypothesis for a psychologist—the constituents of the regnancy are capable of achieving consciousness. (7) To explain a conscious event as well as to explain a behavioral event, however, one must take account of more variables than are, at the moment, present in consciousness. Therefore, it is necessary to conceptualize unconscious regnant processes. (8) In formulating regnant phenomena, constructs derived from subjective experience are at present more useful than those derived from physiological investigations. It should be understood, however, that every psychological term employed refers to some hypothetical physical variable. (9) A man's life is a long history of successive regnancies, each regnancy being at once a culmination, an assimilation, and a prophecy. (10) A regnancy is an utterly hypothetical, or metaphysical, unit, since it is impossible to catch and inspect a single one of them. (11) A single regnancy is organized and successive regnancies are linked together by the endurance of a particular directional tension—to be called a *need*. (12) A need is a force which (if uninhibited) promotes activity which (if competent) brings about a situation that is opposite (as regards its relevant dynamical properties) to the one which aroused it. (13) Successive stimuli may be bound together by a similarity of signification into a single stimulus-gestalt, to be called a *press*. (14) The endurance of a certain kind of press-perception in combination with a certain kind of need organizes regnancies into a convenient temporal unit, to be called an *event*. (15) A need may be internally evoked in a pressless environment. When this happens, the persistence of the directional tension alone determines the duration of the event. (16) For a personologist an *event* is the most actual "thing" there is, and is the proper matter for analysis. (17) The dynamical structure of an event is given by the particular press-need combination which is exemplified. This is called its *thema*. (18) Endopsychic events and pure phantasies of exopsychic events should be recognized. These also have their *themas*. (19) A thematical (dynamic) analysis is merely one of several different modes of describing an event. (20) An abstract biography, or *psychograph*, may be written in terms of the characteristic *themas* and thematic relations occurring during each stage of a subject's development. (21) A single meeting, or a series of recurrent associations between a subject and a particular object (a thing, an animal, a human, or an institution), is to be called a *relational*. An enduring relational may be analyzed into its constituent events. The principal relationals may be taken as the basis for a psychograph.

REFERENCES

Allport, G. W., & Vernon, P. E. The field of personality. *Psychol. Bull.*, 1930, 27, 677–730.

Bridges, J. W. *Psychology, normal and abnormal.* New York: Appleton, 1930. Pp. 552.

Boring, E. G. *The physical dimensions of consciousness.* New York: Century, 1933. Pp. 251.

Köhler, W. The new psychology and physics. *Yale Rev.*, 1930, 19, 560–576.

Lewin, K. Vectors, cognitive processes, and Mr. Tolman's criticism. *J. Gen. Psychol.*, 1933, 8, 318–345.

MacCurdy, J. T. *Common principles in psychology and physiology.* London: Cambridge University Press, 1928. Pp. xvii + 284.

Menninger, K. A. *The human mind.* New York: Knopf, 1930. Pp. xiv + 447.

Mivart, S. G. Address to the British Association. 1879. Reprinted in *Essays and Criticisms* (Vol. 2). London, 1892.

Ritter, W. E. Individual and person. *Amer. J. Sociol.*, 1929, *35*, 271–274.

Schoen, M. *Human nature*. New York: Harper, 1930. Pp. xviii + 504.

Tolman, E. C. *Purposive behavior in animals and men*. New York: Century, 1932. Pp. xiv + 463.

Wheeler, R. H. *The science of psychology*. New York: Crowell, 1929. P. 600.

Whitehead, A. N. *Symbolism, its meaning and effect*. New York: Macmillan, 1927. Pp. x + 88.

Whitehead, A. N. Process and reality. New York: Macmillan, 1929. Pp. xii + 545.

Yoakum, C. S. The definition of personality. *Rep. British Asso. Adv. Sci.*, 1924, 422.

25

Studies of Stressful
Interpersonal Disputations

HENRY A. MURRAY

Between me and the substance of all that I can say in the allotted time are several pages of writing, the contents of which may be summarized as follows:

1. A short introduction with a barely discernible thread of humor;
2. A prosaic survey of the seven major components of what some of us have called the "multiform system of assessment" which is old hat to most of you;
3. A passage in which it is pointed out that two of the essential components of this system have been grievously neglected by most psychologists in their investigations of normal personalities, one being the collection by various means of an abundance of experiential, biographical data from each subject, and the other being a serious, systematic attempt to construct a coherent formulation of each personality;
4. The Jeremiad of an aging psychologist who views with sorrow and misgivings the apparent accentuation of certain powerful forces that are keeping a multiplicity of his colleagues dissociated from the nature and experiences of actual people by binding their energies to an enthralling intellectual game played with abstract counters of dubious importance and of spurious relevance to human life.

INTEGRATION PLAN

Having been led to the belief that this dissociation, if prolonged, would seriously impede the full future development of psychology, I am eager to propose a remedy which could be instituted at numerous centers in this country on a scale that might be just sufficient to make a decisive, vital difference in the evolution of our discipline. The suggested remedy

From H. A. Murray, Studies of Stressful Interpersonal Disputations. *American Psychologist*, 1963, 18, 28–36. Copyright 1963 by the American Psychological Association and reproduced by permission of publisher and author.

consists of integrating the endeavors of experimental specialists with those of personologists engaged in a multiform assessment program. That is, instead of choosing either to learn a lot about a single area of human activity or to learn a little about a lot of areas, everybody chooses both, and can attain both by a division of interrelated labors.

There are only two rules to this integration plan, as I shall call it, the first being that all experimenters will use the same population of thoroughly assessed subjects, no matter how many other subjects they may need. The enormous advantage of this arrangement is that each experimenter, without any expenditure of his own time, will have at his disposal to help him in interpreting his findings, not only the results of other experiments, but the massive collection of data (several hundred rank orders, for example) obtained by the assessment process. The second rule—with even greater potentialities for a sophisticated science of psychology as well as for broadening the horizon of every student—calls for two series of meetings of experimentalists and personologists: one series to formulate the personality of each subject as a unit, and another series to attempt plausible explanations of the variant individual responses in each experiment taken as a unit. The aim would be to test the most promising of these plausible explanations, and in due course to attain the enviable position of being able to predict the critical reactions of each individual subject with a fair measure of accuracy and precision.

To be a little more specific, let me outline one possible version of the integration plan. First there will be four variously trained and variously experienced personologists (members or research associates of a department of psychology) who are engaged in a three-year program of intensive study of 25 preselected subjects. They will be assisted in the assessment process by second-year graduate students who will administer, as part of their technical training course, some of the simpler tests and questionnaires. Then there will be several graduate students of more advanced standing, seven in number, let us say, each of whom is planning an experiment to be performed for a PhD degree. Their interests may vary all the way from those of a physiological psychologist in search of more precise knowedge respecting the temporal correlates of marked changes in the heart rate to those of an investigator of higher mental processes who wishes to test certain propositions as to the power of a subject to recall different parts of a dyadic conversation in which he has actively participated.

Now, as it happens, a few of us at Harvard—research fellows for the most part—found that these two experimental aims and five others could be pursued in unison as interdependent parts of a single chain of linked procedures. The topics of the other five studies, each concerned with a different aspect of a stressful, two-person disputation, were as follows: (a) the determinants of variations among judges in estimating degree of anxiety and of anger; (b) personological and situational determinants of degree of anxiety and of anger; (c) personological correlates of variations of mentational and linguistic style under stress; (d) typological differences as manifested in retrospectively experiencing and reporting a stressful, verbal interaction; and (e) apperceptions and evaluations of an alter before and after meeting him and being exposed to his insulting criticisms.

Now, as partial demonstration of how researches such as these can be readily coordinated, let me outline as briefly as possible the series of techniques that was carried out by a number of us at the Annex (as I shall call our workshop in Cambridge, Massachusetts), first in 1957 with the compliance of 23 comprehensively assessed college sophomores, and then, in a more refined way, in 1960 with a comparable aggregate of 21 subjects. Imagine that you are one of these volunteer subjects.

Experimental Procedures

First, you are told you have a month in which to write a brief exposition of your personal philosophy of life, an affirmation of the major guiding principles in accord with which you live or hope to live.

Second, when you return to the Annex with your finished composition, you are informed that in a day or two you and a talented young lawyer will be asked to debate the respective merits of your two philosophies. You are given a copy of his philosophy and he is given a copy of your philosophy. You are told that a moving picture will be taken of this debate.

Third, on arriving at the Annex on the appointed day, you are given these directions: The debate will be limited to three 6-minute periods separated by two shorter silent periods, in which to rest or collect your thoughts. The first period will be for mutual orientation, for asking and answering questions, clarifying certain points. In the second period the young lawyer will present his criticisms of your philosophy and your task will be to defend it as logically as possible. In the third and final period it will be your turn to call attention to whatever weaknesses you have noted in the lawyer's philosophy. At this point you are introduced to the young lawyer, and in his company escorted to the brilliantly lighted room where the debate will take place in front of a one-way mirror and a hole in the wall for the lens of a moving picture camera with sound track. Before sitting down next to each other, the leads of a cardiotachometer (which records instantaneous heart rates and respirations) are strapped to your chest and to the lawyer's chest by Paul Gross.

Fourth, a signal is given and the discussion starts, continuing through three differentiated periods as you were told it would. In the second period, however, the lawyer's criticism becomes far more vehement, sweeping, and personally abusive than you were led to expect. The directions given to the lawyer were the same as you received, except that he was told to anger you and, adhering to a rehearsed and more or less standardized mode of attack, he will almost certainly succeed in doing this, having been successful in all the dyads we have witnessed. Dyad is the convenient four-letter word we use to refer to each of these 18-minute two-person interactions, plus four inactive periods amounting to 9 minutes, i.e., about 27 minutes in all.

Fifth, after the termination of the debate, you are taken to a room where you are left alone with the instruction to write down as much as you are able to recall of what was said by the lawyer and by yourself, word for word if possible and in proper sequence.

Sixth, as soon as you have reached the end of your memories of the verbal interactions, you are escorted to the room of an interviewer (Alden Wessman), where you are encouraged to relax, and to say what comes to mind while you relive in your imagination the dyad as you experienced it, chronologically from start to finish. When you are through with this— about 30 minutes later, let us say—you are asked certain questions designed to obtain as valid estimates as you both *can* give and *will* give of the intensity of certain variables, such as felt anxiety, felt anger, involvement in the task, liking or disliking the lawyer, respecting or disrespecting his ability or views. A final short questionnaire covering these and other points completes your set of exercises for that day. The interviewer is left with a tape recording of the whole proceeding.

At four appointed times subsequent to your participation in the stressful dyad, you will be called back to the Annex. On two occasions there will be another verbal memory test similar to the one I have described, the aim of which is to measure the percentage of different classes of speech units in the dyad that are recalled by each subject after 2 weeks and after 8 weeks. In addition to these sessions there will be two interviews, in one of which you will again be asked to relive the experience of the dyad and to report it as you go along. In the other interview, the plan of which was both conceived and executed with extraordinary cleverness by Gerhard Nielsen, you will witness and become involved in two or three showings of the sound film of your own dyad. You will see yourself making numerous grimaces and gestures of which you were unconscious at the time, and you will hear yourself uttering incongruent, disjunctive, and unfinished sentences. You are likely to be somewhat shocked by your performance and will be moved to identify with yourself as you were feeling and thinking during those stressful moments; and when the experimenter, *this* experimenter, stops the film at critical points, and asks you what you associate with this and that physiognomic movement or with this and that verbal expression, you are likely to become uncommonly communicative and your free associations may lead you back to childhood memories. Counting the other two reliving interviews and the three memory sessions, you will spend about 8 hours all told trying to recapture various aspects of those 18 minutes under stress.

I have devoted more minutes than I can well afford to this account of how we secured reports of your subjective experience of the dyad as a whole and in detail, because nothing more about the phenomenology of it all will be said this morning, and I wanted to assure you that we considered the covert, inner aspect of that event as essential and revealing as its overt, outer aspect.

Raw data. The dyad in which you participated has perished as an event in time and you are through with it and we with you, in a sense and for a while. But we are in no sense through with the imperishable data pertinent to that event which you have left behind with us, the nature of which I have already briefly indicated: (*a*) a cardiotachometric tracing of your heart and respiration rates, (*b*) a sound film portraying your physical expressions and your verbal interactions with the lawyer, (*c*) a typed record of the exchange of words, (*d*) a tape recording of the debate giving both voice and words, and (*e*) a series of typed protocols of everything that you said about the dyad as you retrospectively relived it. So far as I know, these interrelated temporal records of your discussion are more precise and more complete than those of any other dyadic event in human history. But *cui bono?* As they stand they are nothing but raw data, meaningless as such; and the question is what meaning, what intellectual news, can be extracted from them?

CERTAIN METHODOLOGICAL PRINCIPLES

Besides presenting a plan for coordinating the aims and efforts of experimental specialists and personological generalists, and besides describing a series of procedures as an example of how seven different experimental projects can be coordinated, I had another purpose for this paper to which I shall now attend, namely, to set forth a few of the strategic methodological principles, or aims, which guided the ordination (designing, planning) of our interlocked techniques. These principles will be illustrated by references to what we have learned so far regarding the determinants of variations of the heart rate during a dyadic verbal transaction of varying stressor potency.

1. *Make the experimental conditions as natural as possible.* Although some degree of artificiality is unavoidable in the design of an experiment, we have assumed (without unequivocal evidence) that the wanted range of emotional, conational, and mentational involvement of the subjects (and hence sufficient elevations of the heart rate) is more frequently obtained when the experimental conditions (the directions if any, the setting, the successive stimulus situations, etc.) are naturalistic

(i.e., comparable to those that occur, commonly or exceptionally, in everyday life) and, conversely, that the degree of such involvement is generally less when artificiality is conspicuous and a subject has reason to say to himself, "this is nothing but an experiment, an attempt to show that I can be excited by these means." We have also assumed that the reactions of a subject (including changes of his heart rate) will be less natural (less representative of those that occur in everyday life) if his freedom of action is impeded, either, say, by strapping him to an array of instruments and telling him not to move, or by providing him with no opportunity for effective mental action, no problem to solve, or no way of altering the course of events by verbal means; or by limiting each of the subject's responses to a mere choice between two or more predetermined alternatives, instead of expecting him to *compose* adequate responses. It is not unlikely that the change of heart rate after stimulation varies in direction or degree according to whether a subject is set (*a*) to inhibit or (*b*) to actuate, either all impulses or impulses of a certain class.

As to the naturalness of our experimental conditions, it may be said that heated arguments are common in the ordinary course of social events and dyadic discussions before a camera are daily occurrences on TV programs; but that an unwanted and unnecessary degree of artificiality was introduced in most of the dyads by the suddenness, intensity, and irrationality of the lawyer's criticisms in the second of the active phases of the dyad.

2. *Aim at a temporal, holistic model of the observed event by obtaining synchronized recordings of the occurrence and intensity of each of the most influential participating variables.* "Holistic model" in this sentence means (*a*) a sufficiently complete model *of* the whole (entire) event, one which includes all parts (variables) that are of noteworthy relevance and significance, and (*b*) a model of the event *as* a whole, one which represents the interdependence of the parts (variables) and in so doing exhibits whatever degree of unity or disunity may prevail. Pertinent to this principle is our assumption that variations in the heart rate are determined by the interaction of several different variables. The importance of synchronized temporal records of the occurrence and intensity of each of the relevant variables is obvious, since only in this way can one discover what intrasubject, sequential (cause and effect), or concomitant relationships among the variables recur with dependable regularity. Furthermore, we should not lose sight of the basic tenet that time is an inherent component or attribute of every process and that the history of an event *is* the event.

In charting changes in the intensity of a variable, such as anxiety or anger, or changes in the heart rate or speech rate, a good deal may depend on the duration of the time unit that is represented by a single figure (the average of all measures obtained during that temporal segment). In representing changes in heart rate, for example, the choice of a short micro time unit of 5 seconds (with one point indicating the average interval between six successive beats if the rate is 60 beats per minute) will generally eliminate the effects of respiration (occurring at the rate of roughly 12 a minute); and a choice of a large micro time unit of 30 seconds will generally result in the obliteration of the effects of gross muscular motility if the frequency and magnitude of these movements remain constant; and the choice of a large macro time unit of 6 minutes will obliterate the effects of changes of stimulation during the course of that phase, and so forth. Some of these points will be demonstrated later.

3. *Assume that every psychological variable is a hypothetical (theoretical) construct, the activity of which can be inferred only on the basis of one or more of its subjective and/or objective manifestations.* For centuries every psychological variable was conscious by definition; but within the last half century most psychologists have come round to Freud's conception of unconscious psychic processes; and a host of psychologists have been persuaded, first of all, by Pavlov and Watson, to study organisms who are unable to report whatever awareness of interior mental experiences they may have. As a result many psychologists are now accustomed to the practice of inferring (on the basis of more or less rigorously defined criteria) the operation of imperceptible central (psychic) variables. In view of the prevalent American bias in favor of "behavioral" psychology I am strongly disposed to stress the understanding to be gained from the development of a sophisticated "experiential" psychology.

4. *Attempt to explain the reactions, especially the variant reactions of every individual subject.* We do not say that every person is unique, but say, instead, that every person is in certain very general respects like *all* other persons, in certain less general respects like *some* other persons (persons of this or that sex, age, culture, status, vocation, type, etc.), and in certain particular respects like no other person. As usual, we take note of whatever is common to all subjects, and then of whatever is common to this and to that aggregate or class of subjects, and, finally, we investigate in great detail whatever eccentric or hitherto unknown particularities are manifested by different individuals. From endeavors to understand these unique features have come the greater portion of our "new ideas." But these endeavors, I believe, would have had little chance of bearing fruit if we had had to deal with subjects whose lives and personalities were unexplored by us. Here, then, is another good reason for adhering to the practice of performing experiments only on thoroughly assessed persons.

Now, to illustrate the application of the third principle (variables as theoretical constructs), I shall present an outline of our conception of anger, and then to illustrate the second principle (synchronized temporal tracings) I shall describe one of our ways of estimating the degree of anger.

Theoretical and Operational Definition of Anger

Anger was defined as an hypothetical state of excitation in certain not-yet-definitely-localized, subcortical regions of the brain (say, in the hypothalamus and limbic systems) which, if sufficiently intense, produces various manifestations of which the following could be discriminated in our data:

1. Covert manifestations: (*a*) experienced, or felt, anger, (*b*) agressive words or images of aggressive actions invading the stream of consciousness, and (*c*) certain "emotional" qualities of the temporal structure of mentation; the avowals of all of which by the subject (at various times in the three postdyadic interviews) are ordinarily but not always modulated by some degree of inhibition (suppression).

2. Physiological manifestations: autonomic excitations, including changes of the heart rate and respiration rate as recorded on the polygraph by the cardiotachometer, the nature of which changes seems to depend on the character of the situation.

3. Overt manifestations: (*a*) physiognomic and motoric phenomena which can be seen in the silent moving picture and analyzed in great detail by means of a perceptoscope projecting one frame at a time; (*b*) verbal productions of an oppositional, rude, critical, aggressive, or insulting nature which can be read in the typed protocol; (*c*) vocal qualities, such as louder and more rapid speech which, in conjunction with the verbal productions, can be heard in the playback of the magnetic tape recording of the dyad; and, finally, (*d*) temporal patterns of these motoric, verbal, and vocal manifestations, which can be synchronously seen and heard in the sound movie in conjunction with the behavior of the alter, or lawyer; all of which manifestations of central processes are modulated to some degree by the subject's efforts to control and to conceal them.

To be complete, this scheme would have to be supplemented by the addition of physical (muscular) endeavors, such as fighting, and by further specifications here and there, for example as to the qualities of voice and flow of speech which may be recorded instrumentally, or discriminated without instruments even when one does not understand the language spoken by the subject. But these supplementations are not pertinent to our data which allows for only four completely independent sources of information (cf. 1, 2, 3a, and 3b) which may be compared in respect to their dependability as indices of central anger.

Here I shall limit myself to estimations of anger based on observations of the sound movie which combines the vocal qualities of speech with two of the independent sources of information (physiognomic movements and verbal productions). These estimates were made from moment to moment independently and simultaneously by six psychologists (Arthur Couch, Paul Gross, Kenneth Keniston, David Ricks, Bernard Rosenthal, and myself), each of whom held a dial whose movements produced tracings on a polygraph, that could be synchronized with the tracings of the heart rate, as well as with the speech units produced by the two debates.

The overt manifestations of five other, preselected psychological variables (the subject's level of anxiety, gross motility, vocal-verbal intensity, and task involvement, and the potency of the lawyer's criticisms and insults) were estimated, one by one, in a similar fashion, two of these variables by six judges and three by two judges. I shall not discuss, at this time, the question of the determinants of the unreliability of these estimates, but return to the second methodological principle that I mentioned, which calls for a temporal record of each variable, and illustrate the difference in amount of information gained between choosing a macro or a meso time unit for each point that is represented in a graph by showing two records of the heart rate, before, during, between, and after the dyadic interactions.

Figure 25-1 shows first, the average basal heart rate (74) for all subjects and then seven average dyadic heart rates plotted against time. (The average of about 12 afternoon pulse rates, as counted by each subject on different days under resting conditions, was taken as that subject's basal heart rate.) The three black circles give the average HR (absolute heart rate) for each of the periods of active verbal interchanges (a 6-minute time segment). The white circles give the average HR for each of the verbally

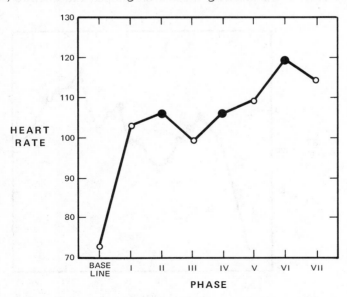

Figure 25-1. Average heart rate during stressful dyad (with seven points).

inactive periods: predyadic first, postdyadic last, and two intradyadic rest periods. Time units of this percentage of total time (about four to six minutes in this case) are called by us macro units and each circle is called a macro figure. What can we learn from this macrotemporal chart?

1. Note the relatively great elevation of the heart rate (above the average basal rate of 74) before the start of the dyad, an index of a high degree of anticipatory central excitation, and then note a similar anticipatory rise before Phase 6, the phase in which the subject had been instructed to criticize the lawyer's views.

2. Note the increase of heart rate during the transition from an overtly inactive state to an overtly active state in all three instances. Micro analyses show that this occurred in 18 of our 21 subjects.

3. Note that the average heart rate in the sixth phase, when most of the subjects were criticizing the lawyer, was considerably higher than it was in Phase 4, when they were *being* criticized.

4. Note the surprising and in-this-graph-unexplainable fact that the average heart rate in the fourth phase (when the subjects were insulted) was no higher than it was in the second phase during which the interpersonal atmosphere was friendly.

Figure 25-2 is a *meso*temporal chart which exhibits 17 successive figures, one for the first, or predyadic, phase, then one for each of 15 subphases (9 active and 6 inactive) of the dyad proper, and finally one for the

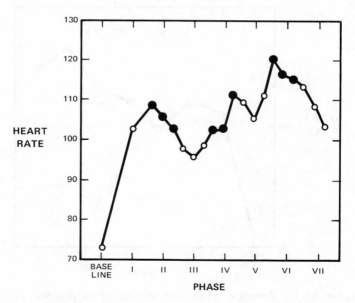

Figure 25-2.   Average heart rate during stressful dyad (with 17 points).

seventh, or postdyadic, phase. Each black circle is the average for a 2-minute time unit (instead of for a 6-minute time unit), a choice of temporal segment which certainly gives you a more intelligible picture of what generally occurred during those stressful proceedings.

1. Take note of some new information: first, the fall of the heart rate during Phase 2 and again during Phase 6, one reasonable explanation of which would be in terms of homeostatic principles, namely that an elevated heart rate always tends to fall as the person becomes habituated to the existing situation, provided the stressor potency of the situation does not increase. During the first two-thirds of Phase 4 the subjects were confronted by a series of unexpected provocations in the form of personally offensive criticisms from the lawyer, and consequently the existing HR level did not fall, but was sustained during the middle subphase and in the last phase ascended sharply. The low HR level during the first subphase of Phase 4 as compared to the level during the initial but unaggressive subphase of Phase 2 might be partly explained by the low level in the middle of resting Phase 3 (the level from which the heart rate had to rise) as compared to the higher level of Phase 1, the predyadic phase. And the lower HR level during the middle subphase of Phase 4 as compared to the level in the third subphase might be partly explained by the fact that subjects talked far less in the first two subphases of Phase 4 than they did during any other period of the dyad; since, according to our micro findings, the HR level is lower, as a rule, when subjects are listening than it is when they are talking. Another possible explanation that needs to be explored through micro analyses is that the eruption of covert anger (which came suddenly in the first subphase of Phase 4 when conditions more or less prohibited its ample expression) produced momentary increase in blood pressure (the noradrenalin effect) and a consequent decrease in the heart rate in some subjects.

2. Again note that the rate was high at the end of Phase 4, by which time most subjects had become engaged in self-defensive refutations and still higher in Phase 6 when they were both most talkative and most offensively aggressive. Taking this covariation of heart rate and vigorous verbal activity in conjunction with the fall in level during the first two-thirds of each resting period, as well as with the other pertinent facts that I have mentioned (e.g., the rise of the heart rate at the end of each of three inactive periods, and the additional rise beyond this point, in all instances, as the subject went from inaction to interaction), the data exhibited in our graphs all point to a positive correlation of the heart rate with (a) anticipated interactivity of a certain sort and (b) with the first phase of actual interactivity. After that, if the intensity level of the interactivity decreases or remains constant, the heart rate will decline; but if the intensity level increases the heart rate will rise or remain constant. Viewing these facts

within a functional frame of reference, we might say that the circulatory system of the majority of our subjects was overprepared (by nervous excitement) for Phase 2 and for Phase 6 (i.e., the subjects anticipated, consciously or unconsciously, more stressors, more demands for quick, difficult, and effective responses, than they subsequently encountered), and as they came to the realization that the situational demands were not so pressing (less than they were physiologically prepared to meet), their heart rates fell to a level that was appropriate to the apperceived current state of affairs. This well-known habituational, or homeostatic, fall of the heart rate, particularly in Phase 2, was the cause of numerous negative intrasubject correlations between heart rate and anxiety (nervous excitement); because, since the subjects were not filmed during any of the inactive periods, the judges had no grounds for inferring a high level of anxiety at the very start of the interaction. Generally speaking, the judges started Phase 2 (the first phase to be observed in the movie) at zero and moved up as signs of nervousness appeared and reappeared and their confidence in the significance of these signs became less wavering. Therefore, while the judges' tracings for anxiety were mounting ("catching up" to the subject's current emotional state) the subject's heart rate was declining. This was but one of many unexpected complications we encountered.

My first reason for showing the two graphs of average heart rate changes during the dyad was to illustrate the general principle (which applies to data such as ours) that, above an ascertainable low limit, the shorter the time segment which is represented by a single figure, the greater will be the amount of usable information to be gained by mere inspection. My second reason was to point out the suitability of the synchronized mesotemporal graphs of our major variables: They present nine opportunities for intersubject correlations between the rank orders of the average subphase intensities of the variables and eight opportunities for intrasubject correlations of their concurrently changing intensities between subphases. Besides these we have the opportunity afforded by the macrotemporal graphs for three more sets of intersubject intercorrelations and finally a set of intercorrelations based on average variable intensities for the total dyad, yielding in all 13 intersubject correlation coefficients for each pair of variables. Finally, to end this paper with a little meat to chew on, it was my intention to summarize the unexpected results of the execution, by Paul Gross and others, of some of the just-enumerated possible correlations for comparison with the information gained through a close inspection of the mesotemporal graph (Figure 25-2).

The first surprise, if not distress, was occasioned by the finding that the elevated heart rate, calculated in the manner I described earlier, was correlated to a significant degree with *none* of our major variables, in *contrast* to the absolute heart rate which correlated positively with all our "activity" variables, in two instances at the 5% level of significance. This result, which at first blush runs counter to accepted principles of measurement in physiology, constitutes a riddle for which I have no ready answer, except to report that the correlation of −.78 between basal heart rate and elevated heart rate might conceivably be the key to its solution. In any case, the average of 13 rank order correlations were significantly positive between absolute heart rate and both of our two measures of manifest drive, or need achievement, in the dyad (the apparent degree of continuous concentration and emotional-mentational-verbal energy devoted to the accomplishment of the assigned task): (*a*) *vocal-verbal intensity*, aver. +.45 (range from +.19 to +.59, with all but one over +.34); and (*b*) *task-involvement*, aver. +.42 (range from +.31 to +.56). The fact that these correlations are all positive, that they are consonant with all the data presented by the graphs, and that they make functional sense, suggests that individual differences among our subjects in respect to basal heart rate and degree of sensitivity of the neurocardiac system were not so great or influential as to cancel the possibility of demonstrating a consistent relationship between motivation and heart rate under the stressful conditions that existed in the dyads. The comparably high heart rates of surgeons while performing major operations could likewise be attributed to this functional relationship. Also positive, but to no significant degree, are the correlations between HR and (*c*) *manifest anger*, aver. +.30 (range from +.11 to +.49), and (*d*) *gross muscular motility*, aver. +.29 (range from +.16 to +.35). Most surprising was the absence of any correlation with (*e*) *anxiety*, aver. −.03 (range +.15 to −.28), and a not-yet-explained, slightly negative correlation with *press* (the alter's *vocal-verbal* intensity and *aggressiveness*), aver. −.26 (range +.04 to −.58). The averages of the intrasubject correlations were also significantly positive for absolute heart rate and vocal-verbal intensity, gross muscular motility, and task-involvement, in that order, and insignificantly positive for press and anger. The correlation with anxiety was in this case slightly negative.

As to anxiety, we might first of all raise the question of whether this is the most appropriate term to apply, say, to a surgeon at the start of a difficult emergency operation. His nervousness is not morbid anxiety in the Freudian sense (fear of conscience), nor is it associated with any tendency to escape, to withdraw, or to avoid, in the usual sense: Surgery is his chosen profession and here is his opportunity to save a life and thus to achieve an all-important result. It might be said, however, that he is bent on avoiding disaster for both his patient and himself. But, regardless of these and other objections, I shall continue to use the term "anxiety" for the duration of this paper to stand for a nervous apprehension of the forthcoming possibility of experiencing some sort of acute pain, distress, failure, exposure, shame, or disgrace. Now, despite the fact that none of our rank order correlations between heart rate and anxiety were positive, it is clear from the

graph that the effect of predyadic anxiety (nervous excitement) on the
heart rate (elevating it 33 points on the average) is greater than that of
any other definable variable, that is to say, heart rate and anxiety *are* in
fact positively correlated, as effect and cause, or cause and effect, in all subjects. The contradiction can be explained, in functional terms, by assuming
that anxiety (situational fear) is a mobilization of energy for emergency
action in a situation that is apprehended as perilous. If the anxiety is high
and a resulting drive to overt action is correspondingly high, particularly if
the drive is combined with anger as well as an increase of gross motility,
the heart rate will be in the highest range, and since the signs of anxiety
will be largely obscured or inhibited by the vigorous and focused ongoing
activity (verbal in our experiments), the subject will be given a rather low
rating on anxiety and a very high rating on both vocal-verbal intensity and
task involvement (see the curve of Tandy in Figure 25-3). If, on the other
hand, an equally high degree of anxiety results in a form of action which
may be termed "surrender and submission," with extrapunitiveness replaced
by a mild intrapunitiveness, the heart rate will fall and remain at a low
level, as one can see in the case of Keeper, also represented in Figure 25-3.

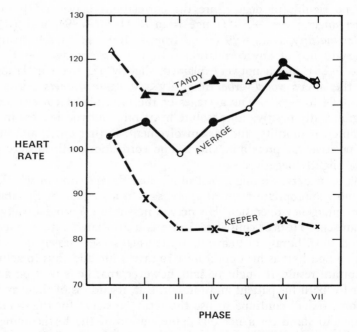

Figure 25-3.   Average heart rate of two deviant cases compared to
group average.

Keeper will receive low ratings on vocal-verbal intensity and high ratings on manifest anxiety. This, in brief, is a partial explanation of the absence of positive correlations between heart rate and anxiety.

And now I have come to the end of my allotted time, with only a few seconds in which to show one last figure (Figure 25-4) in which the average heart rates of seven subjects with the highest drive ratings are compared with the average heart rates of seven subjects with the lowest drive ratings.

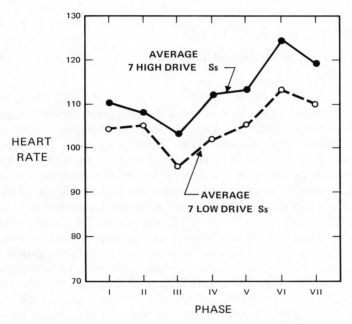

Figure 25-4.   Average heart rate for seven subjects with highest drive and seven subjects with lowest drive.

26

The Validity of
Thematic Projective
Technique Interpretations

KENNETH B. LITTLE
& EDWIN S. SHNEIDMAN

Several studies have been made in the attempt to establish a quantitative index of the validity, in clinical usage, of thematic projective techniques (Calvin, 1950; Combs, 1946; Davenport, 1952; Harrison, 1940; Hartmann, 1949; Saxe, 1950). The major problem in such investigations is the difficulty of establishing a set of measurement dimensions which will cover all, or even most, of the information available in the responses of the subject. Until this can be done a projective technique cannot be considered a *test* in the usual psychometric sense, and no unique validity coefficient (or unique set of validity coefficients) can be determined. An alternative approach, however, is to consider the projective technique protocol merely as a sample of the subject's verbal behavior from which inferences of various sorts may be made by the interpreting clinician. These inferences can be compared with a criterion and an interpreter-protocol index of agreement obtained. The central tendency of such indices among competent interpreters working with a variety of protocols might legitimately be considered the "validity" of the projective technique itself.

The present paper is a report of an initial study of the range and magnitudes of interpreter-protocol validity coefficients using a number of interpreters and the thematic test protocols of a single subject.[1] In addition, the attempt was made to determine the types of inferences made from thematic protocols and the relation between the types of inferences made and their accuracy.

From K. B. Little, and E. S. Shneidman, *The Validity of Thematic Projective Technique Interpretations*. *Journal of Personality*, 1955, 23, 285–294. Reprinted by permission of author and publisher.

This investigation was supported by a research grant from the National Institute of Mental Health, of the National Institutes of Health, Public Health Service and was administered by the University of Southern California, Los Angeles.

[1] A further study is currently being made using a variety of protocols, projective techniques, and interpreters to increase the representativeness of the results.

PROCEDURE

Seventeen psychologists, all familiar with thematic projective technique interpretation (as indicated by their having published one or more books or articles on the subject), were presented with the Thematic Apperception Test (TAT) and the Make A Picture Story (MAPS) protocols of one subject who was identified to them as male, age 25, and single. Each of the judges wrote an essay-form personality description of this subject on the basis of his analysis of the protocols.[2] These reports were then separated, by the present investigators, into discrete statements about the subject. In all, 802 nonduplicated items were secured by this means. For each of the statements describing the subject another statement contradictory to the original was constructed. For example, the statement "He has a very high IQ" was paired with the statement "He is of average intelligence." Of this total item population of 1604, 150 items were selected on a systematic sampling basis as representative of the personality attributes asserted, or implicitly denied, about the subject. These 150 items were returned to the original test interpreters, who sorted them into a forced quasi-normal distribution—a Q-sort (Stephenson, 1953)—on the basis of their truth or falsity for the subject. The resulting distributions of items were intercorrelated giving a 17-by-17 test-interpreter correlation matrix. The range of correlations was from .02 to .68, with a mean of .44.

The same 150 items were also submitted to 29 competent clinicians who independently performed Q-sorts of them on the basis of a complete clinical record (minus the test protocols and reports) of the subject. All of these criterion judges had had at least five years of professional experience, and three had had personal contact with the subject as therapists or consultants. They were of various doctrinaire hues—psychoanalytic, nondirective, neo-Freudian, eclectic, etc. The clinical record contained reports of medical examinations, social history, therapy-interview notes, laboratory data, reports of consultations, course-of-treatment notes, etc. The criterion-judge distributions of items were intercorrelated, giving a 29-by-29 criterion correlational matrix with a range from .04 to .76 and a mean of .52. In addition, each of the test-interpreter distributions was correlated with each of the criterion-judge distributions, giving a 17-by-29 test-interpreter versus criterion-judge correlation matrix. These correlations ranged from −.07 to .70, with a mean of .45.[3]

[2] The two test protocols and 17 interpretations—together with other test materials and case history data—are presented in *Thematic test analysis* (Sheidman, 1951).

[3] More detailed correlation tables of intercorrelation have been deposited as Document No. 4472 with the ADI Auxiliary Publication Project, Photoduplication Service, Library of Congress, Washington 25, D.C. A copy may be secured by citing the document no., and remitting $1.25 for photoprints or $1.25 for a 35 mm. microfilm. Make checks or money orders payable to Chief, Photoduplication Service, Library of Congress.

RESULTS

Criterion Analysis

An initial attempt at a cluster analysis (Tryon, 1939) of the correlations among the criterion judges indicated that all had very similar correlation profiles and could properly be considered members of a single cluster. A centroid factor analysis performed independently confirmed this in that there was a large general factor that could not be eliminated by any form of orthogonal rotation. None of the remaining four factors had loadings exceeding .38. It was decided, therefore, to use the first centroid factor as the best estimate of the criterion judge consensus inasmuch as it accounted for 90 per cent of the total communality among them. Table 26-1 gives the loading of each criterion judge on this factor.

TABLE 26-1.   General Factor Loadings of the Twenty-nine Criterion Judges

Judge	Factor Loading	Judge	Factor Loading	Judge	Factor Loading
1	.744	11	.772	21	.689
2	.740	12	.696	22	.744
3	.710	13	.209	23	.745
4	.800	14	.803	24	.789
5	.754	15	.725	25	.738
6	.777	16	.492	26	.741
7	.610	17	.791	27	.734
8	.833	18	.764	28	.718
9	.884	19	.835	29	.601
10	.833	20	.798		

To identify the criterion, factor scores were computed for each of the 150 items as the sum of the individual weighted scores assigned to it by the criterion judges. The appropriate weights were derived by the Gengerelli method (Gengerelli, 1948). The factor scores of the items were then ranked in order of magnitude and the upper and lower 8 per cent tabulated. Table 26-2 presents the 12 items with the highest ("most true") factor scores and the 12 items with the lowest ("most false") factor scores.

The items presented in Table 26-2 seem to be largely dynamic-descriptive but with a diagnostic flavor. There is little emphasis upon either etiology or symptomatology but rather a cross-sectional picture of the subject's present psychological state.

TABLE 26-2. Identifying Items of the Criterion General Factor

Most True Items	*Most False Items*
1. He is in the early stages of paranoid schizophrenia.	1. He is not a particularly sick individual.
2. He has an enormous amount of hostility.	2. He has satisfactory interpersonal relationships.
3. His deep conflict in the sexual area is between sexual impulses and superego restraints.	3. His thought processes are orderly and well knit.
4. He has strong latent homosexual impulses.	4. He is not a schizoid individual.
5. He feels fearful.	5. He has very little guilt feelings concerning his aggressive impulses.
6. His aggressive impulses are both externally and internally directed.	6. He perceives the world as largely friendly.
7. He is concerned with "good" versus "bad."	7. He does not have much anxiety.
8. He identified more with his mother than with his father.	8. He does not show any evidence of hallucinatory behavior.
9. He lacks positive interpersonal relationships.	9. He seems little concerned with his bodily well being.
10. He feels depressed.	10. He is little concerned with physical violence.
11. He never adequately learned social skills.	11. There are no paranoid ideas of reference or malign influences.
12. He avoids social disapproval by engaging in solitary activity.	12. His superego is relatively mature.

Test Interpretation Analysis

Three groups of judges were isolated from a cluster analysis of test-interpreter intercorrelations. These three clusters included 15 of the 17 judges; the remaining two (numbers 16 and 17) could not properly be placed in any single cluster and are classified as residuals. Table 26-3 gives the estimated correlations of each test judge with the cluster domains (analogous to factor loadings) and also an estimate of the communalities or extent to which each judge shares common sources of variance with the other judges. Table 26-4 presents the estimated correlations among the cluster domains.

A comparison was made between the theoretical correlations among the test judges (computed from the cluster loadings and the correlations among the cluster domains) and the empirical correlations. The distribution of differences between the theoretical correlations and their corresponding empirical correlations is not significantly different from the normal curve of error. Consequently, the hypothesis that the three clusters account for all the general sources of variance among the test judges cannot be rejected.

TABLE 26-3.   Estimated Correlations of Each Test Interpreter with
Each of the Cluster Domains

CLUSTERS

Cluster Domain	A						B			C						Resid.	
	1	2	3	4	5	6	7	8	9	10	11	12	13	14	15	16	17
C_A	.83	.77	.74	.77	.78	.80	.52	.43	.39	.74	.75	.65	.64	.67	.71	.49	.57
C_B	.69	.52	.51	.54	.58	.49	.69	.65	.55	.40	.44	.21	.29	.26	.20	.16	.57
C_C	.76	.75	.66	.68	.74	.75	.29	.34	.13	.82	.82	.73	.77	.71	.75	.64	.48
h^2	.69	.59	.55	.59	.61	.64	.48	.42	.30	.67	.67	.53	.59	.50	.56	.41	.32

TABLE 26-4.   Estimated Correlations among the Cluster Domains

Cluster Domain	C_A	C_B	C_C
C_A	1.00	.71	.93
C_B	.71	1.00	.40
C_C	.93	.40	1.00

Identification of the clusters—the task of describing what the judges of one cluster have in common that sets them apart from the members of the other clusters—was made in the following fashion. The three estimated cluster scores of each of the 150 items were computed as the simple average of the scores assigned to it by the judges in each cluster. The items were then ranked in order of magnitude of their cluster scores for each of the three clusters, and the upper and lower 16 per cent of items examined. Considerable overlap was present, as would be expected from the magnitude of the correlations among the cluster domains. However, it was possible to isolate certain items that ranked high on one cluster and low, or moderately low, on the other two. Conversely, items were isolated that ranked low on one cluster and high or moderately high on the other two. These cluster-defining items are presented in Table 26-5.

The judges of cluster A are characterized by a preference for what is commonly called "dynamic" type items. These items are assertions about the nature of the intrapsychic conflicts, their genetic development, and the subject's affective response to them. A diagnosis for the subject appears only by implication. The judges of cluster C, on the other hand, show a preference for items describing the psychopathology presented by the subject with emphasis upon disorders of intellectual functioning. Cluster B is less clear-cut, possibly because it was the smallest and least homogeneous of the three. However, in the formal characteristics of the defining items it resembles strongly cluster C. The difference between the judges of cluster B and those of cluster C seems to be one of diagnostic conclusion rather than of conceptual framework with the latter asserting that the subject was psychotic and the former disagreeing.

TABLE 26-5.   Identifying Items for Three Clusters of Thematic-Test Interpreters

CLUSTER A

Most true	Most false
He has incestuous desires that have precipitated intense conflict in him.	He has little conflict over his incestuous sexual impulses.
One of the main factors in his personality development was an extremely hostile, dominant mother.	He has satisfactory interpersonal relationships.
He lacks positive interpersonal relations.	He has resolved the conflict between his sexual needs and his interpretation of his mother's standards.
His deep conflict in the sexual area is between sexual impulses and superego restraints.	He shows little guilt over his incestuous sexual impulses.
He feels deprived of the oral gratifications of childhood.	
His aggression is aroused by illicit sexuality.	
Sexuality is strongly rejected by him.	
He suffers from feelings of rejection.	

CLUSTER B

Most true	Most false
His principal conflict is in the sexual area.	He displays certain catatonic features.
His reaction to sex is shame.	An acute break with reality has probably occurred.
He does not show any indication of hallucinatory behavior.	There are some indications that he has cosmic delusions.
He is probably not disoriented.	He is entirely out of contact with reality.
His thinking processes are well preserved.	He seldom uses self-punishment mechanisms.
He is not confused.	

CLUSTER C

Most true	Most false
An acute break with reality has probably occurred.	His thought processes are orderly and well knit.
His thinking is characterized by highly symbolic autistic processes.	He has the well preserved mind of a person who is not psychotic.
His verbal peculiarities are many and rather striking.	His thinking processes are well preserved.
There is some straining for effect in his use of language.	He is not confused.
He is in the early stages of paranoid schizophrenia.	There are no paranoid ideas of reference or malign influences.

Test Interpreter versus Criterion Analysis

The general results of the comparison of the test interpreters with the criterion may be anticipated from an examination of the items defining each. However, a more precise estimate of the extent of the agreement of each test interpreter with the criterion was made by inserting his correlations with the criterion judges' into the criterion matrix as a thirtieth variable and computing his first centroid loading. These loadings, which may be considered as correlations with the criterion general factor, are presented in Table 26-6. They range from .215 to .755, with a mean of .605. The test judges of cluster A have an average of .688; the judges of cluster B, .310; and the judges of cluster C, .698. An analysis of variance of these coefficients indicates that there is no significant difference between the mean validity figures for clusters A and C but that the mean validity figure for cluster B is significantly lower than the other two. A further finding from the analysis was that there was no significant difference between the mean validity coefficients of clusters A and C and the average general factor loading of the criterion judges (Table 26-1).

TABLE 26-6.   Thematic-Test Interpreter Loadings on the Criterion General Factor

	Judge	Factor loading		Judge	Factor loading
	1	.710		10	.755
	2	.738		11	.694
Cluster A	3	.662	Cluster C	12	.716
	4	.650		13	.654
	5	.660		14	.682
	6	.705		15	.697
	7	.315		16	.533
Cluster B	8	.399	Residuals	17	.465
	9	.215			

DISCUSSION

The results presented in the preceding section indicate that even among expert thematic projective-technique interpreters a wide range of validity coefficients may be obtained. The distribution, however, is skewed markedly towards the upper end. Two major categories of interpreters occur, who show a slight preference for describing the subject in terms of "dynamic" characteristics and those who show a slight preference for describing the subject in terms of standard psychopathology and diagnosis. The term "slight preference" is used advisedly here since the method of identifying the clusters is one that emphasizes differences rather than similarities. The rather strong agreement among the clusters is apparent from the size of the correlations among the cluster domains. The group of judges that show a slight preference for emphasis upon psychopathology can further be divided into two subgroups differing in the diagnostic conclusion they reached.

The rather peculiar finding that the two major clusters of test interpreters correlated with the criterion general factor as well as did the criterion judges themselves needs further study. The implication is that test interpreters working from a TAT and MAPS protocol can describe a person as accurately as can clinicians working from the elaborate data of a clinical folder. However ego-syntonic such a conclusion is, it must be viewed with considerable reservation. The present study indicates only the degree of agreement with a clinical criterion that *can* be achieved by competent thematic-test interpreters; it cannot be claimed that the same level of validity will occur with other cases. The subject selected for this study was chosen on the basis of the completeness of the clinical data available about him; there is no assurance that his thematic protocols were not unusually revealing. In addition, the areas of personality description included in the content of the Q-sort items were selected by the test interpreters themselves. In other areas, or on other levels of description, different results might occur.

A word should be said about the criterion at this point. In view of the range of theoretical orientations among the criterion judges, we had expected a diversity of opinion about the subject similar to that found among the test interpreters. The most feasible explanation of the marked agreement would seem to be the quasi-factual nature of many of the Q-sort items for the criterion judges. Practically all of the items required that the test interpreters make an extended series of deductions based up clues in the protocols, their own previous experience, knowledge of personality theory, etc. For the criterion judges these same items would involve a much shorter chain of inferences. If, for example, the report of a psychiatric consultant in the clinical record contained the statement, "The patient is markedly disoriented for time and space," little disagreement would occur among the criterion judges as to the truth value of the Q-sort item, "The subject is or has been disoriented in the psychiatric sense."

The wide range of validity coefficients for the test interpreters who emphasized psychopathology (clusters B and C) is explicable on the above rationale. Items describing symptoms, diagnosis, etc., would be the very ones the criterion judges would consider as having very high, or very low, truth values, thus the possibility of disagreement or of being "wrong" is magnified, as is the possibility of agreement or being "right."

As a final observation, the general results indicate the usefulness of Stephenson's Q-technique for dealing with some of the problems of the validation of projective techniques in that it allows the individual case to be described by the quantitative methods of nomothetic statistics.

SUMMARY

The validity of inferences made from thematic projective techniques was tested using an interpreter population of 17 experts working with the TAT and MAPS protocols of one subject. The criterion was the consensus, in the form of a general factor, of 29 clinicians on the basis of a complete clinical record of the same subject. The results indicated that the test interpreters formed into clusters on the basis of their relative preference for "dynamic" type inferences or for inferences as to the psychopathology presented by the subject. The latter group of interpreters divides into two further groups on the basis of the diagnostic conclusion reached. Validity coefficients for these experts vary from .215 to .755, with a mean of .605. For the cluster of interpreters who made predominantly "dynamic" type inferences, and for the larger of the other two clusters, the mean validity coefficients were not significantly different from the average general factor loading of the criterion judges. The results were discussed and certain restrictions and limitations indicated.

REFERENCES

Calvin, J. S. An attempted experimental validation of the TAT. *J. clin. Psychol.*, 1950, 6, 337–381.

Combs, A. W. The validity and reliability of interpretation from autobiography and the TAT. *J. clin. Psychol.*, 1946, 2, 240–247.

Davenport, Beverly F. The semantic validity of TAT interpretation. *J. consult. Psychol.*, 1952, 16, 171–175.

Gengerelli, J. A. A simplified method for approximate multiple regression coefficients. *Psychometrika*, 1948, 13, 135–146.

Harrison, R. Studies in the use and validity of the TAT with mentally disturbed patients. II. A quantitative validity study. III. Validation by the method of "blind analysis." *Charact. & Pers.*, 1940, 9, 122–138.

Hartmann, A. A. An experimental examination of the TAT in clinical diagnosis. *Psychol. Monogr.*, 1949, 63, No. 8. Pp. 48.

Saxe, C. H. A quantitative comparison of psychodiagnostic formulations from the TAT and therapeutic contacts. *J. consult. Psychol.*, 1950, 14, 116–127.

Shneidman, E. S. (Ed.) *Thematic test analysis.* New York: Grune & Stratton, 1951.

Stephenson, W. S. *The study of behavior.* Chicago: University of Chicago Press, 1953.

Tryon, R. C. *Cluster analysis.* Ann Arbor, Mich.: Edwards Brothers, 1939.

27

The Role of Need-Attitudes
in Adjustment

JAY L. CHAMBERS
& LOUIS J. BROUSSARD

PROBLEM

A previous study (Chambers, 1960) investigated the attitudes of normal and paranoid schizophrenic men toward needs of the Murray (1953) need system. For the present study, the need-attitudes of two new clinical groups were measured by the same technique previously described. Cluster analyses of the need-attitudes of the two groups of the previous study and the two groups of the present study were examined by a method designed to reveal quantitative similarities and differences between cluster configurations. It was expected that a systematic comparison of the need-attitude clusters of normal and maladjusted groups would provide indications of the role of need-attitudes in adjustment.

METHOD

Subjects

Normal subjects for the study were obtained from Americus and Albany, Georgia, from Lexington, Kentucky and from the rural areas surrounding these three communities. Clinical subjects were obtained from five different Veterans Administration and state mental hospitals and from several out-patient clinics located in different cities. The clinical patients were selected on the basis of a clear cut psychiatric diagnosis. The normal subjects had no history of mental disorder or severe emotional disturbance.

Each of the four groups in the present study was composed of 100

From J. L. Chambers, and J. L. Broussard, The Role of Need-Attitudes in Adjustment. *Journal of Clinical Psychology*, 1960, *16*, 383–387. Reprinted by permission of author and publisher.

adult males. The normal subjects had an average age of 34 and a mean education level of 12.4 years. An alcoholic group had an average age of 39 and a mean education level of 11.7 years. A paranoid schizophrenic group had an average age of 38 and a mean education level of 11.5 years. A chronic undifferentiated schizophrenic group had an average age of 35 and a mean education level of 11.2 years. The standard deviations for age ranged from 7.8 to 10.8 years for the four groups while the standard deviations for education levels ranged from 2.3 to 2.9 years.

Some significant differences in age and education occurred between groups. The most reliable mean difference in age ($t > .01$) was five years between normals and alcoholics and the most reliable mean difference in education ($t > .01$) was 1.2 years between normals and undifferentiated schizophrenics. The possible effects of differences in age and/or education must be considered in interpreting the data although no effects attributable to these factors were readily discernible.

Picture Identification Test

Briefly, this test (Chambers, 1960) gives quantifiable measures of the frequency a S attributes need descriptions to his own selections of liked and disliked photographs of people. Consistent sorting of a need description with liked pictures was considered evidence of a positive attitude of the S toward that need. Consistent sorting of a need description with disliked photographs was taken as evidence of a negative attitude of the S toward the need. S's sorting scores for the 21 Murray needs were ordered from most positive to most negative scores. The rank of a need was taken as an index of the relative strength of the S's attitude toward the need. Interpreting rank scores of the needs as indices of attitudes toward needs seemed more defensible than a claim that the needs per se were being measured.

A measure of variability (from chance sorting) and a measure of consistency (tendency to sort more with liked than disliked photographs) were both computed for each subject. Two equivalent forms of the test were used. In each group, half of the subjects took one form and the other half took the alternate form. The combined data from both tests were used in the analyses.

RESULTS

Previous study indicated that a configural approach was the most fruitful for revealing the significance of the various need-attitudes for the different groups. Intercorrelations between all 21 need-attitude scores and the variability and consistency measures were computed for the alcoholic and for the chronic undifferentiated schizophrenic groups. The correlation matrix for each group represented average correlations (via the Z transformation) of two samples with 50 Ss per sample.

The two matrices were cluster analyzed. Tables 27-1 and 27-2 present the cluster analyses for the alcoholic and chronic undifferentiated schizo-

TABLE 27-1.   Cluster Analysis of Need-Attitudes of 100 Alcoholic Males

	Need-Attitude	Avg. r	Need-Attitude	Avg. r
			Deference	−.39
	Harmavoidance	+.36	Nurturance	−.37
Cluster 1	Inferiority-avoidance	+.32	Variability	−.31
	Defendance	+.23	Affiliation	−.29
	Succorance	+.21	Achievement	−.24
			Order	−.23
			Understanding	−.23
	Sex	+.25	Deference	−.35
	Harmavoidance	+.24	Understanding	−.31
Cluster 2	Autonomy	+.23	Order	−.30
	Exhibition	+.22	Nurturance	−.28
	Aggression	+.19	Achievement	−.25
			Affiliation	−.41
Cluster 3	Inferiority-avoidance	+.32	Nurturance	−.37
	Rejection	+.28	Variability	−.30
			Understanding	−.19
	Aggression	+.34		
Cluster 4	Autonomy	+.26	Abasement	−.32
	Sex	+.21	Blamavoidance	−.25
	Exhibition	+.35		
Cluster 5	Play	+.30	Understanding	−.39
	Sex	+.28	Order	−.35
			Deference	−.25
Cluster 6	Succorance	+.26	Affiliation	−.19
	Consistency	+.24	Dominance	−.19
	Succorance	+.25		
Cluster 7	Abasement	+.24	Counteraction	−.28
	Inferiority-avoidance	+.24		
	Blamavoidance	+.20		
	Succorance	+.26		
Cluster 8	Harmavoidance	+.24	Dominance	−.31
	Abasement	+.23		
	Defendance	+.19		

TABLE 27-2.   Cluster Analysis of Need-Attitudes of 100 Chronic
Undifferentiated Schizophrenic Males

	Need-Attitude	Avg. r	Need-Attitude	Avg. r
Cluster 1	Defendance	+.30	Deference	—.36
	Harmavoidance	+.28	Nurturance	—.32
	Autonomy	+.27	Order	—.30
	Inferiority-avoidance	+.27	Achievement	—.28
	Aggression	+.25	Understanding	—.28
	Succorance	+.21	Affiliation	—.26
Cluster 2	Autonomy	+.28	Nurturance	—.34
	Aggression	+.26	Achievement	—.33
	Play	+.24	Order	—.32
			Understanding	—.31
Cluster 3	Autonomy	+.35	Deference	—.40
	Sex	+.25	Achievement	—.37
			Order	—.33
Cluster 4	Inferiority-avoidance	+.25	Dominance	—.21
	Abasement	+.19	Order	—.20
Cluster 5	Succorance	+.32	Counteraction	—.31
	Harmavoidance	+.30		
Cluster 6	Exhibition	+.28	Achievement	—.27
	Aggression	+.25		
Cluster 7	Exhibition	+.26	Abasement	—.26
	Aggression	+.25		
Cluster 8	Aggression	+.25	Blamavoidance	—.24
	Autonomy	+.22		
Clustre 9	Succorance	+.20	Variability	—.25
			Order	—.24
Cluster 10	Rejection	+.24	Deference	—.32
			Nurturance	—.29
Cluster 11	Harmavoidance	+.30	Deference	—.30
	Consistency	+.19		

phrenic groups respectively. The procedure was an exact replica of the
cluster analyses of need-attitude data for normal and paranoid schizophrenic Ss presented previously (Chambers, 1960). It was possible, therefore, to reexamine the previous data and compare the need-attitude clusters
of each of three clinical groups with those of normals.

A quantitative method was devised to show how each of the clinical
groups had the same or different cluster combinations for the test vari-

ables as were found for normals. The method is illustrated as follows. First, each variable appearing in the alcoholics' clusters was checked to see with which other variables it combined. For example, Harmavoidance, in alcoholic cluster 1, correlated with 10 other variables in that cluster and these were all recorded along with any new combinations appearing in alcoholic clusters 2 and 8 where Harmavoidance was also present. The normal cluster correlations for Harmavoidance were likewise recorded and then the two sets of correlations were compared to see which correlations were shared and which were unshared by the two groups. Unshared correlations were classified according to whether normals had the combination and alcoholics lacked it or vice versa. All the other need-attitudes were analyzed the same way. Cluster combinations of each of the three clinical groups were compared with those of normals.

DISCUSSION

Several questions and hypotheses were suggested by the data. First, why do some need-attitudes cluster with a number of others for a particular group while other need-attitudes show few or no cluster combinations? One possible answer is that the more widely a need-attitude is interrelated in the cluster system of a group, the more the group has prepared for the satisfaction, expression, inhibition, or channeling of the need. The combinations of a widely related need-attitude would thus represent a complex system devised to cope with problems associated with the need. If this proposition is valid, normals should be most concerned with such needs as Aggression, Autonomy, Exhibition, and Sex since they have the most cluster combinations for these needs. Normals have the least number of cluster combinations for and should therefore be least concerned with needs for Counteraction, Inferiority-avoidance, Sentience, and Succorance (Chambers, 1960).

Second, it may be assumed that the need-attitude system of normals reflects more realistic and mature solutions for adaptation to our culture than the systems developed by any of the clinical groups. The kinds of departures that clinical groups make from the normal pattern can thus be used as indicators of maladaptive attempts to cope with need problems. For therapeutic change, therefore, clinical groups should unlearn their own peculiar attitude patterns and learn the normal patterns they lack.

If the above speculations are applied to the alcoholic clusters, data suggest that alcoholics require the most unlearning for Succorance and Inferiority-avoidance needs as they hold 14 and 11 need-attitude combinations for these needs which normals do not hold. Alcoholics have the most new learning to do for Blamavoidance and Play needs as they lack 9 and 8 normal attitude combinations for these needs. Lacking normal attitudes to enable them to enjoy ordinary relaxation (n Play) and lacking normal checks and controls from superego or blame avoidance attitudes, inebriates may find that alcohol artificially induces an acceptable and pleasurable escape from their ineffective efforts to cope with problems of dependency (n Succorance) and inadequacy (n Inferiority-avoidance).

Similar analyses applied to the other clinical groups indicate that paranoid schizophrenics and chronic undifferentiated schizophrenics show similarities in their new learning and unlearning requirements. Both groups of schizophrenics have the most new learning requirements for Blamavoidance and Exhibition needs and both need to unlearn attitudes connected with Inferiority-avoidance. The most striking difference between the two schizophrenic groups is with regard to attitudes related to n Succorance. Chronic undifferentiated schizophrenics have devised a complex but abnormal system of attitudes to cope with Succorance needs (13 non-normal need-attitude combinations) whereas the paranoids show no special concern with this need (0 non-normal need-attitude combinations).

Attending to the similarities between the two schizophrenic groups, one could rationalize that delusions of persecution may represent the schizophrenics' primitive substitutes for normal attitudes controlling Blamavoidance needs. Delusions of grandeur might represent primitive substitutes for the lack of normal controlling attitudes for exhibitionistic needs. Autistic withdrawal may reflect the schizophrenics' extensive but abnormal defense preparations to avoid exposure of inferiority feelings.

Theoretically, the most pathological need-attitude problems for any group would center around those needs showing the most deviations from normal standards based on both new learning and unlearning requirements. Accordingly, the three most troublesome needs for alcoholics were: Succorance (17 unshared need-attitude combinations), Harmavoidance (15), and Defendance (14). The three most troublesome needs for paranoid schizophrenics were: Aggression and Blamavoidance (14 unshared combinations), and Achievement (13). The four most troublesome needs for chronic undifferentiated schizophrenics were: Succorance (17 unshared combinations), Harmavoidance (15), Exhibition and Order (12 each). This view of the data shows that alcoholics and chronic undifferentiated schizophrenics were similarly oriented around problems of passivity and fearfulness (n Suc and n Har) while the paranoid's problems were oriented more toward active striving (n Ach), hostility (n Agg), and guilt (n Bla).

SUMMARY

Cluster analyses of the need-attitudes of normal and paranoid schizophrenic males from a previous study and alcoholic and chronic undifferentiated schizophrenic males from the present study were examined by a method designed to reveal quantitative similarities and differences between cluster configurations.

Some theoretical propositions as to the role of need-attitudes in adjustment were formulated as follows: (a) The more widely a need-attitude is interrelated with other attitudes in the cluster system of a group, the more extensive the preparations of the group for coping with problems associated with the need. (b) If the need-attitude cluster system of normals is accepted as the most desirable model, clinical groups should learn the normal patterns they lack and unlearn their peculiar need-attitude patterns.

The data, interpreted according to the above hypotheses, suggested that, in order to conform to normal patterns, alcoholics required most change in attitudes associated with Succorance, Harmavoidance, and Defendance needs; paranoid schizophrenics required most change in attitude patterns related to Aggression, Blamavoidance, and Achievement needs; chronic undifferentiated schizophrenics required most change in attitude patterns related to Succorance, Harmavoidance, Exhibition, and Order needs.

REFERENCES

Chambers, J. L. & Broussard, L. J. Need-attitudes of normal and paranoid schizophrenic males. *J. clin. Psychol.*, 1960, 16, 233–237.

Murray, H. A. *Explorations In Personality*. New York: Oxford University Press, 1953.

PHENOMENOLOGICAL-
HUMANISTIC
THEORIES

VII

IT CAN BE ARGUED that until recent years psychology has been dominated by two major forces, the Behavioristic school, modeled largely on the physical sciences, and the Freudian school, heavily ladened with the mechanistic emphasis of early biological science. It is apparent, as Maslow and others have pointed out, that relatively recent psychological literature has seen the rise of a new movement, a *Third Force*, which can be termed humanistic or phenomenological-humanistic psychology. This new approach is a relatively nonmechanistic, somewhat holistic, positive view dealing almost exclusively with human behavior and emphasizing higher, rather than basic, needs.

To hold, however, that humanism is a single school of thought is somewhat fallacious, since, in reality, it represents a coming together of a number of related but different lines of thought. Included are orientations commonly termed holism, particularly the organismic approach, phenomenology, and self theory. Holistic approaches are treated elsewhere (Section IX). Here, we will deal primarily with phenomenological and self approaches. As a major aspect of the humanistic movement, phenomenology has a long history, dating from its originator, Edmund Husserl, and his predecessors, Stumpf and Brentano. Self theory, which places the integration of personality in a hypothetical coordinating center termed the self or self-concept, also boasts a long history, dating to the soul theory of ancient Greek and later philosophies.

Among current leaders of the phenomenological-humanistic movement, two stand out, Carl Rogers and Abraham Maslow. Rogers has presented a theoretical system consisting of interrelated theories of personality, psychotherapy, interpersonal relationship, and the "fully functioning person." In addition, he has been a pioneer in carrying out and influencing others to carry out carefully designed research in psychotherapy. Since both the theory of personality and the theory of psychotherapy dictate the importance of the self-concept (the individual's perception of his own characteristics), much of the research relating to Rogerian theory (and other self theories) has involved the measurement and investigation of this construct.

The papers presented here deal with both Rogerian theory and related research. The first paper serves as an example of Rogers's theoretical writings and presents, clearly and concisely, a partial statement of his theory of psychotherapy. The second paper, by Butler and Haigh, is an outstanding example of the pioneering research efforts of the Rogers group. The study employs a research method, Q-technique, which, since the efforts of Butler and Haigh, has become a widely used research tool, both in studies of the therapeutic process and in studies of self-concept generally. While the original article was published in 1954, Dr. Butler has been kind enough to provide us with a recent, previously unpublished, addendum in which additional data analyses are reported. These analyses provide stronger support than was previously available for the conclusions reached by Butler and Haigh.

The Q-technique is by no means the only measure of self-concept employed in the empirical literature. In fact, numerous inventories and checklists have been used. The Viney article provides insight into the number and diversity of the available measures and raises certain points concerning the unity of measures of self-regard.

Unlike Rogers, Maslow has taken almost exclusively a theoretical approach to personality, deemphasizing empirical research. In representing Maslow's theory, which is undergoing continual change and extension, we have chosen two recent papers. The first, originally given at a Duke University symposium, deals primarily with the application of Maslow's humanistic orientation to an understanding of neurosis. It will be apparent, however, that the content of the paper is far broader than the phenomena of neurosis. The second Maslow article is a previously unpublished paper which Dr. Maslow has kindly permitted us to print here. It deals succinctly with the meanings of transcendence, a current topic and one central to Maslow's theoretical thinking. The final article (by Gourevitch & Feffer) represents an attempt by others to deal empirically with one of Maslow's constructs, the need hierarchy.

28

The Necessary and Sufficient
Conditions of Therapeutic
Personality Change

CARL R. ROGERS

For many years I have been engaged in psychotherapy with individuals in distress. In recent years I have found myself increasingly concerned with the process of abstracting from that experience the general principles which appear to be involved in it. I have endeavored to discover any orderliness, any unity which seems to inhere in the subtle, complex tissue of interpersonal relationship in which I have so constantly been immersed in therapeutic work. One of the current products of this concern is an attempt to state, in formal terms, a theory of psychotherapy, of personality, and of interpersonal relationships which will encompass and contain the phenomena of my experience.[1] What I wish to do in this paper is to take one very small segment of that theory, spell it out more completely, and explore its meaning and usefulness.

THE PROBLEM

The question to which I wish to address myself is this: Is it possible to state, in terms which are clearly definable and measurable, the psychological conditions which are both necessary and sufficient to bring about constructive personality change? Do we, in other words, know with any

From C. R. Rogers, The Necessary and Sufficient Conditions of Therapeutic Personality Change. *Journal of Consulting Psychology*, 1957, *21*, 95–103. Copyright 1957 by the American Psychological Association, and reproduced by permission of publisher and author.

[1] This formal statement is entitled "A theory of therapy, personality and interpersonal relationships, as developed in the client-centered framework," by Carl R. Rogers. The manuscript was prepared at the request of the Committee of the American Psychological Association for the Study of the Status and Development of Psychology in the United States. It will be published by McGraw-Hill in one of several volumes being prepared by this committee. Copies of the unpublished manuscript are available from the author to those with special interest in this field.

358

precision those elements which are essential if psychotherapeutic change is to ensue?

Before proceeding to the major task let me dispose very briefly of the second portion of the question. What is meant by such phrases as "psychotherapeutic change," "constructive personality change"? This problem also deserves deep and serious consideration, but for the moment let me suggest a common-sense type of meaning upon which we can perhaps agree for purposes of this paper. By these phrases is meant: changes in the personality structure of the individual, at both surface and deeper levels, in a direction which clinicians would agree means greater integration, less internal conflict, more energy utilizable for effective living; change in behavior away from behaviors generally regarded as immature and toward behaviors regarded as mature. This brief description may suffice to indicate the kind of change for which we are considering the preconditions. It may also suggest the ways in which this criterion of change may be determined.[2]

THE CONDITIONS

As I have considered my own clinical experience and that of my colleagues, together with the pertinent research which is available, I have drawn out several conditions which seem to me to be *necessary* to initiate constructive personality change, and which, taken together, appear to be *sufficient* to inaugurate that process. As I have worked on this problem I have found myself surprised at the simplicity of what has emerged. The statement which follows is not offered with any assurance as to its correctness, but with the expectation that it will have the value of any theory, namely that it states or implies a series of hypotheses which are open to proof or disproof, thereby clarifying and extending our knowledge of the field.

Since I am not, in this paper, trying to achieve suspense, I will state at once, in severely rigorous and summarized terms, the six conditions which I have come to feel are basic to the process of personality change. The meaning of a number of the terms is not immediately evident, but will be clarified in the explanatory sections which follow. It is hoped that this brief statement will have much more significance to the reader when he has completed the paper. Without further introduction let me state the basic theoretical position.

For constructive personality change to occur, it is necessary that these conditions exist and continue over a period of time:

1. Two persons are in psychological contact.

---

[2] That this is a measurable and determinable criterion has been shown in research already completed. See Rogers & Dymond, 1954, especially chapters 8, 13, and 17.

2. The first, whom we shall term the client, is in a state of incongruence, being vulnerable or anxious.

3. The second person, whom we shall term the therapist, is congruent or integrated in the relationship.

4. The therapist experiences unconditional positive regard for the client.

5. The therapist experiences an empathic understanding of the client's internal frame of reference and endeavors to communicate this experience to the client.

6. The communication to the client of the therapist's empathic understanding and unconditioned positive regard is to a minimal degree achieved.

No other conditions are necessary. If these six conditions exist, and continue over a period of time, this is sufficient. The process of constructive personality change will follow.

A Relationship

The first condition specifies that a minimal relationship, a psychological contact, must exist. I am hypothesizing that significant positive personality change does not occur except in a relationship. This is of course an hypothesis, and it may be disproved.

Conditions 2 through 6 define the characteristics of the relationship which are regarded as essential by defining the necessary characteristics of each person in the relationship. All that is intended by this first condition is to specify that the two people are to some degree in contact, that each makes some perceived difference in the experiential field of the other. Probably it is sufficient if each makes some "subceived" difference, even though the individual may not be consciously aware of this impact. Thus it might be difficult to know whether a catatonic patient perceives a therapist's presence as making a difference to him—a difference of any kind—but it is almost certain that at some organic level he does sense this difference.

Except in such a difficult borderline situation as that just mentioned, it would be relatively easy to define this condition in operational terms and thus determine, from a hard-boiled research point of view, whether the condition does, or does not, exist. The simplest method of determination involves simply the awareness of both client and therapist. If each is aware of being in personal or psychological contact with the other, then this condition is met.

This first condition of therapeutic change is such a simple one that perhaps it should be labeled an assumption or a precondition in order to set it apart from those that follow. Without it, however, the remaining items would have no meaning, and that is the reason for including it.

The State of the Client

It was specified that it is necessary that the client be "in a state of incongruence, being vulnerable or anxious." What is the meaning of these terms?

Incongruence is a basic construct in the theory we have been developing. It refers to a discrepancy between the actual experience of the organism and the self picture of the individual insofar as it represents that experience. Thus a student may experience, at a total or organismic level, a fear of the university and of examinations which are given on the third floor of a certain building, since these may demonstrate a fundamental inadequacy in him. Since such a fear of his inadequacy is decidedly at odds with his concept of himself, this experience is represented (distortedly) in his awareness as an unreasonable fear of climbing stairs in this building, or any building, and soon an unreasonable fear of crossing the open campus. Thus there is a fundamental discrepancy between the experienced meaning of the situation as it registers in his organism and the symbolic representation of that experience in awareness in such a way that it does not conflict with the picture he has of himself. In this case to admit a fear of inadequacy would contradict the picture he holds of himself; to admit incomprehensible fears does not contradict his self concept.

Another instance would be the mother who develops vague illnesses whenever her only son makes plans to leave home. The actual desire is to hold on to her only source of satisfaction. To perceive this in awareness would be inconsistent with the picture she holds of herself as a good mother. Illness, however, is consistent with her self concept, and the experience is symbolized in this distorted fashion. Thus again there is a basic incongruence between the self as perceived (in this case as an ill mother needing attention) and the actual experience (in this case the desire to hold on to her son).

When the individual has no awareness of such incongruence in himself, then he is merely vulnerable to the possibility of anxiety and disorganization. Some experience might occur so suddenly or so obviously that the incongruence could not be denied. Therefore, the person is vulnerable to such a possibility.

If the individual dimly perceives such an incongruence in himself, then a tension state occurs which is known as anxiety. The incongruence need not be sharply perceived. It is enough that it is subceived—that is, discriminated as threatening to the self without any awareness of the content of that threat. Such anxiety is often seen in therapy as the individual approaches awareness of some element of his experience which is in sharp contradiction to his self concept.

It is not easy to give precise operational definition to this second of the six conditions, yet to some degree this has been achieved. Several research workers have defined the self concept by means of a Q sort by the individual of a list of self-referent items. This gives us an operational picture of the self. The total experiencing of the individual is more difficult to capture. Chodorkoff (2) has defined it as a Q sort made by a clinician who sorts the same self-referent items independently, basing his sorting on the picture he has obtained of the individual from projective tests. His sort thus includes unconscious as well as conscious elements of the individual's experience, thus representing (in an admittedly imperfect way) the totality of the client's experience. The correlation between these two sortings gives a crude operational measure of incongruence between self and experience, low or negative correlation representing of course a high degree of incongruence.

The Therapist's Genuineness in the Relationship

The third condition is that the therapist should be, within the confines of this relationship, a congruent, genuine, integrated person. It means that within the relationship he is freely and deeply himself, with his actual experience accurately represented by his awareness of himself. It is the opposite of presenting a facade, either knowingly or unknowingly.

It is not necessary (nor is it possible) that the therapist be a paragon who exhibits this degree of integration, of wholeness, in every aspect of his life. It is sufficient that he is accurately himself in this hour of this relationship, that in this basic sense he is what he actually is, in this moment of time.

It should be clear that this includes being himself even in ways which are not regarded as ideal for psychotherapy. His experience may be "I am afraid of this client" or "My attention is so focused on my own problems that I can scarcely listen to him." If the therapist is not denying these feelings to awareness, but is able freely to be them (as well as being his other feelings), then the condition we have stated is met.

It would take us too far afield to consider the puzzling matter as to the degree to which the therapist overtly communicates this reality in himself to the client. Certainly the aim is not for the therapist to express or talk out his own feelings, but primarily that he should not be deceiving the client as to himself. At times he may need to talk out some of his own feelings (either to the client, or to a colleague or supervisor) if they are standing in the way of the two following conditions.

It is not too difficult to suggest an operational definition for this third condition. We resort again to Q technique. If the therapist sorts a series of items relevant to the relationship (using a list similar to the ones developed by Fiedler [1950; 1953] and Bown [1954]), this will give his perception of his experience in the relationship. If several judges who have observed the interview or listened to a recording of it (or observed a sound movie of it) now sort the same items to represent *their* perception of the relationship, this second sorting should catch those elements of the therapist's behavior and inferred attitudes of which he is unaware, as well as those of which he is aware. Thus a high correlation between the therapist's sort and the observer's sort would represent in crude form an operational definition of the therapist's congruence or integration is the relationship; and a low correlation, the opposite.

Unconditional Positive Regard

To the extent that the therapist finds himself experiencing a warm acceptance of each aspect of the client's experience as being a part of that client, he is experiencing unconditional positive regard. This concept has been developed by Standal (1954). It means that there are no *conditions* of acceptance, no feeling of "I like you only *if* you are thus and so." It means a "prizing" of the person, as Dewey has used that term. It is at the opposite pole from a selective evaluating attitude—"You are bad in these ways, good in those." It involves as much feeling of acceptance for the client's expression of negative, "bad," painful, fearful, defensive, abnormal feelings as for his expression of "good," positive, mature, confident, social feelings, as much acceptance of ways in which he is inconsistent as of ways in which he is consistent. It means a caring for the client, but not in a possessive way or in such a way as simply to satisfy the therapist's own needs. It means a caring for the client as a *separate* person, with permission to have his own feelings, his own experiences. One client describes the therapist as "fostering my possession of my own experience . . . that [this] is *my* experience and that I am actually having it: thinking what I think, feeling what I feel, wants what I want, fearing what I fear: no 'ifs,' 'buts,' or 'not reallys.'" This is the type of acceptance which is hypothesized as being necessary if personality change is to occur.

Like the two previous conditions, this fourth condition is a matter of degree,[3] as immediately becomes apparent if we attempt to define it in terms of specific research operations. One such method of giving it definition would be to consider the Q sort for the relationship as described under

---

[3] The phrase "unconditional positive regard" may be an unfortunate one, since it sounds like an absolute, an all or nothing dispositional concept. It is probably evident from the description that completely unconditional positive regard would never exist except in theory. From a clinical and experiential point of view I believe the most accurate statement is that the effective therapist experiences unconditional positive regard for the client during many moments of his contact with him, yet from time to time he experiences only a conditional positive regard—and perhaps at times a negative regard, though this is not likely in effective therapy. It is in this sense that unconditional positive regard exists as a matter of degree in any relationship.

Condition 3. To the extent that items expressive of unconditional positive regard are sorted as characteristic of the relationship by both the therapist and the observers, unconditional positive regard might be said to exist. Such items might include statements of this order: "I feel no revulsion at anything the client says"; "I feel neither approval nor disapproval of the client and his statements—simply acceptance"; "I feel warmly toward the client—toward his weaknesses and problems as well as his potentialities"; "I am not inclined to pass judgment on what the client tells me"; "I like the client." To the extent that both therapist and observers perceive these items as characteristic, or their opposites as uncharacteristic, Condition 4 might be said to be met.

Empathy

The fifth condition is that the therapist is experiencing an accurate, empathic understanding of the client's awareness of his own experience. To sense the client's private world as if it were your own, but without ever losing the "as if" quality—this is empathy, and this seems essential to therapy. To sense the client's anger, fear, or confusion as if it were your own, yet without your own anger, fear, or confusion getting bound up in it, is the condition we are endeavoring to describe. When the client's world is this clear to the therapist, and he moves about in it freely, then he can both communicate his understanding of what is clearly known to the client and can also voice meanings in the client's experience of which the client is scarcely aware. As one client described this second aspect: "Every now and again, with me in a tangle of thought and feeling, screwed up in a web of mutually divergent lines of movement, with impulses from different parts of me, and me feeling the feeling of its being all too much and suchlike— then whomp, just like a sunbeam thrusting its way through cloudbanks and tangles of foliage to spread a circle of light on a tangle of forest paths, came some comment from you. [It was] clarity, even disentanglement, an additional twist to the picture, a putting in place. Then the consequence —the sense of moving on, the relaxation. These were sunbeams." That such penetrating empathy is important for therapy is indicated by Fiedler's research (1950) in which items such as the following placed high in the description of relationships created by experienced therapists:

The therapist is well able to understand the patient's feelings.
The therapist is never in any doubt about what the patient means.
The therapist's remarks fit in just right with the patient's mood and content.
The therapist's tone of voice conveys the complete ability to share the patient's feelings.

An operational definition of the therapist's empathy could be provided in different ways. Use might be made of the Q sort described under

Condition 3. To the degree that items descriptive of accurate empathy were sorted as characteristic by both the therapist and the observers, this condition would be regarded as existing.

Another way of defining this condition would be for both client and therapist to sort a list of items descriptive of client feelings. Each would sort independently, the task being to represent the feelings which the client had experienced during a just completed interview. If the correlation between client and therapist sortings were high, accurate empathy would be said to exist, a low correlation indicating the opposite conclusion.

Still another way of measuring empathy would be for trained judges to rate the depth and accuracy of the therapist's empathy on the basis of listening to recorded interviews.

The Client's Perception of the Therapist

The final condition as stated is that the client perceives, to a minimal degree, the acceptance and empathy which the therapist experiences for him. Unless some communication of these attitudes has been achieved, then such attitudes do not exist in the relationship as far as the client is concerned, and the therapeutic process could not, by our hypothesis, be initiated.

Since attitudes cannot be directly perceived, it might be somewhat more accurate to state that therapist behaviors and words are perceived by the client as meaning that to some degree the therapist accepts and understands him.

An operational definition of this condition would not be difficult. The client might, after an interview, sort a Q-sort list of items referring to qualities representing the relationship between himself and the therapist. (The same list could be used as for Condition 3.) If several items descriptive of acceptance and empathy are sorted by the client as characteristic of the relationship, then this condition could be regarded as met. In the present state of our knowledge the meaning of "to a minimal degree" would have to be arbitrary.

Some Comments

Up to this point the effort has been made to present, briefly and factually, the conditions which I have come to regard as essential for psychotherapeutic change. I have not tried to give the theoretical context of these conditions nor to explain what seem to me to be the dynamics of their effectiveness. Such explanatory material will be available, to the reader who is interested, in the document already mentioned (see footnote 1).

I have, however, given at least one means of defining, in operational terms, each of the conditions mentioned. I have done this in order to stress the fact that I am not speaking of vague qualities which ideally should be present if some other vague result is to occur. I am presenting conditions which are crudely measurable even in the present state of our technology, and have suggested specific operations in each instance even though I am sure that more adequate methods of measurement could be devised by a serious investigator.

My purpose has been to stress the notion that in my opinion we are dealing with an if-then phenomenon in which knowledge of the dynamics is not essential to testing the hypotheses. Thus, to illustrate from another field: if one substance, shown by a series of operations to be the substance known as hydrochloric acid, is mixed with another substance, shown by another series of operations to be sodium hydroxide, then salt and water will be products of this mixture. This is true whether one regards the results as due to magic, or whether one explains it in the most adequate terms of modern chemical theory. In the same way it is being postulated here that certain definable conditions precede certain definable changes and that this fact exists independently of our efforts to account for it.

THE RESULTING HYPOTHESES

The major value of stating any theory in unequivocal terms is that specific hypotheses may be drawn from it which are capable of proof or disproof. Thus, even if the conditions which have been postulated as necessary and sufficient conditions are more incorrect than correct (which I hope they are not), they could still advance science in this field by providing a base of operations from which fact could be winnowed out from error.

The hypotheses which would follow from the theory given would be of this order:

If these six conditions (as operationally defined) exist, then constructive personality change (as defined) will occur in the client.

If one or more of these conditions is not present, constructive personality change will not occur.

These hypotheses hold in any situation whether it is or is not labeled "psychotherapy."

Only Condition 1 is dichotomous (it either is present or is not), and the remaining five occur in varying degree, each on its continuum. Since this is true, another hypothesis follows, and it is likely that this would be the simplest to test:

If all six conditions are present, then the greater the degree to which Conditions 2 to 6 exist, the more marked will be the constructive personality change in the client.

At the present time the above hypothesis can only be stated in this general form—which implies that all of the conditions have equal weight. Empirical studies will no doubt make possible much more refinement of this hypothesis. It may be, for example, that if anxiety is high in the client, then the other conditions are less important. Or if unconditional positive regard is high (as in a mother's love for her child), then perhaps a modest degree of empathy is sufficient. But at the moment we can only speculate on such possibilities.

SOME IMPLICATIONS

Significant Omissions

If there is any startling feature in the formulation which has been given as to the necessary conditions for therapy, it probably lies in the elements which are omitted. In present-day clinical practice, therapists operate as though there were many other conditions in addition to those described, which are essential for psychotherapy. To point this up it may be well to mention a few of the conditions which, after thoughtful consideration of our research and our experience, are not included.

For example, it is *not* stated that these conditions apply to one type of client, and that other conditions are necessary to bring about psychotherapeutic change with other types of client. Probably no idea is so prevalent in clinical work today as that one works with neurotics in one way, with psychotics in another; that certain therapeutic conditions must be provided for compulsives, others for homosexuals, etc. Because of this heavy weight of clinical opinion to the contrary, it is with some "fear and trembling" that I advance the concept that the essential conditions of psychotherapy exist in a single configuration, even though the client or patient may use them very differently.[4]

It is *not* stated that these six conditions are the essential conditions for client-centered therapy, and that other conditions are essential for other types of psychotherapy. I certainly am heavily influenced by my own experience, and that experience has led me to a viewpoint which is termed

[4] I cling to this statement of my hypothesis even though it is challenged by a just completed study by Kirtner (1955). Kirtner has found, in a group of 26 cases from the Counseling Center at the University of Chicago, that there are sharp differences in the client's mode of approach to the resolution of life difficulties, and that these differences are related to success in psychotherapy. Briefly, the client who sees his problem as involving his relationships, and who feels that he contributes to this problem and wants to change it, is likely to be successful. The client who externalizes his problem, feeling little self-responsibility, is much more likely to be a failure. Thus the implication is that some other conditions need to be provided for psychotherapy with this group. For the present, however, I will stand by my hypothesis as given, until Kirtner's study is confirmed, and until we know an alternative hypothesis to take its place.

"client centered." Nevertheless my aim in stating this theory is to state the conditions which apply to *any* situation in which constructive personality change occurs, whether we are thinking of classical psychoanalysis, or any of its modern offshoots, or Adlerian psychotherapy, or any other. It will be obvious then that in my judgment much of what is considered to be essential would not be found, empirically, to be essential. Testing of some of the stated hypotheses would throw light on this perplexing issue. We may of course find that various therapies produce various types of personality change, and that for each psychotherapy a separate set of conditions is necessary. Until and unless this is demonstrated, I am hypothesizing that effective psychotherapy of any sort produces similar changes in personality and behavior, and that a single set of preconditions is necessary.

It is *not* stated that psychotherapy is a special kind of relationship, different in kind from all others which occur in everyday life. It will be evident instead that for brief moments, at least, many good friendships fulfill the six conditions. Usually this is only momentarily, however, and then empathy falters, the positive regard becomes conditional, or the congruence of the "therapist" friend becomes overlaid by some degree of facade or defensiveness. Thus the therapeutic relationship is seen as a heightening of the constructive qualities which often exist in part in other relationships, and an extension through time of qualities which in other relationships tend at best to be momentary.

It is *not* stated that special intellectual professional knowledge—psychological, psychiatric, medical, or religious—is required of the therapist. Conditions 3, 4, and 5, which apply especially to the therapist, are qualities of experience, not intellectual information. If they are to be acquired, they must, in my opinion, be acquired through an experiential training—which may be, but usually is not, a part of professional training. It troubles me to hold such a radical point of view, but I can draw no other conclusion from my experience. Intellectual training and the acquiring of information has, I believe, many valuable results—but becoming a therapist is not one of those results.

It is *not* stated that it is necessary for psychotherapy that the therapist have an accurate psychological diagnosis of the client. Here too it troubles me to hold a viewpoint so at variance with my clinical colleagues. When one thinks of the vast proportion of time spent in any psychological, psychiatric, or mental hygiene center on the exhaustive psychological evaluation of the client or patient, it seems as though this *must* serve a useful purpose insofar as psychotherapy is concerned. Yet the more I have observed therapists, and the more closely I have studied research such as that done by Fiedler and others (Fiedler, 1953), the more I am forced to the conclusion that such diagnostic knowledge is not essential to psychotherapy.[5] It

---

[5] There is no intent here to maintain that diagnostic evaluation is useless. We have ourselves made heavy use of such methods in our research studies of change in personality. It is its usefulness as a precondition to psychotherapy which is questioned.

may even be that its defense as a necessary prelude to psychotherapy is simply a protective alternative to the admission that it is, for the most part, a colossal waste of time. There is only one useful purpose I have been able to observe which relates to psychotherapy. Some therapists cannot feel secure in the relationship with the client unless they possess such diagnostic knowledge. Without it they feel fearful of him, unable to be empathic, unable to experience unconditional regard, finding it necessary to put up a pretense in the relationship. If they know in *advance* of suicidal impulses they can somehow be more acceptant of them. Thus, for some therapists, the security they perceive in diagnostic information may be a basis for permitting themselves to be integrated in the relationship, and to experience empathy and full acceptance. In these instances a psychological diagnosis would certainly be justified as adding to the comfort and hence the effectiveness of the therapist. But even here it does not appear to be a basic precondition for psychotherapy.[6]

Perhaps I have given enough illustrations to indicate that the conditions I have hypothesized as necessary and sufficient for psychotherapy are striking and unusual primarily by virtue of what they omit. If we were to determine, by a survey of the behaviors of therapists, those hypotheses which they appear to regard as necessary to psychotherapy, the list would be a great deal longer and more complex.

Is This Theoretical Formulation Useful?

Aside from the personal satisfaction it gives as a venture in abstraction and generalization, what is the value of a theoretical statement such as has been offered in this paper? I should like to spell out more fully the usefulness which I believe it may have.

In the field of research it may give both direction and impetus to investigation. Since it sees the conditions of constructive personality change as general, it greatly broadens the opportunities for study. Psychotherapy is not the only situation aimed at constructive personality change. Programs of training for leadership in industry and programs of training for military leadership often aim at such change. Educational institutions or programs frequently aim at development of character and personality as well as at intellectual skills. Community agencies aim at personality and behavioral change in delinquents and criminals. Such programs would provide an opportunity for the broad testing of the hypotheses offered. If it is found that constructive personality change occurs in such programs when the hypothesized conditions are not fulfilled, then the theory would have to be revised.

---

[6] In a facetious moment I have suggested that such therapists might be made equally comfortable by being given the diagnosis of some other individual, not of this patient or client. The fact that the diagnosis proved inaccurate as psychotherapy continued would not be particularly disturbing, because one always expects to find inaccuracies in the diagnosis as one works with the individual.

If however the hypotheses are upheld, then the results, both for the planning of such programs and for our knowledge of human dynamics, would be significant. In the field of psychotherapy itself, the application of consistent hypotheses to the work of various schools of therapists may prove highly profitable. Again the disproof of the hypotheses offered would be as important as their confirmation, either result adding significantly to our knowledge.

For the practice of psychotherapy the theory also offers significant problems for consideration. One of its implications is that the techniques of the various therapies are relatively unimportant except to the extent that they serve as channels for fulfilling one of the conditions. In client-centered therapy, for example, the technique of "reflecting feelings" has been described and commented on (Rogers, 1951, pp. 26–36). In terms of the theory here being presented, this technique is by no means an essential condition of therapy. To the extent, however, that it provides a channel by which the therapist communicates a sensitive empathy and an unconditional positive regard, then it may serve as a technical channel by which the essential conditions of therapy are fulfilled. In the same way, the theory I have presented would see no essential value to therapy of such techniques as interpretation of personality dynamics, free association, analysis of dreams, analysis of the transference, hypnosis, interpretation of life style, suggestion, and the like. Each of these techniques may, however, become a channel for communicating the essential conditions which have been formulated. An interpretation may be given in a way which communicates the unconditional positive regard of the therapist. A stream of free association may be listened to in a way which communicates an empathy which the therapist is experiencing. In the handling of the transference an effective therapist often communicates his own wholeness and congruence in the relationship. Similarly for the other techniques. But just as these techniques *may* communicate the elements which are essential for therapy, so any one of them may communicate attitudes and experiences sharply contradictory to the hypothesized conditions of therapy. Feeling may be "reflected" in a way which communicates the therapist's lack of empathy. Interpretations may be rendered in a way which indicates the highly conditional regard of the therapist. Any of the techniques may communicate the fact that the therapist is expressing one attitude at a surface level, and another contradictory attitude which is denied to his own awareness. Thus one value of such a theoretical formulation as we have offered is that it may assist therapists to think more critically about those elements of their experience, attitudes, and behaviors which are essential to psychotherapy, and those which are nonessential or even deleterious to psychotherapy.

Finally, in those programs—educational, correctional, military, or industrial—which aim toward constructive changes in the personality structure and behavior of the individual, this formulation may serve as a very tentative criterion against which to measure the program. Until it is much further tested by research, it cannot be thought of as a valid criterion, but, as in the field of psychotherapy, it may help to stimulate critical analysis and the formulation of alternative conditions and alternative hypotheses.

SUMMARY

Drawing from a larger theoretical context, six conditions are postulated as necessary and sufficient conditions for the initiation of a process of constructive personality change. A brief explanation is given of each condition, and suggestions are made as to how each may be operationally defined for research purposes. The implications of this theory for research, for psychotherapy, and for educational and training programs aimed at constructive personality change, are indicated. It is pointed out that many of the conditions which are commonly regarded as necessary to psychotherapy are, in terms of this theory, nonessential.

REFERENCES

Bown, O. H. An investigation of therapeutic relationship in client-centered therapy. Unpublished doctor's dissertation, Univer. of Chicago, 1954.

Chodorkoff, B. Self-perception, perceptual defense, and adjustment. *J. abnorm. soc. Psychol.*, 1954, 49, 503–512.

Fiedler, F. E. A comparison of therapeutic relationships in psychoanalytic, non-directive and Adlerian therapy. *J. consult. Psychol.*, 1950, *14*, 436–445.

Fiedler, F. E. Quantitative studies on the role of therapists' feelings toward their patients. In O. H. Mowrer (Ed.), *Psychotherapy: theory and research.* New York: Ronald Press, 1953.

Kirtner, W. L. Success and failure in client-centered therapy as a function of personality variables. Unpublished master's thesis, University of Chicago, 1955.

Rogers, C. R. *Client-centered therapy.* Boston: Houghton Mifflin, 1951.

Rogers, C. R., & Dymond, Rosalind F. (Eds.) *Psychotherapy and personality change.* Chicago: University of Chicago Press, 1954.

Standal, S. The need for positive regard: a contribution to client-centered theory. Unpublished doctor's dissertation, University of Chicago, 1954.

29

Changes in the Relation between Self-concepts and Ideal Concepts Consequent upon Client-centered Counseling

JOHN M. BUTLER
& GERARD V. HAIGH

I. INTRODUCTION

This chapter reports a study which grows out of the theoretical interest which has been focused upon the self-concept as a useful construct in understanding the dynamics of personality and of behavior. The self-concept, or self-structure, is defined by Rogers (1951) as an organized, fluid but consistent, conceptual pattern of the characteristics of the "I" or the "me" which are admissible into awareness, together with the values attached to those concepts. Since this self-concept is seen as the criterion determining the "repression" or awareness of experiences and as exerting a regulatory effect upon behavior (Rogers, 1951, chap. 11), its relevance to any study of counseling or psychotherapy is clear. How such a seemingly intangible notion is to be used in an objective fashion is less clear.

Theoretical Assumptions of This Study

Let us first consider the basic logic involved in arriving at some operational use of this construct. We start with the notion of Rogers that the self-concept consists of an organized conceptual pattern of the "I" or "me" together with the values attached to those concepts. This implies

From J. M. Butler and G. V. Haigh, Changes in the Relation between Self-concepts and Ideal Concepts Consequent upon Client-centered Counseling, In Rogers & Dymond, *Psychotherapy and personality change*, pp. 55–75. Reprinted by permission of author and publisher.

The Addendum was prepared by Dr. Butler for this book and is included with permission of author and publisher.

that many single self-perceptions, standing in relation each to the other, exist for the same individual. It is quite possible for the individual to order these self-percepts along a subjective or psychophysical continuum from "unlike me" to "like me." Thus, if a given characteristic such as "intelligence" is held by the individual to apply to himself, this characteristic may be perceived by the individual to be more or less like himself than another characteristic, such as "introversion." Thus, if asked, the individual may say, "It is more characteristic of me that I am intelligent than it is that I am introverted. However, I am both intelligent and introverted." To put this in terms of the logic of science, we may say that the fundamental relation involved is the transitive asymmetrical relation, in which if A is greater than B, and B greater than C, then A is greater than C. Thus one assumption is that the individual is able to make this type of judgment about his self-perceptions and to order them along a continuum.

This subjective scale does not, however, yield any clues as to the values attached to the self-concepts. For instance, an individual might say, "I am intelligent and glad of it" (or "I am not stupid and glad of it"). He might say, "I am introverted and am unhappy about it" (or "I am not extroverted and am unhappy about it"). In order to take care of this criss-cross of metrics, we introduce the notion of the ideal self-concept. This is here defined as the organized conceptual pattern of characteristics and emotional states which the individual consciously holds as desirable (and undesirable) for himself. The assumption is that the individual is able to order his self-perceptions along a continuum of value from "what I would most like to be" to "what I would least like to be" or, more briefly, from "like my ideal" to "unlike my ideal." This subjective scale could then yield a distribution of the same characteristics or self-perceptions which were ordered along the scale of "like me" to "unlike me."

The discrepancy between the placements of a given characteristic on the self scale and the ideal scale would yield an indication of self-esteem. It would indicate operationally not only the way in which the individual perceived himself as possessing this given characteristic but the degree to which he values this state. The discrepancies between self and ideal on all these characteristics would yield an index of self-esteem or self-value.

The Instrument

These assumptions about the ordering of characteristics were implemented by means of a list of self-referent statements. A set of one hundred such statements was taken at random from available therapeutic protocols (actually the statements were selected on an accidental sampling rather than a strictly random basis), reworded for clarity, and give to both control and client subjects. The subjects were required to sort the items on the metrics "like-me" to "unlike-me" and "like-ideal" to "unlike-ideal." The sort was a forced normal sort with nine piles.[1] The subjects were given the following instructions:

1. *Self-sort*. Sort these cards to describe yourself as you see yourself today, from those that are least like you to those that are most like you.

2. *Ideal sort*. Now sort these cards to describe your ideal person—the person you would most like within yourself to be.

The nature of the items to be sorted on these two scales may be suggested by these illustrations: "I am a submissive person"; "I am a hard worker"; "I am really disturbed"; "I am afraid of a full-fledged disagreement with a person"; "I am likeable."

It should be noted that the forced sorting of these items into an approximately normal distribution is not a fundamental requirement. Transitive asymmetrical relations when applied to self-concepts and ideal concepts basically imply ranking. The form of the distribution and the sorting of the items into nine piles represents the somewhat arbitrary introduction of a set number of ties into what is essentially a ranking situation. Since our concern was with the correlation between sorts, it is believed that neither the number of ties nor the form of distribution is a matter of serious concern as long as the joint distribution is normal. Indeed, we are of the opinion that the prescribed conditions are an advantage. Psychophysical considerations lead one to expect that forcing a sort leads to finer differentiations than uncontrolled sorting, whereas forcing a nontied ranking of as many as one hundred items might lead to fatigue and carelessness.

The Rationale of the Hypotheses

The hypotheses of this study may be stated very briefly, but it may be well to preface them with a statement of their rationale. We hold that a discrepancy between the self-concept and the concept of the desired or valued self reflects a sense of self-dissatisfaction, which in turn generates the motivation for coming into counseling. Such a discrepancy ordinarily exists when an individual comes for help. It is our hypothesis that this self-dissatisfaction is reduced as a result of counseling. Self-ideal discrepancies in an individual are a product or outcome of experiences which indicate to him that his self-organization is unsatisfactory. Also, the reduction of such discrepancies, consequent upon counseling, is based theoretically on the

---

[1] This is "Q-technique" as developed by Stephenson (1953). To the best of our knowledge the first studies using Q-technique to assess counseling are those by Margaret W. Hartley in an unpublished Ph.D. dissertation, "A Q-Technique Study of Changes in the Self-concept during Psychotherapy" (University of Chicago, 1951), and an unpublished analysis by Thomas E. Jeffrey of data by Haigh entitled "A Quantitative Analysis of the Effect of Client-centered Counseling" (1949).

disorganization and reorganization of both self and ideal structures under the conditions of counseling. The immediate goal of the counselor is to create conditions under which the client can relax his defenses and assimilate experiences into new conceptual patterns. These new patterns are consistent with a wider range of experiences than the conceptual patterns which existed when the client came in. The reduction of discrepancies between self and ideal, therefore, is a result or outcome of fundamental experiences in relationship with a counselor. During the counseling process itself such discrepancies may become greater before they become less. Our basic hypothesis is, then, that a reduction of self-ideal discrepancies is a consequence of the self-concept and the ideal concept coming to rest on a broader base of available experience than before. It is in this way that they become more consistent with each other.

The Q-technique used in this study, with its sortings for the self-characteristics and their perceived values, is clearly in harmony with this theory of the dynamics of inner reorganization. Hence it seems justifiable to regard an increase in the correlation between self and ideal sorts as an operational indication of an increased congruence between the concept of self and the concept of the valued person.

It is recognized that in one respect the method used may not always reflect accurately this fundamental change which is hypothesized. It is possible for a client, either prior to or following therapy, to sort the cards so as to indicate a small self-ideal discrepancy, when, as judged by other criteria, a large discrepancy exists. He may, in other words, be sufficiently motivated by defensive needs that he pictures himself as being very much like the self he values, when, at a deeper level, he feels that he does not resemble his ideal self. The reverse—that is, the picturing of a discrepancy between self and ideal where no such discrepancy exists—is less likely to occur. While recognizing this possibility of a "defensive" type of sorting, it is our hypothesis that the changes indicated in the foregoing paragraph will be evident operationally in the group as increased self-ideal correlations.

It is a part of our theoretical expectation that self-concepts will change as a function of counseling more than ideal concepts. By their very nature it seems probable that ideal concepts are largely general societal concepts, whereas self-concepts may be more idiosyncratic. This notion is borne out by pilot studies which indicate that the correlations between the self-concepts held by different clients are low (of the order of .20), whereas the correlations between the ideal concepts held by different clients are higher (of the order of .50). However, ideal concepts can be expected to show change to the extent that they are introjected (Rogers, 1951, chap. 11). As one client put it after a twentieth-interview sorting of his ideal self: "I am just realizing there are a lot of things I want to be that others [parents] wouldn't approve of. Until now I've acted on the basis of what I ought to be; I've wanted to be what I ought to be. Now I want to be what

I want to be." It is clear that his concept of the desired self is undergoing change in an idiosyncratic direction.

Hypotheses

On the basis of the preceding considerations, we hypothesize that (*a*) client-centered counseling results in a decrease of self-ideal discrepancies and that (*b*) self-ideal discrepancies will be more clearly reduced in clients who have been judged, on experimentally independent criteria, as exhibiting definite improvement. The first hypothesis is without restriction. The second, in being restricted to the subclass of clients evaluated as "successful," does not require a generalized effect of counseling upon the client population.

II. FINDINGS FROM THE CLIENT GROUP AS A WHOLE

We will consider now the evidence from the client group which bears on the first hypothesis. The design of the research and the method of data collection have been described previously. The correlations were computed between the self-sorts and the ideal sorts for the twenty-five clients in the first block (Block I) who had completed six or more counseling interviews and for whom follow-up tests (administered six months to one year after completion of counseling) were available. This group will hereafter be referred to as the *client group*. We will be concerned, in this study, with the sortings made by each client for self and ideal at each of three points— pre-counseling, post-counseling, and follow-up. Table 29-1 gives the self-ideal correlations for these clients at these three points.

The Self-Ideal Relationship before Counseling

From Table 29-1 it can be seen that the pre-counseling self-ideal correlations range from −.47, a very marked discrepancy between self and ideal, to .59, a considerable degree of congruence. The mean z of the array, using Fisher's method (Tippett, 1937, p. 176) is −.01, and the corresponding r is the same, −.01. This is obviously not a significant correlation, and the calculation of the t ratio confirms this. The standard error determined from the observed distribution of z is .07, and the t ratio for testing the hypothesis that the mean z of the client population is zero is −.14, a statistically nonsignificant result.

It is a question, however, whether this zero-order correlation means that there is nothing but a random relationship between self and ideal, or

TABLE 29-1. Self-Ideal Correlations in the Client Group

Client	Pre-counseling r	Post-counseling r	Follow-up r
Oak	.21	.69	.71
Babi	.05	.54	.45
Bacc	−.31	.04	−.19
Bame	.14	.61	.61
Bana	−.38	.36	.44
Barr	−.34	−.13	.02
Bayu	−.47	−.04	.42
Bebb	.06	.26	.21
Beda	.59	.80	.69
Beel	.28	.52	−.04
Beke	.27	.69	−.56
Bene	.38	.80	.78
Benz	−.30	−.04	.39
Beri	.33	.43	.64
Beso	.32	.41	.47
Bett	−.37	.39	.61
Bico	−.11	.51	.72
Bifu	−.12	−.17	−.26
Bime	−.33	.05	.00
Bina	−.30	.59	.71
Bink	−.08	.30	−.20
Bira	.26	−.08	−.16
Bixy	−.39	−.39	.05
Blen	.23	.33	−.36
Bajo	.16	.29	.47
Mean z	−.01	.36	.32
Corresponding r	−.01	.34	.31

whether there might be significant association between self and ideal, which is for some clients positive and for some negative, with a resulting mean in the neighborhood of zero. In order to test this possibility, which appears probable from inspection, we use the chi square, which, according to Tippett (1937, p. 179), is a proper test of association for a group of correlations. We use the formula

$$x^2 = \Sigma(z\sqrt{N-3})^2,$$

with n degrees of freedom, where n is the number of clients and N is the number of items sorted in each Q-sort. For these pre-counseling self-ideal correlations of the client group the value of chi square for magnitude of association is 245.5, which is well beyond the value at the 1 per cent level of significance, 44.31. This result indicates both that there is association between self and ideal in the client group and that there are significant individual differences in self-ideal correlation in this population. The latter conclusion may be also stated as indicating that there are distinct sub-populations in the client population.

Thus our finding in regard to the pre-counseling status of our client group may be stated as follows: The relationship between self and ideal, prior to counseling, is of a zero order, but this lack of correlation is not randomness of association but is due to the fact that there is a wide range of significant associations between self and ideal in the individuals or sub-populations composing the group.

It is interesting to speculate, in passing, as to the relationship between the self-ideal congruence and "adjustment" or "integration." There might be a temptation to see this as a direct relationship. It is unlikely that this is the case and more likely that certain subclasses of individuals will be found who, exhibiting certain types of high and low items in their sortings and certain magnitudes of correlations between self and ideal, will have a specifiable relationship to "adjustment" or "integration." In brief, certain patterns of the self-ideal Gestalt may be discovered to indicate certain patterns or types of personality integration. It is possible that factor analysis of the self-ideal sortings may isolate such fundamental patterns. Such studies are now under way.

The Self-Ideal Relationship at Follow-up

The self-ideal relationship of the client group at follow-up may also be observed in Table 29-1. The range now is even wider, from $-.56$ to $.78$, from a very sharp discrepancy to a very substantial similarity. The mean z is now $.32$, and the corresponding r is $.31$. The ratio of the mean z to its standard error, obtained from the observed values of z, is 3.39 and is well beyond the 1 per cent level of significance for 24 degrees of freedom.[2]

To test again for the significance of individual differences, we use the formula suggested by Tippett (p. 180) for use when the mean correlation has been found to be significant, namely,

$$x^2 = (N - 3)\Sigma(z - \bar{z})^2,$$

with $n - 1$ degrees of freedom, where n and N have the same meaning as before, and $\bar{z}$ denotes the mean value of z. The value of chi square so obtained is 518.7, which is far beyond the 1 per cent level of 42.98. This latter

[2] One-tailed tests are used for all tests of directional hypothesis in this study. Thus one-tailed tests are used for comparing pre-counseling and follow-up results on the clients and for comparisons of mean gains as between controls and clients. Two-tailed tests are used for comparing controls with controls.

result is similar to the result obtained at the pre-counseling testing in suggesting that there are true individual differences in the magnitude of self-ideal correlations. However, these individual differences are now found in terms of a deviation aound an estimated mean z of .32 instead of a hypothesized mean z of zero.

Thus we may say of our clients at the time of the follow-up study: There is now a significant degree of congruence between the perception of the self and the perception of the valued self. There is also a wide and significant range of individual differences in the degree of self-ideal similarity which exists.

A Comparison of the Pre-counseling and Follow-up Results

We come now to one of the crucial aspects of the evidence bearing upon the first hypothesis, the question as to whether there has been a significant decrease in the discrepancy between the self-concept and the wanted self over the period from pre-counseling to follow-up. The mean pre-counseling self-ideal correlation was $-.01$, and the follow-up correlation, .31—a mean difference of .32. Expressed in terms of z, the mean difference is .33. The ratio of the mean difference z to its standard error of .11, based on observed z's, is 3.0, which is well beyond the 1 per cent level of significance for 24 degrees of freedom. This would indicate a significant change in the hypothesized direction.

It is of interest, though it does not bear directly upon the hypothesis, that there has also been a marked increase in the degree of variation of correlations over this period. The variances of the pre-counseling and follow-up correlations, when transformed to z's, are .11 and .22, respectively. The t ratio for comparison of related variances (Walker & Lev, 1953, p. 190) is approximately 1.84 and is significant at the 5 per cent level.

Since there might be some question as to whether the data meet the assumptions necessary for using the t test for paired differences, it was decided to use a nonparametric statistic as well. The sign test (Walker & Lev, 1953, p. 431) was run on the differences. There were nineteen increases (positive differences) in self-ideal correlations and six decreases (negative differences). This result is significant at better than the 1 per cent level, thus confirming the findings from the t test.

From these results it seems doubtful that the number of increases in self-ideal correlation from pre-counseling to follow-up, the amount of such increase, and the increase in the variance are based on random changes. Rather it appears that directional changes of a significant sort are evident and that these provide confirmation of the hypothesis that the discrepancy between self and ideal will be reduced over therapy.

The Post-counseling Findings

It will have been noted that the foregoing comparisons have been made between the pre-counseling and the follow-up correlations. It was felt that the sortings made at the conclusion of counseling might be considered by some to be contaminated by the "hello-goodbye" effect described by Hathaway (1948).

Consideration of the results at the end of counseling, however, only confirms the other picture. The mean post-counseling correlation for the total client group is .34 (see Table 29-1), which is close to the mean of .31 at follow-up. Thus the increase in congruence over counseling was from an r of $-.01$ to .34—a difference of .35, as compared to a difference of .32 over the whole period from precounseling to follow-up. The number of increases in self-ideal correlation from the pre-counseling to the post-counseling testing was twenty-three and, of decreases, two. This result is significant at the 1 per cent level of significance. Over the period from post-counseling to follow-up there were twelve increases in self-ideal correlation, twelve decreases, and one tie, indicating no trend during the follow-up period.

If the "hello-goodbye" effect was a factor in the behavior of these clients, it did not seem to affect their self and ideal sorts to an appreciable degree unless one wishes to postulate that it persisted during the six- to twelve-month follow-up period.

III. FINDINGS FROM THE CONTROL GROUPS

We now turn our attention to the equivalent-control group. This control group was selected to be roughly equivalent to the client group with respect to age, sex, socioeconomic status, and student-nonstudent status. Control-group subjects were tested at the same intervals as clients. At the time this analysis was begun, only sixteen of the controls had completed their testing, and these subjects comprise our group. It will be recalled that the rationale of the research design in regard to this group is as follows: The test scores of these individuals will indicate whether there is change as a result of the passage of time, the experience with the test, and the influence of random variables in a group which is in age, sex, and status similar to the client group.

This rationale leaves untouched the question of whether motivation for counseling rather than counseling itself produces congruence between self and ideal measurements. To answer this question, the own-control procedure was used, in which half the clients underwent a sixty-day control period prior to counseling. The test scores over this sixty-day period will indicate whether test results of clients change as a result of motivation for counseling per se. Obviously, if change occurs in the client group which is greater than that which occurs in the equivalent-control group or in the own-control period, then it is reasonable to attribute this degree of change to our experimental variable, client-centered counseling.

The Self-Ideal Relationship at Pre-counseling

The data from the equivalent-control group are given in Table 29-2. It will be seen that at the pre-counseling point the self-ideal correlations range from −.01 to .86. The mean z of the array is .66, with a corresponding r of .58. The ratio of the mean z to its standard error, based on the observed distribution, is 6.4. This is significant beyond the 1 per cent level. It is obvious that there is, on the average, much more congruence between self and ideal in the controls than was found in the clients. This is in accordance with theoretical expectations.

In order to determine whether there were significant individual differences in the magnitude of the self-ideal correlations, the chi square was utilized in the same way as with the client group. The value of chi square was 247.06—far above the 1 per cent value, which is 30.58. We therefore conclude, as in the case of the client group, that there are distinct sub-

TABLE 29-2.   Self-Ideal Correlations in the Control Group

Client	Pre-counseling r	Follow-up r
Aban	.80	.50
Abor	.00	.30
Acro	.86	.89
Agaz	.75	.83
Akim	.84	.86
Akor	.48	−.03
Ajil	.49	.45
Afit	.73	.71
Abul	.58	.77
Adis	.42	.65
Abri	.35	.30
Abbe	.35	.36
Acme	.80	.65
Abco	.65	.76
Abet	−.01	.43
Adir	.30	.07
Mean z	.66	.68
Corresponding r	.58	.59

classes of individual self-ideal relations in the control population. Whether these subclasses are the same as those in the client population cannot be ascertained from the data here presented. However, studies designed to provide answers to this question are now in progress.

The Self-Ideal Relationship at Follow-up

For the follow-up testing of the controls the range of the self-ideal correlations is from $-.03$ to $.89$. The mean z of the array is $.68$, with a corresponding r of $.59$. The standard error of the mean z, based on the observed distribution, is $.11$, and the t ratio is 6.3, which indicates a 1 per cent level of significance. The chi square for individual differences in magnitude of self-ideal correlations is 272.28, with the 1 per cent value being 30.58.

The variances of the pre-counseling and follow-up correlations, when transformed to z's, are $.17$ and $.19$, respectively. The t ratio for comparing related variances is $.28$ and is not significant for 14 degrees of freedom.

The picture at this final testing point is, it is evident, very similar to what it was at the pre-counseling point.

Inspection of the data from pre-counseling to follow-up in these control individuals shows a considerable degree of consistency, though there are some sharp individual changes which indicate that alteration in self-ideal congruence does occur at times in the absence of therapy. The over-all findings are, however, clear, as is indicated in the following paragraphs by both the t ratio and the Wilcoxon sign test, both showing that no significant change has occurred in the control group.

The differences between the mean z's of the pre-counseling and the follow-up correlations of the controls is $.02$, with the standard error of the difference being $.08$. The t ratio is $.25$, which is not significant. Therefore, there is no reason to believe that the control correlations, pre-counseling and follow-up, are from populations with different means and variances.

There were nine increases and seven decreases in self-ideal correlations from the pre-counseling to the follow-up testing. The Wilcoxon signed ranks test (Walker & Lev, 1953, p. 433) was used to test the paired differences, since it is sensitive to the magnitude of differences. The sum of the ranks corresponding to the negative differences is 63.5. The sum of the negatively signed ranks for the 5 per cent level of significance is 30, and the obtained sum is, therefore, not significant.

A Comparison of Change in Clients and Equivalent Controls

We have established that there are nonrandom increases in the self-ideal correlations of the client group from the pre-counseling to follow-up and that similar increases cannot be regarded as established for the control group. The results for the comparisons of variances are similar. Nevertheless, the results are ambiguous, since it might be held that there is a combined effect of testing and counseling leading to a conclusion of definite increases where none exists. To test this possibility, we must ask whether the increase in the self-ideal correlations in the client group is significantly greater than the increase found in the control group. The mean gain in z for the client group is .33 and for the control group .02; the mean difference is .31, with a standard error of .13. The t ratio is 2.38 and is significant at the 2.5 per cent level of significance.

When the nonparametric Mann-Whitney test (Walker & Lev, 1953, p. 434) is applied to the paired differences of r's for the pre-counseling and the follow-up testing of the control and client groups considered together, the sum of the ranks for the control group is 245.5. This sum is significant at the 1 per cent level, indicating a true change in the client group over and above the change found in the control group.

Findings from the Own-Control Group

Do clients motivated for counseling show alteration in the relationship between self and ideal simply as the result of the passage of time? The data on this point come from the own-control group, the findings from which are presented in integrated fashion by Grummon in a later chapter.[3]

We are now in a position to assemble the findings which relate to our present concern.

The fifteen members of the client group who formed the own-control group were tested at the time they requested counseling and again at the pre-counseling point. They then went into counseling and, like the others, were tested at the post-counseling point and at follow-up. The relationship between self and ideal sortings for these fifteen clients at the pre-wait point is indicated by a mean z of $-.01$. At the pre-counseling point the relationship is still the same, $-.01$. It is clear that no change has occurred during the control period.[4]

The Testing of the First Hypothesis

We are now in a position to assemble the findings which relate to our first hypothesis—that client-centered counseling results in a decrease of self-ideal discrepancies. It has been shown that:

1. Both clients and controls exhibit significant individual differences at each point tested. The degree of self-ideal congruence has wide range in each group.

[3] In C. R. Rogers and R. F. Dymond, eds., *Psychotherapy and Personality Change*. Chicago, University of Chicago Press, 1954. —Ed. note.
[4] The finding is quite different for those applicants who did *not* continue in therapy after the sixty-day period.

2. The mean correlation of self and ideal in the client group at pre-counseling is −.01, which is not a significant degree of congruence.
3. The mean correlation of self and ideal in the client group at follow-up is .31, a significant relationship. This is a significant increase in self-ideal congruence, whether judged by the *t* test or by the sign test.
4. The finding is similar at the post-counseling point.
5. The mean correlation of self and ideal in the equivalent-control group at pre-counseling is .58, a significant congruence.
6. The mean correlation for this group at follow-up is .59, indicating no significant change over time.
7. The own-control group has a mean correlation of self and ideal of −.01 at pre-wait and −.01 at pre-counseling, indicating no change during the control period.
8. The change in the client group is significantly greater than the change found in the equivalent-control group or in clients in the own-control period. The difference is significant at the 2.5 per cent level in terms of the *t* test and at better than the 1 per cent level in terms of the sign test.

These findings lead us to infer that significant increases in the self-ideal correlations in the client group are consequent upon client-centered counseling.

IV. FINDINGS REGARDING DEFINITELY IMPROVED CLIENTS

We turn now to our second hypothesis—that the self-ideal discrepancies will, as a result of counseling, be more clearly reduced in those clients who have been judged, on independent criteria, as showing definite improvement. In terms of its rationale, this hypothesis states that, if the relationship between the self-concept and the ideal concept exists as theorized, the changes in this relationship should be more marked in a group in which the process of therapy has clearly occurred.

The Selection of the Improved Group

The client group was classified by using two criteria of success which were experimentally independent of each other and of the self-ideal correlations. One criterion was an over-all rating of success by the counselor of each client made at the conclusion of counseling; the rating was on a nine-point scale, with the highest scale value being 9. Another criterion was a judgment based on blind analyses of Thematic Apperception Test (TAT) protocols. The TAT-derived judgments were on a seven-point scale. Those clients were selected for the "improved" group who received counselor ratings of 5 with an improvement shown in TAT ratings or who received ratings of 6 or above and whose TAT ratings were no lower for the follow-up protocol than for pre-counseling. There was general positive agreement between the TAT and the counselor rating, since, of the sixteen clients chosen by these criteria, eleven showed improvement from pre-counseling to follow-up on the TAT ratings. One additional client included in the improved group has a counselor rating below 5. He was included because, although the counselor made a low rating on the basis of a judgment that the absolute level of inner adjustment was low at termination, the counselor had also predicted that the adjustment level would rise, since an integrative process had definitely been set in motion. Since the client's TAT rating exhibited a rise in scale value, he was included in the improved category. This gave a group of seventeen clients, who will be termed "definitely improved."

Of the eight remaining clients, none showed improvement on the TAT, and only two had counselor ratings above 5. These two showed a decrease on the TAT scale.

A Comparison with the Control Group

Before counseling, the improved group (see data in Table 29-3) has much the same statistical characteristics as the total group. The mean z between pre-counseling selves and ideals is .02, with the corresponding r having the same value. The mean z is not significantly different from zero for the pre-counseling correlations. As before, the chi-square value for association and for individual differences is highly significant, being 164.03, with 17 degrees of freedom. At the follow-up testing the mean r between self and ideal is .44, the corresponding z being .47. The t ratio for testing the hypothesis that the population mean correlation coefficient is zero is approximately 4.7, far beyond the 1 per cent level of significance. The chi-square value for individual differences is 277.32 for 16 degrees of freedom and again is greater than the 1 per cent value of chi square. It will be seen that the total picture is similar to that found in the client group as a whole, except that the increase in the mean correlation is greater.

Let us look at this group in relation to the equivalent-control group. One would expect, if the independent criteria of success and improvement were at all valid, that a significant difference would obtain between the mean gain for this client subgroup, selected on the basis of success and improvement, and the mean gain for the control group. This, indeed, is the case. The difference between the mean gain in z's for the improved client group (.45) and the control group (.02) is .43, with the standard error being .13. The t ratio is 3.31 and is significant at the 1 per cent level. The Mann-Whitney test is also significant at the 1 per cent level. We conclude that, for clients judged on experimentally independent bases as im-

TABLE 29-3.   Self-Ideal Correlation in the Improved Client Group

| Client | Pre-counseling r | Follow-up r | Counselor's Rating | TAT Rating | |
				Pre-counseling	Follow-up
Oak	.21	.71	8	3	4
Babi	.05	.45	8	4	5
Bacc	−.31	−.19	6	3	4
Bame	.14	.61	6	4	4
Barr	−.34	.02	6	4	4
Bebb	.06	.21	6	2	2
Beda	.59	.69	6	4	6
Beel	.28	−.04	7	2	4
Bene	.38	.78	9	4	5
Benz	−.30	.39	7	3	5
Beri	.33	.64	7	2	3
Beso	.32	.47	5	5	6
Bett	−.37	.61	7	4	4
Bico*	−.11	.72	7		
Bime†	−.33	.00	4	4	5
Bina	−.30	.71	7	2	5
Bink	−.08	−.20	7	4	6
Mean z	.02	.47			
Corresponding r	.02	.44			

* Blind TAT ratings are not available, but a complete TAT analysis yielded a judgment of improvement.

† Counselor rated absolute adjustment level as low but held that an integrative process had begun in counseling which would result in post-counseling improvement.

proving in adjustment, the correlation between measured self and measured ideal increases between pre-counseling testing and follow-up testing and that the increase is a product of the counseling situation.

A Comparison with the Unimproved Group

Another comparison is that between the definitely improved group and the subgroup which is not definitely improved. One would expect that, if the criteria of success and improvement were related to the level of self-ideal correlation, the improved subgroup of clients could be distinguished from the less improved group by comparing them on the follow-up self-ideal correlations. This was tested by means of the Mann-Whitney test, and it was found that the sum of ranks of the less improved group was 65.5, which is significant at the 1 per cent level against a one-sided hypothesis. Thus the distribution of self-ideal correlations in the subgroup classified as improved is not from the same population as the distribution of correlations in the subgroup classified as less improved. The same test was applied to the pre-counseling self-ideal correlations classified according to whether the individual was judged as improved or less improved. The sum of ranks for the less improved group was 89, a nonsignificant result. Thus we may say that the improved group is not significantly different from those judged as less improved at the pre-counseling point. At the follow-up point, however, the difference is significant, the improved group showing a greater self-ideal congruence.

Curiously enough, when we compare magnitude of the increases in the self-ideal correlations from pre-counseling to follow-up, we do not find a significant difference between the two groups. The Mann-Whitney test was applied to the differences in the self-ideal correlations between the pre-counseling and follow-up testings when classified as improved and less improved. The sum of ranks for the negative differences was 83.5, which is not significant at the 12 per cent level.

Improvement, then, is related to final level of self-ideal correlations but not to increase in self-ideal correlations. This puzzling finding seems, on examination of the data, to be due to a defensive sorting of the cards by individuals whose final adjustment was no better or even worse than at the pre-counseling period. For example, gains of 44, 82, and 89 correlation points were made by three of the eight individuals classified as less improved. It appears that in some instances where both counselor ratings and TAT ratings give evidence of little or no improvement, defensive mechanisms are set in operation which produce sharp increases in self-ideal congruence—increases which are similar to those achieved by clients whose improvement is confirmed by evidence from other sources. In spite of these exceptions, the mean changes are in line with those hypothesized.

This finding also raises interesting questions about the relationship between the adjustment of an individual and the correlation between self and ideal. It is quite certain that a correlation of unity between self and ideal would not indicate perfect adjustment. Indeed, the only self-ideal correlation above .90 was achieved by an individual (in another study) who was clearly paranoid. Tentatively the speculation would seem warranted that extremely high self-ideal correlations are likely to be products of defensive sortings.

The Testing of the Second Hypothesis

The following evidence bears on the second hypothesis. A group selected as definitely improved, by criteria independent of the self and the ideal sorts, was found (1) to exhibit a more marked increase in congruence of self and ideal than the total client group; (2) to exhibit a significantly greater increase in such congruence than the equivalent-control group; (3) to be significantly different from the less improved subgroup at the follow-up point, though not at the pre-counseling point; and (4) to show no significant difference in magnitude of increases from the less improved subgroup.

All these findings except the last give definite confirmation to the hypothesis that a more improved group of clients exhibits a greater decrease in self-ideal discrepancies than a group of less improved clients or a group of controls. The final finding suggests that we are dealing with a complex rather than a simple relationship.

V. SUMMARY

In this chapter we have reported our investigation of the hypothesis that client-centered counseling results in an increase in congruence between the self and the self-ideal concepts in the client. It was also part of our hypothesis that this reduction would be especially marked in those cases judged independently as exhibiting improvement.

The total client group shows, at the outset, a generally large discrepancy between self and ideal, as these concepts are measured by Q-sorts under the associated conditions of instruction. The relationship approximates a zero correlation, indicative of low self-esteem and a decided degree of internal tension. By the end of counseling the discrepancy between self and ideal had decreased for a majority of clients, and the mean correlation was .34. At the follow-up point this reduction in the discrepancy had remained constant, suggesting that it was not due to a temporary "hello-goodbye" effect.

A comparison of the self-ideal discrepancy of the clients at the pre-counseling point and at the follow-up point indicates a statistically significant change. The variance within the group has also increased during this period, indicating, perhaps, a differential reduction in self-ideal discrepancies.

The control group at the outset exhibits a small discrepancy between self and ideal, relative to the client group, represented by a mean correlation of .58. There is no significant change in this discrepancy over time, and at the follow-up point the mean correlation is .59. The differences between the changes in the client group and in the control group are so large as to be clearly nonrandom in character.

An own-control group of fifteen of the clients were tested before and after a sixty-day period of no counseling, prior to the beginning of counseling. The relationship between self and ideal was approximately zero, and the motivation for counseling and personal reorganization produced no change during this control period, the correlation at the end of the period being again zero.

In order to test the second hypothesis, a group of seventeen "definitely improved" clients was selected on two criteria which were experimentally independent of each other and of this study. For this group the reduction in self-ideal discrepancy from pre-counseling to follow-up is even more marked than for the client group as a whole. The gain was also significantly greater than for the controls and for the "not definitely improved" group. Even at follow-up time, however, this group still showed a discrepancy between self and ideal greater than that found in the controls, suggesting that self-esteem and degree of internal comfort were still less than optimal.

Some evidence was presented suggesting that defensiveness may, under certain conditions, bring about an increase in self-ideal congruence not confirmed by other evidence.

In our opinion the results discussed here indicate that low correlations between self and ideal are based on a low level of self-esteem related to a relatively low adjustment level and that a consequence of client-centered counseling for the clients in this study was, on the average, a rise in the level of self-esteem and of adjustment.

REFERENCES

Cattell, R. B. On the Disuse and Misuse of P, Q, and O Techniques in Clinical Psychology, *Journal of Clinical Psychology*, VII (1951), 203–215.

Cronbach, Lee J., & Gleser, Goldine C. *Similarity between Persons and Related Problems of Profile Analysis.* (Technical Report No. 2.) Urbana, Ill.: Bureau of Research and Service, College of Education, University of Illinois, 1952.

Hathaway, S. R. Some Considerations Relative to Nondirective Counseling as Therapy, *Journal of Clinical Psychology*, IV (1948), 226–231.

Rogers, Carl R. *Client-centered Therapy.* Boston: Houghton Mifflin, 1951.

Stephenson, William. *The Study of Behavior: Q-Technique and Its Methodology.* Chicago: University of Chicago Press, 1953.

Tippett, L. H. C. *The Methods of Statistics.* London: William & Norgate, 1937.

Walker, H., & Lev, J. *Statistical Inference.* New York: Holt, 1953.

Addendum

Since the above was written more information has been accumulated on the relation between self and ideal concepts in client-centered psychotherapy. In particular it has been shown that for the items used in the above study, self-ideal correlations have a mean approximating zero for many client groups and that clients change systematically in self-ideal correlation whereas various types of control groups do not. Descriptively the change occurring in clients is an increase in both the mean and variance of the self-ideal correlations.

The mean self-ideal correlations for six different client and control groups are shown in Table 29-4. The results shown there support the hypothesis that changes in self-ideal correlation are due to psychotherapy whereas those of people not in psychotherapy do not change as a result of a systematic influence. This statement holds whether the controls are subjects who have had no therapy and do not expect to or whether they are clients on a waiting list.

Another aspect of systematic change is afforded by sub-groups 1a and 1b of Table 29-4. These clients were independently rated as definitely im-

TABLE 29-4. Mean Self-Ideal Correlation for Six Groups

Group	Type of Therapy	N	S_0I_0*	S_1I_1	S_2I_2	S_1S_2
I. Unlimited Therapy	Client-centered	29		−.04	.32	.49
1a Definitely improved		20		−.02	.52	.43†
1b Not definitely improved		9		−.08	.05	.63
II. (10 weeks of therapy)	Client-centered	43		.04	.26	
III. Normal Controls	None	16		.58	.59	
IV. Client Controls (10 wk wait)	None	20	−.04	.03		
V. Time Limited	Client-centered	20		.05	.44	
VI. Time Limited	Adlerian	14		.05	.35	

* Subscript of zero indicates prewait; of one, pretherapy test; of two, posttherapy.

† Mann-Whitney U test (U = 40) on combined ranks of improved and not-improved groups sig. at 1% level.

This section of the paper was not published with the original article, but was supplied by Dr. Butler for original publication in this volume.

proved (1a) or not definitely improved (1b) using a combination of TAT ratings and therapist success ratings (Butler & Haigh, 1954, p. 69). The self-sort before psychotherapy was correlated with the self-sort after therapy. The mean of these self-self correlations was .43 for the definitely improved group and .63 for the not definitely improved group. The Mann-Whitney U test (U = 40) on the combined ranks of the self-self correlations for the improved–not improved groups was significant at the 1 per cent level. Thus the not definitely improved group showed less mean change in self-self correlations than did the definitely improved group. Furthermore, the correlation between self and ideal in the definitely improved group exhibited a mean increase of .54; the increase for the not definitely improved group was .13. These results are compatible with the hypothesis that self and ideal concepts change more for definitely improved groups than for others and that the change is in the direction from self toward ideal rather than in a change from ideal to self. In general, clients do not lower their self-aspirations; they move toward realizing them.

Table 29-5 shows the z-transformed self-ideal correlation of 12 clients from group 1 who served as their own controls. They had a mean wait period of 63 days before entering therapy and were tested at a mean of 64 days after entering therapy. All testings were between the sixth and eighth interviews. If therapy was having a systematic effect upon self concepts, a self-self correlation over the wait period should be higher (show less change) than a self-self correlation spanning the equivalent in-therapy period. As Table 29-4 shows, this is indeed the case. Nine of the twelve wait period correlations are higher than the equivalent in-therapy correla-

TABLE 29-5.   Own-Control Sub-Group of Group 1 Z-Transformed Correlations of Self-Descriptions at Three Testing Points

Client	S_0S_1*	S_1S_2
1	.89†	.50
2	1.02	.80
3	1.10	.97
4	1.10	.91
5	.85	.71
6	.74	.73
7	.73	.55
8	1.04	.74
9	.79	1.03
10	.45	.27
11	.64	.70
12	.64	.64

* Subscript of zero indicates prewait sort; one, pretherapy; two, sort between 6th and 8th interviews.

† Wilcoxon signed ranks statistic T = 11, sig. at the 2.5% level.

tions. The Wilcoxon signed ranks test yielded a T statistic significant at the 2.5 per cent level. It appears, therefore, that self-concepts changed more during the therapy period, than during the equivalent wait period. The results of Table 29-4 and Table 29-5 are consistent with the hypothesis that self and ideal concepts tend to become more similar over therapy without regard to the extent of "success" or "improvement" and that such changes do not appear in a systematic fashion for in groups of persons not in psychotherapy. It seems safe to conclude, therefore, that psychotherapy, whether client-centered or Adlerian, constitutes a systematic influence that is reflected in increasing correspondence between self and ideal concepts as therapy progresses. Since definitely improved clients seem to show more of an increase in the correspondence of self and ideal concepts than not definitely improved clients, differentiation with regard to both process and outcome would probably yield more differentiated results. Indeed, Rice and Wagstaff (1967) have shown that increase in self-ideal correlations has a complex relation to outcome when stratified according to productive psychotherapy process. They found one subclass of clients whose therapist success ratings were low and positive change in self-ideal correlations was high. Such clients exhibited unproductive therapy process whereas those clients exhibiting productive therapy process also showed positive change in self-ideal correlation and had relatively low therapist success ratings and low or negative change in self-ideal correlations. Therefore some clients, a small minority, to be sure, are "false positives"; however, these are counterbalanced by clients who are "false negatives," clients with high therapist ratings and good therapy process who have low or negative change in self-ideal correlation. It appears, therefore, that inferences based on overall group results mirror the essential truth that clients in client-centered therapy and Adlerian therapy tend to move toward increased correspondence of self and ideal and that such changes reflect, overall, an increase in personal well-being. They do not in themselves mirror the well-known clinical observation that some clients become more defensive during therapy and that other clients seem to change more with respect to interpersonal behavior than with respect to self-concept.

The self and ideal self-descriptions of the clients reported by Butler and Haigh (1954) were later factor analyzed at pretherapy and follow-up testing points. The follow-up testing points ranged from 6 months to 18 months after therapy. The shortest period between pretherapy and follow-up testing points was 7.5 months; the longest, over 3 years. Factor approximations were obtained by best fitting the obtained self and ideal descriptions in the sense of least squares (Harman, 1960, p. 360). The approximations yielded weights for each item so that the items could be arranged in order of magnitude of the weights and then into actual Q-sort arrays of the kind made by the clients and controls. That factor approximations can be arranged like actual Q-sorts is one of the methodological advantages of Q-sorts. Factor approximations result in new Q-sorts that can be empirically correlated like actual Q-sorts.

The variance of ideal descriptions of the client and control groups at both testing points was largely accounted for by one factor so the first centroid factor of each group at each testing point was considered to be a general ideal factor. (The approximations of each of the four first centroid factors, when arranged into Q-sort arrays, all had empirical intercorrelations of .90 or higher.) Because of the high intercorrelations, the approximation of the pretherapy client ideal factor was taken to represent the general or culturally common ideal that accounted for most of the variance of the intercorrelations of the ideal factors. Some of the relationships between factors are shown in Table 29-6.

The general ideal factor can be characterized by the items most like the hypothetical ideal person represented by the factor approximation. The items characterizing the positive pole of the ideal were:

I feel emotionally mature, I am intelligent, I understand myself, I feel adequate, I have warm emotional relationships with others, I am self-reliant, I am

TABLE 29-6.   Correlations of Various Approximated Factors with
the Approximated Client Pretherapy Ideal Factor

A	Client Ideal Factor, Posttherapy		.92
	Control Ideal Factor, Pretherapy		.90
	Control Ideal Factor, Posttherapy		.90
B	Control Self Factor, First Testing		.77
	Control Self Factor, Second Testing		.84
C	Client Self Factors, Pretherapy		
		A	.17
		B	.40
		C	−.11
		D	−.03
		E	−.04
		F	−.09
		G	−.44
		H	.46
		J	.03
		K	−.12
		L	.07
D	Client Self Factors, Posttherapy		
		A	.80
		B	−.44
		C	−.40
		D	.34

a responsible person, I usually like other people, I am liked by most people who know me, I am tolerant, I am a rational person, I take a positive attitude toward myself.

The items characterizing the positive pole of the general ideal were quite different from those characterizing the positive pole of the pretherapy self-factor approximations. Even the approximated self-factor with the highest correlation with the approximated ideal factor (self-factor H of Table 29-6) was characterized on the positive pole by items such as:

I am confused, I am really self-centered, I often feel humiliated, and I need someone else to push me through on things.

The remaining characterizing items were all more positive and had to do more with social stimulus value except for the item "I have warm emotional relationships with others." None of the remaining characterizing items had to do with feelings of inner comfort, competence, or security.

The items characterizing the approximation of the self-factor with the lowest correlation with the approximation of the general ideal factor included:

I often feel guilty, I am worthless, I am a hostile person, I often feel resentful, I have a hard time controlling my sexual desires, I am often down in the dumps, I feel insecure within myself, I am afraid of a full-fledged disagreement with another person.

The only characterizing item that could be construed as favorable was "I am a rational person."

Clearly both of these pretherapy self-factors were distinctly unlike the general ideal factor.

The general ideal factor, although it might well be subscribed to by a majority of people in Western culture, is far from being the stereotype defined in English and English (1958) as "a relatively rigid and oversimplified or biased perception or conception of an aspect of reality, especially of persons or social groups . . . ." The general ideal obtained from both clients and controls delineates a person for whom inner security, positive attitudes toward self and others, intelligence and competence blend harmoniously.

The high correlations of section A in Table 29-6 show that the general ideal factor, common to *all* of the ideal descriptions of both groups is stable to a degree unprecedented in verbal inventories, not changing (or changing minimally) over time for the controls and over therapy for the clients. That is to say, the common factor variance is stable. The unique factor variance of the ideal descriptions, in general more than 50 per cent of the total common factor variance, is not so stable, as is shown by the stability coefficients of individual clients and controls which ranged from near zero to a maximum of .64.

The factoring of the self-descriptions of the normal controls also yielded but one common factor at each testing point. The Q-sorts resulting from the approximations of each control self factor correlated highly with the approximation of the general ideal factor as is shown in section B of Table 29-6. The results on the normal controls indicate that most of what is common to their self-descriptions (and this is about 25 per cent of the common factor variance) is also common to the general ideal factor. But this general ideal is shared by the Group I clients studied by Butler and Haigh (1954).

The low self-ideal correlations of clients before therapy shown in Table 29-4 indicate that the self-descriptions of the clients have little in common with their own ideal descriptions and with the general ideal factor.

The factor analytic results on the self-descriptions of the clients (sections C and D, Table 29-6) are quite different from those of the normal controls. The number of pretherapy factors was 11 using the criterion of a normal distribution of residuals. The Q arrays resulting from approximating these self factors had a mean correlation of $-.01$ with the general ideal factor, the range of correlation running from $-.44$ to $.46$. Relatively little of the pretherapy common factor variance was accounted for by each of the obtained pretherapy self factors.

By the time of the follow-up testings 7.5 months to 3 years later, the number of self factors was reduced to four using the same criterion. It is significant that more than 50 per cent of the common factor variance was accounted for by follow-up self factor A. The least squares approximation to this factor correlated almost as highly ($.80$) with the approximation to the general ideal factor as the approximations of the self factors of the normal controls. That is, most of the common factor variance of the follow-up self-descriptions was accounted for by one factor with much in common with the general ideal factor.

DISCUSSION

The results reported here buttress the conclusion of Butler and Haigh (1954) that the changes in self-ideal correlations of the Group 1 clients were indeed attributable to the effects of psychotherapy. And the results reported here cannot be vitiated by arguments that the self-self and self-ideal correlations are biased estimations of population correlations. Here the correlations have been treated as descriptive statistics, no more, no less. The question asked was whether subjects under a systematic influence, the psychotherapeutic situation, changed self- and ideal-descriptions as a result of that influence. It was answered by testing nonparametrically whether arrays of correlations before and after psychotherapy could be considered as coming from the same populations of arrays. The answer was in the negative for clients and in the positive for controls. The answer to the question did not depend upon the bias or lack of it in the individual correlations considered as estimators of population correlations.

The implications of the results given here are clear. At pretherapy the client self-descriptions have little in common with each other, and what they do have in common differs from the general ideal factor shared by clients and normal controls. At follow-up the self-descriptions have a much higher degree of similarity and what is similar to them is also similar to the general ideal factor. The self-descriptions of the normal controls at the two testing points have overall relatively high similarity: what they have in common is similarity to the general ideal factor.

From a factor analytic perspective the clients have changed over therapy to more closely resemble the normal controls, who in general have not changed, with respect to what was initially common to them. Further support for the hypothesis that the changes are due to therapy itself comes from the finding that systematic changes were not found for groups of matched client controls, own-controls, and normal controls. Finally, the fact that clients in Adlerian therapy showed significant increase implies that increase in self-ideal correspondence due to client-centered therapy is not unique to that one approach.

One of the most significant results is that self factors are not stable over therapy whereas the ideal factor is stable over therapy for clients and over time for controls. Since client self-factor A, accounting for most of the follow-up common factor variance, correlates highly with the general ideal factor, Rogers' (1951) hypothesis that client-centered therapy results in higher self-ideal congruence is strongly supported. The hypothesis of increase in self-ideal congruence is that self concepts change to correspond more to relatively stable ideal concepts.

That self-ideal congruence increases over psychotherapy and that the increase in self-ideal congruence is attributable to psychotherapy is reassuring. However, the nature of the ideal factor should be even more reassuring. The items characterizing this factor show that the ideal factor representing one aspect of the aspirations of both clients and controls is an ideal of a relatively self-actualizing person. This self-actualizing person is not afraid of experiencing, thinking, feeling, and acting, has productive relationships and is competent. The items provide us with a picture of a person with considerable affective and cognitive complexity, and, therefore, of a person who lives in a more complex world than the self-limited person who guards against many kinds of thoughts and feelings, whose behavior is self-maintaining rather than self-enhancing. It seems, therefore, that increase in self-ideal congruence implies a change from a self-limiting toward a self-actualizing life style. Since there is evidence that increase in self-ideal congruence is associated with several criteria of improvement, the contention that increase in self-ideal congruence implies increased individuality rather than increased conformity is not without support.

REFERENCES

Butler, J. M. Self-Concept Change in Psychotherapy. *University of Chicago Counseling Center Discussion Paper.* Chicago: University of Chicago Library. 1960, Vol. VI, No. 16.

Butler, J. M. Adience, self-actualization, and drive theory. In J. Wepman & R. Heine (Eds.) *Concepts of Personality.* Chicago: Aldine, 1963. (a)

Butler, J. M. Self-Concept Change in Psychotherapy. *Proceedings, XVII Congress Internationale de Psychologie.* Amsterdam: North Holland Publishing Company, 1963. (b)

Butler, J. M. Self Ideal Congruence in Psychotherapy. *Psychotherapy: Theory, Research and Practice,* 5, 13–17, 1968.

Butler, J. M. & Haigh, G. V. Changes in the relation between self-concepts and ideal concepts consequent upon client-centered counseling. In C. R. Rogers & R. F. Dymond (Eds.) *Psychotherapy and Personality Change.* Chicago: University of Chicago Press, 1954.

Butler, J. M., Rice, L. N., & Wagstaff, A. K. On the naturalistic definition of variables: An analogue of clinical analysis. In H. H. Strupp & L. Luborsky (Eds.) *Research in Psychotherapy II.* Washington, D.C.: American Psychological Association, 1962.

English, H. B. & English, A. C. *A Comprehensive Dictionary of Psychological and Psychoanalytical Terms.* New York: Longmans, Green, 1958.

Harman, H. H. *Factor Analysis.* Chicago: University of Chicago Press, 1960.

Rice, L. N. & Wagstaff, A. K. Client voice quality and expressive style as indexes of productive psychotherapy. *Journal of Consulting Psychology,* 31, 557–563, 1967.

Rogers, C. R. Perceptual reorganization in client-centered psychology, In R. R. Blake & G. V. Ramsey (Eds.) *Perception: An Approach to Personality.* N.Y.: Ronald Press, 1951.

Shlien, J. M., Mosak, H. H., & Dreikurs, R. Effect of time limits, a comparison of two psychotherapies. *Journal of Counseling Psychology,* 9, 31–34, 1962.

30

Congruence of Measures
of Self-Regard

LINDA L. VINEY

The variable, attitude to self, has been operationally defined under a variety of headings, but the validity of the resulting measures is rarely demonstrated. A concurrent criterion of self-regard is not available in the literature so that it is necessary to clarify the meaning of the different scores by finding the areas of their overlap. Selection of the self-acceptance measures for this comparison was guided by reported research results. The Phillips Self-Acceptance Inventory (1951), Berger Self-Acceptance Scale (1952), Brownfain Inventory (1952), Butler and Haigh Q-Sort (1954), Buss and Guerjoy adjectives (1957), and Gough Adjective Check List (1955) were excluded because the relationships of these scales to the Index of Adjustment and Values (I.A.V.) self-regard scales have been demonstrated (Cowen, 1956; Crowne, Stephens, & Kelly, 1961; Omwake, 1954). The I.A.V. II and D scales, therefore, were employed as marker variables.

Use of the I.A.V. was first reported by Bills, Vance and McLean in 1951. A test manual has been published subsequently (Bills, 1958). The test form contains a list of 49 trait words for each of which the S is required to answer three questions in terms of five-point rating scales. The questions are: how often are you this sort of person (I), how do you feel about being this way (II), and how much of the time would you like this trait to be characteristic of you? (III). Two self-regard measures are derived from this process, II giving a direct estimate of self-satisfaction, and the discrepancy score of self minus ideal (III-I) or (D) being regarded as a measure of self-acceptance. High scores for II indicate the high self-regard of the S but high scores for D indicate low or negative self-regard.

Another approach to self attitudes has been made by R. B. Cattell (1957). At the apex of his system of motivation components is the self-sentiment, "the factor and system of attitudes centered on the conceived, contemplated self and directed to maintaining its physical, social and moral

From L. Viney, Congruence of Measures of Self-Regard. Reprinted from *The Psychological Record*, Volume 16, 1966, pp. 487–493 by permission of publisher and author.

integrity as a basis for other sentiment and ergic satisfactions" (p. 900).

Five characteristic measures were examined in the present experiment, four being scales of the Motivation Analysis Test (M.A.T.) (Cattell & Horn, 1964). Four sets of items make up the M.A.T., from groupings of which the four scores are assessed. The first measure (USS) was derived from the Uses and Estimates subtests and represented an unintegrated self-sentiment reflecting the level of unconscious concern about the self-concept. High scores suggest strong unconscious motivation. The second measure (ISS) was provided by the Word Association and Information subtests and was an indication of the extent of conscious motivation connected with the self-concept. High scores suggest high conscious interest. MSS was a measure of the total motivation involved, much motivation being shown by high scores. The fourth measure was the conflict score (CSS) which yielded a high score to indicate a high degree of conflict in the dynamic area of the self-concept. All four measures are statistically related by the nature of the techniques used to derive them from the raw data.

The independent self-sentiment measure employed in this study was Factor U.I. (Q) 18 or the Q_3 scale from the Sixteen Personality Factor Questionnaire (16 P.F.). The items contributing to this score were derived from Form A of the 16 P.F. The Australian Tabular Supplement of the 16 P.F. (A.C.E.R. 1963) was used to obtain appropriate norms for scores. High scores indicate high self-sentiment formation, sometimes described as "controlled exacting will-power" (Cattell & Eber, 1957, p. 18). Q_3 represents the strength of dynamic investment and aspiration level achieved in the self-sentiment, and is related to measures of consideration for others, persistence, foresight, conscientiousness, leadership qualities, mechanical success and lack of accident proneness. It has the highest loading in Cattell's second order factor of general anxiety. He has hypothesized that Q_3 measures the extent to which the person is able to achieve the self-sentiment behavior which society prescribes (Cattell, 1957). Smith (1958) compared six measures of self-concept discrepancy and instability with Q_3 and found only one of the six correlations to be significant. Nine more relationships were tested in the present experiment.

Another questionnaire measure of the self-acceptance variable is the Sa scale of the California Psychological Inventory (C.P.I.). Gough (1956) has claimed that the scale assesses factors such as a sense of personal worth, self-acceptance, and the capacity for independent acting and thinking. High scores are gained by Ss who are intelligent, outspoken, cool, versatile, witty, aggressive, self-centered, and have more confidence. Those with low scores are methodical, conservative, dependable conventional easy-going, quiet, self-abasing, passive in action, and narrow in interests. The main method of validation of the C.P.I. to data has been factor analysis. The factors isolated by Mitchell (1960) agree in the main with those extracted by Crites et al. (1961) and he found that the C.P.I. and the 16 P.F., each taken in their entirety, have high loadings on a number of common factors (Mitchell, 1961). The Sa scale correlates significantly with scale II of the I.A.V. (Gough, 1956). These relationships were retested in the present experimental design.

The measures listed above provide little scope for the S to perform with reference to his individual phenomenal field, since his score is the result of limited responses to limited stimuli. The investigator, in effect, determines much of the structure of the self attitude expressed. Shlien (1961) has devised an abstract measure of self-acceptance for which the content is not so determined, the Abstract Apparatus (A.A.). The apparatus of the A.A. consists of two transparent curved circles of plexiglass which can be moved by the S so that they are opposite ($r = -1.00$) or completely overlapping ($r = +1.00$), or at any intermediate position. The S moves the two circles representing his self and his ideal-self until he is satisfied with their overlap. On the back of the stand, hidden from his view, are pointers, one attached to each circle arm so that they indicate the angle of separation between the circles. The self-acceptance score which Shlien employs is the cosine of the angle between the two vectors which is represented as a coefficient of correlation. The higher the score, the greater the correspondence between self and ideal circles and, presumably, the greater the self-acceptance within the individual.

Shlien (1961) has provided another measure of self-acceptance which is relatively unstructured. This is a Q-sort for which the items are not supplied, nor is any particular form of distribution required. The S is asked to make up a set of 25 statements about himself, and he ranks them for self and ideal. The Ideo-Q-sort (I-Q) is the rank correlation coefficient (Kendall's tau is appropriate) between self and ideal sorts or rankings. Shlien reported a positive relationship between the I-Q and the I.A.V. D score and between his two abstract measures. This I-Q measure of correspondence between self-concept and ideal-self yields a high score when correspondence is great.

Ten measures were intercorrelated in this experiment. The aim was exploratory, the plan being to analyse and interpret the resulting correlation matrix and to extract factors if appropriate. In calculating the coefficients 45 null hypotheses were tested, comprising intercorrelations between these measures:

    a. Index of Adjustment and Values, Column II (II)
    b. Index of Adjustment and Values, Discrepancy Score (D)
    c. Motivation Analysis Test, Unintegrated Self-Sentiment (USS)
    d. Motivation Analysis Test, Integrated Self-Sentiment (ISS)
    e. Motivation Analysis Test, Total Motivation within Self-Sentiment
       (MSS)

    f. Motivation Analysis Test, Total Conflict within Self-Sentiment (CSS)

    g. Sixteen Personality Factor Questionnaire, U.I. 18 (Q_3)

    h. California Psychological Inventory, Self-Acceptance Scale (Sa)

    i. Shlien's Abstract Apparatus (A.A.)

    j. Shlien's Ideo-Q-Sort (I-Q)

METHOD

Data was collected from 40 male and female Ss between the ages of 16 and 25 years. During the administration of the tests the Ss were asked to remain anonymous. Each S first was presented with an omnibus questionnaire providing data for USS, ISS, MSS, CSS, Sa and Q_3 scores; when this was completed the I.A.V. was administered. This task in some cases took up to two hours, during which the S may have gained a way of describing his self-concept which was not uniquely his own. The learning of such a style was not, however, apparent in performances on the two abstract tests then administered. The A.A. was individually administered, and then each S was given the 25 blank cards to be filled in and ranked at his own pace.

RESULTS

From the collection of data it was apparent that the relationships between some of the variables were not amenable to analysis by means of the Pearson Product Moment Correlation Coefficient because of curved regression lines in the plottings of the relationships and the lack of homoscedasticity inherent in them (Guilford, 1956). Spearman's rho who used as an approximation of Pearson's r, as the conversion cannot be applied to this small sample. A formula for a statistic with the same form of distribution as Student's t (Siegel, 1956) was used to gauge the significance of the coefficients.

Table 30-1 shows the resulting correlation matrix. Only nine coefficients were found to be significant, seven with a probability of .01 or less, and two with a probability of up to .05. All correlations, however, were in the direction which would be predicted from the description of the measures given by their authors. Positive and negative polarities of self-regard were found to be consistent over the different scales.

Factors were extracted by the principle axes method which ensures the smallest number of orthogonal factors with the maximal amount of

TABLE 30-1.   Intercorrelations of Self-Regard Measures

| | I.A.V. | | M.A.T. | | | | 16 P.F. | C.P.I. | Shlien Tests | |
	II	D	USS	ISS	MSS	CSS	Q_3	Sa	A.A.	I-Q
II	.	−.249	.197	−.025	.162	.161	.377**	.199	−.023	.374**
D		.	.130	.115	.134	.195	−.162	−.189	−.124	−.230
USS			.	.385**	.416**	.649**	.163	.214	.073	−.049
ISS				.	.587**	−.337*	.158	.161	.207	.089
MSS					.	.316*	.170	.208	.000	−.065
CSS						.	.082	.229	−.227	.015
Q_3							.	−.092	.059	.597**
Sa								.	−.151	−.023
A.A.									.	−.100
I-Q										.

* $p < .05$
** $p < .01$

variance. Since the size of the sample was small for such a procedure, Humphrey's rule was applied as the criterion for sufficient factors (Fruchter, 1954). The four significant factors were rotated for meaningful interpretation.

DISCUSSION

Interpretation of the correlation matrix was attempted at several levels, the first question to be answered being whether relationships reported in the literature were supported. The answer was not encouraging: not one of the intercorrelations retested was represented by a significant coefficient in this matrix. Bills (1958) reported a significant correlation between the two I.A.V. variables which the present coefficient did not bear out. Neither was his correlation between II and Sa borne out. The relationship between Q_3 and the M.A.T. variables found by Cattell (1957) was not supported. The findings of Shlien (1961) concerning the I-Q were contradicted by the small non-significant correlations in the matrix between I-Q and D and I-Q and A.A. The lack of relationship between the two abstract measures was particularly surprising, although it is probable that this wider selection of Ss would better reflect the true relationship than that tested by Shlien.

The larger of the correlation clusters in the matrix was that of the six coefficients between the four M.A.T. variables. These coefficients were interrelated statistically through the scoring methods used, so that they had no psychological meaning. The only other cluster is of more interest. The three variables significantly related were II, Q_3 and I-Q. Correlations with the marker variable I.A.V. II suggested the possibility of correlations with other tests to which II has been related. None of these results which led to the refutations of the three null hypotheses would have been specifically predicted from examination of the relevant literature, although they would have been predicted from the notion that tests which are presented with similar aims and rationales may measure similar variables. Some consistency has been demonstrated here in the measurement of self-regard, since the authors of the intercorrelating tests, Bills, Cattell and Shlien, work within different frames of theoretical reference.

The rotated loadings and communalities on the four orthogonal factors extracted are shown in Table 30-2. Factor I appeared to represent the extent of Dynamic Investment in the Self, high loadings of the Cattell motivation tests yielding this impression with the self-abasement vs. self-centered confidence of the Sa score. Although Cattell's Q_3 measure might be expected to load highly on a factor of this description, the negligible loadings of the remaining tests supported this name. Tests contributing to the next factor, I-Q, Q_3, II and D, suggested a title of Self-Ideal Discrepancy since, again with the exception of Q_3, they were the representatives of the discrepancy self-regard measures in use. The A.A. too, was designed on the discrepancy model, but from its low communality in this analysis it would appear to have a high specific variance, contributing to Factor III only.

This factor was the most difficult to identify. The high positive loading of ISS indicated high conscious motivation about the self, while the high negative loading of CSS indicated low conflict in that area. What Shlien's A.A. measures is unclear, but in view of the procedure involved a hypothesis of Awareness of Self-Acceptance was postulated for Factor III. Factor IV was defined as Conformity of Self-Concept, because the polarities represented in the high loadings were between conventionality and

TABLE 30-2. Rotated Orthogonal Factor Loadings for An Analysis of Measures of Self-Regard

	I	II	III	IV	h^2
II	−.256	−.670	−.226	−.186	.600
D	−.252	.533	.102	.586	.701
USS	−.849	.000	−.068	.072	.731
ISS	−.499	−.062	.794	−.072	.888
MSS	−.782	−.005	.288	.036	.696
CSS	−.640	.108	−.698	.054	.911
Q_3	−.191	−.778	.031	.382	.788
Sa	−.416	−.059	−.055	−.774	.778
AA	.054	−.039	.583	−.073	.350
I-Q	.032	−.821	−.084	.220	.731

outspoken confidence (Sa), high and low self-regard (D), and success and failure in achievement of the self-concept laid down by society.

The validities of several self-acceptance measures have been placed in considerable doubt by the intercorrelations obtained in this study. However, descriptions of orthogonal factors underlying these relationships suggest that such lack of congruence may be overcome by specification of the aspect of self-regard to be measured.

REFERENCES

A.C.E.R. 1963. *Tabular supplement to the* 16 *P.F.* Melbourne: A.C.E.R.

Berger, E. M. 1952. The relation between expressed acceptance of self and expressed acceptance of others. *J. abnorm. soc. Psychol.*, 47, 778–782.

Bills, R. E. 1958. *Manual for the index of adjustment and values.* Auburn: Alabama Polytech. Inst.

Bills, R. E., Vance, E. L., & McLean, D. S. 1951. An index of adjustment and values. *J. consult. Psychol.*, 15, 257–261.

Brownfain, J. J. 1952. Stability of the self-concept as a dimension of personality. *J. abnorm. soc. Psychol.*, 47, 597–606.

Buss, A. H., & Guerjoy, H. 1957. The scaling of terms used to describe personality. *J. consult. Psychol.*, 21, 361–369.

Butler, J. M., & Haigh, G. V. 1954. Changes in the relationship between self-concepts and ideal concepts. In C. R. Rogers & R. F. Diamond (Eds.) *Psychotherapy and personality change.* Chicago: University of Chicago Press.

Cattell, R. B. 1957. *Personality and motivation structure and measurement.* New York: World.

Cattell, R. B., & Eber, H. W. 1957. *Handbook for the sixteen personality factor questionnaire.* Illinois: I.P.A.T.

Cattell, R. B., & Horn, J. L. 1964. *The motivation analysis test.* Illinois: I.P.A.T.

Cowen, E. L. 1956. An investigation of the relationship between two measures of self-regarding attitudes. *J. clin. Psychol.*, 12, 156–160.

Crites, J. O., Bechtoldt, H. P., Goodstein, L. D., & Heilbrun, A. B., Jr. 1961. A factor analysis of the California Psychological Inventory. *J. appl. Psychol.*, 45, 408–414.

Crowne, D. P., Stephens, M. W., & Kelly, R. 1961. The validity and equivalence of tests of self-acceptance. *J. Psychol.*, 51, 101–112.

Fruchter, B. 1954. *Introduction to factor analysis.* New York: Van Nostrand.

Gough, H. G. 1965. *The adjective check list manual.* California: Consult. Psychol. Press, Inc.

Gough, H. G. 1956. *The California psychological inventory.* California: Consult. Psychol. Press Inc.

Guilford, J. P. 1956. *Fundamental statistics in psychology and education.* New York: McGraw-Hill.

Mitchell, J. V., Jr. 1961. Statistical relationships between the score categories of the 16 P.F. and C.P.I. inventories. *Amer. Psychologist, 16,* 386.

Mitchell, J. V. 1962. An analysis of the factorial dimension of the Bills Index of Adjustment and Values. *J. soc. Psychol., 58,* 331–337.

Omwake, Katherine T. 1954. The relation between acceptance of self and acceptance of others shown by three personality inventories. *J. consult. Psychol., 18,* 443–446.

Phillips, E. L. 1951. Attitudes towards self and others: A brief questionnaire report. *J. consult. Psychol., 15,* 79–81.

Shlien, J. M. 1961. Toward what level of abstraction in criteria? *Research in psychotherapy,* 2.

Siegel, S. 1956. *Nonparametric statistics for the behavioural sciences.* New York: McGraw-Hill.

Smith, G. M. 1958. Six measures of self-concept discrepancy and instability: their interrelations, reliability and relations to other personality measures. *J. consult. Psychol., 22,* 101–113.

31

Neurosis as a Failure
of Personal Growth

A. H. MASLOW

Rather than trying to be comprehensive, I have chosen to discuss only a few selected aspects of this topic, partly because I have been working with them recently, partly also because I think they are especially important, but mostly because they have been overlooked.

The frame of reference which we in this symposium have all taken for granted today considers the neurosis to be, from *one* aspect, a describable, pathological state of affairs which presently exists, a kind of disease or sickness or illness, on the medical model. But we have learned to see it also in a dialectical fashion, as simultaneously a kind of moving forward, a clumsy groping forward toward health and toward fullest humanness, in a kind of timid and weak way, under the aegis of fear rather than of courage, and *now* involving the future as well as the present.

All the evidence that we have (mostly clinical evidence, but already some other kinds of research evidence) indicates that it is reasonable to assume in practically every human being, and certainly in almost every newborn baby, that there is an active will toward health, an impulse toward growth, or toward the actualization of human potentialities. But at once we are confronted with the very saddening realization that so few people make it. Only a small proportion of the human population gets to the point of identity, or of selfhood, full humanness, self-actualization, etc., even in a society like ours which is relatively one of the most fortunate on the face of the earth. This is our great paradox. We all here have the impulse towards full development of humanness. Then why is it that it doesn't happen more often? What blocks it?

This is our new way of approaching the problem of humanness, i.e., with an appreciation of its high possibilities and, simultaneously, a deep disappointment that these possibilities are so infrequently actualized. This

From A. H. Maslow, Neurosis as a Failure of Personal Growth. Reprinted by permission of the author and publisher from *Humanitas, Journal of the Institute of Man*, III (2), Fall, 1967, 153–169.

A lecture at an Institute of Man symposium, Duquesne University, November 18, 1966.

attitude contrasts with the "realistic" acceptance of whatever happens to be the case, and then of regarding that as the norm, as, for instance, Kinsey did, and as the TV pollsters do today. We tend then to get into the situation that Dr. Barton pointed out to us this morning in which normalcy from the descriptive point of view, from the value-free science point of view —that this normalcy or averageness is the best we can expect, and that therefore we should be content with it. From the point of view that I have outlined, normalcy would be rather the kind of sickness or crippling or stunting that we share with everybody else and therefore don't notice. I remember an old textbook of abnormal psychology that I used when I was an undergraduate, which was an awful book, but which had a wonderful frontispiece. The lower half was a picture of a line of babies, pink, sweet, delightful, innocent, lovable. Above that was a picture of a lot of passengers in a subway train, glum, grey, sullen, sour. The caption underneath was very simply, "What happened?" This is what I'm talking about.

I should mention also—I feel a little self-conscious about this after Dr. Gendlin's address—but I should mention also that part of what I have been doing and what I want to do here now comes under the head of the strategy and tactics of research and of preparation for research and of trying to phrase all of these clinical experiences and personal subjective experiences that we've been discussing today in such a way that we can learn more about them in a scientific way, that is, checking and testing and making more precise, and seeing if it's really so, and were the intuitions correct, etc., etc. For this purpose and also for those of you who are primarily interested in the philosophical problems which are involved in this day's discussions, I would like to present briefly a few theoretical points which are relevant for what follows. This is the age-old problem of the relationship between facts and values, between *is* and *ought*, between the descriptive and the normative—a terrible problem for the philosophers who have dealt with it ever since there were any philosophers, and who haven't got very far with it yet. I'd like to offer some considerations that I would like you to mull over which have helped me with this old philosophical difficulty, and perhaps might do the same for you, a third horn to the dilemma, you might say.

FUSION-WORDS

What I have in mind here is the general conclusion that I have already written about (Maslow, 1963b), which comes partly from the Gestalt psychologists and partly from clinical and psychotherapeutic experience, namely, that, in a kind of a Socratic fashion, facts often point in a direction, i.e., they are vectorial. Facts just don't lie there like pancakes, just doing nothing; they are to a certain extent signposts which tell you what to do, which make suggestions to you, which nudge you in one direction rather than another. They "call for," they have demand character, they even have "requiredness," as Köhler called it (Köhler,1938). I get the feeling very frequently that whenever we get to know enough, that then we know what to do, or we know much better what to do; that sufficient knowledge will often solve the problem, that it will often help us at our moral and ethical choice-points, when we must decide whether to do this or to do that. For instance, it is our common experience in therapy, that as people "know" more and more consciously, that their solutions, their choices become more and more easy, more and more automatic. This is why I would reject entirely Sartre's kind of arbitrariness. I think it's a profound mistake to think of us as being confronted only with arbitrariness, with choices we make by fiat, by sheer, unaided acts of will, and without any help from the nature of reality or from the essential nature of human nature.

I am suggesting something other than that. I am suggesting that there are facts and words which themselves are both normative and descriptive simultaneously. I am calling them for the moment "fusion-words," meaning a fusion of facts and values, and what I have to say beyond this should be understood as part of this effort to solve the *is* and *ought* problem.

I myself have advanced, as I think we all have in this kind of work, from talking in the beginning, in a frankly normative way, for example, asking the questions—what is normal, what is healthy? My former philosophy professor, who still feels fatherly toward me in a very nice way, and to whom I still feel filial, has occasionally written me a worried letter scolding me gently for the cavalier way in which I was handling these old philosophical problems, saying something like, "Don't you realize what you have done here? There is 2000 years of thought behind this problem and you just go skating over this thin ice so easily and casually." And I remember that I wrote back once trying to explain myself, saying that this sort of thing is really the way a scientist functions, and that this is part of his strategy of research, i.e., to skate past philosophical difficulties as fast as he can. I remember writing to him once that my attitude as a strategist in the advancement of knowledge had to be one, so far as philosophical problems were concerned, of "determined naivete." And I think that's what we have here. I felt that it was heuristic, and therefore all right, to talk about normal and healthy and what was good and what was bad, and frequently getting very arbitrary about it. I did one research in which there were good paintings, and bad paintings, and with a perfectly straight face I put in the footnote, "Good paintings are defined here as paintings that I like." The thing is, if I can skip to my conclusion, that this turns out to be not so bad a strategy. In studying healthy people, self-actualizing people, etc., there has been a steady move from the openly normative and the frankly personal, step by step, toward more and more descriptive, objective words, to the point there is today a standardized test of self-actualization (Shostrom,

1963). Self-actualization can now be defined quite operationally, as intelligence used to be defined, i.e., self-actualization is what that test tests. It correlates well with external variables of various kinds, and keeps on accumulating additional correlational meanings. As a result, I feel heuristically justified in *starting* with my "determined naivete." Most of what I was able to see intuitively, directly, personally, is being confirmed now with numbers and tables and curves.

FULL-HUMANNESS

And now I would like to suggest a further step toward the fusion-word "fully-human," a concept which is still more descriptive and objective (than the concept "self-actualization") and yet retains everything that we need of normativeness. This is in the hope of moving thus from intuitive heuristic beginnings toward more and more certainty, greater and greater reliability, more and more external validation, which in turn means more and more scientific and theoretical usefulness of this concept. This phrasing and this way of thinking was suggested to me about fifteen or so years ago by the axiological writings of Robert Hartman (Hartman, 1959) who defined "good" as the degree to which an object fulfills its definition or concept. This suggested to me that the conception of humanness might be made, for research purposes, into a kind of quantitative concept. For instance, full humanness can be defined in a cataloguing fashion, i.e., full humanness is the ability to abstract, to have a grammatical language, to be able to love, to have values of a particular kind, to transcend the self, etc., etc. The complete cataloguing definition could even be made into a kind of check list if we wanted to. We might shudder a little at this thought, but it could be very useful if only to make the theoretical point for the researching scientist that the concept *can* be descriptive and quantitative—and yet also normative, i.e., this person is closer to full humanness than that person. Or even we could say: This person is *more* human than that one. This is a fusion-word in the sense that I have mentioned above; it is really objectively descriptive because it has nothing to do with my wishes and tastes, my personality, my neuroses; and my unconscious wishes or fears or anxieties or hopes are far more easily excluded from the conception of full humanness than they are from the conception of psychological health.

If you ever work with the concept of psychological health—or any other kind of health, or normality—you will discover what a temptation it is to project your own values and to make it into a self-description or perhaps a description of what you would like to be, or what you think people *should* be like, etc., etc. You'll have to fight against it all the time, and you'll discover that, while it's *possible* to be objective in such work, it's certainly difficult. And even then, you can't be really sure. Have you fallen into sampling error? After all, if you select persons for investigation on the basis of your personal judgment and diagnosis, such sampling errors are more likely than if you select by some more impersonal criterion (Maslow, 1961).

Clearly, fusion-words are a scientific advance over more purely normative words, while also avoiding the worse trap of believing that science *must* be *only* value-free, and non-normative, i.e., non-human. Fusion concepts and words permit us to participate in the normal advance of science and knowledge from its phenomenological and experiential beginnings on toward greater reliability, greater validity, greater confidence, greater exactness, greater sharing with others and agreement with them (Maslow, 1965).

Other obvious fusion-words are such as: mature, evolved, developed, stunted, crippled, fully-functioning, graceful, awkward, clumsy, and the like. There are many, many more words which are less obviously fusions of the normative and the descriptive. And we may one day have to get used to thinking of fusion-words as paradigmatic, as normal, usual and central. Then the more purely descriptive words and the more purely normative words would be thought of as peripheral and exceptional. I believe that this will come as part of the new humanistic Weltanschauung which is now rapidly crystallizing into a structured form.[1]

For one thing, as I have pointed out (Maslow, 1954), these conceptions are too exclusively extra-psychic and don't account sufficiently for the quality of consciousness, for intra-psychic or subjective abilities, for intance, to enjoy music, to meditate and contemplate, to savor flavors, to be sensitive to one's *inner voices*, etc. Getting along well within one's inner world may be as important as social competence or reality competence.

But more important from the point of view of theoretical elegance and research strategy, these concepts are less objective and quantifiable than is a list of the capacities that make up the concept of humanness.

I would add that I consider none of these models to be *opposed* to the medical model. There is no need to dichotomize them from each other. Medical illnesses diminish the human being and therefore fall on the continuum of greater to lesser degree of humanness. Of course, though the medical illness model is necessary (for tumors, bacterial invasions, ulcers, etc.), it is certainly not sufficient (for neurotic, characterological or spiritual disturbances).

HUMAN DIMINUTION

One consequence of this usage of "full-humanness" rather than "psychological health" is the corresponding or parallel use of "human diminu-

[1] I consider the "degree of humanness" concept to be more useful also than the concepts of "social competence," "human effectiveness" and similar notions.

tion," instead of "neurosis," which is anyway a totally obsolete word. Here the key concept is the loss or not-yet-actualization of human capacities and possibilities, and obviously this is also a matter of degree and quantity. Furthermore, it is closer to being externally observable, i.e., behavioral, which of course makes it easier to investigate than, for example, anxiety or compulsiveness or repression. Also it puts on the same continuum all the standard psychiatric categories, all the stuntings, cripplings and inhibitions that come from poverty, exploitation, maleducation, enslavement, etc., and also the newer value pathologies, existential disorders, character disorders that come to the economically privileged. It handles very nicely the diminutions that result from drug-addiction, psychopathy, authoritarianism, criminality, and other categories that cannot be called "illness" in the same medical sense as can, e.g., brain tumor.

This is a radical move away from the medical model, a move which is long overdue. Strictly speaking, neurosis means an illness of the nerves, a relic we can very well do without today. In addition, using the label "psychological illness" puts neurosis into the same universe of discourse as ulcers, lesions, bacterial invasions, broken bones, or tumors. But by now, we have learned very well that it is better to consider neurosis as rather related to spiritual disorders, to loss of meaning, to doubts about the goals of life, to grief and anger over a lost love, to seeing life in a different way, to loss of courage or of hope, to despair over the future, to dislike for oneself, to recognition that one's life is being wasted, or that there is no possibility of joy or love, etc., etc.

These are all fallings away from full-humanness, from the full blooming of human nature. They are losses of human possibility, of what might have been and could yet be perhaps. Physical and chemical hygiene and prophylaxes certainly have some little place in this realm of psychopathogenesis, but are as nothing in comparison with the far more powerful role of social, economic, political, religious, educational, philosophical, axiological and familial determinants.

SUBJECTIVE BIOLOGY

There are still other important advantages to be gained from moving over to this psychological-philosophical-educational-spiritual usage. Not least of these, it seems to me, is that it encourages the *proper* conceptual use of the biological and constitutional base which underlies any discussion of Identity or of The Real Self, of growth, of uncovering therapy, of full-humanness or of diminution of humanness, of self-transcendence, or any version of these. To say it briefly, I believe that helping a person to move toward full-humanness proceeds inevitably via awareness of one's identity (among other things). A very important part of this task is to become aware of what one *is*, biologically, temperamentally, constitution-ally, as a member of a species, of one's capacities, desires, needs, and also of one's vocation, what one is fitted for, what one's destiny is.

To say it very bluntly and unequivocally, one absolutely necessary aspect of this self-awareness is a kind of phenomenology of one's own inner biology, of that which I have called instinctoid (Maslow, 1965), of one's animality and species-hood. This is certainly what psychoanalysis tries to do, i.e., to help one to become conscious of one's animal urges, needs, ten-sions, depressions, tastes, anxieties. So also for Horney's distinction between a real self and a pseudo-self. Is this also not a subjective discrimination of what one truly is? And what *is* one truly if not first and foremost one's own body, one's own constitution, one's own functioning, one's own species-hood? (I have very much enjoyed, *qua theorist*, this pretty integration of Freud, Goldstein, Sheldon, Horney, Cattell, Frankl, May, Rogers, Murray, etc., etc., etc. Perhaps even Skinner could be coaxed into this diverse com-pany, since I suspect that a listing of all his "intrinsic reinforcers" for his human subjects might very well look much like the "hierarchy of instinc-toid basic needs and metaneeds" that I have proposed!)

I believe it is possible to carry through this paradigm even at the very highest levels of personal development, where one transcends one's own personality (Maslow, 1964). I hope to make a good case soon for accept-ing the probable instinctoid character of one's highest values, i.e., of what might be called the spiritual or philosophical life (Maslow, 1967). Even this personally discovered axiology I feel can be subsumed under this cate-gory of "phenomenology of one's own instinctoid nature" or of "subjective biology" or "experiential biology" or some such phrase.

Think of the great theoretical and scientific advantages of placing on one single continuum of degree or amount of humanness, not only all the kinds of sickness the psychiatrists and physicians talk about but also all the additional kinds that existentialists and philosophers and religious thinkers and social reformers have worried about. Not only this, but we can also place on the same single scale all the various degrees and kinds of health that we know about, plus even the health-beyond-health of self-transcendence, of mystical fusion, and whatever still higher possibilities of human nature the future may yet disclose.

INNER SIGNALS

Thinking in this way has had for me at least the one special advan-tage of directing my attention sharply to what I called at first "the impulse voices" but which had better be called more generally something like the "inner signals" (or cues or stimuli). I had not realized sufficiently that in most neuroses, and in many other disturbances as well, the inner signals become weak or even disappear entirely (as in the severely obsessional person) and/or are not "heard" or *cannot* be heard. At the extreme we have the experientially-empty person, the zombie, the one with empty insides. Recovering the self *must*, as a *sine qua non*, include the recovery of the ability to have and to cognize these inner signals, to know what and whom one likes and dislikes, what is enjoyable and what is not, when to eat and when not to (Schachter), when to sleep, when to urinate, when to rest.

The experientially-empty person, lacking these directives from within, these voices of the real self, must turn to outer cues for guidance, for instance eating when the clock tells him to, rather than obeying his appetite (he has none). He guides himself by clocks, rules, calendars, schedules, agenda, and by hints and cues from other people.

In any case, I think the particular sense in which I suggest interpreting the neurosis as a failure of personal growth must be clear by now. It is a falling short of what one could have been, and even one could say, of what one *should* have been, biologically speaking, that is, if one had grown and developed in an unimpeded way. Human and personal possibilities have been lost. The world has been narrowed, and so has consciousness. Capacities have been inhibited. I think for instance of the fine pianist who couldn't play before an audience of more than a few, or the phobic who is forced to avoid heights or crowds. The person who can't study, or who can't sleep, or who can't eat many foods has been diminished as surely as the one who has been blinded. The cognitive losses, the lost pleasures, joys, and ecstasies,[2] the loss of competence, the inability to relax, the weakening of will, the fear of responsibility—all these are diminutions of humanness.

I've mentioned some of the advantages of replacing the concepts of psychological illness and health with the more pragmatic, public and quantitative concept of full or diminished humanness, which I believe is also biologically and philosophically sounder. But before I move on, I'd like to note also that diminution can of course be either reversible or irreversible, e.g., we feel far less hopeful about the paranoid person than we do about say a nice, lovable hysterical. And of course also diminution is dynamic, in the Freudian style. The original Freudian schema spoke of an intrinsic dialectic between the impulse and the defenses against this impulse. In this same sense, diminution leads to consequences and processes. It is only rarely a completion or a finality in a simple descriptive way. In most people these losses lead not only to all sorts of defensive processes which have been well described by Freudian and other psychoanalytic groups, for instance, to repression, denial, conflict, etc. They also lead to coping responses as I stressed long ago (Maslow & Mittelmann, 1941).

[2] What it means for one's style of life to lose peak-experiences has been very well set forth in Colin Wilson's *Introduction to the New Existentialism* (Wilson, 1967).

Conflict itself is, of course, a sign of relative health as you would know if you ever met really apathetic people, really hopeless people, people who have given up hoping, striving and coping. Neurosis is by contrast a very hopeful kind of thing. It means that a man who is frightened, who doesn't trust himself, who has a low self-image, etc., yet reaches out for the human heritage and for the basic gratifications to which every human being has a right simply by virtue of being human. You might say it's a kind of *timid* and ineffectual striving toward self-actualization, toward full humanness.

Diminution can, of course, be reversible. Very frequently, simply supplying the need gratifications can solve the problem, especially in children. For a child who hasn't been loved enough, obviously the treatment of first choice is to love him to death, to just slop it all over him. Clinical and general experience is that it works—I don't have any statistics, but I would suspect 9 out of 10 times. So is respect a wonderful medicine for counteracting a feeling of worthlessness. Which, of course, brings up the obvious conclusion that, if "health and illness" on the medical model are seen as obsolete, so also must the medical concepts of "treatment" and "cure" and the authoritative doctor be discarded and replaced.

THE JONAH COMPLEX

In the time I have left I'd like to turn to one of the many reasons for what Angyal (1965) called the evasion of growth. Certainly everybody in this room would like to be better than he is. We have, all of us, an impulse to improve ourselves, an impulse toward actualizing more of our potentialities, toward self-actualization, or full humanness, or human fulfillment, or whatever term you like. Granted this for everybody here, then what holds us up? What blocks us?

One such defense against growth that I'd like to speak about specially-because it hasn't been noticed much—I shall call the Jonah Complex.[3]

In my own notes I had at first labelled this defense the "fear of one's own greatness" or the "evasion of one's destiny" or the "running away from one's own best talents." I had wanted to stress as bluntly and sharply as I could the non-Freudian point that we fear our best as well as our worst, even though in different ways. It is certainly possible for most of us to be greater than we are in actuality. We all have unused potentialities or not fully developed ones. It is certainly true that many of us evade our constitutionally suggested vocations (call, destiny, task in life, mission). So often

---

[3] This name was suggested by my friend, Professor Frank Manual, with whom I had discussed this puzzle.

we run away from the responsibilities dictated (or rather suggested) by nature, by fate, even sometimes by accident, just as Jonah tried—in vain—to run away from *his* fate.

We fear our highest possibilities (as well as our lowest ones). We are generally afraid to become that which we can glimpse in our most perfect moments, under the most perfect conditions, under conditions of greatest courage. We enjoy and even thrill to the godlike possibilities we see in ourselves in such peak moments. And yet we simultaneously shiver with weakness, awe and fear before these very same possibilities.

I have found it easy enough to demonstrate this to my students simply by asking, "Which of you in this class hopes to write the great American novel, or to be a Senator, or Governor, or President? Who wants to be Secretary-General of the United Nations? Or a great composer? Who aspires to be a saint, like Schweitzer, perhaps? Who among you will be a great leader?" Generally everybody starts giggling, blushing, and squirming until I ask, "If not you, then who else?" Which of course is the truth. And in this same way, as I push my graduate students towards these higher levels of aspiration, I'll say, "What great book are you now secretly planning to write?" And then they often blush and stammer and push me off in some way. But why should I not ask that question? Who else will write the books on psychology except psychologists? So I can ask, "Do you not plan to be a psychologist?" "Well, yes." "Are you in training to be a mute or an inactive psychologist? What's the advantage of that? That's not a good path to self-actualization. No, you must want to be a first-class psychologist, meaning the best, the very best you are capable of becoming. If you deliberately plan to be less than you are capable of being, then I warn you that you'll be deeply unhappy for the rest of your life. You will be evading your own capacities, your own possibilities."

Not only are we ambivalent about our own highest possibilities, we are also in a perpetual and I think universal—perhaps even *necessary*—conflict and ambivalence over these same highest possibilities in other people, and in human nature in general. Certainly we love and admire good men, saints, honest, virtuous, clean men. But could anybody who has looked into the depths of human nature fail to be aware of our mixed and often hostile feelings toward saintly men? Or toward very beautiful women or men? Or toward great creators? Or toward our intellectual geniuses? It is not necessary to be a psychotherapist to see this phenomenon—let us call it "Counter-valuing." Any reading of history will turn up plenty of examples, or perhaps even I could say that any such historical search might fail to turn up a single exception throughout the whole history of mankind. We surely love and admire all the persons who have incarnated the true, the good, the beautiful, the just, the perfect, the ultimately successful. And yet they also make us uneasy, anxious, confused, perhaps a little jealous or envious, a little inferior, clumsy. They usually make us lose our aplomb, our self-possession and self-regard. (Nietzsche is still our best teacher here.)

Here we have a first clue. My impression so far is that the greatest people, simply by their presence and by being what they are, make us feel aware of our lesser worth, whether or not they intend to. If this is an unconscious effect, and we are not aware of why we feel stupid or ugly or inferior whenever such a person turns up, we are apt to respond with projection, i.e., we react as if he were *trying* to make us feel inferior, as if we were the target (Huxley, 1963). Hostility is then an understandable consequence. It looks to me so far as if conscious awareness tends to fend off this hostility. That is, if you are willing to attempt self-awareness and self-analysis of your *own* counter-valuing, i.e., of your unconscious fear and hatred of true, good, beautiful, etc., people, you will very likely be less nasty to them. And I am willing also to extrapolate to the guess that if you can learn to love more purely the highest values in others, this might make you love these qualities in yourself in a less frightened way.

Allied to this dynamic is the awe before the highest, of which Rudolf Otto (1958) has given us the classical description. Putting this together with Eliade's insights (Eliade, 1961) into sacralization and desacralization, we become more aware of the universality of the fear of direct confrontation with a god or with the godlike. In some religions death is the inevitable consequence. Most preliterate societies also have places or objects that are taboo because they are too sacred and *therefore too dangerous*. In the last chapter of my *Psychology of Science* (Maslow, 1966) I have also given examples mostly from science and medicine of desacralizing and resacralizing and tried to explain the psychodynamics of these processes. Mostly it comes down to awe before the highest and best (I want to stress that this awe is intrinsic, justified, *right*, suitable, rather than some sickness or failing to get "cured of").

But here again my feeling is that this awe and fear need not be negative alone, something to make us flee or cower. There are also desirable and enjoyable feelings capable of bringing us even to the point of highest ecstasy and rapture. Conscious awareness, insight and "working through," a la Freud, is the answer here too I think. This is the best path I know to the acceptance of our highest powers, and whatever elements of greatness or goodness or wisdom or talent we may have concealed or evaded.

A helpful sidelight for me has come from trying to understand why peak-experiences are ordinarily transient and brief (Maslow, 1962). The answer becomes clearer and clearer. *We are just not strong enough to endure more!* It is just too shaking and wearing. So often people in such ecstatic moments say, "It's too much," or "I can't stand it," or "I could die." And as I get the descriptions, I sometimes feel, "Yes, they *could* die." Delirious happiness cannot be borne for long. Our organisms are just too weak for any large doses of greatness, just as they would be too weak to endure hour-long sexual orgasms, for example.

The word "peak-experience" is more appropriate than I realized at first. The acute emotion must be climactic and momentary and it *must* give way to non-ecstatic serenity, calmer happiness, and the intrinsic pleasures of clear, contemplative cognition of the highest goods. The climactic emotion can not endure, but B-Cognition *can* (Maslow, 1964; 1966).

Doesn't this help us to understand our Jonah complex? It is partly a justified fear of being torn apart, of losing control, of being shattered and disintegrated, even of being killed by the experience. Great emotions after all can in *fact* overwhelm us. The fear of surrendering to such an experience, a fear which reminds us of all the parallel fears found in sexual frigidity, can be understood better I think through familiarity with the literature of psychodynamics and depth psychology, and of the psychophysiology and medical psychomatics of emotion.

There is still another psychological process that I have run across in my explorations of failure to actualize the self. This evasion of growth can also be set in motion by a fear of paranoia. Of course this has been said in more universal ways. Promethean and Faustian legends are found in practically any culture.[4] For instance, the Greeks called it the fear of *hubris*. It has been called "sinful pride," which is of course a permanent human problem. The person who says to himself, "Yes, I will be a great philosopher and I will rewrite Plato and do it better," must sooner or later be struck dumb by his grandiosity, his arrogance. And especially in his weaker moments, will say to himself, "Who? Me?" and think of it as a crazy fantasy or even fear it as a delusion. He compares his knowledge of his inner private self, with all its weakness, vacillation, and shortcomings, with the bright, shining, perfect and faultless image he has of Plato. Then, of course, he'll feel presumptuous and grandiose. (What he doesn't realize is that Plato, introspecting, must have felt just the same way about himself, but went ahead anyway, overriding his doubts about himself.)

For some people this evasion of one's own growth, setting low levels of aspiration, the fear of doing what one is capable of doing, voluntary self-crippling, pseudo-stupidity, mock-humility are in fact defenses against grandiosity, arrogance, sinful pride, hubris. There are people who cannot manage that graceful integration between the humility and the pride which is absolutely necessary for creative work. To invent or create you must have the "arrogance of creativeness" which so many investigators have noticed. But, of course, if you have *only* the arrogance without the humility, then you are in fact paranoid. You *must* be aware not only of the godlike possibilities within, but also of the existential human limitations. You must be able simultaneously to laugh at yourself and at all human pretensions. If you can be amused by the worm trying to be a god (Wilson, 1959), then

---

[4] Sheldon's excellent book on this subject (Sheldon, 1936) is not quoted often enough on this subject, possibly because it came before we were quite ready to assimilate it.

in fact you may be able to go on trying and being arrogant without fearing paranoia or bringing down upon yourself the evil eye. This is a good technique.

May I mention one more such technique that I saw at its best in Aldous Huxley, who was certainly a great man in the sense I've been discussing, one who was able to accept his talents and use them to the full. He managed it by perpetually marvelling at how interesting and fascinating everything was, by wondering like a youngster at how miraculous things are, by saying frequently, "Extraordinary! Extraordinary!" He could look out at the world with wide eyes, with unabashed innocence, awe and fascination, which is a kind of admission of smallness, a form of humility, and then proceed calmly and unafraid to the great tasks he set for himself.

Finally, may I refer you to a paper of mine (Maslow, 1963a) relevant in itself, but also as the first in a possible series. Its name, "The need to know and the fear of knowing," illustrates well what I want to say about *each* of the intrinsic or ultimate values that I've called Values of Being (B-Values). I am trying to say that these ultimate values, which I think are also the highest needs (or metaneeds, as I'm calling them (Maslow, 1967) in a forthcoming publication) fall, like all basic needs, into the basic Freudian schema of impulse *and* defense against that impulse. Thus it is certainly demonstrable that we need the truth and love it and seek it. And yet it is just as easy to demonstrate that we are also simultaneously *afraid* to know the truth. For instance, certain truths carry automatic responsibilities which may be anxiety-producing. One way to evade the responsibility and the anxiety is simply to evade consciousness of the truth.

I predict that we will find a similar dialectic for each of the intrinsic Values of Being, and I have vaguely thought of doing a series of papers on, e.g., "The love of beauty and our uneasiness with it." "Our love of the good man and our irritation with him." "Our search for excellence and our tendency to destroy it," etc., etc. Of course, these counter-values are stronger in neurotic people, but it looks to me as if all of us must make our peace with these mean impulses within ourselves. And my impression so far is that the best way to do this is to transmute envy, jealousy, *presentiment*, and nastiness into humble admiration, gratitude, appreciation, adoration, and even worship via conscious insight and working through. (Maslow, Rand, & Newman, 1960.) This is the road to feeling small and weak and unworthy and *accepting* these feelings instead of needing to protect a spuriously high self-esteem by striking out (Horney, 1950).

And again I think it is obvious that understanding of this basic existential problem should help us to embrace the B-Values not only in others, but also in ourselves, thereby helping to resolve the Jonah complex.

REFERENCES

Angyal, A. *Neurosis and Treatment: A Holistic Theory*. Wiley, 1965.

Eliade, M. *The Sacred and the Profane*. Harper & Row, 1961.

Frankl, V. Self-transcendence as a human phenomenon, *Journal of Humanistic Psychology*, 1966, 6, 97–206.

Goldstein, K. *The Organism*. American Book Company, 1939.

Hartman, R. The science of value. In *New Knowledge in Human Values*, A. H. Maslow (Ed.) Harper & Row, 1959.

Henle, M. (Ed.) *Documents of Gestalt Psychology*, University of California Press, 1961.

Horney, K. *Neurosis and Human Growth*. Norton, 1950.

Huxley, L. *You Are Not the Target*. Farrar, Straus, & Giroux, 1963.

King, C. D. The meaning of normal, *Yale Journal of Biology and Medicine*, 1945, *17*, 493–501.

Köhler, W. *The Place of Values in a World of Facts*. Liveright, 1938.

Maslow, A. H. *Motivation and Personality*. Harper & Row, 1954.

Maslow, A. H. Some frontier problems in mental health, in A. Combs (Ed.). *Personality Theory and Counseling Practice*, University of Florida Press, 1961.

Maslow, A. H. Lessons from the peak-experiences, *Journal of Humanistic Psychology*, 1962, 2, 9–18.

Maslow, A. H. The need to know and the fear of knowing, *Journal of General Psychology*, 1963, 68, 111–125. (a)

Maslow, A. H. Fusions of facts and values, *American Journal of Psychoanalysis*, 1963, 23, 117–131. (b)

Maslow, A. H. *Religions, Values, and Peak-Experiences*. Ohio State University Press, 1964.

Maslow, A. H. Criteria for Judging Needs to be Instinctoid. In M. R. Jones (Ed.) *Human Motivation: A Symposium*. University of Nebraska Press, 1965, 33–47.

Maslow, A. H. *The Psychology of Science: A Reconnaissance*. Harper & Row, 1966.

Maslow, A. H. The biological rooting of the spiritual life. *The Humanist*, 1967.

Maslow, A. H. Beyond Self-actualization. In J. Bugental (Ed.) *The Challenge of Humanistic Psychology*. McGraw-Hill, 1967.

Maslow, A. H. & Mittelmann, B. *Principles of Abnormal Psychology*. Harper & Row, 1941.

Maslow, A. H. with Rand, H., & Newman, S. Some parallels between the dominance and sexual behavior of monkeys and the fantasies of patients in psychotherapy, *Journal of Nervous & Mental Disease*, 1960, *131*, 202–212.

Otto, R. *The Idea of the Holy*. Oxford University Press, 1958.

Sheldon, W. H. *Psychology and the Promethean Will*. Harper & Row, 1936.

Shostrom, E. *Personal Orientation Inventory* (POI) Educational & Industrial Testing Service, 1963.

van Kaam, A. *Existential Foundations of Psychology.* Duquesne University Press, 1966.

Weiss, F. A. Emphasis on health in psychoanalysis, *American Journal of Psychoanalysis*, 1966, 26, 194–198.

Wilson, C. *The Stature of Man.* Houghton Mifflin, 1959.

Wilson, C. *Introduction to the New Existentialism.* Houghton Mifflin, 1967.

32

Various Meanings of "Transcendence"

A. H. MASLOW

1. Transcendence in the sense of: loss of self-consciousness, of self-awareness, of depersonalization and of self-observing, of the kind characteristically seen in the adolescent. It is, in principle, the same kind of self-forgetfulness which comes from getting absorbed, fascinated, concentrated. In this sense, meditation or concentration on something outside one's own psyche can produce self-forgetfulness and therefore loss of self-consciousness, and therefore in this particular sense of transcendence of the ego or of the conscious self. At least, it can be seen as a precursor of the experience of self-transcendence. In teaching, this is where I start from because it is shared by all my listeners.

2. In the Metapsychological sense: of transcending one's own skin and body and bloodstream, as in identification with the B-values so that they become intrinsic to the Self itself. (See Maslow, 1967, for more detail.)

3. Transcendence of time: example—my experience of being bored in an academic procession and feeling slightly ridiculous in cap and gown, and suddenly slipping over into being a symbol under the aspect of eternity rather than just a bored and irritated individual in the moment and in the specific place. My vision or imagining was that the academic procession stretched way, way out into the future, far, far away, further than I could see, and it had Socrates at its head, and the implication was, I suppose, that many of the people far ahead had been there and in previous generations, and that I was a successor and a follower of all the great academics and professors and intellectuals. Then the vision was also of the procession stretching out behind me into a dim, hazy infinity where there were people not yet born who would join the academic procession, the procession of scholars, of intellectuals, of scientists and philosophers. And I thrilled at being in such a procession and felt the great dignity of it, of my robes, and even of myself as a person who belonged in this procession. That is, I became a symbol; I stood for something outside my own skin. I was not exactly an individual. I was also a "role" of the eternal teacher. I was the Platonic essence of the teacher.

Published here by permission of the author.

This kind of transcendence of time is also true in another sense, namely that I can feel friendly, in a very personal and affectionate way, with Spinoza, Abraham Lincoln, Jefferson, William James, Whitehead, etc., as if they still lived. Which is to say that in specific ways they *do* still live. This would be in the sense that I would like to retain the names on the Board of Editors of the *Journal of Humanistic Psychology* of those former editors who had died. In the sense that they still inspire, they live and they belong in the roster of editors. I, myself, would be sentimental enough to add to the Board of Editors Socrates, Spinoza, Bergson, Whitehead, James, etc.

In still another sense, one can transcend time, namely in the sense of working hard for not yet born great-grandchildren or other successors. But this is in the sense in which Allen Wheelis, in his novel, *The Seeker*, had his hero on the point of death thinking that the best thing he could do would be to plant trees for future generations.

4. Transcendence of culture. In a very specific sense, the self-actualizing man, or the transcendent self-actualizing man, is a universal man. He is a member of the human species. He is rooted in a particular culture but he rises above that culture and can be said in various ways to be independent of it and to look down upon it from a height, perhaps like a tree which has its roots in the soil but whose branches are spread out very high above the soil, and able to look down upon the soil in which the roots are rooted. I have written about the resistance to enculturation of the self-actualizing person. One can examine one's own culture in which one is rooted in a detached and objective way of a certain kind. This parallels the process in psychotherapy of simultaneously experiencing and of self-observing of one's own experience in a kind of critical or editorial or detached and removed way so that one can criticize it, approve or disapprove of it and therefore assume control, and therefore the possibility of changing it. This attitude toward one's culture, and toward the parts of it which one has consciously accepted, is quite different from the unthinking and blind, unaware, unconscious total identification with one's culture in a nondiscriminating way.

5. Two attitudes toward one's past are possible. One may be said to be a transcendent attitude. One can have a B-cognition of one's own past. That is, one's own past can be embraced and accepted into one's present self. It can *now* exist ahistorically and therefore be worked with, changed, reconstructed. This means full acceptance. It means forgiving one's self via understanding one's self. It means the transcendence of remorse, regret, guilt, shame, embarrassment and the like.

This is different from viewing one's past as something before which one was and is helpless, something that happened *to* me, situations in which I was only passive and completely determined by outside determinants and which I can no longer do anything about. In a certain sense this is like taking responsibility for one's past. It means "having become retrospectively an agent as well as now being an agent." It means seeing in an Olympian nonevaluating way the *necessity* of what happened, and therefore of being "reconciled" with it, as one can be with death or with evil. It implies also seeing how one brought about one's own past. In these senses, one can relate impersonally to one's own past as coolly as to someone else's past, thereby "transcending" it.

6. We transcend ego, self, selfishness, ego-centering, etc., when we respond to the demand-character of external tasks, causes, duties, responsibilities to others and to the world of reality. When one is doing one's duty, this also can be seen to be under the aspect of eternity and can represent a transcendence of the ego, of the lower needs of the self. Actually, of course, it is ultimately a form of metamotivation, and identification with what "calls for" doing. This is a sensitivity to extra-psychic requiredness. This in turn means a kind of Taoistic attitude. The phrase "being in harmony with nature" implies this ability to yield, to be receptive to, to respond to, to live with extra-psychic reality as if one belonged with it, or were in harmony with it. We then transcend our own "selfish" wishes, becoming receptive to the demand-character of non-self.

7. The mystical experience. Mystic fusion, either with another person or with the whole cosmos or with anything in between. I mean here the mystical experience as classically described by the religious mystics in the various religious literatures, to the extent that these *may* be found to be different from my own descriptions of peak-experiences.

8. One transcends death, pain, sickness, evil, etc., when one is at a level high enough to be reconciled with the necessity of death, pain, etc. From a Godlike or Olympian point of view, all these are necessary, and can be understood as necessary. If this attitude is achieved, as for instance it can be in the B-cognition, then bitterness, rebelliousness, anger, resentment may all disappear or at least be much lessened.

9. (Overlaps with above.) The word "transcendence" can describe accepting the natural world, letting it be itself in the Taoistic fashion, the transcending the lower needs of the self, that is, of one's selfish within-the-skin demands, of one's egocentric judgments upon extra-psychic things as being dangerous or not dangerous, edible or not edible, useful or not useful, etc. This is the ultimate meaning of the phrase "to perceive the world objectively and impersonally." This is one necessary aspect of B-cognition. B-cognition implies a transcendence of one's ego, lower needs, selfishness, etc. (This is of course a totally different and new conception of "objectivity.")

10. Transcendence of the We-They polarity and enmity. Transcendence of the Zero-Sum game as between persons. This means to ascend up to the level of synergy (interpersonal synergy, synergy of social institutions or of cultures). (See Maslow & Gross, 1964.)

11. Transcendence of the basic needs (either by gratifying them so

that they disappear normally from consciousness, *or* by being able to give up the gratifications and to "conquer" the needs). This is another way of saying "to become primarily metamotivated." It implies identification with the B-values.

12. Identification-love is a kind of transcendence, e.g., for one's child, or for one's beloved friend. This means "unselfish." This means transcendence of the selfish Self. It implies also a wider circle of identifications, i.e., with more and more and more people approaching the limit of identification with *all* human beings, i.e., specieshood, brotherhood. This can also be phrased as the more and more inclusive Self. The limit here is identification with the human species. This can also be expressed intrapsychically, phenomenologically, as experiencing one's self to be one of the band of brothers, to belong to the human species.

13. All examples of Angyal-type homonomy, either high or low.

14. "Getting off the merry-go-round." Walking through the abbatoir without getting bloody. To be clean even in the midst of filth. To transcend advertising means to be above it, to scorn it, to be unaffected by it, to be untouched, perhaps not even to notice it. In this sense one can transcend all kinds of bondage, slavery, etc., in the same way that Frankl, Bettelheim, et al., could transcend even the concentration camp situation. Here I can use the example of *The New York Times* front page picture sometime in 1933 of an old Jewish man with a beard being paraded before the jeering crowd in Berlin in a garbage truck. It was my impression that he had compassion for the crowd and that he looked upon them with pity and perhaps forgiveness, thinking of them as unfortunate and sick and subhuman. Being independent of other people's evil or ignorance or stupidity or immaturity even when this is directed toward oneself, is possible, though very difficult. And yet one *can*, in such a situation, gaze upon the whole situation, including oneself in the midst of the situation, as if one were looking upon it objectively, detachedly from a great and impersonal or suprapersonal height.

15. Transcending the opinions of others, i.e., of reflected appraisals. This means a self-determining Self. It means to be able to be unpopular when this is the right thing to be, to become an autonomous, self-deciding Self; to write one's own lines; to be one's own man. To be not manipulable or seduceable. These are the resisters (rather than the conformers) in the Asch-type experiment. Resistance to being rubricized, to be able to be role-free, i.e., to transcend one's role and be a person rather than being the role. This includes resisting suggestion, propaganda, social pressures, being outvoted, etc.

16. Transcending the Freudian superego and coming up to the level of intrinsic conscience, and intrinsic guilt, deserved and suitable remorse, regret, shame.

17. Transcendence of one's own weakness and dependency, to tran-

scend being a child, to become one's own mother and father to one's self, to become parental and not only filial, to be able to be strong and responsible in addition to being dependent. To transcend one's own weakness, and to rise to being strong. Since we always have both of these within us simultaneously, this is really a matter of degree in large part. But after all, it can be said meaningfully, of some individuals, that they are primarily weak, and that they primarily relate to all other human beings as the weak relate to the strong, and that all mechanisms of adaptation, coping mechanisms, defense mechanisms, are the defenses of weakness against strength. It's the same for dependency and independence. It's the same for irresponsibility and responsibility. It's the same for being the captain of the ship, or the driver of the car on the one hand, and of being merely the passenger on the other hand.

18. Transcending the present situation in the sense of Kurt Goldstein "to relate to existence also in terms of the possible as well as the actual." This is to rise above being stimulus-bound and here-now, situation-bound, and actuality-bound. Goldstein's reduction to the concrete can be transcended. Perhaps the best phrase here is to rise to the realm of the possible as well as of the actual.

19. Transcendence of dichotomies (polarities, black and white oppositions, either-or, etc.). To rise from dichotomies to superordinate wholes. To transcend atomism in favor of hierarchical-integration and holism. To bind together separate things into an integration. The ultimate limit here is the holistic perceiving of the cosmos as a unity. This is the ultimate transcendence, but any step along the way to this ultimate limit is itself a transcendence. Any dichotomy may be used as an example; for instance, selfish versus unselfish, or masculine versus feminine, or parent versus child, teacher versus student, etc. All these can be transcended so that the mutual exclusiveness and oppositeness and Zero-Sum game quality is transcended, in the sense of rising above to a higher viewpoint where one can see that these mutually exclusive differences in opposites can be coordinated into a superordinate unity which would be more realistic, more true, more in accord with actual reality.

20. Transcendence of the D-realm into the B-realm. (Of course this overlaps with every other kind of transcendence. As a matter of fact, every kind of transcendence overlaps with every other kind.)

21. Transcendence of one's own will (in favor of the spirit of "not my will be done but Thine"). To yield to one's destiny or fate and to fuse with it, to love it in the Spinozistic sense or in the Taoistic sense. To embrace, lovingly, one's own destiny. This is a rising above one's own personal will, being in charge, taking control, *needing* control, etc.

22. The word transcend also means "surpass" in the sense simply of being able to do more than one thought one could do, or more than one had done in the past, e.g., simply to be able to run faster than one used to,

or to be a better dancer or pianist, or a better carpenter, or whatever. Someone has called this "the demonstration in the realm of the possible of what had been considered impossible."

23. Transcend also means to become divine or Godlike, to go beyond the merely human. But one must be careful here not to make anything extrahuman or supernatural out of this kind of statement. I am thinking of using the word "metahuman" or "B-human" in order to stress that this becoming very high or divine or Godlike is part of human nature even though this is not often perceived. It is still a potentiality of human nature.

24. "Transcending" is sometimes used to mean, to rise above dichotomized nationalism, patriotism, or ethnocentrism, in the sense of them against us, or of we-they, or Ardrey's enmity-amity complex. Use here Piaget's example of the little Genevan boy who couldn't imagine being both Genevan and Swiss. He could think of being only either Genevan or Swiss. It takes more development in order to be able to be more inclusive and superordinate, more holistic, more integrative. My identification with nationalism, patriotism, or with my culture does not necessarily mitigate against my identification, and more inclusive and higher patriotism with the human species or with the United Nations. As a matter of fact, such a superordinate patriotism is of course not only more inclusive, but therefore more healthy, more fully-human, than the strict localism which is regarded as antagonistic or as excluding others. That is, I can be a good American, and of course *must* be an American (that's the culture I grew up in, which I can never shake off and I don't want to shake off) in favor of being a world citizen. Stress that the world citizen who has no roots, who doesn't belong any place, who is utterly and merely cosmopolitan, is not as good a world citizen as one who grew up in a family, in a place, in a home, with a particular language, in a particular culture, and therefore has a sense of belongingness on which to build toward higher need and meta-need levels. To be a full member of the human species does not mean repudiating the lower levels; it means rather including them in the hierarchical integration, e.g., cultural pluralism, enjoying the differences, enjoying different kinds of restaurants with different kinds of food, enjoying travel to other countries, enjoying the ethnological study of other cultures, etc., while yet accepting one's own roots.

25. Transcendence can mean to live in the Realm of Being, speaking the language of Being, B-cognizing, high-plateau-living. It can mean the serene B-cognition as well as the climactic peak-experience kind of B-cognition. After the insight or the great conversion or the great mystic experience or the great illumination or the great full awakening, one can calm down as the novelty disappears, and as one gets used to good things or even great things, one can learn to live casually in heaven and to be on easy terms with the eternal and the infinite. One can get over being surprised and startled and then live calmly and serenely among the platonic

essences, or among the B-values. The phrase to use here for contrast with the climactic or emotionally poignant great insight and B-cognition would be "plateau-cognition." [1] Peak-experiences must be transient, and in fact *are* transient so far as I can make out. And yet an illumination or an insight remains with the person. He can't really become naive or innocent again or ignorant again in the same way that he was. He cannot un-see. He can't become blind again. And yet there must be a language to describe getting used to the conversion or the illumination or to living daily or even lounging in the Garden of Eden. Such an awakened person normally proceeds in a unitive way or in a B-cognizing way as an everyday kind of thing, certainly whenever he wishes to. This serene B-cognition or plateau-cognition can come under one's own control. One can turn it off or on as one pleases.

26. The (transient) attainment of full-humanness or perfection or of finality or being an end is an example of transcendence. Coming to an end-state or a total completion is one kind of transcendence.

27. (Which may be the same as some of the above.) The attainment of Taoistic (B-level) loving objectivity is the transcendence of non-involved, neutral, laissez faire, non-caring, spectator-type objectivity (which itself transcends the purely egocentric and immature lack of objectivity).

28. Transcending the split between facts and values. Fusion of facts and values in which they become one (see Maslow, 1963).

29. A transcendence of negatives (which include evil, pain, death, etc., but also include more than that) is seen in the report from the peak-experiences in which the world is accepted as good, and in which one is reconciled to the evils that one perceives. But this is also a transcendence of inhibitions, of blocks, of denials, of refusals.

30. Transcendence of space. This can be in the very simplest sense of getting so absorbed in something that one forgets where one is. But it can also rise to the very highest sense in which one is identified with the whole human species and therefore in which one's brothers on the other side of the earth are part of oneself, so that in a certain sense one's self is on the other side of the earth as well as being here in space. The same is true for the introjection of the B-values since they are everywhere. Since they are then defining characteristics of the self, then one's self is everywhere too.

31. Overlapping with several of the above is the transcendence of effort and of striving, of wishing and hoping, of any vectorial or intentional or directional characteristics. In the simplest sense this is of course the sheer enjoyment of the state of gratification, of hope fulfilled and attained, of being there rather than of striving to get there, of having arrived rather than of traveling toward. This is also in the sense of "being fortuitous" or of Mrs. Garrett's use of the phrase, "high carelessness." It is the Taoistic

---

[1] (I forget where I first saw this phrase.)

feeling of letting things happen rather than of making them happen, and of being perfectly happy and accepting of this state of non-striving, non-wishing, non-interfering, non-controlling, non-willing. This is the transcendence of ambition, of efficiencies. This is the state of having rather than of not having. Then of course one lacks nothing. This means it is possible to go over to the state of happiness, of contentment, of being satisfied with what is. Pure appreciation. Pure gratitude. The state and the feeling of good fortune, good luck, the feeling of grace, of gratuitous grace. The simplest example I can think of is the pleasure of soaking in a hot tub. Certainly one is not then going anyplace.

32. Being in an end-state means the transcendence of means in various senses. (But this has to be very carefully spelled out.)

33. Specially noteworthy for research purposes as well as for therapeutic purposes is the transcendence of fear into the state of not-fearing or of courage (these are not quite the same thing).

34. Also useful would be Bucke's (1923) use of cosmic consciousness. This is a special phenomenological state in which the person somehow perceives the whole cosmos, or at least the unity and integration of it and of everything in it, including his self. He then feels as if he belongs by right in the cosmos. He becomes one of the family rather than an orphan. He comes inside rather than being outside looking in. He feels simultaneously small because of the vastness of the universe, but also he feels important because he is there in it by absolute right. He is part of the universe rather than a stranger to it or an intruder in it. The sense of belongingness can be very strongly reported here, as contrasting with the sense of ostracism, isolation, aloneness, of rejection, of not having any roots, of belonging no place in particular. After such a perception, apparently one can feel permanently this sense of belonging, of having a place, of being there by right, etc. (I have used this cosmic consciousness type of B-cognition in the peak-experience to contrast with another type, namely, that which comes from narrowing down consciousness and zeroing in in an intense absorption and fascination with one person or one thing or one happening which somehow then *stands for* the whole world, the whole cosmos. I have called this the narrowing-down kind of peak-experience and B-cognition.)

35. Perhaps a special and separate statement ought to be made of the transcendence in the particular meaning of having already achieved intro-jection of and identification with B-values, and therefore with the state of being *primarily* motivated by them thereafter.

36. One can even transcend individual differences in a very specific sense. The highest attitude toward individual differences is to be aware of them, to accept them, but also to enjoy them and finally to be profoundly grateful for them as a beautiful instance of the ingenuity of the cosmos, i.e., the recognition of their value and wonder at them. This is certainly a higher attitude and I suppose therefore a kind of transcendence. But also,

and quite different from this ultimate gratitude for individual differences is the other attitude of rising above them in the recognition of the essential commonness and mutual belongingness and identification with all kinds of people in ultimate humanness or specieshood, in the sense that everyone is one's brother or sister. Then individual differences and even the differences between the sexes have been transcended in a very particular way. That is, at different times one can be very aware of the differences between individuals; but at another time one can wave aside these individual differences as relatively unimportant for the moment by contrast with the universal humanness and *similarities* between human beings.

37. A particular kind of transcendence useful for certain theoretical purposes is the transcendence of human limits, imperfections, shortcomings, and finiteness. This comes either in the acute end experiences of perfection or in the plateau-experiences of perfection, in which one can *be* an end, a god, a perfection, an essence, a Being (rather than a Becoming), sacred, divine. This can be phrased as a transcendence of ordinary, everyday humanness in favor of extraordinary humanness or metahumanness or some such phrasing. This can be an actual phenomenological state; it can be a kind of cognizing; it can also be a conceived limit or ideal of philosophy as, for instance, the platonic essences or ideas are. In such acute moments, or to some extent in plateau-cognition, one becomes perfect, or can see oneself as perfect, e.g., in that moment I can love all and accept all, forgive all, be reconciled even to evil that hurts me. I can understand and enjoy the way things are. And I can even then feel some subjective equivalent of what has been attributed to the gods only, i.e., omniscience, omnipotence, ubiquity, all-loving, etc. In a certain sense one can *become* in such moments a god, a sage, a saint, a mystic.

38. Transcendence of one's own credo, or system of values, or system of beliefs. This is worth discussing separately because of the special situation in psychology in which the first force, the second force and the third force have been seen as mutually exclusive by many. Of course this is erroneous. Humanistic psychology is inclusive rather than exclusive. It is epi-Freudian and epi-positivistic. These two points of view are not so much wrong or incorrect as they are limited and partial. Their essence fits very nicely into a larger and inclusive structure. Of course integrating them into this larger and more inclusive structure certainly changes them in some ways, corrects them, points to certain mistakes, but yet includes their most essential, though partial, characteristics. There can be the enmity-amity complex among intellectuals, in which loyalty to Freud or to Clark Hull, or for that matter to Galileo or Einstein or Darwin, can be a kind of local excluding-others type of patriotism in which one forms a club or fraternity as much to keep other people out as to include some in. This is a special case of inclusiveness or hierarchical integration or holism, but it is useful to make a special point of it for psychologists, as well as for philosophers,

scientists, and other intellectual areas where there is a tendency to divide into so-called "schools of thought." This is to say that one can take either the dichotomous or the integrative attitude toward a school of thought.

39. One Freudian equivalent of the word "transcend" can have special theoretical and research usefulness I think. It can be used as a near-synonym for the concept "post-ambivalence," i.e., transcending (rising above or maturing beyond) ambivalence about love, sex, parents, authority, violence, etc. This is about as close as one can get in the Freudian system of thought to a concept of maturity or health. Freud's definition "to be able to love and to work" is not very useful because both can be done ambivalently.

SUMMARY STATEMENT [2]

Transcendence refers to the very highest and most inclusive or holistic levels of human consciousness, behaving and relating, as ends rather than as means, whether to oneself, to significant others, to human beings in general, to other species, to nature, or to the cosmos. (Holism in the sense of hierarchical integration is assumed; so also is cognitive and value isomorphism.)

[2] It should be stressed that all of these meanings of "transcendence" are natural-istic, empirical and not supernatural or supermundane. There is no overlap here with the common use in theology of the word "transcendent God" to mean wholly *other* than human nature or Nature in general. I use the word transcendent to mean wholly *within* Nature and human nature, and I mean to include whatever can be called sacred, divine, religious, etc., as being transcendent and yet *within* the world and within human nature.

REFERENCES

Bucke, R. *Cosmic Consciousness*. New York: Dutton, 1923.

Maslow, A. H. Fusions of facts and values. *American Journal of Psychoanalysis*, 1963, 23, 117–131.

Maslow, A. H. A theory of metamotivation: The biological rooting of the value-life. *Journal of Humanistic Psychology*, 1967, 7.

Maslow, A. H., & Gross, L. Synergy in the society and in the individual. *Journal of Individual Psychology*, 1964, 20, 153–164.

33

A Study of Motivational Development

VIVIAN GOUREVITCH
& MELVIN H. FEFFER

A. INTRODUCTION AND PROBLEM

In a previous investigation of the relationship between motivation and social adequacy among normal adults (Gourevitch, 1959), support was found for the notion that the more socially adequate adult is characterized by a greater preference for symbolic, internalized kinds of gratification such as self-approval and self-actualization. The argument was advanced that his more effective social functioning is due to a lesser dependence upon concrete support from the environment, made possible by his development of an internal source of support. This idea is consistent with Maslow's theory of a motivational hierarchy (Maslow, 1954) in which it is proposed that self-actualization and esteem needs appear later in an individual's development than do physiological and love needs, and that mature psychological health is dependent upon the development and active fulfillment of these "higher" needs. In the investigation of adults, however, it was only possible to test hypotheses relevant to the upper level of motivational development because almost all of these subjects gave evidence of some familiarity with "higher" needs, and thus could not be differentiated in terms of different levels of development. For a test of the hierarchical notion as it applies to the course of development from one level of motivation to another, the addition of younger subjects seemed necessary. Accordingly, for the present study a group of 68 children ranging in age from six to 13 years was added

From V. Gourevitch, & M. H. Feffer, A Study of Motivational Development. *Journal of Genetic Psychology*, 1962, 100, 361–375. Reprinted by permission of authors and publisher.

This investigation was supported by the Dementia Praecox Research Project, Worcester State Hospital, and a research grant (M-896) from the National Institute of Mental Health, Public Health Service.

The investigators are indebted to a number of persons for their contributions. Dr. D. Broverman read the present paper and made many helpful suggestions. The administration of the tests was carried out by Dr. Sybil Speier, and Mr. B. D'Agostino. Subjects were obtained through the help of the Worcester Boys Club and Mr. H. Blaukopf at the Jewish Community Center.

to the sample of adults already studied, and the developmental implications of the hierarchy were tested on this combined sample.

The motivational hierarchy formulated for the study of adults was retained in the present investigation. This hierarchy preserves the essential order of development proposed by Maslow, but also includes areas of gratification—pleasure in objects, play, and self-expression—which Maslow assigns to a category of "unmotivated" behavior because such behaviors generally involve no "striving." The conceptual difficulty is avoided if motivation is conceived in terms of the reinforcement value of certain events, as Rotter (1954) has done, without reference to the internal drive state of the organism. Bindra (1951) offers a similar interpretation of motivation in terms of reinforcement categories. These theorists define reinforcement in empirical terms as a stimulus which increases (decreases, or maintains at a given level) the probability of a class of responses, further classifying such stimuli in terms of content categories. These approaches, then, emphasize what is generally regarded as the goal or goal-object of motivation, rather than its energizing aspects. Such a formulation permits the classification of play and other pleasurable and expressive activities as reinforcing events, and hence as goals or objects of motivation. The motivational hierarchy used here was, therefore, formulated in terms of different content categories of reinforcement, representing the different levels of development hypothesized. The levels are distinguished as follows: 1. Concrete, internal reinforcement (*e.g.*, physiological satisfactions, physical comfort and safety, freedom from fear and anxiety *per se*). 2. Concrete, external reinforcement (*e.g.*, money, material goods, affection, belongingness, concrete praise and reward). 3. Abstract, external reinforcement (*e.g.*, social approval and esteem, popularity, prestige, fame). 4. Abstract, internal reinforcement (*e.g.*, self-respect and self-approval, self-actualization). In this context, the dimension "concrete-abstract" refers to the type of reinforcer, *i.e.*, tangible events such as eating or being praised (concrete), or intangible events such as approval or esteem (abstract). The dimension "internal-external" refers to the locus of the reinforcer—whether it is essentially internal as in physical comfort and self-respect, or essentially external as in possessions and social esteem.

The hierarchy, from 1 to 4 as shown, is intended to reflect the hypothetical progress of an individual from concrete, primary reinforcement to the acquisition of abstract, secondary reinforcers. Quantitative and qualitative aspects of the development are conceived as follows: Quantitatively, it is presumed that with expanding social experience secondary reinforcers of all kinds will be acquired, yielding a general increase in the number of effective reinforcers with age. Qualitatively, the individual attains a new level of development when he acquires secondary reinforcers belonging to that level. Reinforcers at a new level rest, of course, upon the previously established reinforcement of earlier levels. Maslow's theory of "prepotency" also carries this implication in its contention that higher level motivation rests upon the gratification of lower level needs. Development is thus viewed as a cumulative process, including both a horizontal expansion in the number of reinforcers, and vertical growth represented by the addition of new sources of reinforcement at progressively higher levels of the hierarchy. The individual thus acquires with motivational development multiple supports for his behavior in the form of additional reinforcers at attained levels, as well as acquiring new reinforcers at more "abstract" levels which render his behavior less dependent upon the immediate circumstances in his environment. Such development would seem to lead to the increased stability and independence which characterize mature as opposed to immature behavior.

The theory predicts, then, a general increase in the number of effective reinforcers with age, coupled with the appearance of reinforcers belonging to progressively higher levels of the proposed hierarchy. That is, older age groups are expected to show a greater number of reinforcers than younger age groups, and older age groups are expected to differ increasingly from younger groups at successive levels of the motivational hierarchy.

B. METHOD

The subjects were 68 boys ranging in age from six to 13 years and 36 male adults with a mean-age of 36.0 years. Table 33-1 shows the number of subjects at different age levels, and the mean and standard deviation of vocabulary standard scores at each level, as measured by the WISC Vocabulary test among the children and by the WAIS Vocabulary test among the

TABLE 33-1. Number of Subjects and Mean Vocabulary Score at Each Age Level

Age group	N	Mean vocabulary score[a]	Vocabulary SD
6–7 yrs	16	12.1	2.46
8–9 yrs	20	11.5	3.14
10–11 yrs	20	11.4	1.96
12–13 yrs[b]	12	9.8	4.00
Adults			
Mean age = 36.0 yrs	36	13.2	2.49

[a] Vocabulary scores are scaled scores achieved on the WAIS Vocabulary by the adults and on the WISC Vocabulary by the children. WISC means are based on a total of 62 children: one subject in the 10–11 year group, four in the 8–9 year group, and one in the 6–7 year group were not given the WISC Vocabulary.

[b] One 14-year-old child is included in this group.

adults. The boys were obtained from two community centers. The adults were members of two Protestant churches and had volunteered their services in order to earn money for their respective churches. Both samples of subjects are characterized by a middle class socio-economic background.

The necessary measures of motivation were obtained from fantasy material produced by the subjects on the Role-Taking Task (RTT), which has been described in detail elsewhere (Feffer, 1959). In this test, adapted from Schneidman's Make a Picture Story (MAPS) test, the subject is asked to place at least three figures in a scene and tell a story about them as in the standard MAPS administration. After the stories are completed, each scene is again set up and the subject is asked to take, successively, the roles of each of the different actors in his stories, retelling the story from each actor's point of view. Two stories with their accompanying roles were used in the present study. All subjects were given the living-room scene as a background for their first story and used a scene of their choice for the second story. Adults told an additional story using a work-shop scene which was omitted from the comparisons of the present study. Testing sessions were recorded and a verbatim transcript was made of each subject's performance.

The method of scoring RTT protocols for motivation and the reliability of the procedure have been given in detail in the previous study of adults (Gourevitch, 1959). Split-half reliability, computed on the basis of odd and even roles and corrected by Spearman-Brown formula, ranged from .72 to .93 for the four different levels of motivation. Scoring reliability, based on the scores assigned to each level by two independent scorers, ranged from .71 to .96 for the four levels. Briefly, the scoring method consists of assigning to the appropriate level of the hierarchy—1, 2, 3, or 4— each reinforcement clearly discernible in the behavior sequences and character descriptions given by the subject in the course of telling his stories and taking the roles of his various actors. Descriptive statements and accounts without readily interpretable motivational implications are not scored. Sample statements assigned to each of the levels are shown below. The samples have been chosen to illustrate the diversity of content included at any given level, and the range of sophistication of expression. Only the type and locus of the reinforcement implied by the subject's statement are considered in assigning the statement to a given level.

1. Concrete, Internal Reinforcement

Statements assigned to this level reflect a concern with physiological satisfactions, safety, or the release of tension for its own sake. For example:

What he wants is some ice cream. . . . It's so hot he takes off his shirt to cool off. . . . He hides from the man with the gun because he doesn't want to get shot. . . . She puts on a temper tantrum to wear off some of the frustration she feels.

2. Concrete, External Reinforcement

This level reflects a concern with pleasurable objects and material goods, concrete reward, or affection and belongingness. For example:

He wants Santa to bring him a new bicycle. . . . After supper he likes to watch TV. . . . He hopes his team will win the prize. . . . They want a summer cottage for weekends. . . . He only gets into fights because he craves attention and affection.

3. Abstract, External Reinforcement

This category is concerned with generalized esteem and Popularity. For example:

He doesn't want the other boys to think he's a sissy. . . . He wants everybody to think he's a good citizen of the U.S. . . . He wishes he had an education so he could make a name for himself. . . . Keeping up with the Joneses is primary in their thinking.

4. Abstract, Internal Reinforcement

This category reflects an active concern with self-actualization and the intrinsic satisfactions of achievement. Also included in this category are statements concerned with self-respect, integrity and moral rightness. For example:

He's practicing with his bat and ball because he wants to become a baseball player when he grows up. . . . He likes his work, it's a real challenge to him. . . . Even though he's a cripple he wants to make something of himself, become a real person. . . . She thinks you ought to be a good mother and teach your son the right things. . . . He doesn't believe he should soft-soap or walk around any issue in the department just to please his boss.

The classification of statements as shown above yields four raw scores for each subject, representing the number of his responses assigned to each of the four levels. A fifth raw score, Motivation R, represents the sum of the four categories or the total number of scorable motivation responses. The RTT protocols were scored in this fashion and sets of raw scores were obtained for each of the subjects without any knowledge of other variables of the study. Mean raw scores for the different age groups are shown in Table 33-2.

TABLE 33-2. Raw RTT Motivation Scores of Age Groups

RTT variable	Means			Standard deviations		
	Adults (N = 36)	10–14 yrs (N = 32)	6–9 yrs (N = 36)	Adults (N = 36)	10–14 yrs (N = 32)	6–9 yrs (N = 36)
RTT Verbal Production, number of words	1,677	1,195	897	980	826	695
Motivation R	18.25	10.25	5.97	12.24	4.61	3.62
Level 1	4.89	3.47	2.67	2.96	3.06	2.48
Level 2	10.53	6.19	3.06	8.54	3.45	2.32
Level 3	.83	.13	.03	1.07	.42	.16
Level 4	2.00	.50	.22	1.83	.98	.58

Since the RTT is a verbal task, a check was made on the relationship of the motivation scores to verbal intelligence. In the previous investigation of adults, it was found that RTT motivation scores were not significantly related to verbal intelligence as measured by the WAIS Vocabulary test. Correlations ranged from .05 to .19. A check on the children's group of the present study revealed correlations between WISC Vocabulary raw scores and raw motivation scores of the order of .43 and .38, for Levels 1 and 2 respectively. When sheer verbal productivity on the RTT is held constant by partial correlation, these relationships are reduced to .38 between WISC and Level 1 motivation and .36 between WISC and Level 2 scores. Therefore, although among the children the RTT motivation scores appear to have some relationship to verbal intelligence, there is no differential relationship with higher level and lower level motivation scores. That is, differential scoring at the higher motivational level cannot be attributed to the selective influence of verbal ability. Too few children received scores at the Abstract Levels 3 and 4 to warrant the above procedures. However, a *t*-test comparison revealed that the mean WISC score of the children who gave some Abstract level motivation (37.6) is not significantly higher than the mean WISC score of the children who gave no such motivation (32.8). Among both children and adults, then, it seems clear that developmentally high motivation scores on the RTT cannot be attributed to the selective influence of verbal intelligence, at least as this is measured by standard vocabulary tests.

In the previous investigation of adults, all the various RTT motivation scores were found to be highly related to the subjects' verbal productivity (number of words) in the Role-Taking situation. Although the children's motivation scores showed a much lower order of relationship to their verbal productivity, some of these relationships also reached significance. In addition, as Table 33-2 reveals, the adults were considerably more productive than the children. It seemed necessary, therefore, to control the motivational scores for RTT verbal productivity. Since discrete age groups were to be compared, the usual partial correlation procedure was not feasible. A method suggested by Cronbach (1949) was used which may be called the "roving median" technique. The pooled sample of children and adults were divided into eight groups representing different degrees of RTT verbal productivity, subjects within each group manifesting roughly equal verbal productivity. For each such group, the median score on each of the motivation variables was obtained. The median score for a given variable was then subtracted from each member's raw score for that variable, yielding a set of deviation scores for each subject which represented the discrepancy, plus or minus, between his raw scores and the median raw scores of his productivity group. For convenience, a constant was added to the deviation scores to eliminate minus signs. All comparisons between children and adults were made in terms of these scores. For the comparisons between older and younger children, similar scores were obtained by dividing the pooled sample of younger and older children into productivity groups. All scores used in the test of the hypotheses were, therefore, controlled for the influence of RTT verbal productivity.

C. RESULTS

The results were analyzed by both parametric and nonparametric methods. For both analyses, three sets of comparisons were made: (1) adults with total children, (2) adults with older children (10–13 years), and (3) older children (10–13 years) with younger children (6–9 years).

Table 33-3 shows the results of t tests comparing the mean RTT motivation scores of the different age groups. Even when scores are controlled for verbal productivity, Motivation R shows the expected increase with age. Adults have a significantly higher Motivation R than children, and the Motivation R of older children is significantly greater than that of younger children. None of the groups differs significantly in Level 1 motivation, the lowest level of the hierarchy. For all groups, the absolute differences are greatest at Level 2, which is the most frequent score at all ages (see Table 33-2), but the great variability of the Level 2 scores among the adults renders these differences considerably less reliable than the smaller differences found at Levels 3 and 4. Thus, in the comparison of adults with total children, the most significant differences appear at Levels 3 and 4, the highest levels of the hierarchy, and the order of differentiation is, as hypothesized, increasingly sharp at successive levels from 1 to 4. The probability of this order arising by chance is 1/24, or less than .05. As would be expected, the differences are less marked when adults are compared only with the older children of the group (10–13 years), though here also, the reliability of these differences follows the same pattern of increasing significance from Level 1 to Level 4 of the hierarchy. In the comparison of older with younger children, a significant difference is obtained only at Level 2, scores at Levels 3 and 4 failing to discriminate significantly between the two groups although the differences are in the hypothesized direction. There were very few scores at Levels 3 and 4 among both groups of children (see Table 33-2). Eleven children received a single score at one of these levels, and five children, four of whom were in the older age group, received more than one such score. With these few exceptions, Level 2 constituted the "upper" motivational level among the children, and a significant difference between the older and younger children at this level is in accord with the hypothesis.

In Table 33-4, the same age groups are compared in terms of individuals falling above and below the medians of the various RTT motivation variables. The resulting χ^2 values confirm the findings obtained by t test

TABLE 33-3. t-Test Comparison of Age Groups on RTT Motivation

RTT motivation variable	Adults vs. Total Children			Adults vs. 10–13 yr. children			10–13 yr. vs. 6–9 yr. children		
	Diff. between means	SE Diff.	t	Diff. between means	SE Diff.	t	Diff. between means	SE Diff.	t
Motivation R	6.01	1.30	4.64c	4.98	1.67	2.98b	3.18	.94	3.40b
Level 1	.38	.48	.79	.63	.61	1.03	−.08	.65	−.12
Level 2	3.40	1.08	3.14b	2.59	1.27	2.04a	2.43	.74	3.26b
Level 3	.56	.14	4.11c	.53	.16	3.21b	.10	.08	1.25
Level 4	1.22	.29	4.16c	1.19	.33	3.56b	.25	.20	1.22

Note: All differences were computed by subtracting the mean of the younger group from the mean of the older group.

[a] Significant at the .05 level.
[b] Significant at the .01 level.
[c] Significant at the .001 level.

TABLE 33.4. χ^2 Comparison of Age Groups on RTT Motivation

RTT motivation variable	Adults (N=36) % above median	Children (N=68) % above median	χ^2	Adults (N=36) % above median	10–13 yrs (N=32) % above median	χ^2	10–13 yrs (N=32) % above median	6–9 yrs (N=36) % above median	χ^2
Motivation R	77	40	10.78c	64	47	1.99	63	36	4.72a
Level 1	59	50	.56	59	45	1.10	41	47	.30
Level 2	66	39	5.80a	58	44	1.44	71	31	8.87b
Level 3	33	4	15.95c	33	6	4.84a	9	3	—
Level 4	64	18	22.54c	64	22	12.13c	25	17	.31

Note: Frequencies used in computing χ^2 have been converted to percentages to facilitate the comparison of different groups.

[a] Significant at the .05 level.
[b] Significant at the .01 level.
[c] Significant at the .001 level.
[d] At these levels, the median score was zero and comparisons were necessarily made between individuals above the median and individuals at the median.

with two exceptions. When individuals are compared rather than means, the adults and older children (10–13 years) differ significantly only at Levels 3 and 4 of the hierarchy. The two groups do not differ significantly in Motivation R and in Level 2 scores, suggesting that the significant differences found between the means of these high variables may be due to a few scores among the adults or a few low scores among the older children, or both. An inspection of the distribution of Motivation R scores revealed two very high adult scores, but an omission of these subjects did not substantially reduce the significance of the difference between the mean Motivation R scores of adults and older children. However, an inspection of the distribution of scores at Level 2 revealed that four adults had scores so high as to be discontinuous with the rest of the distribution and one of the older children had a score so low as to be discontinuous with the rest of the distribution. When these five subjects were omitted and new means and variances were computed for the remaining adults and older children, the difference between the means of the two groups at Level 2 was reduced from 2.59 to .49, and the corresponding t value became .54 or insignificant. This finding suggests that the difference between adults and older children at Level 2 is exaggerated by the use of a t test, and is probably better represented by the χ^2 value of 1.44, which is not significant.

D. DISCUSSION

By both methods of analysis, the findings confirm the hypothesis of a developmental hierarchy of motivation as proposed. Over the three groups studied, there is an increase with age in the sheer number of reinforcers appearing in the RTT fantasy material of these subjects, suggesting the quantitative expansion hypothesized to occur in motivational development. Further, adults differ increasingly from children at successive levels of the proposed hierarchy. The three age groups studied reveal approximately equal Level 1 motivation, or approximately equal concern with concrete, internal reinforcement. This need not be surprising. There are decided limits to quantitative expansion in a realm comprised of such reinforcers as food, drink, physical comfort and safety, and it may be that this limit is reached at an earlier age than that represented by the youngest group of this study. Thereafter, changes may occur in what constitutes acceptable food and drink, or in what seems to threaten physical safety, but there is apparently little increase in the number of such reinforcers. At Level 2 of the hierarchy, both adults and older children reveal significantly more reinforcers than do the younger children, apparently reflecting more sources of reinforcement in the external world of objects and people. Concrete reinforcement of this kind seems to approach an asymptote at the age level represented by the 10- to 13-year-old group, as the adults do not show a clear-cut increase over this group in Level 2 motivation. At the abstract levels, 3 and 4, differences between adults and children were highly significant. Abstract reinforcement in the form of one's own judgment of approval or the imagined judgment of other was rare among the children, while 83 per cent of the adults gave evidence of familiarity with this kind of reinforcement.

These findings suggest a course of motivational development which has implications for a number of areas. If, for example, the pre-adolescent child cannot typically be counted upon to respond to "abstract" reinforcement, it becomes wasteful for teachers to try to educate him in learning "for learning's sake," wherein he is expected to "realize himself," compete only with himself, etc. If he applies himself to the task of learning, it will more likely be because this task involves enjoyable concrete operations, or is rewarded by concrete symbols of achievement.

In the area of social adaptation, motivational development undoubtedly plays a crucial role. If normal development follows the course suggested by the findings of this study, the plight of the adult who has failed to fully attain this development is immediately apparent. Such an individual is likely to be unduly dependent upon concrete reinforcement from the environment, and consequently unduly vulnerable to adverse shifts and changes in this environment. This may be one explanation of the low frustration tolerance, dependency, and instability which characterize some behavior disorders. Such individuals have frequently been regarded as showing disturbance in "superego functioning" or as lacking "internalized values," etc. In terms of the present framework, they may be regarded as lacking the stable sources of internal reinforcement which are necessary for the independent and self-disciplined functioning which our society demands.

Further investigation will require some behavioral validation of the RTT motivation scores, as of course, reinforcers and reinforcement are not directly measured by the RTT and have not been measured in the present study. Only the subjects' reported perceptions and interpretations of fantasied behavior have been measured. The conclusions drawn rest upon the assumption that such interpretations are necessarily made in terms of reinforcers with which the subject is familiar, and that the absence of mention of a whole class of reinforcers constitutes evidence that this class of reinforcers is not significant in the subject's experience. Such methods and assumptions are obviously unnecessary for observable responses and observable reinforcers, but there seems to be no more direct way of measuring the reinforcing responses which occur covertly within an individual's own response system, although the importance of such responses has been recognized by a number of writers—for example, Mowrer and Ullman (1945), Dollard and Miller (1950), and Skinner (1957). All of the projective techniques, of course, attempt some assessment of an individual's covert, symbolic responses. The RTT has certain advantages in this respect. Requiring the subject to take the roles of the various actors in his stories necessarily obliges him to deal with the supposed covert responses of each actor. It is a common occurrence to have a seemingly flat story "blossom" in the role-taking portion of the test to reveal feelings, thoughts, perceptions and interpretations which could never have been surmised from the initial story. RTT protocols are especially rich in such material.

The RTT scoring system for motivation has a precedent in the McClelland (McClelland, Atkinson, Clark, & Lowell, 1953) scoring of achievement motivation. The RTT scoring system is more comprehensive and, obviously, the classification of motives is quite different from McClelland's. In the RTT system, "achievement" may be classified at Level 2 if, for example, it is seen by the subject as a means of making more money, or at Level 3 if it is seen as conferring status, or at Level 4 if it is seen as an opportunity for self-actualization.

Some of the methodological difficulties encountered in the development of the RTT motivational scoring system may be worth considering for the sake of the general questions they raise about measures obtained from fantasy material. With the RTT, it soon became apparent that it was a hazardous procedure to relate any one of the motivation scores to a criterion and ignore the other motivation scores. For example, a hypothesized relationship was found between social adequacy and Level 4 motivation, but upon further investigation it appeared that scores at Level 2 and Level 1 were even more highly related to social adequacy (Gourevitch, 1959). All of the scores were related to the subjects' verbal productivity—more productive subjects having higher scores at every level—and verbal productivity itself was related to social adequacy. When verbal productivity was partialed out, many significant correlations disappeared. Similar findings have been reported recently by Lindzey and Silverman (1959) in a study of TAT verbal productivity. It is not uncommon to read reports of research in which measures of a single motive obtained from fantasy material are related to some variable with no concern for other motives which may appear in the same material, much less for the subjects' general productivity. Experience with the RTT suggests that such relationships cannot be confidently interpreted at face value. Verbal productivity is a variable for which there is no ready interpretation—it is not related to intelligence among our subjects—and partialing out such a variable may not always be the wisest course, but certainly scores obtained from fantasy material should be examined for its influence.

E. SUMMARY

A hierarchy of motivation, following Maslow's (1954) general scheme, was formulated in terms of four levels of development. Successive levels of the hierarchy were intended to reflect the hypothetical progress of an individual in the gradual acquisition of learned or "secondary" reinforcers, culminating in his development of a source of symbolic, internalized reinforcement such as is manifested in self-approval and self-actualization. Motivational development was regarded as a cumulative process, reflected in a general quantitative increase of effective reinforcers with age, as well as in qualitative development from one level to another in the proposed hierarchy. Older age groups were expected, therefore, to show a greater number of reinforcers than younger age groups, and older age groups were expected to differ increasingly from younger age groups at successively higher levels of the hierarchy.

Three age groups, comprising a total of 104 subjects, were studied: adults (mean age 36.0 years), older children (10–13 years), and younger children (6–9 years). Motivation was assessed from fantasy material produced by the subjects on the Role-Taking Task. The scoring system developed for this instrument yields a score for each of the four levels of the proposed motivational hierarchy. The scores were controlled for the verbal productivity of the subjects, and comparisons were made between the three age groups at each level of the hierarchy. The results confirmed the broad outlines of the hierarchy as proposed. There was a general increase with age in the number of "reinforcers" appearing in the Role-Taking protocols. None of the groups differed significantly at the "earliest" or lowest level of the hierarchy. Older children differed significantly from the younger children at the second level of the hierarchy, and adults differed significantly from older children at the third and fourth levels of the hierarchy. As hypothesized, adults differed increasingly from both groups of children at successively higher levels of the hierarchy. Such increasing differences were not found, however, between the older and younger children. The symbolic reinforcement represented by the third and fourth levels of the hierarchy was rarely mentioned by the children, and there were no significant differences between the two age groups at these levels. The second level of the hierarchy seemed to constitute the effective "upper" level of motivation among both groups of children.

Possible implications of the findings in the areas of education and social adaptation were considered. The limitations of the Role-Taking Task as a measure of motivation, and the general difficulty of assessing reinforcement at symbolic levels, were discussed. Experience with the Role-Taking Task suggests that scores derived from fantasy material should be examined for the influence of verbal productivity.

REFERENCES

Bindra, D. *Motivation*. New York: Ronald Press, 1959.

Cronbach, L. J. Statistical methods applied to Rorschach scores: A review. *Psychol. Bull.*, 1949, 46, 393–429.

Dollard, J., & Miller, N. E. *Personality and Psychotherapy*. New York: McGraw-Hill, 1950.

Feffer, M. H. The cognitive implications of role-taking behavior. *J. Pers.*, 1959, 27, 152–168.

Ferster, C. B., & Skinner, B. F. *Schedules of Reinforcement*. New York: Appleton-Century-Crofts, 1957.

Gourevitch, V. Motivation and social adequacy. Unpublished doctoral dissertation, Teachers College, Columbia University, 1959.

Lindzey, G., & Silverman, M. Thematic apperception test: Techniques of group administration, sex differences, and the role of verbal productivity. *J. Pers.*, 1959, 27, 311–323.

Maslow, A. H. *Motivation and Personality*. New York: Harper, 1954.

McClelland, D. C., Atkinson, J. W., Clark, R. A., & Lowell, E. L. *The Achievement Motive*. New York: Appleton-Century-Crofts, 1953.

Mowrer, O. H., & Ullman, A. D. Time as a determinant in integrative learning. *Psychol. Rev.*, 1945, 52, 61–90.

Rotter, J. B. *Social Learning and Clinical Psychology*. New York: Prentice-Hall, 1954.

Skinner, B. F. *Verbal Behavior*. New York: Appleton-Century-Crofts, 1957.

EXISTENTIALIST CONCEPTIONS OF MAN

EXISTENTIAL PSYCHOLOGY originated as a reaction to nineteenth-century philosophy and as a protest against the world situation in the nineteenth and twentieth centuries. Political democracy and economic prosperity had failed, by the turn of the century, to fulfill optimistic beliefs in progress and the ability of the individual to improve society as a whole by his initiative. Impersonal mass society and technology robbed the individual of authentic status. Nineteenth-century philosophic preoccupation with reality as an object of consciousness had fragmented man in its emphasis upon rationality as his basic nature and in its failure to deal with the more immediate and subjective character of existence. In response to this twofold situation—rationalistic philosophy and the anomic consequences of an impersonalized society—existentialism developed as a philosophy of the crisis in the relationship of individuals to societies. Existential psychology, more specifically, focuses on the alienation of modern man and his search for meaning in life.

Existential psychologists have found scientific and experimental techniques inappropriate to the study of man. They have been highly critical of attempts to treat man as comparable to any other natural object, thus eliminating the most essential human characteristics—man's awareness of himself (existence) and his self-directed, goal-oriented strivings (continued becoming). It is essential, they maintain, to focus on human behavior as it appears in real life, without necessarily renouncing one's identity as a scientist. Yet the original, spontaneous way of being-in-the-world is not the scientific mode; concrete daily experience is not scientific. But the scientific mode of existence must not lose contact with the spontaneous "lived" mode of existence. The world of primary experience, from which science emerges and upon which it is nourished, is composed of different kinds of meanings from those which science imparts. We can fully understand the scientific mode of existence only if we are able to first grasp the primary mode of being-in-the-world. A man's role as a scientist is second to, and presupposes, his first role, that of a man. Thus, the scientist must adapt his methods to behavior as it actually appears instead of arbitrarily adapting behavior to scientific methods.

Kierkegaard provided the philosophical basis for existential psychology. He died in 1838, and his work went virtually unnoticed until the turn of the century. Husserl was a German philosopher whose phenomenological method directly influenced present theory. Jaspers and Heidegger were two professors of philosophy profoundly influenced by Kierkegaard. Heidegger is the godfather of Daseinsanalysis (existential analysis). For him, the possibility of death stands for all possibility in life, and thus it enhances man's awareness of his existence. Binswanger, advancing from Heidegger's analysis, has elaborated in great detail the variety of possible modes in which one's relations to the world may be experienced. Frankl, taking his departure from Jaspers, has emphasized, in his logotherapy, the human being's need to realize his unique possibilities through his love and the discovery of and devotion to his particular self requirements. Both show the human potentialities and powers for transcending constricted modes of existence. Boss has tried to combine the techniques of psychoanalysis and the ideas of Heidegger. Rollo May is the most prominent American existential psychologist. As will become clear, the movement is not unified, nor does it have one spokesman.

As the papers in this section demonstrate, existentialism has not generated a consistent and internally coherent system of postulates and constructs which could be compared with most of the other personality theories presented in this volume. Apart from explicitly philosophical concerns, existentialism has found its widest employment in the therapeutic setting, e.g., in Frankl's logotherapy and in Daseinsanalysis. But as the Crumbaugh and Maholick paper shows, not all of its propositions are outside the range of empirical test.

On this particular matter, it is difficult to imagine the work of Crumbaugh and Maholick arousing much interest or excitement among existential psychologists or psychiatrists. Their views are basically alien to the positivistic interpretations of science and materialistic views of reality. Yet, in many ways, their approach parallels the indigenous American pragmatic philosophy, especially in relation to the nature of truth. A wedding of European existentialism and American pragmatism may eventually prove to be richly productive. Furthermore, existential philosophy does speak with directness and immediacy to the American of his contemporary experience, however poetic or awkward its metalanguage may be. Existentialism has been called a crisis philosophy. This is particularly appropriate to our troubled present. As Buber has remarked, only when one lives on "the sharp edge of existence" can one see clearly. Certainly, contemporary society is living on such an edge.

34

An Appraisal
of Existential Analysis

EUGEN KAHN

I

If one plans a discussion of *Daseinsanalysis*, it is necessary to go back to Existentialism, from which it springs. Mentioning Existentialism makes it inevitable that one say something of its founder, Soren Kierkegaard.

Soren Kierkegaard's father had been a poor lad who had attained a fortune as a merchant. He died in 1838 in his 80's.[1] Before he died—the writer does not know how long before—he told his son the following story: he had worked as a shepherd in his youth. Once while minding his sheep in complete loneliness, he cursed God. He was never able to get over this sin. He was a sober, maybe even melancholy, man. Throughout his life, he could never enjoy himself. It would be vain to inquire into how far this curse motivated his unhappiness or how much, perhaps, the curse was motivated by an unfortunate personality make-up. It may be taken for granted that Soren Kierkegaard—always a devout man of high sensitivity—was immensely impressed with his father's confession; he was perhaps unable ever to rid himself entirely of its impact.[2]

Soren Kierkegaard was born in 1813. He died in 1855. Because of his father's means, he was never compelled to work for a living. He studied theology and became a minister, though he never had a parish. He studied for the most part in his homeland, Denmark, and for a time in Berlin with his foremost interest in philosophy. He began to write in his early life, em-

From E. Kahn, An Appraisal of Existential Analysis. Reprinted by permission of *The Psychiatric Quarterly*, 1957, 31, 203–227, and the author.

From Baylor University—College of Medicine, Department of Psychiatry, Houston 25, Texas.

Part I of a two-part discussion of *Daseinsanalysis*, appearing in successive issues of *The Psychiatric Quarterly*.

[1] He apparently was in his late 50's when Soren Kierkegaard was born.

[2] "Scripture teaches that God visits the sins of the fathers upon the children unto the third and fourth generation; verily, life is telling this in a loud voice" (Kierkegaard).

phasizing the role of the individual and the fact of his existence in opposition to the teaching of the Protestant clergy of his time. Of Kierkegaard's person and personal life, it should be added that he was a hunchback and that for some time he was engaged to a young girl whom he probably loved very dearly. Nevertheless, he broke off the engagement in 1834, but appeared disappointed and dismayed, as the young lady did not show any tendency to re-approach him but married somebody else. For all that seems to be known, Kierkegaard did not have any other dealings with women. He lived as an unhappy, lonely creature, reminding one of his father. However, he wrote most amply,[3] mostly under pseudonyms, using a variety of them during his literary career. His writings are very hard to understand. He sometimes gets himself into very long and involved sentences. Often he appears extremely bitter, in spite of apparent humor, or rather biting wit. It is the interjection of ironic and witty remarks which makes the understanding of his productions still more difficult. However, it may well be that the translations are not perfect in all places.

In the original writings of Kierkegaard that the present writer has himself seen and according to various interpretations and reports, one may venture to say that whatever he wrote was the expression of a haunted person, of a profoundly unhappy human being who, devout as he was, never stopped searching God and who seems to have suffered feelings of guilt for his philosophical inquisitiveness. One may refrain from deciding whether his writings are more often a fusion or a confusion of religion and philosophy. He is the first one to write strictly about existence, about individual existence. He is familiar with the fundamental existential experience: dread.[4] Dread is experienced in the face of Nothing. Whatever excursions into philosophy he made; whatever ideas he expounded about existence, about dread, about fear, about Nothing, his experiential center, if one may call it so, was made and remained the Deity. This haunted man was running, and working, himself mercilessly to death. At the age of 42, he broke down on the street; he was taken to a hospital where he died shortly afterward. Nobody had minded him and his work much while he was alive; nobody minded them for years to come after his death. His most eminent literary contemporary compatriot, Heiberg, "blackballed" him. It must be remembered that Kierkegaard stood up in arms against his then all-too-quiet Protestant chruch, as well as against the leading philosophers of his time.

It was only around the turn of this century that a few people took notice of Kierkegaard's work. Most outstanding among them were Karl

---

[3] Kierkegaard wrote about boredom, dread, melancholy and despair. He stated that "in the beginning was boredom." He called melancholy his "intimate, confidential friend"; he said: "The man who is plagued by grief and worry, knows the causes of grief and worry. If, however, you ask a melancholic man what there is that makes him so melancholic, he will reply: 'I do not know. I cannot tell.' "

[4] Danish: *angest*; German: *Angst*.

Jaspers and Martin Heidegger who are both profoundly influenced by Kierke-gaard's, and incidently by Nietzsche's, thought. Their interpretations of both Kierkegaard and Nietzsche differ considerably. Both Jaspers and Heidegger were professors of philosophy, in Heidelberg and Freiburg (Germany), respectively. Both were dismissed from their universities as will be noted briefly.

"The Kierkegaard-Renaissance is one of the strangest phenomena of our time," Heinemann writes, ". . . he was a proleptic man, who, as a single individual, experienced in the middle of the last century something which has become common experience in our own day, and who had the power of expressing it in a most interesting, paradoxical and challenging manner. The literary representation of his thought is, moreover, so enig-matic, obscure and sometimes mysterious that his writings make the im-pression of great profundity and offer an occasion for indefinite new inter-pretations."

II

Karl Jaspers, born in 1883, is a venerable figure of considerable im-portance in German psychiatry and philosophy. He read law for a year be-fore going into medicine, where he turned to psychiatry immediately after finishing medical school. On the staff of the Psychiatric University Clinic in Heidelberg, he published outstanding and unusually stimulating papers, and in 1913, his *General Psychopathology*. This book, showing the rare erudition of its author, in particular in psychology and philosophy, became a sort of psychopathological *Bible* for psychiatrists of the German lan-guage; its fifth edition appeared in 1948. Jaspers soon began to teach and to work in the philosophical faculty in Heidelberg, in which he attained a full professorship in 1921. He wrote a *Psychologie der Weltanschaungen* and a *Philosophie* in three volumes. The second volume of Jaspers' *Philoso-phie* bears the title *Existenzerhellung*.[5]

Jaspers had married a Jewish girl. Hence, in 1937, he was dismissed from the university and could not publish anything again before 1945. Since then, he has published a number of papers and republished some of his books. Reinstated as professor in Heidelberg, he soon accepted a call to the University of Basel, Switzerland, where he is still teaching and writing.

Fully aware of the development of the masses and their aspirations, Jaspers seems to appeal to the individual and his existence. He does not give any definition of existence, and in his philosophizing, has a peculiar atti-tude of *"Schweben,"* [6] assuming that it is not feasible to come to grips with

[5] Clarification of existence.
[6] "Floating."

the problems involved in the way one can with less ethereal problems. He says: "A philosophy of existence is a way of thinking which uses and transcends all material knowledge in order that man may again become himself." In 1950, Jaspers declared that his philosophy was not—or rather was no longer—a philosophy of existence, but was a philosophy of reason. There will be no more detailed discussion of Jaspers' work here, as, in spite of the great impact his *Psychopathology* exerted in psychiatry, his philosophy did not influence the psychiatric existential analysts with whom this paper will deal. It might be noted, though, that Jaspers sees in Heidegger's attempt "regardless of the value of his concrete discussions principally a philosophical error." [7] Accordingly, Jaspers considers Ludwig Binswanger's particular existential analytic attitude and aspect "a philosophical and scientific error." [8]

III

An interpolation about Edmund Husserl (1859–1938) appears indicated. Husserl was Heidegger's teacher. Heidegger was Husserl's successor as professor in Freiburg in 1929. A philosopher of high significance in Germany, Husserl lost many of his pupils when he published his *Ideas About a Pure Phenomenology*. Husserl wanted to get directly to "the things themselves." [9] He tried to analyze what was immediately given in consciousness. He tried to deal with the essence of the given material and did not pay any attention, so it appears, to the existence of the world—apart from the actual matter he was investigating. It has been said that existentialists and others found it impossible to follow him because he considered essence to be prior to existence. It is held, however, that there cannot be any essence unless there is some existence and unless there is something and/or someone existent that, due to its existence, is capable of being endowed with essence.

It has been claimed that Husserl's phenomenological method has profoundly influenced contemporary philosophical thought. As it is, the phenomenological methods used by philosophers and psychologists appear to be definitely different from Husserl's. Jaspers, for example, writes that he uses the word phenomenology and the phenomenological method in his *General Psychopathology* in the sense originally used by Husserl, that is, " 'descriptive psychology' of manifestations of consciousness," while for Husserl, it later became "*Wesensschau*" (intuition). It is outside the present writer's competence to participate in these particular discussions of the

---

[7] "*Unbeschadet des Wertes seiner konkreten Ausführungen halte ich den Versuch im Prinzip für einen philosophischen Irrweg*" (Jaspers).

[8] "*ein philosophischer und ein wissenschaftlicher Irrtum*" (Jaspers).

[9] "*zu den Sachen selbst*" (Husserl).

philosophers. Yet mention of their dissensions seems indicated. The dispute leads some writers to a pretty free use of the word and concept, phenomenology. All manner of verbosities and mental gyrations have been called phenomenological.

Husserl had to leave Germany under the Nazi regime.

IV

Martin Heidegger (1889–), who is considered the godfather of *Daseinsanalyse* (existential analysis) had been professor of philosophy in Marburg an der Lahn before he was called to Freiburg to succeed Husserl in 1929. He had been educated as a Jesuit novice, but obviously became estranged from the Roman Catholic church. He appeared for a time to be wholeheartedly Nazi, as rector of the University of Freiburg, with the consequence that he was dismissed in 1945. He is now again lecturing at that university.

Heidegger published, in 1927, the book, *Sein und Zeit* [10] that made him famous. Heidegger seems to have admired Kierkegaard greatly; later, it is true, he considered Kierkegaard to have been a religious writer rather than a philosophical thinker.[11] Like Kierkegaard, he approaches existence from, and as, individual existence. *Dasein*, about which more will be said later, always refers to the human individual; it actually means for Heidegger a human mode of individual existence. Hence early in *Sein und Zeit* he writes, "Human existence is a being which does not only exist among other beings. It is rather characterized as a being that in its Being is concerned about this Being itself." [12] And, "The Being itself to which human existence can refer in this or that way and to which it always refers in some way is called existence." [13]

This may sound less strange if one tries to clarify some of Heidegger's terminology. It has already been remarked that by *Dasein* [14] he means the individual mode of human existence; *Dasein* will, in the following discussion be rendered, for brevity's sake as human existence; the reference to the

[10] *Being and Time.*

[11] *According to Löwith.*

[12] "*Das Dasein ist ein Seiendes, das nicht nur unter anderen Seienden vorkommt. Es ist vielmehr dadurch gekennzeichnet, dass es diesem Seienden in seinem Sein um dieses Sein selbst geht*" (Heidegger).

[13] "*Das Sein selbst, zu dem sich das Dasein so oder so verhalten kann und immer irgendwie verhaelt, nennen wir Existenz*" (Heidegger).

[14] The German word *Dasein*, noun with capital "D," is generally used in the German language to denote existence or life. Heidegger uses *Dasein* with the special meaning mentioned. So do his followers, although, at a closer view, not all of them really mean exactly what Heidegger does. Writers who are not existentially oriented usually take the word in its general meaning. The use of the word *Dasein* is no certificate of existentialism.

individual should always be kept in mind. The German words *sein, Sein, seiend* and *Seiendes* mean: "to be," "Being," "being," and "existent," respectively. The word *sein* is the infinitive that corresponds to "to be"; it is spelled with a small "s" unless it begins a sentence, which will be avoided here. The word *Sein*, always spelled with a capital "S," is a noun; it means existence per se, the existence due to which all existing things—living and not living—exist; the sentence just quoted "The Being itself to which human existence can refer in this or that way and to which it always refers in some way is called existence," may be quite understandable now, although at first sight it may have looked odd.

The word *seiend* is the present participle of the verb *sein; seiend* is related to *sein* as "being" with a small "b," is related to "to be." From this present participle, *seiend*, the noun *Seiend* is derived. It can be used for people (male and female) and things (neuter); in order to avoid confusion, *Seiend* will be translated as "the existent." "Existent" will be used only as a noun. If an attribute (adjective) is needed, "being," as well as "existing," is available. One might now slightly change the sentence quoted first: "Human existence is an existent which does not only exist among other existents, it is rather characterized as an existent that in its Being it is concerned about this Being itself." There is no doubt that many a sentence of Heidegger's must be read repeatedly and carefully before it actually "gets home."

Human existence, as he wants to have it understood, is *"geistig,"* [15] Heidegger says. It does not occupy any space like physical things, but has *Spielraum*, in which there is direction and distance. Human existence is thrown into its world or rather into its being-in-the-world. Its being-in-the-world is occasionally equated with human existence. This world is always "world-with"; other existents belong to the world in which I exist. The relation of human existence to its world is care, taking care, which in a broader sense might be interpreted as responsibility. "I myself am the existent that we call human existence; I am human existence as a possibility of existence concerned to be this existent." [16] This very "I" refers to and "means the existent that is concerned about the existence of the existent that it is." [17] "In saying 'I' human existence expresses itself as being-in-the-world." [18]

The "Time" of human existence is not "a one after the other," it is rather temporality [19] and temporalization. [19] Temporality means "the future that has been being and is being present." [20] As human existence, I am still

---

[15] Spiritual.

[16] *"das Seiende, das wir Dasein nennen, bin ich je selbst und zwar als Seinkönnen, dem es darum geht, dieses Seiende zu sein"* (Heidegger).

[17] *"meint das Seiende, dem es um das Sein des Seienden, das es ist, geht"* (Heidegger).

[18] *"Im Ich-sagen spricht sich das Dasein als In-der-Welt-sein aus"* (Heidegger).

[19] *"Zeitlichkeit und Zeitigung"* (Heidegger).

[20] *"gewesend-gegenwärtigende Zukunft"* (Heidegger).

my past, my past belongs to me, is part of me, in my present; yet from my present, I am reaching into the future, anticipating—expecting, planning, hoping—in a manner that makes my past and my present and my future one—not one time, but one temporality. "Temporality is the Existential sense of care." [21]

The notions of care and time will be more easily comprehended through the "myth of Care" which Wild has translated from *Sein und Zeit:* "Once when Care was crossing a river she saw a sounding piece of earth. Taking it up thoughtfully, she began to form it. As she was wondering what she would make, Jupiter appeared. Care asked him to bestow spirit on it and he readily agreed, but when Care wished to have her name given to the creature, Jupiter forbade this and said his name should be used. While Care and Jupiter were arguing over this, Earth also arose and sought to have her name imposed, since she had given it a piece of her body. They turned to Saturn to judge between them, and he rendered the following judgement in all fairness: 'You, Jupiter, because you have given the spirit, shall take the spirit at death. You, Earth, since you have given the body, shall have the body returned. But Care, since she first formed this being, shall possess him as long as he lives. Now since there is disagreement over the name, let him be called "homo" because he is made out of "earth" (humus).' "

Saturn is Time! In the threefold structure of Time, "All the manifestations of human existence are filled with care. In whatever he does, man is led by a devotion to something. He is a center of care" (Wild). For Heidegger, the myth of Care appears to have the implication that "homo," man, is human existence as well as human being. Thus he can say, as already quoted: "I myself am the existent that we call human existence. . . ."

Like Kierkegaard, Heidegger distinguishes between dread [22] and fear.[23] In fear, there is always some threat. In dread, that "springs from human existence itself," [24] threat is nowhere and everywhere; it signifies facing "nothing" or "nothingness." However, can "nothing" be faced? Can "nothing" be the content of dread? Can "nothing" exist? Can "nothing" whose existence, whose possibility appears questionable, be at the root of dread? One might conjecture that "nothing" is only created by dread. This may well be what Heidegger has in mind. It is characteristic of his dealing with language that he never says, "Nothing" exists, but formulates, "Nothing is nothinging." [25] It is left to the human being to consider that he came from "nothing" and will go to "nothing"; thus when he, or rather human existence, is grasped by dread without any primary threat, he may come to using this "nothing," secondarily elaborated, to give this errie dread a cause and content. Dread is thought to represent an existential crisis.

[21] *"Zeitlichkeit ist der Seinssinn der Sorge"* (Heidegger).
[22] *Angst.*
[23] *Furcht.*
[24] ". . . *entspringt aus dem Dasein selbst"* (Heidegger).
[25] *"Das Nichts nichtet"* (Heidegger).

Human existence, exposing itself to crises and going through them, is called "authentic existence." [26] Such human existence remains authentic in its communication with other human existences: "Human existence always has the existential mode of being together." [27] There, is in spite of communication and togetherness, always a certain distance between authentic human existences. There is another mode of being, "unauthentic existence," [28] everyday life in which all and sundry participate. Here "Everyone is the other one and nobody is himself." [29] This is called the existence of *Man*, which in this context might best be translated as Tom, Dick and Harry.[30]

Thrown into its existence in the world, human existence dreads the existence in the world. In a certain way, human existence dreads itself. This makes sense in view of its coming from and going to "nothing," and of Heidegger's remark: "Dread isolates and manifests human existence as *solus ipse.*' " [31] Furthermore, human existence is "existence to death," [32] or as Bollnow words it, "To exist means to be faced with death." [33] Human existence is unfinished as long as it exists. "The death of human existence is the possibility of being unable to exist further." [34] As all existence is possibility, death belongs to the possibilities of existence; this concerns authentic human existence. In unauthentic existence, in everyday life, death is not "a mode of being" [35] that is faced, but "a certainty that is avoided." [36]

"Time" is, as has been said, not a "one after the other" but, as the present writer would call it, the trinity of past, present and future. In its temporality and temporalization, human existence remains unfinished as long as there are possibilities, that is, as long as there is a future: "Only the existent 'between' birth and death represents the whole that we search." [37] "The attainment of the wholeness of human existence is also loss of the existence of human existence." One might perhaps say: When human existence has run its whole course it is over.

[26] *"eigentliches Dasein"* (Heidegger).
[27] *"Sofern Dasein überhaupt ist, hat es die Seinsart des Miteinanderseins"* (Heidegger).
[28] *"uneigentliches Dasein"* (Heidegger).
[29] *"Jeder ist der andere und keiner er selbst"* (Heidegger).
[30] The German *man* might in this context be translated as "the common man." This would however lead to confusion between the English "man" (German *Mann, Mensch*) and the German *man*, which is a pronoun.
[31] *"Die Angst vereinzelt und erschliesst so das Dasein als 'solus ipse' "* (Heidegger).
[32] *"Sein zum Tode"* (Heidegger).
[33] *"Existieren bedeutet im Angesicht des Todes stehen"* (Bollnow).
[34] *"Sein (des Daseins) Tod ist die Möglichkeit des Nicht-mehr-sein-könnens"* (Heidegger).
[35] *"eine Seinsweise"* (Heidegger).
[36] ". . . *kennt die Gewissheit des Todes und weicht dem Gewisssein doch aus"* (Heidegger).
[37] *"Erst das Seiende 'zwischen' Geburt und Tod stellt das gesuchte Ganze dar"* (Heidegger).

There is public time, "world time" (*Welt-Zeit*). We are dealing with world time when we look at the clock, and if we say "now."

V

In the preceding section, there has been an attempt to give a condensed picture of Heidegger's *Sein und Zeit* or rather of a few of the many ideas contained in it. Heidegger coined the term existential analy*tics*. He writes in *Sein und Zeit:* "All efforts of existential analy*tics* aim at one goal, to find a possibility of answering the quest for the sense of Being itself." [38]

Heidegger has, in a number of points, changed his attitudes and/or his interpretation. In the discussion among philosophers, he has been reproached about these changes. He has been blamed in particular for the introduction of the notion of "ek-sistence." One of his critics, Heinemann, states that Heidegger has rejected existentialism and "has risen again as an 'ek-sistentialist.' " Heinemann quotes from a later paper of Heidegger's: "The essence of man consists in ek-sistence. It is this that matters essentially, i.e., from the point of view of Being, in so far as Being itself installs man as ek-sistent as guardian of the truth of Being." [39]

There does not seem to be even *one* interpretation of "ek-sistence" among philosophers. In ek-sistence, Heidegger tries to conceive of man's ability to look at himself and at the "truth," which presumably is, or is meant to be, the truth of his existence. Despite a lively, partly outspoken, antagonistic discussion among philosophers, the continuing interest of Heidegger in Being and its sense is denied by nobody. It is not up to this writer to decide against earlier or later concepts and interpretations. After all, every thinker is, in the writer's belief, entitled to, and justified in discarding former, and presenting new, ideas. Heidegger has let it be known that nobody really understands him.[40] The writer could scarcely claim that he, of all people, might understand him. As it is, there are no limits to any interpretation as, curiously enough, people generally find what they are seeking. In Heidegger's case, everything would be definitely easier if there

---

[38] "*Alle Bemühungen der existentialen Analytik gelten dem einen Ziel, eine Möglichkeit der Beantwortung der Frage nach dem Sinn von Sein überhaupt zu finden*" (Heidegger). Heidegger uses "*existentiale analytik*" and "*Daseinsanalytik*" as synonyms. Both terms here are rendered as "existential analy*tics*."

[39] "*Das Wesen des Menschen beruht in der Ek-sistenz. Auf diese kommt es wesentlich, d.h. vom Sein selbts her an, insofern das Sein den Menschen als den ek-sistierenden zur Wächterschaft für die Wahrheit Seins in diese selbst ereignet*" (Heidegger). This sentence is quoted by Heinemann; it is taken from Heidegger's paper, "*Platons Lehre von der Wahrheit*," *Jahrbuch für geistige Überlieferung*, 1941. The English translation is from Heinemann.

[40] It is of some interest that Heidegger occasionally defended himself against the reproach that his *Sein und Zeit* was atheistic.

were not that sore spot which Blackman touched in observing ". . . a greater tenderness with common sense might better serve the cause of a 'guardian of Being.'"

The writer is not going to go into detail about Heidegger's rough handling of the German language. Yet one cannot avoid thinking *"Quod licet Jovi, non licet bovi"* when one studies the vast liberties some of his psychiatric pupils permit themselves with the same language.

Heidegger has objected to being classified as an existentialist. He considers, and wants others to consider, his philosophy as fundamental ontology. It appears to be useless, at least here, to argue about this. It is more appropriate to understand with Bollnow: "There is . . . no pure existential philosophy. . . . It is according to its essence a transition, leading into a deepened concept of philosophizing." [41] Bollnow writes: "The thinking of the existing thinker is determined through the definite task and difficulties of his life. Hence the purpose of his thinking is not this very purpose itself; his thinking rather serves his very existing." [42] According to the same author, who does not restrict himself in his book to Heidegger's work ". . . existence in the meaning of existential philosophy has nothing to do with an outer existence. Existence rather refers to a last inner core of man, to a last, unconditional center." [43] With unmistakable reference to Kierkegaard, Bollnow gives the opinion that this philosophy stems "from a definite attitude toward Christianity . . . one may understand the interest in existence from the care for the salvation of the soul." [44]

While Jaspers states: "I am only in communication with the other," [45] Heidegger writes: "Human existence is essentially Being-with." [46] Even Being-alone is Being-With. To this observation, which first does not appear plausible, Bollnow remarks: "Only a creature is able to be alone that is according to its nature living with others." [47] The present writer might express the same thus: Only a creature whose natural life is lived with others is able to experience loneliness.

---

[41] *"Es gibt . . . gar keine reine Existenzphilosophie . . . Sie ist ihrem Wesen nach ein Durchgang, der in eine vertiefte Auffassung des Philosophierens hineinführt"* (Bollnow).

[42] *"Der existierende Denker ist ein solcher, dessen Denken durch die bestimmten Aufgaben und Schwierigkeiten seines Lebens bestimmt sind, dessen Denken also nicht Selbstzweck ist, sondern im Dienst seines Existierens steht"* (Bollnow).

[43] *"Existenz im Sinne der Existenzphilosophie (hat) mit einer solchen äusseren Existenz nichts zu tun. Sie bezeichnet vielmehr im vollen Gegensatz dazu einen letzten inneren Kern des Menschen, ein letztes, unbedingtes Zentrum"* (Bollnow).

[44] *"Aus einer bestimmten Auffassung des Christentums herausgewachsen . . . darf man das Interesse am Existieren von der Sorge ums Seelenheil her verstehen"* (Bollnow). (See footnote 40.)

[45] *"Ich bin nur in Kommunikation mit Anderen"* (Jaspers).

[46] *"Dasein ist wesentlich Mitsein"* (Heidegger).

[47] *"Allein sein kann nur ein Wesen, das seiner Natur nach in Gemeinschaft lebt"* (Bollnow).

VI

When Heidegger discusses human existence, he does not seem to think of the body. As already mentioned, he considers human existence to be "spiritual." He expounds about dread and care in their relations to human existence; there is a remarkable passage in *Sein und Zeit*: "Dread is often 'physiologically' conditioned . . . Physiological precipitation of dread is possible only because human existence is dreading in the ground of its Being." [48] There may be several interpretations of this passage. The writer understands it in the sense that human existence, *Dasein*, is considered to have a sort of priority: Only "because" human existence is there, can anything physiological—in this instance precipitation of dread—happen, and this only because dread appears to be an essential mode of human existence. This attitude of Heidegger has allowed some of his pupils to go "back stage" every time they want to interpret anything phenomenologically. This will be seen in the further discussion. It has, indeed, with several of these pupils, gone so far that they propose and pretend to solve or dissolve the body-mind dualism through making *Dasein* into the very ruling aspect of the human individual—a sort of commanding general who disposes of physical properties and psychological attitudes and performances in a manner that permits the adept to interpret, and thus to understand completely, practically every experience of the human individual. The writer for one, doubts that Heidegger ever meant it this way.

What Heidegger considers the goal of his existential analytics [49] to be has already been discussed. This must be referred to when one now turns to dealing with existential analysis [50] as developed and propagated by Ludwig Binswanger. He defines Heidegger's existential analytics as the "philosophic-phenomenological clarification of the a priori or transcendental structure of human existence as being-in-the-world." [51] Binswanger defines existential analysis as "the empirical-phenomenological, scientific analysis of actual ways and *Gestalten* of human existence." [52] Existential analysis as developed in the hands of Binswanger and his pupils purports to be a method of interpretation, of hermeneutics, based on the presupposition of a certain

---

[48] "*Oft ist die Angst 'physiologisch' bedingt . . . Physiologische Auslösung der Angst wird nur möglich, weil das Dasein im Grund seines Seins sich ängstet*" (Heidegger).

[49] Heidegger's *Daseinsanalytik* or *existenziale Analytik*. (See footnote 38.)

[50] Binswanger's *Daseinsanalyse*.

[51] "*die philosophisch-phänomenologische Erhellung der apriorischen oder transcendentalen Struktur des Daseins als In-der-Welt-sein.*"

[52] "*die empirisch-phänomenologische, wissenschaftliche Analyse faktischer Daseinsweisen und Daseinsgestalten*" (Binswanger). One may remind the reader here that, for Heidegger, *Dasein* always refers to a human mode of individual existence, which for the sake of brevity and readability is rendered as "human existence."

"a priori structure of human existence as being-in-the-world." [53] This a priori structure is taken over from Heidegger's thoughts and formulations.

Binswanger emphasizes that he accepts "Being-in-the-world as existence in which human existence is concerned about myself. But [he understands] this self not only as the actual I-myself of human existence as mine or thine or his, but also as the we-our-selves a priori to that I-myself as ontologic possibility, as 'our' human existence, as primal meeting." [54] Binswanger concedes the "overwhelming impression" which *Sein und Zeit* made on him. But he soon notices "that the loving existence-together, love, stands in the cold outside of the doors of this project of Being." [55] Binswanger sees a contrast between care and love. On the ground of care there is "the nothing—eerie, overwhelming and overpowering," [56] on the ground of love there is "homey security, protecting home . . ." [57] Binswanger considers love the ontological opposite of care. He sees "in the eternity-aspect of *de facto* love a structural moment essentially immanent in love." [58] As already indicated, he declares Being-together as the very ground or foundation of love. He says many things about love, about "human existence as the we-ness of love." [59] "Love conquers 'space' and 'time' and 'history,' for it is not 'worlding' but eterning." [60] Binswanger says: "I can die only as an individual, but not as the thou of an I. Even if I die as an individual, I am, in dying, thine, a part of our we-ness." [61] Care does not have the aspect of eternity that love has. Yet, in the Being-in-the-world of the patient with a flight of ideas, Binswanger sees "The best example for the fact that both care and love belong equally to the full phenomenon of human existence . . . and that wherever either emancipates itself from the whole, the other 'gets altered' so that human existence becomes strange (alien) to itself and we talk about alienation, human existence in the form of estrange-

[53] *"apriorische Struktur des Daseins als In-der-Welt-sein."*

[54] "In-der-Welt-sein als ein Sein, darin es dem Dasein um es selbst geht, dass wir dieses Selbst aber nicht nur in dem faktischen Ich-selbst des Daseins als je meinem, deinem, seinem zu erblicken vermögen, sondern auch in den jenem Selbst vorgelagerten Möglichkeiten des Wir-selbst, des Daseins als 'unserem,' als Urbegegnung" (Binswanger).

[55] "dass das liebende Miteinander-sein, die Liebe, frierend ausserhalb dieses [Heidegger's] Seinsentwurfes steht" (Binswanger).

[56] "das 'unheimliche,' überwältigende und übermächtigende Nichts" (Binswanger).

[57] " 'heimliche' Geborgenheit, schützende Heimat." The play with the words "heimlich" and "unheimlich" cannot be rendered in English as is regrettably the case with a great number of words and phrases in both Daseinanalytik and Daseinsanalyse.

[58] "in dem Ewigkeitsaspekt der Liebe tatsächlich ein ihr wesenhaft immanentes Strukturmoment" (Binswanger).

[59] "Dasein als Wirheit der Liebe" (Binswanger).

[60] "Liebe an und für sich überschwingt wie 'dem Raum' und 'die Zeit' so auch 'die Geschichte'; denn sie 'weltet' nicht, sondern ewigt" (Binswanger).

[61] "Sterben kann ich nur als Individuum, aber nicht als Du eines Ich. Wenn ich als Individuum auch sterbe, so bin ich doch noch im Sterben, ja jetzt erst recht, der Deine, Glied unserer Wirheit" (Binswanger).

ment, alienation, of insanity. The whole of psychopathology can (and must) be understood and described from the viewpoints of these two constituents of human existence, viz. care and love." [62]

There is another digression from his teacher, Heidegger, which Binswanger stresses: ". . . If we talk of human existence, in fundamental opposition to Heidegger we *never* mean human existence, as mine, thine, or his, but human existence in general, or the human existence of mankind if one wants to say so . . ." [63] It may help to understand the preceding and some of the following quotations from Binswanger when one of his much-emphasized observations is rendered in a somewhat simplified manner: It is not due to language and consciousness that man is man; it is primarily existence-with which makes man; only on this basis, do language and self-consciousness become possible.

"Body and soul," we are told, "are abstractions from the inseparable unity of Being-human, seen from the anthropological viewpoint." [64] Admitting that body and soul are abstractions, one must wonder why the modes of Being as offered by Binswanger should and could be anything else but abstractions from the anthopological or any other viewpoint. Binswanger writers that plurality, duality and singularity are fundamental modes of Being-human: "Only in these modes and their special modifications and interweavings ('complexions'), is human existence really by itself. Where one cannot speak of an I, a thou, a dual we, a he or she nor of a plural we or they, there human existence is no longer 'by itself' but 'beside itself.' " [65] " 'Between' Being-by-itself and Not-being-here is Being-beside-itself as we call the 'furor of passion,' of anger, of rage, of jealousy, of despair of any kind. There human existence is no longer entirely by itself, here it approaches naked existence, horror." [66]

[62] "das beste Beispiel dafür, dass zum vollen Phänomen des menschlichen Daseins Sorge und Liebe zusammenghören . . . und dass, wo das eine sich vom Ganzen emanzipiert, das andere sich 'alteriert,' so dass das Dasein sich selber fremd (aliéné) wird, und wir von alienation, Dasein in der Gestalt der Entfremdung, des Wahnsinns sprechen. Die ganze Psychopathologie kann (und muss) von diesen beiden Konstituentien des Dasiens, der Sorge und der Liebe, aus verstanden und beschrieben werden" (Binswanger).

[63] ". . . wenn wir von Dasein sprechen, meinen wir ja in fundmentalem Gegensatz zu Heidegger, nie nur das Dasein als je meines, deines oder seines, sondern das menschliche Dasein überhaupt, oder, wenn man will, das Dasein der Menschheit" (Binswanger).

[64] "Leib und Seele sind lediglich Abstraktionen aus der untrennbaren Einheit des Menschseins, aus dem Sein als anthropologischem" (Binswanger).

[65] "Nur in diesen Modi, ihren speziellen Abwandlungen und Verflechtungen ('Komplexionen') ist das Dasein wirklich bei sich. Wo von keinem Ich, keinem Du, keinem dualen Wir, keinem Er oder Sie und keinem pluralen Wir die Rede sein kann, da ist das Dasein nicht mehr 'bei sich,' sondern 'ausser sich' " (Binswanger).

[66] "Gleichsam 'zwischen' dem Bei-sich-sein und dem Nicht-da-sein des Daseins steht das Ausser-sich-sein, wie wir die 'Raserei der Leidenschaft' nennen. Hier ist das Dasein nicht mehr ganz bei sich, hier nähert es sich dem nackten Dasein, dem Grauen" (Binswanger).

Binswanger observes that "cognition of human existence can never come to 'an end' " [67] and "that cognition of human existence is based not on logical reflection, but on imaginative intuition of *Gestalten* and on the imaginative cognition of the change of *Gestalten*." [68] In other words: We shall never get close to his thinking when we approach it with logical reflection. If we desire to gain any understanding of his elaborations we have to accept his intuition and the products of his intuition.

Binswanger defends himself against the reproach that he has misunderstood and supplemented Heidegger's teachings. He missed the anthropological aspect in Heidegger's thought and tried to add it. He considers Heidegger's existential analy*tics* as fundamental for psychiatry. Binswanger has attempted to plan a "building" [69] of psychiatry in which Heidegger's existential analy*tics*, Heidegger's *Daseinsanaly*tik,[70] is said to be the "foundation." [71] Upon this foundation, in an architectural sense, the first story consisting of Binswanger's existential analy*sis, Daseinsanaly*se,[72] is to be erected. In the upper stories, clinical psychiatry and psychopathology, plus all auxiliary sciences, would be assigned their places. Binswanger apparently sees in his existential analy*sis* a step forward into anthropology. He has reported that existential analy*sis* grew out of the wish to clarify "the conceptual bases of the psychological and psychotherapeutic observations, thought and actions of the psychiatrist at the 'sick bed.' " [73] One wonders how logical reflections, concepts, observations, thoughts and actions were taken care of by intuition. Anyway—slowly—so Binswanger tells us, he came to believe that there were psychotherapeutic possibilities in existential analy*sis*, namely when some patients seemed to show an understanding of the new manner of being understood; "when the experience of insight into their own structure of human existence and the pertinent knottings, bendings and shrinkings" [74] seemed to carry a certain therapeutic effect.

Binswanger, after him, Boss, Kuhn and others, went under full sail into this apparently new understanding and published a number of books and papers, some, if not most, of them based on their interpretations of patients, or on what the authors chose to consider, the human existences

---

[67] "*dass Daseinerkenntnis schon ihrem Wesen nach niemals an ein Ende gelangen kann*" (Binswanger).

[68] "*Dass das Wesen der Daseinserkenntnis keineswegs auf der logischen Reflexion, sondern auf der imaginativen Gestaltenschau und imaginativen Erkenntis von Gestaltwandel (beruht)*" (Binswanger).

[69] "*Gebäude.*"

[70] See page 459.

[71] "*Grundriss.*"

[72] See pages 465–470.

[73] "*die begrifflichen Grundlagen dessen, was der Psychiater in psychologischer und psychotherapeutischer Hinsicht 'am Krankenbett' wahrnimmt, überlegt und tut*" (Binswanger).

[74] Dass "*das Erlebnis der Einsicht in die eigene Daseinsstruktur und ihre konstitutionell oder geschichtlich bedingten Verknotunger, Verbiegungen oder Schrumpfungen . . . oft schon allein einen psychotherapeutischen Effekt hat*" (Binswanger).

of patients. As the understanding of the working of existential analysis may best be won from such publications, some of the published material will be presented in the following, first from Binswanger.

VII

In his study on flight of ideas, Binswanger deals with three patients in three chapters. He first states that flight of ideas is a certain way of experiencing, and wonders about the "form of being-human in which something like flight of ideas is at all possible, i.e., which is, clinically speaking, the anthropological structure of 'mania.' " [75] He sees, in or behind the thinking in flight of ideas, a leveling of order in which the individual's or rather the *Dasein's*, world becomes smaller, but in which the manic "sprints" [76] or even jumps when the healthy person moves warily in small steps. The existence of the manic has the "structure of festivity." [77] "In the anthropological structure of the manic-depressive forms of being-human this experience of rising and of its opposite, of falling or sinking, plays a central role, so much so that dreams, in which the experience of one's own rising or the rising of something and then of sinking occurs first can be considered as manic-depressive 'psychoses' *in nuce.*" [78] While the world of the manic appears to be smaller—to the manic—he himself behaves like a powerful man, using big gestures and big words.[79]

Referring to Heidegger's observations concerning physiological precipitation of dread,[80] Binswanger remarks that "the manic excitation does not make the ecstasis of victory and the festive jubilation, but only makes it come out of man.[81] He adds a footnote, "All 'the brain' or 'the organism' is able to achieve, here too, is only the physiological 'precipitation' of ontological-anthropological moments of structure." [82]

[75] ". . . *diejenige Form des Menschseins, in der so etwas wie Ideenflucht überhaupt möglich ist, klinisch gesprochen die anthropologische Struktur der 'Manie'* " (Binswanger).

[76] "*springt.*"

[77] "*Struktur der Festlichkeit*" (Binswanger).

[78] "*In der anthropologischen Struktur der manisch-depressiven Formen des Menschseins spielt dieses Erlebnis des Steigens und seines Gegenteils, des Fallens oder Sinkens, eine zentrale Rolle, sodass man Träume, in denen zuerst das Erlebnis des eigenen Steigens oder des Steigens von etwas und dann des Sinkens vorkommt, als manisch-depressive 'Psychosen' in nuce auffassen kann*" (Binswanger).

[79] Binswanger here uses the adjectives "*grossmächtig,*" "*grosszügig,*" and "*grossmäulig.*"

[80] See page 461.

[81] ". . . *die manische Erregung (macht nicht) den Siegestaumel und Festesjubel, sie lockt ihn nur aus dem Menschen heraus*" (Binswanger).

[82] "*Was 'das Gehirn' oder 'der Organismus' überhaupt zu leisten vermag, ist auch hier nur die physiologische 'Auslösung' ontologischantropologischer Strukturmomente*" . . ." (Binswanger).

Dealing with two different patients in the second and third chapter, Binswanger is desirous of establishing a world of optimism, that is the world of the optimist where things are light, volatile. The optimist is correlated to this world, the optimist in the sense of an individuality with flight of ideas, i.e., with a "style of thinking" [83] corresponding to, or correlated to, that world of optimism. We are then told about melancholy and mania: In the first "the *Dasein* may stand still under its burden of guilt, grief and dread . . . in mania . . . decisions are reached in springing . . ." [84] The writer cannot go into all details; he must particularly desist from a detailed report on what Binswanger does with the word "big-mouthed" [85] which for him has great importance in the manic person. It is characteristic that, in interpreting his three cases of flight of ideas, Binswanger not only discusses various kinds of flights of ideas as he finds them established in clinical psychopathology, but broadens out into an interpretation of the manic-depressive psychosis and of schizophrenia. In this repect, he writes, for example, "that the 'manic-depressive psychosis' does not teach us anything anthropologically new about 'man' but that it rather answers our question, 'what is man?' in more conspicuous form and in more outspoken extremes." [86] Binswanger sees "manic-depressive man . . . on the ground of his existential 'insecurity' and 'lack of protection,' the creature that doubts everything." [87] The "manic-depressive" says yes and no to life —"I love to live but life is not important for me." [88] Furthermore, "the manic and the depressive form of existence represent, despite their inner contrariness, only two kinds of one and the same existential attitude, two contrasting attempts, at self-concealment and at self-flights." [89] Apparently, Binswanger wants to say that the manic runs from the problems of existence to the joy of life and is happy in his very existence, while the depressive is defeated by the problems of existence, and wonders whether he belongs to it (to existence) at all.

In the life of the schizophrenic there is no "springing," but "some

[83] "*Denkstil.*"

[84] ". . . (*erfährt*)*unter dem Lastcharakter des Daseins, unter Schuld, Leid und Angst, einen völligen Stillstand . . .; in mania . . . decisions . . . are reached in springing . . .*" (Binswanger).

[85] "*grossmäulig*" (Binswanger).

[86] ". . . *dass das 'manisch-depressive Irresein' anthropologisch uns über 'den Menschen' nichts Neues lehrt, dass es uns vielmehr nur in auffälligerer Form und in deutlicheren Extremen eine Antwort gibe auf die Frage, 'was der Mensch ist'* " (Binswanger).

[87] "*Vielmehr ist der manisch-depressive Mensch . . . das auf Grund seiner existentiellen 'Unsicherheit' und 'Ungesichertheit' an allem zweifelnde Wesen*" (Binswanger).

[88] "*Ich lebe zwar gerne, das Leben ist aber für mich nichts wichtiges*" (Binswanger).

[89] "*Die manische und die depressive Form der Existenz stellen also bei aller inneren Gegensätzlichkeit doch nur zwei Arten ein und derselben inneren Haltung dar, zwei zu einander gegensätzliche Versuche der Selbstverdeckung und der Selbstflucht . . .*" (Biswanger).

sort of development in a life history"; [90] this development occurs along a straight, if often broken, line. The manic-depressive goes through his *Dasein* "in rhythmic-concentric motion." [91] "We call the man healthy who is able to go his way 'between' the two extremes. The way of life of the healthy does not resemble either the circle or the 'straight line' but the spiral." [92]

Binswanger has published several cases of schizophrenic patients. In those that the writer has had the opportunity to read, there was no existential analytic therapy done or even planned. These patients were analyzed phenomenologically in Binswanger's manner under viewpoints which might be called existential-analytical or ontological or anthropological, according to the thought or intuition the author followed or wanted to convey in each particular instance. He attempts to show the profound change in the human existence of the pertinent patients. One of them, Lola Voss,[93] a Latin American girl in her 20's, behaved oddly from the age of 12 or before. She felt insecure, hated to be alone, and developed obsessive-compulsive notions and actions early in her teens. She was extremely superstitious. In her early 20's there was a paranoid development. She suffered indescribable fears; she mistrusted people; people wanted to kill her. She was extremely unhappy. A feeling of eeriness overcame her that she was unable to describe. Later the eeriness made way for a feeling of secrecy [94] in which everything was evil and threatening her. Binswanger's interpretation is condensed here: Lola's ideal was to have peace. She was unable to attain this ideal; instead, behind the picture of obsessions and delusions, she underwent a complete "voiding" of her human existence; she lived in the present, perhaps somewhat ailing from the past, but not really seeing any future for herself. The patient became increasingly "less human": finally she sank down into animal-like voraciousness.

In a short paper, Binswanger reported the case of a middle-aged American woman, Mary, who described herself as living in two worlds and at two speeds. One of these worlds was her marriage and her home in which the role of an understanding husband appeared to be paramount. The other world was the world of sensuality, in which she gave in to any desire and went through some "romance" at least once annually.

[90] *"er entwickelt sich irgendwie lebensgeschichtlich"* (Binswanger).

[91] *"in rhythmisch-konzentrischer Bewegung"* (Binswanger).

[92] " *'Gesund' nennen wir, wer seinen Weg 'zwischen' beiden Extremen hindurch zu nehmen vermag. Der Lebensweg des Gesunden gleicht weder dem Kreis noch der 'Geraden,' sondern der Spirale"* (Binswanger).

[93] The case of Lola Voss has been critically analyzed in an excellent lecture by Theodor Spörri. This analysis, the script of which the writer was permitted to read, has, regrettably, not been published so far. It should be noted that this patient was fluent only in Spanish. One may have some doubts whether the phenomena Binswanger undertook to interpret in his manner could be satisfactorily understood, because of mutual language difficulties.

[94] There Binswanger plays a little with the German words *unheimlich* (eerie) and *heimlich* (secret). See footnote 56.

In the first world of relative stability, there was, according to Binswanger's interpretation, "the mode of temporalization of the authentic present that temporalizes itself equally from the future and from the past." [95] Here the patient thinks, acts and experiences with deliberation at a relatively low speed. The patient calls the other world "the world of sensuality, of heightened speed, . . . the world of rapid burning, comparing it with a big flame which burns a candle faster than a small flame does." [96] Binswanger makes the interpretation that the "spiritual" [97] (Binswanger's quotation marks) world of lower speed is spatially characterized by rising vertically, while the sensual world of higher speed is characterized by running or riding horizontally. He conjectures that human existence of this kind "must be called disproportioned from the 'humanistic,' dissociated from the psychopathological, viewpoint." [98] Binswanger writes that this patient, Mary, "shows like most polymorphous schizophrenics, cyclothymic features," but he finds and interprets her utterances differently from those of manic-depressive patients. He discovers the "symptom of queerness" [99] in this patient, and believes, "that we are able to understand the symptom of queerness, i.e., that we can refer it to an alteration in the basic structure of human existence." [100] It can scarcely be denied that one can refer everything to anything if one has made one's mind up to do so.

It should be mentioned that in his case presentations, Binswanger usually gives an extensive case history, a psychopathological discussion and analysis which are followed by his existential-analytical discussions and elaborations. As it seems very difficult, if at all possible, to keep them apart, it happens that existential-analytical and psychopathological terms get somewhat mixed. It is always obvious that the existential-analytical pattern or mode is seen—presumably in many instances intuited—by the author first and that the pertinent considerations are shaped according to this pattern.

In another schizophrenic patient, Ellen West, Binswanger is anxious to show how a human existence, formerly flexible, is sinking and drowning while time is crawling and ultimately getting rigid. Here Binswanger observes: " 'Pressing' upon human existence, the past robs it of every view into the future . . . Where the past of lived life has become overpowering,

[95] *"den Zeitigungsmodus der eigentlichen Gegenwart, die sich gleicherweise aus der Zukunft wie aus der Gewesenheit zeitigt"* (Binswanger). The present writer here translates *Gewesenheit*, literally *"been-ness,"* as *"past."*

[96] *"Die Welt des 'Sensualismus' der erhöhten Geschwindigkeit . . . die Welt der raschen Verbrennung, derart wie eine grosse Flamme eine Kerze rascher aufbraucht als eine kleine"* (Binswanger).

[97] *"geistig."* See footnote 15.

[98] *" 'humanistisch' als unproportioniert, psychopathologisch als dissoziiert bezeichnet werden muss"* (Binswanger).

[99] *"das Symptom der Verschrobenheit"* (Binswanger).

[100] *"dass wir auch das Symptom der Verschrobenheit daseinsanalytisch verstehen, d. h. auf eine Veränderung der Grundstruktur des Daseins zurückführen können"* (Binswanger).

and where the life still to be lived is dominated by the past, we talk about old age." [101] In Ellen West, Binswanger says human existence has become emptied in her youth, "existential aging had preceded biological aging, and existential death, 'to be among people like a corpse' [patient's remarks], had preceded the biological end of life." [102] Binswanger's interpretation continues: "Ellen West's world underwent an obvious change from the liveliness, width, brightness and colorfulness of the ether over the dimness, mistiness, rotting, decomposition and putrefaction to the narrowness, darkness and grayness of dead earth. The existential analytical precondition of the possibility of this change is an obvious unitary phenomenon. This phenomenon is the phenomenon of temporalization." [103] The schizophrenic process is seen as "a process of existential voiding and improverishment in the sense of an increasing rigidity ('congealment') of the free self into a less and less free ('more dependent') object that is strange to itself." [104]

These are only a few examples of Binswanger's very copious writings. When his writings are called copious, it is meant that he wrote many papers and several books. The books, as well as the papers, are, as a rule, rather long. That this author gives all those who want to believe a profusion of material is clear. It is to be wondered at that he has not been criticized more. Binswanger starts from "a certain way of experiencing," [105] the flight of ideas. In this discussion, as in others, there is much talk about experiencing—normal or pathological—although it is emphasized that existential analysis is neither psychology nor psychopathology. In the work on flight of ideas, the following terms occur: human existence, life, form of life, way of life [106] without clear definition of any of them. There is the *ad hoc* production "bigmouthed form of existence," [107] there are the manic, the depressive and the manic-depressive man.[108] There is also the manic

---

[101] "*Indem die Vergangenheit auf das Dasein 'drückt,' benimmt sie ihm jede Aussicht auf die Zukunft. Wo aber die Vergangenheit, das gelebte Leben, übermächtig geworden ist, das noch zu lebende Leben von der Vergangenheit beherrscht wird, sprechen wir von Alter*" (Binswanger).

[102] "*Das existentielle Altern war dem biologischen Altern vorausgeeilt, wie auch der existentielle Tod, das 'wie eine Leiche unter Menschen sein,' dem biologischen Lebensende vorausgeeilt war*" (Binswanger).

[103] "*die existential-analytische Voraussetzung dafür, dass die Welt Ellen West's eine so eindeutige Wandlung von der Lebendigkeit, Weite, Helle und Farbigkeit des Äthers über die Verdüsterung, Vernebelung, Verdorrung, Moderung und Faulung zur Enge, Dunkelheit und Grauheit der Verschalung und Vererdung der toten Erde durchzumachen vermag, ist, dass dieser Wandlung ein eindeutiges, einheitliches Phänomen zugrundeliegt. Dieses Phänomen aber ist das Phänomen der Zeitigung*" (Binswanger).

[104] "*ein existentieller Entleerungs-oder Verarmungsprozess, und zwar im Sinne einer zunehmenden Erstarrung ('Gerinnung') des freien Selbst zu einem immer unfreieren ('unselbständigeren') selbstfremden Gegenstand*" (Binswanger).

[105] "*eine bestimmte Erlebensweise*" (Binswanger).

[106] *Dasein, Leben, Lebensform, Lebensweg* (Binswanger).

[107] "*grossmäulige Existenzform*" (Binswanger).

[108] *der manische, der depressive und der manisch-depressive Mensch* (Binswanger).

form of being-human [109] and the manic being in-the-world.[110] Also, the *"ideenflüchtige Individualität"* is to be found. There is, last but not least, the joy of existence, the *Daseinsfreude*; in respect to conditions of confusion with flight of ideas,[111] one reads: "Language as a tool of thinking is turned into verbosity or rather bombast as a toy of the joy of existence." [112]

One may wonder whether something like this did not happen to the author—who rejoiced after finding a tool or toy that, in his conviction, made it possible and permissible to give free rein to his intuitive phenomenology or phenomenological intuition. The observer or critic who has been informed that phenomenology is dealing with reality, with the data as given immediately, wonders about the cheerful subjectivity with which allegedly phenomenologically immediate data appear, are followed and juggled around *ad libitum auctoris.*

[109] *"manische Form des Menschseins"* (Binswanger).
[110] *"das manische In-der-Welt-sein"* (Binswanger).
[111] *"verworrene Ideenflucht"* (*ideenflüchtige Verwirrtheit, Kraepelin*).
[112] *"Anstelle der Sprache als eines Werkzeugs des Denkens trit dann der Wort-oder richtiger Lautschwall als ein Spielzeug der Daseinsfreude"* (Binswanger).

BIBLIOGRAPHY

Binswanger, Ludwig, Über Ideenflucht. Orrell-Füssli. Zürich. 1933.
Binswanger, Ludwig, Grundformen und Erkenntnis menschlichen Daseins. Neihaus. Zürich. 1942.
Binswanger, Ludwig, Studien zum Schizophrenieproblem.
    Erste Studie: Der Fall Ellen West. Schweiz. Arch. Neur. u. Psychiat., 53, 54, 55, 1945.
    Zweite Studie: Der Fall Jürg Zünd, *Ibid.*, 56, 58, 59, 1947.
    Dritte Studie: Der Fall Lola Voss., *Ibid.*, 63, 1949.
Binswanger, Ludwig, Symptom und Zeit. Schweiz. Med Wochenschr., 81, 1951.
Binswanger, Ludwig, Daseinsanalytik und Psychiatrie. Nervenarzt, January 1951.
Blackwell, H. J. Six Existentialist Thinkers. Macmillan. New York. 1952.
Bollnow, O. F. Existentialismus. Kohlhammer-Stuttgart. 1950.
Boss, Medard, Sinn und Gehalt Sexueller Perversionen. Huber. Bern. 1947.
Boss, Medard, Der Traum und seine Auslegung. Huber. Bern-Stuttgart. 1953.
Boss, Medard, Einführung in die Psychosomatische Medizin. Huber. Bern-Stuttgart. 1954.
Heidegger, Martin, Sein und Zeit. Niemeyer-Halle. 1. Auflage. 1927.
Heidegger, Martin, Was Heisst Denken? Niemeyer-Tübingen, 1954.
Heinemann, F. H. Existentialism and the Modern Predicament. Harper. New York. 1953.
Jaspers, Karl, Allgemeine Psychopathologie. 5. Ed. Springer. Berlin. 1948.

Kierkegaard, Søren, Der Begriff der Angst (1. dänische Auflage. 1844.) Deutsche Übersetzung von Em. Hirsch. Diederichs. Düsseldorf. 1952.

Kuhn, Roland, Mordversuch eines depressiven Fetischisten und Sodomisten an einer Dirne. Monatsschr. Psychiat. u. Neurol., *116*, 1948.

Kuhn, Roland, Daseinsanalyse im psychotherapeutischen Gespräch. Schweiz. Arch. Neurol. u. Psychiat., *67*, 1951.

Kuhn, Roland, Zur Daseinanalyse der Anorexia nervosa. Nervenarzt., January 1951, March 1953.

Kuhn, Roland, Zur Daseinsstruktur einer Neurose. Jahrb. Psychol. u. Psychother., 1954.

Kuhn, Roland, Der Mensch in der Zwiesprache des Kranken mit seinem Arzte und das Problem der Übertragung. Monatsschr. Psychiat. u. Neurol., *129*, 1955.

Löwith, Karl, Heidegger—Denker in dürftiger Zeit. Fischer. Frankfurt am Main. 1953.

Schneider, Kurt, Klinische Psychopathologie. 3 ed. Thieme. Stuttgart. 1950.

Spörri, Theodor, Kritik der Daseinsanalyse vom strukturanalytischen Standpunkt aus. Vortrag, 1955.

Wild, John, The Challenge of Existentialism. Indiana University Press. 1955.

35

Dynamics, Existence and Values

VIKTOR E. FRANKL

Psychoanalysis, especially in its former, early stages of development, has often been blamed for its so-called pansexualism. I doubt whether in previous times, or even in Freud's time, this reproach has ever been legitimate and validated. Nowadays, however, during the most recent history of psychoanalysis, one can scarcely find any pansexualism in the strict sense of the term.

However, there is something different that seems to me to be an even more erroneous assumption underlying each of the psychoanalytic theories —and, unfortunately, psychoanalytic practice—which we may call "pandeterminism." By this is meant any view of man which disregards or neglects the intrinsically human capacity of free choice and, instead, interprets human existence in terms of mere dynamics.[1]

Man as a finite being, which he basically is, will never be able to free himself completely from the ties which bind him in many respects incessantly to the various realms wherein he is confronted by unalterable conditions. Nevertheless, ultimately there is always a certain residue of freedom left to his decisions. For within the limits—however restricted they may be —he can move freely; and only by this very stand which he takes again and again, toward whatsoever conditions he may face, does he prove to be a truly human being. This holds true with regard to biological and psychological as well as sociological facts and factors. Social environment, hereditary endowment, and instinctual drives can limit the scope of man's freedom, but in themselves they can never totally blur the human capacity to take a stand toward all those conditions, to choose an option.

Let me illustrate this by a concrete example. Some months ago I was sitting with a famous American psychoanalyst in a Viennese coffee-house. As this was a Sunday morning and the weather was fine I invited him to

From V. E. Frankl, Dynamics, Existence and Values. *Journal of Existential Psychiatry*, 1961, 2, 5–16. Reprinted by permission. © 1961 by Libra Publishers, Inc.
[1] The word "dynamism" often serves as no more than a euphemistic substitution for the term "mechanism." However, I do not believe that even the orthodoxically Freudian psychoanalysts have remained or will remain forever the "incorrigible mechanists and materialists" which they have been designated by a clearcut statement once made by no less than Sigmund Freud.

472

join me on a trip to climb mountains. He refused passionately, however, by pointing out that his deep reluctance against mountain climbing was due to early childhood experiences. His father had taken him as a boy on walking trips of long duration, and he soon began to hate such things. Thus he wanted to explain to me by what infantile conditioning process he was incapacitated to share my hobby of scaling steep rocky walls. Now, however, it was my turn to confess; and I began reporting to him that I, too, was taken on week-end trips by my father and hated them because they were fatiguing and annoying. But in spite of all that, as for myself, I went on to become a climbing guide in an Alpine club.

Whether any circumstances, be they inner or outer ones, have an influence on a given individual or not, and in which direction this influence takes its way—all that depends on the individual's free choice. *The conditions do not determine me but I determine whether I yield to them or brave them.* There is nothing conceivable that would condition a man wholly, i.e., without leaving to him the slightest freedom. Man is never fully conditioned in the sense of being determined by any facts or forces. Rather *man is ultimately self-determining*—determining not only his fate but even his own self for man is not only forming and shaping the course of his life but also his very self. To this extent man is not only responsible [2] for what he does but also for what he is, inasmuch as *man does not only behave according to what he is but also becomes according to how he behaves.* In the last analysis, man has become what he has made out of himself. Instead of being fully conditioned by any conditions he is rather constructing himself. Facts and factors are nothing but the raw material for such self-constructing acts, of which a human life is an unbroken chain. They present the tools, the means, to an end set by man himself.

To be sure, such a view of man is just the reverse of that concept which claims that man is a product or effect of a chain of diverse causes. On the other hand, our assertion of *human existence as a self-creating act* corresponds to the basic assumption that a man does not simply "be," but always decides what he will be in the next moment. In every moment the human person is steadily molding and forging his own character. Thus, every human being has the chance of changing at any instant. There is the freedom to change, in principle, and no one should be denied the right to make use of it. Therefore, we never can predict a human being's future except within the large frame of a statistical survey referring to a whole group. On the contrary, an individual personality is essentially unpredictable. The basis for any predictions would be represented by biological,

---

[2] Of course, man's responsibility is as finite as his freedom; for, though man is a spiritual being, he remains a finite being. E.g., I am not responsible for the fact that I have grey hair; however, I am certainly responsible for the fact that I did not go to the hairdresser to have him tint my hair (which under the same "conditions" a number of ladies might have done). So even there a certain amount of freedom is left to everyone, even if only the choice of the color of his hair.

psychological or sociological influences. However, one of the main features of human existence is the capacity to emerge from and rise above all such conditions—to transcend them. By the same token, man is ultimately transcending himself. The human person then transcends himself insofar as he reshapes his own character.

Let me cite the following case. It concerns Dr. J., the only man I have ever encountered in my whole life whom I would dare to qualify as a mephistophelic being, a satanic existence. At that time he was generally called the mass murderer of *Steinhof*—the name of the large mental hospital in Vienna. When the Nazis had started their euthanasia program, he held all the strings in his hands and was so fanatic in the job assigned to him that he tried not to let one single psychotic individual escape the gas chamber. The few patients who did escape were, paradoxically, Jews. It happened that a small ward in a Jewish home for aging people remained unknown to Dr. J.; and though the Gestapo which supervised this institution had strictly forbidden the admission of any psychotic patients, I succeeded in smuggling and hiding such cases there by issuing false diagnostic certificates. I manipulated the symptomatology in these cases so as to indicate aphasia instead of schizophrenia, and the like. I also administered illegal metrazol shocks. So these Jewish patients could be rescued, whereas even the relatives of Nazi party functionaries were "mercy"-killed. When I came back to Vienna—after having myself escaped from being sent to the gas chamber in Auschwitz—I asked what had happened to Dr. J. "He had been imprisoned by the Russians in one of the isolation cells of *Steinhof*," they told me. "The next day, however, the door of this cell stood open and Dr. J. was never seen again." Later I was convinced that like others he had by the help of his comrades found his way to South America. More recently, however, I was consulted by a former high-ranking Austrian diplomat who had been imprisoned behind the Iron Curtain for many years, first in Siberia, and then in the famous Ljubljanka prison in Moscow. While I was examining him neurologically he suddenly asked me whether I happened to know Dr. J. After my affirmative reply he continued: "I made his acquaintance in Ljubjanka. There he died, at the age of about forty years, from a cancer of the urinary bladder. Before he died, however, he showed himself to be the best comrade you can imagine! He gave consolation to everybody. He lived up to the highest conceivable moral standard. He was the best comrade I ever met during my long years of prison!"

This is the story of Dr. J., "the mass murderer of *Steinhof*." *How can you dare to predict the behavior of man!* What you may predict are the movements of a machine, of an apparatus, of an automaton. More than that, you may even try to predict the mechanisms or "dynamisms" of the human psyche as well; but *man is more than psyche:* man is spirit. By the very act of his own self-transcendence he leaves the plane of the merely biopsychological and enters the sphere of the specifically human which I call the noölogical dimension. Human existence is, in its essence, noëtic. A *human being is not one thing among others: things are determining each other—but man is self-determining.* In actuality, man is free and responsible, and these constituents of his spirituality, i.e., freedom and responsibility, must never be clouded by what is called the reification or depersonalization of man.

By the process of reification or depersonalization the subject is made an object. The human person when being dealt with merely in terms of a psychic mechanism ruled by the law of cause and effect loses his intrinsic character as a subject who is ultimately self-determining (according to a statement of Thomas Aquinas the person is *dominium sui*). In this way an essential characteristic of human existence, freedom of will, has been totally overlooked in any exclusively psychodynamic interpretation of the human being. The subject who "wills" has been made an object that "must"!

However, freedom, in the last analysis (phenomenological analysis, I mean!), is the subjective aspect of a total phenomenon and, as such, would still have to be completed by its objective aspect, which can be designated as responsibility. The freedom to take a stand as emphasized above is never complete if it has not been converted and rendered into the freedom to take responsibility. The specifically human capacity to "will" remains empty as long as it has not yet been complemented by its objective counterpart, to will what I "ought." What I ought, however, is the actualization of values, the fulfillment of the concrete meaning of my personal existence. The world of meanings and values may rightly be termed *logos*. Then, *logos* is the objective correlate to the subjective phenomenon called human existence. Man is free to be responsible, and he is responsible for the realization of the meaning of his life, the *logos* of his existence.

But we have still to pose the question in what regard or to what extent the values to be actualized or the meanings to be fulfilled have any "objective" character. Now, what we mean by this term "objective" is to say that values are necessarily more than a mere self-expression of the subject himself. They are more than a mere expression of one's inner life, whether in the sense of sublimations or secondary rationalizations of one's own instinctual drives as Freudian psychoanalysis would explain them, or in the sense of inherent archetypes of one's collective unconscious as Jungian psychology would assume (they, too, are mere self-expressions— namely, of mankind as a whole). If meanings and values were just something emerging from the subject himself—that is to say, if they were not something that stems from a sphere beyond man and above man—they would instantly lose their demanding force. They could no longer be a real challenge to man, they would never be able to summon him up, to call him forth. If that, for the realization of which we are responsible, is to keep its obligative character then it must be seen in its objective character.[3]

This objective character inherent in meanings and values and accounting for their obligative character can no longer be recognized if we see in them "nothing but" a subjective design, or even a projection of instincts or archetypes. Thus we can understand that alongside the reification and depersonalization of the human person, i.e., alongside the *objectification of existence*, there always takes place another process, i.e., a subjectification of meaning and values, the *subjectification of logos*.

It was *psychoanalysis* that brought about this twofold process, inasmuch as an exclusively psychodynamic interpretation of the human person must result in an objectification of something that is intrinsically subjective; whereas at the same time an exclusively psychogenetic interpretation of meaning and values must result in the subjectification of something that is intrinsically objective.

It seems to me to be one of the great merits and achievements of *ontoanalysis* (Erwin Straus, 1958; Ludwig Binswanger, 1958; Jordan Scher, 1960; etc.) to offer a corrective to the first aspect of the twofold mistake committed by psychoanalysis as delineated above. This newer school of thinking has helped to reinstate the human person as a phenomenon that eludes any attempt to grasp its essence in terms of a fully conditioned and wholly predictable thing among and like other things. Thus the fully subjective character is being preserved or regained, among others, by ontoanalysis as against psychoanalysis.

However, the other aspect of the same process, the depreciation of the objective character of meaning and values, the subjectification of the objective, had not yet been rectified. By ontoanalysis *the subjective*, i.e., existence, was *resubjectified*. It is *logotherapy* that has regarded and considered its own task and purpose now to *reobjectify the objective*, i.e., *logos*! Only then will the unabridged phenomenon of the human being in its double aspect be restored: existence in its subjectivity, and *logos* in its objectivity.

For logotherapy, however, meaning is not only an "ought" but also a "will": logotherapists speak of man's "will to meaning." This logotherapeutic concept should not leave the impression with the reader that he has to deal with just an idealistic hypothesis. Let us recall the results of experiments as reported by J. M. Davis, William F. McCourt, and P. Solomon, referring to the effects of visual stimulation on hallucinations during sensory deprivation. The authors finally come to the following conclusion: "Our results are consistent with the hypothesis which emphasizes the parameter of meaning. Hallucinations occur as a result of isolation from mean-

---

[3] This pertains also to that entity to which we are responsible: if the conscience or that Being of whom this conscience is experienced to be the voice—is reduced to superego (thus being interpreted in terms of an introjection of one's father image, or its projection) the obligative character of such an instance would evaporate.

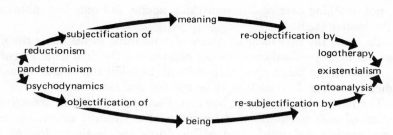

ingful contact with the outside world. *What the brain needs* for normal functioning *is* a continuous *meaning*ful contact with the outside world (1960)."

This has been noted by logotherapists long before. We have known the detrimental impact of what we call a man's "existential vacuum," i.e., the result of the frustration of the above mentioned "will to meaning." The feeling of a total and ultimate meaninglessness of one's life often results in a certain type of neurosis for which logotherapy has coined the term "noögenic" neurosis; that is to say a neurosis of which the origin is a spiritual problem, a moral conflict or the existential vacuum. But other types of neuroses are also invading this vacuum! So that no psychotherapy can be completed, no neurosis of whatsoever kind can be completely and definitely overcome, if this inner void and emptiness in which neurotic symptoms are flourishing has not been filled up by supplementary logotherapy, be it applied unconsciously or methodically.

By this I do not want to give the impression that the existential vacuum in itself represents a mental disease: the doubt whether one's life has a meaning is an existential despair, it is a spiritual distress rather than a mental disease. Thus logotherapy in such cases is more than the therapy of a disease; it is a challenge for all counseling professions. The search for a meaning to one's existence, even the doubt whether such a meaning can be found at all, is something human and nothing morbid.

From the above it can easily be seen how much mental health is based on the presence of an adequate state of tension, like that which arises from the unbridgeable gap between what a man has achieved and what he should accomplish. The cleavage between what I am and what I ought to become is inherent in my being human and, therefore, indispensable to my mental well being. Therefore, we should not be timid and hesitant in confronting man with the potential meaning to be actualized by him, nor evoking his will to meaning out of its latency. Logotherapy attempts to make both events conscious to man: (1) the meaning that, so to speak, waits to be fulfilled by him, as well as (2) his will to meaning that, so to speak, waits for a task, nay, a mission to be assigned to him. Inasmuch as logotherapy makes the patient aware of both facts it represents an essentially analytical procedure for it makes something conscious; however, not anything psychic but something noëtic, not only the subhuman but the human itself.

To make the patient again aware of a meaning in his life is the ultimate asset in all psychotherapy simply because it is the final requirement in every neurosis. To be charged with the task to fulfill the unique meaning assigned to each of us is nothing to be avoided and feared at all.

The homeostasis principle, however, that underlies the dynamic interpretation of man maintains that his behavior is basically directed toward the gratification and satisfaction of his drives and instincts, toward the reconciliation of different aspects of his own such as id, ego, and superego, and toward adaptation and adjustment to society, in one word, toward his own bio-psycho-sociological equilibrium. But human existence is essentially self-transcendence. By the same token, it cannot consist in self-actualization; man's primary concern does not lie in the actualization of his self but in the realization of values and in the fulfillment of meaning potentialities which are to be found in the world rather than within himself or within his own psyche as a closed system.

What man actually needs is not homeostasis but what I call *noödynamics*, i.e., that kind of appropriate tension that holds him steadily oriented toward concrete values to be actualized, toward the meaning of his personal existence to be fulfilled. This is also what guarantees and sustains his mental health whereas escaping from any stress situation would even precipitate his falling prey to the existential vacuum.

What man needs is not a tensionless state but the striving and struggling for something worth longing and groping for it. What man needs is not so much the discharge of tensions as it is the challenge by the concrete meaning of his personal existence that must be fulfilled by him and can only be fulfilled by him alone. In neurotic individuals, this is not less but even more valid. Integration of the subject presupposes direction toward an object. The tension between subject and object does not weaken but strengthens health and wholeness. If architects want to strengthen a decrepit arch they *increase* the load that is laid upon it for thereby the parts are joined more firmly together. So if therapists wish to foster their patients' mental health they, too, should not be afraid to increase the burden of one's responsibility to fulfill the meaning of his existence.

REFERENCES

Arnold, M. B., & J. A. Gasson. *The Human Person*, New York: Ronald Press, 1954. Chapter 16, Logotherapy and Existential Analysis.
Binswanger, L. In *Existence*, R. May, E. Angel, & H. F. Ellenberger (Eds.). New York: Basic Books, 1958.

Davis, J. M., W. F. McCourt, & Solomon P. *The American Journal of Psychiatry*, 116, 889–892, 1960.

Frankl, V. E. *The Doctor and the Soul, An Introduction to Logotherapy.* New York: Knopf, 1955, 1957.

Frankl, V. E. *From Death-Camp to Existentialism, A Psychiatrist's Path to a New Therapy.* Preface by Gordon W. Allport. Boston: Beacon Press, 1959.

Frankl, V. E. Logotherapy and the Collective Neuroses. In *Progress in Psychotherapy*, Vol. IV, J. H. Masserman & J. L. Moreno (Eds.). New York: Grune & Stratton, 1959.

Frankl, V. E. In *Critical Incidents in Psychotherapy*, S. W. Standal and R. J. Corsini (Eds.). Englewood Cliffs: Prentice-Hall, 1959.

Frankl, V. E. Group therapeutic experiences in a concentration camp, *Group Psychotherapy*, 7, 81–90, 1954. (Paper read before the Second International Congress of Psychotherapy in Leiden, Netherlands, on September 8, 1951.)

Frankl, V. E. "On Logotherapy and Existential Analysis," *American Journal of Psychoanalysis*, 10, 28–37, 1958. (Paper read before the Association for the Advancement of Psychoanalysis in New York on April 17, 1957.)

Frankl, V. E. The spiritual dimension in existential analysis and logotherapy. *Journal of Individual Psychology*, 15, 157–165, 1959. (Paper read before the Fourth International Congress of Psychotherapy in Barcelona, Spain, on September 5, 1958.)

Frankl, V. E. Beyond self-actualization and self-expression. *Journal of Existential Psychiatry*, 1, 5–20, 1960. (Paper read before the Conference on Existential Psychiatry in Chicago on December 13, 1959.)

Frankl, V. E. Paradoxical intention, a logotherapeutic technique. *American Journal of Psychotherapy*, 14, 520–535, 1960. (Paper read before the American Association for the Advancement of Psychotherapy in New York on February 26, 1960.)

Frankl, V. E. Logotherapy and the challenge of suffering. *Review of Existential Psychology and Psychiatry*, 1, 3–7, 1961. (Paper read before the Conference on Existential Psychotherapy in New York on February 27, 1960.)

Freud, S. *Schriften*, Londoner Ausgabe, XVII, 29.

Polak, P. Frankl's existential analysis. *American Journal of Psychotherapy*, 3, 617–622, 1949.

Scher, J. M. The concept of the self in schizophrenia. *Journal of Existential Psychiatry*, 1, 64–88, 1960.

Straus, E. In *Existence*, R. May, E. Angel and H. F. Ellenberger (Eds.). New York: Basic Books, 1958.

Tweedie, D. F. *Logotherapy and the Christian Faith, An Evaluation of Frankl's Existential Approach to Psychotherapy*, Grand Rapids, Mich.: Baker Book House, 1961.

Ungersma, A. J. *The Search for Meaning*, Philadelphia: The Westminster Press, 1961.

Weisskopf-Joelson, E. Logotherapy and existential analysis. *Acta Psychotherapeutica*, 6, 193–204, 1958.

36

The Concept of Man in Logotherapy

VIKTOR E. FRANKL

According to a statement made by Gordon W. Allport (Frankl, 1962), logotherapy is one of the schools of existential psychiatry. In this respect, however, logotherapy "is a notable exception," as Professor Robert C. Leslie (1963) of the Pacific School of Religion, Berkeley, California, has pointed out; for, "although a good deal of attention is being given in the psychotherapeutic world to existentialism as a new movement rivaling Freudian psychoanalysis and Watsonian behaviorism, specific elaborations of an existentialist psychotherapy are difficult to find." Logotherapy, however, is the only one of all existential psychiatries to succeed in developing a therapeutic technique (Crumbaugh, 1965), to quote from a paper read by Godfryd Kaczanowski, the Clinical Director of the Ontario Hospital, before the Conference on Existential Psychiatry (Kaczanowski, 1962).

But there is no technique without a theory of man and a philosophy of life underlying it. The only question is whether or not this theory and this philosophy are right, more specifically, whether or not the concept of man underlying a therapeutic technique does justice to the humanness of the patient, in other words, whether or not it includes the human dimension.

Insofar as logotherapy (Frankl, 1964a) is concerned its concept of man is based on three pillars: (1) freedom of will; (2) will to meaning; and (3) meaning of life. They are opposed to those three principles which characterize the bulk of current approaches to man, namely, (1) pan-determinism (Frankl, 1961a), as I am used to call it; (2) homeostasis theory; and (3) reductionism, an approach, that is, which—rather than taking a human phenomenon at its face value—traces it back to sub-human phenomena.

Pan-determinism accounts for the fact that the majority of psychologists are preferring either "the machine model," or "the rat model"

From V. E. Frankl, The Concept of Man in Logotherapy. *Journal of Existentialism*, 1965, 6, 53–58. Reprinted by permission of Libra Publishers, Inc.

Lecture sponsored by the Philosophy and Psychology Department, Georgetown University, Washington, D.C., in the series of 175th Anniversary Lectures and delivered on February 27th, 1964.

(Allport, 1960). As to the first, I deem it to be remarkable a fact that man, as long as he regarded himself as a creature, interpreted his existence in the image of God, his creator; but as soon as he started considering himself as a creator, henceforth interpreted his existence merely in the image of his own creation, the machine, that is to say, along the lines of LaMettrie's book title, *"L'homme Machine."* Now we may understand how justified Stanley J. Rowland, Jr. (Rowland, 1962) was in contending that "the major chasm" is not "between religion and psychiatry" but rather "between those who" take "a methodological and mechanistic approach and those who" take "an existential approach, with special emphasis on the question of life's meaning."

However, pan-determinism not only contradicts religion but also interferes with education. Time and again we are confronted, particularly in the academic youth, with boredom and apathy. I would say, boredom means the incapacity to take an interest whereas apathy might well be defined as the incapacity to take the initiative. In my opinion, however, it is small wonder that "on almost every campus from California to New England, student apathy was the one subject mentioned most often" when Eduard D. Eddy (1959) and two associates carefully studied twenty representative colleges and universities in the United States, interviewing hundreds of administrators, faculty, and students. Because if one continues teaching young people that man is nothing but the battleground of the clashing claims of personality aspects such as id, ego and superego, or if one continues preaching that man is nothing but the victim of conditions and determinants, be they biological, psychological or sociological in nature and origin, we cannot expect our students to behave like free and responsible beings. They rather become what they are taught to be, i.e., a set of mechanisms. Thus a pan-deterministic indoctrination makes young people increasingly susceptible of manipulation.

Is this to imply that I deny that man is subject to conditions and determinants? How could this be possible? After all, I am a neurologist and psychiatrist and as such, of course, I am fully aware of the extent to which man is not at all free from conditions and determinants. But apart from being a worker in two fields (neurology and psychiatry) I am a survivor of four camps, that is, concentration camps, and as such I bear witness of the inestimable extent to which man, although he is never free from conditions and determinants, is always free to take a stand to whatever he might have to face. Although he may be conditioned and determined, he is never fully determined, he is not pan-determined.

Man's intrinsically human capacity to take a stand to whatever may confront him includes his capacity to choose his attitude toward himself, more specifically, to take a stand to his own somatic and psychic conditions and determinants. By so doing, however, he also rises above the level of somatic and psychic phenomena and thereby opens up a dimension of its own, the dimension of those phenomena which, in an at least heuristic counterdistinction to the somatic and psychic ones, are termed noëtic phenomena, or, as I am used to call this dimension, the noölogical dimension. Man passes this dimension whenever he is reflecting upon himself—or rejecting himself; whenever he is making himself an object—or making objections to himself; whenever he displays his being conscious of himself—or whenever he exhibits his being conscientious. Indeed, conscience presupposes the distinctly human capacity to rise above oneself in order to judge and evaluate one's own deeds in moral terms. And this is certainly something which is not accessible to a beast. A dog which has wet the carpet may well slink under the couch with its tail between the legs; but this is no manifestation of conscience but rather the expression of fearful expectation of punishment and, thus, might well be the result of conditioning processes.

By opening up the noölogical dimension man becomes capable to put a distance between himself and his own biological and psychological make-up. In logotherapy, we speak of the specifically human capacity of self-detachment. This quality, however, not only enables a human being victoriously to overcome himself in a heroic way but also empowers him to deal with himself in an ironic way. In fact, humor also falls under the category of definitely human phenomena and qualities. After all, no beast is capable of laughing.

In logotherapy, both the capacity of self-detachment and a sound sense of humor are being utilized in the form of a specifically logotherapeutic technique which is called paradoxical intention (Frankl, 1960a). The patient is, then, encouraged to do, or wish to happen, the very things he fears. In this context, I refer to an article whose author is the Clinical Director of the Connecticut Valley Hospital, Hans O. Gerz (1962, 1964). The therapeutic results he could obtain by this logotherapeutic technique are surprising and astonishing, indeed. Even purely Freudian psychoanalysts, after having used paradoxical intention successfully, admit that it constitutes a very helpful short-term procedure although they are still struggling for an explanation in psychodynamic terms. In communist countries, too, logotherapy in general and the paradoxical intention technique in particular have been introduced and acclaimed although being interpreted as a "neurophysiologically oriented approach." However this might be, the Director of the Neurologic-Psychiatric Clinic of Karl Marx University in Leipzig, D. Müller-Hegemann (1963) "has observed favorable results which justify further studies along these lines." The same holds for Stanislav Kratochvil (1961) of Czechoslovakia.

In context with logotherapy, logos means meaning as well as spirit. Spirit, however, is not conceived with a religious connotation but rather in the sense of noëtic phenomena or the noölogical dimension (Grollman, 1964; Leslie, 1965; Tweedie, 1961; 1963). By making therapeutic use of a noëtic phenomenon such as man's capacity of self-detachment paradoxical intention is logotherapy at its best.

Once more the noölogical dimension was mentioned; but what was the reason that I spoke of a dimension rather than a stratum? Conceiving of man in terms of strata, for example, along the lines of the concepts propounded by Nicolai Hartmann and Max Scheler would disregard and neglect what I should like to call, human coexistence of anthropological wholeness and unity on the one hand and ontological differences on the other hand; or, as Thomas Aquinas put it, the *"unitas multiplex"* quality of existence. By anthropological wholeness and unity I mean that man is not composed of somatic, psychic and noëtic components; while by ontological differences I wish to indicate that the somatic, psychic and noëtic modes of being are qualitatively rather than quantitatively different from each other (Hegel, 1964). This coexistence of both unity and multiplicity in man is taken into account by an anthropological theory which I have developed in logotherapy and called dimensional ontology.

There are two laws of dimensional ontology. Its first law reads: One and the same thing projected into different dimensions lower than its own, yields contradictory pictures.

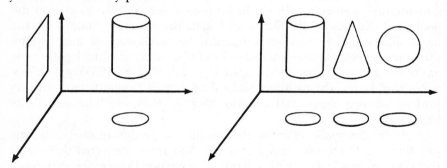

Imagine a cylinder, say, a cup. Projected out of its three-dimensional space down into the horizontal and vertical two-dimensional planes it yields in the first case a circle and in the second one a rectangle. These pictures contradict one another. What is even more important, the cup is an open vessel contrary to the circle which is a closed figure. Another contradiction.

Let us proceed to the second law of dimensional ontology which reads: Different things projected into one and the same dimension lower than their own, yield ambiguous pictures.

Imagine a cylinder, a cone and a sphere. The shadows they cast upon the horizontal plane depict them as three circles which are indiscriminate, interchangeable and ambiguous inasmuch as we cannot infer whether they belong to a cylinder, a cone or a sphere.

Let's see how this may be applied to man; how it may be fertilized in an anthropology *"ordine geometrico,"* to use the term coined by Spinoza

(1843). Once that we have projected man, for instance, into the biological and psychological dimensions we obtain contradictory results since in the one case we obtain a biological organism in contrast to the other one in which a psychological mechanism is the result; but however the bodily and mental aspects of human existence might contradict one another, this contradiction no longer contradicts the oneness of man. Dimensional ontology has not the answer to the mind-body problem; but it does explain why this problem is unsolvable.

Alongside the problem mind versus body there is the problem determinism versus indeterminism, the problem of freedom of choice, and this problem, too, may be approached along the lines of dimensional ontology. Once that man has been projected into a dimension lower than his own he, too, seems to be a closed system, be it of physiological reflexes or psychological reactions and responses to stimuli. What disappears is the essential openness of human existence, the fact that being human is directed, and pointing, to something, or someone, other than itself; but in terms of dimensional ontology we at least understand why this self-transcendent quality of man, as I am used to call it, of necessity disappears. Now the apparent closedness of man in the biological and psychological dimensions is well compatible with his humanness which is located in the noölogical dimension. By the same token, the scientific findings in the lower dimensions as they are unearthed by psychoanalytic and psychodynamic research are not invalidated but rather overarched by logotherapy; or, as the Norwegian psychotherapist Bjarne Kvilhaug (1963) put it in a paper read before the Austrian Medical Society of Psychotherapy with regard to learning theory and behavior therapy, they are "humanized" by logotherapy.

As to the applicability of the second law of dimensional ontology, just think of Dostoevsky and Bernadette Soubirous. Projected down into the plane of psychiatry, in this frame of reference Dostoevsky is nothing but an epileptic and the visions of Bernadette Soubirous nothing but hysteric hallucinations. There is no possibility to discern Dostoevsky from any epileptic and Bernadette Soubirous from any hysteric patient. What Dostoevsky is apart from being an epileptic and what Bernadette Soubirous may be irrespective of hysteric symptoms is not accessible to psychiatry. An artistic achievement and accomplishment and a religious encounter and experience elude the conceptual network of psychiatric categories. Their place is beyond psychiatry. What might hide behind pathology is unknown to the psychiatrist.

As compared with ontoanalysis, logotherapy, as the very name betrays, is more than mere analysis in that it is therapy. And it is not only concerned with ontos but also with logos, that is to say, meaning. What in logotherapy is called the will to meaning indeed occupies a central place in this system. It refers to the fact which reveals itself to a phenomenological analysis, namely, that man is basically striving for finding and fulfilling meaning and purpose in life.

Today, the will to meaning is often frustrated. In logotherapy, we speak of existential frustration. Patients who fall under this diagnostic category usually complain of a sense of futility and meaninglessness or emptiness and void. In logotherapy, this condition is termed existential vacuum. It constitutes the mass neurosis of our age. In a recent publication, a Czechoslovakian psychiatrist, Stanislav Kratochvil (1961), has pointed out that existential frustration makes itself noticeable even in communist countries.

In cases in which existential frustration eventuates in neurotic symptomatology, we have to deal with a new type of neurosis which we call noögenic neurosis (Frankl, 1965). In order to substantiate this concept, Crumbaugh and Maholick (Crumbaugh, 1965), the Directors of a Research Center in the USA, have devised their P(urpose) I(n) L(ife) Test and tried it on 225 subjects.[1] "The results," the authors say in a paper which has been published in the *Journal of Clinical Psychology*, "consistently support Frankl's hypothesis that a new type of neurosis—which he terms noögenic neurosis—is present in the clinics alongside the conventional forms. There is evidence," the authors conclude, "that we are in truth dealing with a new syndrome." As to the frequency of its occurrence, let me refer to the statistical research conducted by Werner in London, Langen and Volhard in Tübingen, Prill in Würzburg, and Niebauer in Vienna. They estimate that about 20% of neuroses are noögenic in nature and origin.

It goes without saying that meaning and purpose in life are no matter of prescription. It is not the job of a doctor to give meaning to the patient's life. But it may well be his task through an existential analysis to enable the patient to find meaning in life. And in my opinion meaning is something to be found rather than to be given (Frankl, 1960b). As if it could be given in an arbitrary way! Again it was Crumbaugh and Maholick (Crumbaugh, 1963) who, to my knowledge for the first time, have pointed to the fact that finding meaning in a situation has something to do with a Gestalt perception. This assumption is confirmed by the Gestaltist Wertheimer's explicit statement that a quality of "requiredness" is inherent in the situation and, what is even more, "the demands and 'requirements' " of the situation "are objective qualities" (Wertheimer, 1961).

According to logotherapeutic teachings, there is no life situation conceivable which would really lack meaning. This is due to the fact that even the negative aspects of human existence such as suffering, guilt and death can still be turned into something positive, provided that they are faced with the right attitude (Frankl, 1961b). Needless to say that possible

---

[1] Author's note: This test has now been administered to 1,200 subjects, with the same results.

meaning may be seen in *necessary* suffering only, whereas accepting avoidable pain would form some sort of masochism rather than heroism. As a matter of fact, unavoidable suffering is inherent in the human condition and the therapist should take heed not to reinforce the patient's evasive denial of this existential fact.

REFERENCES

Allport, Gordon W. *Personality and Social Encounter*. Boston: Beacon Press, 1960.

Crumbaugh, James C., & Leonard T. Maholick. The Case for Frankl's "Will to Meaning." *Journal of Existential Psychiatry 4*, 43, 1963.

Crumbaugh, James C., & Leonard T. Maholick. An Experimental Study in Existentialism: The Psychometric Approach to Frankl's Concept of Noögenic Neurosis. *Journal of Clinical Psychology 20*, 200, 1964.

Crumbaugh, James C. The Application of Logotherapy. *Journal of Existentialism 5*, 20, 1965.

Eddy, Eduard D. The College Influence on Student Character. Washington: American Council on Education, 1959.

Frankl, Viktor E. Paradoxical Intention: A Logotherapeutic Technique. *American Journal of Psychotherapy 14*, 520, 1960. (a)

Frankl, Viktor E. Beyond Self-Actualization and Self-Expression. *Journal of Existential Psychiatry, 1*, 5, 1960. (b)

Frankl, Viktor E. Dynamics, Existence and Values. *Journal of Existential Psychiatry 2*, 5, 1961. (a)

Frankl, Viktor E. Logotherapy and the Challenge of Suffering. *Review of Existential Psychology and Psychiatry 1*, 3, 1961. (b)

Frankl, Viktor E. *Man's Search for Meaning: An Introduction to Logotherapy*. Preface by Gordon W. Allport. Boston: Beacon Press, 1962.

Frankl, Viktor E. Existential Dynamics and Neurotic Escapism. *Journal of Existential Psychiatry 4*, 27, 1963.

Frankl, Viktor E. Philosophical Foundations of Logotherapy. In *Phenomenology: Pure and Applied*. Edited by Erwin W. Straus. Pittsburgh: Duquesne University Press, 1964. (a)

Frankl, Viktor E. Existential Escapism. *Motive 24*, 11, 1964. (b)

Frankl, Viktor E. *The Doctor and the Soul: From Psychotherapy to Logotherapy*. (2nd, expanded ed.) New York: Knopf, 1965.

Frankl, Viktor E. *Psychotherapy and Existentialism*. New York: Simon and Schuster, 1968.

Frankl, Viktor E. *The Will to Meaning*. New York, New American Library, 1970.

Gerz, Hans O. The Treatment of the Phobic and the Obsessive-Compulsive Patient Using Paradoxical Intention Sec. Viktor E. Frankl. *Journal of Neuropsychiatry 3*, 375, 1962.

Gerz, Hans O. Paper read before the Symposium on Logotherapy, 6th International Congress of Psychotherapy, London, 1964.

Grollman, Earl A. Viktor E. Frankl: A Bridge between Psychiatry and Religion. *Conservative Judaism 19,* 19, 1964.

Hegel, G. W. Friedrich. *Einleitung in die Phänomenologie des Geistes.* Frankfurt am Main: Insel-Verlag, 1964.

Kaczanowski, G. Conference on Existential Psychiatry, Toronto, May 6, 1962.

Kratochvil, Stanislav. K psychoterapii existencialni frustrace. *Československa psychiatrie 17,* 186, 1961.

Kvilhaug, Bjarne. Paper read before the Austrian Medical Society of Psychotherapy on July 18th, 1963.

Leslie, Robert C. Book review in *Journal of Religion and Health 2,* 169, 1963.

Leslie, Robert C. *Jesus and Logotherapy: The Ministry of Jesus as Interpreted Through the Psychotherapy of Viktor Frankl.* New York-Nashville: Abingdon Press, 1965.

Müller-Hegemann, D. Methodological Approaches in Psychotherapy. *American Journal of Psychotherapy 17,* 554, 1963.

Rowland, Stanley J., Jr. Viktor Frankl and the Will to Meaning. *The Christian Century 79,* 722, 1962.

Spinoza, Benedictus De *Opera Quae Supersunt Omnia.* Leipzig: Tauchnitz, 1843.

Tweedie, Donald F. *Logotherapy and the Christian Faith: An Evaluation of Frankl's Existential Approach to Psychotherapy.* Grand Rapids: Baker Book House, 1961.

Tweedie, Donald F. *The Christian and the Couch: An Introduction to Christian Logotherapy.* Grand Rapids: Baker Book House, 1963.

Wertheimer, M. Some Problems in the Theory of Ethics. In *Documents of Gestalt Psychology* (M. Henle, Ed.). Berkeley: University of California Press, 1961.

37

An Experimental Study
in Existentialism:
The Psychometric Approach
to Frankl's Concept
of "Noogenic" Neurosis

JAMES C. CRUMBAUGH
& LEONARD T. MAHOLICK

PROBLEM

Frankl's (1955; 1958; 1959; 1960) method of psychotherapeusis, *logotherapy*, is an application of the principles of existential philosophy to clinical practice. His basic contention is that a new type of neurosis is increasingly seen in the clinics today in contrast to the hysterias and other classical patterns, and that this new syndrome—which he terms *noogenic* neurosis, and which supposedly constitutes about 55 per cent of the typical present-day case load (Frankl, 1960)—arises largely as a response to a complete emptiness of purpose in life. The chief dynamic is "existential frustration" created by a vacuum of perceived meaning in personal existence, and manifested by the symptom of boredom. According to Frankl, the essence of human motivation is the "will to meaning" (*Der Wille zum Sinn*); when meaning is not found, the individual becomes "existentially frustrated." This may or may not lead to psychopathology, depending upon other dynamic factors,

From J. C. Crumbaugh, and L. T. Moholick. An Experimental Study in Existentialism. *Journal of Clinical Psychology*, 1964, 20, 200–207. Reprinted by permission of authors and publisher.

An abridged version of this paper was delivered before the Section on Methodology and Social Psychology of The Southern Society for Philosophy and Psychology, at the annual meeting in Miami, April 12, 1963. We are indebted to J. L. Chambers, Ph.D., Research Director of the Mix Memorial Fund of Americus, Georgia, for a critical reading of this paper and valuable pertinent comments.

488

but he feels that the incidence of clinical cases thus rooted is of major significance.[1]

The fact that existentialism accepts intuitive as well as rational and empirical knowledge in arriving at values and meanings has been anathema to American behavioral scientists, who have tended to write it off as a conglomeration of widely divergent speculations with little thread of consistency or operational sense. If, however, one may, by approaching mental illness from this frame of reference, specify a symptomatic condition which is measurable by an instrument constructed from this orientation, but which is not identical with any condition measured from the usual orientations, then there is evidence that we are in truth dealing with a new and different syndrome. Frankl has specified such a condition, but has made only rather informal and loosely quantitative attempts to measure it (as will be shown later).

Kotchen (1960) has published a quantitative attack upon the relation of mental illness to existential concepts. He analysed the literature for the traits pertinent to mental health as conceived by the existential writers, found seven characteristics of the kind of life meaning which is supposed to be present in good mental health (such as uniqueness, responsibility, etc.), and then constructed an attitude scale with items representing each of these seven categories. He predicted that the level of mental health operationally defined by the nature of each of five population samples of 30 cases each, from locked-ward patients in a mental hospital to Harvard summer school students, would agree with the scoring level of the questionnaire. The prediction was affirmed at a generally satisfactory level of statistical significance. His scale, however, had some open-end items which could be quantified only by a rating code, and three items applied only to hospital patients and had to be omitted from the scoring. Further, his samples were composed entirely of males, and this is an area in which there may well be sex differences, as will be seen later.

The purpose of the present study is to carry further the quantification of the existential concept of "purpose" or "meaning in life," in particular to measure the condition of existential frustration described by Frankl, with a view to determining whether his *noogenic* neurosis exists apart from

---

[1] Noogenic neurosis should not be identified with *existential vacuum*. The former, according to Frankl, is an illness, while the latter is a human condition. In those cases which show pathology (by which Frankl means "symptoms"), the term *noogenic neurosis* applies, while cases lacking symptoms of pathology are victims of *existential vacuum* and/or frustration of the *will to meaning*. His insistence upon drawing a distinction here is due in large measure to his claim that treatment of neuroses (whether they be somatogenic, psychogenic or noogenic) should be limited to M.D.'s, while treatment of existential vacuum should be open to psychologists, social workers, educators and pastoral counselors as well. Apart from this policy, however, Frankl would certainly agree with the broader use of his concept of noogenic neurosis as implied in the present paper, which he has read and approved with the exception of the above point.

the usual neuroses as dynamically conceived. We may rationally define the phrase, "purpose in life" as the ontological significance of life from the point of view of the experiencing individual. Operationally we may say that it is that which is measured by our instrument (Ebel, 1961, p. 643), and this is the frame of reference adopted herein. The task then becomes one of showing that the instrument measures something which is (a) what Frankl is referring to by the phrase in question, (b) different from the usual pathology, and (c) identifiable as a distinguishing characteristic of pathological groups in contrast to "normal" populations.

SUBJECTS

A total of 225 subjects comprised five subpopulations as follows: Group I, 30 "high purpose" nonpatients, composed of six Junior League females and 24 Havard summer school graduate students (14 males and 16 females).[2] Group II, 75 undergraduate college students, nonpatients (44 males and 31 females).[3] Group III, outpatients of various cooperating psychiatrists in private practice in Georgia,[4] a total of 49 (25 male and 24 female) cases of mixed diagnoses. Group IV, outpatients of the Bradley Center, Inc. (a privately endowed nonprofit outpatient psychiatric clinic), a total of 50 (22 male and 28 female) cases of mixed diagnoses. Group V, hospitalized patients, all alcoholics, a total of 21 (14 males and 7 females). Ages ranged from 17 to over 50, all groups except the undergraduate college students being pretty well mixed, but with averages near 30.

MATERIALS

1. The "Purpose in Life" Test (PIL). An attitude scale was specially designed to evoke responses believed related to the degree to which the individual experienced "purpose in life." The a priori basis of the items was a background in the literature of existentialism, particularly in logotherapy, and a "guess" as to what type of material would discriminate pa-

[2] Our gratitude is due Dr. Viktor Frankl for permission to administer our scale to his Harvard seminar, summer 1961, as well as for his cooperation in administering our pilot version of the PIL to his Vienna classes, and for his great encouragement throughout this study.

[3] We are also grateful for the cooperation of Mr. Ed Shivers who arranged for the administration of the PIL, A-V-L and Frankl Questionnaire to students at MacAlester College.

[4] We wish to express appreciation to the following Georgia psychiatrists who kindly gathered data upon their own patients: Alfred Agren, M.D.; R. E. Felder, M.D.; Sidney Isenberg, M.D.; Harry R. Lipton, M.D.; Joseph Skobba, M.D.; Carl A. Whitaker, M.D.

tients from nonpatients. The structure of all items followed the pattern of a seven-point scale as follows:

I am usually:

1	2	3	4	5	6	7
completely bored			(neutral)			exuberant, enthusiastic

A pilot study was performed using 25 such items; on the basis of the results half were discarded and new items substituted. Twenty-two then stood up in item analysis, and these were utilized in the present study.[5]

The scale was designed on the unorthodox principle that, while theoretically a subject cannot accurately describe his real attitudes and these must be arrived at indirectly, in practice—and particularly in this attitude area—he can and will give a pretty reliable approximation of his true feelings from conscious consideration. This is also the theory upon which Kotchen (1960) proceeded. If this assumption be wrong, it would show up both in low reliability and in low validity as measured against an operational criterion of either mental health or "life purpose."

The PIL was so designed that each item becomes a scale within the scale. This is similar to the Likert technique except that the quantitative extremes of each item were in the present case set by qualitative phrases which seemed *a priori* to be identified with quantitative extremes of attitude. It was felt that if these choices were wrong, low item validity would eliminate them, whereas if they were right, the scale would be less monotonous and would stimulate more meaningful responses. The score was simply the sum of individual ratings assigned to each of the items. The direction of magnitude was randomized for the items, in order that position preferences and the "halo" effect might be minimized.

2. *The Frankl Questionnaire.* To demonstrate his thesis, Frankl utilized a rather informal series of questions [5] which he evaluated clinically, apparently depending heavily upon Item 3 to determine the percentage of "existentially frustrated" individuals. For the present study Frankl translated his questionnaire into English and the present experimenters quantified it by assigning a value of "1" to item choices which seemed to represent the least degree of purpose or meaning in life, a value of "2" to intermediate responses, and "3" to responses which appeared to involve the greatest degree of purpose. For example, Item 3 ("Do you feel that your life is without purpose?") was scored as follows: 1 = frequently (*haüfig*); 2 =

[5] A duplicated copy of a more detailed version of this paper, giving full tables of results was well as copies of the Frankl Questionnaire and the Purpose in Life Test, will be sent upon request. Address the writers c/o The Bradley Center, Inc., 1327 Warren Williams Road, Columbus, Georgia.

seldom (*selten*); 3 = never (*niemals*). Six of the 13 items (Nos. 1, 3, 7, 8, 10, 11) could be similarly quantified, and a total score was obtained from the sum of these six.

3. *The Allport-Vernon-Lindzey Scale of Values* (A-V-L). This best-known measure of values was administered and scored according to the published instructions. Scores were then computed as deviations from the published sex norms, and the deviations were then coded for IBM processing.

4. *The Minnesota Multiphasic Personality Inventory.* Administered and scored according to published instructions. Only the "T" scores were recorded.

PROCEDURE

The Purpose in Life Test was administered to all five groups of Ss. The Frankl Questionnaire and the Allport-Vernon-Lindsey Scale of Values were given only to Groups II, III and V, while the MMPI was administered only to Group IV (being part of the regular intake battery at the Bradley Center). Because of the extensive tests already required of the latter it was not possible to add the Frankl or A-V-L scales, and pressure of time also prevented their administration to Group I. All of these measures are virtually self-administering, and both patients and nonpatients experienced no difficulty in following the printed directions. Each Bradley Center patient (Group IV) was further evaluated by the therapist's ratings, after the first therapeutic session, of each PIL item as he thought the patient should have rated himself if he were accurate in judgment.

RESULTS

The Purpose in Life Test. There is significant discrimination between patients and nonpatients, and a progressive decline in mean scores from Group I through Group V, both for the total scores and for most of the individual items (Table 37-1).[5] An item analysis (Pearson r's between the total score and the score on each item, $N = 225$) revealed a correlation range of from −.06 (Item 19) to .82 (Item 9), 17 items being above .50 and 20 above .40. The reliability of the PIL revised total score, determined by the odd-even method (Pearson r, $N = 225$) is .81, Spearman-Brown corrected to .90.

TABLE 37-1. Results of the Purpose in Life Test (PIL). Scores are Sum of Ratings for all 22 Items.

Total Score	Nonpatients				Patients						Diff. in M between patients & nonpatients
	Group I		Group II		Group III		Group IV		Group V		
	M	SD	M	SD	M	SD	M	SD	M	SD	
Males	122.86	10.04	116.14	13.17	98.24	20.06	100.45	17.41	87.50	17.63	21.19**
Females	126.50	12.90	117.84	15.04	105.50	24.02	101.96	18.67	93.72	13.40	18.37**
Both	124.78	11.80	116.84	14.00	101.80	22.38	101.30	18.14	89.57	16.60	19.66**

** Difference significant at $p = .01$.

The most appropriate norms (means, rounded to the nearest whole number) for the PIL (based on the "revised" total score, N = 47 female nonpatients, 58 male nonpatients, 59 female patients, 61 male patients) are: Nonpatients, 119, patients, 99; females, 111, males, 107. Patients are more variable than nonpatients. Being a patient drops the scores of males more than those of females: The norm for female nonpatients is 121, for female patients, 102; while that for male nonpatients is 118, for male patients, 97. The sex difference, while not significant, is suggestive. Females are more variable than males (except in Group V, alcoholics), and the instrument proved to predict more efficiently for males.

The following cutting scores half way between patient and nonpatient norms for each sex were employed: For females, 111.5; for males, 107.5. At these cutting points the predictive power of the PIL revised total score was: For females, 65.4% correct classifications (of which 34.6% were patients and 30.8% were nonpatients); for males, 75.4% correct classifications (of which 35.6% were patients and 39.8% were nonpatients).

A partial "concurrent" validation of the PIL revised total score against one type of criterion, the ratings assigned by patients' therapists of each PIL item as the therapists thought the patients should have rated themselves in order to be accurate yielded an r of .27 (Pearson product-moment, N = 39). The PIL scores were not related to the subject's age, but it should be noted that the extremes of age are not covered in the population samples. In particular, a significant relationship at the upper level may have been missed.

The Frankl Questionnaire. The total score norms are 15.7 for non-patients and 13.7 for patients, with an over-all range of 8 to 19. The predictive power of the total score (using a cutting score of 14.5, half way between patient and nonpatient norms) was 66.9% correct classifications (of which 26.5% were patients and 40.4% nonpatients). This total score correlated .68 (Pearson product-moment, N = 136) with the total score of the PIL.

The A-V-L. Of the six value scales, none discriminated adequately between patients and nonpatients, although the social scale gave a difference at the 5% level of confidence. There was little relationship between any of the A-V-L scales and the PIL.

The MMPI. Since data were available only on Group IV, no comparison of patients and nonpatients could be made, but the published norms are well known. Of all the scales, only the K (Validity) and D (Depression) scores showed any substantial relationship to the PIL (respectively .39 and −.30, Pearson product-moment, N = 45). Since the K scale is a measure of defensiveness, the indication is that subjects who have a high degree of "purpose in life" tend to have adequate defenses; they also tend to be less depressed than others.

DISCUSSION

The Purpose in Life Test distinguished significantly between patient and nonpatient populations (Table 37-1), and also showed—in most of its items individually as well as in the total score—a consistent progression of scoring from the nonpatient group that was considered most highly motivated (Group I) to the most seriously ill patient group (Group V). This is consistent with predictions from the orientation of *construct validity* (Chronbach, 1955).

The much greater variability of patients (Table 37-1) suggests that some patients become such because of loss of "purpose in life" while others break down because of dynamic factors as conventionally conceived. Possession of a substantial degree of "purpose" seems to be one of the usual properties of normal function, but there may or may not be a lack of it in the abnormal personality. All of this is consistent with Frankl's belief that a new type of neurosis is present in the clinics alongside the conventional forms.

The study of *concurrent validity* in correlating the PIL scores with therapists' ratings of "purposefulness" in patients yielded only very modest success. This was at least partially due to making the ratings after the first therapy session, which proved too soon for the therapist to know the patient's dynamics well. To have made them after a number of sessions, however, would have confounded the effects of therapy (if any) with the increased knowledge of the patient. Further, the obtained relationship is probably somewhat lower than the true value because of restriction of the range of variability through use of only patients in the sample, but it was not possible to secure such ratings upon the nonpatients.

The high relationship between the PIL and the Frankl Questionnaire indicates that the PIL gets at essentially the same functions which Frankl describes as "existential frustration" (since his questionnaire may be presumed to represent his effort to define operationally what he is talking about). This, he holds, is the basic ingredient of *noogenic* neurosis.

The low relationships between the PIL and the A-V-L scales suggest that "purpose or meaning in life" in not just another name for values in the usual sense. Frankl (1958) insists that it represents a basic human motivating force best described as spiritual.

The low relationships between the PIL and the MMPI scales indicate that the PIL's significant discrimination between normal and pathological populations is not just another measure of the usual forms of pathology. Once again Frankl's hypothesis of a new type of neurosis is supported. Because of restriction of the range of variability by the use of only patients

(Group IV) in the sample, the true relationships may be somewhat greater, but only for the K and D scales could they be large enough to indicate appreciable overlapping measures. And some overlap would be predicted, since Frankl postulates that *noogenic* factors may cause a breakdown of defenses and thus affect the patient's other dynamic mechanisms. The tendency of highly depressed patients to show a loss of life purpose and meaning is clearly observable in the clinic.

This raises the question of whether the PIL is an indirect measure of depression. The limited though significant correlation with the D scale suggests that the test is not primarily this, and it is probable that the causes of both depression and lack of life meaning and purpose are complex and variable. It is likely that lack of meaning can be both a cause and an effect of depression, and that both lack of purpose and depression can result from other causes. Depression, for example, could be due to an abundance of meaning but a deficience in techniques of acquiring meaningful ends, while lack of meaning and purpose may be present in a rhathymic (far from depressed) personality who drifts aimlessly because of lack of organization in life experience. From the orientation of psychopathology as behavior disorder, herein adopted, that which makes a trait a reflection of pathology in its incapacitating effect upon the individual's ability to adjust efficiently to life problems. Lack of purpose or meaning implies a failure to perceive an integrated pattern of goals and values in life, with a consequent dissipation of energies which can only be debilitating. Existence may become boring and not worth the struggle to overcome obstacles. Needs still operate within, and the individual may be highly frustrated, but he has no organized frame of reference from which to perceive meaning in the elements of experience, and consequently he can perceive no active attack upon the causes of frustration. So he drifts along in constant search of new diversion to ease tensions he is often unaware of having. Depression, often interpreted dynamically as a hostile aggression against real or imagined causes of frustration, similarly represents an ineffectual means of dealing with the situation. Lack of purpose is probably a more generic term than depression, for the latter represents a relatively specific and inadequate technique of adjustment to conflict. Loss of meaning and purpose may follow failure of any adjustment technique.

Some variables which it was impossible to control in the available samples of patients and nonpatients require discussion. The question arises whether the differential in PIL scores between population samples is a reflection of educational levels rather than psychopathology, since the nonpatient samples were college students while the patients were of mixed educational level. Exact educational status was available only for our own patients (Group IV), but they seemed typical of *private* psychiatric outpatients: Two-thirds attended college; 18% held a Master's degree or higher; the mean is one year of college. Although this still leaves a little educational balance in favor of the nonpatient samples, the correlation between the PIL and educational level for Group IV in only .19 (Pearson product-moment, N = 49). Further, Snavely (1962) found that freshmen score significantly *higher* than seniors on the PIL. Thus it would seem unlikely that the patient-nonpatient differences could be attributed to education.

It may be suspected that such variables as intelligence and socioeconomic class correlate with the PIL scores and are significantly different from patient to nonpatient samples. There is, of course, some relationship between education, intelligence and socio-economic class; and it would seem probable that the latter two variables follow education fairly closely in the present samples. It seems very possible that the extremes of intelligence do correlate with the presence of purpose and meaning in life, since there is a known tendency for people of genius level to achieve much (and logically, therefore, to have found much meaning and purpose), while it is difficult to see how the mentally retarded can integrate their lives very well around purposeful goals. The present samples of both patients and nonpatients were, however, composed primarily of subjects of higher average education with few at either extreme, and the known substantial relationship between education and intelligence suggests that the latter was not appreciably different, at least between Groups II (nonpatient college students) and III (private outpatients) where the PIL differences are greatest. Therefore it seems unlikely that the differences between patients and nonpatients are due primarily to those variables.

One might ask whether the PIL responses of Frankl's Harvard class were influenced by his teaching. These students were all professional people functioning at high level (ministers, teachers, social service workers and the like), and it is probable that they already had highly purposive orientations to life. His instruction likely did not change this much, because it was slanted entirely to the theoretical side and not toward helping lost students find themselves. Further it is improbable that such basic attitudes toward life would be changed by anything in the few weeks devoted to the course, though a response set could have been established toward "purposive" goals. But the Junior Leaguers who form part of Group I score similarly, and the group level probably reflects genuine purposiveness.

There is a question of the possible influence of social desirability upon the PIL answers. The moderate relationship between the K scale of the MMPI and the PIL scores could be interpreted as indicating the subject's defensive effort to make himself look purposive. As previously noted, it seems likely that individuals of genuinely high level of purpose would have strong defenses which would be reflected in the K scale. It also could be true, however, that highly defensive individuals exercise their defenses in responding to the PIL items. It is obvious that the instrument could not be used in a competitive situation, since, like other "self" tests, it could be either willfully or through unconscious motivation distorted in the direction of desirable or purposive responses. But the findings in relation to most such measures have been that there is relatively little willful distortion in most noncompetitive situations. Unconscious distortion would probably reflect the presence of at least some degree of emotional disturbance and should be present more often in patients than in nonpatients. This would partially account for the greater patient variability which has been found, and suggests that the patient-nonpatient differences have been somewhat affected by spuriously high or purposive scores among the patients. But this is on the side of "safety" in that instead of spurious differences between these populations being created by this effect, the obtained differences are reduced, which encourages the belief that the significances can be depended upon.

SUMMARY

The question of the existence of Frankl's *noogenic* neurosis—breakdown due to "existential frustration" or a lack of perceived meaning or "purpose" in life—was attacked psychometrically, through an attitude scale designed to measure the degree of awareness of such meaning among different populations. The concept of "purpose in life" was operationally defined as what the instrument measures; thus the problem became the threefold one of showing that its scores represent (a) what Frankl is describing, (b) something different from the usual neuroses, and (c) a characteristic of psychopathological as distinguished from "normal" groups.

The results of 225 subjects, comprising two nonpatient and three patient samples, consistently support the *noogenic* hypothesis: (a) The relationship between the scale and a questionnaire designed by Frankl to describe the factors involved in the concepts was high; (b) the relationship of the scale to an established measure of traditionally conceived psychopathology, the MMPI, was low; and (c) the scale significantly distinguished patient from nonpatient populations, showing a predicted progressive drop in scores to match the level of pathology assumed by the nature of the group.

Further study of *noogenic* neurosis by the Purpose in Life Test and other methods is needed in order to answer a number of questions which present data treat only partially, to define the dynamic properties which would make possible diagnostic isolation of this syndrome, and to determine the variables which affect it. The work reported herein is considered primarily heuristic and exploratory rather than definitive.

REFERENCES

Cronbach, L. J., & Meehl, P. E. Construct validity in psychological tests. *Psychol. Bull.*, 1955, 52, 281–302.

Ebel, R. L. Must all tests be valid? *Amer. Psychologist*, 1961, 10, 640–647.

Frankl, V. E. *The doctor and the soul*. New York: Knopf, 1955.

Frankl, V. E. The will to meaning. *J. pastoral Care*, 1958, 12, 82–88.

Frankl, V. E. *From death-camp to existentialism*. Boston: Beacon Press, 1959.

Frankl, V. E. Beyond self-actualization and self-expression. *J. existent. Psychiat.*, 1960, 1, 5–20.

Garrett, H. E. *Statistics in psychology and education* (3rd ed.). New York: Longmans, Green & Co., 1947.

Kotchen, T. A. Existential mental health: An empirical approach. *J. indiv. Psychol.*, 1960. 16, 174–181.

Snavely, H. R. An unpublished special course project, Carleton College, 1962.

HOLISTIC APPROACHES | IX

THE DISTINCTION among phenomenological-humanistic, existential, and what we are here calling
holistic approaches often becomes blurred. In fact, it is
readily possible to justify grouping under quite different
category systems the theorists whom we have chosen to
place under these three classifications; and similarities
across categories are not difficult to discover. Many theorists under all three orientations, for example, emphasize
positive, teleological (goal-oriented) motivation.

Let us, however, attempt to justify our selection of
categories. As we have seen in earlier sections, the phenomenological-humanistic and existential schools emphasize, among other points, the differentiation of human
from animal behavior (man having, for example, unique
higher needs), the central significance of self-conceptualiz-
ing behavior, and, to a lesser extent, the holistic functioning of the human organism. Theories covered in the
present section differ from the existential and humanistic
in placing considerable emphasis on the uniqueness of human behavior and the centrality of self-awareness (though
both are present in some nonholistic theories). At the
same time, the holistic theories stress more strongly than
existential and humanistic theories the postulate that virtually no event in the universe, and particularly no human
behavior, can be validly considered apart from the whole
of which it is an element. This, then, is what holism is all
about. One part or component of the system does not
function without affecting or being affected by the entire
system. Nor does behavior occur in a vacuum, with a given
behavior involving only one small part of the organism
(i.e., the responding element, such as an arm, finger, or
voice) and one small part of the environment (i.e., the
stimulus).

502

The holistic position can readily be seen as comprising two major schools, organismic theory and field theory. The *organismic* orientation stresses the holistic nature of all that goes on within a single organism. Both the psychological and physical aspects of the organism are included in the whole, and each individual behavior is a function of the ongoing interaction of the physical and psychological. The *field* theoretical orientation does not restrict itself to the physical boundaries of the organism, as does the organismic position. In fact, some field theories deemphasize the importance of holism within the organism, stressing, instead, the holistic interaction of organism and environment in determining behavior.

The historical antecedents of the holistic positions are multiform and interacting. Intraorganismic holism can be traced to the unitary soul of Aristotle and, via Spinoza's holistic treatment of the soul-body relationship, to the nineteenth-century philosophical holism of John Dewey and his functionalist school and the psychological holism of William James. The late nineteenth and early twentieth century saw a number of other names associated with this branch of holism. R. H. Wheeler and J. R. Cantor became quite widely known as proponents of the organismic viewpoint, and Adolph Meyer, a functionalist psychiatrist, developed his psychobiology, which was essentially a holistic approach to psychiatry. In addition, we should mention General Jan Smuts, who coined the term "holism," and Helen Flanders Dunbar, who initiated the school of psychosomatic medicine, which holds that psychological processes can produce physical symptoms.

Despite this rather lengthy list of prominent names, the man most commonly associated with organismic theory is Kurt Goldstein, a German-educated neurologist. Goldstein's theoretical and methodological writings, stemming largely from his work with brain-damaged individuals, are by far the most thorough and extensive treatments in the field of organismic psychology. We have chosen for inclusion here a paper in which Goldstein presents some of the important concepts from his theory and applies the organismic orientation to psychotherapeutic treatment.

The field theoretical orientation shares some of the historical antecedents of organismic psychology, but is primarily a descendant of Gestalt psychology and the field theory of the physical sciences. Physical field theory is most strongly represented by Einstein's theory of relativity but is traced to the early work of Faraday and others in electromagnetic fields. Gestalt psychology, clearly influenced by the field theory of physics, began with the reaction of Wertheimer, and shortly of Koffka and Köhler, against the elementism of the Wundtian approach. The perception of any object or *figure*, Gestalt psychology held, is partially a function of the surrounding environment or *ground*. This holistic approach to perception has had many lines of influence in psychology, including the development of field theories of personality.

Two major field theories are included here. The first is that of Kurt Lewin, who is one of the most widely renowned of all theorists in the history of psychology, influencing experimental, social, personality, and clinical psychologists. Lewin had worked for a time with Wertheimer and Köhler in Berlin and eventually came to the United States, convinced that an extention of Gestalt psychology to personality—a field theory of personality—would be both possible and useful. The theory which he constructed, and which has had such widespread influence, is represented here by two articles. The first is an exceptionally clear presentation and defense, by Lewin, of the principle of contemporaneity in field theory. This principle, misinterpreted and criticized by many, states that a given behavior (action or action pattern) is dependent only upon the psychological field which surrounds and includes the individual *at the time* of occurrence of that behavior. The mathematical treatment included in the article is, if followed closely, quite simple and straightforward, and provides an example of Lewin's approach to psychological theory. The second article, by Mary Henle, follows an earlier series of studies concerning the Lewinian concept of valence and its effect on task substitution. Simply stated, valence is the Lewinian value concept. The valence of an object is its perceived value for need satisfaction. In addition to dealing with the problem of substitute values, the Henle experiments provide an excellent opportunity for consideration and discussion of methodological issues.

The second field orientation included here, that of Gardner Murphy, might better be called an *integrative field approach*, as Murphy's work has characteristically gone far beyond a simple statement of field principles. The basic tenet of Murphy's approach is that it is the cross-organization and interaction of the organism-environment field which is the critical focus of personality theory and research. Murphy is known not only for his personality theory, but also for his closely related theoretical and empirical work in perception, social psychology, self-deception and psychical (parapsychological) phenomena, such as ESP. We have chosen for inclusion here three recent papers.[1] The first two provide examples of Murphy's recent theoretical thinking and demonstrate his outstanding ability to meaningfully integrate diverse bodies of knowledge. The final paper is one of Murphy's most recent published researches and demonstrates his capacity not only as an integrative theorist, but also as a careful and effective experimentalist.

[1] The editors are indebted to Dr. Murphy for his kindness in supplying several unpublished papers, one of which, "Encounter with Reality," is included here.

38

The Concept of Health,
Disease and Therapy:
Basic Ideas for an
Organismic Psychotherapy

KURT GOLDSTEIN

The problems of health, disease and therapy are so manifold that nobody will expect me to cover them in all their aspects. To do this even superficially is rather difficult because, from the organismic point of view which underlies my presentation, we have to consider *all* the usually distinguished appearances of illness—bodily disease, functional and organic disease of the nervous system—and we are thus confronted with an enormous number of facts. Therefore, I shall restrict myself to a presentation of the essentials of my ideas, and hope that you will not mind if I deal with some phenomena in an aphoristic way.

My concept of the nature of health, disease and therapy originated from practical work with patients with chronic diseases of the nervous system or damage of the brain—particularly when after World War I, I had the task of helping brain injured soldiers by the thousands, who had been for many years under my care. Very soon I realized that helping them was possible only by a new concept of the functioning of the organism, which put in the foreground not the various separate symptoms—as was customary —but stressed more the modification of the total personality and the attitude of the individual toward his disturbances. This "organismic" approach—the usefulness of which I have attempted to prove in my book, *The Organism* (Goldstein, 1938) gave not only a better basis for treatment of the disturbances in special performance fields, such as, disturbances of language, and the like, but also brought much insight into the nature of what we call "health," "disease" and "therapy." There can scarcely be found more appropriate material to define these so important categories of

From K. Goldstein, The Concept of Health, Disease, and Therapy: Basic Ideas for an Organismic Psychotherapy. Originally published in *American Journal of Psychotherapy*, 1954, 8, 745–764. Reprinted by permission of publisher.

Read before the Association for the Advancement of Psychotherapy, January 29, 1954.

life than that revealed by the observation of human beings who, by the nature of their pathological condition—defects of the brain cortex—are destined never to become totally "normal" even under most adequate therapy.

The general results to which I came in treating brain injured persons proved to be useful when applied to conditions of bodily disturbances of all kinds and to the symptom complexes we call neuroses and psychoses.

Before I go into this matter, I wish to make a remark concerning *terminology*. We should distinguish between the "condition of being sick" and "disease" as a cause of becoming sick. We are interested here in the phenomenon of "being sick," in the patient's appearance and his feelings while he is in this condition, we are interested in how the function of the organism—organic and psychologic—is modified, and how the organism returns to "health."

Let us begin with a very simple observation. Take an individual suffering from a common cold. He may have various little disturbing symptoms, such as headache, a little temperature, etc. In his everyday life, he may not show any essential deviation from the norm. He may not feel quite at ease, but, at the same time, he may not feel "sick." Should the same individual enter a situation where he has to do some difficult and, at the same time, very important work—for instance, take an examination the passing of which is essential for his whole future—we may face a totally different picture. The individual then may display a number of physical and mental symptoms, such as, sweating, trembling, increase of pulse rate, etc.; he may not be able to answer questions which under other conditions he could answer without any difficulty. He may feel himself seriously handicapped, more and more embarrassed. He may appear distracted, confused, be in a "state of disorder" physically and mentally. He is in a condition which I have called "catastrophic." This condition can be observed very frequently in brain-injured individuals. It represents the essential characteristics of the situation of being sick: disordered behavior which makes the individual *unable to use his remaining capacities* and so to come to terms with the demands of his environment, and the *experience of anxiety*. As the result of analysis of many observations I came to the conclusion that the anxiety of the sick individual—and so also anxiety in general—is not a reaction of the individual to the experience of failure and the anger involved in it, but that the behavior disorder *and* the anxiety are the concomitant objective and subjective expressions of the danger in which the organism finds itself (Goldstein, 1951, p. 91). Not all danger brings about this condition; catastrophe and anxiety occur when the organism is no longer able to actualize its "essential capacities"—or, as I also say, when it is no longer able to realize itself, at least to an essential degree. This inability to "realize one's nature" is the danger which characterizes the condition we call anxiety; in other words, when existence is endangered by the failure (Goldstein, 1938,

p. 291). It is important that you do not misunderstand the word "existence." It means here simply a condition of "not being able to actualize one's essential capacities." When an individual is able to do that, he feels he exists—he feels well. I could show by a great number of examples that a trend to realize its essential capacities, i.e., its own nature, is the basic trend of every organism, and so also of the human organism (Goldstein, 1951, p. 291). When the patient is unable to do that, he experiences threat to his existence, breakdown, catastrophe, anxiety.

From the above it is understandable that the breakdown can be the effect of very different causes, psychological or bodily. Furthermore, an event can be evaluated as a cause of a breakdown and anxiety only if one considers it in relation to the personality in question, the tasks he is confronted with and to the demands arising from life which, he feels, is his own and worthwhile to live. For one individual, failing in an examination may not represent any danger; for another, it may spell disaster for his whole future. It is the latter type who is likely to break down.

The observations on a special kind of brain injured (Goldstein, 1936) became important for our knowledge of the structure of the catastrophic condition and anxiety because these patients, due to their mental defect, are unable to offer to themselves an account of anything and so also not of the origin of their catastrophes. Thus it became evident that anxiety is not a pathological reaction of the individual to the situation or danger, but, like the disorder itself, a biological expression of the danger to the existence of the organism. This corresponds to the phenomenological analysis of the phenomenon of anxiety in normals, a phenomenon which has been described by philosophers as the experience of a state in which we face "nothingness"; more concretely, a state in which we face the danger of not being able to fulfill, our essential nature.

If we characterize "being sick" as disordered functioning of the organism combined with anxiety, and "health" as orderly functioning and normal physical and psychological reactions to environment, we may object, that normal healthy life is not at all always ordered, nor anxiety alien to normal life. Certainly, in normal life incongruities often arise between the capacities of the individual and the tasks imposed by the constellation of the environment; such environment may contain factors which are not in keeping with the capacities of the organism, and which may expose it to danger. Shocks and anxiety belong to normal life, as philosophers like Kierkegaard, Pascal, and others have seen very clearly. But, as a matter of fact, incapacity to solve problems, does not usually put us in a state of anxiety.

As a rule, we are able to overcome arising anxiety by the use of our mental capacities, by foresight in avoiding catastrophes and courage in bearing them. From the impossibility of the brain-injured to react in this way we may assume that this normal behavior is related to that special mental capacity we call "capacity of abstraction"; it is this capacity in which our research showed the brain-injured referred to is damaged. What we call courage (Goldstein, 1951, p. 113) is, in the final analysis, but an affirmative answer to the normal shocks of existence which are born by necessity for the sake of realization of our individual nature. Individuals differ as to how much anxiety they can sustain. The more they are able to do that, the less they are hindered in the way of self-realization. We shall see how significant the consideration of this ability to bear anxiety is, when we try to understand the condition of brain injured as well as neurotics and how much this factor determines our procedure in therapy. If any cause produces such danger that actualization of essential capacities (or those considered essential by the individual) becomes impossible and the individual is not able to bear the arising anxiety, a state of "being sick" sets in.

How does the organism recover from the condition of being sick? The individual feels healthy when disorder and anxiety have disappeared or become bearable, so that he can fulfill his essential nature in spite of some symptoms. If we are dealing with a transient condition it is self-evident how recovery occurs; but it is different if restitution of the defect which produces the condition of being sick is impossible. Then the situation of disorder and anxiety becomes more or less persistent, as, for instance, in brain injury, chronic heart failure, or severe neurosis. But even under these conditions, after a certain time, the patients are again in an orderly setting, even the brain-injured person (Goldstein, 1928, pp. 217–241; 1936, pp. 586–610). In spite of remaining defects, he fulfills a number of tasks so that, superficially, he may not appear so very different from the normal. This state is reached by characteristic changes of behavior, all of which have in common that they are suited to protect the individual against occurrence of the "catastrophic condition."

I can give you here only a hint of the various ways in which this is achieved. I have described this behavior change on another occasion in detail (Goldstein, 1951). Such an individual will be inclined to avoid company and situations which may present him with demands that are beyond his capacity. He keeps busy, as much as possible, with things he is capable of doing. These activities may not have a great value in themselves, but they are apt to protect the individual against danger and anxiety. One of the outstanding features is an excessive and fanatical orderliness. Everything has to be in a definite order. All activities have to be organized in a precise way, as to space and time. In their way of living, these patients cannot stand any vacuum. A particularly interesting phenomenon is the frequently observed unawareness of the defect. The more complete the defect, the more evident in the patient is this lack of awareness.

We observe all these modifications of behavior not only in certain cases of brain injury, but in all patients with organic disease. The adaptive change takes place when the hindrance to self-realization becomes excessive and the arising anxiety appears unbearable, as in severe tuberculosis, carcinoma, paresis, etc. (Goldstein, 1952, p. 245). Observation of certain types of brain-injured person leaves no doubt that these protective mechanisms develop without the patient's awareness as to how or even that they develop. The mental defect in such cases is of such a kind that a deliberate creation of this behavior is impossible. We can assume that it originates by a biological adaptation of the organism to its defect, indeed, under the influence of the trend to self-realization. In this "passive" way, protective mechanisms develop also in children, at a time when the capacity of abstraction is not yet fully developed.

At this point you will certainly have realized that the peculiarities of behavior mentioned have a great similarity with those we observe in chronic states of neuroses and psychoses: on the one hand, withdrawal and passivity; on the other—abnormal continuous orderliness; lack of awareness of the real defect, and the like. In grown-up neurotics, such protective mechanisms developed in childhood neurosis, may appear in form of "habits" of different kinds. Karen Horney was right when she assumed that many of the symptoms neurotics show correspond to protective mechanisms developed in infancy. But in neurotics, besides these protective mechanisms, other mechanisms develop in a more active way, as a protection against the current conflict. I think we should distinguish the latter from the passive "protective mechanisms" by terming them "defense mechanisms."

The mechanisms which Anna Freud has analyzed in so instructive a way in *The Ego and the Mechanisms of Defense* (1937) resemble in many respects those we observe in organic patients. They represent a mixture between protective and defense mechanisms (Goldstein, 1936; 1952). Such a mixture can be observed particularly in the neurotic conditions of children, at an age where the capacity for abstraction has not yet fully developed. The distinction between protective and defense mechanisms seems particularly significant for psychotherapy as they require different handling.

Following our concept about the nature of sickness we can say that the patients mentioned above are now in a "more healthy" state and there is no doubt they also *feel* so. Indeed, this state does *not* represent restitution to normalcy. It goes along with more or less outspoken restriction of the individual's capacities, of his nature. The restrictions find an expression in a change, a shrinkage of the patient's world in comparison with this individual's world as it existed before. Life may be more secure in this condition through the exclusion of some demands with which the individual would not be able to cope adequately, and of some inner conflicts which may produce anxiety. But under circumstances life may remain so restricted that the individual may feel doubtful whether it is still worth living.

A severely brain-injured individual, due to his mental defect, does not recognize this shrinkage of his world and his personality, especially when we arrange a custodial environment which allows the patient to get as much personal satisfaction as he needs. He may not recognize that by this "custody" we exclude him, in a high degree, from the normal communion with his fellow men. If he should become aware of his factual position, this awareness alone might hurl him back into catastrophe. As a matter of fact, this may happen easily if the patient is approached by somebody who does not realize his vulnerability in this respect. The occurrence of such shocks during treatment, when the brain-injured has to face demands he as yet cannot fulfill—because otherwise retraining would not be possible—is avoided, more or less successfully, by the transference situation, about which we shall talk later.

Living under restricted conditions is not satisfactory either for a mentally normal individual suffering from a severe bodily disease, or for the neurotic or the psychotic. If, in addition, such an individual gets the feeling that he will have to keep on living in this way for the rest of his life, then he may come to the conclusion that there is no other way out for him than suicide. Suicide then appears to him as the only means of protecting himself against the horrifying affliction of not being able to carry on with tasks which to him are essential; it appears as the only way of escaping the perpetual catastrophes and anxiety and, particularly, the exclusion from *his* world. Then we meet the apparent paradox (but, from our point of view, a logical conclusion) that an individual prefers death to a life so shrunken that it appears to him no longer suitable to realize his true nature. He prefers destruction of his physical existence to a life which is so inadequate that to him it means non-existence.

In situations in which "health" could be reached only with severe restrictions of the way of living, there is but one way out of the dilemma. The individual must *voluntarily bear some conflicts*, some suffering and anxiety. There remains only the choice between this, and the restrictions which may make life not worth living any more. If the patient is able to make this choice, he may still suffer, but may no longer feel sick; i.e., though somewhat disordered and stricken by some anxiety, he is, at least, able to realize his essential capacities, to a considerable degree.

While stressing the significance of this choice for regaining "health," we admit that health is not an objective condition which can be understood by the methods of natural science alone. It is, rather, a state related to a lofty mental attitude by which the individual has to value what is essential for his life. *"Health" appears thus as a value; its value consists in the individual's capacity to actualize his nature to a degree that, for him at least, it is essential.* "Being sick" appears as a loss or diminution of value; the value of self-realization, of existence. The central aim of "therapy"—in cases in which full restitution is not possible—appears to be a transformation of the patient's personality in such a manner, as to enable him to make the right choice, this choice must be capable of bringing about a new orientation, an orientation which is adequate enough to his nature to make life appear worth living again.

It has often been demanded that psychotherapy keep *free from values*. As far as the therapist's attitude toward the failures of the patient is concerned, this demand is certainly correct. The therapist is not supposed to impose his own values upon the patient; but that does not mean that the problem of value has to be, or even can be, avoided totally. Freud as a typical positivist believes that therapy should be based on scientific methods and concepts alone. "All that is outside of science is delusion, particularly religion." Whether or not Freud's own attitude is free of value judgments, is debatable. I think that belief in science alone is also based on a value judgment. Freud's stress on the significance of pleasure as driving force of man is certainly based on his special estimation of it for normal life, on the value he sees in the relief of tension. But, however that may be, Freud himself was not at all certain that treatment can be based on science alone. The following quotations demonstrate this clearly.

"*Weltanschauung*," he writes, "based upon science has essentially negative characteristics, such as, that it limits itself to truth, and rejects illusions. Those of our fellow-men who are dissatisfied with this state of affairs, and who crave for a more temporary peace of mind, may look for it where they can find it. We shall not blame them for doing so; but we cannot help them . . ."

In spite of this emphasis on the scientific approach, on another occasion—in a paper published in 1937—Freud admits that one is obliged, for the sake of therapy, to use also other factors. He even goes so far as to say that we must use (I quote) "a bit of magic" and adds the German words "*es muss doch dann die Hexe dran*." ("Thus we see we cannot get along without the witch.") The "witch" in question is the use of non-psychological and non-scientific factors for the purpose of helping to solve human conflicts. Freud assumes, e.g., that the constitutional strength of the instinct, (i.e., a biological condition) has to be accepted without having been proved scientifically by methods of natural science is of crucial importance from the beginning, if one wants to understand why this ego is hampered in overcoming its conflicts.

It depends upon various factors how efficient an individual is in making the aforementioned *choice* and in enduring conflict and anxiety.

Firstly, it depends upon the structure of the premorbid personality—particularly the nature of his "inborn character." Here the intrinsic courage of the individual is of paramount importance; incidentally, this applies not only to pathological but also to normal situations of anxiety.

Secondly, it depends upon whether the personality is involved in what we call "pathology" in its totality, or whether an essential part of it has remained "normal." This difference shows up in neurotics, on the one hand, and, on the other hand, in patients suffering from organic brain defects and from schizophrenia. In both latter conditions the whole personality is affected, and the use of the abstract capacity (Goldstein, 1936; 1952) which is of considerable significance for the aforementioned choice—is reduced.

Under these conditions, all that the patient can do is to try out which of the possible ways of behavior may best bring about "order" and satisfactory use of his capacities; the brain-injured does it by sticking to what he can do in the protective environment—the schizophrenic by a more or less complete withdrawal from our world and by building up his own world.

Finally, the choice is dependent upon past experiences and their influence on the patient's current condition; particularly with regard to how much they interfere with solving the current conflict.

How can we help the patient to find the new orientation of his personality which will bring about the condition of "health?"

Our first task is to help the patient in his search for the causes which have previously produced disorder and anxiety. The conflict with which the patient and we are concerned, is always a current conflict. We don't doubt, however, that the current conflict also depends upon the after-effects of previous experiences, physical and psychic alike. Here those protective mechanisms which have developed in childhood to protect the individual against anxiety can have a disastrous after-effect. Their persistence shows, as we have already mentioned, in some traits of the neurotic's behavior, where it may produce conflicts. Thus, unearthing of previous events and experiences is of paramount significance for psychotherapy. But the material which comes to the fore in the utterances of the patient has to be scrutinized and used with the greatest care. What can be uncovered at present does not at all correspond to the real previous experiences, not even to the fantasies which have played a great role in childhood.

I am sorry that I cannot discuss this important point in detail. This would involve the consideration of a number of complex problems. I should like, however, at least to point them out. There is, e.g., the problem of the *essential difference in the structure* between the experiences of the infant and those of the grown-up. This makes it difficult for the latter to recall the previous experiences. Recollection presupposes a similarity between the situation in which the organism was at the time of the experience, and the condition in which it is when remembrance is taking place. As I have explained on another occasion (Goldstein, 1938, p. 320), the feelings and attitudes which are predominant in childhood usually cannot be re-experienced by the grown-up, because they cannot as a rule, be made conscious. Another important factor is that the after-effects of childhood experiences undergo, during the years of development, systematic modifications by maturation of the personality and by the cultural influences under which the child grows up. We owe it to an excellent paper of Schachtel

(Schachtel, 1947) that we have now more insight into this very complex phenomenon. Finally, it should not be forgotten that after-effects of previous experiences normally become effective (or not effective) only according to their significance (or non-significance) for self-realization.

I am very doubtful whether *repression*, as understood by Freud, plays an essential role in forgetting in childhood (Goldstein, 1938, pp. 315–322). I think much that is called repression is the effect of the modification of behavior of the child due to the change of personality by maturation and by influences from the outer world. These factors create new patterns which determine the behavior of the organism. *Elimination of some* (called repression) occurs when the maturing organism readapts itself to the environment and gains new patterns, of which those that appear to be "repressed" actually are no longer a part. The former reactions have not been "forgotten" through repression. Rather, they cannot be remembered because they are no longer part of the attitudes of later life and, therefore, cannot become effective. They can be revived or recalled under definite conditions, conditions similar to those under which they originated, such as, for example, is the case in the psychotherapeutic situation, in free associations and in dreams. However, what comes now to the fore as recollection cannot be considered as equal to what the child has experienced. Many mistakes of interpretation originate from overlooking this difference.

A particular difficulty for the interpretation of utterances of adults as "childhood experiences" arised from the *ambiguity of language*. The same word may have a different meaning in different situations, not only in a general sense, but also, especially, when used by the child. As the *objects* in infancy are experiences in a way which differs in principle from that had by adults, so also the same *words* in adults, may correspond to totally different experiences in the child. Now, the patient has no other means to refer to his previous experiences than using the language of the grown-up. This language, however, is particularly unfit to describe the childhood experiences, because it is—as a rule—built according to the demands of the objective world of the grown-ups, and cannot well describe feelings, attitudes, etc., which are predominant in infancy and childhood. When the patient speaks of father, mother, child, sexuality, incest, etc., we must not forget that the words may give a wrong impression as to what actually was going on in the child.

Finally, we must mention that recollection is often impeded by the anxiety and catastrophes which arise from becoming aware of the dangerous conflict which some experiences entail. The patient does not like to give up his previously acquired protective mechanisms. It is one of the most important parts of therapy to overcome this resistance, not only because this alone makes it possible for the patient to become aware of his conflicts; but also because the treatment of resistance brings to the patient insight into the psychic processes underlying these conflicts.

Recollection of dangerous experiences takes place, if the patient is protected against anxiety attached to the recollection. This protection is achieved through the development of that relationship between the patient and the physician which we call *transference*. Because of its great significance I should like to make a few remarks about it.[1] Transference—since Freud—has been considered an essential tool of treatment of neurotics. It also plays a great role in the treatment and retraining of patients with organic brain lesions. Here, too, it is a prerequisite of success. The catastrophic conditions mentioned above appear in these patients so frequently, even in their everyday life—particularly in the situation of retraining, where demands are made of the patient he cannot meet—that in the beginning retraining may appear difficult, even scarcely possible. *All retraining has to begin with the development of transference.* The confidence in the physician's capacity and willingness to help enables the patient not to be afraid that he may do something that he himself considers as "probably wrong."

The development of the transference-relationship is not as easily accomplished as it may seem. It presupposes that (1) the physician knows the patient in all respects; (2) he as able to get the confidence of the patient; (3) he has considered the special defect, e.g., in language, of the *patient in all details*; (4) he has studied the patient's premorbid personality; (5) he has evaluated the change of his personality caused by brain damage; (6) he has envisioned the manner of the patient's relationship to other people, particularly the relationship between him and the members of his family; the previous and present conflicts about them, etc.; finally, (7) that he has considered the patient's fears and hopes for the future, as well as the possibilities for self-realization, in spite of the defect. The therapist has to judge how much "catastrophe" the patient will be able to take.

All these considerations involve matters which we meet, in a similar form, also in the treatment of neurotics. The similarity is understandable because in both conditions we are dealing with the same dynamic problem: the individual's reaction to "unbearable" conflicts. It does not matter whether the conflict is due to an organic defect or to a psychological cause. One can learn much about the problem of transference in general from the experiences with organic patients.

Now, there may be doubt whether "transference" as described in the therapy of organic patients is the same as Freud has defined it. It is generally known that Freud stresses particularly the fact that the relationship between the patient and the therapist represents a repetition of the patient's experiences with his parents. He spoke of a *transference neurosis* in which the patient under the influence of the instinct of repetition reproduces the difficulties of the relationship of the infant toward his parents. This repetition is considered a means of making the patient aware of the nature of conflict in general and of some of his basic conflicts in particular. Thus the

[1] For a more detailed discussion of this subject see Goldstein, 1954.

patient may learn, by re-experiencing of the relationship, and with the help of the therapist, how to handle conflicts in general and, so also, those underlying his neurosis.

There has been an increasing discussion about the value and the necessity of transference neurosis for the treatment of neuroses and, also about the danger connected with it.

I cannot discuss here the usefulness or disadvantage of transference neurosis. I do not even feel competent to do so, because in the form of psychotherapy which I have practiced for decades transference neurosis plays a very small role. This is due not only to the fact that I am using a more active procedure in my therapy, but also to my intentional avoidance of all factors which may foster it. I do not think that an outspoken transference-neurosis is at all necessary. Moreover, I consider it as a potential complication of the treatment. I do not wish to be misunderstood in this respect. I do not maintain that a recollection by the patient of his relationship toward his parents and a corresponding ambiguous attitude toward his physician do not occur, or should not occur; certainly, it is a frequent phenomenon and the basis of resistance which is useful in so far as it offers the therapist an occasion to discuss some of the patient's conflicting childhood situations. However, all of this can be handled without the development of an outspoken transference-neurosis and, I think, in a much shorter and easier way. It gives me satisfaction to know that my experiences go parallel with those of some well known psychoanalysts. Franz Alexander (Goldstein, 1938) says that "the emphasis is no longer on the transference neurosis, the transference relationship becomes the axis of the therapy." It corresponds to my own experiences when he further stresses the fact that "the therapist should always be in control of the transference neurosis, avoiding a more extensive neurosis and restricting the growth of it to those facets which reflect the conflict."

With that, indeed, a part of the treatment procedure in psychoanalysis, usually considered very important, is eliminated or at least reduced, in as much as the transference neurosis is a means of bringing to the fore much of the so-called "unconscious" material. Judging from my experience, the usual transference relationship is a sufficient basis for free associations and their use as a basis for discussion of the important problems. I have the feeling that much of what the patient utters in transference neurosis and what used to be considered as recollection from infancy, is not of much significance as is frequently assumed. When one assumes (as I do) that the conflict is always a current one, many of the patient's recollections produced by free association are more or less meaningless as far as his improvement is concerned.

The avoidance of the development of transference-neurosis shortens the treatment considerably, also because it facilitates the disentanglement of the transference. The latter will be the easier the more one makes the patient realize from the beginning that anything beyond friendship must be excluded; and the friendship relationship will develop easier when the physician does not behave like a powerful God or a representative of a powerful doctrine which alone can cure the patient. The more the entire treatment is arranged and experienced as a "common enterprise" (in which the physician can help the patient because he has been trained in handling difficult problems)—the better for both parts.

In this respect I find myself again in agreement with some analysts, such as Ferenczi, Reich, Rank, F. Alexander, Frieda Fromm-Reichmann— who emphasized that it is not necessary to reach all "repressed" experiences. Alexander says that eliciting memories by free association may not be so much the cause of the therapeutic progress as its results. I do not wish to make the impression as though I did not consider recollection of previous experiences and conflicts very important; indeed, I believe that more important than the contents are often the attitudes—a fact stressed, as far as I can see, first, particularly by Max Friedemann.

The discussion of what is more important for the success in treatment, the contents or the dynamics of disturbances, brings us to the problem of transference in schizophrenics. Freud thought that treatment of schizophrenics in the form of psychoanalysis was hardly feasible, because the development of transference in these patients was very difficult, or even impossible. As a matter of fact, this is true whenever one tries to proceed in psychoses in a similar way as one does in neuroses. What is the cause of it? Is not the lack of success perhaps due to the fact that this procedure may fit the structure of the neurotic conflict but not of the conflict in schizophrenia? On the basis of the psychological studies by Vigotsky, Hanfmann, Kasanin, Bolles, myself, and others (Vigotsky, 1934, et al.; Goldstein, 1938), I am inclined to assume that the center of the psychological deviation in schizophrenia—at least in some types of the disease—is the anxiety originating from the patient's concept of the "dangerousness" of *our* world. To avoid this anxiety, the patient has to withdraw from this world. That is achieved by the elimination of the approach to the environment with an abstract attitude. As protection against his anxiety (generated by the "dangers" of our world) he develops an abnormally concrete behavior, by which a good deal of our world is eliminated from his experiences, but with it also a good deal of its "dangers." Because the schizophrenic is aware of his conflicts—as especially Paul Federn has pointed out—it becomes easily understandable that any transference relationship to a member of this dangerous world will by all means be avoided. The patient withdraws and resists every communication.

Our explanation of the origin of withdrawal and the difficulty in building up a transference relationship finds its confirmation in the observation that touching upon some conflicts, may immediately produce anxiety and withdrawal in a patient with whom a transference relationship had been already developed (Goldstein, 1938). The use of language, which is so important for the development of any human relationship and, also so important for the establishment of transference in the therapy of neuroses, can only be a hindrance in the treatment of schizophrenics. We know of observations which show clearly that the schizophrenic does not want to understand our language, and that he changes his language in a way that we cannot understand him. He is protected against any approach by language through the elimination of the abstract attitude, which concerns in the same way language as the attitude toward our world in general (Goldstein, 1948). That takes away from language much of its usability as a means of communication with us. As I have tried to show, many of the peculiarities of the language of the patients lose their obstruse character and become understandable when one analyzes them from this point of view (Goldstein, 1944).

From what was said, it becomes evident that the development of transference in schizophrenia must be enormously hampered. We may now ask whether the consideration of this knowledge cannot help us to find another way for establishing transference.

The transference relation is based on communication, and communication presupposes a communion which alone leads people toward understanding each other. Let us consider the possibilities for such a communion. In general, we say that all one has to do is to avoid the difficulties which arise from differences of personality or language, and from all the common causes of antagonistic attitudes between man. But this is not enough. We must give up the use of an abstract attitude in our approach to the patient. We must proceed in a concrete, direct way. The physician's entire behavior must make the patient feel that there is not much difference between our world and his world, that the physician is not in opposition to the patient's world, and that the patient, therefore, does not have to be afraid of us. Under such conditions there is a good prospect that the patient may be inclined to give up more and more of his withdrawal as a defense that is no more longer necessary. The patient will explain without great anxiety his difficulties and will accept with more greater willingness the help of the therapist.

I admit that this is a very crude description of the development of transference in schizophrenics; in fact it is as such an extremely difficult job. It needs not only knowledge, endurance and courage but also deep devotion to the work. I should like to recommend, for more detailed an account of the procedure, especially the publications of Frieda Fromm-Reichmann. The recommendations she offers are in many details very similar to those we give for treatment of organic patients. This confirms my original assumption that the basis of the development of transference is in both conditions similar, the common factor being the direct, concrete relationship between physician and patient. Needless to say that in view of the different causes of both conditions, and the different etiology of the special symptoms in organic brain disease and in schizophrenia, the routine in transference differs in spite of the basic similarity.

I have the impression that the successes of therapists like Klaesi, Frieda Fromm-Reichmann, Rosen and others are based on the development of that kind of transference which I have described above.

I must come to an end, although I feel that to prove the usefulness of my concept I should have touched upon many more problems that confront us in therapy.

I would have wanted to say something about the *problem of release of tension in psychotherapy*. It happens in every psychotherapy that the patient is sometimes, often acutely, so overwhelmed by conflicts and by anxiety that the therapeutic management of the symptoms is in the immediate foreground. This alone may sometimes prevent the patient's death. Only after release of tension, planned psychotherapy can be continued. Under dangerous conditions it is justified, even mandatory, to use the *physiochemical* approach besides psychotherapy. In some situations even shock therapy may be indicated. However, all this is allowed only if we explain to the patient why we apply these procedures, and if he understands that we consider them not as therapy by which he can be cured, but as an emergency action to prevent acute disaster. Otherwise the application of these methods may obstruct the effect of psychotherapy. When the patient experiences improvement after shock therapy, he should know that this is not "the cure."

The application of methods for the release of tension represents another even more serious problem, especially when it is considered as *goal* of therapy. In organic patients there is often no other way open than this. In neurotics the situation is essentially different. Certainly, we should try to eliminate unnecessary tension also in treatment of neurotic patients; but one should not even attempt to eliminate all tension. How far we should go, which tension we should not touch, has to be always decided with respect to the patient's total personality. The decision should be made by considering in which way the highest degree of self-realization may be reached in the individual concerned. The release of tension should not be in the foreground of the thinking of either of the therapist or of the patient.

To mention only one example: Sex difficulties should not be treated only with the intention of restoring orgasm. While absence of orgasm in the patient may produce great suffering, we must not view the problem of his sexual difficulties from the point of how many orgasms he may have in a week (as it may be suggested by the evaluation of the orgasm by Kinsey and his co-workers). Only the orgasm embedded in a right relationship to the partner, in a right form of self-realization, can be considered as an expession of "improvement" in a neurosis. How often do we observe a severe neurotic condition in a woman in spite of a normal orgasm!

The tendency to put release of tension in the foreground of treatment originated from a wrong interpretation of life, an interpretation which overlooked the significance of tension for human existence, so that it, consequently could arrive at the formula that death is "the" goal of all life. The assumption of the death instinct is a logical consequence of the overrating of the pleasure principle (Goldstein, 1938, p. 382).

I have scarcely been able to touch on the problem of the contents of the conflicts in neuroses and psychoses and to show what role the social factor plays in the fulfillment of self-realization and, therefore, in health and therapy. A discussion of it would reveal the great impediment to therapy originating from the uncertainty and inconsistency of our civilization and the lack of a value system which the individual could accept wholeheartedly, and which would make his life worth living despite all necessary sacrifices. Very little can be found in our civilization which will allow for a satisfactory self-realization. I want to draw your attention to one special sacrifice demanded by our economic system which to me seems particularly unfortunate for therapy, namely, the transformation of "work" into "having a job." Work can be very helpful as a value, as a means to actualizing one's personality, as enabling one to bear all necessary sacrifices. But in the moment when "earning money" for the purpose of "making a living" becomes paramount, the individual is often forced to separate his work from his personality. This is more so as unfortunately the amount of earned money often influences the individual's social-actualization. From this situation a disunity of the personality originates. There are many other peculiarities of the modern social structure which also tend to produce a split in the personality, so that self-realization often becomes difficult.

Ichheizer (1943) has published an interesting study on the difference of the interpretation of "personality" as it functions in everyday life, and the frame of reference within which the psychologist considers "personality." The difference between the "occupational" and the "private" personality produces, he writes, a split, from which inevitable tensions arise. These tensions are deeply increased by the fact that traditional ideology and traditional education posit the unity of personality as an ideal, which the actual conditions of modern life and the existing social system make the realization of this ideal impossible. Here the profound relation between disease and therapy on the one hand and the general attitude toward life and the society in which the individual lives, on the other, becomes evident.

From this point of view, therapy appears to be more than a means of helping individuals to overcome personal conflicts. It must be considered, at the same time, as an attempt, among others, to diminish the disturbing effect on the individual of a society which is not organized adequately to fit human nature. Therapy's hope lies, to a high degree, in a better organization of society. Therapy today is not a completely satisfying activity, and often it is doomed to remain patch-work. Like any other helping procedure it presupposes belief that conditions can be changed for the better, which represents an optimistic attitude in spite of all the insight into the enormous difficulties and all the doubt regarding the prospects of the effort. This optimism alone can help the therapist to bear his own sacrifice and his inability to do a better job—without being too much disturbed in his own self-realization.

From all that follows that all treatment of a condition in which a full restitution cannot be achieved, consists in a transformation of the individual. This change will enable him to find a new adjustment to the environment, i.e., to find a world which allows him to realize his remaining capacities to a degree and proves that life is still worth living. This success never takes place without restrictions. The patient has to learn that achieving this demands the endurance of some conflicts, anxiety and restriction of his world; that such endurance is necessary to protect him against unbearable difficulties and conflicts. It will help him to be successful, when he becomes aware that his situation is in principle not different from that present in normal beings; that restrictions are an unavoidable necessity of human existence. They are, so to say, the price man has to pay for his being an individual. The more the patient will *accept this role without resentment*, the more he will be able to realize himself, the more happy (or less unhappy) he will be, the more "healthy"—even in spite of irreparable defects.

BIBLIOGRAPHY

Kurt Goldstein "Beobachtungen ueber die Veraenderungen d. Gesamtverhaltens bei Gehirnschaedigung." *Mtschr. g. Psych. u. Neur.*, Vol. 68, 1928.

Kurt Goldstein The Modifications of Behavior Consequent to Cerebral Lesions. *Psychiatr. Quart.*, Vol. X, 1936.

Kurt Goldstein *Der Aufbau d. Organismus.* Nijhoff, Haag, 1934. English version. *The Organism*, Amer. Book Co., 1938.

Kurt Goldstein *Language and Thought in Schizophrenia.* Ed. by Kasanin. University of Calif. Press, 1944, pp. 17–40.

Kurt Goldstein *Language and Language Disturbances*, Grune & Stratton, New York, 1948.

Kurt Goldstein *Human Nature in the Light of Psychopathology.* Harvard University Press, 1951.

Kurt Goldstein The Effect of Brain Damage on the Personality. *Psychiatry*, 1952, p. 245.

Kurt Goldstein "Transference in the Treatment of Organic and Functional
    Nervous Diseases." Read at the Intern. Congress for Psychotherapy,
    Zurich, 1954.
Ichheizer Misinterpretat. of Personality in Everyday Life and the Psychologists
    Frame of Reference. *Character and Personality*, Vol. XII, 1943, p. 195.
E. G. Schachtel On Memory and Childhood Amnesia. *Psychiatry*, Vol. X, p. 1,
    1947.
L. Vigotsky Thought in Schizophrenia. *Arch. Neurol. and Psych.*, Vol. 31,
    1934.—Hanfmann and Kasanin *Journ. Psychol.* 1937, p. 521.—E. Hanf-
    mann Analysis of the Thinking Disorder in a Case of Schizophrenia.
    Arch. Neurol. and Psych., Vol. 41, 1939, p. 568.—Kasanin *Language
    and Thought in Schizophrenia*, Coll. Pap. of various authors. Univ. of
    Calif. Press, 1944.—K. Goldstein The Significance of Psychol. Research
    in Schizophrenia. *Jour. Nerv. and Ment. Dis.*, Vol. 97, 1943.—M. Bolles
    and K. Goldstein A Study of Impairment of Abstr. Attitude in Schizo-
    phr. Patient *Psychiatr. Quart.*, Vol. 12, 1938, p. 42.

39

Defining the
"Field at a Given Time"

KURT LEWIN

I. FIELD THEORY AND THE PHASE SPACE

The history of acceptance of new theories frequently shows the following steps: At first the new idea is treated as pure nonsense, not worth looking at. Then comes a time when a multitude of contradictory objections are raised, such as: the new theory is too fancy, or merely a new terminology; it is not fruitful, or simply wrong. Finally a state is reached when everyone seems to claim that he had always followed this theory. This usually marks the last state before general acceptance.

The increasing trend toward field theory in psychology is apparent in recent variations of psychoanalysis (Kardiner, Horney) and also within the theory of the conditioned reflex. This trend makes the clarification of the meaning of field theory only the more important, because, I am afraid, those psychologists who like myself, have been in favor of field theory for many years have not been very successful in making the essence of this theory clear. The only excuse I know of is that this matter is not very simple. Physics and philosophy do not seem to have done much analytical work about the meaning of field theory that could be helpful to the psychologist. In addition, methods like field theory can really be understood and mastered only in the same way as methods in a handcraft, namely, by learning them through practice.

Hilgard and Marquis (1940), in a recent publication, quote from a letter of Clark Hull the following sentence: "As I see it, the moment one expresses in any very general manner the various potentialities of behavior as dependent upon the simultaneous status of one or more variables, he has the substance of what is currently called field theory."

From K. Lewin, Defining the "Field at a Given Time," Psychological Review, 1943, 50, 292–310. Copyright 1943 by the American Psychological Association, and reproduced by permission of publisher.

This is the third paper given at a Symposium on Psychology and Scientific Method held as part of the Sixth International Congress for the Unity of Science, University of Chicago, September, 1941. The first paper is by Egon Brunswik and the second by C. L. Hull.

It is correct that field theory emphasizes the importance of the fact that any event is a resultant of a multitude of factors. The recognition of the necessity of a fair representation of this multitude of interdependent factors is a step in the direction toward field theory. However, this does not suffice. Field theory is something more specific.

To use an illustration: Success in a certain sport may depend upon a combination of muscular strength, velocity of movement, ability to make quick decisions, and precise perception of direction and distance. A change in any one of these five variables might alter the result to a certain degree. One can represent these variables as five dimensions of a diagram. The resultant of any possible constellation of these factors for the amount of success can be marked as a point in the diagram. The totality of these points then is a diagrammatic representation of this dependence, in other words, of an empirical law.

Physics frequently makes use of such representation of a multitude of factors influencing an event. To each of certain properties, such as temperature, pressure, time, spacial position, one dimension is coordinated. Such a representation in physics is called "phase space." Such a phase space may have twenty dimensions if twenty factors have to be considered. A phase space is something definitely different from that three-dimensional "physical space" within which physical objects are moving. In the same way the psychological space, the life space or psychological field, in which psychological locomotion or structural changes take place, is something different from those diagrams where dimensions mean merely gradations of properties.

In discussing these questions with a leading theoretical physicist, we agreed that the recognition of a multitude of factors as determining an event, and even their representation as a phase space, does not presuppose field theory. In psychology, Thurstone's factor analysis deals with such relations of various factors. Any character profile recognizes the multitude of factors. Field theorists and non-field theorists can both avail themselves of these useful devices, but not everybody who uses them is therefore a field theorist.

What is field theory? Is it a kind of very general theory? If one proceeds in physics from a special law or theory (such as the law of the free-falling body) to more general theories (such as the Newtonian laws) or still more general theories (such as the equations of Maxwell), one does *not* finally come to field theory. In other words, field theory can hardly be called a theory in the usual sense.

This fact becomes still more apparent when we consider the relation between the correctness or incorrectness of a theory and its character as a field theory. A special theory in physics or psychology may be a field theory, but nevertheless wrong. On the other hand, a description of what Hans Feigl calls an "empirical theory on the lowest level" may be correct without being field theory (although I do not believe that a theory on the higher levels of constructs can be correct in psychology without being field theory).

Field theory, therefore, can hardly be called correct or incorrect in the same way as a theory in the usual sense of the term. *Field theory is probably best characterized as a method:* namely, a method of *analyzing causal relations and of building scientific constructs.* This method of analyzing causal relations can be expressed in the form of certain general statements about the "nature" of the conditions of change. To what degree such a statement has an "analytical" (logical, *a priori*) and to what degree it has an "empirical" character do not need to be discussed here.

II. THE PRINCIPLE OF CONTEMPORANEITY AND THE EFFECT OF PAST AND FUTURE

One of the basic statements of psychological field theory can be formulated as follows: Any behavior or any other change in a psychological field depends only upon the psychological field *at that time.*

This principle has been stressed by the field theorists from the beginning. It has been frequently misunderstood and interpreted to mean that field theorists are not interested in historical problems or in the effect of previous experiences. Nothing can be more mistaken. In fact, field theorists are most interested in developmental and historical problems and have certainly done their share to enlarge the temporal scope of the psychological experiment from that of the classical reaction-time experiment, which lasts only a few seconds, to experimental situations, which contain a systematically created history through hours or weeks.

If a classification of the field theoretical principle of contemporaneity could be achieved, it would, I feel, be most helpful for an understanding among the various schools in psychology.

The meaning of this far-reaching principle can be expressed rather easily by referring to its application in classical physics.

A change at the point x in the physical world is customarily characterized as dx/dt; that is to say, as a differential change in the position of x during a differential time-period dt. Field theory states that the change dx/dt at the time t depends only on the Situation S^t at that time t (Figure 39-1).

$$(1) \qquad \frac{dx}{dt} = F(S^t)$$

It does not depend, in addition, on past or future situations. In other words, the formula (1) is correct, but not the formula (1a).

$$(1a) \qquad dx = F(S^t) + F^1(S^{t-1}) + \ldots + F^2(S^{t+1}) + \ldots$$

Of course, there are cases in physics where one can state the relation between a change and a past situation S^{t-n} (where $t - n$ is a time not immediately preceding t; $|t - n| > dt$). In other words, there are occasions where it is technically possible to write:

$$(2) \qquad \frac{dx}{dt} = F(S^{t-n})$$

However, that is possible only if it is known how the later situation S^t depends on the previous situation S^{t-n}; in other words, if the function F in the equation

$$(3) \qquad S^t = F(S^{t-n})$$

is known. Such knowledge presupposes usually (a) that both situations are "closed systems" which are genidentic (Lewin, 1922); (b) that the laws are known which deal with the change of all points of the previous situation S^{t-n} and also the laws dealing with the changes in the situations between the previous situation S^{t-n} and the later situation S.

The meaning of linking a change to a past situation by formula (2) might be clarified best by pointing out that it is possible in a similar way to link a present change to a future situation S^{t+n} and to write:

$$(2a) \qquad \frac{dx}{dt} = F(S^{t+n})$$

This is possible whenever we have to deal with a "closed system" during the time-period t until $t + n$, and if the laws of the on-going changes during this period are known.

The possibility of writing this functional equation does not mean that the future situation S^{t+1} is conceived of as a "condition" of the present change dx/dt. In fact, the same dx/dt would occur if the closed system would be destroyed before the time $(t + n)$. In other words, the change dx/dt depends on the situation (S^t) at that time only (in line with formula [1]). The technical possibility of expressing this change mathematically as a function of a future or a past time does not change this fact.[1]

The equivalent to dx/dt in physics is the concept "behavior" in psychology, if we understand the term behavior to cover any change in the

---

[1] Frequently an occurrence is said to be caused by the "preceding conditions." This term seems to have been misunderstood by psychologists to refer to a distant past situation (S^{t-n}), although it should refer to the present situation, or at least to the "immediately preceding situation" (S^{t-dt}). We will come back to this question.

psychological field. The field theoretical principle of contemporaneity in psychology then means that the behavior b at the time t is a function of the situation S at the time t only (S is meant to include both the person and his psychological environment),

$$(4) \qquad\qquad b^t = F(S^t)$$

and not, in addition, a function of past or future situations S^{t-n} or S^{t+n} (Figure 39-2). Again, it is possible to relate the behavior b indirectly to either a past situation (S^{t-n}) or a future situation (S^{t+n}); but again, this can be done only if these situations are closed systems, and if the changes in the intermediate periods can be accounted for by known laws. It seems that psychologists are increasingly aware of the importance of this formula.

III. HOW TO DETERMINE THE PROPERTIES OF A FIELD AT A GIVEN TIME

If one has to derive behavior from the situation at that time, a way has to be found to *determine* the character of the "situation at a given time." This determination implies a number of questions which are, I think, interesting both psychologically and philosophically.

To determine the properties of a present situation or—to use a medical terminology—to make a diagnosis, one can follow two different procedures: One may base one's statement on conclusions from history (*anamneses*), or one may use diagnostic *tests of the present*.

To use a simple example: I wish to know whether the floor of the attic is sufficiently strong to carry a certain weight. I might try to gain this knowledge by finding out what material was used when the house was built ten years ago. As I get reliable reports that good material has been used, and that the architect was a dependable man, I might conclude that the load probably would be safe. If I can find the original blueprints, I might be able to do some exact figuring and feel still more safe.

Of course, there is always a chance that the workmen have actually not followed the blueprints, or that insects have weakened the woodwork, or that some rebuilding has been done during the last ten years. Therefore, I might decide to avoid these uncertain conclusions from past data and to determine the present strength of the floor by testing its strength now. Such a diagnostic test will not yield data which are absolutely certain; how reliable they are depends upon the quality of the available test and the carefulness of testing. However, the value of a present test is, from the point of view of methodology, superior to that of an *anamneses*. An *anamneses* includes logically two steps: namely, the testing of certain properties in the past (of the quality, size, and structure of the woodwork) and the proof that nothing unknown has interfered in the meantime; in other words that we have to deal with a "closed system." Even if a system is left untouched by the outside, inner changes occur. Therefore, in addition, the laws governing these inner changes have to be known (see above) if the properties of a situation are to be determined through an *anamneses*.

Medicine, engineering, physics, biology are accustomed to use both methods, an inquiry into the past and a test of the present. But they prefer the latter whenever possible.[2]

Psychology has used diagnosis by *anamneses* rather excessively, particularly in classical psychoanalysis and other clinical approaches to problems of personality. Psychology of perception and psychology of memory have been relatively free from the historical type of diagnosis. Experimental psychology, on the whole, has shown a progressive trend toward testing the present situation.

The method of determining the properties of a situation (S^t) by testing them at that time t avoids the uncertainties of historical conclusions. It does not follow, however, that this method eliminates considerations of time-periods altogether. A "situation at a given time" actually does not refer to a moment without time extension, but to a certain time-period. This fact is of great theoretical and methodological importance for psychology.

It may be helpful to go back for a moment to the procedure in physics. If the vertical lines in Figure 39-1 represent the socalled physical "world-lines," a "situation" means a cut through these lines at a given time t. A description of such a situation has to include (1) the relative position of the parts of the field at that time; (2) the direction and the velocity of the changes going on at that time. The first task is fulfilled by ascribing certain scalar values to the different entities; the second, by ascribing certain vectors to them. The second task contains a difficulty which I would like to discuss.

To describe the direction and velocity of a change going on at a given moment, it is necessary to refer to a certain period of events. Ideally, a time-differential should suffice for such determination. Actually, one has to observe a macroscopic time-interval or at least the position at the beginning and at the end of such interval to determine that time-differential. In the

---

[2] There are cases where a historical procedure is preferable. For instance, the hunger of a rat can probably be better determined by the duration of starvation than by a physiological or psychological test of the hunger at the time t. This conclusion from the past to the present can be made, however, only during periods and in settings where a "closed system" (no interference from outside can be enforced; e.g., for animals which during this period do the same amount of work, which have been on a known diet, etc. The difficulties of this type of control have led Skinner (1938) to link the problem of drive strength to properties of present consumption.

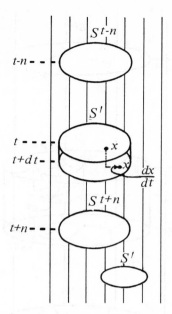

Figure 39-1. S during $t - n$ until $t + n$ is a "closed system"; but S is not genidentic with S'.

$$\frac{dx}{dt} \text{ indicates the velocity of } x.$$

simplest case the velocity at a given time is assumed to equal the average velocity during that macroscopic time-interval. I will not attempt to follow up the details of this procedure in physics. If sufficient laws are known, certain indirect methods like those based on the Dopler effect permit different procedures.

However, it remains a basic fact that the adequate description of a situation at a moment is impossible without observation of a certain time-period. This observation has to be interpreted (according to the "most plausible" assumption and our knowledge of the physical laws) in a way which permits its transformation into a statement of the "state of affairs at the time t."

In psychology a similar problem exists. The person at a given time may be in the midst of saying "a." Actually such a statement implies already that a certain time-interval is observed. Otherwise, only a certain position of mouth and body could be recorded. Usually the psychologist will not be satisfied with such a characterization of the ongoing process. He likes to know whether this "a" belongs to the word "can" or "apple" or to what word it does belong. If the word was "can," the psychologist wants to

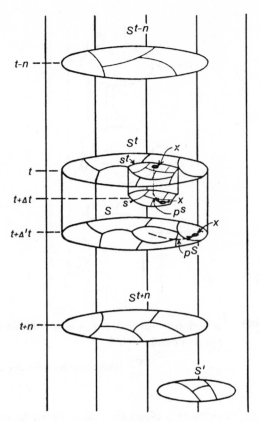

Figure 39-2.   S during $t - n$ until $t + n$ is a "closed system"; but S is
not genidentic with S'. $s^{t,tt\Delta t}$ is a small time-field-unit
which extends over a relatively small area and includes
the relatively small time-period t until $t + \Delta t$. $S^{t,tt+\Delta't}$ is
a larger time-field-unit covering a larger area and in-
cluding the longer period t until $t + \Delta't$. p^s and P^s
indicate the change in position of x during the small and
the large time unit.

know whether the person was going to say: "I cannot come back" or "I can
stand on my head if I have to." The psychologist even likes to know
whether the sentence is spoken to an intimate friend as a part of a conversation about personal plans for the future or whether this sentence is
part of a political address and has the meaning of an attempt to retreat
from an untenable political position.

In other words, an adequate psychological description of the character
and the direction of an ongoing process can and has to be done on various
microscopic and macroscopic levels. To each "size of a unit of behavior" a

different "size of situation" can be coordinated. That the individual in our example is saying "a," can be made sure without taking into account much of the surrounding of the individual. To characterize the sentence as a part of a political retreat, much more of the surrounding has to be considered.

Without altering the principle of contemporaneity as one of the basic propositions of field theory, we have to realize that to determine the psychological direction and velocity of behavior (*i.e.*, what is usually called the "meaning" of the psychological event), we have to take into account in psychology as in physics a certain time-period. The length of this period depends in psychology upon the scope of the situation. As a rule, the more macroscopic the situation is which has to be described the longer is the period which has to be observed to determine the direction and velocity of behavior at a given time (Figure 39-2).

In other words, we are dealing in psychology with "situational units" which have to be conceived of as having an extension in regard to their field dimensions and their time dimensions. If I am not mistaken, the problem of time-space-quanta, which is so important for modern quantum theory in physics (Reichenbach, 1942), is methodologically parallel (although, of course, on a more advanced level) to the problem of "time-field-units" in psychology.

The concept of situations of different scope has proved to be very helpful in solving a number of otherwise rather puzzling problems. Tolman (1932), Muenzinger (1939), and Floyd Allport (1942), have stressed that a psychological description has to include the macroscopic as well as the microscopic events. Barker, Dembo, and Lewin (1941) distinguish and treat mathematically three sizes of units of processes and corresponding sizes of situations. They have handled certain problems of measuring the strength of frustration during extended periods by referring to overlapping situations in regard to two different sizes of time-field-units. Lippitt and White (Lippitt, 1940), in their study of social atmosphere, distinguish still larger periods of events. They have shown that the beginning and end of these macroscopic units can be determined rather precisely and with very satisfactory reliability. However, I will not discuss these questions here where we are interested in methodological problems only.

IV. THE PSYCHOLOGICAL PAST, PRESENT, AND FUTURE AS PARTS OF A PSYCHOLOGICAL FIELD AT A GIVEN TIME

The clarification of the problem of past and future has been much delayed by the fact that the psychological field which exists at a given time contains also the views of that individual about his future and past. The individual sees not only his present situation; he has certain expectations, wishes, fears, daydreams for his future. His views about his own past and that of the rest of the physical and social world are often incorrect, but nevertheless constitute, in his life space, the "reality-level" of the past: In addition, a wish-level in regard to the past can frequently be observed. The discrepancy between the structure of this wish- or irreality-level of the psychological past and the reality-level plays an important role for the phenomenon of guilt. The structure of the psychological future is closely related, for instance, to hope and planning (Barker, Dembo, & Lewin, 1941).

Following a terminology of L. K. Frank (1939), we speak of "time perspective" which includes the psychological past and psychological future on the reality-level and on the various irreality-levels. The time perspective existing at a given time has been shown to be very important for many problems such as the level of aspiration, the mood, the constructiveness, and the initiative of the individual. Farber (1940) has shown, for instance, that the amount of suffering of a prisoner depends more on his expectation in regard to his release, which may be five years ahead, than on the pleasantness or unpleasantness of his present occupation.

It is important to realize that the psychological past and the psychological future are simultaneous parts of the psychological field existing at a given time t. The time perspective is continually changing. According to field theory, any type of behavior depends upon the total field, including the time perspective at that time, but not, in addition, upon any past or future field and its time perspectives.

It may be illustrative to consider briefly from this field theoretical point of view the methodological problems connected with one of the basic concepts of the conditioned reflex theory, namely, the concept of "extinction." An individual has experienced that after a certain stimulus, let us say the ringing of a bell, food will appear. Being hungry, the individual eats. After a number of such experiences, the individual will show certain preparatory actions for eating as soon as the eating bell rings. The individual is then said to be "conditioned." Now, the situation is secretly changed by the experimenter and the eating bell is not followed by food. After a while the individual catches on and does not show the preparatory action for food when the bell rings. This process is called "extinction."

"Habits" of a person at a given time can and have to be treated as parts of the present field. Whether they should be represented partly as cognitive structure or resistance to change of cognitive structure, partly as a building up or fixation of valences (Lewin, 1942a), or whether they have to be conceptualized in other ways is not a problem here. Habits of action (Schwarz, 1927; Lewin, 1942b), as well as of thinking, are dealt with in field theoretical research. They are closely related to problems of ideology (Kalhorn, 1941) and expectation.

As Tolman (1932), Hilgard and Marquis (1940), and others have correctly pointed out, conditioning as well as extinction are both related to changes in the reality level of the psychological future. Field theorists have to distinguish in regard to conditioning and extinction two types of problems. The one type deals with such a question as how expectation is affected by perception on the one hand, and memory on the other. What changes in the perceived structure of the psychological present lead to a change in the structure of the psychological future, and what are the laws governing the interdependence of these two parts of the psychological field? The studies on level of aspiration have provided some knowledge about the factors which influence the structure of the future reality-level. Korsch-Escalona (1939) has made a step toward a mathematical treatment of the effect of the future reality-level on the forces which govern present behavior. Study of the level of aspiration has also given us considerable insight into the effect of the psychological past (namely of previous success or failure) on the psychological future. This question is obviously closely related to extinction.

The methodological position of these types of problems is clear: They deal with the interdependence of various parts of the psychological field existing at a given time t. In other words, they are legitimate field theoretical questions of the type $b^t = F(S^t)$.

The second type of questions, treated in the theory of conditioned reflex, tries to relate a later situation S^4, (for instance, during extinction) to a previous situation S^1 during learning or to a number of similar or different previous situations S^1, S^2, S^3, . . .: it relates behavior to the number of repetitions. In other words, these questions have the form $b^t = F(S^{t-n})$ or $b^t = F(S^{t-n}, S^{t-m}, . . .)$. Here field theory demands a more critical and more analytical type of thinking. One should distinguish at least two types of problems:

(a) How the perceived psychological situation will look at the time S^4 depends obviously upon whether or not the experimenter will provide food and on similar external physical or social conditions. Everybody will agree, I suppose, that these factors cannot possibly be derived from the psychological field of the individual at the previous time, even if all the psychological laws were known. These factors are alien to psychology.

(b) There remain, however, legitimate psychological questions in this second type of problem. We can keep the boundary conditions of a life space constant or change them in a known way during a certain period and investigate what would happen under those conditions. These problems lie definitely within the domain of psychology. An example is the problem of restructurization of memory traces. We know that these processes depend on the state of the individual during the total period S^{t-n} until S^t (Fig. 39-2) and are different, for instance, during sleep and while being awake. Doubtless the experiments on conditioned reflex have given us a wealth of material in regard to this type of problem. They will have to be treated finally in the way which we discussed in the beginning, namely, as a sequence of relations between a situation S^t and the immediately following situation S^{t+dt}.

On the whole, I think the psychological trend is definitely going in this direction. For instance, the goal gradient theory has been formulated originally as a relation between behavior and past situations. Straight, analytical thinking demands that such a statement should be broken up into several propositions (Lewin, 1938), one of which has to do with the intensity of goal striving as a function of the distance between individual and goal. This is identical with a statement about certain force fields and is probably correct. A second proposition implied in the goal gradient theory links the present behavior to the past situation S^{t-n}. The specific form is, to my mind, unsatisfactory. But even if it should be correct, it should be treated as an independent theory. Hull's formulation of a "Gradient of Reinforcement Hypothesis" is a step in this direction.

BIBLIOGRAPHY

Allport, F. H. Methods in the study of collective action phenomena. *J. soc. Psychol.*, SPSSI Bulletin, 1942, *15*, 165–185.

Barker, R., Dembo, T., & Lewin, K. Frustration and regression; Studies in topological and vector psychology II. *Univ. Ia Stud. Child Welf.*, 1941, *18*, 1–314.

Brunswik, E. Organismic achievement and environmental probability. *Psychol. Rev.*, 1943, *50*, 255–272.

Farber, M. L. Imprisonment as a psychological situation. Unpublished Ph.D. Thesis, State University of Iowa, 1940.

Festinger, L. A theoretical interpretation of shifts in level of aspiration. *Psychol. Rev.*, 1942, *49*, 235–250.

Frank, L. K. Time perspectives. *J. soc. Phil.*, 1939, *4*, 293–312.

Hilgard, E. R., & Marquis, D. G. *Conditioning and learning.* New York, London: D. Appleton-Century Co., 1940.

Hull, C. L. The problem of intervening variables in molar behavior theory. *Psychol. Rev.*, 1943, *50*, 273–291.

Kalhorn, J. Ideological differences among rural children. Unpublished Master's Thesis, State University of Iowa, 1941.

Korsch-Escalona, S. The effect of success and failure upon the level of aspiration and behavior in manic-depressive psychoses. In Lewin, K., Lippitt, R., & Korsch-Escalona, S., Studies in topological and vector psychology I. *Univ. Ia. Stud. Child Welf.*, 1939, *16*, no. 3, 199–303.

Lewin, K. Der *Begriff der Genese in Physik, Biologie und Entwicklungsgeschichte.* [The concept of genesis in physics, biology and theory of evolution.] Berlin: Julius Springer, 1922.

Lewin, K. The conceptual representation and the measurement of psychological forces. *Contr. psychol. Theor.*, 1938, *1*, no. 4. P. 247.

Lewin, K. Field theory and learning. In *41st Yearbook of the National Society for the Study of Education*, Part II, 1942, pp. 215–239. (a)

Lewin, K. The relative effectiveness of a lecture method and a method of group decision for changing food habits. Committee on Food Habits, National Research Council, 1942. (b)

Lippitt, R. An experimental study of the effect of democratic and authoritarian group atmospheres. *Univ. Ia. Stud. Child Welf.*, 1940, 16, no. 3, 44–195.

Muenzinger, K. F. *Psychology: the science of behavior.* Denver: World Press, 1939. Pp. 270.

Reichenbach, H. *From Copernicus to Einstein.* New York: Alliance Book Corp., New York Philosophical Library, 1942.

Schwarz, G. IV. Über Ruckfalligkeit bei Umgewohnung. I, II. [On relapses in re-learning.] *Psychol. Forsch.*, 1927, 9, 86–158; 1933, 18, 143–190.

Skinner, B. F. *The behavior of organisms; an experimental analysis.* New York: D. Appleton-Century Co., 1938.

Tolman, E. C. *Purposive behavior in animals and men.* New York: Century Co., 1932. Pp. xiv, 463.

40

The Influence
of Valence on Substitution

MARY HENLE

In a previous paper (Henle, 1942) experiments on the influence of valence on substitution were reported. Evidence will now be presented which permits a further analysis of this influence, and which further clarifies the relation between valence and other determinants of substitution.

The problem of substitution arises when an individual is denied some satisfaction: can some other satisfaction be substituted for the original one, so that it will take the place of the original, and the individual will no longer seek the satisfaction which was denied him? The problem may be translated into an experimental one by presenting a task to a subject, interrupting it before completion, and introducing as a substitute for the unfinished task another task which the subject is permitted to complete. The substitute value of this completed task for the interrupted one must then be determined.

Experimental investigations of substitution have taken their departure from Lewin's theoretical formulation of the problem (Lewin, 1935; 1936). Lewin assumes that when a subject is given a task to perform in an experimental situation there is aroused in him an intention ("quasi-need") to complete it. Corresponding to the intention, a system under tension is set up which initiates activity directed to the satisfaction of the need—thus to the completion of the task. Completion of the task releases the tension of the system corresponding to it. If, however, the subject is unable to complete the task, the system in question remains under tension. The residual tension of such a system may manifest itself in a variety of ways, one of which has been found by Ovsiankina (1928) to be a tendency of the subject to resume the unfinished task. A tendency to resume an unfinished task may, therefore, be regarded as a criterion of the existence of a system under tension.

Received in the Editorial Office on September 23, 1943, and published immediately at Provincetown, Massachusetts. Copyright by The Journal Press.

From M. Henle, The Influence of Valence on Substitution. *Journal of Psychology*, 1944, *17*, 11–19. Reprinted by permission of author and publisher.

In an experiment on substitution, a second task is offered to the subject in place of the interrupted one. Completion of it may not only release the tension corresponding to this task itself; it may also release the tension of the need to complete the original unfinished task. Then the second task is said to have *substitute value* for the first. In such a case the individual will no longer show a tendency to resume the unfinished task since the system corresponding to it is no longer under tension, and the dynamic basis for resumption has thus been removed. Therefore *non-resumption of the interrupted task* becomes the behavioral criterion of the substitute value of the substituted task for the interrupted one. If the interrupted task fails to be resumed in a statistically significant percentage of cases after completion of the substituted task, and if conditions of the experiment are such that it would be resumed on the whole in the absence of the substitute, the latter will be said to have substitute value for the interrupted task.[1]

In the investigation cited above, the writer found that the higher the valence of the tasks employed (that is, the greater their attractiveness or interest for the subject), the less the possibility of substitution of one for another. A task of medium valence was found to have substitute value for a similar interrupted one in a significantly high percentage of cases, whereas under otherwise like conditions, substitution could not be demonstrated when tasks of high valence were used.

In these experiments, the two tasks of the experimental series, the interrupted and the substituted task, were chosen to be similar to each other. This procedure was followed because similarity has been shown to be a condition of substitution: it has been found that a task will have substitute value for an interrupted one similar to it, but not, other things being equal, for a dissimilar task (Lissner, 1933). The present experiments continue the investigation of the effect of valence on substitute value in series of dissimilar tasks. They were performed to determine whether, by proper manipulation of valences, substitution of dissimilar tasks could be demonstrated.

A finding of Lissner's suggests the possibility of demonstrating substitution with dissimilar tasks. In investigating the influence of difficulty on substitute value, Lissner found that an interrupted task followed by a completed task dissimilar to it, but of the same level of difficulty, was resumed less frequently than an interrupted task for which no substitute at all was offered.[2] On the other hand, an interrupted task followed by a dissimilar

---

[1] Further discussion of this criterion of substitute value, and particularly of the necessity of employing a statistical criterion at the present stage of our knowledge of substitution, is to be found in the writer's earlier paper on substitution (Henle, 1942, p. 48 ff.).

[2] The difference approaches statistical significance, as tested by the χ^2 criterion (corrected by Yates's correction). This result requires confirmation, however, in view of Ovsiankina's finding that unfinished tasks followed by dissimilar completed ones

task which was easier than itself was resumed in approximately the same percentage of cases as an interrupted task for which no substitute of any kind was offered. This finding suggests that, by the proper manipulation of relations of difficulty, substitution of dissimilar tasks might be demonstrated conclusively. In connection with the present problem, it raises the question of whether relations of valences within an experimental series might not also be manipulated so as to make possible the substitution of dissimilar tasks. The experiments now to be reported were performed to answer this question.

PROCEDURE

The subject (S) sat facing the experimenter (E) at a table on which were displayed the experimental tasks. After some preliminary conversation to establish rapport with S, E started the experiment by explaining to S the requirements of each of the tasks. Five or six of the following tasks were used: jigsaw puzzle, pencil maze, anagrams, letter cancellation, mosaic, city naming, card sorting, modelling from plasticine. When S understood each of the tasks, E went on to determine their relative valences with the following words: *"Now here's what I'd like to know about these tasks. If you had your choice of all of them, which one would you most like to do?"* If necessary, the question was repeated, but no additional explanations were given. When S had made his choice, he was asked in turn for his second, third, fourth, and fifth choices. The order of preferences so obtained was taken as the rank order of valences of the tasks for the particular subject.

The valences of the tasks determined which ones were to be used with each S. Thus valence was held constant in each experiment, although the specific tasks used varied from subject to subject. For purposes of the present experiment the variation in the tasks used was of no importance; previous investigation has shown that with tasks of the kind employed here (all *"Endhand-lungen"* or tasks with definite goals; cf. Zeigarnik, 1927), the particular tasks used make no difference for the occurrence of substitution if only their difficulty and their valence are controlled (Henle, 1942).

E selected the task of appropriate valence and presented it to S with the words: *"I'm working on a couple of these now, so I've already picked out the ones I want you to do."* S was ordinarily allowed to work on his

---

are resumed in a very high percentage of cases. Although Ovsiankina did not specifically investigate the effect of the difficulty of the completed task on the frequency of resumption of the incomplete task, there is no indication in her paper of any consistent difference in the difficulty of the two tasks. Yet, if Lissner's finding is correct, we must assume that the completed task in Ovsiankina's series was almost always easier than the interrupted one.

task until he was well along with it.[3] At a point when he was judged to be involved in the task, *E* interrupted by presenting another task and saying: "*Will you do this one now please.*" When *S* had completed this substituted task, *E* said that this was the last task. She said she had some questions to ask *S*, but first had to complete the notes she had been taking during the experiment. She started writing, thus leaving *S* an unoccupied period in which to resume the interrupted task if he desired. Other tasks were also present with which *S* could occupy himself if he did not resume the interrupted task. At least two minutes were allowed for resumption. If at the end of one minute *S* had not resumed the incomplete task, *E* said: "*I'll be a minute or two, so just do anything you like while I'm writing.*" This remark frequently had the effect of causing a subject to resume a task which he had wanted to resume, but failed to do so because he thought *E* did not want him to. After the two minutes allowed for resumption *E* asked questions to supplement information obtained from observation of *S*'s behavior about any possible tendency to resumption on *S*'s part. In most cases, *S* was also asked to indicate again his preferences among the experimental tasks. In this way any cases could be eliminated in which changes of valence had occurred, so that the conditions of the experiment were no longer fulfilled.

Three categories were employed in scoring the records: resumption, tendency to resumption, and non-resumption. A subject was said to show *resumption* of the unfinished task if he returned to it and carried on the work in the direction of the original goal. If he did something about the unfinished task, but without a view to reaching the original goal, or if he reported that he had wanted to resume the task, but did not actually resume it, the subject was said to show a *tendency to resumption*. The category of *non-resumption* was reserved for cases in which no resumption or tendency to resumption could be detected.

The χ^2 criterion was used to determine the significance of differences.[4] In the statistical treatment of results the categories of resumption and tendency to resumption were grouped together since they appeared psychologically to belong together. For it is likely that in a perfectly free experimental situation in which the subject was guided solely by his own wishes with respect to resumption, the difference between resumption and

---

[3] Occasionally it was necessary to interrupt *S* earlier in the work to prevent him from reaching a sub-goal through the completion of some clearly defined part of the task. That such part completions may have substitute value for the task as a whole has been shown by Ovsiankina (1928).

[4] χ^2 was calculated directly from the observed values according to the formula given by Fisher (1930) for fourfold tables:

$$\chi^2 = \frac{(ad - bc)^2 \, (a + b + c + d)}{(a + b) \, (c + d) \, (a + c) \, (b + d)}$$

where *a*, *b*, *c*, and *d* are the four observed values.

Whenever a value less than 5 appeared in any compartment of the table, Yates's correction (Rider, 1939) was used. Where frequencies are small, the probabilities obtained by the use of the uncorrected χ^2 may deviate considerably from the true ones.

tendency to resumption would tend to disappear, and the tendency to resumption would more frequently be expressed in outright resumption.

Fifty college undergraduates served as subjects in the experiments reported here. Each subject was used in one experiment only. Statistical comparisons of the results of these experiments with those reported in the previous paper (Henle, 1942) will be made, since the two series of experiments were performed under like conditions.

RESULTS

In Experiment I the first task presented to S was one of middle valence (S's third choice). This task was interrupted and was followed by the task of highest valence (S's first choice). Results of this experiment are presented in Table 40-1. Resumption plus tendency to resumption occurred in 41 per cent of the cases, non-resumption in 59 per cent.

These results are to be compared with those of experiments previously reported (Henle, 1942, p. 59) in which a task was interrupted, and no substitute was offered in its place. In these experiments non-resumption occurred respectively in 5 per cent and 8 per cent of the cases, as compared with 59 per cent in the present experiment. The differences are statistically significant, with P-coefficients below .01 in both cases. On the other hand, the results of Experiment I show good agreement with those of an earlier experiment (Henle, 1942, p. 60) in which substitution was demonstrated.[5] These statistical comparisons indicate, then, that in Experiment I the completed task had substitute value for the unfinished one in a statistically significant percentage of cases.

This result is confirmed by the results of five S's which could not be included in Table 40-1 because changes in the valence of the tasks occurred during the course of the experiment. For these S's a task of lower valence was interrupted and followed by one of higher valence (though the in-

TABLE 40-1.   Resumption (R), Tendency to Resumption (TR), and Non-Resumption (NR) Obtained in Experiment I in Which the Task of Highest Valence Was Offered in Place of the Interrupted Task of Middle Valence

	N		%	
R	3		18	
TR	4		24	
R + TR		7		41
NR	10		59	
Total	17		100	

[5] In this experiment, resumption plus tendency to resumption occurred in 52 per cent of the cases, non-resumption in 48 per cent.

tended sequence of middle and highest valence was not produced). Of these five S's, three failed to resume the interrupted task. When the results of these S's are combined with those of the S's of Experiment I, resumption plus tendency to resumption still occurred in 41 per cent of the cases, non-resumption in 59 per cent.

Previous experiments (Lissner, 1933), as stated above, have established similarity as a condition of substitution. The present results show, however, that when the valences of tasks are properly manipulated, substitution can also be demonstrated with dissimilar tasks. The meaning of this finding for a theory of the conditions of substitution will be discussed below.

Experiment II was performed to investigate further the effects of varying relations of valences within an experimental series. In Experiment II the valence relations of Experiment I were reversed. The task of highest valence (S's first choice) was first presented. This task was interrupted, and was followed by the task of middle valence (S's third choice out of five tasks or his third or fourth choice when six experimental tasks were used), which S was allowed to carry to completion. Table 40-2 contains the results of Experiment II. Resumption plus tendency to resumption occurred in 81 per cent of the cases, non-resumption in only 19 per cent. These results are significantly different from those of Experiment I.

Substitution has not been demonstrated in Experiment II. This is shown by the fact that the results of this experiment show good and excellent agreement respectively with previous experiments in which no substitute was offered, and only poor agreement with the previous experiment where substitution was demonstrated.

These results are confirmed by those of seven S's for whom valence changes occurred. For them the experiment consisted in an interrupted task of higher valence followed by a completed one of lower valence (but not highest followed by middle valence, as intended). Of these S's only two failed to resume the interrupted task. When these results are combined with those of Experiment II, the results are essentially unchanged. Thus the percentage of resumption plus tendency to resumption is 79, while non-resumption occurred in 21 per cent of the cases.

TABLE 40-2. Results of Experiment II: Task of Highest Valence Interrupted and Followed by Completed Task of Middle Valence

	N		%	
R	7		33	
TR	10		48	
R + TR		17		81
NR	4		19	
Total	21		100	

Taken together, the results of Experiments I and II are in agreement with the previous finding that the higher the valence of the interrupted task, the less is the likelihood that another task will have substitute value for it. They show further that when dissimilar tasks are used, a substituted task will have substitute value for an interrupted one of lower valence than itself, but not for one whose valence is higher. This second generalization may hold within limits set by the first, and it may break down when valences are very high.

It will be noted that the findings for valence as a condition of substitute value are similar to those for difficulty. Lissner has found that in series of similar tasks, the greater the difficulty of the substituted task, the higher its substitute value. In the case of dissimilar tasks, Lissner's findings suggest that a substituted task will have substitute value for an interrupted task of equal or lower difficulty, but not for one of greater difficulty.

It might be objected that what is important for substitute value is not the relation of the two valences, as suggested here, but rather the valence of the interrupted task alone. Thus it might be that when this task is of middle valence, substitution will occur, whereas when it is of high valence substitution will not appear regardless of the valence of the substituted task. There are several reasons for discarding this interpretation. In the first place, substitution is not easily demonstrated with dissimilar tasks. Besides, we are dealing here with relative valences of tasks only; the absolute valences are unknown. What is held constant from subject to subject is not the absolute valence of the tasks employed, but rather the relation of valences. Furthermore, the results of S's for whom valence changes occurred suggest that the important thing is the relation of valences. Those results confirmed the findings of the main experiments when the relations of valences of the experimental tasks were the same as in the main experiments, even though the interrupted task did not possess the same (relative) valence as those in Experiments I and II. Further experiments of this kind, in which valences other than the middle and highest valences are employed, would settle the point.

DISCUSSION

How can we explain the occurrence of substitution with the dissimilar tasks of Experiment I? Similarity has been shown to be a condition of substitution only to the extent to which it is a condition of pair formation between tension systems corresponding to the two tasks of the experimental series (Henle, 1942). Other conditions favoring such pair formation are also conditions of substitution. Thus the important condition of substitution appears to be not similarity *per se*, but rather pair formation (or specific communication) of tension systems. It may, then, be that such communication of tension systems exists in Experiment I, even though the tasks are to all appearances dissimilar.

It is apparent that the intentions to complete the particular experimental tasks are not the only needs (or quasi-needs) operating in the experimental situation. Other more inclusive needs are also called into play: for example, a desire to do well in the experiment, as well as the still more inclusive need for superiority; a desire to do tasks that are "fun," or a more comprehensive need for construction, etc. It may be, then, that the completed task in Experiment I releases the tension corresponding to the interrupted task by releasing the tension of a superordinate need. Such an interpretation could be applied not only to the present results, but also to Lissner's findings on difficulty as a condition of substitute value.

If this interpretation is correct, it might be possible to use the method of substitution to investigate certain aspects of the organization of needs within the personality.

More specifically, it may be that Experiment I employs tasks which are psychologically similar with respect to some superordinate goal to which both are means, in spite of their objective dissimilarity. It is clear that similarity cannot be defined in terms of piecemeal identity of parts (Goldmeier, 1937); and it is equally clear that the aroused needs of the individual have a part in determining what similarities exist for him. For example, a building block will be more similar to a missile than to other construction materials when the child's need for aggression is aroused. Systematic experiments on the rôle of needs in defining similarities need to be done. With respect to the present problem, if the tasks employed here may be considered similar with respect to some larger goal, then the law of similarity as a condition of substitution need not be modified in the light of these results.

In any case, the problem which is raised by the results of the present experiments is that of determining how large a unit is necessary to describe adequately the behavior of the subjects in the experimental situation. It is suggested that here the relevant segment of behavior does not consist simply of activity directed to satisfy a quasi-need to complete a particular task, but must be thought of as activity directed to a more inclusive goal.

REFERENCES

Fisher, R. A. *Statistical Methods for Research Workers.* London: Oliver & Bond, 1930.

Goldmeier, E. Über Ähnlichkeit bei gesehenen Figuren. *Psychol. Forsch.*, 1937, 21, 146–208.

Henle, M. An experimental investigation of dynamic and structural determinants of substitution. *Contrib. Psychol. The.*, 1942, 2, No. 7.

Lewin, K. *A Dynamic Theory of Personality*. New York: McGraw-Hill, 1935.

Lewin, K. *Principles of Topological Psychology*. New York: McGraw-Hill, 1936.

Lissner, K. Die Entspannung von Bedürfnissen durch Ersatzhandlungen. *Psychol. Forsch.*, 1933, *18*, 218–250.

Ovsiankina, M. Die Wiederaufnahme unterbrochener Handlungen. *Psychol. Forsch.*, 1928, *11*, 302–379.

Rider, P. R. *An Introduction to Modern Statistical Methods*. New York: Wiley, 1939.

Zeigarnik, B. Über das Behalten von erledigten und unerledigten Handlungen. *Psychol. Forsch.*, 1927, 9, 1–85.

41

Pythagorean Number Theory and
its Implications for Psychology

GARDNER MURPHY

When Lois and I had the delightful course by Ruth Benedict at Columbia entitled "The Religions of Preliterate Peoples," we learned the following from the philosophy of the Dakotahs:

As the units of time are four, the day, the night, the month and the year, and as the seasons of man's life are four, infancy, childhood, adulthood and old age, and as the fingers are four, and the toes are four, and the sum of the thumbs and big toes is four (!). . . .

We decided we were encountering a number-obsessed people. Perhaps we ourselves are another number-obsessed people. I thought I would explore this question. Numbers are vital to our life. It may be worth while to understand their role in our thinking.

It is not my intention to regale you, like Major General Stanley, with "many cheerful facts about the square of the hypotenuse." Rather, I hope to direct your attention to the "golden numbers" of arithmetic and geometry, inclining to the view that "God made the whole numbers, man everything else." I shall ask you to accept from me a few little signposts planted by Egyptians in the earth to mark distances; a few little numbers that make for Mendeleev the all-or-none difference between one traditional atom and another; a few little odd facts about black-body radiations that give us Planck's world of the quantum and discontinuity; a few little reminders that we must, in two profound meanings of the term, find "safety in numbers"; and a few unanswerable questions, I believe, as to where number cathexis carries us from the soundest reality testing to the wildest extravaganza of irrationality.

Not much is known about Pythagoras, nor about any of his immediate followers. They shared the fascination and the excitement of those

From G. Murphy, Pythagorean Number Theory and its Implications for Psychology. *American Psychologist*, 1967, 22, 423–431. Copyright 1967 by the American Psychological Association, and reproduced by permission of publisher and author.

Presidential Address presented to Division 24 at the meeting of the American Psychological Association, New York, September 1966.

who made discoveries that transcend the world of ordinary communication, and maintained the secret fraternity of their silence through the whole great period of their discoveries. They taught a wide variety of things that puzzle you and me. The basic thing about them for the history of science is that they discovered the role of number in that vast enterprise which we call science; together with the atomists on the one hand and the Platonists on the other, they defined the basis for an ordered cosmic structure, an ordered structure of human individuality, and a social order.

We may make many mistakes as to what they taught, but this is of secondary importance. The main thrust of what they taught is very plain, and the danger is not that we falsely attribute this or that to them, but that we go wrong in our own contemporary thinking about what numbers are; how they can be used; where they hold a priceless key to reality; and where they lead us off into a solipsistic world in which the manipulation of numbers bends back upon itself in a self-contained world of fantasy, remote from that numbered world which it is our scientific task to perceive and to use.

Absolutely nothing that I shall say will be new to the mathematical specialist. But there is enough, I believe, of direct importance for psychologists in the rich Pythagorean tradition to be worth our spending an hour with it, and it is only in these terms that I ask for your attention.

HERACLITUS, DEMOCRITUS, AND PYTHAGORAS

There are three great personalities from pre-Socratic philosophy to whom I would invite your attention: (a) There is Heraclitus, the man who said that we never step twice into the same river, and the man who, in the expanding trade between Greeks and Mesopotamians, reminded us that all things can be changed into gold, or into fire, and back again. He taught that strife is the father of all things, and above all, that all things flow. (b) There was the atomist, Democritus, who conceived the world to be made of minute moving particles, some larger, some smaller, some constituting what we call our bodies, some what we call our minds. He laid the foundation for all modern material atomism. (c) There was Pythagoras, of the Island of Samos, who fled a local despot and set up his school in Croton in the south of Italy about 530 B.C. His school was a fraternity, or secret society, lost in the immensities of number and of measurement, and like many Greek schools, concerned both with cosmic and with human problems; both with epistemology and with aesthetics and ethics. He taught that quantity, and specifically, number, was the key to all reality, and it is for this that we revere him.

MATHEMATICS AND BEAUTY

Two great discoveries heralded the arrival of Pythagorean number theory: (*a*) in tuning the lyre it was discovered that there is a certain unity or blending of tone when one string is twice as long as another, the octave; that there is a good, acceptable, sweet chord when the ratio of length is three to two, and again that good chords are produced by relations such as four to three. Using four strings, it was found that the combinations one to two, three to two, and four to three were especially delicious to the lover of tone. (*b*) There was something about simple numbers that gave beauty. More complex numerical relationships appeared when the lyre was not quite properly tuned, and the relation was something like fifteen to eight. These, when simultaneously struck, gave a discord. There was thus a direct relationship between arithmetical simplicity on the one hand, and beauty on the other hand. It was not far from this to a doctrine of harmony in nature, for example, in the courses of the stars or the rhythms and ordered time relations of pageantry and the dance, and the basic physiological rhythms of life.

You will notice that in this conception of order there is a preoccupation and fascination with whole numbers. Of course, the mystic three, the mystic four, the mystic seven, are virtually universal human concerns. There is luck in odd numbers, specifically three and seven; and bad luck in thirteen, etc., according to the culture. This feeling that numbers are almost persons, almost benign and malignant entities in nature adds to the emotional investment or cathexis in the number system as a whole. A child is early aware that he has two hands, two eyes, etc. He must "count out"; he must reestablish rhythm after falling or sobbing or getting lost in his own little diadic patty-cake of life.

This idea of the sacredness of number was, of course, enormously accentuated with the discovery of the amazing fact that the right triangle, familiar from Egyptian measurements of the land, was so invested with nature's universal harmonies that the square of the hypotenuse was exactly equal to the sum of the squares on the other two sides; not somewhere near it, not by an approximation to a 1% error, not probabalistically, or in terms of averages, but literally, absolutely, eternally, and indisputably, as a necessary numerical relationship.

Many a Greek temple showed likewise a subtle and marvelous concern with the manipulation of arithmetical relations between columns, capitals, the interspaces between columns, and the relations of lengths and widths appreciated by the beauty-loving eye long before they are discovered by the individual to be based upon numerical realities. In other words, the world of geometry speaks to us in the same language as the world of the musician's lyre, and both speak in terms of the basic numerical relationships of the body. Music and the time arts, geometry and the space arts, gave the Pythagoreans boldness to speculate that order, rhythm, balance, numerical simplicity are likewise the clue to the ordering of human affairs through systems of morals, politics, and law.

Another celebrated discovery of the Pythagoreans related to the interdependence of the integers which add up to ten. Imagine the front elevation of a traditional pile of cannon balls with 1 at the top, 2 in the line below, 3 below that, and 4 at the base. The total is 10; 10 contains in rational order the first four cardinal numbers. But the form of the two-dimensional figure, if properly ordered, is an equilateral triangle, so that the 3 enters into the company of the 10 in an especially intimate way.

If you think that "this way madness lies," I will not dispute you. I learned once from a numerologist in New Haven why the prevailing color on the face of the earth is green. Count out from the sun: the sun is one; Mercury, two; Venus, three; the earth, four. Now count the colors of the rainbow: red is one; orange, two; yellow, three; and green, four. Does it not follow that in the kingdom of the number four the earth must be green? Or does it? If it is not self-evident to you, you are lacking in that fine flavor of number mysticism which stretches all the way from the greatest mathematical genius to the schizoid confusion of symbols with the things symbolized.

But this is not the only kind of passion with which the lovers of number are tortured. Deep in our culture is the belief that numbers have distinctive qualities, like people: the clean, square four, and the ragged, cruel, unfortunate thirteen. They have family resemblances and tribal affinities. Indeed, who can quite say that they have not? In anthropology we encounter the moieties, and the people who live on one or the other side of the river; and in the number world we have the odds and the evens, the prime numbers and those that can be factored, and countless other categories. These qualities often lead to their being loved and hated, sought and avoided.

THE "PERSONALITIES" OF NUMBERS

Let me see if I can persuade you that there are, in our tradition, easily recognizable and very intense feelings about the qualities and the importance of the individual integers. Take them, then, from 1 to 10. One is, of course, the center and root of all numerical thinking. There is no number at all if the one is itself uncertain. "One is one and all alone and evermore shall be so." Two represents the fundamental duality—the male and the female, the Yang and the Yin, the odd and the even—as bases of the eternal polarities based on opposition or directionality. Three is the great tripod, the universal system in which simple opposition is transcended—the father, the mother, and the child; the trinity of body, mind, and spirit; Osiris, Isis, and Horus; of course, three is lucky; "third time never fails."

The four is a pair of pairs; the consummation of the polarities, north, south, east, west. Five is a hand, a fist full of fingers, the combination of the polarity and the mystic triad so structured in its "fearful symmetry" that it appears in evolution as the five-toed form from which endless diversification has appeared in feet, paws, and hands. There are countless creatures to whom this supple and majestic symmetry is essential for balance, for locomotion, and for grasping. How much is biology, how much culture; how much the inscrutable "fiveness" of elementary symmetry? Six is another kind of two and three—not a simple summation, but a multiplication which appears in the hexagonal cell of the insects' constructions, and appears in the perfect cube, because there are really three dimensions, and there really are six basic faces of the simplest reality. Mathematicians, with their theories of the group, have done many wonderful things with boxes of sixes. Now as we go on, we realize another enormously mysterious and mystifying number—the seven, which is a six plus a one, a four plus a three, and you know intuitively why there had to be seven heavenly bodies to constitute the harmony of the spheres, seven wonders of the ancient world, seven candles in the mystic candelabra. Seven is a lucky number. More than that, it is a number fundamental in that kind of human constructiveness which gives symmetry and asymmetry their equal power. Another challenging relation of two and three appears in the eight, which is a two to the third power; and the sublime rhythm which represents the number of the muses, the three times three, the nine.

You have only now to put your two hands together and find suddenly the root of all Western numerical construction, the decimal or digital system. As Frank Lorimer says, a decade is a "two hands of years, and a century is a two hands of two hands of years." Alone in its oddity stands 11, claiming its arch intimacy with the 10 on the one side and the tremendous 12 on the other; the 12, with its facets of 2 and 3, its divisibility into all the fundamental forces we have tried to describe. When this magnificence has been exhausted, is there anything strange about the threatening quality of the lonely, residual 13? It negates the supreme 12, and in utter Satanism, rejects the sublime unity of the number ritual which all the foregoing have laid down.

I will not hold you longer on this point, but ask you to play this game in your own way, remembering the sacredness of the "score," the diabolism of "40 stripes save 1," the 70 years which define the span of man's life, the

144,000 of the majestic vision of the Revelation, and so on, to your heart's content. I read from the Family Section of *Grit* for July 3, 1966:

No. 40 Plays Unusual Role
The number 40 has played a role of great importance in world history.
Jesus fasted 40 days. Moses spent 40 days and 40 nights on Mount Sinai at the time he got the Ten Commandments . . .
A quarantine extends to 40 days. In old English law, the privilege of sanctuary was for 40 days. . . ."

From the sublime to the ridiculous: I myself discovered, at the age of 5, a basic numerical clue to human personality: I discovered that there were odd-numbered people—generous, friendly, free-roving, simple, direct, earthy, lovable people; and that there were even-numbered people—restrained, orderly, correct, demanding, and ultimately inscrutable people. The odd-ball, minority-group kinds of people with Irish names like myself were comfortable in their oddness. Most of the Anglo-Saxons who lived in the little Massachusetts town which was my home were even-numbered in every respect —in their politics, their religion, their philosophy of life, the way they said "good morning," and the way they called in the dog. Think back. Did you not also make a great discovery about numbers and people? And when you took statistics, did you really find all numbers equal, or some "more equal than others?"

NUMBERS IN WESTERN PHILOSOPHY

Aristotle, of course, had the theory of the golden mean. He was speaking a language already somewhat familiar to his fourth-century audience who flourished long after the time of the Pythagoreans. But Aristotle had virtually no interest in mathematics; virtually no understanding of the Pythagorean vision. Despite his brilliant derivation of an ethical system from the theory of the golden mean, he left the main course of Greek thought to develop number theory in other directions. The Platonists, however, through the extraordinary mathematical cosmogony of the *Timaeus* saw the implications for man's moral and ideal fulfillment. Plato indeed made a journey to the Pythagorean establishment in southern Italy, and came back a man broadened in terms of his mathematics. Over the gate of the Academy the inscription was written: "Only Mathematicians' Enter Here," and in one of his wisest intellectual bouts with an especially alert questioner, Socrates himself is reported to have said: "They err not only with respect to lack of knowledge in general, but in particular with respect to that kind of knowledge which is called measuring."
If we think of Socrates and Plato as drawing away from crass mathematical atomism and the early forms of a hard-boiled physicalist scientific

naturalism we wholly miss the boat, and flounder helplessly in a sea of confusion. For the whole point, from the Greek outlook, was to find the value of numbers as guides to order, and not only to physical but to aesthetic and ideal order. Naturally, this led to mystical applications which neither the Pythagoreans nor the Platonists shunned. It is not, however, with these mystical applications that we are here concerned, except insofar as we must note that preoccupations with numbers and attribution of vast importance to them in the basic cosmic and human meanings was inevitably associated with the conception of cognitive drives as superior to the simpler physical or physiological drives, and to the idea, especially associated with Plato, that man is most completely man when he thinks in terms of generalizations and abstractions representing a pure, cognitive attachment to the known or knowable world, man being driven on by an orderly nature of the knowing process syntonic with—we might almost say isomorphic with—the ordered nature of the world which he hopes to know.

GALILEO

Pythagorean number theory was kept alive in the West largely through Plato's *Timaeus*. The historian and the philosopher are concerned to know how it fared in the great Catholic system of St. Thomas Aquinas and his intellectual descendants in northern Italy at the time of the Renaissance. One of the questions which the scholars, acting as subjects in the celebrated Würzburg experiments, were asked to reflect about and answer, was couched in the words: "Was the Pythagorean theorem known to the Middle Ages?" The most important question for us is whether it was known when modern science took shape. Part of the answer lies in the fact that at the University of Padua in northern Italy mathematics was flourishing in Renaissance times, and the great Galileo Galilei was Professor of Mathematics at Padua. So sure was he of the soundness of a mathematical approach to reality that he apparently belittled his own experiments as being necessary only for beginners who did not see the inner necessity of nature's laws. You will recall that Kurt Lewin opposed an Aristotelian to a Galilean principle in the sense that the latter looks for laws having "exceptionless validity," that is, the necessity of mathematical logic. This does not cover all the historical facts; for Galileo, hearing of a telescope in the Netherlands, pushed telescopic observation about Jupiter's moons and other objects to a point where it intrigued and shocked the classicists of his day. He and his pupil, Torricelli, exchanged messages with lanterns to see whether the speed of light was actually infinite, and as Conant has reminded us, he speculated on the failure of hand pumps which had to draw water more than about 25 feet, looking for empirical considerations (mistakenly as it happened) in the tendency of the column of water to break of its own weight. It is true that he had earlier begun his mathematical investigations by watching the swinging of a lamp in the cathedral at Pisa, and that his approach to the laws of the falling body is a clean-cut instance of an empirical determination of something which followed of necessity from the mathematics of the relation of velocity to acceleration, a straight question of arithmetic and geometry. Galileo, in short, married empiricism to mathematical deduction. But so had Pythagoras; so had the great astronomers of Egypt. Mathematics was a tool which operated when continually fed with good raw material. It is possible, but likewise it is idle, to say that the development of science could have been carried through without benefit of Pythagoras. The empirical fact stands clear: Pythagorean thinking was of the very essence of the applied mathematics which we find in the history of science. It was because number theory and its application to arithmetic and geometry was clear and exciting that empirical observations took the shape which we call science.

Historians of psychology have not forgotten that as Galileo's thought was causing an electrical storm in Western Europe, Descartes invented analytical geometry; that amazing science which showed that an orderly equation derived from the study of conic sections will lay out for you upon a plane the exquisite three-petal and four-petal roses which are inherent in the bare abstractions of an equation. Certainly nothing could more dramatically satisfy the triumphant Pythagorean prediction that the world of beauty, the beauty of music, of architecture, and indeed of the very structure and symmetry of human thought, lies in the ordered relations of the numbers themselves. Newton carried the torch further, and with the impact of his thinking the eighteenth century became the intellectualist century, or the century of the enlightenment. Voltaire, armed with mathematics in one hand and scepticism in the other, gave us the ordered, but essentially non-human universe in which Laplace could conceive of "celestial mechanics," and of a "system of the world." The physician, David Hartley, having reference to Newton's Laws of the Pendulum, which in turn went back to Galileo's Laws of the Pendulum, created an "association psychology" based squarely upon the elementary mathematics of the sine wave incorporated in the functions of the "white medullary substance of the brain."

HERBART

But it was Herbart who saw the radical implications. It was he who conceived of elementary concepts, or psychic atoms, pushing upon one another like the molecules in a gas; he saw them colliding and interfering with each other's movements, and under other conditions coalescing or structuring themselves into larger wholes. He saw the mind as a dynamic system of energies running an ordered course; he saw the difference between the ideas at a conscious level upon which we can make direct observations, and those below threshold which act, in the darkness of unconsciousness, exactly as if they were in the light of consciousness. He saw how the phenomena of conflict, and likewise the phenomena of assimilation, integration, and the apperception mass realize, in an ordered and predictable way, the structural potentialities from which dynamic potentialities must emerge. All this he did, of course, with the aid of a well-defined conception of energies, and with the benefit of the new differential and integral calculus which came from Newton and from Leibnitz. A giant, indeed, he was, with but few equals in either ancient or modern times—who saw the necessity of formal assumptions about elements, their relations, their energies, their dynamic interdependence, their capacities for synthesis. He went on, in a life of intense usefulness, to build educational institutions to make more rational the ordered acquisition of facts and ideas in the mind of the child. It was to a large degree from Herbart that Fechner derived his conception of the threshold, and the rich system of psychophysical method and psychological measurement which dominated experimental psychology in its opening decades. It was from this kind of a systematic experimental quantitative psychology that a psychology of individual differences was built.

Indeed, in his presidential address to the American Psychological Association in 1956, Cronbach showed the massive place of quantitative method in the whole structure of modern psychology. Cronbach's analysis implied that systematic quantitative thinking was even more of the basic substance or essence of modern psychology than was experimental or other inductive methodology. As the slogan of the Psychometric Society expresses it, the trend and aim of scientific psychology is to create a "quantitative rational science," and of course, the realization of this whole trend in our own day lies in the preoccupation with the construction of mathematical models.

NUMBER IN MODERN PSYCHOLOGY

No form of psychology can escape this mathematical thrust. We may think of it as the very essence of the modern quest for truth, almost as Plato did; or we may think of it as a force which, hand in hand with materialist atomism and mechanism, debases our ideal and distorts our vision. But normative judgments of these types do not seem to impede too greatly the spread of mathematics which is so deeply ingrained in our modern way of thinking. Indeed Freud, whose thinking is as radically qualitative as any you could devise, made more and more of the economic principle with its quantitative approach to the resolution of conflict, and his invention of the polarities and of systems of three's may well represent the same cathexis upon numbers, the same love of abstract quantitative relationships, which is the very essence of Pythagoreanism.

Gestalt psychology began protesting against atomism and mechanism, yet found very early in Köhler's doctrine of the physical gestalt, the tendency of organismic operations to take the simplest mathematical form, leading on to the generalization of the principles of prägnanz and the law of closure, which tell us why, in a complex and heterogeneous field, the relatively simple, ordered, symmetrical, rhythmic, or structured will tend to press its way in, and to press out the components of randomness, confusion, or noise, which have the same stimulus intensity, but are doomed to vastly less effective roles in biological and psychological life. The mathematical obsession, or aspiration—however you view it—has seeped and percolated, pressed forward and invaded everything in psychology. Laws, however stated, soon became quantitative laws; as in Thorndike's dictum: "Whatever exists must exist in some quantity, and therefore can be measured."

In Heinz Werner's magnificent developmental system, at first the global or undifferentiated world is not ready for number; at the second level it is a world of identifiable and measurable components; at the third level these components find articulate and structured relations, one with another, and we have the quantitative, the quasi-geometrical system which universal science would expect. We look everywhere now for isomorphism between physical, physiological, and psychological realities, assuring ourselves—possibly correctly, though we do not know for sure—that number and number systems apply equally to the object, to the subject, to the cosmos, and to the person, to the infinitely large and to the infinitely small.

I have moved ahead rapidly in praise of the Pythagoreans because I believe that we seldom realize the enormous dependence upon them which is characteristic of our work as psychologists, and the enormous strength of the preoccupation with numbers which feed in, together with a reality principle, to make psychology one special kind of number system. I would simply ask, as objectively as I know how, and without knowing the answer: "Are we overinvested in number?" There is not the slightest doubt that number theory and number preoccupation helps us towards the discovery of many kinds of reality. There is likewise no doubt that number leads into various types of mysticism which become so fascinating, so enriching, and so sustaining that one finds it difficult indeed to come back to the world of plain things and the immediate world to be dealt with. Number mysticism makes us believe that symmetry, order, rhythm have direct predictive power as to what will be actually observed. It has often led us astray. The colossal achievement of Fechner, for example, produced a colossal scientific and a colossal mystical output. Several decades of cautious inductive work have shown the great limitations in time and place upon Fechner's generalizations.

DISCONTINUITY

But I have another grave question to put regarding the adequacy of the formulation which I have used. I have not distinguished between number theory and quantitative theory. Of course, all of us must recognize the principles of continuity and discontinuity. We know that people, for example, come in whole numbers, and we laugh when the statistician tells us that there are 2.3 children in the average family, or that you have a certain fractional chance of dying of cancer. The very nature of the mathematical operations, however, which have followed from the practical art of measurement, and likewise from the beautiful methods of Newton and his followers, have represented the real as continuous and continuity as the only modality of a true science. We teach our pupils about continuities, linear relationships, normal curves. Nature may hate a vacuum, but not more intensely than we hate the gaps which would appear from discontinuous distributions, or in particular from true quantum principles. The profound revolution in physics, coming from Max Planck's discovery of a constant "h" in black-body radiation, which has served as a prototype for unit thinking, whole number thinking in so much of modern physics, has almost completely passed psychology by. We have, in our devotion to the mathematics of the continuum, forgotten—or almost forgotten—the Pythagoreans' adoring attitude toward whole numbers. We have forgotten that nature—that is, the siderial universe, and our own Mother Earth—and life, including amoeba and man, that psychology—including perception, memory, emotion, and thought—often come in chunks. Very often when properly observed, these identifiable chunks are discontinuous from other chunks. Some of these chunks happen to be called whole individuals, and we have idiographic as well as nomothetic methods to employ. But there are many discontinuities also *within* the individual, many potential "split brain monkeys" lurking within our own inner selves and sometimes becoming painfully manifest.

The quantum principle, dating from the year 1900, may manifest itself in large units, or in small. Planck's discovery appears to indicate that action comes in unit packages, as we might expect from the new electron theory which just preceded it. I do not believe we have yet fully grasped the importance of this principle in behavior study, or in the analysis of our immediate awareness. The all-or-nothing law in neurophysiology and the related all-or-nothing law which applies to rods, cones, and receptors generally, gives discrete psychophysiological units which are concealed behind the misleading appearance of continuity. S. S. Stevens won the Warren Prize for demonstrating the quantal basis of pitch. As Mary Shirley showed, growth is a matter of "saltatory" chunks, unit spurts, behind the maturation process. Affectivity, fears, rages, and other dynamic processes come in quantum terms when first excited, and it may well be that the affective life really comes in psychophysiological integer units too. There are, in personality structure and in the social order, stupid stubborn lines which say: "Thou shalt not cross." In fact, everywhere in society there are discontinuities so enormous that you can wonder, when you look at them, how a speaker could have taken two-thirds of his time assuming the universality of continuities.

The heart of the difficulty appears to lie in misunderstanding the process of abstracting. Whole numbers are an abstraction. The "threeness" which is present in three apples and three pears is not apprehended at the lowest sensory level, but at the level of cognition. If, by using the word *real* we mean that you can operate rationally, construct systems, and make predictions on the basis of whole numbers thus abstracted, the numbers are certainly real. They are, of course, one step away from sensory reality; one step towards some other kind of reality. If you speak of the square root of three, you are carrying out a further abstraction: You are asking what can happen if two equal quantities multiplied by one another give three; then you can perfectly well go on to emphasize that the square roots of negative numbers—which involve a still *further* abstracting process—can be multiplied by one another and come back giving the less puzzling reality of a whole negative number. There may be abstractions upon abstractions, and the abstracting process can itself be real. Sometimes after many such abstractions we come back and stub our toes upon simple sensory realities which have been predicted through these abstractions. I am not inveighing against the abstractions as unreal, or the process of manipulating them as scientifically unsound. On the contrary, I am endeavoring to justify higher-order abstractions by the same process of legitimization which applies to simpler, lower-order abstractions.

But there is always, in science, a further empirical test. If you come back from a simple factoring job with two answers, one of which is the square root of a positive number, and the other of which is the square root of a negative number, you have every reason to say that the intellect must choose one as a real answer to your problem and reject the other. In exactly the same way if the real examination of evidence shows discontinuity as one possibility, and continuity as another, it is an empirical question which one will fit the facts. I am raising the question whether we are aware of this in contemporary psychology. We have a strong tendency to believe that continuities are in some sense real, that linear relations and normal distributions, multiple-factor analysis, and most of the machinery of calculation, and inherently the normalization, the linearization, the adjustment of data through the use of inverse squares, and of logarithmic restatement of bizarre distribution forms, are all carried out in the name of intelligibility, and ultimately in the name of truth. The result is, of course, that we force data sometimes slightly, but sometimes profoundly, into channels which are conceived to make them more real, but can only in fact make them less real in the sense of confronting nature as she is. My statistical friends frequently remind me that the fundamental methods of dealing with discontinuous data in the biological sciences are very primitive and grossly incomplete. The result is that we forget the quantum principle which Schrödinger emphasizes in his definition of life and of evolution; we turn away from the discontinuities and the pure numbers, the step functions, or jump processes with which nature is so full—so full indeed that the theory of the electron, the theory of the cell, the theory of the individual, would all be utterly confused if we insisted upon continuities. What we have done, in the light of mathematics since the seventeenth century, is to defy the fundamental sense in Pythagorean number theory and to rely almost wholly upon those higher-order abstractions which make use of continuities, linearities, and "normalities" which nature so often contradicts. It is not the mathematics that is intellectually crippling, nor can mathematics ever take the side of one metaphysical proposition against another; but the use of mathematics can become blind, as can any tool revealed by the sociology of knowledge.

MODERN "NUMBER MYSTICISM"

My task has been to suggest our enormous emotional investment or cathexis in numbers; not just the danger of looking for discontinuities and quantum principles when they do not exist, but the very much greater danger that we look for higher-order abstractions relating to numbers rather than respecting empirical stepwise or quantum numerical realities with which nature is shot through. It is only the empirical use of Pythagorean number theory, only the investigation of the tough problem whether nature is working in terms of units or continua, that can save us from the pitfalls inherent in the assumptions of modern psychology. Fifty years ago psychology unwittingly turned at the crossroads in the direction of continuity theory, but the issue is not really closed and if wrong decisions have been made they can be reconsidered.

Over and above the general cathexis upon numbers and ways of manipulating them, psychology is, of course, shot through with preference for specific numbers. A p value, for example, at a significance level of .05 is significant, but at .06 is not significant, I suppose because few of us have six fingers. Here we have misplaced the discontinuity, that is, where there is a real continuity we have made a gulf between the .05 and the .06, or indeed for certain problems, the .01 rather than the .02. When I was a graduate student at Columbia, a critical ratio had to be three and a doctor's dissertation had to report a nonsignificant difference between two means if the critical ratio was only 2.7. There had to be 30 subjects to make possible the use of a Pearson correlation coefficient. Despite the nonlinearities with which nature is so replete, we may not use the assumptions about eta or nonlinear relations unless we have really massive evidence against linearity.

It would, of course, take us further into metaphysics to ask whether there is more than our own human ways of thinking that produces this universality of mathematical laws to be found in science—whether, in short, the world is, in reality, ordered mathematically. If you are as much of a Pythagorean as I am, you have to believe that it is; but if you are as critical as you ought to be, you have to balk. Neither science nor metaphysics is ready to say anything final on this issue.

There is, however, one profound question from the time of the Pythagoreans, and very much alive today, which we do have to attempt briefly to answer in conclusion. This is the question of the isomorphism, the ultimate unity of the rhythms and symmetries, the quantitative laws of our life, and the rhythms and symmetries of stars and oceans, cells and electrical particles which emerge from scientific study. Research in the biology and psychology of the last few decades has shown a rich abundance of quantitatively known behavior principles, principles of perception, memory, and thought which make up, as I said, a fair part of modern psychology. As in the case of Fechner's "outer psychophysics" and "inner psychophysics," and as in the case of Köhler's physical *Gestalten*, the laws which describe the *within* also describe the *without*.

ISOMORPHISM

It is not simply a question of one system of realities fitting another. It is a question, apparently, of their being one and the same. Isomorphism or identity of form forces us to the recognition that the same reality of adaptation, or learning, or forgetting, or generalization, or whatever it is, appears in different levels of observation because it is simply the same reality which is refracted through different media. That the curve of forgetting looks like the curve of declining gas pressure as more and more elements are lost is not an odd coincidence, but a statement that parabolic declines of this sort are a mathematical necessity for particles free from outside interference. James Miller and his collaborators have been undertaking, with some success, to show that the same basic laws apply at different levels in nature, and as in Herbert Spencer's and Heinz Werner's broad evolutionary schemes, we may say that the mathematical order is the same in all these different contexts for the simple reason that there are cosmic universals relating to observable realities in general, and to the mathematics of their change in time. Psychology will thus become isomorphic with physiology, with psychoanalysis, with linguistic and moral change and development insofar as there are observables subject to the same possibilities of measurement. If this be mystical, make the most of it. If it be materialistic, make the most of it. This is not the first time in history that the mystical and the materialistic have both been suspected under the cover of a very broad groping generalization. Such ideas are fascinating, but, of course, likewise dangerous. Pythagoreans had to flee despots because their secret society was dangerous. But my point is that they really *were* dangerous. There is no deity that we worship more abjectly today than number theory in its two-theory form, the quantum and the continuity form. It would be wise to know at which shrine we are worshipping in each of our scientific endeavors, and to know, in the last analysis, what we think of the strange prophetic figure who defined both these deities, and apparently worshipped them both. I should like to conclude with a quotation from one of the great biologists of this century, D'Arcy Thompson (1952):

A "principle of discontinuity," then, is inherent in all our classifications, whether mathematical, physical or biological; and the infinitude of possible forms, always limited, may be further reduced and discontinuity further revealed by imposing conditions—as, for example, that our parameters must be whole numbers, or proceed by *quanta*, as the physicists say. The lines of the spectrum, the six families of crystals, Dalton's atomic law, the chemical elements themselves, all illustrate this principle of discontinuity. In short, nature proceeds *from one type to another* among organic as well as inorganic forms; and these types vary according to their own parameters, and are defined by physico-mathematical conditions of possibility. In natural history Cuvier's "types" may not be perfectly chosen nor numerous enough, but *types* they are; and to seek for stepping-stones across the gaps between is to seek in vain, for ever [p. 1094].

REFERENCES

No. 40 plays unusual role. *Grit*. (Family section) 1966, July 3, 26.
Thompson, D'A. W. *On growth and form*. Vol. 2. (2nd ed.) Cambridge: Harvard University Press, 1952.

42

Encounter with Reality

GARDNER MURPHY

Last time I suggested that man is skillful indeed in deceiving himself by rejecting the evidence from his senses; yet that he can learn through the use of his muscles to welcome more evidence. Today I shall expand this theme, arguing that the experimental psychology of the messages from the interior of the body is rapidly writing a new chapter in the psychology of personality. Most of these suggestions will appear in a forthcoming book entitled *Encounter with Reality*. I hope for your critical suggestions, especially from the perception and cognition research people here.

Any psychology of perception concerned *exclusively* with the response to the structure of the external environment is just half of the total world with which perception is concerned. Eddington notes that the human body is, in a sense, half way between the smallest, and the largest things of which we have knowledge, namely, the electron and the sidereal universe; in the sense that the body contains about 10^{29} electrical particles, and the number in the human body would have to be raised to about 10^{29} to represent the number of particles in the universe. However this may be, man is, in a sense, the measure of all things; at least, from his own point of view, a geometric mean between the infinitely little and the infinitely big.

We can no longer in these days of biology, medicine, and Claude Bernard's "inner environment," write as if reality were simply a knowable thing or process *outside of us*. The knowing process reaches in, and finds that there is just as much complexity, just as much that eludes us, yet calls for scrutiny, as there is at the astronomical level. The reflector telescope is a powerful engine, but so is the electron microscope. That is what is meant by saying that exactly half of the problem of the real lies within.

Here Bleuler with his magnificent introduction to the world of self-deception, the inner world which he called "de-realist," somehow missed the boat. For him the process of "autistic thinking" is the process by which a real outer world is distorted or "de-realized" by inner dynamics. But we likewise distort our view of the *inner* world; indeed, the inner world is both

From Murphy, G. Encounter with Reality. Paper presented at George Washington University, Washington, D.C., November 17, 1967. Published here by permission of the author. See Gardner Murphy and Herbert E. Spohn, Encounter with Reality. Boston, Houghton Mifflin, 1968.

the "distorter" and the "distorted." And to add another paradox, the inner world, as Hebb and Berlyne and many others are showing, has its own craving for reality, and may sweep away the illusions begotten by defective perceptual processes. There is no eternal alliance between the "inner" and the "unreal." The problem of learning to perceive, to understand, and to use the *inner real* is as fundamental as the problem of coping with the *outer real*. Cognitive confusion is a failure of the knowing process, and it fails just as much through defect in grasping what is within, as through defect in grasping what is without.

Fully as important as the feedback studies from striped muscles, which I mentioned earlier, and probably even *more* important, are the studies of the process of getting direct information from one's own brain rhythms, first the *alpha* and then apparently a wide gamut of EEG responses. Joe Kamiya, of Langley Porter at San Francisco, has developed operant control of one's own alpha. The subject begins by blindly striving to get into the right internal state, and is taught to succeed as if this were a motor skill. Kamiya is rapidly moving into a systematic study of the processes of inner control. Here again feedback is important. Its limits, in opening up man's control, are hard to define. Kamiya, moreover, is systematically comparing each EEG rhythm with its own internally recognizable psychological process; the pattern that prevails while perceiving, remembering, experiencing affect and effort, etc.

The thoughtful critic may reply that from the very beginning the world within is a world of *disorder*, while the world from without is a world of *order*, as know by science. Surely, however, this world within is being rapidly sorted out with all the remarkable techniques of modern genetics, embryology, physiology, biochemistry, and "input" from inner vegetative and muscular sources. Surely it has been found that the world without owes its orderliness in considerable degree to the imposition upon it of those structured thinking principles which have arisen just as much from the inner necessities as from the outer pressures.

EGO ON THE BRIDGE BETWEEN INNER AND OUTER

Similarly, the question may be raised: If both "outer" and "inner" are subject to systematic and objective scrutiny, where is the "knowing" consciousness located and what are the conditions under which objectivity about both worlds of information may be achieved? In partial answer we may rely upon David Rapaport's formulation of the issue. The ego—the organized expression of human individuality—utilizes the instinctual energies, but at the same time guides the executive functions which make possible both the mastery of impulse within and of behavior without. It can achieve autonomy only if the turbulent surge of the world within can be kept at bay, while at the same time the overwhelming and crushing weight of external stimulation can be blocked. It can succeed only if firm testing of reality—sifting, sorting, and controlling of its energies, development of buffer systems equal to the stress—can be built up through the long social-ization process. There is a tiny node of security, and even of power, for the ego, if it can keep at bay both of the crushing systems which strive to im-pose their massive force upon it.

It is a delicate balance that the ego maintains. Harold Voth, in con-templating the modern typologies which have classified personalities in terms of their closeness to the outer environment or their tendency to fall back upon the inner environment, has developed the concepts "ego dis-tant" and "ego close." He has shown, by systematic clinical interviewing, and by means of the Rorschach test, and especially by means of the Auto-kinetic test, that subjects can be arranged in a series from extremely "ego close" to extremely "ego distant." In the Autokinetic test ego-distant peo-ple can build their far-away fantasies as the light moves; ego-close people, concerned with the outer reality of a stationary light, keep the movement severely limited, or block the movement altogether. Of this, more later.

In American life it has been rather bad form to uphold too vigorously the reality of the world within, for two reasons: (1) the strenuous tasks of a geographically expanding and industrially growing society make external contacts more reputable than internal; (2) the fact that instruments de-vised to make observation more accurate—the extended eye of the micro-scope, the extended ear of the hearing aid, the resonator, the electronic pick up—have given us more precision up to the present moment, than the sensory processes within us have so far discovered alone.

Perhaps this is because we *wish it to be so*. Perhaps by means of the mechanisms of turning away, undoing, denial, and the other principles by which we refuse close attention, and especially close analysis, we turn from that which threatens the integrity of our ego, including this world of inner experience. It may indeed be, by virtue of the very principles just quoted above from David Rapaport, that we stand on guard not only against the massive force of the inner world, but against getting acquainted with its inhabitants, its component parts. Perhaps we would feel overwhelmed if we knew the inhabitants too closely. Perhaps the process of placing a taboo, especially upon the broad gamut of the experiences which Freud calls libid-inal, would make the process of differentiation a sin or a crime, or at least an expression of bad taste. Perhaps condemnation is added to initial clumsi-ness and to the negative reinforcements or punishments which have come when one sees that which is socially disreputable, or at least personally re-pugnant to parents. We think, for example, of the little boy in Hans Anderson's story of the "Emperor's New Clothes." There is surely more to it than this: Perhaps all these factors and more too, are involved in our habitual denial of reality to the very real *real* of the inner world.

Certainly related to all these mechanisms, by which we keep ourselves from sharp perception of the inner world stands the process which Else Frenkel-Brunswik called "tolerance and intolerance of ambiguity." To some of us an illusion or even a mild hallucination is mildly intriguing, or a bit challenging. To others, because the thing is both real and unreal, it is ambiguous; and because ambiguous, intolerable. The horseman shown in a pattern of lights may be shown as he jumps from one point to another with the throwing on or off of the requisite electrical switches. To some, because it is well-known that this horseman is "really" sitting there in the etched outline of the figure, and it is certain that he can *not* be jumping, the experience is disagreeable indeed. If a careful count is made, the horseman spends a good deal less time in the air for such an observer than for the observer who has less intolerance of ambiguity. The concept of intolerance of ambiguity is a convenient one in the classification of persons for whom the real is the objective external order with "no nonsense about it," while the kind of flexibility described here under the term "intolerance of ambiguity" is convenient in reference to the habit of assigning a large number of experiences to the doubtful region of a sort of second-class reality.

HOW THE "INNER" IS PERCEIVED

But there is another reason for failure to evaluate and even to observe the world within. This lies in the nature of the thresholds of perception. It is a habit of psychologists to define thresholds in terms of the amounts of stimulation required to set a sensory process going. The "all-or-none law" often means in practice that the impact of a given energy upon a receptor fails to achieve a value starting the wave of excitation passing along the afferent fiber towards the brain; while a bit more would have done the trick, triggering the nerve fiber, getting the message through to the second component in the relay, and perhaps the third, and perhaps the fourth. Different receptors have different thresholds—the thresholds for pain, for example, are very low—and the threshold varies from one part of the body to another. Now the different limits are rather high in the inner sensory life of man, at least for the warmth, cold, and pressure detected in the interior, and for those diffuse experiences associated with hunger, thirst, oxygen need, sex need, and fatigue, malaise, and the stimuli associated with "mood." The affective states are much like these inner sensations in some ways. They are "massive" rather than "precise"; they are like the "protopathic" rather than the "epicritic" experiences found when a severed nerve in the arm makes possible a differentiation of sensations. The experiences of disgust, delight, surprise, amusement seem like varieties of sensations, and the sexual has often been called "sensuous" on the grounds that sensory values make up a large part of the experience.

It is worth noting in this connection, however, that Soviet physiologists have made precise studies of numerous "interoceptors" in the visceral organs of animals and man. Such interoceptors differ anatomically and respond selectively to differing types of stimulation. In an early attempt at demonstrating interoceptive two-point discrimination, Marakov found that human subjects could differentiate rapid, successive electrical stimulation of gastric mucosa 8 cm. apart. It should be clear, therefore, that an anatomical and physiological basis for fairly fine discrimination of interoceptive sensation exists. It may be that our high threshold levels for such sensation and its differentiation are in part functional for reasons suggested above.

A great deal of the inner sensory world varies hour by hour through a range well below thresholds for good description, as our moods vary. Even moods which last so long that we call them "temperament" are like inner sensations but crude, coarse, hard to observe, and certainly hard to evaluate. When we try to report on what we mean by a cheerful temperament, or what we mean if we say that this morning we are cheerful but by afternoon we will be glum again, we seem to be dealing with complex *interpretations* rather than with descriptions of sensory data. Schachter reported that the same biochemical and physiological upheaval was *perceived* by different observers with different meanings, and so constituted different emotions. We may in fact have a great deal of massive, sub-threshold excitation going on all the time. Relatively little of it takes sensory form even when the trained observer tries to find evidence of specific "organic" sensations. A person may act as if he were thirsty, or a habitual smoker may act in an obvious way with reference to his tobacco need, without having been conscious of the need state. Clark Hull's pipe-smokers, after the smoking "satisfaction" from sham pipes which they thought were filled, "lit up" as they left the laboratory. A person may, even without benefit of repression, respond to massive visceral tension—appetitive or aversive—while not knowing at all (at the conscious level) that this is so.

INTEROCEPTIVE STIMULATION AND THE "SENSE OF REALITY"

Now there is a very special reason for considering here these rich and varied types of sub-threshold inner excitation. For the "sense of reality" is to a large degree determined by the elaboration of this kind of sensory experience. From Pierre Janet and his "memories which are too real" to the modern psychoanalytically oriented psychiatrist's concern with "unreality feelings" as related to "depersonalization," there is evidence that awareness of the real is itself partly an expression of the subthreshold condition in the interior of the trunk, especially the cardiovascular and gastrointestinal systems. A swimming head or a growling stomach may mean that "nothing is real today." At another extreme, the experience of intense or incandescent reality, associated with some types of religious or esthetic mysticism and with some modern drug investigations, may accentuate the sharpness of definition to a point where both the inner and the outer cosmos of reality reach by a wide margin their highest intensity, their sharpest definition, as the "very real," just because the exteroceptive definition of the world is both controlled and submerged by the messages from within.

A medical friend, experimenting with drugs which enabled the red blood cells to carry far more oxygen than usual, coined the expression "ferric consciousness," (pertaining to iron) by which he intended to convey that the sharpness, the intensity, the meaning of reality was no longer dependent upon sheer neurophysiological function, but was expressly the product of the *iron* of the red blood cells capable of carrying this overload of oxygen. For him, from the flattest to the sharpest affective level in daily life is but a hand's breadth compared to the *ocean-like* distance between nonferric and ferric consciousness. This fancy, or whimsy, led him to choose a chemical symbol to show how far his psychological state differed from those known to most men.

But whereas the reality described by such mystics depends partly on inner processes, it is usually not directly experienced as an inner process. Rather, it tends to be oriented to an outer cosmos. When one looks more closely, one begins to doubt whether these experiences of supernal reality could be as intense if the experiencer were *looking* at his interoceptive activities. He would, at any rate, have to learn to observe them by lowering their thresholds, and by developing a progressive conceptual differentiation, like a tea taster, or a wine sampler, learning to pick out faint elements of "aroma" or "bouquet," which are beyond the capacity of the novice. It is possible that this type of analytical and perceptual training would actually weaken or destroy the perceptual wholes, or at any rate, their meaning. Here again, it is too early to be sure. We have not trained the experiencer to describe this kind of experience as the tea taster and wine sampler are trained. What is more safely said is that we differentiate, look at, and compare piece by piece and phase by phase, while the interoceptive world is generally massive, relatively undifferentiated, and relatively unchallenging to the perceptive eye of curiosity. The exteroceptive is easy to *share*, the interoceptive hard to share.

INTERNAL SCANNING

But evidence has been coming in to indicate that many of us carry out a continuous process of internal scanning, exactly as we carry out the process of external scanning. The most obvious case is the infant's or child's —or adult's—watching his own dream, a process recognized by the brilliant insight of Kleitman as he observed horizontal rapid eye movements behind the eye lids of a sleeping infant. We know today that dreams are scanned just as outer worlds are scanned, and that memory materials are scanned by horizontal eye movement, very much in the way that the hallucinatory material of dreams is scanned. We know indeed that the power and the delicacy of visual seeking and scanning movements is employed with regard to those maps and designs for living which some of us utilize in planning the day or the life well in advance. We know that failure to relax and to go to sleep is often expressed in the inability or unwillingness to give up the eager nervous eye movements directed towards the precious things of the imagination which we cannot give up or even allow to go to their rest.

There may be a paradox here. We are beginning to concern ourselves with internal scanning, but we are *still* describing exteroceptive organs. We look within; we look at dreams and memories. But when we want more evidence than sight can afford, we listen, as did Socrates, to an inner voice. We bring back the voice of father and mother. Or indeed, when we become frightened or anxious, we may, in auditory hallucinations, make real to ourselves the threats or accusations which once came from without and now come from within us. Somehow, then, though we are talking about an inner world, the machinery of exteroception is involved.

Even this statement, however, seems to miss a fundamental point. It is not literally the eyes or the ears that perform the act of scanning. It is a more central, or organismic *act* of attending. *Look* at some bright object in the room, but attend to something quite different. You will find—and many a laboratory investigator has confirmed and made more specific what you can observe in the first ten seconds of your own experiment—that to attend is a more complex process than to look or to listen. You look at the foci but *attend* to the verbal explanation. It makes use of the peripheral machinery in the organs of sense, but the central process is to attend, as James has pointed out, by *drawing objects into the center of clearest awareness*. This is what you do with interoceptive material whether you are looking or not. You have some vague internal distress. It may be difficult to tell what it is, or even where it is. But the internist who has to decide whether there is something seriously wrong or not, may have to press, both in a literal and in a metaphorical sense, to find out what it is; and the night after you see him, as you review the experience, you may find yourself, in your internal scanning, doing relatively little with your eyes or ears, and a great deal with the attending processes. Through them you bring back the pressure, strain, warm, cold, and pain experiences which you described as well as you could to the doctor. You recapitulate such sensations, mark off, sunder one from another, emphasize, regroup, reinterpret, making sense as well as you can out of this material by a rich internal scanning, focusing, and reporting process. There seem to be profound individual differences in the disposition to internal scanning, as compared with external. Harold Voth, with his ego-close and ego-distant patients, must offer each one a *near* or a *far-away* handle, so to speak, suitable to his patients' grasping hands.

"INPUT" FROM THE BRAIN

Up to this point we have been describing input from receptors, and have said almost nothing at all about the types of input which have recently yielded to experimental study through *direct stimulation of the brain,* especially in the conscious subject under local anesthesia. Penfield and his collaborators, operating on patients subject to convulsive disorders, have brought back specific memories over and over again from the excitation of the same spot in the cerebral cortex. Most of the studies have to do with patients in whom excision of brain tissue has been determined because of their proneness to convulsions. In general, however, the course of the experimentation seems to run smoothly, with no evidence of any abnormal state in the patient at the time of the electrical excitation. Upon exposure of the temporal lobe cortex to a specific stimulus, one gets the sudden arousal of memories, as for example the following:

J. T. was startled when, as the result of temporal stimulation, he heard, as he lay in the operating room, the voices of his "cousins Bessie and Ann Wheliow," so that he cried out, "Yes, Doctor, yes, Doctor. Now I hear people laughing—my friends, in South Africa." It was obvious that this experience seemed to him different from an ordinary recollection. It forced itself upon his attention suddenly and unexpectedly.

When he reconsidered the matter a fortnight later, he said it had seemed to him that he was with his cousins and that they were all laughing together at something, although he could not say what the subject of their merriment might be. The recollection, as far as it went, was vivid and detailed.

These experiences although the description may suggest a hallucinatory state, are experienced by the subject as vivid memories, more vivid than he could arouse by his own effort. Yet such memories are in no way capable of confusion with the actual "here and now" reality of the operating room, the table on which he lies, and the situation of the experiment involving its conversation with the surgeon. One seems to have here a remarkable instance of direct contact with the past as mediated by memory, which would ordinarily require the roundabout means of a verbal inquiry and similar to the direct excitation of affect through the pleasure centers, as contrasted with the more roundabout way of exciting affect by stimulating the skin or the viscera.

But the concept of making contact with time in an unusual way comprises a deeper and more complex reality, which Penfield and his collaborators have sketched out, namely the fact that there is a general proneness to time disorientation in persons subject to temporal lobe-type convulsions. In his chart, the person in whom these memories were elicited by excitation of regions 15 and 16 was also subject to the experience of "having been there before," known to psychiatry as *déjà vu*. There is much to suggest that the temporal lobe is, in a certain sense, a specialized center for orientation to time, space, and person, and orientation in time has been studied in a variety of ways through the examination of lesions in many patients and through post-mortem examinations of those whose brains did not function properly in time orientation. These feelings of "having been there before" involve indeed, from present evidence, direct light on the mechanism of orientation in time, for the subject may have, at the critical moment of excitation, the feeling that he has gone through this particular experience before and that the surgeon is about to take some specific step. There is, in other words, convincing evidence of time disorientation with its specific cerebral locus, and under conditions where manifestly the patient has not been in that situation before.

Now the important thing for us, from this viewpoint, is the disorder in reality testing which appears: The subjects feels as if all this had happened before, just as he feels on direct excitation of a "memory center" in the temporal lobe that he were reliving a disturbing experience such as the one described earlier. There is, in other words, a disturbance in the ability to estimate his own position in time. It is not just a question of the expansion or contraction of time as we know it from the study of drug effects, such as those from hashish; rather, it is a radical shifting of the person to a different stance, a different point in the time flow. What is often most real in such experiences is denied by the kind of reality emphasized in the study of clock time by the experimental scientist. There are two or more time systems. William James has referred to this kind of double consciousness effect, and it has been rather elaborately studied from the pharmacological point of view.

All this seems to mean that on the screen of reality, used constantly by the subject to check his own position, there may be memory-feedback failures, essentially like the visual-feedback failures mentioned earlier, and also the spatial and other orientation failures for which the proprioceptive system may be responsible. As Snyder and Pronko have shown, the subject who has had long experiences with an unreal visual world may feel certain as to what is real, although it is belied by other lines of evidence from his own sense organs and from those of others. The overwhelming conviction that one system of reality is real, and another less real or not real at all, seems intimately related to a time-space orientation process. We are not quite ready to say that there is a "center for reality testing" nor indeed, in somewhat more mystical language, to say that there is a "reality center." Rather, we are ready to say that reality as encountered may go through myriad qualitative and quantitative changes, and that it will be necessary to incorporate findings of this sort in our ultimate interpretation as to what man really does when he "makes contact with reality." Experiences of *déjà vu* suggest a timing fault with reference to the memory process—a mixed reality of present and past which cannot rationally exist.

As a matter of fact, we learn to duplicate clinical anomalies of this sort by the experimental process of intersecting one time with another, or intersecting time with a space dimension which does not belong to it. An extreme illustration is the commando device of World War II, somewhat similar to the brainwashing device reported in connection with the mainland Chinese techniques of remaking personality: The inquisitor finds a way of consistently denying or misrepresenting memories of the prisoner's past, one's earlier or deeper convictions; skillfully and continuously a different past is fed in. There is no mail; there are no visits to correct the impressions which are funneled in, and a large part of the past is successfully replaced with a pseudo-past which, in time, takes on the quality of reality, because it is consistent within itself and consistent with the immediate exteroceptive environment. Orwell's *1984* is an extrapolation from existing possibilities.

It is possible to formulate, from the viewpoint of "information theory," the quantitative relations between various forms of information input and the corresponding reduction of error. This is important from an engineering and data processing viewpoint, but it will probably turn out to have very much broader psychological implications. It is likely that in the effort to restate the process of communication, in highly abstract quantitative forms, and the attempt to organize education grade by grade and process by process, in terms of feedback theory, there may be a restatement of the modalities by which the individual may approximate to a working truth or reality through some "law of least action." It is indeed possible likewise that each social group, or even humanity at large, may find an individualized path leading towards the reality based upon the specifics and the generalities of such utilization of feedback. It would ill behoove an effort of the present sort to belittle the enormous possibilities which may come our way as a result of these rapid changes.

Yet from the point of view of the psychology of man as far as we understand him today, there is a very large dimension missing in such an approach, a dimension starting with some elementary data of motivation, and extending to a study of the way in which motivation sensitizes us to certain kinds of data processing, including data processing relating to the very nature of the motivation itself. Feedback of this sort could be of huge importance.

J. J. Gibson's extraordinary new book, *The Senses Considered as Perceptual Systems*, pushes hard in the direction of replacing the sensation-centered approach by an information-theory approach. He succeeds remarkably well in writing perceptual theory in information-theory terms. Yet it seems to me that the wedding of information theory with an evolutionary organismic theory does not quit come off. For it remains to work through the relation of the *drive* system, including the *cognitive* drives, to the sensory registration patterns. Indeed the transfer of perceptual habits from one situation to another, so fundamental for personality theory, must wait upon this wedding of the motivational with the informational components in the dynamics of the act of perceiving.

But we have left out the role of the *self*. There are two reasons why the problem of the real enters a new phase with the first reference to the self. Things are not just perceived; they are perceived in relation to the *self*. Things are not just remembered; they are remembered in terms of a place, an act, and a feeling that they belong to the *self*. Things are not just expected or anticipated; they are activities in which the self will be involved. All reality has a self reference. The second reason lies in the fact that the heightening of the sense of reality and the heightening of the sense of self are intimately related. Experiences of depersonalization and derealization are closely related. The concepts and the methods applicable to training in the reduction of self awareness—such as hypnosis, yoga, and the psychedelic drugs—sometimes produce the strange sense that all is unreal, or on the contrary, a sense that all is intensely *real* at a level where we are not sure how useful the epithets *real* and *unreal* are. At any rate, "self" and "real" are two terms that seem to pulsate or whirl in our diction; they refuse to stand put. We cannot talk about the real without talking about the self. This becomes especially clear when we encounter not *loss* of reality or *loss* of selfhood, but a tremendous *intensification* of both in various types of spontaneously or deliberately inculcated awareness of reality. Some people, wishing to drown the awareness of reality, drink; others drink to apprehend a reality not otherwise attainable. William James reminds us that nitrous oxide may yield an enormous intensity of *affirmation*.

As sensory data are used in meaningful integrations called percepts, they have a dynamic exactly such as J. F. Herbart supposed, an internal dynamic or cohesion, resisting disturbance, and an external dynamic, involving outer energy relations. At times these are simple push and pull relations; at times the more integrative and disruptive, or consonant and dissonant relationships. From this point of view, the self is the richest and most complex of the perceptual systems. It is highly flexible, but it is also "ultra-stable." It is attended to a good deal of the time, but it controls behavior even when it is not attended to.

Like other perceptual systems, but to an extraordinarily high degree, it has the capacity to push other perceptual units aside. This, apparently because the love, fear, disgust, and other affectively toned attitudes directed towards it, are of such enormous force. Actually it is the dynamic of love of the image of one's own body, the sound of one's own voice, etc., which makes the self stand out so very prominently. It is not only the thing that is there most of the time in all our waking hours, or years, "overlearned," one might say, but it is likewise dynamically the primary center with reference to which other things are measured ("Man is the measure of all things"). It is also the perceptual unity which is most directly related to what we are carrying out, and therefore has almost unlimited and continuous reinforcement from other activities. This means that the self, by virtue of the cathexis, the investment in it, wins out in most competitions with other investments however precious. This is the case not solely because of some superficial role of daily social reinforcement, however important that may be, but because of the central position of the self image in the world of reality. From this point of view, the whole problem of voluntary attention which we considered, takes on a new light; for that which controls attention is, in large measure, that system of deep strong forces which stands ready forever to defend and enhance the self. One attends in order to defend oneself, to enhance oneself, to keep the world adequate in terms of the needs of the self. Voluntary attention is not just a kind of attention dependent upon the striped musculature such as the external eye muscles; rather, the striped muscles, whatever they may be in all the adjustive systems of the body, are perpetually at work helping to steer in directions which are salutary to the self; that is, response to the deep gratifications which come from all that favors the self or wards off threats against it. Voluntary attention is self-generated. It is not only concerned with the self a large part of the time, but it derives from self. There seems here to be a shortcut into the problem of what is real in this world: That is real which commends voluntary attention.

It is a fundamental thesis of psychoanalysis, confirmed by much experimental evidence that there is grave confusion in the little child between the desirable and the real, and that only slowly and with much distress in the learning process, does one come to the sober reflection that the wished-for is unreal and the ardently-to-be-rejected is the real. It does not take masses of experimental evidence to convince us in general that wishful perceiving, remembering, imagining, and thinking tend not only to bring us pleasant pastures, but that they do actually deceive us not uncommonly; they sing siren songs which we have known to be deceptive, but which we never learn fully to reject. Voluntary attention is then guided by two masters: a reality principle and a wish-fulfilling or primary process principle. Training in reality seeking must, in some measure, be training to accept the former rather than the latter.

But we are speaking as if voluntary attention and the whole massive role of the self which lies behind it were directed mainly to getting a consistent, practical, dependable view of the outer world. It is to almost exactly the same degree directed to getting a consistent and workable view of the *inner* world. One checks forever what one sees inside against other things that are to be seen inside, and any and all of these are to be checked against what is seen outside. The memory processes stand on the middle of the bridge, derived as they are both from prior exteroceptive and prior interoceptive experience, and inclining this way and that, now towards an emphasis upon fresh exteroceptive information—the seeking of new information—and at times asking whether one's appraisal of what is within is actually sound, correct, in harmony with what one deeply knows to be true. Here lies much of the problem of objectivity, and of conscience. This is a way of saying that there is the same struggle towards compactness, integration, internal consistency, and ultimate verification in the case of material within, as in the case of material without.

Those processes of active, attentive exploration, which we considered earlier under the terms *seeking* and *scanning*, apply likewise to the process of finding what is deeply acceptable to the self, and rejecting that which threatens it. This requires a "gating" process similar to the gating described earlier, but now organized in terms of a full-dress battle royal between our strongest inner tendencies and those magisterial forces, which, organized around the self, cannot accept any second, or equal terms from a competitor. The battle is usually "won," and the self image somehow maintained. There is, however, at times a vague awareness that something is wrong. There may be sleeplessness, restlessness, a need for drugs, compliments, excitement to keep the accusing voice of self disesteem from entering into clear awareness. Sometimes suspension on a knife-edge results in a sudden reversal of structure, and that which has been rejected and made to play the part of the unreal comes driving back in a whirlwind, and we encounter what Janet called "memories which are too real." For the most part this great overwhelming reversing process does not occur. For most men most of the time, the adage of Nietzsche would seem to suffice: "I did it, said my memory. I could not have done it, said my pride, and in the end my memory yields."

THE SELF AND COGNITIVE CONTROLS

The controls just described are habitual, affect-laden controls belonging to what we have called the self system. They are not altogether independent, however, of "cognitive controls," devices described by G. S. Klein, Riley Gardner, and others, to define the individual modalities of structuring the perceived world, the world remembered, thought about, imagined in a way which organizes, classifies, and makes sense out of the stimulus world in accordance with some personal idiom of interpretation. Objecting to the conception that affects, instincts, or impulses control what will be accepted and what will be rejected, they define the consistent individual differences which enable one individual to exclude what another cannot exclude, or to make fine distinctions when another can only make coarse distinctions in the same cognitive situation. Here they have a place both for blind and unaware modalities of differentiation, integration, emphasis, attention predilections for contrast or assimilation, etc., but also for the establishment of different ground rules which permit one person to go to a higher level before decisions are made, while another prefers to remain at a lower, simpler, or more homeostatic level. Cognitive controls then are ingrained and consistent ways of regulating the impact of information as decisions are made. There is room in the theory both for cognitive controls operating in a "conflict-free ego sphere"—providing for idiosyncrasies in the way in which perceptual, judgmental cognitive issues are handled—and also with reference to the manner in which instinctual or autistic components are allowed to enter the theater of cognitive interplay.

The task of living involves defining for oneself, within a sociocultural norm, a conception of what can be expected, a conception of how far it can be modified, a conception of how it can be transfigured by creative imagination. Reality is being perpetually edited. It is this editing of the real, this calling into existence of that which was only potentially there, and of turning back again into the potential that which a minute ago was real, that is the process both of facing the real and of creating the real.

From the present viewpoint there is always more. There is more stuff. There are more processes. There are more systems. There are more legitimate forms of conceptualization and abstraction as we discover more and more. The endless seeking, searching, scanning processes increase both the range and the depth of the real, both the number and variety of real things, and the levels of structure which the architecture of the universe may allow us to observe, until we strive to observe even the apex of the pyramid, the top architectural plan of the real as a whole. It is profoundly satisfying and self enhancing to do this, and this may be one of the things which make the cosmic experiences more joyous. If this should involve both the increasing range or extensity of the things and processes that are swept within our ken, and at the same time a deepening understanding of the problem of reality itself, we can literally say that there is some progress towards the real.

DETERMINANTS OF REALITY SEEKING

We believe the process is quite complex, and that the half-dozen factors which we have struggled to develop, even when used in combination, will still prove insufficient to do justice to the subtleties of this reality-seeking process. But we can make a preliminary inventory. The process certainly includes at least seven phases: (1) an expression of curiosity; (2) a shortcut to practical advantage; (3) the reassertion of ego and superego against the more primitive or infantile primary process thinking; (4) a step to regain one's position with the social group by accepting the truth for which they—our social environment—stand; (5) this is partly like the reversal of perspective which we saw above with the Necker cubes, or a case of figure-ground reversal based on satiation or boredom; but (6) at times, it is a fairly pure operant. Having tried everything else, we may try giving the situation a fresh looking over. (7) Certainly there is some of Sokolov's principle of pressure to reduce the gap between the inner model and the outer, or more broadly, the struggle towards achievement of an isomorphism of the inner and outer worlds, sheer strain or pressure in the sense of the exteroceptively challenging and inviting, all that it shares with the little inner homunculus isomorphic with it.

It is this aspect of self correction that offers the core possibility for greater human reality contact, greater penetration of realities, and the potentialities which may become realized. It is recognition, as William James said, that there is "always more," outgrowing the bonds of present self limitation for the apprehension of present reality, and developing that openness upon which the germinal—or not yet germinal—potentialities for new reals may come into existence. Just as we saw, with reference to generalized consequences of proprioceptive feedback, so we find here in more general terms that there can be progressive transfer and generalization to wider modes of apprehension.

It may be, as Berlyne suggests, that this is a matter of increasing arousal-alerting activation. One might think here of a very generalized physiological or biochemical increase in arousal level, like the strychninization that Sherrington described as having a generalized overall facilitating effect upon the central nervous system functions. It may be that there is such a thing as developing this kind of reality orientation. In fact it is even possible that the affirmation of nitrous oxide described above or the "wild surmise" of the climber of high peaks, or the mystic sense of "unutterable revelation" may all be connected with this kind of reality resonance—not only the real which can be independently shown to be real by other more sober methods, but the real which comes into existence as evolution goes on.

There may then be an increasingly generalized sensitization to the real, both in the sense of increased motivation or "love of the real," and in the sense of movement towards greater discriminating power, ultimately greater perceptual skill in making such contacts. It is likely that the development of such increasing skills will depend both upon the use of all the available help from learning theory in the generalization of these feedback skills, of discriminative skills generally, and also in the discovery of devices controlled from without or from within, by which the reality hunger and the reality contact skill can be intensified. Insofar as the correction of errors enters into the total progress, we seem to be on familiar territory, in the sense that this is a component in all learning. The unsuccessful components in the complex skill are dropped out. But in keeping with the evidence of recent decades we would believe that reward is, for the most part, more effective than punishment. It is not in stubbing one's toes on a tough unreality, or a plainly bad reality-seeking technique, that the chief learning lies. Rather, the main driving force is that which comes from the positive reinforcement of the satisfactions, the self enhancements that follow. Reality seeking can therefore become habitual not only at the segmental level, but at the level of a highly generalized attribute. Reality seeking may become a quality of the person as a person.

43

Development and Transfer
of Attentional Habits

GARDNER MURPHY,
JOHN F. SANTOS,
& CHARLES M. SOLLEY

The habits of attending which we develop have important implications for the effectiveness of a variety of behavior which we must perform each day. It is obviously necessary to be alert and attentive to the proper cues in order to learn in academic settings, avoid dangers, achieve our goals, and reduce our needs (Berlyne, 1954; Solley & Murphy, 1960). This is not to say, however, that our attentional habits cannot result in the avoidance or perceptual blurring of stimuli which are unimportant, unappealing or distasteful to us. In either case, we must learn to scan and search the environment for relevant cues which will be pursued or avoided, depending upon our current needs and other conditions existing in the internal and external environments. It also seems likely that the acts of searching, scanning, and attending will be influenced by the events which follow this behavior. Thus rewarding certain acts of scanning and attending should increase the probability that these acts will occur in the future and should also increase the potency of stimuli which are perceived as a result of the scanning and attending.

The present study was intended to demonstrate that attentional acts can be influenced by reinforcing events. An attempt was made to condition attentional shifts selectively to certain objects by giving verbal reinforcements more frequently in connection with the presentation of these objects than others which were only infrequently reinforced. The extent to which the effects developed in the conditioning phase of the experiment

From G. Murphy, J. F. Santos, and C. M. Solley, Development and Transfer of Attentional Habits. *Perceptual and Motor Skills*, 1968, 26, 515–519. Reprinted by permission of authors and publisher.

This research was performed at The Menninger Foundation and was supported by a research grant (M-715-C) from the National Institute of Mental Health, of the National Institute of Health, Public Health Service.

influence perceptual performance in a later task was also investigated. It was hypothesized (1) that during the course of conditioning Ss would shift their attention more and more often to objects which were frequently associated with verbal reinforcement to the relative neglect of infrequently reinforced objects and (2) that Ss would locate frequently reinforced objects more rapidly than infrequently reinforced objects in a subsequent search task.

METHOD

Subjects

Ss in this study were 16 fourth-grade girls from a Catholic parochial grammar school.

Apparatus

Conditioning panel. The conditioning panel (CP) was constructed from a 3-ft. square plywood board which was painted gray, and which had 6-in. square windows located 2 in. from the edges of each corner. The windows were 19 in. apart and were situated 13 in. from the center of the board. A 7-in. × 6-in. × 4-in. white compartment, also made of plywood, was attached behind each window. Within each compartment was a 7-w bulb which would be activated by means of a programmer which utilized a tape recorder and a four-channel frequency-selective amplifier. Four sine waves (1,000, 3,000, 5,000 and 7,000 cps) were recorded in a random series on a tape with only the restriction that no successive repetitions were allowed. The tones were on for 2 sec. and off for 1 sec. They were taped in series of 40 (10 of each tone) with 30-sec. delays between successive series. The taped signals were fed into the amplifier selectively to activate one of four relays connected to the lights in the compartments. When activated, the lights illuminated a small toy camel, elephant, lion, or sheep, all of which were painted white.

Search panel. The search panel (SP) consisted of a 4-ft. × 4-ft section of pegboard which had been painted white. On the pegboard were 100 S-shaped metal pegs placed in holes approximately 3 in. apart so that they formed a 35-in. × 27-in. rectangle with 10 rows and 10 columns. A total of 40 different human and animal plastic figures of the dime store type were attached in a random fashion on the pegs. These figures varied slightly in size but all were approximately 2-in. × 2-in. and were painted white to blend in with the SP and make their detection more difficult.

Procedure

Ss were seated approximately 4 ft. front and center of the CP, which was placed on top of a 30-in. high desk. Ss were told that the task involved a game in which figures would light up on the CP, and they were to identify the lighted figures as quickly as possible. The tape recorder was then started and each figure was illuminated and identified 20 times for a total of 80. S was allowed a minute rest interval after 40 trials. One E explained the task to Ss and differentially reinforced their attentional shifts and identifications of the 4 figures with verbalizations such as "uh-huh," and "that's good," "fine," "you're doing swell." "couldn't fool you that time," etc. Verbal encouragement was given such that attentional shift to one figure was reinforced approximately 90% of the time and the shifts to the other three figures were reinforced approximately 10% of the time. A counterbalanced experimental design provided that each figure should be 90% reinforced once in each position on the CP when 16 Ss had been tested. Each S, however, was so reinforced for only one position on the panel.

The second E handled the apparatus, observed and noted general behavior, and tallied the number of times that Ss attended to each position on the CP during the 2-sec. light-off phase. Attentional shifts were measured by means of eye movements, when Ss looked toward the windows on the CP.

Immediately following the conditioning phase of the experiment S was introduced to the search task and was told that it would be similar to a game of "hide and seek." One E explained that S would now have to locate each of the 4 test figures, one at a time, on a board among many other figures. The search figure was to be identified by pointing as soon as it was located. Thirty-nine irrelevant figures and one of the test figures were placed on the SP which was situated 90° to the right of the conditioning panel and 4 ft. from S. The first E showed Ss the figures to be located, one at a time, and removed the previous figure after each trial. The next figure was placed in its proper position while S was made to look away. These positions were predetermined by using a table of random numbers to obtain coordinates which localized 4 positions within each quadrant. Quadrant refers here to the 4 divisions which were formed when imaginary lines were drawn between hook columns 5 and 6 and hook rows 5 and 6. Each S was required to locate each figure once in each quadrant of the SP for a total of 16 trials. The order of figure location varied systematically over 16 trials for each S (e.g., camel, elephant, lion, sheep, S, C, E, L, L, S, C, E, E, L, S, C). The second E observed general behavior of Ss during the search task and measured recognition latency with a stop watch.

RESULTS

Table 43-1 shows the frequency of inter-trial eye movements to the four figures during the first and second series of 40 trials, and the changes from the former to the latter. These data are shown separately for subgroups reinforced for different positions on the CP and are pooled over four Ss and four figures. It may be seen that there is an increasing tendency to attend to the reinforced figure during the inter-trial intervals. Of course, there are certain preferences which Ss brought into the experiment as a result of previous experiences and learning and these would influence the extent to which changes in attentional shifts would be possible within a limited number of trials. The data do not accurately reflect initial preferences because they are confounded with early conditioning effects, but the results do suggest a greater initial tendency to attend to upper rather than lower positions. The strongest preference seems to be for the upper left position while the weakest preference appears to be for the lower left position. Reinforcement apparently alters these position preferences by the second series of 40 trials, in the direction of the reinforced figure. As a matter of fact, 14 out of 16 Ss began attending more frequently to the position of the reinforced figure. These results are significant at the .05 level when evaluated by a sign test.

Table 43-2 gives the median search latencies for animal figures whose verbal recognition was followed 90% or 10% of the time by reinforcement. These results show that the median search latencies are lower for all of the animals following 90% reinforcement. These data are confounded, how-

TABLE 43-1. Frequency of Inter-trial Eye Movements to Positions on the Conditioning Panel During Conditioning Trials

90% Reinforced Position	Trial Series	Positions on Conditioning Panel			
		Upper Left	Upper Right	Lower Left	Lower Right
Upper Left	First	22	14	6	10
	Second	31	9	3	12
	Change	9	−5	−3	2
Upper Right	First	19	18	5	3
	Second	18	36	2	7
	Change	−1	18	−3	4
Lower Left	First	16	18	10	12
	Second	13	15	24	13
	Change	−3	−3	14	1
Lower Right	First	13	12	8	9
	Second	12	12	2	22
	Change	−1	0	−6	13

TABLE 43-2.   Median Search Latencies (in sec.) for 90% and 10% Reinforced Figures

Figure	90% reinforced	10% reinforced
Camel	6.50	9.75
Elephant	4.75	7.00
Sheep	6.75	10.75
Lion	7.50	7.75

ever, inasmuch as the experimental design allows each S to contribute more than one score, e.g., S who was 90% reinforced for camel was also reinforced 10% for elephant, sheep, and lion.

A statistical test can be applied to the number of Ss whose median search time for the 90% reinforced figure exceeded their median search time for the 10% reinforced figure as compared to Ss for whom the opposite was true. For 12 Ss the median was lower for the 90% figure and for 4 Ss the opposite was true. These numbers are significantly different, when evaluated by a sign test, at the .05 level of confidence.

DISCUSSION

The results of the present experiment suggest that attentional acts are conditionable and that these acts have a facilitory effect upon performance in a subsequent search task.

The increased occurrence of reinforced responses between trials presents no particular problems on the assumption that looking or seeking responses directed toward the reinforced stimulus are developed or strengthened. However, the manner in which all of this may influence search latency in a subsequent task is more complicated and difficult to explain. In the search task Ss have to make frequent shifts in order to locate the goal object. The shifts continue until the final one which is followed by successful recognition. It seems likely that frequent reinforcement may produce a lowering of perceptual thresholds, along with a high articulation of percepts, a greater clarity of images and memory for frequently reinforced stimuli and a stronger tendency to react to them. In observing Ss during the experiment it was obvious that, when they reached a frequently reinforced figure, they tended to stop searching immediately whereas they would often look past infrequently reinforced figures. The children also tended to do obvious "double-takes" on frequently reinforced figures but never on the others. Thus, it seems that the former figures had become strongly reinforcing goal objects in and of themselves, with an acquired capacity for effectively stopping the search pattern.

The present research is obviously preliminary and needs to be expanded, especially to situations where attentional shifts away from as well as toward certain objects are reinforced. Such a procedure might succeed in producing an extinction of attentional shifts toward certain stimuli, thus raising the recognition threshold for those objects and negatively influencing search-discrimination time. In fact, if this procedure were carried far enough it might be possible to demonstrate the development of perceptual insensitivities which would vary as a function of level of conditioning. Obviously insensitivities of this type mght result from the *attractive* influence of certain stimuli which cause other stimuli to be partly or completely neglected. However, they could also be due to the *repulsive* influence of certain stimuli which prompt a search for other stimuli to their own partial or complete neglect. A combination of high levels of attractiveness of certain stimuli along with high levels of repulsivity in other stimuli could lead to extremes of insensitivity, "scotoma" or functional blindness for the latter.

REFERENCES

Berlyne, D. E. An experimental study of human curiosity. *British Journal of Psychology*, 1954, 45, 180–191.

Solley, C. M., & Murphy, G. *Development of the perceptual world*. New York: Basic Books, 1960.

LEARNING THEORY | X

THE BASIC THESIS of the learning theory approach to personality has been that the individual is minimally equipped by heredity for either behavior or personality. The infant has few Freudian instincts, no Jungian archetypes, and no phenomenological self-actualization motive. The behavior he will eventually exhibit and the personality to be inferred from that behavior must be *learned*. Just what is learned and how learning takes place is a function of the particular type of learning theory and of the individual theorist.

Presented here are four articles relevant to the learning theory approach. The first, by O. Hobart Mowrer, is concerned with the basis for anxiety, a major construct in theories of personality and psychopathology. The article is of value not only in its presentation of a straightforward early learning theory viewpoint concerning this important construct, but in that Mowrer also reviews other approaches to the topic.

Major changes in the thinking of some learning theorists during the past few years is exemplified by a second Mowrer article in which he rejects the earlier view that psychopathology is based on the learning of abnormal emotions. To replace this earlier stimulus-response (S-R) viewpoint, Mowrer opts for choice-mediated behavior as a basis for pathological symptomatology. Socially unacceptable behavior, he holds, results in guilt, emotional disturbance and defensive symptomatic behavior.

A second major learning theorist has been Neal E. Miller, who, for his innovative work in the experimental psychology of drives, reinforcement, conflict and related areas, is among the most widely respected of contemporary American psychologists. Working with John Dollard, Miller provided, in 1950, the most thorough and explicit of all learning theories of personality. Since that time, however, his thinking has changed markedly and his work has gone far beyond the original book. As a result, we have chosen to present here a concise but most informative paper in which Miller details results of some of his recent investigations in the learning of glandular and visceral responses. Of particular interest for personality and psychopathology are the noted implications of this work for psychosomatic symptoms.

In our final selection, Broen and Storms demonstrate how basic learning theory, with qualifications and extensions, can be applied to specific psychopathological syndromes. Their article is of particular interest because it attempts to explain and predict, using the relatively simple constructs of learning theory, the symptomatic behaviors associated with one of the most complex of psychological disorders, schizophrenia.

44

A Stimulus-Response Analysis
of Anxiety and Its Role
as a Reinforcing Agent

O. HOBART MOWRER

Within recent decades an important change has taken place in the scientific view of anxiety (fear),[1] its genesis, and its psychological significance. Writing in 1890, William James (1890) stoutly supported the then current supposition that anxiety was an *instinctive* ("idiopathic") reaction to certain objects or situations, which might or might not represent real danger. To the extent that the instinctively given, predetermined objects of anxiety were indeed dangerous, anxiety reactions had biological utility and could be accounted for as an evolutionary product of the struggle for existence. On the other hand, there were, James assumed, also anxiety reactions that were altogether senseless and which, conjecturally, came about through Nature's imperfect wisdom. But in all cases, an anxiety reaction was regarded as phylogenetically fixed and unlearned. The fact that children may show no fear of a given type of object, *e.g.*, live frogs, during the first year of life but may later manifest such a reaction, James attributed to the "ripening" of the fear-of-live-frogs instinct; and the fact that such fears, once they have "ripened," may also disappear he explained on the assumption that all instincts, after putting in an appearance and, as it were, placing themselves at the individual's disposal, tend to undergo a kind of obliviscence or decay unless taken advantage of and made "habitual."

Some years later John B. Watson (1928) demonstrated experimen-

From O. H. Mowrer, A Stimulus-Response Analysis of Anxiety and Its Role as a Reinforcing Agent. *Psychological Review*, 1939, 46, 553–565. Copyright 1939 by the American Psychological Association, and reproduced by permission of publisher and author.

This paper, in substantially its present form, was presented before the Monday Night Group of the Institute of Human Relations, Yale University, March 13, 1939.

[1] Psychoanalytic writers sometimes differentiate between anxiety and fear on the grounds that fear has a consciously perceived object and anxiety does not. Although this distinction may be useful for some purposes, these two terms will be used in the present paper as strictly synonymous.

tally that, contrary to the Jamesian view, most human fears are specifically relatable to and dependent upon individual experience. Starting with the reaction of infants to loud sounds or loss of physical support, which he refused to call "instinctive" but did not hesitate to regard as "unlearned" or "reflexive," Watson was able to show, by means of Pavlov's conditioning technique, that an indefinitely wide range of other stimuli, if associated with this reaction, could be made to acquire the capacity to elicit unmistakably fearful behavior. This was an important discovery, but it appears to have involved a basic fallacy. Watson overlooked the fact that "loud sounds" are intrinsically *painful*, and he also overlooked the fact that "loss of physical support," although not painful in its own right, is almost certain to be followed by some form of stimulation (incident to the stopping of the body's fall) that is painful. The so-called fearful reaction to loss of support—if not confused with an actual pain reaction—is, therefore, in all probability itself a learned (conditioned) reaction, which means that, according to Watson's observations, human infants show no innate *fear* responses whatever, merely innate *pain* responses.

Freud seems to have seen the problem in this light from the outset and accordingly posited that *all* anxiety (fear) reactions are probably learned; [2] his hypothesis, when recast in stimulus-response terminology, runs as follows. A so-called "traumatic" ("painful") stimulus (arising either from external injury, of whatever kind, or from severe organic need) impinges upon the organism and produces a more or less violent defence (striving) reaction. Furthermore, such a stimulus-response sequence is usually preceded or accompanied by originally "indifferent" stimuli which, however, after one or more temporally contiguous associations with the traumatic stimulus, begin to be perceived as "danger signals," *i.e.*, acquire the capacity to elicit an "anxiety" reaction. This latter reaction, which may or may not be grossly observable, has two outstanding characteristics: (i) it creates or, perhaps more accurately, consists of a state of heightened tension (or "attention") and a more or less specific readiness for (expectation of) the impending traumatic stimulus; and (ii), by virtue of the fact that such a state of tension is itself a form of discomfort, it adaptively motivates the organism to escape from the danger situation, thereby lessening the intensity of the tension (anxiety) and also probably decreasing the chances of encountering the traumatic stimulus. In short, *anxiety (fear) is the conditioned form of the pain reaction*, which has the highly useful function of motivating and reinforcing behavior that tends to avoid or prevent the recurrence of the pain-producing (unconditioned) stimulus.

---

[2] Freud (1936) has explicitly acknowledged the possibility of anxiety occurring, especially in birds and other wild animals, as an instinctive reaction; but he takes the position that in human beings, instinctive anxiety (not to be confused with "instinctual" anxiety, *i.e.*, fear of the intensity of one's own organic impulses) is probably nonexistent or is at least inconsequential.

In the mentalistic terminology that he characteristically employs, Freud (1936) has formulated this view of anxiety formation and its adaptational significance as follows:

Now it is an important advance in self-protection when this traumatic situation of helplessness [discomfort] is not merely awaited but is foreseen, anticipated. Let us call the situation in which resides the cause of this anticipation the danger situation; it is in this latter that the signal of anxiety is given. What this means is: I anticipate that a situation of helplessness [discomfort] will come about, or the present situation reminds me of one of the traumatic experiences which I have previously undergone. Hence I will anticipate this trauma; I will act as if it were already present as long as there is still time to avert it. Anxiety, therefore, is the expectation of the trauma on the one hand, and on the other, an attenuated repetition of it (pp. 149–150).

Affective [anxiety] states are incorporated into the life of the psyche as precipitates of primal traumatic experiences, and are evoked in similar situations like memory symbols (p. 23). Anxiety is undeniably related to expectation; one feels anxiety *lest* something occur (pp. 146–147).

According to views expressed elsewhere by Freud, expectation and anxiety lie along a continuum, with the former merging into the latter at the point at which it becomes uncomfortably intense, *i.e.*, begins to take on motivational properties in its own right. The preparatory, expectant character of anxiety is likely, however, to be obscured by the fact that danger situations sometimes arise and pass so quickly that they are over before the anxiety reaction—involving, as it does, not only an augmentation of neuromuscular readiness and tension but also a general mobilization of the physical energies needed to sustain strenuous action—has had an opportunity to occur. The result is that in situations in which danger is so highly transitory, as, for example, in near-accidents in motor traffic, anxiety is commonly experienced, somewhat paradoxically, *after* the danger is past and therefore gives the appearance of being indeed a useless, wasted reaction (*cf.* James). It must not be overlooked, however, that situations of this kind are more or less anomalous. The fact that in a given situation the element of danger disappears before flight, for which the anxiety-preparedness is most appropriate, has had time to occur, does not, of course, mean that anxiety-preparedness in the face of danger is not in general a very adaptive reaction.[3]

As early as 1903, Pavlov (1938a) expressed a point of view that bears a striking resemblance to the position taken by Freud in this connection. He said: "The importance of the remote signs (signals) of objects can be easily recognized in the movement reaction of the animal. By means of distant and even accidental characteristics of objects the animal seeks his food, avoids enemies, etc." (p. 52). Again, a quarter of a century later, Pavlov (1938b) wrote as follows:

[3] *Cf.* the discussion of the 'startle pattern' by Landis and Hunt (1939).

It is pretty evident that under natural conditions the normal animal must respond not only to stimuli which themselves bring immediate benefit or harm, but also to other physical or chemical agencies—waves of sound, light, and the like—which in themselves only *signal* the approach of these stimuli; though it is not the sight and sound of the beast of prey which is in itself harmful to the smaller animal, but its teeth and claws (p. 14).

Although both Pavlov and Freud thus clearly recognize the biological utility of anticipatory reactions to danger signals, there is, however, an important difference in their viewpoints. Pavlov emphasizes the mechanism of simple stimulus substitution (conditioning). According to his hypothesis, a danger signal (the conditioned stimulus) comes to elicit essentially the *same* "movement reaction" that has previously been produced by actual trauma (the unconditioned stimulus). It is true that the blink of the eyelids to a threatening visual stimulus is not greatly unlike the reaction made to direct corneal irritation. A dog may learn to flex its leg in response to a formerly neutral stimulus so as to simulate the flexion produced by an electric shock administered to its paw. And a small child may for a time make very much the same type of withdrawal reactions to the sight of a flame that it makes to actual contact with it. However, any attempt to establish this pattern of stimulus substitution as the prototype of all learning places severe restrictions on the limits of adaptive behavior: it implies that the only reactions that can become attached to formerly unrelated stimuli (*i.e.*, can be learned) are those which already occur more or less reflexly to some other type of stimulation.

According to the conception of anxiety proposed by Freud, on the other hand, a danger signal may come to produce any of an infinite variety of reactions that are wholly unlike the reaction that occurs to the actual trauma of which the signal is premonitory. Freud assumes that the first and most immediate response to a danger signal is not a complete, overt reaction, as Pavlov implies, but an implicit state of tension and augmented preparedness for action,[4] which he calls "anxiety." This state of affairs, being itself a source of discomfort, may then motivate innumerable random acts, from which will be selected and fixated (by the law of effect) the behavior that most effectively reduces the anxiety. Anxiety is thus to be regarded as a motivating and reinforcing (fixating) agent, similar to hunger, thirst, sex, temperature deviations, and the many other forms of discomfort that harass living organisms, which is, however, presumably distinctive in that it is derived from (based upon anticipation of) these other, more basic forms of discomfort.[5]

By and large, behavior that reduces anxiety also operates to lessen the danger that it presages. An antelope that scents a panther is likely not only

[4] *Cf.* the revised theory of conditioning proposed by Culler (1938).
[5] Freud has never explicitly formulated this view in precisely these words, but it is clearly implied in various of his writings.

to feel less uneasy (anxious) if it moves out of the range of the odor of the panther but is also likely to be in fact somewhat safer. A primitive village that is threatened by marauding men or beasts sleeps better after it has surrounded itself with a deep moat or a sturdy stockade. And a modern mother is made emotionally more comfortable after her child has been properly vaccinated against a dreaded disease. This capacity to be made uncomfortable by the mere prospect of traumatic experiences, in advance of their actual occurrence (or recurrence), and to be motivated thereby to take realistic precautions against them, is unquestionably a tremendously important and useful psychological mechanism, and the fact that the forward-looking, anxiety-arousing propensity of the human mind is more highly developed than it is in lower animals probably accounts for many of man's unique accomplishments. But it also accounts for some of his most conspicuous failures.

The ostrich has become a proverbial object of contempt and a symbol of stupidity because of its alleged tendency, when frightened, to put its head in the sand, thereby calming its emotional agitation but not in the slightest degree altering the danger situation in its objective aspects. Such relevant scientific inquiry as has been carried out indicates, however, that infra-human organisms are ordinarily more realistic in this respect than are human beings. For example, if a dog learns to avoid an electric shock by lifting its foreleg in response to a tone, it will give up this response entirely when it discovers that the tone is no longer followed by shock if the response is not made. Human beings, on the other hand, are notoriously prone to engage in all manner of magical, superstitious, and propitiatory acts, which undoubtedly relieve dread and uncertainty (at least temporarily) but which have a highly questionable value in controlling real events.[6] The remarkable persistence of such practices may be due, at least in part, to the fact that they are followed relatively promptly by anxiety-reduction, whereas their experienced futility at the reality level may come many hours or days or even months later.[7] The persistence of certain forms of "unrealistic" anxiety-reinforced behavior may also be due to the fact that in most societies there seem always to be some individuals who are able and ready to derive an easy living by fostering beliefs on the part of others in "unrealistic" dangers. For the common man protection against such "dangers" consists of whatever type of behavior the bogey-makers choose to say is "safe" (and which furthers their own interests).

Yet other forms of "unrealistic" anxiety-reinforced behavior are to be observed in the symptomatic acts of the psychoneuroses. According to

---

[6] Under some circumstances, e.g., when warriors are preparing for battle, malevolent incantations or similar anxiety-reducing magical procedures may, of course, be objectively efficacious, not, to be sure, in the supposed magical way, but in that they alter human conduct in crucial life situations (i.e., make the warriors bolder and better fighters).

[7] Cf. Hull's concept of the "goal gradient" (Hull, 1932).

Freud, anxiety is in fact "the fundamental phenomenon and the central problem of neurosis" (Freud, 1936, p. 111). He further says:

> Since we have reduced the development of anxiety to a response to situations of danger, we shall prefer to say that the symptoms are created in order to remove or rescue the ego from the situation of danger. . . . We can also say, in supplement to this, that the development of anxiety induces symptom formation—nay more, it is a *sine qua non* thereof, for if the ego did not forcibly arouse the pleasure-pain mechanism through the development of anxiety, it would not acquire the power to put a stop to the danger-threatening process elaborated in the id (Freud, 1936, pp. 112–113).

Willoughby (1935), in a scholarly, well-documented paper, has previously stressed the similarity of magical rites (including religion) and neurotic symptoms and has shown that both types of behavior spring from the common propensity of human beings to deal with their anxieties unrealistically, *i.e.*, by means which diminish emotional discomfort but do not adaptively alter external realities. This excellent study has, in the present writer's opinion, only one important weakness: it takes as its point of departure what Freud has called his "first theory" of anxiety formation (1894), which he subsequently abandoned for the one outlined above. In brief, Freud's earlier supposition was that anxiety arose whenever a strong organic drive or impulse was prevented from discharging through its accustomed motor outlets. According to this view, inhibition was the primary state, anxiety the resultant. In all his more recent writings, on the other hand, Freud takes the position, here also adopted, that anxiety (as a reaction to a "danger signal") is primal and that inhibition, of anxiety-arousing, danger-producing impulses,[8] is a consequence (Freud, 1936). Reaction mechanisms (magic, symptoms, etc.) that contribute to this end tend, for reasons already given, to be reinforced and perpetuated. Willoughby's analysis is not of necessity predicated upon Freud's original view of anxiety formation and would seem to gain rather than lose cogency if based instead upon his more recent formulations.

Magical and neurotic practices constitute a very perplexing and challenging problem from the point of view of traditional psychological theory;

---

[8] One of Freud's most fundamental discoveries, basic to the understanding of reaction-formation, repression, projection, and other neurotic mechanisms, is that organic impulses, even though they are not consciously experienced and identified, may function as "danger signals" and thereby evoke anxiety. This relatively simple yet frequently misapprehended finding (Freud has himself contributed to the confusion by sometimes speaking as if anxiety *is* the "danger signal," instead of a *reaction* to it) can be readily translated into Pavlovian terminology by saying that an organic need, or drive, which has in the past led to overt behavior that was severely punished will tend upon its recurrence, even at low intensities, to elicit a conditioned pain (anxiety) reaction. Yet, as will be shown in a later paper on the so-called "experimental neurosis," Pavlov and his followers have largely ignored this possibility of internal, as well as external, stimuli acquiring "signal" value, *i.e.*, becoming "conditioned," and have consequently made apparent mysteries of some laboratory observations which, when viewed more broadly, seem completely intelligible.

but, as Allport (1937) has recently pointed out, so also do many other types of human activity that are commonly regarded as both rational and normal. Allport rightly stresses the inadequacies of the conditioned-reflex concept as a comprehensive explanation of learning and personality development in general. He also justly criticizes the view that all human conduct is to be accounted for in terms of trial-and-error striving to eliminate immediately felt organic needs. The plain fact is that much of modern man's most energetic behavior occurs when his organic needs are ostensibly well satisfied. In an attempt to account for this state of affairs, without, on the other hand, falling back on a forthright mentalistic type of approach, Allport elaborates the view, previously advanced by Woodworth, that habits themselves have an on-going character, independent of the motivation that originally brought them into being, and that this type of habit-momentum constitutes a form of self-sustained motivation. Allport calls this the principle of "functional autonomy" and relies heavily upon it in developing his system of the "psychology of personality."

In the estimation of the present writer, "functional autonomy" is on a par with "perpetual motion." Its author clearly perceives an important psychological problem, but it seems unlikely that his is a scientifically tenable solution to it. The position here taken is that human beings (and also other living organs to varying degrees) can be motivated either by organic pressures (needs) that are currently present and felt or by the mere anticipation of such pressures and that those habits tend to be acquired and perpetuated (reinforced) which effect a reduction in *either* of these two types of motivation. This view rests upon and is but an extended application of the well-founded law of effect and involves no assumptions that are not empirically verifiable. It has the further advantage that it is consistent with common-sense impressions and practices and at the same times serves as a useful integrational device at the scientific level.

The present analysis of anxiety (anticipation, expectancy) and its role in shaping both "adaptive" and "mal-adaptive" behavior in human beings is also consistent with the growing tendency to eliminate the distinction between learning through "punishment" and learning through "reward." The earlier view was that so-called punishment "stamped out" habits and that reward "stamped" them in. This distinction now appears to have been spurious and to have depended upon a selectivity of emphasis or interest (Mowrer, 1938). If an individual is motivated by an internal discomfort or need (produced by his own metabolic processes), and if another individual provides the means of eliminating it, and if, in the process, the first individual acquires new behavior, this is called learning through "reward." But if a second individual supplies the need (by inflicting or threatening to inflict some form of discomfort), and if the affected individual supplies the means of eliminating this discomfort (by flight, inactivity, propitiation, compliance, or the like), and if, in the process, this individual acquires new behavior, then this is called learning through "punishment." The truth of the matter seems to be that all learning presupposes (i) an increase of motivation (striving) and (ii) a decrease of motivation (success) and that the essential features of the process are much the same, regardless of the specific source of motivation or of the particular circumstances of its elimination.[9]

There is, however, one practical consideration to be taken into account. Although learning through "punishment" does not seem to differ basically from learning through "reward," inter-personal relationships are likely to be affected very differently in the two cases. If the method of "reward" is employed, inter-personal relationships are likely to be made more "positive" (*i.e.*, approach tendencies will be strengthened); whereas, if the method of "punishment" is employed, inter-personal relationships are likely to be made more "negative" (*i.e.*, avoidance tendencies will be strengthened). From a purely social point of view, it is therefore preferable to employ the method of "reward," whenever this is possible; but "punishment" may have to be resorted to if no *organic* needs are present to be "rewarded" or if means of rewarding them are not available. Punishment (or the threat of punishment, *i.e.*, anxiety) is particularly convenient in that it can be produced instantly; but this advantage is accompanied by disadvantages which cannot be safely disregarded (Mowrer, 1940).

Even the practical basis for distinguishing between learning through reward and through punishment just suggested becomes tenuous when one considers the type of situation in which one person withholds from another an expected reward. This, in one sense, is a form of "punishment," and yet its effectiveness is based upon the principle of "reward." This complicated state of affairs seems especially likely to arise in the parent-child relationship and has implications that have been but slightly explored in stimulus-response terms.

SUMMARY

In contrast to the older view, which held that anxiety (fear) was an instinctive reaction to phylogenetically pre-determined objects or situations, the position here taken is that anxiety is a learned response, occurring to "signals" (conditioned stimuli) that are premonitory of (*i.e.*, have in the

---

[9] According to this point of view, old habits are eliminated, not by being "stamped out" or extracted, as it were, "by the roots," but by the functional superimposition of new, more powerful, antagonistic habits (Mowrer, 1938). Anxiety may thus be said to exercise an "inhibitory" effect (see foregoing discussion of Freud's "first theory" of anxiety) upon established behavior trends mainly through its motivation and reinforcement of opposing behavior trends. In this way emphasis falls primarily upon the positive, habit-forming consequences of anxiety and only secondarily and indirectly upon its negative, inhibitory functions.

past been followed by) situations of injury or pain (unconditioned stimuli). Anxiety is thus basically anticipatory in nature and has great biological utility in that it adaptively motivates living organisms to deal with (prepare for or flee from) traumatic events in advance of their actual occurrence, thereby diminishing their harmful effects. However, experienced anxiety does not always vary in direct proportion to the objective danger in a given situation, with the result that living organisms, and human beings in particular, show tendencies to behave "irrationally," *i.e.*, to have anxiety in situations that are not dangerous or to have no anxiety in situations that are dangerous. Such a "disproportionality of affect" may come about for a variety of reasons, and the analysis of these reasons throws light upon such diverse phenomena as magic, superstition, social exploration, and the psychoneuroses.

Moreover, by posting anxiety as a kind of connecting link between complete wellbeing and active organic discomfort or injury, it is possible to reconcile the fact that much, perhaps most, of the day-to-day behavior of civilized human beings is not prompted by simultaneously active organic drives and the fact that the law of effect (principle of learning through motivation-reduction) is apparently one of the best-established of psychological principles. This is accomplished by assuming (i) that anxiety, *i.e.*, mere anticipation of actual organic need or injury, may effectively motivate human beings and (ii) that reduction of anxiety may serve powerfully to reinforce behavior that brings about such a state of "relief" or "security." Anxiety, Although derived from more basic forms of motivation, is thus regarded as functioning in an essentially parallel manner as far as its role as an activating and reinforcing agent is concerned. This analysis is consistent with the common sense view in such matters and does not conflict with any known empirical fact. Finally, it has the advantage of being open to objective investigation and of giving rise to a host of problems that have scarcely been touched experimentally (Mowrer, 1940).

REFERENCES

Allport, G. W. *Personality*. New York: Henry Holt and Company, 1937. Pp. 588.

Culler, E. A. Recent advances in some concepts of conditioning. *Psychol. Rev.*, 1938, *45*, 134–153.

Freud, S. *The problem of anxiety*. New York: Norton and Co., 1936. Pp. 165.

Hull, C. L. The goal gradient hypothesis and maze learning. *Psychol. Rev.*, 1932, 39, 25–43.

Landis, C. & Hunt, W. A. *The startle pattern*. New York: Farrar & Rinehart, 1939. Pp. 168.

James, W. *Principles of psychology*, Vol. II. New York: Henry Holt and Company, 1890. Pp. 704.

Mowrer, O. H. Preparatory set (expectancy)—A determinant in motivation and learning. *Psychol. Rev.*, 1938, *45*, 61–91.

Mowrer, O. H. Preparatory set (expectancy)—Some methods of measurement. *Psychol. Monogr.*, 1940, *52*, No. 2.

Pavlov, I. P. *Conditioned reflexes*. (Translated by Anrep.) England: Oxford University Press: Humphrey Milford, 1938. Pp. 430. (a)

Pavlov, I. P. *Lectures on conditioned reflexes*. (Translated by Gantt.) New York: International Publishers, 1938. Pp. 414. (b)

Watson, J. B. Experimental studies on the growth of the emotions. Pp. 37–57, *Psychologies of 1925*, Worcester, Mass.: Clark University Press, 1928, pp. 412.

Willoughby, R. R. Magic and cognate phenomena: An hypothesis. Pp. 461–519, in A *Handbook of Social Psychology*, Worcester, Mass.: Clark University Press, 1935, pp. 1195.

45

The Basis of Psychopathology:
Malconditioning or Misbehavior?

O. HOBART MOWRER

The view most often espoused by those who have approached the domain of psychopathology from the standpoint of learning theory is that the afflicted individual's basic trouble lies in some anomaly in his emotional (or attitudinal) life and that any irregularities in overt behavior are merely symptomatic of the underlying affective problem. More specifically, the assumption has been that psychoneurotic individuals have suffered from traumatic emotional malconditioning of some sort as a result of physical accidents or overly harsh, perverse "training" at the hands of others. Irrational or irresponsible behavior on the part of the victims of such unfortunate treatment is thus merely an expression of the irrationality and abnormality of their emotions. This then is supposed to be the essence of "neurosis" and "mental illness" in the most pervasive sense of these terms.

Despite the great insight and practical control which this essentially Freudian way of conceptualizing the problem is supposed to have provided, sober appraisal of our situation suggests, in point of fact, that it has contributed very little to the more effective management and prevention of psychopathology. A plausible case indeed can be made for the surmise that this theoretical position merely reinforces a perception which the neurotic is himself almost certain to have. He will be quick to tell you how bad he feels, and he will not be averse to the suggestion that others are somehow responsible for his present unfortunate state and thus ought to treat him in such a way as to make him feel better. He will readily fall in with the idea, which flows naturally from the foregoing assumptions, that he himself is not responsible for what he now does. This type of theory—to the effect that so-called neurotic individuals act strangely or compulsively or irrationally because their emotions have been perverted and warped—is thus part and parcel of the "disease" itself and by no means its cure. Increasingly, we are getting reports of iatrogenic (treatment-exacerbated) personality dis-

From O. H. Mowrer, The Basis of Psychopathology: Malconditioning or Misbehavior? *Journal of the National Association of Women Deans and Counselors*, Vol. 29, 1966, Winter, Number 2, 51–58. Reprinted by permission of author and publisher.

order. Social institutions, such as the home and the church, which have assimilated this philosophy are afflicted by a mysterious, creeping paralysis and loss of confidence to such a degree that our whole society is commonly said to be sick (LaPiere, 1959; Schoek & Wiggins, 1962).

I. A NEW CONCEPTION OF EMOTIONAL DISTURBANCE

Where then can we find a sounder and more effective way of thinking about this type of problem? On the basis of various clinical reports and experimental studies (Mowrer, 1964), the induction is emerging that so-called emotional disturbance, discomfort, or "dis-ease" is the lawful, well-learned, and eminently normal result of abnormal (in the sense of socially and morally deviant) behavior and not the other way round. Once an individual becomes fearful and guilt-ridden because of his misconduct, he *may* develop symptoms which reflect his inner malaise and apprehension; but this does not mean that his emotional responses are the original source of his difficulty.

Our thesis is that in psychopathology the basic cause of disorder is deliberate, choice-mediated behavior of a socially disapproved, reprehensible nature which results in emotional disturbance and insecurity because the individual is now objectively guilty, socially vulnerable, and, if caught, subject to criticism or punishment. The symptoms which then ensue represent ways in which the individual is trying to defend himself against and hide his disturbing and suspicion-arousing emotions of moral fear and guilt. Thus, a deliberate misdeed is the original, or primary, cause; and emotional disturbance follows which may then produce symptoms of a more or less behavioral type. That is, we assume that emotional disturbance is the *second* in a three-link chain of consequences rather than the original or *first* link in a two-link chain.

To be more precise, we perhaps should say that both approaches imply three links in the chain of circumstances which eventuates in the more manifest aspects of what we call psychopathology. If one wishes, one can easily think of emotional disturbance or disturbing emotions as the second link in both frames of reference; but in the one case the first link would be the foolish, unthinking, harmful behavior of others, whereas in the other case the first link is the foolish, unthinking, harmful behavior of the individual himself. This is the distinction behind the suggestion of certain contemporary writers that in neurosis and functional psychosis, the element of personal responsibility is probably far greater than has been commonly supposed. If this be true, there is also a corresponding opportunity, indeed obligation, for the individual to help himself if he has fallen into a pathological state.

Or one might take the position that it is not the emotions experienced by patients in mental hospitals which constitute their "craziness." Given their personal history and life style, the presumption is that in the absence of gross neurological lesions, toxic states, and hormonal disorders, their emotions (however turbulent and painful) are, in an ultimate sense, reasonable and proper. What is "crazy" is the previous behavior of these persons and the ways in which they (and very likely their therapists are now dealing with the resulting emotional "dis-ease."

This perception of the situation is in direct contrast to the still widespread view that the essence of mental illness lies in the inappropriate, disproportional, and irrational nature of the individual's emotional reactions. Our assumption is rather that it is the individual's behavior, both originally and now symptomatically, that has been "off" and that his emotions are and have been in no way unsuited to the circumstances when the latter are fully known and understood. By this route we arrive at the view that the therapy of choice is necessarily behavior therapy, in the sense of changing the behavior which originally got the individual into trouble and changing what the individual has since been trying to do about his trouble or his emotions. This approach is manifestly different from the view that a neurotic's trouble is that he is *having* trouble—emotional trouble or troubling emotions—a view which still dominates large segments of both psychiatric and psychological precept and practice. Our assumption is that the capacity to be "troubled" in this way is the hallmark of the individual's basic humanity and potentially his salvation and deliverance.

The "sick" individual's problem lies not in how he is feeling but in what he perhaps is or has been doing. Further, no therapy can be ultimately successful which involves a direct attack (by chemical or whatever other means) upon the patient's emotions as such. They can be effectively modified only through systematic changes in behavior. As Glasser (1966) succinctly says, "No one can help another person *feel* better." Neurotic persons do not act irresponsibly because they are sick; instead, they are sick of themselves and feel bad because they act badly, irresponsibly. So the strategy of choice for the therapist is to help the other person become more responsible, even though it may temporarily hurt. This is in direct contradiction to the more traditional, but manifestly unsatisfactory, view that human beings become emotionally ill because they have been morally overtrained and are, in consequence, trying to be "too good."

II. CHOICE, RESPONSIBILITY, AND IDENTITY CRISIS

If others are truly responsible for our emotional difficulties, then it would perhaps follow that we could recover only through treatment (that is, a so-called "corrective emotional experience") which would likewise have to come from without. This is tantamount to saying that psychopathology is due to false, unrealistic guilt—a mere guilt complex; but a revolution is now in progress which puts the responsibility—both for one's having gotten into a neurotic impasse in the first place and for one's getting out of it—much more squarely upon the individual himself. Here, we are assuming that psychopathology involves real guilt, and the fear of being "found out" generated by actions which the individual's reference group condemns and negatively sanctions.

This view attributes to human beings the capacity for choice: capacity to choose either to behave or not to behave; and, having chosen misbehavior, the further capacity to choose either to conceal or reveal this fact. Manifestly, we do not, cannot choose or control our emotions directly or voluntarily. Given the appropriate or conditioned stimulus, they occur automatically, reflexly. So the question of control and choice exists only at the level of overt, voluntary behavior. This is why behavior therapy opens up vistas and potentialities which are forever closed if one thinks of the problem of psychopathology as essentially emotional. But in recent decades there has been some question as to whether the concept of choice or volition is justified even in respect to overt, instrumental behavior. We must pause momentarily to consider this matter, for the validity of our whole analysis hinges upon it.

Much of the skepticism concerning the possibility of human freedom of choice comes from stimulus-response psychology, or primitive behaviorism, which holds that given a specific stimulus, the organism (be he man or mouse) must give whatever response happens to be most directly connected or conditioned to the stimulus. On the basis of evidence which has been reviewed elsewhere in detail, it can now be maintained with good reason that stimuli never produce or cause behavioral, as opposed to emotional, responses in the manner implied by the stimulus-response connectionism or reflexology. A stimulus may provide an image or memory of a particular response, but the presence of this stimulus does not at all mean that the subject is obliged or forced (Loeb, 1918) to make a particular response or, indeed, any response at all. A given stimulus may remind the subject of a certain possibility; but whether the individual responds to this suggestion and "yields to the temptation" is dependent upon prudential factors (hopes and fears) which are complexly determined by the individual's total life experience, knowledge (including that which is gained vicariously), and objectives—in a word, by "character." Whatever else Gestalt psychologists may have meant when they spoke of an organism's responding as a whole, totally rather than segmentally, this is surely an important part of what they should have meant.

In the foregoing analysis, we are not repudiating determinism in the sense of denying that the universe, including the principles governing the human mind, is orderly and lawful; but we are saying that the *overt* response is in progress. The reflexological, connectionistic model of behavior Their occurrence is dependent not merely upon the presence or absence of any given stimulus or upon a particular pattern or concatenation of stimuli comprising a situation but also upon everything which, as Kreshevsky (1932) has phrased it, the organism "brings to" the situation and, we might add, upon the sensory feedback information provided while a response is in progress. The reflevological, connectionistic model of behavior postulated by Pavlov, Watson, Thorndike, and others is grossly inadequate (that is, not isomorphic or iconic) for the reality it is supposed to represent. Instead, we must have a model which at least recognizes the reality of mediating processes and higher order habits (even Russian reflexologists are now speaking of the *second* signal system) which make possible the deliberate weighing and balancing of alternate possibilities. (Miller, Galanter, & Pribram, 1960) Thinking about the problem in this way largely resolves the conflict between determinism and teleology or purpose. In effect, we have now discovered in contemporary learning theory the mechanics of teleology. As long as we respond to the circumstances of our existence with flexibility and intelligence rather than in a fixed and essentially stupid manner, don't we have all the freedom we need or should desire?

What choice or choices do people make which precipitate the state ambiguously known as neurosis? Manifestly, this term is a medical euphemism and does not mean what it literally seems to mean, namely, an "osis" or disorder of the nerves or nervous system. The term *psychosis* comes closer to carrying the implication in point here; and it might be good if this term gradually replaced the term *neurosis*. However, Erikson (1958) has suggested an even more appropriate expression—*identity crisis*. It fits in nicely with the answer to the question: What is it that human beings do which leads to the personal condition with which we are here concerned? The answer to this may be: They choose to do socially forbidden things, and then they hide and deny what they have done. They refuse to say who they really are and deny their true identity to others.

Francis Thompson ends the first stanza of *The Hound of Heaven* with: "All things betray thee, who betrayest Me." If we for long deny who we are to others (that is, betray them), the time comes when we no longer know ourselves (Jourard, 1964). This is the state of psychic nonbeing or anxiety commonly called neurosis or psychosis and which could so much more pertinently and precisely be called identity crisis.

This way of thinking represents a radical departure from the prevailing medical emphasis. In mental hospitals, both public and private, the doctor typically tries to reassure the patient and make him feel better by saying something like this: "Now you should realize, first of all, that you do have a disease, and this is just like any other disease or sickness of an organic nature which you might have. It is not associated with anything you have done or not done. You are in no way responsible for it, and you can't do anything about it yourself. You should not worry or blame yourself for anything; instead, just relax and leave everything to us. We understand these things and will completely take over the treatment. Simply do as you are told." If it is true that the individual does have a responsibility, perhaps a sizable one, for both the cause and the cure of the condition, how tragically nonfunctional this approach is! It has served to create what someone has aptly called "the healing industry," but it has not accomplished much else.

Understandably, there is growing skepticism concerning the appropriateness of the medical model of illness, sickness, and treatment in the whole psychiatric area (Glasser, 1965; Szasz, 1961). However, while probably willing enough to accept this development, psychologists must decide whether they will continue to keep the patient in another deterministic frame of reference—not that of "disease" but of stimulus-response bondage —or liberate him, in the sense of granting him a significant role in both the production and the elimination of his difficulties.

The simple, unelaborated stimulus-response learning model can only make man a robot, but this model is inherently unsatisfactory and is being replaced by a model in which freedom of choice is a definite, though qualified, possibility. The real elements of determinism, compulsion, constraint, or necessity come not so much from the biological, neurological, or even psychological nature of the individual himself as from the conceptualization of man as a social being operating within a social system, and this system puts very definite and inevitable constraints and restraints upon him.

In such a system the individual still has a number of choices. He can choose, within limits, the particular social system in which he wishes to function. He can also choose whether he is going to function honestly or dishonestly within a given system. If he chooses to be dishonest, there is an inevitable consequence: He becomes prey to that special variety of fear and personal misery which we call guilt; and if he does not deal with this in a realistic and constructive way, either by confession or restitution, he will soon be dealing with it in symptomatic ways. This is not the place to elaborate on the meaning of the latter term (Mowrer, 1964, Chap. 11); but so-called "symptoms" represent an effort on the part of the guilty, uneasy, dis-easy, apprehensive, or anxious individual to deny and hide such feelings lest they arouse suspicion (Why are you so fearful?) and an effort to lessen the subjective intensity of such feelings because they are inherently unpleasant and painful. Hence, the appropriateness of referring to symptoms as "defenses," not against a fear of a return of repressed impulses of sex and hostility, as Freud supposed, but against the danger of having one's guilty secrets known to others and against the subjective experience of the emotion of guilt by the individual himself.

Thus one arrives at the view that there is no possibility of a successful private treatment of neurosis either in a religious or a secular context (Mowrer, 1963) for the reason that privacy, concealment, secrecy, and defensiveness are the essence of the difficulty. Both psychiatrists and psychologists have made the error of engaging in treatment procedures which are more congruent with the premises of the disease than those of health. It is not surprising that such procedures have been salable, for they promise the neurotic an opportunity to get well on his own terms. But neither should it surprise us that such procedures have not been truly effective, for they have not adequately recognized the real nature of an identity crisis.

In the final analysis, a rational and effective behavior therapy must involve admission of, rather than denial of, who one genuinely is to the significant others in one's life and rectification of and restitution for past deviations and errors. Thus, one must traverse the same path which led him into neurosis in the first place but now in the reverse direction. If it is by sinning and then trying to conceal the sinning that one progressively destroys his social relatedness, his identity, the only possibility of recovering it is to move back in the opposite direction toward openness, cooperation, the community, and fellowship.

III. PSYCHOLOGICAL SCIENCE, ANCIENT WISDOM—AND FOLLY

Is the foregoing the shape of science in the domain of psychopathology or an awful retrogression? In the biblical story of the temptation and fall of man, man sins and then hides his sin. If, after violating the one rule that had been put upon him, man had gone to God (his "significant others") and admitted his mistake, the outcome would presumably have been quite different. But instead, after eating the forbidden fruit, man and woman decided to deny and conceal what they had done. Banishment from Paradise was their penalty, just as loss of peace of mind and a pervasive insecurity is the price that is exacted of us if we violate our social obligations and then pretend that we have not done so. We are "banished" and no longer belong because we have disqualified ourselves for the privilege of membership and group participation. But we alone know this; and our neurosis consists of this knowledge, the fear of being "found out" which it engenders, and the constant vigilance which is needed lest this should happen.

If man is truly free, why should he choose to violate rules? Rational rules involve a restriction which has the effect of ensuring a long-term advantage of some sort; and whenever an individual is not experienced or intelligent enough to see the logic of a rule, he is uunderstandably tempted to violate it. In Paradise, it was no imposition upon Adam and Eve to be forbidden to eat a certain fruit, but it was an affront to their vanity and pride to be told there was something they should not do. So they ate. Then, instead of admitting what they had done, each denied it. Because they both refused to confess and to accept the responsibility for their mistake, they found no restoration, no redemption, no recovery, no reconciliation, and no return to innocence.

This biblical story is one of the great allegories of all time. It is like a finely cut diamond: No matter how one turns and looks at it, it reflects a bright and illuminating light. The particular facet of the story which we have chosen suggests that most current efforts to help neurotic individuals to recover are to no avail because we do not sufficiently recognize man's true nature and destiny.

We shall use this classical conception of Genesis as the standard of comparison for latter-day theories and practices in this domain (Meehl, et al., 1958). However, the conception of neurosis and recovery which will be taken as a kind of bench mark is not conventionally religious. In one sense, of course, this approach is deeply and inveterately religious. One of the roots of the word *religion* is the Latin term *ligare*, from which come our words *ligament* and *ligature*. Thus, religion literally implies a binding-to, a connectedness, a relationship, or a belonging; and in this sense, we shall assume that the normal, healthy man is necessarily "religious" and that an abnormal, sick one is suffering from a tragic form of brokenness and alienation.

In the institutional sense, religion—particularly Protestant religion—suffers from some of the same presuppositions that have so seriously handicapped secular therapeutic approaches. Perhaps the most fatal of these is the assumption that in an identity crisis the individual's emotions are in some way out of kilter, inappropriate, and disordered. An excellent case can be made for the alternative view that the neurotic is suffering not from an emotional disorder but from a disorderly, irresponsible way of life. It is in itself "neurotic" to view emotions as the source of the trouble. Thus, much of contemporary religion is itself sick, just as psychiatry, clinical psychology, and the neurotic himself are sick (Mowrer, 1961a, b).

But is it true, is it fair to say that contemporary Protestantism stresses wrong emotions as the source of suffering? Protestantism takes a dim view of an individual's own efforts and actions as a means of salvation, and now we find that many ministers have become so advanced in their thinking that they don't even mention sin and guilt. All is forgiveness and love —first love of God, then of one's fellowmen, and then of oneself. What is "love"? As ordinarily understood it is an emotion. If you don't have it or can't experience it, you are as helpless as if you have a negative emotion like anxiety and want to get rid of it. Operationally, such a theology hamstrings the lost, alienated, and suffering individual about as effectively as do the doctrines of disease in psychiatry or of reflexology in psychology. The main difference is that in the religious context one is supposed to see a theologian for help instead of a secular healer of some sort.

This approach exemplifies the much discussed, but seldom actualized, Protestant doctrine of "the priesthood of all believers"—everyone's ability and obligation to be a priest-therapist to himself and to others. There is excellent biblical support for this view. In Judaism, one appears before God on the Day of Atonement only after having spent a week making right one's transgressions against one's fellowmen during the preceding year. In the New Testament we read: "So if you are offering your gift at the altar, and there remember that your brother has something against you, leave your gift there before the altar and go; first be reconciled to your brother, and then come and offer your gift." (Matthew 5:23–24)

There is a familiar couplet that goes:

> I sought my soul, I sought my God;
> but neither could I see;
> But then I sought my brother,
> and then I found all three.

This may not be exalted poetry, but it is excellent psychology and theology. It puts behavior—interpersonal, social, and moral behavior—first and says that everything else will follow from this. Why have professional psychologists and religionists been so reluctant to acknowledge and emphasize this time-honored approach? Can it be that we dislike it precisely because it gives the layman more freedom, responsibility, and power than we wish him to have? Does it make him too independent of us? If there is even a trace of professional chauvinism in this important area, we should surely divest ourselves of it as promptly and completely as possible. Behavior therapy can, hopefully, be a useful instrument to this end.

REFERENCES

Erikson, E. H. *Young Man Luther*. New York: Norton, 1958.

Glasser, W. *Reality Therapy: A New Approach to Psychiatry*. New York: Harper & Row, 1965.

Glasser, W. "Reality Therapy: A New Approach." *Morality and Mental Health*. (Edited by O. Hobart Mowrer.) Chicago: Rand McNally & Co., 1966.

Jourard, Sidney M. *The Transparent Self*. Princeton, N.J.: Van Nostrand, 1964.

Kreshevsky, I. " 'Hypotheses' in Rats." *Psychological Review* 39: 516–32; 1932.

LaPiere, R. *The Freudian Ethic*. New York: Duell, Sloan & Pearce, 1959.

Loeb, J. *Forced Movements, Tropisms, and Animal Conduct*. Philadelphia: J. B. Lippincott Co., 1918.

Meehl, P. E., et al., *What, Then, Is Man?* St. Louis: Concordia Publishing House, 1958.

Miller, G. A.; Galanter, E.; & Pribram, K. H. *Plans and the Structure of Behavior.* New York: Holt, Rinehart and Winston, 1960.

Mowrer, O. Hobart. "The Rediscovery of Moral Responsibility." *Atlantic Monthly 208*: 88–91; 1961. (a)

Mowrer, O. Hobart. *The Crisis in Psychiatry and Religion.* Princeton, N.J.: Van Nostrand Co., 1961. (b)

Mowrer, O. Hobart. "Payment or Repayment? The Problem of Private Practice." *American Psychologist 18*: 577–80; 1963.

Mowrer, O. Hobart. *The New Group Therapy.* Princeton, N.J.: Van Nostrand Co., 1964.

Schoeck, H., & Wiggins, J. W. *Psychiatry and Responsibility.* Princeton, N.J.: D. Van Nostrand Co., 1962.

Szasz, Thomas S. *The Myth of Mental Illness.* New York: Harper & Row, 1961.

46

Learning of Visceral and
Glandular Responses

NEAL E. MILLER

There is a strong traditional belief in the inferiority of the autonomic nervous system and the visceral responses that it controls. The recent experiments disproving this belief have deep implications for theories of learning, for individual differences in autonomic responses, for the cause and the cure of abnormal psychosomatic symptoms, and possibly also for the understanding of normal homeostasis. Their success encourages investigators to try other unconventional types of training. Before describing these experiments, let me briefly sketch some elements in the history of the deeply entrenched, false belief in the gross inferiority of one major part of the nervous system.

HISTORICAL ROOTS AND MODERN RAMIFICATIONS

Since ancient times, reason and the voluntary responses of the skeletal muscles have been considered to be superior, while emotions and the presumably involuntary glandular and visceral responses have been considered to be inferior. This invidious dichotomy appears in the philosophy of Plato (1), with his superior rational soul in the head above and inferior souls in the body below. Much later, the great French neuroanatomist Bichat (2) distinguished between the cerebrospinal nervous system of the great brain and spinal cord, controlling skeletal responses, and the dual chain of ganglia (which he called "little brains") running down on either side of the spinal cord in the body below and controlling emotional and visceral responses. He indicated his low opinion of the ganglionic system by calling it "vegetative"; he also believed it to be largely independent of the cerebrospinal system, an opinion which is still reflected in our modern name for it, the autonomic nervous system. Considerably later, Cannon (3) studied the

From N. E. Miller, Learning of Visceral and Glandular Responses. Science, 31 Jan., 1969, 163, 434–445. Copyright 1969 by the American Association for the Advancement of Science. Reprinted by permission of publisher and author.

sympathetic part of the autonomic nervous system and concluded that the different nerves in it all fire simultaneously and are incapable of the finely differentiated individual responses possible for the cerebrospinal system, a conclusion which is enshrined in modern textbooks.

Many, though not all, psychiatrists have made an invidious distinction between the hysterical and other symptoms that are mediated by the cerebrospinal nervous system and the psychosomatic symptoms that are mediated by the autonomic nervous system. Whereas the former are supposed to be subject to a higher type of control that is symbolic, the latter are presumed to be only the direct physiological consequences of the type and intensity of the patient's emotions (see, for example, 4).

Similarly, students of learning have made a distinction between a lower form, called classical conditioning and thought to be involuntary, and a superior form variously called trial-and-error learning, operant conditioning, type II conditioning, or instrumental learning and believed to be responsible for voluntary behavior. In classical conditioning, the reinforcement must be by an unconditioned stimulus that already elicits the specific response to be learned; therefore, the possibilities are quite limited. In instrumental learning, the reinforcement, called a reward, has the property of strengthening any immediately preceding response. Therefore, the possibilities for reinforcement are much greater; a given reward may reinforce any one of a number of different responses, and a given response may be reinforced by any one of a number of different rewards.

Finally, the foregoing invidious distinctions have coalesced into the strong traditional belief that the superior type of instrumental learning involved in the superior voluntary behavior is possible only for skeletal responses mediated by the superior cerebrospinal nervous system, while, conversely, the inferior classical conditioning is the only kind possible for the inferior, presumably involuntary, visceral and emotional responses mediated by the inferior autonomic nervous system. Thus, in a recent summary generally considered authoritative, Kimble (5) states the almost universal belief that "for autonomically mediated behavior, the evidence points unequivocally to the conclusion that such responses can be modified by classical, but not instrumental, training methods." Upon examining the evidence, however, one finds that it consists only of failure to secure instrumental learning in two incompletely reported exploratory experiments and a vague allusion to the Russian literature (6). It is only against a cultural background of great prejudice that such weak evidence could lead to such a strong conviction.

The belief that instrumental learning is possible only for the cerebrospinal system and, conversely, that the autonomic nervous system can be modified only by classical conditioning has been used as one of the strongest arguments for the notion that instrumental learning and classical conditioning are two basically different phenomena rather than different manifestations of the same phenomenon under different conditions. But for many years I have been impressed with the similarity between the laws of classical conditioning and those of instrumental learning, and with the fact that, in each of these two situations, some of the specific details of learning vary with the specific conditions of learning. Failing to see any clear-cut dichotomy, I have assumed that there is only one kind of learning (7). This assumption has logically demanded that instrumental training procedures be able to produce the learning of any visceral responses that could be acquired through classical conditioning procedures. Yet it was only a little over a dozen years ago that I began some experimental work on this problem and a somewhat shorter time ago that I first, in published articles (8), made specific sharp challenges to the traditional view that the instrumental learning of visceral responses is impossible.

SOME DIFFICULTIES

One of the difficulties of investigating the instrumental learning of visceral responses stems from the fact that the responses that are the easiest to measure—namely, heart rate, vasomotor responses, and the galvanic skin response—are known to be affected by skeletal responses, such as exercise, breathing, and even tensing of certain muscles, such as those in the diaphragm. Thus, it is hard to rule out the possibility that, instead of directly learning a visceral response, the subject has learned a skeletal response the performance of which causes the visceral change being recorded.

One of the controls I planned to use was the paralysis of all skeletal responses through administration of curare, a drug which selectively blocks the motor end plates of skeletal muscles without eliminating consciousness in human subjects or the neural control of visceral responses, such as the beating of the heart. The muscles involved in breathing are paralyzed, so the subject's breathing must be maintained through artificial respiration. Since it seemed unlikely that curarization and other rigorous control techniques would be easy to use with human subjects, I decided to concentrate first on experiments with animals.

Originally I thought that learning would be more difficult when the animal was paralyzed, under the influence of curare, and therefore I decided to postpone such experiments until ones on nonparalyzed animals had yielded some definitely promising results. This turned out to be a mistake because, as I found out much later, paralyzing the animal with curare not only greatly simplifies the problem of recording visceral responses without artifacts introduced by movement but also apparently makes it easier for the animal to learn, perhaps because paralysis of the skeletal muscles removes sources of variability and distraction. Also, in certain experiments I made the mistake of using rewards that induced strong unconditioned responses that interfered with instrumental learning.

One of the greatest difficulties, however, was the strength of the belief that instrumental learning of glandular and visceral responses is impossible. It was extremely difficult to get students to work on this problem, and when paid assistants were assigned to it, their attempts were so half-hearted that it soon became more economical to let them work on some other problem which they could attack with greater faith and enthusiasm. These difficulties and a few preliminary encouraging but inconclusive early results have been described elsewhere (9).

SUCCESS WITH SALIVATION

The first clear-cut results were secured by Alfredo Carmona and me in an experiment on the salivation of dogs. Initial attempts to use food as a reward for hungry dogs were unsuccessful, partly because of strong and persistent unconditioned salivation elicited by the food. Therefore, we decided to use water as a reward for thirsty dogs. Preliminary observations showed that the water had no appreciable effects one way or the other on the bursts of spontaneous salivation. As an additional precaution, however, we used the experimental design of rewarding dogs in one group whenever they showed a burst of spontaneous salivation, so that they would be trained to increase salivation, and rewarding dogs in another group whenever there was a long interval between spontaneous bursts, so that they would be trained to decrease salivation. If the reward had any unconditioned effect, this effect might be classically conditioned to the experimental situation and therefore produce a change in salivation that was not a true instance of instrumental learning. But in classical conditioning the reinforcement must elicit the response that is to be acquired. Therefore, conditioning of a response elicited by the reward could produce either an increase or a decrease in salivation, depending upon the direction of the unconditioned response elicited by the reward, but it could not produce a change in one direction for one group and in the opposite direction for the other group. The same type of logic applies for any unlearned cumulative aftereffects of the reward; they could not be in opposite directions for the two groups. With instrumental learning, however, the reward can reinforce any response that immediately precedes it; therefore, the same reward can be used to produce either increases or decreases.

The results are presented in Figure 46-1, which summarizes the effects of 40 days of training with one 45-minute training session per day. It may be seen that in this experiment the learning proceeded slowly. However, statistical analysis showed that each of the trends in the predicted rewarded direction was highly reliable (10).

Since the changes in salivation for the two groups were in opposite directions, they cannot be attributed to classical conditioning. It was noted,

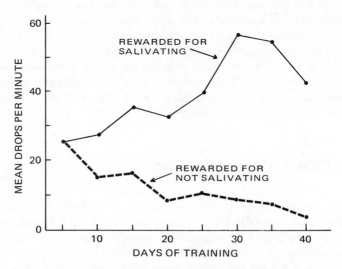

Figure 46-1. Learning curves for groups of thirsty dogs rewarded with water for either increases or decreases in spontaneous salivation. (From Miller and Carmona, 1957)

however, that the group rewarded for increases seemed to be more aroused and active than the one rewarded for decreases. Conceivably, all we were doing was to change the level of activation of the dogs, and this change was, in turn, affecting the salivation. Although we did not observe any specific skeletal responses, such as chewing movements or panting, which might be expected to elicit salivation, it was difficult to be absolutely certain that such movements did not occur. Therefore, we decided to rule out such movements by paralyzing the dogs with curare, but we immediately found that curare had two effects which were disastrous for this experiment: it elicited such copious and continuous salivation that there were no changes in salivation to reward, and the salivation was so viscous that it almost immediately gummed up the recording apparatus.

HEART RATE

In the meantime, Jay Trowill, working with me on this problem, was displaying great ingenuity, courage, and persistence in trying to produce instrumental learning of heart rate in rats that had been paralyzed by curare to prevent them from "cheating" by muscular exertion to speed up the heart or by relaxation to slow it down. As a result of preliminary testing, he selected a dose of curare (3.6 milligrams of d-tubocurarine chloride per kilogram, injected intraperitoneally) which produced deep paralysis for at least 3 hours, and a rate of artificial respiration (inspiration-expiration ratio 1:1; 70 breaths per minute; peak pressure reading, 20 cm-H_2O) which maintained the heat at a constant and normal rate throughout this time.

In subsequent experiments, DiCara and I have obtained similar effects by starting with a smaller dose (1.2 milligrams per kilogram) and constantly infusing additional amounts of the drug, through intraperitoneal injection, at the rate of 1.2 milligrams per kilogram per hour, for the duration of the experiment. We have recorded, electromyographically, the response of the muscles, to determine that this dose does indeed produce a complete block of the action potentials, lasting for at least an hour after the end of infusion. We have found that if parameters of respiration and the face mask are adjusted carefully, the procedure not only maintains the heart rate of a 500-gram control animal constant but also maintains the vital signs of temperature, peripheral vasomotor responses, and the pCO_2 of the blood constant.

Since there are not very many ways to reward an animal completely paralyzed by curare, Trowill and I decided to use direct electrical stimulation of rewarding areas of the brain. There were other technical difficulties to overcome, such as devising the automatic system for rewarding small changes in heart rate as recorded by the electrocardiogram. Nevertheless, Trowill at last succeeded in training his rats (11). Those rewarded for an increase in heart rate showed a statistically reliable increase, and those rewarded for a decrease in heart rate showed a statistically reliable decrease. The changes, however, were disappointingly small, averaging only 5 percent in each direction.

The next question was whether larger changes could be achieved by improving the technique of training. DiCara and I used the technique of shaping—in other words, of immediately rewarding first very small, and hence frequently occurring, changes in the correct direction and, as soon as these had been learned, requiring progressively larger changes as the criterion for reward. In this way, we were able to produce in 90 minutes of training changes averaging 20 percent in either direction (12).

KEY PROPERTIES OF LEARNING: DISCRIMINATION AND RETENTION

Does the learning of visceral responses have the same properties as the learning of skeletal responses? One of the important characteristics of the instrumental learning of skeletal responses is that a discrimination can be learned, so that the responses are more likely to be made in the stimulus situations in which they are rewarded than in those in which they are not.

After the training of the first few rats had convinced us that we could produce large changes in heart rate, DiCara and I gave all the rest of the rats in the experiment described above 45 minutes of additional training with the most difficult criterion. We did this in order to see whether they could learn to give a greater response during a "time-in" stimulus (the presence of a flashing light and a tone) which indicated that a response in the proper direction would be rewarded than during a "time-out" stimulus (absence of light and tone) which indicated that a correct response would not be rewarded.

Figure 46-2 shows the record of one of the rats given such training. Before the beginning of the special discrimination training it had slowed its heart from an initial rate of 350 beats per minute to a rate of 230 beats per minute. From the top record of Figure 46-2 one can see that, at the beginning of the special discrimination training, there was no appreciable reduction in heart rate that was specifically associated with the time-in stimulus. Thus it took the rat considerable time after the onset of this stimulus to meet the criterion and get the reward. At the end of the discrimination training the heart rate during time-out remained approximately the same, but when the time-in light and tone came on, the heart slowed down and the criterion was promptly met. Although the other rats showed less change than this, by the end of the relatively short period of discrimination training their heart rate did change reliably ($P < .001$) in the pre-

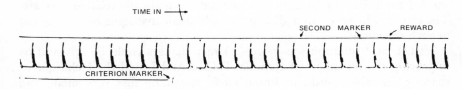

BEGINNING OF DISCRIMINATION TRAINING

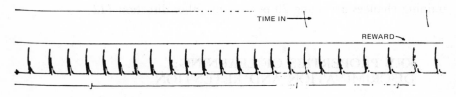

AFTER 45 MINUTES OF DISCRIMINATION TRAINING

Figure 46-2.   Electrocardiograms at the beginning and at the end of discrimination training of curarized rat rewarded for slow heart rate. Slowing of heart rate is rewarded only during a "time-in" stimulus (tone and light). (From DiCara and Miller, 1967)

dicted direction when the time-in stimulus came on. Thus, it is clear that instrumental visceral learning has at least one of the important properties of instrumental skeletal learning—namely, the ability to be brought under the control of a discriminative stimulus.

Another of the important properties of the instrumental learning of skeletal responses is that it is remembered. DiCara and I performed a special experiment to test the retention of learned changes in heart rate (13). Rats that had been given a single training session were returned to their home cages for 3 months without further training. When curarized again and returned to the experimental situation for nonreinforced test trials, rats in both the "increase" and the "decrease" groups showed good retention by exhibiting reliable changes in the direction rewarded in the earlier training.

ESCAPE AND AVOIDANCE LEARNING

Is visceral learning by any chance peculiarly limited to reinforcement by the unusual reward of direct electrical stimulation of the brain, or can it be reinforced by other rewards in the same way that skeletal learning can be? In order to answer this question, DiCara and I (14) performed an experiment using the other of the two forms of thoroughly studied reward that can be conveniently used with rats which are paralyzed by curare—namely, the chance to avoid, or escape from, mild electric shock. A shock signal was turned on; after it had been on for 10 seconds it was accompanied by brief pulses of mild electric shock delivered to the rat's tail. During the first 10 seconds the rat could turn off the shock signal and avoid the shock by making the correct response of changing its heart rate in the required direction by the required amount. If it did not make the correct response in time, the shocks continued to be delivered until the rat escaped them by making the correct response, which immediately turned off both the shock and the shock signal.

For one group of curarized rats, the correct response was an increase in heart rate; for the other group it was a decrease. After the rats had learned to make small responses in the proper direction, they were required to make larger ones. During this training the shock signals were randomly interspersed with an equal number of "safe" signals that were not followed by shock; the heart rate was also recorded during so-called blank trials—trials without any signals or shocks. For half of the rats the shock signal was a tone and the "safe" signal was a flashing light; for the other half the roles of these cues were reversed.

The results are shown in Figure 46-3. Each of the 12 rats in this experiment changed its heart rate in the rewarded direction. As training progressed, the shock signal began to elicit a progressively greater change in

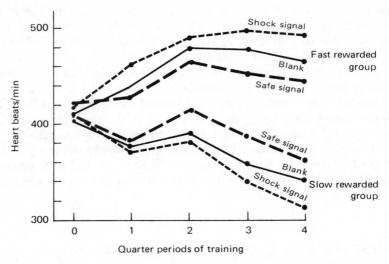

Figure 46-3.   Changes in heart rate during avoidance training. (From DiCara and Miller, 1968)

the rewarded direction than the change recorded during the blank trials; this was a statistically reliable trend. Conversely, as training progressed, the "safe" signal came to elicit a statistically reliable change in the opposite direction, toward the initial base line. These results show learning when escape and avoidance are the rewards; this means that visceral responses in curarized rats can be reinforced by rewards other than direct electrical stimulation of the brain. These rats also discriminate between the shock and the "safe" signals. You will remember that, with noncurarized thirsty dogs, we were able to use yet another kind of reward, water, to produce learned changes in salivation.

TRANSFER TO NONCURARIZED STATE: MORE EVIDENCE AGAINST MEDIATION

In the experiments discussed above, paralysis of the skeletal muscles by curare ruled out the possibility that the subjects were learning the overt performance of skeletal responses which were indirectly eliciting the changes in the heart rate. It is barely conceivable, however, that the rats were learning to send out from the motor cortex central impulses which would have activated the muscles had they not been paralyzed. And it is barely conceivable that these central impulses affected heart rate by means either of inborn connections or of classically conditioned ones that had been acquired when previous exercise had been accompanied by an increase in heart rate and relaxation had been accompanied by a decrease. But, if the changes in heart rate were produced in this indirect way, we would expect that, during a subsequent test without curare, any rat that showed learned changes in heart rate would show the movements in the muscles that were no longer paralyzed. Furthermore, the problem of whether or not visceral responses learned under curarization carry over to the noncurarized state is of interest in its own right.

In order to answer this question, DiCara and I (*15*) trained two groups of curarized rats to increase or decrease, respectively, their heart rate in order to avoid, or escape from, brief pulses of mild electric shock. When these rats were tested 2 weeks later in the noncurarized state, the habit was remembered. Statistically reliable increases in heart rate averaging 5 percent and decreases averaging 16 percent occurred. Immediately subsequent retraining without curare produced additional significant changes of heart rate in the rewarded direction, bringing the total overall increase to 11 percent and the decrease to 22 percent. While, at the beginning of the test in the noncurarized state, the two groups showed some differences in respiration and activity, these differences decreased until, by the end of the retraining, they were small and far from statistically reliable ($t = 0.3$ and 1.3, respectively). At the same time, the difference between the two groups with respect to heart rate was increasing, until it became large and thus extremely reliable ($t = 8.6$, d.f. $= 12$, $P < .001$).

In short, while greater changes in heart rate were being learned, the response was becoming more specific, involving smaller changes in respiration and muscular activity. This increase in specificity with additional training is another point of similarity with the instrumental learning of skeletal responses. Early in skeletal learning, the rewarded correct response is likely to be accompanied by many unnecessary movements. With additional training during which extraneous movements are not rewarded, they tend to drop out.

It is difficult to reconcile the foregoing results with the hypothesis that the differences in heart rate were mediated primarily by a difference in either respiration or amount of general activity. This is especially true in view of the research, summarized by Ehrlich and Malmo (*16*), which shows that muscular activity, to affect heart rate in the rat, must be rather vigorous.

While it is difficult to rule out completely the possibility that changes in heart rate are mediated by central impulses to skeletal muscles, the possibility of such mediation is much less attractive for other responses, such as intestinal contractions and the formation of urine by the kidney. Furthermore, if the learning of these different responses can be shown to be specific in enough visceral responses, one runs out of different skeletal movements each eliciting a specific different visceral response (*17*). Therefore, experiments were performed on the learning of a variety of different visceral responses and on the specificity of that learning. Each of these experiments was, of course, interesting in its own right, quite apart from any bearing on the problem of mediation.

SPECIFICITY: INTESTINAL VERSUS CARDIAC

The purpose of our next experiment was to determine the specificity of visceral learning. If such learning has the same properties as the instrumental learning of skeletal responses, it should be possible to learn a specific visceral response independently of other ones. Furthermore, as we have just seen, we might expect to find that, the better the rewarded response is learned, the more specific is the learning. Banuazizi and I worked on this problem (18). First we had to discover another visceral response that could be conveniently recorded and rewarded. We decided on intestinal contractions, and recorded them in the curarized rat with a little balloon filled with water thrust approximately 4 centimeters beyond the anal sphincter. Changes of pressure in the balloon were transduced into electric voltages which produced a record on a polygraph and also activated an automatic mechanism for delivering the reward, which was electrical stimulation of the brain.

The results for the first rat trained, which was a typical one, are shown in Figure 46-4. From the top record it may be seen that, during habituation, there were some spontaneous contractions. When the rat was rewarded by brain stimulation for keeping contractions below a certain amplitude for a certain time, the number of contractions was reduced and the base line was lowered. After the record showed a highly reliable change indicating that relaxation had been learned (Figure 46-4, second record from the top), the conditions of training were reversed and the reward was delivered whenever the amplitude of contractions rose above a certain level. From the next record (Figure 46-4, middle) it may be seen that this type of training increased the number of contractions and raised the base line. Finally (Figure 46-4, two bottom records) the reward was discontinued and, as would be expected, the response continued for a while but gradually became extinguished, so that the activity eventually returned to approximately its original base-line level.

After studying a number of other rats in this way and convincing ourselves that the instrumental learning of intestinal responses was a possibility, we designed an experiment to test specificity. For all the rats of the experiment, both intestinal contractions and heart rate were recorded, but half the rats were rewarded for one of these responses and half were rewarded for the other response. Each of these two groups of rats was divided

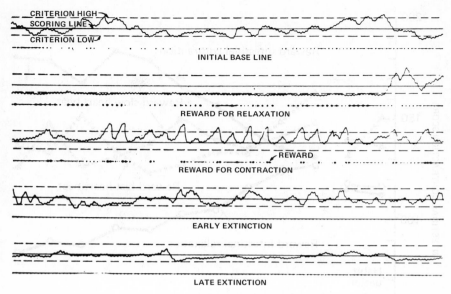

CRITERION HIGH
SCORING LINE
CRITERION LOW

INITIAL BASE LINE

REWARD FOR RELAXATION

REWARD

REWARD FOR CONTRACTION

EARLY EXTINCTION

LATE EXTINCTION

Figure 46-4. Typical samples of a record of instrumental learning of an intestinal response by a curarized rat. (*From top to bottom*) Record of spontaneous contraction before training; record after training with reward for relaxation; record after training with reward for contractions; records during nonrewarded extinction trials. (From Miller and Banuazizi, 1968)

into two subgroups, rewarded, respectively, for increased and decreased response. The rats were completely paralyzed by curare, maintained on artificial respiration, and rewarded by electrical stimulation of the brain.

The results are shown in Figures 46-5 and 46-6. In Figure 46-5 it may be seen that the group rewarded for increases in intestinal contractions learned an increase, the group rewarded for decreases learned a decrease, but neither of these groups showed an appreciable change in heart rate. Conversely (Figure 46-6), the group rewarded for increases in heart rate showed an increase, the group rewarded for decreases showed a decrease, but neither of these groups showed a change in intestinal contractions.

The fact that each type of response changed when it was rewarded rules out the interpretation that the failure to secure a change when that change was not rewarded could have been due to either a strong and stable homeostatic regulation of that response or an inability of our techniques to measure changes reliably under the particular conditions of our experiment.

Each of the 12 rats in the experiment showed statistically reliable changes in the rewarded direction; for 11 the changes were reliable beyond

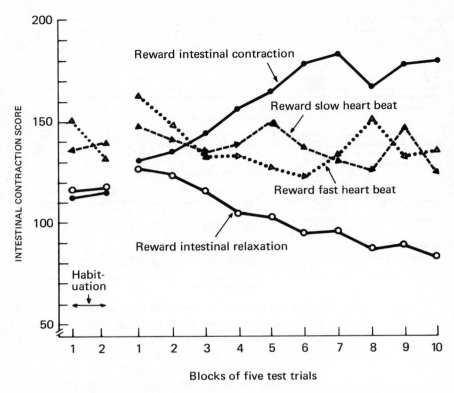

Figure 46-5.   Graph showing that the intestinal contraction score is changed by rewarding either increases or decreases in intestinal contractions but is unaffected by rewarding changes in heart rate. (From Miller and Banuazizi, 1968)

the $P < .001$ level, while for the 12th the changes were reliable only beyond the .05 level. A statistically reliable negative correlation showed that the better the rewarded visceral response was learned, the less change occurred in the other, nonrewarded response. This greater specificity with better learning is what we had expected. The results showed that visceral learning can be specific to an organ system, and they clearly ruled out the possibility of mediation by any single general factor, such as level of activation or central commands for either general activity or relaxation.

In an additional experiment, Banuazizi (19) showed that either increases or decreases in intestinal contraction can be rewarded by avoidance of, or escape from, mild electric shocks, and that the intestinal responses can be discriminatively elicited by a specific stimulus associated with reinforcement.

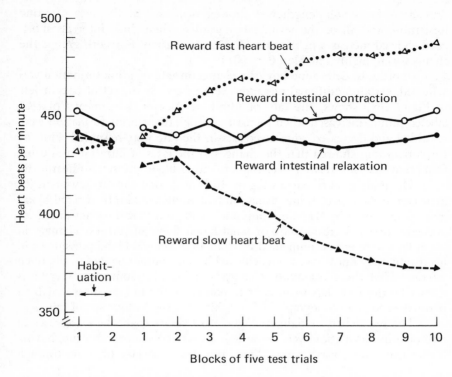

Figure 46-6. Graph showing that the heart rate is changed by reward-ing either increases or decreases in heart rate but is un-affected by rewarding changes in intestinal contractions. Comparison with Figure 46-5 demonstrates the specificity of visceral learning. (From Miller and Banuazizi, 1968)

KIDNEY FUNCTION

Encouraged by these successes, DiCara and I decided to see whether or not the rate of urine formation by the kidney could be changed in the curarized rat rewarded by electrical stimulation of the brain (20). A catheter, permanently inserted, was used to prevent accumulation of urine by the bladder, and the rate of urine formation was measured by an elec-tronic device for counting minute drops. In order to secure a rate of urine formation fast enough so that small changes could be promptly detected and rewarded, the rats were kept constantly loaded with water through infusion by way of a catheter permanently inserted in the jugular vein.

All of the seven rats rewarded when the intervals between times of urine-drop formation lengthened showed decreases in the rate of urine formation, and all of the seven rats rewarded when these intervals shortened showed increases in the rate of urine formation. For both groups the changes were highly reliable ($P < .001$).

In order to determine how the change in rate of urine formation was achieved, certain additional measures were taken. As the set of bars at left in Figure 46-7 shows, the rate of filtration, measured by means of ^{14}C-labeled inulin, increased when increases in the rate of urine formation were rewarded and decreased when decreases in the rate were rewarded. Plots of the correlations showed that the changes in the rates of filtration and urine formation were not related to changes in either blood pressure or heart rate.

The middle set of bars in Figure 46-7 shows that the rats rewarded for increases in the rate of urine formation had an increased rate of renal blood flow, as measured by ^{3}H-p-aminohippuric acid, and that those rewarded for decreases had a decreased rate of renal blood flow. Since these changes in blood flow were not accompanied by changes in general blood pressure or in heart rate, they must have been achieved by vasomotor changes of the renal arteries. That these vasomotor changes were at least somewhat specific is shown by the fact that vasomotor responses of the tail, as measured by a photoelectric plethysmograph, did not differ for the two groups of rats.

The set of bars at right in Figure 46-7 shows that when decreases in rate of urine formation were rewarded, a more concentrated urine, having higher osmolarity, was formed. Since the slower passage of urine through

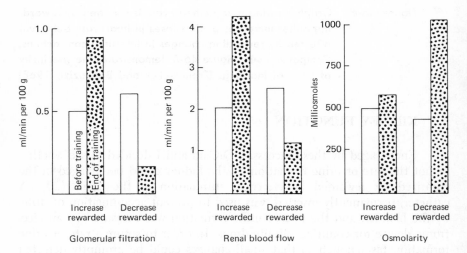

Figure 46-7.   Effects of rewarding increased rate of urine formation in one group and decreased rate in another on measures of glomerular filtration, renal blood flow, and osmolarity. (From Miller and DiCara, 1968)

the tubules would afford more opportunity for reabsorption of water, this higher concentration does not necessarily mean an increase in the secretion of antidiuretic hormone. When an increased rate of urine formation was rewarded, the urine did not become more diluted—that is, it showed no decrease in osmolarity; therefore, the increase in rate of urine formation observed in this experiment cannot be accounted for in terms of an inhibition of the secretion of antidiuretic hormone.

From the foregoing results it appears that the learned changes in urine formation in this experiment were produced primarily by changes in the rate of filtration, which, in turn, were produced primarily by changes in the rate of blood flow through the kidneys.

GASTRIC CHANGES

In the next experiment, Carmona, Demierre, and I used a photo-electric plethysmograph to measure changes, presumably in the amount of blood, in the stomach wall (21). In an operation performed under anesthesia, a small glass tube, painted black except for a small spot, was inserted into the rat's stomach. The same tube was used to hold the stomach wall against a small glass window inserted through the body wall. The tube was left in that position. After the animal had recovered, a bundle of optical fibers could be slipped snugly into the glass tube so that the light beamed through it would shine out through the unpainted spot in the tube inside the stomach, pass through the stomach wall, and be recorded by a photocell on the other side of the glass window. Preliminary tests indicated that, as would be expected, when the amount of blood in the stomach wall increased, less light would pass through. Other tests showed that stomach contractions elicited by injections of insulin did not affect the amount of light transmitted.

In the main experiment we rewarded curarized rats by enabling them to avoid or escape from mild electric shocks. Some were rewarded when the amount of light that passed through the stomach wall increased, while others were rewarded when the amount decreased. Fourteen of the 15 rats showed changes in the rewarded direction. Thus, we demonstrated that the stomach wall, under the control of the autonomic nervous system, can be modified by instrumental learning. There is strong reason to believe that the learned changes were achieved by vasomotor responses affecting the amount of blood in the stomach wall or mucosa, or in both.

In another experiment, Carmona (22) showed that stomach contractions can be either increased or decreased by instrumental learning.

It is obvious that learned changes in the blood supply of internal organs can affect their functioning—as, for example, the rate at which urine was formed by the kidneys was affected by changes in the amount of blood that flowed through them. Thus, such changes can produce psychosomatic symptoms. And if the learned changes in blood supply can be specific to a given organ, the symptom will occur in that organ rather than in another one.

PERIPHERAL VASOMOTOR RESPONSES

Having investigated the instrumental learning of internal vasomotor responses, we next studied the learning of peripheral ones. In the first experiment, the amount of blood in the tail of a curarized rat was measured by a photoelectric plethysmograph, and changes were rewarded by electrical stimulation of the brain (23). All of the four rats rewarded for vasoconstriction showed that response, and, at the same time, their average core temperature, measured rectally, decreased from 98.9° to 97.9° F. All of the four rats rewarded for vasodilatation showed that response and, at the same time, their average core temperature increased from 99.9° to 101° F. The vasomotor change for each individual rat was reliable beyond the $P < .01$ level, and the difference in change in temperature between the groups was reliable beyond the .01 level. The direction of the change in temperature was opposite to that which would be expected from the heat conservation caused by peripheral vasoconstriction of the heat loss caused by peripheral vasodilatation. The changes are in the direction which would be expected if the training had altered the rate of heat production, causing a change in temperature which, in turn, elicited the vasomotor response.

The next experiment was designed to try to determine the limits of the specificity of vasomotor learning. The pinnae of the rat's ears were chosen because the blood vessels in them are believed to be innervated primarily, and perhaps exclusively, by the sympathetic branch of the autonomic nervous system, the branch that Cannon believed always fired nonspecifically as a unit (3). But Cannon's experiments involved exposing cats to extremely strong emotion-evoking stimuli, such as barking dogs, and such stimuli will also evoke generalized activity throughout the skeletal musculature. Perhaps his results reflected the way in which sympathetic activity was elicited, rather than demonstrating any inherent inferiority of the sympathetic nervous system.

In order to test this interpretation, DiCara and I (24) put photocells on both ears of the curarized rat and connected them to a bridge circuit so that only differences in the vasomotor responses of the two ears were rewarded by brain stimulation. We were somewhat surprised and greatly delighted to find that this experiment actually worked. The results are

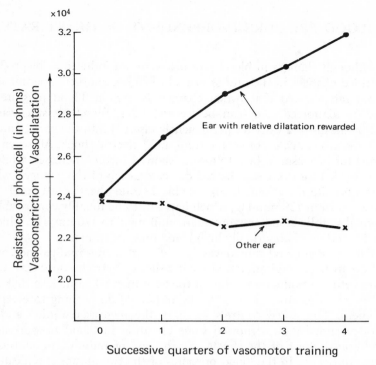

Figure 46-8. Learning a difference in the vasomotor responses of the two ears in the curarized rat. (From data in DiCara and Miller, 1968)

summarized in Figure 46-8. Each of the six rats rewarded for relative vasodilatation of the left ear showed that response, while each of the six rats rewarded for relative vasodilatation of the right ear showed that response. Recordings from the right and left forepaws showed little if any change in vasomotor response.

It is clear that these results cannot be by-products of changes in either heart rate or blood pressure, as these would be expected to affect both ears equally. They show either that vasomotor responses mediated by the sympathetic nervous system are capable of much greater specificity than has previously been believed, or that the innervation of the blood vessels in the pinnae of the ears is not restricted almost exclusively to sympathetic-nervous-system components, as has been believed, and involves functionally significant parasympathetic components. In any event, the changes in the blood flow certainly were surprisingly specific. Such changes in blood flow could account for specific psychosomatic symptoms.

BLOOD PRESSURE INDEPENDENT OF HEART RATE

Although changes in blood pressure were not induced as by-products of rewarded changes in the rate of urine formation, another experiment on curarized rats showed that, when changes in systolic blood pressure are specifically reinforced, they can be learned (25). Blood pressure was recorded by means of a catheter permanently inserted into the aorta, and the reward was avoidance of, or escape from, mild electric shock. All seven rats rewarded for increases in blood pressure showed further increases, while all seven rewarded for decreases showed decreases, each of the changes, which were in opposite directions, being reliable beyond the $P < .01$ level. The increase was from 139 mm-Hg, which happens to be roughly comparable to the normal systolic blood pressure of an adult man, to 170 mm-Hg, which is on the borderline of abnormally high blood pressure in man.

Each experimental animal was "yoked" with a curarized partner, maintained on artificial respiration and having shock electrodes on its tail wired in series with electrodes on the tail of the experimental animal, so that it received exactly the same electric shocks and could do nothing to escape or avoid them. The yoked controls for both the increase-rewarded and the decrease-rewarded groups showed some elevation in blood pressure as an unconditioned effect of the shocks. By the end of training, in contrast to the large difference in the blood pressures of the two groups specifically rewarded for changes in opposite directions, there was no difference in blood pressure between the yoked control partners for these two groups. Furthermore, the increase in blood pressure in these control groups was reliably less $(P < .01)$ than that in the group specifically rewarded for increases. Thus, it is clear that the reward for an increase in blood pressure produced an additional increase over and above the effects of the shocks per se, while the reward for a decrease was able to overcome the unconditioned increase elicited by the shocks.

For none of the four groups was there a significant change in heart rate or in temperature during training; there were no significant differences in these measures among the groups. Thus, the learned change was relatively specific to blood pressure.

TRANSFER FROM HEART RATE TO SKELETAL AVOIDANCE

Although visceral learning can be quite specific, especially if only a specific response is rewarded, as was the case in the experiment on the two ears, under some circumstances it can involve a more generalized effect.

In handling the rats that had just recovered from curarization, DiCara noticed that those that had been trained, through the avoidance or escape reward, to increase their heart rate were more likely to squirm, squeal, defecate, and show other responses indicating emotionality than were those that had been trained to reduce their heart rate. Could instrumental learning of heart-rate changes have some generalized effects, perhaps on the level of emotionality, which might affect the behavior in a different avoidance-learning situation? In order to look for such an effect, DiCara and Weiss (26) used a modified shuttle avoidance apparatus. In this apparatus, when a danger signal is given, the rat must run from compartment A to compartment B. If he runs fast enough, he avoids the shock; if not, he must run to escape it. The next time the danger signal is given, the rat must run in the opposite direction, from B to A.

Other work had shown that learning in this apparatus is an inverted U-shaped function of the strength of the shocks, with shocks that are too strong eliciting emotional behavior instead of running. DiCara and Weiss trained their rats in this apparatus with a level of shock that is approximately optimum for naive rats of this strain. They found that the rats that had been rewarded for decreasing their heart rate learned well, but that those that had been rewarded for increasing their heart rate learned less well, as if their emotionality had been increased. The difference was statistically reliable ($P < .001$). This experiment clearly demonstrates that training a visceral response can affect the subsequent learning of a skeletal one, but additional work will be required to prove the hypothesis that training to increase heart rate increases emotionality.

VISCERAL LEARNING WITHOUT CURARE

Thus far, in all of the experiments except the one on teaching thirsty dogs to salivate, the initial training was given when the animal was under the influence of curare. All of the experiments, except the one on salivation, have produced surprisingly rapid learning—definitive results within 1 or 2 hours. Will learning in the normal, noncurarized state be easier, as we originally thought it should be, or will it be harder, as the experiment on the noncurarized dogs suggests? DiCara and I have started to get additional evidence on this problem. We have obtained clear-cut evidence that rewarding (with the avoidance or escape reward) one group of freely moving rats for reducing heart rate and rewarding another group for increasing heart rate produces a difference between the two groups (27). That this difference was not due to the indirect effects of the overt performance of skeletal responses is shown by the fact that it persisted in subsequent tests during which the rats were paralyzed by curare. And, on subsequent retraining without curare, such differences in activity and respiration as were present earlier in training continued to decrease, while the differences in heart rate continued to increase. It seems extremely unlikely that, at the end of training, the highly reliable differences in heart rate ($t = 7.2; P < .0001$) can be explained by the highly unreliable differences in activity and respiration ($t = .07$ and 0.2, respectively).

Although the rats in this experiment showed some learning when they were trained initially in the noncurarized state, this learning was much poorer than that which we have seen in our other experiments on curarized rats. This is exactly the opposite of my original expectation, but seems plausible in the light of hindsight. My hunch is that paralysis by curare improved learning by eliminating sources of distraction and variability. The stimulus situation was kept more constant, and confusing visceral fluctuations induced indirectly by skeletal movements were eliminated.

LEARNED CHANGES IN BRAIN WAVES

Encouraged by success in the experiments on the instrumental learning of visceral responses, my colleagues and I have attempted to produce other unconventional types of learning. Electrodes placed on the skull or, better yet, touching the surface of the brain record summative effects of electrical activity over a considerable area of the brain. Such electrical effects are called brain waves, and the record of them is called an electroencephalogram. When the animal is aroused, the electroencephalogram consists of fast, low-voltage activity; when the animal is drowsy or sleeping normally, the electroencephalogram consists of considerably slow, higher-voltage activity. Carmona attempted to see whether this type of brain activity, and the state of arousal accompanying it, can be modified by direct reward of changes in the brain activity (28, 29).

The subjects of the first experiment were freely moving cats. In order to have a reward that was under complete control and that did not require the cat to move, Carmona used direct electrical stimulation of the medial forebrain bundle, which is a rewarding area of the brain. Such stimulation produced a slight lowering in the average voltage of the electroencephalogram and an increase in behavioral arousal. In order to provide a control for these and any other unlearned effects, he rewarded one group for changes in the direction of high-voltage activity and another group for changes in the direction of low-voltage activity.

Both groups learned. The cats rewarded for high-voltage activity showed more high-voltage slow waves and tended to sit like sphinxes, staring out into space. The cats rewarded for low-voltage activity showed much more low-voltage fast activity, and appeared to be aroused, pacing restlessly about, sniffing, and looking here and there. It was clear that this type of training had modified both the character of the electrical brain waves and the general level of the behavioral activity. It was not clear, however, whether the level of arousal of the brain was directly modified and hence modified the behavior; whether the animals learned specific items of behavior which, in turn, modified the arousal of the brain as reflected in the electroencephalogram; or whether both types of learning were occurring simultaneously.

In order to rule out the direct sensory consequences of changes in muscular tension, movement, and posture, Carmona performed the next experiment on rats that had been paralyzed by means of curare. The results, given in Figure 46-9, show that both rewarded groups showed changes in the rewarded direction; that a subsequent nonrewarded rest increased the number of high-voltage responses in both groups; and that, when the conditions of reward were reversed, the direction of change in voltage was reversed.

At present we are trying to use similar techniques to modify the func-

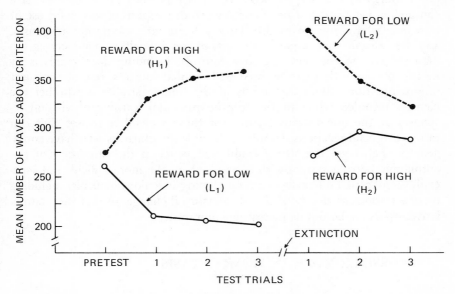

Figure 46-9. Instrumental learning by curarized rats rewarded for high-voltage or for low-voltage electroencephalograms recorded from the cerebral cortex. After a period of non-rewarded extinction, which produced some drowsiness, as indicated by an increase in voltage, the rats in the two groups were then rewarded for voltage changes opposite in direction to the changes for which they were rewarded earlier. (From Carmona, 1967)

tions of a specific part of the vagal nucleus, by recording and specifically rewarding changes in the electrical activity there. Preliminary results suggest that this is possible. The next step is to investigate the visceral consequences of such modification. This kind of work may open up possibilities for modifying the activity of specific parts of the brain and the functions that they control. In some cases, directly rewarding brain activity may be a more convenient or more powerful technique than rewarding skeletal or visceral behavior. It also may be a new way to throw light on the functions of specific parts of the brain (30).

HUMAN VISCERAL LEARNING

Another question is that of whether people are capable of instrumental learning of visceral responses. I believe that in this respect they are as smart as rats. But, as a recent critical review by Katkin and Murray (31) points out, this has not yet been completely proved. These authors have comprehensively summarized the recent studies reporting successful use of instrumental training to modify human heart rate, vasomotor responses, and the galvanic skin response. Because of the difficulties in subjecting human subjects to the same rigorous controls, including deep paralysis by means of curare, that can be used with animal subjects, one of the most serious questions about the results of the human studies is whether the changes recorded represent the true instrumental learning of visceral responses or the unconscious learning of those skeletal responses that can produce visceral reactions. However, the able investigators who have courageously challenged the strong traditional belief in the inferiority of the autonomic nervous system with experiments at the more difficult but especially significant human level are developing ingenious controls, including demonstrations of the specificity of the visceral change, so that their cumulative results are becoming increasingly impressive.

POSSIBLE ROLE IN HOMEOSTASIS

The functional utility of instrumental learning by the cerebrospinal nervous system under the conditions that existed during mammalian evolution is obvious. The skeletal responses mediated by the cerebrospinal nervous system operate on the external environment, so that there is survival value in the ability to learn responses that bring rewards such as food, water, or escape from pain. The fact that the responses mediated by the autonomic nervous system do not have such direct action on the external environment was one of the reasons for believing that they are not subject to instrumental learning. Is the learning ability of the autonomic nervous system something that has no normal function other than that of providing my students with subject matter for publications? Is it a mere accidental by-product of the survival value of cerebrospinal learning, or does the instrumental learning of autonomically mediated responses have some adaptive function, such as helping to maintain that constancy of the internal environment called homeostasis?

In order for instrumental learning to function homeostatically, a deviation away from the optimum level will have to function as a drive to motivate learning, and a change toward the optimum level will have to function as a reward to reinforce the learning of the particular visceral response that produced the corrective change.

When a mammal has less than the optimum amount of water in his body, this deficiency serves as a drive of thirst to motivate learning; the overt consummatory response of drinking functions as a reward to reinforce the learning of the particular skeletal responses that were successful in securing the water that restored the optimum level. But is the consummatory response essential? Can restoration of an optimum level by a glandular response function as a reward?

In order to test for the possible rewarding effects of a glandular response, DiCara, Wolf, and I (32) injected albino rats with antidiuretic hormone (ADH) if they chose one arm of a T-maze and with the isotonic saline vehicle if they chose the other, distinctively different, arm. The ADH permitted water to be reabsorbed in the kidney, so that a smaller volume of more concentrated urine was formed. Thus, for normal rats loaded in advance with H_2O, the ADH interfered with the excess-water excretion required for the restoration of homeostasis, while the control injection of isotonic saline allowed the excess water to be excreted. And, indeed, such rats learned to select the side of the maze that assured them an injection of saline so that their glandular response could restore homeostasis.

Conversely, for rats with diabetes insipidus, loaded in advance with hypertonic NaCl, the homeostatic effects of the same two injections were reversed; the ADH, causing the urine to be more concentrated, helped the rats to get rid of the excess NaCl, while the isotonic saline vehicle did not. And, indeed, a group of rats of this kind learned the opposite choice of selecting the ADH side of the maze. As a further control on the effects of the ADH per se, normal rats which had not been given H_2O or NaCl exhibited no learning. This experiment showed that an excess of either H_2O or NaCl functions as a drive and that the return to the normal concentration produced by the appropriate response of a gland, the kidney, functions as a reward.

When we consider the results of this experiment together with those of our experiments showing that glandular and visceral responses can be instrumentally learned, we will expect the animal to learn those glandular and visceral responses mediated by the central nervous system that promptly restore homeostasis after any considerable deviation. Whether or not this theoretically possible learning has any practical significance will depend on whether or not the innate homeostatic mechanisms control the levels closely enough to prevent any deviations large enough to function as a drive from occurring. Even if the innate control should be accurate enough to preclude learning in most cases, there remains the intriguing possibility that, when pathology interferes with innate control, visceral learning is available as a supplementary mechanism.

IMPLICATIONS AND SPECULATIONS

We have seen how the instrumental learning of visceral responses suggests a new possible homeostatic mechanism worthy of further investigation. Such learning also shows that the autonomic nervous system is not as inferior as has been so widely and firmly believed. It removes one of the strongest arguments for the hypothesis that there are two fundamentally different mechanisms of learning, involving different parts of the nervous system.

Cause of psychosomatic symptoms. Similarly, evidence of the instrumental learning of visceral responses removes the main basis for assuming that the psychosomatic symptoms that involve the autonomic nervous system are fundamentally different from those functional symptoms, such as hysterical ones, that involve the cerebrospinal nervous system. Such evidence allows us to extend to psychosomatic symptoms the type of learning-theory analysis that Dollard and I (7, 33) have applied to other symptoms.

For example, suppose a child is terror-stricken at the thought of going to school in the morning because he is completely unprepared for an important examination. The strong fear elicits a variety of fluctuating autonomic symptoms, such as a queasy stomach at one time and pallor and faintness at another; at this point his mother, who is particularly concerned about cardiovascular symptoms, says, "You are sick and must stay home." The child feels a great relief from fear, and this reward should reinforce the cardiovascular responses producing pallor and faintness. If such experiences are repeated frequently enough, the child, theoretically, should learn to respond with that kind of symptom. Similarly, another child whose mother ignored the vasomotor responses but was particularly concerned by signs of gastric distress would learn the latter type of symptom. I want to emphasize, however, that we need careful clinical research to determine how frequently, if at all, the social conditions sufficient for such theoretically possible learning of visceral symptoms actually occur. Since a given instrumental response can be reinforced by a considerable variety of rewards, and by one reward on one occasion and a different reward on another, the fact that glandular and visceral responses can be instrumentally learned opens up many new theoretical possibilities for the reinforcement of psychosomatic symptoms.

Furthermore, we do not yet know how severe a psychosomatic effect can be produced by learning. While none of the 40 rats rewarded for speeding up their heart rates have died in the course of training under curarization, 7 of the 40 rats rewarded for slowing down their heart rates have died. This statistically reliable difference (chi square $= 5.6$, $P < .02$) is highly suggestive, but it could mean that training to speed up the heart helped the rats resist the stress of curare rather than that the reward for slowing down the heart was strong enough to overcome innate regulatory mechanisms and induce sudden death. In either event the visceral learning had a vital effect. At present, DiCara and I are trying to see whether or not the learning of visceral responses can be carried far enough in the noncurarized animal to produce physical damage. We are also investigating the possibility that there may be a critical period in early infancy during which visceral learning has particularly intense and long-lasting effects.

Individual and cultural differences. It is possible that, in addition to producing psychosomatic symptoms in extreme cases, visceral learning can account for certain more benign individual and cultural differences. Lacey and Lacey (34) have shown that a given individual may have a tendency, which is stable over a number of years, to respond to a variety of different stresses with the same profile of autonomic responses, while other individuals may have statistically reliable tendencies to respond with different profiles. It now seems possible that differential conditions of learning may account for at least some of these individual differences in patterns of autonomic response.

Conversely, such learning may account also for certain instances in which the same individual responds to the same stress in different ways. For example, a small boy who receives a severe bump in rough-and-tumble play may learn to inhibit the secretion of tears in this situation since his peer group will punish crying by calling it "sissy." But the same small boy may burst into tears when he gets home to his mother, who will not punish weeping and may even reward tears with sympathy.

Similarly, it seems conceivable that different conditions of reward by a culture different from our own may be responsible for the fact that Homer's adult heroes so often "let the big tears fall." Indeed, a former colleague of mine, Herbert Barry III, has analyzed cross-cultural data and found that the amount of crying reported for children seems to be related to the way in which the society reacts to their tears (35).

I have emphasized the possible role of learning in producing the observed individual differences in visceral responses to stress, which in extreme cases may result in one type of psychosomatic symptom in one person and a different type in another. Such learning does not, of course, exclude innate individual differences in the susceptibility of different organs. In fact, given social conditions under which any form of illness will be rewarded, the symptoms of the most susceptible organ will be the most likely ones to be learned. Furthermore, some types of stress may be so strong that the innate reactions to them produce damage without any learning. My colleagues and I are currently investigating the psychological variables involved in such types of stress (36).

Therapeutic training. The experimental work on animals has developed a powerful technique for using instrumental learning to modify glandular and visceral responses. The improved training technique consists of moment-to-moment recording of the visceral function and immediate reward, at first, of very small changes in the desired direction and then of progressively larger ones. The success of this technique suggests that it should be able to produce therapeutic changes. If the patient who is highly motivated to get rid of a symptom understands that a signal, such as a tone, indicates a change in the desired direction, that tone could serve as a powerful reward. Instruction to try to turn the tone on as often as possible and praise for success should increase the reward. As patients find that they can secure some control of the symptom, their motivation should be strengthened. Such a procedure should be well worth trying on any symptom, functional or organic, that is under neural control, that can be continuously monitored by modern instrumentation, and for which a given direction of change is clearly indicated medically—for example, cardiac arrhythmias, spastic colitis, asthma, and those cases of high blood pressure that are not essential compensation for kidney damage (37). The obvious cases to begin with are those in which drugs are ineffective or contraindicated. In the light of the fact that our animals learned so much better when under the influence of curare and transferred their training so well to the normal, nondrugged state, it should be worth while to try to use hypnotic suggestion to achieve similar results by enhancing the reward effect of the signal indicating a change in the desired direction, by producing relaxation and regular breathing, and by removing interference from skeletal responses and distraction by irrelevant cues.

Engel and Melmon (38) have reported encouraging results in the use of instrumental training to treat cardiac arrhythmias of organic origin. Randt, Korein, Carmona, and I have had some success in using the method described above to train epileptic patients in the laboratory to suppress, in one way or another, the abnormal paroxysmal spikes in their electroencephalogram. My colleagues and I are hoping to try learning therapy for other symptoms—for example, the rewarding of high-voltage electroencephalograms as a treatment for insomnia. While it is far too early to promise any cures, it certainly will be worth while to investigate thoroughly the therapeutic possibilities of improved instrumental training techniques.

REFERENCES AND NOTES

1. *The Dialogues of Plato*, B. Jowett, Transl. (Univ. of Oxford Press, London, ed. 2, 1875), vol. 3, "Timaeus."
2. X. Bichat, *Recherches Physiologiques sur la Vie et le Mort* (Brosson, Gabon, Paris, 1800).
3. W. B. Cannon, *The Wisdom of the Body* (Norton, New York, 1932).
4. F. Alexander, *Psychosomatic Medicine: Its Principles and Applications* (Norton, New York, 1950), pp. 40–41.
5. G. A. Kimble, *Hilgard and Marquis' Conditioning and Learning* (Appleton-Century-Crofts, New York, ed. 2, 1961), p. 100.
6. B. F. Skinner, *The Behavior of Organisms* (Appleton-Century, New York, 1938); O. H. Mowrer, *Harvard Educ. Rev.* 17, 102 (1947).
7. N. E. Miller and J. Dollard, *Social Learning and Imitation* (Yale Univ. Press, New Haven, 1941); J. Dollard and N. E. Miller, *Personality and Psychotherapy* (McGraw-Hill, New York, 1950); N. E. Miller, *Psychol. Rev.* 58, 375 (1951).
8. N. E. Miller, *Ann. N.Y. Acad. Sci.* 92, 830 (1961); N. E. Miller, in *Nebraska Symposium on Motivation*, M. R. Jones, Ed. (Univ. of Nebraska Press, Lincoln, 1963); N. E. Miller, in *Proc. 3rd World Congr. Psychiat., Montreal, 1961* (1963), vol. 3, p. 213.
9. N. E. Miller, in "Proceedings, 18th International Congress of Psychology, Moscow, 1966," in press.
10. N. E. Miller and A. Carmona, *J. Comp. Physiol. Psychol.* 63, 1 (1967).
11. J. A. Trowill, *ibid.*, p. 7.
12. N. E. Miller and L. V. DiCara, *ibid.*, p. 12.
13. L. V. DiCara and N. E. Miller, *Commun. Behav. Biol.* 2, 19 (1968).
14. L. V. DiCara, *J. Comp. Physiol. Psychol.* 65, 8 (1968).
15. L. V. DiCara, *ibid.*, in press.
16. D. J. Ehrlich and R. B. Malmo, *Neuro-psychologia* 5, 219 (1967).
17. "It even becomes difficult to postulate enough different thoughts each arousing a different emotion, each of which in turn innately elicits a specific visceral response. And if one assumes a more direct specific connection between different thoughts and different visceral responses, the notion becomes indistinguishable from the ideo-motor hypothesis of the voluntary movement of skeletal muscles." [W. James, *Principles of Psychology* (Dover, New York, new ed., 1950), vol. 2, chap. 26].
18. N. E. Miller and A. Banuazizi, *J. Comp. Physiol. Psychol.* 65, 1 (1968).
19. A. Banuazizi, thesis, Yale University (1968).
20. N. E. Miller and L. V. DiCara, *Amer. J. Physiol.* 215, 677 (1968).
21. A. Carmona, N. E. Miller, T. Demierre, in preparation.
22. A. Carmona, in preparation.
23. L. V. DiCara and N. E. Miller, *Commun. Behav. Biol.* 1, 209 (1968).
24. L. V. DiCara, *Science* 159, 1485 (1968).
25. L. V. DiCara, *Psychosom. Med.* 30, 489 (1968).
26. L. V. DiCara and J. M. Weiss, *J. Comp. Physiol. Psychol.*, in press.

27. L. V. DiCara and N. E. Miller, *Physiol. Behav.*, in press.
28. N. E. Miller, *Science 152*, 676 (1966).
29. A. Carmona, thesis, Yale University (1967).
30. For somewhat similar work on the single-cell level, see J. Olds and M. E. Olds, in *Brain Mechanisms and Learning*, J. Delafresnaye, A. Fessard, J. Konorski, Eds. (Blackwell, London, 1961).
31. E. S. Katkin and N. E. Murray, *Psychol. Bull.* 70, 52 (1968); for a reply to their criticisms, see A. Crider, G. Schwartz, S. Shnidman, *ibid.*, in press.
32. N. E. Miller, L. V. DiCara, G. Wolf, *Amer. J. Physiol.* 215, 684 (1968).
33. N. E. Miller, in *Personality Change*, D. Byrne and P. Worchel, Eds. (Wiley, New York, 1964), p. 149.
34. J. I. Lacey and B. C. Lacey, *Amer. J. Psychol.* 71, 50 (1958); *Ann. N.Y. Acad. Sci.* 98, 1257 (1962).
35. H. Barry III, personal communication.
36. N. E. Miller, *Proc. N.Y. Acad. Sci.*, in press.
37. Objective recording of such symptoms might be useful also in monitoring the effects of quite different types of psychotherapy.
38. B. T. Engel and K. T. Melmon, personal communication.
39. The work described is supported by U.S. Public Health Service grant MH 13189.

47

Lawful Disorganization:
The Process Underlying
a Schizophrenic Syndrome

WILLIAM E. BROEN, JR.
& LOWELL H. STORMS

This paper is concerned with the question, "Why do different behaviors which are thought of as 'schizophrenic' go together?" Our purpose is to present a possible explanation for the clustering of some schizophrenic behaviors, basing the explanation on a process which is seen as underlying different areas of schizophrenic behavior. The discussion is not intended as a definitive account of all behaviors which occur in persons diagnosed as schizophrenic, partly because much of what will be said requires additional support, and partly because our goal is to emphasize only certain related aspects of the behaviors characteristic of this heterogeneous nosologic category, schizophrenia. We will emphasize behavior changes which are a part of a process which would be expected as a direct result of increased arousal which facilitates the various response tendencies evoked in a situation. These behaviors include the type of disturbances in thought association and conceptualization which have been considered basic or of major importance in schizophrenia (Bleuler, 1950; Cameron, 1939, 1944; Chapman, 1956, 1958, 1961; Meehl, 1962; Payne, 1961). We will also discuss regression, delusions, and hallucinations as related behaviors. We will not emphasize defensive behaviors which serve an anxiety-reducing function. There is little doubt that defensive behaviors are used by schizophrenics. However, defensive behaviors will be seen as probable, but not necessary, correlates of the process which is the focus of this paper. This focus follows

From W. E. Broen, Jr., and L. H. Storms, Lawful Disorganization: The Process Underlying the Schizophrenic Syndrome. *Psychological Review*, 73, 1966, 265–279. Copyright 1966 by the American Psychological Association, and reproduced by permission of publisher and author.

Part of this paper was written while the senior author was a special consultant on a research project supported by Grant No. R-61-2-20 from the California Department of Mental Hygiene.

635

two complementary lines of thought: (*a*) that behavioral deficit in schizophrenia is the result of arousal or anxiety (see literature reviewed in Distler, May, & Tuma, 1964; Lynn, 1963; Mednick, 1958), and (*b*) that behavioral deficit may be related to arousal apart from possible defensive or avoidance functions of the behavior (Fish, 1961; Freeman, 1960; Malmo, 1959).

The basic theoretical account of the arousal-related process to be used here has been presented previously (Broen & Storms, 1961). In this account, a stimulus situation evokes habitual tendencies to respond which vary in strength depending on amount of previous training. Habit strength interacts multiplicatively with arousal (drive) level to yield response strength. When more than one tendency to respond is evoked in a situation, the probability of the dominant response is an increasing function of the differences in response strengths between dominant and competing responses. A response-strength ceiling which is lower than the product of maximum arousal level and maximum habit strength is also postulated. In this account, if arousal level and habit strength of the dominant response are sufficient to raise the strength of the dominant response to its ceiling, further increases in arousal can only facilitate competing responses. The result is a decrease in the relative dominance of the dominant response, with increased probability of competing responses.

The basic relationships in the account are illustrated in Figure 47-1. Note the figure on the left first. This figure is intended to illustrate alternate responses which are evoked in different strengths (e.g., the dominant response "light" and competing response "night" evoked by the stimulus word DARK in a word-association task). When arousal level is increased beyond the level where the strength of the dominant response reaches ceil-

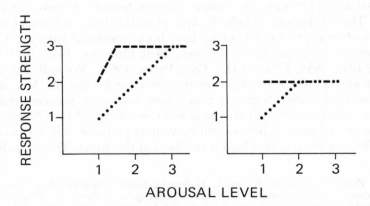

Figure 47-1.   Strengths of dominant (– –) and competing (. . . .) responses as a function of arousal level and level of response-strength ceiling. (Level of response-strength ceiling is 3 in the left figure, 2 in the right.)

ing, the hierarchical order of dominant and competing responses tends to break down. With increasing arousal, the tendency is for alternate responses to become more equal in strength and probability of occurrence (Arousal Level 3 in Figure 47-1).

Normal, appropriate behavior is characterized by dominance of appropriate responses. Thus in an appropriately responding person, an increase in arousal which decreases the frequency of dominant responses usually reduces appropriateness of behavior. This decreased appropriateness will be of a particular type. With decreased hierarchial dominance of appropriate over competing responses, behavior will be characterized by increased fluctuation between appropriate and competing responses. This type of disorganization of normal response hierarchies seems to be common to each of the content areas of schizophrenic behavior we will discuss.

As is illustrated in Figure 47-1, note that the extent of hierarchical disorganization is a function of three variables: (*a*) the strength of dominant and competing responses, (*b*) the level of arousal, and (*c*) the level of response-strength ceiling. If response strengths of dominant and competing responses are low, an increase in arousal may increase the dominance of the appropriate response (as in the increase in arousal from 1 to 1.5 in the left figure). Also, if competing responses are not present, there is no decrement in the relative strength of the appropriate response regardless of arousal level. The effect of individual differences in ceiling level can be seen by comparing the left and right figures. A low ceiling leads to disorganization of a response hierarchy under lower levels of arousal. It is important to note that because of differences in level of ceiling we expect the same type of disorganized behavior to occur at different arousal levels in different persons. While we expect similar changes in behavior to occur across individuals as a function of intraindividual variations in arousal, a specific level of arousal will not be assumed to be related to a specific amount of disorganization of response hierarchies. Not all schizophrenics exhibiting the type of behavior to be discussed here will be expected to be characterized by high levels of arousal.

Some additional comments will aid in translating the account into experimental predictions. The term arousal is used to indicate a dimension of relatively diffuse cortical and physiological activation which may be measured by changes in peripheral physiological indicants such as increases in heart rate, blood pressure, and respiration rate. Extended discussion concerning the concept of arousal or activation as we use the terms can be found in Carlton (1963), Gellhorn (1964), Malmo (1959), Pinneo (1961), and Schnore (1959). The studies we will cite as having varied arousal experimentally use independent variables which are similar to variables which have been shown to lead to the general physiological changes indicative of arousal. A particularly good example of such a variable is induced muscular tension (Pinneo, 1961). Variation in anxiety or psychological stress is also seen as related to arousal variation (Schnore, 1959; Spence, 1958b), although caution is needed in the interpretation of studies using specific methods of varying anxiety which have not been related to physiological indicants of arousal.

We have used three measures of habit strength in making predictions for our own research and in interpreting other research. In experiments in which new S–R connections are trained, the habit strength of a response is assumed to be an increasing function of the number of occurrences of that response during training. Habit strength is also assumed to vary inversely with the amount a stimulus differs from a training stimulus when the subject is familiar with the stimulus alternatives in the experiment. However, these definitions are of little use in many of the studies we will cite because these studies deal with responses with unknown learning histories. In studies using stimuli and responses which are commonly used, for example, associations to familiar words, we will assume that the habit strength of the dominant response is at its maximum, and the average habit strength of a competing response for groups of schizophrenics is a function of the probability of that response as observed in normals.

Response-strength ceiling effects in experiments are predicted on the basis of two assumptions. First, schizophrenics are assumed to have lower average response-strength ceilings than nonschizophrenics. As a result, the response hierarchies of schizophrenics should become disorganized at lower levels of arousal. This assumption is consistent with data suggesting that normals may operate efficiently within a broader range of arousal than schizophrenics (Lynn, 1963; Venables, 1960). Second, we will assume that, in a group of persons who exhibit schizophrenic behavior in hospital environments, the stress of standard experimental situations is sufficient to lead to ceiling effects when familiar associations are tested. With this level of arousal and lower ceilings, schizophrenics should exhibit more of the type of disorganization expected from response-strength ceiling effects than nonschizophrenics.

The implications of the present account overlap in some respects hypotheses proposed by Chapman (1958), Payne (1961), Meehl (1962), especially in his second neurological model, Weckowicz and Blewett (1959), and Stilson and Kopell (1964) in their neurophysiological thinking. The account also has a degree of similarity to Russian thinking concerning a reduction in internal inhibition in some schizophrenics which would selectively facilitate nonreinforced responses and responses to weak stimuli (Lynn, 1963). There is also a great deal of similarity to the neurophysiological theory of schizophrenia proposed by Fish (1961).

Because of common background in extensions or modifications of concepts from Hullian learning theory, this account is also similar in some respects to an account of inappropriate behavior in terms of competing responses raised above threshold by increased drive (Spence, 1956, 1958a; Taylor & Spence, 1952). This threshold theory was used by Mednick

(1958) in a very stimulating account of some aspects of schizophrenia. However, the accounts differ on the basic point of how increased arousal leads to inappropriate behavior and thus also differ in predictions regarding schizophrenic behavior (for discussions of the accounts see Broen & Storms, 1961; Broen, Storms, & Schenck, 1961; DeMille, 1959; Hill, 1957).

It may be useful to note a basic difference between the ceiling account and the threshold account. When response-strength threshold factors, rather than ceiling effects, are seen as leading to decrement in a dominant response, increased arousal is expected to lead to decrement only when response strength is low. In the usual situation where a response which is appropriate has higher habit strength than a competing response, threshold effects would lead to the following:

. . . at very low levels of drive and training a relatively weak-drive group would be expected to perform at a higher level than a somewhat stronger-drive group. On the other hand at higher levels of training and drive the reverse picture would hold; that is, the performance of the higher-drive group should be above that of the relatively weaker-drive group (Spence, 1958a, p. 92).

In contrast, response-strength ceiling effects would lead to dominant-response decrement primarily under higher levels of drive and higher levels of strength of dominant and competing responses. The following discussion of some aspects of schizophrenic behavior is based on the consideration of response-strength ceiling effects.

ASSOCIATION DISTURBANCE

Both clinical and research literature suggest that schizophrenics have different associations in their thought processes or, on a more overt level, different verbal associations from normals or other psychiatric patients (Deering, 1963; Sommer, Dewar, & Osmond, 1960; Storms & Broen, 1964). Looking at the particular nature of this difference, it seems that the schizophrenic's associations are not disconnected, highly irrelevant thoughts. Instead, schizophrenic associations are characterized as "unprecise approximations" which "cannot be dismissed as either 'irrelevant' or 'incoherent' for they are certainly about the general subject and loosely related to one another (Cameron, 1944, pp. 53–54)." Bleuler (1950) described the deviant but related associations another way, characterizing some schizophrenic thinking as "ideas of a certain category . . . thrown into one pot, mixed, and subsequently picked out at random [p. 16]." As a more specific example of schizophrenic "looseness of association," Arieti (1955, p. 4) considers the schizophrenic disorder to be implicit in the answer, "White House," to the question, "Who was the first president of the United States?" Burstein's (1961) study comparing schizophrenics and normals on selecting synonyms from a list of words also suggests that the primary verbal difference between schizophrenics and normals is the schizophrenics' overuse of associations which are inappropriate but related to the stimulus, such as antonyms and homonyms.

This particular form of association disturbance seems to be consistent with the kind of behavior expected under high arousal within the account used in this paper. As has been noted, an increase in arousal beyond the level necessary to raise a dominant response to maximum strength will tend to equalize the response strengths of dominant and competing responses. Thus, the expected form of disturbed behavior would be characterized by increased randomization among the responses in response hierarchies (Bleuler's 1950, "ideas in a certain category") with a consequent increase in the probability of those behaviors which are at relatively low strength in normal response hierarchies. The increase in within-hierarchy, associated-but-deviant responses seems much like the descriptions of the characteristics of associative disturbance in schizophrenia mentioned above.

If schizophrenic associations can be primarily understood as associations under high arousal, the formal account has other implications in addition to the expectation that deviant responses will be loosely relevant. The partial equalization of response strengths of alternate responses under increased arousal also implies an instability of associations. In addition, in schizophrenics, instability of associations should increase with increased arousal level. Greater instability of associative responses in schizophrenics than in normals was found on repeated association tasks by Sommer et al. (1960) and Storms and Broen (1964). This associative instability in schizophrenics does seem to increase under stress conditions, such as time stress and in response to words rated as anxiety producing, and the increase in instability under stress tends to be greater in schizophrenics than in neurotics and normals (Storms & Broen, 1964). The latter result was interpreted as being due to schizophrenics having greater arousal reactivity to stress conditions, or having lower response-strength ceilings, and therefore being more likely to show the response-strength ceiling effects discussed above.

As was noted previously, the account used here also implies that schizophrenic association disturbance should be greatest on tasks where competing responses are present and have relatively high habit strength. This implication is consistent with data indicating that, relative to normals, schizophrenics exhibit greater deficit on tasks requiring the use of words with multiple meanings than on tasks using single-meaning words (Faibish, 1961). In another relevant study, Blaufarb (1962) compared schizophrenics and normals on the meanings associated with proverbs, with the ambiguity of the proverbs varied by two methods of presentation (i.e., presenting proverbs singly, and presenting three proverbs having the same meaning in a group, with the group method assumed to provide a more precise stimulus which would reduce the number of inadequate associations). The performance of schizophrenics was significantly poorer than that of the normals only under the more ambiguous method of presenting proverbs, again suggesting that schizophrenics' associations are most deviant on tasks where competing associations are present.

Paired-associate learning tasks have also been used to investigate the hypothesis that schizophrenics are especially deficient on tasks where competing responses are present in strength. The results are inconsistent but apparently tend to support the hypothesis (Kausler, Lair, & Matsumoto, 1964; Spence & Lair, 1965, support the hypothesis, while Spence & Lair, 1964, report negative results). However, it is difficult to interpret the results of these studies in terms of the relative decrement in dominant response expected from the present account. This is because during training the correct response is not dominant at first and then becomes dominant, but the data are overall measures of performance which do not take variation in dominance into account.

In summary, there is some support for the hypothesis that schizophrenic associations may be influenced by the type of disorganization of response hierarchies expected from ceiling effects: (a) Schizophrenic deviant associations tend to be loosely associated with the stimulus; (b) schizophrenic response hierarchies tend to be unstable, with this instability increasing under stress; and (c) schizophrenic association deficits tend to occur primarily in situations which elicit multiple associations.

CONCEPT DISTURBANCE

Certain changes in conceptual responses are also expected as a result of increased arousal. By "conceptual responses" we mean responses which are appropriate only to specific classes of objects (e.g., using the label "birds" only to designate birds). The same task and arousal conditions which were relevant to the occurrence of "looseness of association" are relevant to concept disturbance. When appropriate conceptual responses are dominant and competing responses are also evoked at high strength, increased arousal may increase the frequency of the competing conceptual responses. As an example, consider a task which has been used in research on concept disturbance (Chapman, 1961). A subject is given cards on which the names of different objects are printed, and he is instructed to select the cards which refer to birds. Some of the cards designate flying insects. When the subject looks at a card designating a flying insect, the response which is appropriate to bird cards (selection) will be evoked in some strength due to mediated generalization. This generalized response tendency will compete with appropriate conceptual responding. Increased arousal which is sufficient to lead to response-strength ceiling effects would increase the frequency of competing responses. Some insect cards would be selected as bird cards. This is an example of an overly broad or overinclusive use of a conceptual response which may result from increased arousal.

Increased arousal may also result in a too narrow or overexclusive use of a conceptual response. Some objects which should be included in a class of objects may be similar in some respects to objects which do not belong in a class. Such objects would evoke competing tendencies not to include them in their appropriate category. With sufficient increase in arousal, these competing tendencies toward inappropriate exclusion would be exacerbated. Note that overexclusive and overinclusive responding are not mutually incompatible. If competing response tendencies to include certain inappropriate objects in a class and to exclude certain appropriate objects are both present, increased arousal may increase both types of conceptual errors.

Deviant breadth of concepts is a commonly noted aspect of schizophrenic behavior. Consistent with the above expectations, schizophrenic concept performance has been characterized both as overexclusive ("concrete") and overinclusive (see literature reviewed by Chapman, 1961; Payne, 1961). Usually studies have found schizophrenic concepts to be either overexclusive or overinclusive, with more recent studies emphasizing overinclusion. A few studies have found schizophrenic conceptual performance to be both overexclusive and overinclusive (Chapman, 1961; Chapman & Taylor, 1957; Zaslow, 1950). In some contrast to the rationale of the present discussion it has been suggested that type of conceptual error in schizophrenics is a function of type of subjects, with organic pathology in "process" schizophrenics leading to overexclusive concepts (e.g., Tutko & Spence, 1962). Subject and task variables may both be important in determining type of conceptual disturbance. Cortical damage in some schizophrenics may lead to overexclusion, while an arousal process in others leads to overexclusion or overinclusion, depending on task conditions.

Within the present account, increased arousal will increase a particular kind of error only in a task which evokes a tendency toward that error in some strength. To the extent that differences between schizophrenics and normals are due to the arousal process, this means that schizophrenics should make the same types of conceptual errors as normals, except that schizophrenics should make more of these errors. Also because exacerbation of errors under arousal depends in part on the strength of error tendency evoked by a task, the frequency of errors across tasks should tend to be correlated for schizophrenics and normals. Evidence on the above points is provided in the study we have used to provide a research example (Chapman, 1961). Chapman used four kinds of conceptual card-sorting tasks and recorded both overinclusive and overexclusive errors. Relevant data from Chapman's study are presented in Table 47-1.

TABLE 47-1.   Mean Errors on Concept-Sorting Tasks for
               Schizophrenics and Normals

Task	Overinclusion errors		Overexclusion errors	
	Normal	Schizophrenic	Normal	Schizophrenic
1	.12	1.61	1.52	2.61
2	.33	2.08	2.94	8.06
3	.42	6.85	.94	2.40
4	2.12	10.57	.61	1.39

Note: Adapted from Chapman (1961).

Note several things in Table 47-1. First, both overinclusion and over-exclusion errors are made by schizophrenics and normals, with schizophrenics making more of both types of errors. Also, in three of the four tasks the dominant error direction (overinclusion versus overexclusion) is the same for both schizophrenics and normals. In addition, note that for overinclusion and overexclusion errors the error frequencies for schizophrenics and normals have 1.0 rank-order correlation across tasks. It may also be of interest to note that in a different content area, syllogistic reasoning, Gottesman and Chapman (1960) found that hierarchies of reasoning errors within tasks were similar for schizophrenics and normals, the difference consisting of a partial randomization of response hierarchies in the schizophrenics. As expected from the paradigm used here, the frequency of a particular type of conceptual error does seem to be a function of the strength of that error tendency in normal response hierarchies. The suggestion that schizophrenic error patterns seem to be exacerbations of normal error patterns (with supporting evidence) has also been made in other papers by Chapman (1958) and by Fey (1951).

We have emphasized the relationship of schizophrenic conceptual errors to the strength of error tendencies in normal response hierarchies. In the paradigm being used here, the strength of an appropriate dominant response also plays a role in determining whether or not competing inappropriate responses will increase under increased arousal. As was seen in the discussion of Figure 47-1, response-strength ceiling effects leading to an increase in competing responses are most likely when dominant response strength is high. Concept research with schizophrenics has usually not emphasized strength of appropriate conceptual responses as an independent variable. The stimuli have tended to be familiar, supposedly eliciting appropriate responses of high strength. Stimulus-generalization studies may provide relevant evidence concerning variation in strength of dominant responses as related to errors. We have some hesitation about citing stimulus-generalization studies in the present context because concepts are usually based on mediated generalization instead of primary stimulus generalization. However, as suggestive evidence, note that in stimulus-generalization tasks, schizophrenics as compared to normals do tend to exhibit reduced frequency of a dominant response primarily where the response is strong—at the training stimulus (Broen & Storms, 1964; Dunn, 1954; Garmezy, 1952; Knopf & Fager, 1959). Recent evidence suggests that the same phenomena may occur in the area of mediated generalization (Chapman & Chapman, 1965; Peastrel, 1964). In these studies, schizophrenic deficit in responses which depended on mediated similarity occurred primarily to stimuli where mediated similarity was greatest.

Consideration of the importance of task variables in determining type of concept disturbance in schizophrenia suggests that the recent emphasis on schizophrenics' overinclusive concepts in the research literature may be a function of task conditions. We hypothesize that overinclusive and underinclusive errors would occur with equal frequency in acute schizophrenics if task conditions were equated. Equating task conditions would involve equating appropriate response strengths and competing response strengths for stimuli where inclusive and exclusive responses are appropriate, and having equal numbers of both classes of stimuli in the study (equal numbers of objects which would be correctly included and excluded).

An additional point is that if schizophrenic conceptual errors are responses which are low in normal response hierarchies, schizophrenic conceptual errors should be associated responses rather than irrelevant responses. Referring back to the research example, this means that if there is overinclusion in selecting objects which are birds, the specific overinclusions would tend to be flying insects rather than irrelevant objects such as articles of clothing. The research evidence indicates that schizophrenic conceptual errors do tend to be associated errors rather than irrelevant errors (Chapman, 1958, 1961; Chapman & Taylor, 1957).

The arousal paradigm also implies that schizophrenics should show more conceptual deficit under increased arousal (except when dominant appropriate responses have low strength—see Figure 47-1—or when an aversive stimulus is used specifically to provide new information or as an incentive—see Cavanaugh, 1958). The most relevant data we know on this point are again from stimulus-generalization studies. Broen, Storms, and Goldberg (1963) tested the generalization of a motor response under different amounts of induced muscular tension (arousal). Increased arousal led to a decrease in the response at its training stimulus (overexclusion) and a facilitation of the response to generalization stimuli (overinclusion). In another relevant study, Broen and Storms 1964) trained schizophrenics to press a lever in one direction in response to one category of pictures (tree with branch angles in a specified range) and to press the lever in the other direction in response to another category of pictures (different branch angles). Lengthy training and probabilistic reinforcement were used to insure that both appropriate and competing responses had high habit strengths. An increase in induced muscular tension reduced the number of appropriate responses and increased the number of competing responses. In accordance with an hypothesis of higher response-strength ceilings in normals, hospitalized nonpsychiatric subjects showed no significant decrement in appropriate responses or increase in competing responses. These two studies are most directly relevant to the effect of arousal on conceptual responses when concepts are defined in terms of a range of stimulus similarity. In these studies the evidence is consistent with the implication from the account that under certain boundary conditions increased arousal tends to increase competing conceptual responses at the expense of appropriate conceptual responses. We expect that increased arousal has similar effects on responses to other types of concepts, such as conceptual groupings determined by functions of objects, but research which would confirm this generalization is certainly needed.

DELUSIONS

We expect that transitory and relatively unstructured delusions will accompany the types of association and concept disturbances we have been discussing. When a person's categorizations are underinclusive and overinclusive, the data which he sees as relevant to a problem will be deviant. In drawing conclusions some relevant data will not be used, and loosely associated data, which are normally excluded as unimportant, will be seen as quite relevant. Delusional conclusions will result. These delusions will be transitory and unstructured because the underlying process involves fluctuations between appropriate and competing associations. It is important to note that increased arousal should lead to a syndrome which includes only transitory and unstructured delusions. Stable delusions may develop later if a particular delusion reduces anxiety. Such stability of thought implies that the current level of arousal is not sufficient to lead to response-strength ceiling effects.

Cameron's (1951) conclusions concerning delusions are quite similar to the implications of the present account. He distinguished two stages in the formation of a delusion—an initial diffuse and unstructured phase and a later restrictive phase. The unstructured delusions are related to anxiety through a causal chain like that in the present account, namely the effect of anxiety in lowering the "relevance-to-irrelevance" ratio of the information on which conclusions are based. The development of structure and stability would occur later if the delusional thinking comes to serve a defensive function.

Relevant research information is sparse but supportive enough to suggest that further investigation based on the implications of the present account may be useful. As expected from the postulated relationship between concept disturbance and delusions, recently admitted schizophrenics who have delusions are significantly more overinclusive in their thinking than either nondeluded schizophrenics or nonschizophrenic patients (Payne, Caird, & Laverty, 1964). The relationship seems to be a function of chronicity and may be reversed in chronic deluded schizophrenics if delusions are the single prominent symptom as would be expected when a delusion serves a defensive function (Silverman, 1964).

HALLUCINATIONS

An arousal-induced disorganization of response hierarchies may also underlie the occurrence of some types of hallucinations. When internal or external cues evoke competing perceptual responses, increased arousal may lead to a relative decrease in the dominance of appropriate perceptual responses, thereby increasing inappropriate perceptions.

The hallucinations which would result from this breakdown in normal response hierarchies would tend to be disorganized and fragmented mixtures of appropriate and inappropriate perceptions. These hallucinations should also increase with increased arousal. In addition, because the hallucinatory perceptions are normally evoked as low-strength competing responses, the misperceptions should have some association to the stimulus situation in which they occur. We will briefly discuss each of these implications in turn.

The expectation that some schizophrenic hallucinations should be disorganized mixtures of appropriate and inappropriate perceptions is different from the rather organized and meaningful reports of hallucinations which are usually presented in abnormal psychology texts. However, there is a fair amount of clinical evidence suggesting that schizophrenic hallucinations are often, even usually, such fragmented mixtures. For example, Kraepelin (1919) and Bleuler (1950) both report rather disorganized and fragmented content in schizophrenic hallucinations. Bleuler emphasizes the varied and abrupt nature of hallucinations and observes that sensory deceptions may occur along with a correct observation of the same event. Discussing hallucinated voices Bleuler (1950) states that: "As a rule . . . the patients hear short sentences or single words which in themselves need not always make sense. It is the patient who usually imputes some meaning to the words or sentences [p. 99]." This meaningful organization of misperceptions may be a secondary process which is learned because it is anxiety reducing. As Kraepelin (1919.) notes: "They [hallucinations] are almost never wanting in the acute and subacute forms of the disease . . . at the beginning these are usually simple noises . . . and then develops . . . the hearing of voices [p. 7]."

The hypothesized relationship between increased arousal and hallucinations seems at first to be contrary to the discussions which have emphasized the causal role of low arousal, primarily being concerned with dreams during sleep (see Evarts, 1962). However, Harris (1959) has emphasized the point that this low-arousal process is different from the process leading to hallucinations in schizophrenia, a suggestion which is supported by physiological differences between dreaming and schizophrenia (Rechtschaffen, Schulsinger, & Mednick, 1964). Other writers point out that high levels of arousal or anxiety may also be associated with hallucinations (Fish, 1961; West, 1962; Zuckerman, Albright, Marks, & Miller, 1962). A high-arousal explanation of schizophrenic hallucinations also seems consistent with differences in frequency of different types of hallucinations. For example, hallucinations seem to have more stressful than nonstressful content (e.g., accusing voices). Stressful thoughts would be expected to lead to higher levels of arousal than nonstressful content, increasing the likelihood of lack of discrimination of the source of the stimulation. We might also consider why unusual perceptions in schizophrenia are so frequently concerned with body sensations (note the MMPI *Sc* scale content) and are more frequently auditory than visual (Malitz, Wilkens, & Esecover, 1962). The explanation may lie in different arousal-producing properties in different sensory modalities. If a particular kind of stimulation leads to more arousal, these stimuli will be more usually misperceived. In line with the dominance of body and auditory hallucinations in schizophrenia, Bernhaut, Gellhorn, and Rasmussen (1953, p. 33) state that ". . . sensory stimuli listed in decreasing order of ability to produce an arousal reaction are: (i) pain (most effective); (ii) proprioception; (iii) auditory stimulation; (iv) optic stimulation (least effective)."

The suggestion that hallucinatory perceptions should be perceptions which are associated with the situation in which they occur also seems consistent with clinical observations and the results of a few relevant experiments. The association is most obvious when the misperception is simply an inaccurate localization of stimulation. For example, patients' own thoughts appear to be spoken out loud, and actual external sounds may be perceived as coming from within (Bleuler, 1950). The view that hallucinations are associated responses also receives some experimental support from studies indicating that auditory hallucinations are more likely in the presence of audible sound (Harris, 1959; Riss, 1959), and from Lindsley's (1963) finding that "in general, the more similar the stimulus was to a human voice, the higher the probability that a given patient would 'talk to it' [p. 295]."

REGRESSION

In normal adults, those responses which are dominant in a situation tend to be appropriate to that situation. Competing responses may also be evoked at some strengths. These competing responses may be of at least two types: (a) responses which had been learned earlier but are no longer appropriate, and (b) responses which are generalized from similar situations. Increased arousal which is sufficient to equalize dominant and competing responses at ceiling strengths will therefore increase the proportion of responses which had been learned earlier in the situation (or related situations). In the sense that the probability of old responses is increased, regression is expected as one aspect of the syndrome of behaviors expected under high levels of arousal. However, the expected behavior is not simply a return to childlike patterns of behaving. The form of regression would be a relatively unstructured mixture of appropriate, generalized, and regressive responses.

There is some evidence that schizophrenic regression is not a simple return to childlike behavior patterns (see literature reviewed in Chapman, Burstein, Day, & Verdone, 1961), and that the lack of subordination of responses which are normally more hierarchically ordered is the form of regression which occurs in schizophrenia (Cameron, 1939). Cameron's conclusions from an object-sorting task he used to study regression provide a good description of the type of regression which occurs in schizophrenia. He observed that the schizophrenics were ". . . unable to organize or subordinate the events occurring simultaneously in their organism—perceptual, memorial, imaginal [p. 269]." While such behavior may have some childlike qualities, it would seem to be more aptly described as a decrement in the normal hierarchical ordering of alternate response tendencies.

Much of the research suggesting that regression can be induced by increased arousal has been done with infrahuman subjects (see Kleemeier, 1942). However, there is considerable clinical literature and some experimental evidence suggesting that increased stress or arousal is related to regression in humans (e.g., Barker, Dembo, & Lewin, 1941; Levin, 1965; Noyes & Kolb, 1958; Rodnick, 1942; Sadler, 1953).

Levin's (1965) study provides an especially rigorous test of a relationship between increased arousal and regression implied by the paradigm used here. In this study, normal subjects first learned to associate numbers to colors. In a second phase the correct associations were changed, and associations were tested under different degrees of arousal (varied by changing degree of induced muscular tension). At the time that arousal was varied, the responses which had previously been correct (regressive responses) were the strongest competing responses. The arousal paradigm implies that when arousal increases the strength of competing responses, the multiplicative effect of arousal should favor the strongest competing response (Levin's regression response) to the point where this response is restricted by the response-strength ceiling. Arousal increased beyond this level would tend to increase the proportion of other, initially weaker, competing responses. In the Levin study when proportion of regression errors to other errors was related to arousal level, the inverted U relationship implied by the present account was found. The proportion of errors which were regressive responses increased as muscle tension increased from zero to low to medium tension, and then decreased under high tension.

Another implication from the theoretical account used in the present paper is that regression is more likely to occur if both presently dominant and older responses have high response strength. Clinical literature and research reports (using animal subjects) have concentrated on only part of this implication, being concerned with the strength of the older or regressive response as a determiner of regression. Most authors have agreed that there is a positive relation between strength of the former response and likelihood of regression (e.g., Fenichel, 1945; Freud, 1949; Martin, 1940).

Thus there is some support for the hypothesis that a form of regression, the destructured mixture of mature, generalized, and previously appropriate behaviors which seems to occur in schizophrenia, may be the result of the same arousal-related process which determines other aspects of a schizophrenic syndrome.

REFERENCES

Arieti, S. *Interpretation of schizophrenia.* New York: Brunner, 1955.

Barker, R., Dembo, T., & Lewin, K. Frustration and regression: An experiment with young children. *University of Iowa Studies in Child Welfare*, 1941, 18, No. 1.

Bernhaut, M., Gellhorn, E., & Rasmussen, A. T. Experimental contributions to problem of consciousness. *Journal of Neurophysiology*, 1953, 16, 21–35.

Blaufarb, H. A demonstration of verbal abstracting ability in chronic schizophrenics under enriched stimulus and instructional conditions. *Journal of Consulting Psychology*, 1962, 26, 471–475.

Bleuler, E. *Dementia praecox or the group of schizophrenias.* New York: International Universities Press, 1950.

Broen, W. E., Jr., & Storms, L. H. A reaction potential ceiling and response decrements in complex situations. *Psychological Review*, 1961, 68, 405–415.

Broen, W. E., Jr., & Storms, L. H. The differential effect of induced muscular tension (drive) on discrimination in schizophrenics and normals. *Journal of Abnormal and Social Psychology*, 1964, 68, 349–353.

Broen, W. E., Jr., Storms, L. H., & Goldberg, D. H. Decreased discrimination as a function of increased drive. *Journal of Abnormal and Social Psychology*, 1963, 67, 266–273.

Broen, W. E., Jr., Storms, L. H., & Schenck, H. U., Jr. Inappropriate behavior as a function of the energizing effect of drive. *Journal of Personality*, 1961, 29, 489–498.

Burstein, A. G. Some verbal aspects of primary process thought in schizophrenia. *Journal of Abnormal and Social Psychology*, 1961, 62, 155–157.

Cameron, N. Deterioration and regression in schizophrenic thinking. *Journal of Abnormal and Social Psychology*, 1939, 34, 265–269.

Cameron, N. Experimental analysis of schizophrenic thinking. In J. S. Kasanin (Ed.), *Language and thought in schizophrenia*. Berkeley, Los Angeles: University of California Press, 1944. Pp. 50–63.

Cameron, N. Perceptual organization and behavior pathology. In R. R. Blake & G. V. Ramsey (Eds.), *Perception—an approach to personality*. New York: Ronald, 1951. Pp. 283–306.

Carlton, P. L. Cholinergic mechanisms in the control of behavior by the brain. *Psychological Review*, 1963, 70, 19–39.

Cavanaugh, D. Improvement in the performance of schizophrenics on concept formation tasks as a function of motivational change. *Journal of Abnormal and Social Psychology*, 1958, 57, 8–12.

Chapman, L. J. Distractibility in the conceptual performance of schizophrenics. *Journal of Abnormal and Social Psychology*, 1956, 53, 286–291.

Chapman, L. J. Intrusion of associative responses into schizophrenic conceptual performance. *Journal of Abnormal and Social Psychology*, 1958, 56, 374–379.

Chapman, L. J. A reinterpretation of some pathological disturbances in conceptual breadth. *Journal of Abnormal and Social Psychology*, 1961, 62, 514–519.

Chapman, L. J., Burstein, A. G., Day, D., & Verdone, P. Regression and disorders of thought. *Journal of Abnormal and Social Psychology*, 1961, 63, 540–545.

Chapman, L. J., & Chapman, J. P. Interpretation of words in schizophrenia. *Journal of Personality and Social Psychology*, 1965, 1, 135–146.

Chapman, L. J., & Taylor, J. A. Breadth of deviant concepts used by schizophrenics. *Journal of Abnormal and Social Psychology*, 1957, 54, 118–123.

Deering, G. Affective stimuli and disturbance of thought processes. *Journal of Consulting Psychology*, 1963, 27, 338–343.

DeMille, R. Learning theory and schizophrenia: A comment. *Psychological Bulletin*, 1959, 56, 313–314.

Distler, L. S., May, P. R. A., & Tuma, A. H. Anxiety and ego strength as predictors of response to treatment in schizophrenic patients. *Journal of Consulting Psychology*, 1964, 28, 170–177.

Dunn, W. L. Visual discrimination of schizophrenic subjects as a function of stimulus meaning. *Journal of Personality*, 1954, 23, 48–64.

Evarts, E. V. A neurophysiologic theory of hallucinations. In L. J. West (Ed.), *Hallucinations*. New York: Grune & Stratton, 1962. Pp. 1–14.

Faibish, G. M. Schizophrenic response to words of multiple meaning. *Journal of Personality*, 1961, 29, 414–427.

Fenichel, O. *The psychoanalytic theory of neurosis*. New York: Norton, 1945.

Fey, E. T. The performance of young schizophrenics and young normals on the Wisconsin Card Sorting Test. *Journal of Consulting Psychology*, 1951, 15, 311–319.

Fish, F. A neurophysiological theory of schizophrenia. *Journal of Mental Science*, 1961, 107, 828–838.

Freeman, T. On the psychopathology of schizophrenia. *Journal of Mental Science*, 1960, 106, 925–937.

Freud, S. *An outline of psychoanalysis.* New York: Norton, 1949.

Garmezy, N. Stimulus differentiation by schizophrenic and normal subjects under conditions of reward and punishment. *Journal of Personality,* 1952, 20, 253–276.

Gellhorn, E. Motion and emotion: The role of proprioception in the physiology and pathology of the emotions. *Psychological Review,* 1964, 71, 457–472.

Gottesman, L., & Chapman, L. J. Syllogistic reasoning errors in schizophrenia. *Journal of Consulting Psychology,* 1960, 24, 250–255.

Harris, A. Sensory deprivation and schizophrenia. *Journal of Mental Science,* 1959, 105, 235–237.

Hill, W. F. Comments on Taylor's "Drive theory and manifest anxiety." *Psychological Bulletin,* 1957, 54, 490–493.

Kausler, D. H., Lair, C. V., & Matsumoto, R. Interference transfer paradigms and the performance of schizophrenics and controls. *Journal of Abnormal and Social Psychology,* 1964, 69, 584–587.

Kleemeier, R. W. Fixation and regression in the rat. *Psychological Monographs,* 1942, 54 (4, Whole No. 246).

Knopf, I. J., & Fager, R. E. Differences in gradients of stimulus generalization as a function of psychiatric disorder. *Journal of Abnormal and Social Psychology,* 1959, 59, 73–76.

Kraepelin, E. *Dementia praecox and paraphrenia.* (Trans. by R. M. Barclay) (Ed. by G. M. Robertson) Edinburgh: Livingstone, 1919.

Levin, I. P. Induced muscle tension and response shift in paired-associate learning. Unpublished doctoral dissertation, University of California, Los Angeles, 1965.

Lindsley, O. R. Direct measurement and functional definition of vocal hallucinatory symptoms. *Journal of Nervous and Mental Disease,* 1963, 136, 293–297.

Lynn, R. Russian theory and research on schizophrenia. *Psychological Bulletin,* 1963, 60, 486–498.

Malitz, S., Wilkens, B., & Esecover, H. A comparison of drug-induced hallucinations with those seen in spontaneously occurring psychoses. In L. J. West (Ed.), *Hallucinations.* New York: Grune & Stratton, 1962. Pp. 50–63.

Malmo, R. B. Activation: A neuropsychological dimension. *Psychological Review,* 1959, 66, 367–386.

Martin, R. F. "Native" traits and regression in the rat. *Journal of Comparative Psychology,* 1940, 30, 1–16.

Mednick, S. A. A learning approach to research in schizophrenia. *Psychological Bulletin,* 1958, 55, 316–327.

Meehl, P. E. Schizotaxia, schizotypy, schizophrenia. *American Psychologist,* 1962, 17, 827–838.

Noyes, A. P., & Kolb, L. C. *Modern clinical psychiatry.* Philadelphia: Saunders, 1958.

Payne, R. W. Cognitive abnormalities. In H. J. Eysenck (Ed.), *Handbook of abnormal psychology.* New York: Basic Books, 1961. Pp. 193–261.

Payne, R. W., Caird, W. K., & Laverty, S. G. Overinclusive thinking and delusions in schizophrenic patients. *Journal of Abnormal and Social Psychology*, 1964, *68*, 562–566.

Peastrel, A. L. Studies in efficiency: Semantic generalization in schizophrenia. *Journal of Abnormal and Social Psychology*, 1964, *69*, 444–449.

Pinneo, L. R. The effects of induced muscle tension during tracking on level of activation and on performance. *Journal of Experimental Psychology*, 1961, *62*, 523–531.

Rechtschaffen, A., Schulsinger, F., & Mednick, S. A. Schizophrenia and physiological indices of dreaming. *Archives of General Psychiatry*, 1964, *10*, 89–93.

Riss, E. Are hallucinations illusions? An experimental study of nonveridical perception. *Journal of Psychology*, 1959, *48*, 367–373.

Rodnick, E. H. The effect of metrazol shock upon habit systems. *Journal of Abnormal and Social Psychology*, 1942, *37*, 560–565.

Sadler, W. S. *Practice of psychiatry*. St. Louis: Mosby, 1953.

Schnore, M. M. Individual patterns of physiological activity as a function of task differences and degree of arousal. *Journal of Experimental Psychology*, 1959, *58*, 117–128.

Silverman, J. Scanning-control mechanism and "cognitive filtering" in paranoid and nonparanoid schizophrenia. *Journal of Consulting Psychology*, 1964, *28*, 385–393.

Sommer, R., Dewar, R., & Osmond, H. Is there a schizophrenic language? *Archives of General Psychiatry*, 1960, *3*, 665–673.

Spence, J. T., & Lair, C. V. Associative interference in the verbal learning performance of schizophrenics and normals. *Journal of Abnormal and Social Psychology*, 1964, *68*, 204–209.

Spence, J. T., & Lair, C. V. Associative interference in paired-associate learning of remitted and nonremitted schizophrenics. *Journal of Abnormal Psychology*, 1965, *70*, 119–122.

Spence, K. W. *Behavior theory and conditioning*. New Haven: Yale University Press, 1956.

Spence, K. W. Behavior theory and selective learning. In M. R. Jones (Ed.), *Nebraska symposium of motivation: 1958*. Lincoln: University of Nebraska Press, 1958. Pp. 73–107. (a)

Spence, K. W. A theory of emotionally based drive (D) and its relation to performance in simple learning situations. *American Psychologist*, 1958, *13*, 131–141. (b)

Stilson, D. W., & Kopell, B. S. The recognition of visual signals in the presence of visual noise by psychiatric patients. *Journal of Nervous and Mental Disease*, 1964, *139*, 209–221.

Storms, L. H., & Broen, W. E., Jr. Verbal associative stability and appropriateness in schizophrenics, neurotics, and normals as a function of time pressure. *American Psychologist*, 1964, *19*, 460. (Abstract)

Taylor, J. A., & Spence, K. W. The relationship of anxiety to level of performance in serial learning. *Journal of Experimental Psychology*, 1952, *44*, 61–64.

Tutko, T. A., & Spence, J. T. The performance of process and reactive schizophrenics and brain injured subjects on a conceptual task. *Journal of Abnormal and Social Psychology*, 1962, *65*, 387–394.

Venables, P. H. The effect of auditory and visual stimulation on skin potential responses of schizophrenics. *Brain*, 1960, *83*, 77–92.

Weckowicz, T. E., & Blewett, D. B. Size constancy and abstract thinking in schizophrenic patients. *Journal of Mental Science*, 1959, *105*, 909–934.

West, L. J. A general theory of hallucinations and dreams. In L. J. West (Ed.), *Hallucinations*. New York: Grune & Stratton, 1962. Pp. 275–291.

Zaslow, R. W. A new approach to the problem of conceptual thinking in schizophrenia. *Journal of Consulting Psychology*, 1950, *14*, 335–339.

Zuckerman, M., Albright, R. J., Marks, C. S., & Miller, G. L. Stress and hallucinatory effects of percepual isolation and confinement. *Psychological Monographs*, 1962, 76(30, Whole No. 549).

SOCIAL LEARNING THEORY: JULIAN B. ROTTER AND ALBERT BANDURA

XI

In 1954, Julian B. Rotter published a volume entitled *Social Learning and Clinical Psychology,* which presented a series of seven postulates, together with a number of corollaries, derived from a combination of systematic studies of learning and clinical experience. Rotter accounted for the addition of the term *social* on the grounds that the theory stressed that the principal modes of human behavior: (1) are learned in social situations; and (2) are bound up with needs which require the mediation of others for their gratification. He also takes pains to point out that the system is "open" rather than "closed," i.e., it is not formulated in precise mathematical terms which permit rigorous deductions regarding particular events. The openness of the system is viewed as an asset rather than a liability, since Rotter feels that his system is maximally sensitive to the development and change in theoretical constructs occasioned by increasing refinement in data collection and analysis.

The heuristic value of Rotter's theory has been demonstrated in a number of studies conducted by Rotter and his students. The article selected for inclusion in this anthology, however, is not concerned with an empirical test on the theory, but rather is devoted to an analysis and clarification of some basic methodological issues in the application of personality theory in general to the measurement of personality variables. Specifically, it is focused upon three aspects of what Rotter identifies as the gap between personality theory and the procedures employed to measure personality variables: (1) the constructs used in theory and those which tests were developed to measure; (2) problems implicit in the test procedure itself; and (3) inferences derived from test behavior. Rotter examines these aspects with reference to social learning theory.

Like Julian Rotter, Albert Bandura is interested in social aspects of learning situations. In the past, he has been critical of approaches to social learning based on Skinnerian or Hullian conceptualizations of behavior theory on the grounds that both systems incorporate an entirely too restricted view of human learning. Bandura charges researchers to devote much more attention to the "social transmission of behavior."

In his analysis of the transmission process, Bandura emphasizes the prominent role displayed by imitative learning. He is not particularly concerned with distinctions between imitation, a term employed in behavior theory, and identification, the term favored by personality theory, because he is convinced that the differences between the two are semantic rather than conceptual. He holds that other terms, like *introjection* and *incorporation,* are similarly based on the common property of the occurrence of matching responses in the subject and model in an imitative social learning situation.

The centrality of imitation in Bandura's social learning theory was demonstrated in an earlier volume on adolescent aggression which he coauthored with Richard H. Walters. Material was provided by TAT stories and interview data from 26 adolescent boys with histories of aggressive antisocial behavior, a matched control group of 26 nonaggressive adolescents, and the parent informants of boys in both groups. Although hypotheses relating to the importance of dependency behavior and its disruption for the development of aggressive tendencies fared less well than the authors anticipated they would, identification is viewed by the authors as indispensable in the child's progression from behavior under the control of fear to more mature behavioral restraint imposed by feelings of guilt or remorse.

Bandura stresses the point that imitation is a fundamental and significant part of many learning situations— a matter which can readily be confirmed by observing learning in naturalistic settings. He also directs attention to the complexity of many social learning situations, particularly with respect to the unit of response acquisition. This he sees as typically molar rather than molecular, patterned rather than segmental, and acquired in its entirety rather than by successive approximation.

A succinct statement of the major features of his approach is given at the conclusion of his contribution to the 1962 *Nebraska Symposium on Motivation*:

. . . the theory of imitative learning which I have described places primary emphasis on contiguous sensory stimulation as a sufficient condition for the acquisition of most forms of mediating responses. To the extent that subject and model characteristics, stimulus programming, motivational variables, reinforcement, and set-inducing operations create conditions which enhance and channel an organism's observing responses, these factors will determine in part the level of imitative learning achieved and the types of models who will be selected as sources of behavior. These latter variables, however, are regarded as facilitative rather than as necessary preconditions for the occurrence of imitative behavior.*

The above quotation also affords a forecast of the research directions which Bandura and his students have pursued for more than a decade, with results that have become assimilated into the general body of well-documented empirical findings of psychological science.

* Bandura, A. Social Learning through imitation. In M. R. Jones (Ed.), *Nebraska Symposium on motivation*. Lincoln: University of Nebraska Press, 1962, p. 264.

48

Some Implications
of a Social Learning Theory
for the Prediction of Goal Directed
Behavior from Testing Procedures

JULIAN B. ROTTER

Many sophisticated observers are aware that a wide gap exists between personality theory and the techniques or procedures used to measure personality variables. The low level of prediction of such testing procedures may well be a function of the failure to apply the theories themselves to the methods of measurement. Particularly, it is a failure to apply an analysis of the determinants of behavior in general to the specific test taking behavior of the subjects (Ss).

The gap itself may be described as having three aspects. The first of these relates to the question of the constucts used in the theory and the constructs which the tests were developed to measure. In many instances rather than devising tests which measure specific theoretical constructs which are carefully defined and for which the test behavior can be understood as a logical referent, the descriptive constructs used to classify test response do not logically relate to the new theoretical constructs but are bent or twisted to measure the new variables. That is, test constructs which were used to classify test responses developed earlier are "translated" to be measures of the new variables. Examples of this are use of Rorschach variables such as color, movement, and shading which arose from imagery-type theory, to measure such constructs as "ego strength," "rigidity," and "tolerance for ambiguity." The Rorschach was not developed to assess such

From J. B. Rotter, Some Implications of a Social Learning Theory for the Prediction of Goal Directed Behavior from Testing Procedures. *Psychological Review*, 1960, 67, 301–316. Copyright 1960 by the American Psychological Association, and reproduced by permission of publisher and author.

I am indebted to Shephard Liverant for his helpful comments and suggestions about this paper.

variables and in translating or twisting older methods of Rorschach scoring to measure these variables it is quite likely that a loss of prediction results.

A second aspect of this gap between personality theory and methods of measurement of personality lies in the testing procedure itself. For example, where the theory may emphasize the significance of differences in behavior in the presence of authority figures vs. peers of males vs. females, the formal test procedure assumes no such variables are important. That is, no difference in interpretation of test results follows from the fact that the examiner may have a different social stimulus value in one case than in another or under one set of conditions rather than another. In such an instance although the theory itself recognizes (and experimental data such as Gibby, Miller, & Walker, 1953, and Lord, 1950, support) the importance of the effect on behavior of the nature of the social stimulus, the test procedure itself does not take it into account. An example would be in the application of Murray's theory (1952) which sees behavior as a function of internal *needs* and environmental *presses*. Tests have been developed using this theory (Thematic Apperception Test, as clinically used; Edwards Personal Preference Schedule) which presume to measure the strength of various needs but fail to account for the test behavior as a function of the testing situation itself (an environmental press) as one of the variables determining the test behavior. Other characteristics of this discrepancy between theory and test taking procedure will be discussed more fully later.

A third aspect of the gap lies in the area of inference from test behavior. The issue here is that there is an absence of logic or contradiction in the assumed relationship between what the S does, or test behavior, and what is inferred from such behavior. Peak (1953) and Butler (1954) among others have discussed this problem earlier. Jessor and Hammond (1957) have noted such a gap in the inferences made from the Taylor Anxiety Scale. Another example could be drawn from the Edwards Personal Preference Schedule (Edwards, 1953) in which Ss are asked to state their preferences for different kinds of goals but there is no theoretical basis provided to allow one to make predictions about *nontest behavior* from such preferences. Of course, it can be assumed that the preferences have some one-to-one relationship with some criterion behavior, but it is unlikely that even the test authors would make such a theoretical commitment. In other words, it is not clear exactly what can be predicted or should be predicted from the test responses. Individuals using such tests, however, can defend themselves by stating that prediction is after all an empirical matter and one has to find out what can or should be predicted. It is likely, however, that the construction of tests which are systematically or theoretically pure, in that they are devised to measure specific variables or to make specific predictions, with the method of measurement and inference consistent with the theory will ultimately provide much better predictions of behavior as well as a test of the utility of the theory itself.

The purpose of this paper is to explicate some of the implications of a social learning theory of personality for the measurement of personality variables. The particular point of emphasis is the measurement of goal directed behavior conceptualized in social learning terms as *need potential*. Secondarily, the paper aims at illustrating the nature of the relationship between testing procedures and inference about behavior more generally.

In social learning theory (Rotter, 1954) the basic formula for the prediction of goal directed behavior is as given below:

$$BP_{x,s_1,R_a} = f(E_{x,R_a,s_1} \ \& \ RV_{a,s_1})$$ [1]

The formula may be read as follows: The potential for behavior *x* to occur in Situation 1 in relation to Reinforcement *a* is a function of the expectancy of the occurrence of Reinforcement *a* following Behavior *x* in Situation 1 and the value of Reinforcement *a*, in Situation 1. Such a formula, however, is extremely limited in application for it deals only with the potential for a given behavior to occur in relationship to a single specific reinforcement. The prediction of responses from personality tests requires a more generalized concept of behavior and the formula for these broader concepts is given below:

$$BP_{(x-n),s_{(1-n)},R_{(a-n)}} = f(E_{(x-n),s_{(1-n)},R_{(a-n)}} \ \& \ RV_{(a-n),s_{(1-n)}})$$ [2]

This may be read: The potentiality of the functionally related Behaviors *x* to *n* to occur in the specified Situations 1 to *n* in relation to potential Reinforcements *a* to *n* is a function of the expectancies of these behaviors leading to these reinforcements in these situations and the values of these reinforcements in these situations. For purposes of simplicity of communication, the three basic terms in this formula have been typically referred to as need potential, freedom of movement, and need value as in the third formula below:

$$NP = f(FM \ \& \ NV)$$ [3]

In this formula the fourth concept, that of the psychological situation, is implicit. The variables referred to above and operations for measurement have been defined and further explicated in a previous publication (Rotter, 1954).

In order to illustrate the social learning theory implications for measurement of personality and for the measurement of goal directed behavior, it seems expedient to consider three basic approaches to this problem based on the number of determinants used theoretically to predict such goal directed behavior and the problems, limitations, and advantages of each approach.

STRENGTH OF NEED AS A BASIS FOR PREDICTING BEHAVIOR

Although many esoteric systems of prediction utilize essentially the strength of need, drive, or instinct approach, this method can be described as the simplest or least complicated approach. Basically a series of constructs are formulated more often on an a priori basis than empirically, or at least on a presumed clinical rather than experimental basis. These descriptive terms may refer to instincts, drives, needs, factors, entities, or vectors of the mind (i.e., the Minnesota Multiphasic Personality Inventory, Edwards Personal Preference Schedule, Rorschach, Humm-Wadsworth, etc.). They all have in common that there is more than one basic characteristic, that these two or more characteristics are in some way measurable along a continuum and presumably the individual's behavior can be predicted from the characteristics which are "stronger" and the characteristics which are "weaker."

Sometimes the personality disposition can be predicted from the strength of other constructs according to either simple or complex statements of relationship formally postulated, hypothesized, or informally asserted. These relationships can become quite complex as in psychoanalysis or quite esoteric as in Szondi's explanation that motivated behavior is a result of the interaction of dominant and recessive genes. Because the methods of measurement in some instances cannot be direct, as in the assessment of unconscious drives in psychoanalysis, an impression of great complexity is given but regarded entirely from the point of view of the prediction of behavior, the system may still have a simple character. The potential for a given kind of behavior is still directly predictable from the strength of the drive, instincts, needs, or energies postulated.

There is another form of this model in which the various drives, dispositions, or needs are considered to interact. For example, the individual may be conceived of as being controlled by his intellect and his emotions, but his behavior must be understood in light of the interactions of these two forces with a third variable, the will as in the Rorschach Test (1942). Again, this makes complex the calculation of strength or weakness but does not change the overall method of making predictions. Whether dealing with will, intellect and emotions or ego, superego and id, the effect of interaction is only to increase or decrease the tendency of one of the needs to function or to strengthen or weaken one of them or perhaps to produce a fourth or fifth additional need. The basic method of prediction stays the same although the calculation of strength or weakness in such a model becomes more difficult.

The obvious problem, of course, for such rudimentary method of prediction is how to predict anything at all. If a system included five instincts or needs and these are ordered on some metric system from high to low, does one assume that the person will always act in the fashion to be predicted from his strongest or highest need? If an S is more oral than anal, does he always act in an oral fashion? Actually the most logical assumption in regard to any specific instance is that he will always act the same way. One might presume on a statistical basis, as it is sometimes done, if the individual is at the 70th percentile on Need A and at the 30th percentile on Need B, 70% of the time he would act in one fashion and 30% of the time in the other over some undefined period of time. However, the only sensible statistical or logical prediction in any specific instance, if no other variables are concerned, is that he would act in accordance with the higher need. This might still give fairly good prediction if only 2 variables are involved, but if 20 variables are involved and many of them are very close in value or "strength," then the amount of error begins to increase. In fact, it becomes a problem to predict even slightly above chance and, indeed, except for some limited and highly controlled experimental situations, this is the problem in psychology now. A recent illustration of this failure is reported in a carefully controlled study by Little and Shneidman (1959) who failed to find much relationship between interpretations of psychological tests (Rorschach, MAPS, TAT, and MMPI) and anamnestic data. Loevinger (1959) summarizing the predictiveness of individual tests in the recent *Annual Review of Psychology* states, "To date the only tests which meet standards for individual prediction are those of general ability" (p. 305). Previous reviewers have made similar statements.

Another problem which arises in the prediction of behavior with this simple model is that it soon becomes apparent that the strength of a wish, need, or drive to achieve some goal such as being taken care of, obtaining love, or injuring someone is not a good predictor of the occurrence of behavior directed towards the achieving of that goal. To some extent this problem can be dealt with by the notion of interaction of needs, but usually in order to account for the discrepancy between need or wish and behavior, constructs of the same order do not provide sufficient explanatory basis. It is actually necessary to postulate some other kinds of internal constructs to account for the discrepancy between what might be called wish, desire, need, or instinct and observable behavior.

In the measurement of these need strengths all varieties of tests and devices have been used. To some extent, the personality questionnaire is utilized a little more by people adopting such a predictive scheme as that described above, but also projective tests, observation, interviewing, and many other techniques of personality measurement have been used in this fashion. Test construction methodologies may currently be more sophisticated in that they control for social desirability of items, motivation, faking, lying, and inability to understand directions. Recent tests may also rely on purification of factors, cross-validation, or item analysis. However, with all these "modern improvements" in test design one is still left with a series of figures which are of doubtful utility for the actual prediction of behavior at a level satisfactory for either practical application or for the clarification of theoretical issues.

THE ADDITION OF AN EXPECTANCY CONSTRUCT IN THE PREDICTION OF GOAL DIRECTED BEHAVIOR

The absence of additional variables explicitly defining the relationship of need and behavior appears to be not so much a matter of simple theoretical structure as it is merely the absence of any real explicit theory about human behavior. The development of a predictive model which recognizes the discrepancy between need and behavior and tries to systematically take it into account represents a second level of sophistication.

At an earlier date perhaps psychoanalysis dealt with this problem most effectively in introducing concepts such as repression, sublimation, suppression, defense, reaction formation, etc., to account for the discrepancy between observed behavior and the presumed internal drive, need, or instinctual urge.

At this level of theorizing some systematic variable is added to the internal motivational state in order to predict behavior. Perhaps another way of saying this is that in addition to some measure of preference or value of a specific goal another systematic concept must be introduced, not only in a hit-or-miss fashion but perhaps directly into our assessment procedure. The psychoanalytic solution has been criticized because many specific concepts are introduced to account for a discrepancy between drives, urges, or needs and observable behavior, but these concepts are not readily measurable. In addition, one does not know when one explanation, i.e., reaction formation, is the explanatory concept or another such as sublimation or simple repression.

In social learning theory (Rotter, 1954) it is presumed that the relationship between goal preference (reinforcement value) and behavior can be determined only by introducing the concept of the individual's expectancy, on the basis of past history, that the given behavior will actually lead to a satisfying outcome rather than to punishment, failure, or, more generally, to negative reinforcement. Since the early formulations of Tolman (1932), expectancy theories have become more and more widely relied upon both in human learning and personality theories. It is possible to conceptualize more specific constructs such as repression and reaction formation as only special cases of an expectancy for severe punishment and that a more general relationship holds which includes perhaps all of these and also expectancies for punishment or failure of which the individual is quite aware. For example, an individual may wish very much to be a good dancer and to dance with members of the opposite sex. He makes no attempts, however, to dance at a party or a dance because he can tell you "but I look like a fool when I go out on the dance floor." We need, in other words, to introduce no specific construct involving the "unconscious" to explain the discrepancy between his wish and his behavior. The S may or may not be aware of expectancies which influence his behavior. Whether or not he is aware of them may affect the degree to which these expectancies change with new experience as well as other variables. The degree of awareness may be an important additional variable; however, the level of expectancy itself is the broader variable which bears a direct relationship to the potential occurrence of a specified behavior.

The question arises, then, of how one takes into account such factors in an actual testing situation. It could be said that no one is really so naive as to believe that the strength of an internal motivational condition or need is a direct predictor of behavior. Somehow or other, whether or not the individual had learned a given behavior or expected it to work is also an important aspect of prediction. However, more often than not this aspect of prediction has been treated as a source of error, something to be eliminated if possible, both in testing or in the validation of a test instrument. As a matter of fact, many currently used instruments attempting to assess the strength of motives, drives, or needs are usually confounded. Although they may be quite sophisticated in methodology, the test items or the test variables usually refer in part to what the individual did, i.e., overt behavior ("I frequently lose my temper"), in part to what he wished ("I would like to have more friends"), and in part to what he expected to be the outcome of his own behavior ("I feel that other people do not appreciate my good intentions"). To some extent these impure items probably add to prediction by providing more than one kind of referent for behavior, but the nonsystematic way in which they are used also limits prediction.

In trying to predict goal directed behavior from tests, two possibilities are open. One of these is to attempt to predict behavior from other behavior which presumably is functionally or predictively related to the test behavior. What this involves is analyzing test situations as behavioral samples under a given set of test conditions. For example, to assess dependent behavior one could use direct observation techniques, perhaps in problem solving situations, which the S is scored for help-seeking behavior (cf. Naylor, 1955). In questionnaires the items should refer to what the S does, not to what he expects, wishes, or feels. The use of behavior samples for predictions or the regarding of all kinds of tests including projective tests essentially as samples of behavior to be analyzed in terms of what the S does under these conditions has been described elsewhere (Rotter, 1954). Like the work sample test in industry it undoubtedly provides the best prediction to a limited specific behavioral criterion since it requires the fewest intermediate constructs and the fewest assumptions regarding the action of other variables.

However, there are many problems, both theoretical and clinical, when it is important to break down this behavioral measure into its major determinants of reinforcement value and expectancy for the occurrence of the reinforcement. For example, in psychotherapy an understanding of how some behavior or group of behaviors may be most readily changed requires analysis into at least these two components. Even when strictly concerned with predictions of behavior in a broad band of life situations, rather than change, analysis into separate determinants may provide greater prediction than a work sample or behavioral technique. In this second alternative it is important either to control or systematically vary the other variable or measure both. For example, Liverant (1958) has measured some needs by presenting pairs of items involving goal preference matched for social desirability, and Jessor and Mandell (Mandell, 1959) are developing a similar test to measure expectancy for success in satisfying the same needs.

In using projective material such as the TAT, Crandall (1951) has demonstrated that expectancy for need satisfaction, for which the term freedom of movement is used in social learning theory, can be reliably measured by selecting particular kinds of referents. The work of Mussen and Naylor (1945), Kagan (1956), and Lesser (1957) gives strong evidence that the relationship between theme counts of aggression on the TAT and overt aggressive behavior depends to a large extent on whether or not that overt behavior is socially acceptable in the Ss' own homes or social climates. The relationship between theme count and overt aggressive behavior appears to hold only when the Ss do not have a high expectancy that aggressive behavior will be punished. Atkinson and Reitman (1956) report that in a number of studies of need achievement, it has become clear that prediction of behavior is enhanced if, in addition to taking a measure of need achievement based upon achievement theme counts in TAT-like material, an additional measure of expectancy for success is also taken into account.

In dealing with this type of testing material the recently published study of Fitzgerald (1958) provides a more systematic analysis. Using a highly reliable sociometric technique of nomination of fraternity brothers as his behavioral criteria and dealing with the need dependency, Fitzgerald found no relationship between theme counts and overt behavior. Presumably, dependent behavior is not socially acceptable among male college students. He had, however, independent interview ratings of need value, that is preference or desire for dependency satisfactions and of freedom of movement, or expectancy that behavior directed toward achieving dependency would be satisfied.

He found that by using these measures he did obtain a significant correlation between theme counts and the *discrepancy* between need value and freedom of movement. More specifically, what he called a conflict score or score indicating the degree to which the individual preferred dependency or desired dependency satisfactions but expected that he could not achieve them correlated with theme counts for dependency.[1] On the other hand, an Incomplete Sentences Blank measure of dependency which utilized behavioral referents as well as reinforcement value and expectancy referents did show a low but significant relationship of the number of completions dealing with dependency with both the sociometric and interview measures of need potential or actual dependent behavior. Although an actual analysis was not made, it seems very likely that the reason for the correlation in the case of the ISB and not the TAT is that at least some of the ISB completions were descriptions of actual behavior. Possibly a purer measure of behavior would have shown a greater relationship to the sociometric and interview rating assessment of actual dependent behavior in life situations.

Should we build two instruments or at least two sets of testing operations to separately assess need value and freedom of movement, or should we attempt to use behavioral measures in order to make our predictions about behavior, we would still be faced with the problem of predicting in a specific situation. Given measures of six behavior potentials, however arrived at, the problem remains that of knowing which of these is likely to be the behavior preferred in some specific situation. One is again forced to predict that the behavior with the highest potential always occurs and one is limited again in prediction to a very low level of accuracy. In the laboratory situation where we can reduce the possible alternatives to two, significant, although not predictive results, are possible. In the life situation where the alternatives are very frequently of a large order, the question arises of whether or not any useful prediction is possible. This leads us to a third level of sophistication, one in which the psychological situation is one of the variables on which prediction is based.

THE PSYCHOLOGICAL SITUATION AS A THIRD DETERMINANT OF GOAL DIRECTED BEHAVIOR

Few would deny that the psychological situation will affect the potential of occurrence of any behavior or class of behaviors. However, the fact that behavior will vary from situation to situation is most often treated

---

[1] Whether or not the relationship between theme count and high reinforcement value and low expectancy is general is not yet known. It appears at this time to possibly depend on whether or not the test material and testing situation is conducive to the free expression of fantasy.

as a source of error, something to be avoided. If possible, one should construct tests or find personality variables which rise somehow above the situation. It is probably no exaggeration to say that thousands of hours of wasted work have been done by psychologists in the vain goal of finding either tests or variables which would, somehow or other, predict regardless of the situation in which the test is given or regardless of the situation in which the predicted behavior is expected to occur.

There are three separate problems here which will be discussed as one basic problem. The first problem is to understand the effect of the testing situation on test results. For example, Sarason (1950) has provided an excellent discussion of some of the influential situational variables in intelligence testing. The second problem is to understand the nature of the criterion situation which affects the criterion measures. The third and ultimately most important problem is to devise our tests with full consideration of the nature of the test situation in order to predict behavior in other situations for which the test was constructed. In other words, we need to devise tests not to predict personality or needs or behavior in the abstract but in specified situations or classes of situations if we want high prediction. *We need to know and take into account the dimensions of situation similarity in devising test procedures.*

Cronbach (1956) has criticized the failure to regard differentially the criterion situations in which tests are applied. In regard to the test situation we have only attempted to standardize the test procedure but usually have ignored the importance of the social context in which the test is given. Perhaps the most important thesis of this paper is that the psychological situation needs to be understood and systematically considered in our predictive formula, not treated as a source of error or something that can be ignored because part of the total situation is standardized.

Recently there have been a number of studies which demonstrate that almost all tests are subject to faking, to instructional variation, to examiner influences, to testing conditions, etc., regardless of the type of test (Borislow, 1958; Green, 1951; Gross, 1959; Mussen & Scodel, 1955; Rotter, 1955). The general inference drawn from these studies is that the tests are poor. Actually the implication of such findings is that we are making inefficient use of our tests. If the test situation for many personality tests is one in which social conformity or acceptability is easily achieved and no other satisfactions are given up in achieving acceptability, then for some purposes this motive should be controlled. However, the test situation can also be utilized to measure the important of social conformity of the individual. *What we call faking is only our recognition of the fact that the S is taking the test with a different purpose or goal than the one the examiner wants him to have.* For some purposes it might be important to understand what kind of goals he exhibits in this kind of situation. More often than not we simply try to control what we should be studying. For example, in giving intelligence tests it might be better to study systematically the effect on performance of encouragement and discouragement rather than to attempt some mythical neutral attitude which is presumably the same for every examiner. Knowledge of the effects of situational variations would be of particular value in understanding the frequently diverse and contradictory results of apparently similar research investigations. For example, Henry and Rotter (1956) found that large, predicted differences were obtained between two comparable groups on the Rorschach test if one group was reminded before the regular instructions that the test had been used frequently to study psychopathology. An obvious implication of this study is that investigators using this same test in the college laboratory and in the clinical setting may well produce diverse results.

Another example of how the situation can be used in testing is provided by the patient who is being assessed for possible benefit from psychotherapy. If the clinic or hospital can provide both male and female therapists and also therapists who rely on support and direction as well as therapists who remain distant and passive, then the testing procedures can be varied so that those situational influences are present. The testing could provide information to indicate what kind of therapy and what kind of therapist is likely to provide *this* patient with the most efficient conditions for relearning. For more conventional purposes of clinical testing, it is still more important to know under what conditions the patient behaves in a paranoid fashion and under what conditions he does not, than it is to know how many percentiles of paranoia he has.

Not only can the test situation itself be analyzed as a behavioral sample but situational referents can be incorporated into the content of items by systematic sampling. For example, questionnaire items can deal with the *conditions* under which the S feels tense, nervous, happy, has headaches, etc. as Mandler and Sarason (1952) have done for some intellectual test taking situations. Similarly, projective methods, particularly TAT-type tests, can systematically vary the situation through the selection of test stimuli as has been done by Crandall (1951) and McClelland, Atkinson, Clark, and Lowell (1953). More recently Murstein (1959) has suggested a conceptual model for stimulus variation with thematic techniques.

The many studies indicating marked effects of testing conditions suggest that it is of great importance in the publication of any test that descriptions of the differences in test results that are likely to be associated with different kinds of testing situations be provided. No test can be adequately understood unless the data regarding its standardization or use includes systematic descriptions of the differences in test results which are a function of different kinds of testing conditions and different kinds of purposes in taking the test for similar samples of Ss. Only when we know whether an S is likely to produce different test results when he is taking the test to demonstrate how imaginative he is as compared to taking it to prove that he needs help will we be adequately able to understand the meaning of test results and to predict future behavior from them.

There have been personality theorists who have made much of the importance of the individual's life space. Kantor (1924) was one of the first to emphasize that the basic datum of psychology is the interaction of an individual and his meaningful environment. For Kantor, people do not have internal characteristics in the same sense as for other theorists; rather they have a reactional biography of interactions with the environment. Lewin (1951) has also emphasized the importance of the life space or psychological situation in the determination of human behavior. Brunswik (1947) has repeatedly called for analyses of and sampling of psychological situations for predictive purposes. Helson (1948) has applied his theory of Adaptation Level to social psychology stating that the effect of the total field can be quantified by careful ordering of the field of exposed stimuli. Recent concern with the importance and need for systematic study of situation variation has been expressed by Allport (1958) and Cronbach (1957).

In a more limited and less systematic way, psychoanalysis has suggested, in a few areas, that certain kinds of goal directed behavior depended upon the psychological situation. This is done in making distinctions between the individual's potential response to authority figures vs. non-authority figures and males vs. females. Beyond this, little systematic analysis of differences in life situations has been made by the traditional analyst. Murray's (1952) formulation of the nature of personality stresses that behavior is a function of the interaction of an individual with a psychological situation which he felt could be categorized as "press." At a more specific level Atkinson and Raphelson (1956) have shown the value of including situational variables in studying achievement behavior. This general point of view has also been represented in sociology by Thomas (1951) and Coutu (1949).

In social learning theory, it has been hypothesized that the situation operates primarily by providing cues for the S which are related to the magnitude of his expectancies for reinforcement for different behaviors. The effect on the value of the reinforcement itself operates through expectancies for associated or subsequent reinforcements which may differ from situation to situation. It has also been hypothesized that situations may be usefully categorized in terms of the predominant reinforcements as culturally determined for any large or small culture group. There are many other possible ways of categorizing situations depending upon the predictive purposes involved.[2] Methods of determining generality or determining

---

[2] Several writers have pointed out the difficulty of identifying situations independently of behavior. That is, how can one describe a situation as one would a physical

the dimensions of similarity among situations have been described in an earlier paper (Rotter, 1955).

Two illustrative studies of an increasing number of experimental analyses of behavior which vary both internal characteristics and the psychological situation systematically in the same study are described below. These studies follow the basic paradigm that the presumed relevant individual (personality) and situational (experimental manipulations) variables can be observed simultaneously and their interaction studied.

ILLUSTRATIVE STUDIES VARYING BOTH THE SITUATION AND INTERNAL CHARACTERISTICS

A recent doctoral dissertation by James (1957) illuminates very clearly the potential of greater prediction when both the situation and the internal characteristic are varied in the same study. The behavior being studied by James involved a variety of learning variables, including acquisition, changes or shifts, extinction, generalization, and recovery of verbalized expectancies for gratification. Two general hypotheses were involved in this study growing out of previous work by Lasko (1952), Phares (1957), Neff (1956), and James and Rotter (1958). Hunt and Schroder (1958) have also dealt with what appears to be a related variable. The first of these hypotheses might be stated as a situational one. That is, that the nature of a learning process differs depending upon whether or not the situation is one in which the reinforcements that occur are a direct outcome of some internal characteristic of the individual such as skill, a physical characteristic, or whatever, versus a situation where the reinforcements are essentially controlled by someone else or by chance or by conditions or powers beyond the S's control. Perhaps a good example of the latter would be a dice game or the winning of a door prize or having soup spilled on one because a

---

stimulus independently of the S's response? The problem is not different from that of describing stimuli along dimensions of color although perhaps vastly complicated in social or other complex situations. In the case of color stimuli ultimately the criteria is a response of the scientist or observer, sometimes a response to an intermediate instrument, and one that is at the level of sensory discrimination and so leads to high observer agreement. In the case of the social situation, the level of discrimination is common sense based on an understanding of the culture rather than the reading of an instrument. As such, reliability may be limited but still be sufficiently high to considerably increase prediction. In this way specific situations could be identified as school situations, employment situations, girl friend situations, etc. For the purpose of generality various kinds of psychological constructs could be devised to arrive at classes of situations which have similar meaning to the S. The utility of such classes would have to be empirically determined depending on the S's response. The objective referents for these situations, which provide the basis for prediction, however, can be independent of the specific S. That is, they can be reliably identified by cultural, common sense terms.

waiter tripped, etc. James utilized line and angle matching tasks reinforcing each S positively on his guesses in six of the eight training trials. He specifically hypothesized when the situation is structured in such a way that the S expects the occurrence of reinforcements to be beyond his control or partly beyond his control, increments and decrements in expectancy for gratification as a result of experience are smaller, the number of unusual shifts, that is, shifts up after failure or down after success, are greater, extinction is faster, and there is less generalization from one task to another and greater recovery following extinction.

The measurement of individual differences in this study followed from the previous work of Phares which suggested that individuals can be differentiated in the degree to which they see the world and the things that happen to them as controlled by others or as determined by chance or unpredictable forces. The second hypothesis, then, was that all the differences which would occur as a result of the situational conditions would also be true of individuals within all groups as a function of their general attitude towards "control of reinforcement."

In order to predict the individual differences in attitude, James enlarged and revised the questionnaire first devised by Phares. This was given to all Ss at the end of each experiment. The results are most striking. All of the predicted outcomes hypothesized above resulting from the differences in instructions or situations were obtained and all were statistically significant with the exception of recovery following extinction, which showed a strong trend in the predicted direction. Similarly, within each group the individuals high as compared to low on the questionnaire differed significantly in exactly the same way as did the groups themselves as a result of the different instructions or situations presented. Although individual prediction was not the concern of his investigation, it is quite clear that a simple formula could be devised which could predict all of the learning variables involved in this study with a fair degree of accuracy. Certainly it is clear that a greater degree of accuracy is possible when both the situational and individual variables are taken into account. Perhaps far more important, this study indicates that various experimental paradigms in studying human learning are likely to produce different kinds of results. Whether or not a given learning task is one in which the S feels that success is dependent upon the experimenter's manipulation (for example, when he is expecting to predict a random sequence of red or green lights) or is the result of his own skill provides a crucial difference in the nature of the learning process itself.

The study of James, however, does not provide a satisfied feeling that it illustrates all of the problems of prediction involving both the individual's characteristics and the situation from which the prediction is made. It gives an almost too simple picture of the interaction of these two variables. Another recent dissertation by Moss (1958) suggests that this relationship can be more complex, and illustrates more clearly the effect of the testing situation on more commonly used types of assessment procedures.

Moss studied a general behavioral characteristic which he called cautiousness. Essentially this was defined as the avoidance of risk, the selection of the safest alternative in a situation where failure or negative reinforcement was possible. He varied the situation by reacting differently to three groups following the administration of a questionnaire which he described as a measure of social acceptability. One group was shown false norms at the conclusion of the questionnaire that indicated that they were in the ninetieth percentile of social acceptability for a college group. Another group of Ss was shown that they were at the tenth percentile, and a third group was given no information about the results of this supposed test of social acceptability. He hypothesized that cautious behavior would increase with negative reinforcement. Immediately following this procedure, the Ss were given two projective type tests and behavior on these tests was analyzed as to degree of cautiousness.

Prior to the giving of the "social acceptability" questionnaire the Ss had been tested on the level of aspiration board. Behavior on the level of aspiration board (Rotter, 1942) was categorized into cautious or noncautious patterns.[3] The general tendency to seek safe alternatives in the obtaining of satisfactions then was measured in a situation in which the S himself has some control over failure or success.

One kind of behavior studied was that of sorting figures taken from the MAPS test. The S was presented the figures and asked to sort them into two piles any way he wished. The procedure was repeated a second time asking for a different kind of sort, and a third time. The sorts themselves were characterized as being safe or cautious in that they dealt with highly objective characteristics of these figures, or less safe in that they dealt with characteristics which were more abstract or had to be read into many of the figures. For example, sorts based on personality characteristics were considered as noncautious as opposed to safer or more cautious sorts such as those into groups of men and women, children and adults, Negroes and whites, etc.

A second kind of behavior studied was the S's response to a series of four TAT pictures. In this case the S's stories were treated as Weisskopf (1950) has treated them with her measure of transcendence. A cautious or safe interpretation was one sticking close to the characteristics of the picture and one in which the theme itself was a common one.

[3] Cautious and noncautious behavior was characterized according to the patterns described by Rotter (1954, pp. 318–324). Patterns 1 and 3 were considered as noncautious and 2, 4, 7, and 8 as cautious patterns. The latter group are characterized by a variety of techniques presumably aimed at avoiding failure to reach explicit goals. Patterns 1 and 3 are characterized by higher expectancies than performance but within "normal" bounds and consequently a higher number of failures to reach one's estimates.

Moss found some differences among his groups in the direction he had hypothesized, that is, that the threatened group, the group that was told that it was at the tenth percentile, showed greater cautiousness than the other two groups. The differences between groups, however, although consistently in the direction he predicted, only approached significance and were not large. However, when Moss divided his Ss within groups into cautious and noncautious on the basis of their level of aspiration patterns, he found some highly significant differences. The cautious Ss showed no significant differences among the three conditions. However, the noncautious Ss showed significant differences between conditions. That is, noncautious Ss in one condition responded differentially from noncautious Ss in another condition. These differences were primarily due to greater noncautious behavior in the no-information group. Differences in test behavior between cautious and noncautious Ss were also highly significant on both tests within the no-information group but not in the other groups.

In spite of the complexity of this study, a few findings seem relatively clear from an analysis of group means as well as significance of differences. Ss who were cautious on the level of aspiration test, which is a somewhat free situation, were also cautious in the other test conditions. Of course, this does not mean that they were cautious in situations which were not perceived by them as evaluation situations. On the other hand, Ss who were noncautious on the level of aspiration test appeared to maintain this greater risk taking behavior under test situations where no information about results was given. However, when they were negatively reinforced, they became more cautious and they also did not appear to be different from cautious Ss under conditions where they were quite successful. Perhaps this is related to the presumed conservatism which follows from success. There was no consistent prediction from the level of aspiration situation to the two "projective tests" which could be made without considering the situation. In at least two of the situations the cautious Ss were not significantly different from the noncautious Ss. On the other hand, the psychological situation or the three different situations seemed to have no effect on the cautious Ss. Only in the interaction of the noncautious Ss with the situational variables was prediction possible from the level of aspiration test.

A similar type of result to that of Moss was recently reported by Lesser (1959). Lesser found that intercorrelations among various measures of aggression were significantly higher under experimental conditions of low anxiety than under conditions of high anxiety about aggression.

James' results suggest a rather simple relationship between dispositional and situational variables, but it is clear from the study of Moss and other studies that a simple additive or multiplicative relationship will not always describe the nature of the interaction. An important implication of this principle is that there is a general lack of efficiency in research studies in which only one set of variables, that is only dispositional or situational, are systematically varied, since the conclusions of the two sets of studies cannot be put together in a simple fashion. Unless both kinds of variables are systematically varied *within the same investigation,* both an understanding of the determinants of behavior and the prediction of it may suffer.

A striking example of the importance of studying the effects of dispositional and situational influences simultaneously is provided by Helson, Blake, Mouton, and Olmstead (1956). In applying Adaptation Level theory to a study of attitude change they found important interactional effects when situations were varied in external influence pressure and individuals were distributed on a measure of ascendancy–submissiveness.

It is true that many of the above propositions are obvious. Most psychologists recognize that there is a difference between overt behavior directed toward certain goals and the desires that individuals have to obtain these goals. Similarly, most psychologists know that the psychological situation is a determinant of the occurrence of a given behavior. The thesis here, however, is not merely that this is the case but that all of these variables must be ordered and studied systematically, in order to make predictions.

SUMMARY

The major contention of this paper has been that the prediction of goal directed behavior of human subjects from test procedures has been and will continue to be at an extremely low hit-or-miss level because of inadequate conceptualization of the problem. Findings are frequently not replicatable because of the failure to systematically differentiate behavior, reinforcement value, and expectancy as internal variables and to recognize that these variables are affected by the psychological situation.

The psychological situation of the patient in the clinic is so different from that of the elementary psychology student taking a test as part of an experiment that it is possible that the kinds of predictions which can be made in one situation would hardly hold in the other. The evidence that faking is possible and that different norms obtain when subjects are job applicants, employees, or volunteers does not necessarily mean that a test is no good. Nor is prediction essentially hopeless because it can be demonstrated that two experimenters, whether the same sex or opposite, or slight changes in the wording of instructions, will differentially affect test or experimental results. All of these things indicate only that the psychological situation, perhaps acting primarily through the expectancies they arouse by the cues present, considerably affect behavior. It is necessary that we do not consider such influence as error to be ignored, as difficulty to be avoided or as the problem of some other profession to investigate. Rather it is necessary to study these influences and consider them regularly and systematically in a predictive schema. That is, for some purposes, factors such as social desirability of items, examiner's behavior, and the subject's goals in the test situation should be controlled, and in other cases they should be allowed to vary. In all cases, however, they must be systematically considered.

Implicit in this entire paper is the belief that a satisfactory theory of goal directed behavior is a primary prerequisite for developing adequate tests. Knowledge of statistics and test construction procedures can be valuable but they cannot supplant an adequate theory of behavior which is applied to the test taking behavior itself.

To arrive at a fully systematic model for relating these general or high order constructs and to coordinate them in turn to lower level sets of content variables, devised for different purposes, will be a long and arduous but rewarding task.

REFERENCES

Allport, G. W. What units shall we employ? In G. Lindzey (Ed.), *The assessment of human motives.* New York: Rinehart, 1958.

Atkinson, J. W., & Raphelson, A. C. Individual differences in motivation and behavior in particular situation. *J. Pers.*, 1956, 24, 349–363.

Atkinson, J. W., & Reitman, W. R. Performance as a function of motive strength and expectancy of goal attainment. *J. abnorm. soc. Psychol.*, 1956, 53, 361–366.

Borislow, B. The Edwards Personal Preference Schedule and fakability. *J. appl. Psychol.*, 1958, 42, 22–27.

Brunswik, E. *Systematic and representative design of psychological experiments.* Berkeley: Univer. California Press, 1947.

Butler, J. M. The use of a psychological model in personality testing. *Educ. psychol. Measmt.*, 1954, 14, 77–89.

Coutu, W. *Emergent human nature.* New York: Knopf, 1949.

Crandall, V. J. Induced frustration and punishment-reward expectancy in thematic apperception stories. *J. consult. Psychol.*, 1951, 15, 400–404.

Cronbach, L. J. Assessment of individual differences. In P. R. Farnsworth and Q. McNemar (Eds.), *Annu. Rev. Psychol.*, 1956. Stanford, Calif.: Annual Review, 1956. Pp. 173–196.

Cronbach, L. J. The two disciplines of scientific psychology. *Amer. Psychologist*, 1957, 12, 671–684.

Edwards, A. L. *Manual of the Edwards Personal Preference Schedule.* New York: Psychological Corp., 1953.

Fitzgerald, B. J. Some relationships among projective test, interview and sociometric measures of dependent behavior. *J. abnorm. soc. Psychol.*, 1958, 56, 199–204.

Gibby, R. G., Miller, N. R., & Walker, E. L. The examiner's influence on the Rorschach protocol. *J. consult. Psychol.*, 1953, *17*, 425–428.

Green, R. F. Does a selection situation induce testees to bias their answers on interest and temperament tests? *Educ. psychol. Measmt.*, 1951, *11*, 503–515.

Gross, L. R. Effects of verbal and nonverbal reinforcement in the Rorschach. *J. consult. Psychol.*, 1959, *23*, 66–68.

Helson, H. Adaptation level as a basis for quantitative theory of frames of reference. *Psychol. Rev.*, 1948, *55*, 297–313.

Helson, H., Blake, R. R., Mouton, Jane S., & Olmstead, J. A. Attitudes as adjustments to stimulus, background, and residual factors. *J. abnorm. soc. Psychol.*, 1956, *52*, 314–322.

Henry, Edith M., & Rotter, J. B. Situational influences on Rorschach responses. *J. consult. Psychol.*, 1956, *20*, 457–462.

Hunt, D. E., & Schroder, H. M. Assimilation, failure-avoidance, and anxiety. *J. consult. Psychol.*, 1958, *22*, 39–44.

James, W. H. Internal versus external control of reinforcement as a basic variable in learning theory. Unpublished doctoral dissertation, Ohio State Univer., 1957.

James, W. H., & Rotter, J. B. Partial and one hundred percent reinforcement under chance and skill conditions. *J. exp. Psychol.*, 1958, *55*, 397–403.

Jessor, R., & Hammond, K. R. Construct validity and the Taylor anxiety scale. *Psychol. Bull.*, 1957, *54*, 161–170.

Kagan, J. The measurement of over aggression from fantasy. *J. abnorm. soc. Psychol.*, 1956, *52*, 390–393.

Kantor, J. R. *Principles of psychology.* Vols. 1, 2. New York: Knopf, 1924.

Lasko, A. A. The development of expectancies under conditions of patterning and differential reinforcement. Unpublished doctoral dissertation, Ohio State Univer., 1952.

Lesser, G. S. The relationship between overt and fantasy aggression as a function of maternal response to aggression. *J. abnorm. soc. Psychol.*, 1957, *55*, 218–222.

Lesser, G. S. Population differences in construct validity. *J. consult. Psychol.*, 1959, *23*, 60–65.

Lewin, K. The nature of field theory. In M. H. Marx (Ed.), *Psychological theory.* New York: Macmillan, 1951.

Little, K. B., & Shneidman, E. S. Congruencies among interpretations of psychological test and anamnestic data. *Psychol. Monogr.*, 1959, *73* (6, Whole No. 476).

Liverant, S. The use of Rotter's social learning theory in developing a personality inventory. *Psychol. Monogr.*, 1958, *72*(2, Whole No. 455).

Loevinger, Jane. Theory and techniques of assessment. In P. R. Farnsworth (Ed.), *Annu. Rev. Psychol.*, 1959. Palo Alto, Calif.: Annual Reviews, 1959. Pp. 287–316.

Lord, E. E. Experimentally induced variations in Rorschach performance. *Psychol. Monogr.*, 1950, *64*(10, Whole No. 316).

McClelland, D. C., Atkinson, J. W., Clark, R. A., & Lowell, E. L. *The achievement motive.* New York: Appleton-Century-Crofts, 1953.

Mandell, Elizabeth E. Construct validation of a psychometric measure of expectancy. Unpublished master's thesis, Univer. Colorado, 1959.

Mandler, G., & Sarason, S. B. A study of anxiety and learning. *J. abnorm. soc. Psychol.*, 1952, 47, 166–173.

Moss, H. The generality of cautiousness as a defense behavior. Unpublished doctoral dissertation, Ohio State Univer., 1958.

Murray, H. A. Toward a classification of interaction. In T. Parsons & E. A. Shils (Eds.), *Toward a general theory of action*. Cambridge: Harvard Univer. Press, 1952.

Murstein, B. I. A conceptual model of projective techniques applied to stimulus variations with thematic techniques. *J. consult. Psychol.*, 1959, 23, 3–14.

Mussen, P. H., & Naylor, H. K. Relationship between overt and fantasy aggression. *J. abnorm. soc. Psychol.*, 1954, 49, 235–239.

Mussen, P. H., & Scodel, A. The effect of sexual stimulation under varying conditions on TAT sexual responsiveness. *J. consult. Psychol.*, 1955, 19, 90.

Naylor, H. K. The relationship of dependency behavior to intellectual problem solving. Unpublished doctoral dissertation, Ohio State Univer., 1955.

Neff, J. Individual differences in resistance to extinction as a function of generalized expectancy. Unpublished doctoral dissertation, Ohio State Univer., 1956.

Peak, Helen. Problems of objective observation. In L. Festinger & D. Katz (Eds.), *Research methods in the behavioral sciences*. New York: Dryden, 1953.

Phares, E. J. Expectancy changes in skill and chance situations. *J. abnorm. soc. Psychol.*, 1957, 54, 339–342.

Rorschach, H. *Psychodiagnostics*. New York: Grune & Stratton, 1942.

Rotter, J. B. Level of aspiration as a method of studying personality: II. Development and evaluation of a controlled method. *J. exp. Psychol.*, 1942, 31, 410–422.

Rotter, J. B. *Social learning and clinical psychology*. New York: Prentice Hall, 1954.

Rotter, J. B. The role of the psychological situation in determining the direction of human behavior. In M. R. Jones (Ed.), *Nebraska symposium on motivation*, 1955. Lincoln: Univer. Nebraska Press.

Sarason, S. The test situation and the problem of prediction. *J. clin. Psychol.*, 1950, 6, 387–392.

Thomas, W. I. (Collected writings) In E. H. Volkart (Ed.), *Social behavior and personality: Contributions of W. I. Thomas to theory and social research*. New York: Social Science Research Council, 1951.

Tolman, E. C. *Purposive behavior in animals and men*. New York: Appleton-Century, 1932.

Weisskopf, E. A. A transcendence index as a proposed measure of projection in the Thematic Apperception Test. *J. Psychol.*, 1950, 29, 379–390.

49

Transmission of Patterns
of Self-Reinforcement
Through Modeling

ALBERT BANDURA
& CAROL J. KUPERS

According to current social-learning theories, new responses are acquired and existing behavioral repertoires are maintained or modified through positive or negative reinforcements administered by external agents. Although the controlling power of external reinforcing stimuli cannot be minimized (Ferster, 1958; Skinner, 1961), self-administered primary and conditioned rewards may frequently outweigh the influence of external stimuli in governing social behavior, particularly in the case of older children and adults.

The latter phenomenon, however, has been virtually ignored both in psychological theorizing and experimentation, perhaps due to the preoccupation with infrahuman learning. Unlike human subjects, rats or chimpanzees are disinclined to pat themselves on the back for commendable performances, or to berate themselves for getting lost in cul-de-sacs. By contrast, people typically make self-reinforcement contingent on their performing certain classes of responses which they have come to value as an index of personal merit. They often set themselves relatively explicit criteria of achievement, failure to meet which is considered undeserving of self-reward and may elicit self-denial or even self-punitive responses; on the other hand,

From A. Bandura, and C. J. Kupers, Transmission of Patterns of Self-Reinforcement Through Modeling. *Journal of Abnormal and Social Psychology*, 1964, 69, 1–9. Copyright 1964 by the American Psychological Association and reproduced by permission of publisher and author.

This investigation was supported in part by Research Grant M-5162 from the National Institutes of Health, United States Public Health Service. The study was conducted while the junior author was the recipient of an undergraduate National Science Foundation research fellowship.

The authors are grateful to Robert Grant, Jefferson Union School District, and to Herbert Popenoe, Los Angeles City School Districts, for their assistance in arranging the research facilities.

they tend to reward themselves generously on those occasions when they attain their self-imposed standards. Since self-administered rewards may serve both as powerful incentives for learning and as effective reinforcers in maintaining behavioral repertoires in humans, it is of considerable interest to determine the manner in which self-reinforcing responses are acquired.

It is likely that self-rewarding responses are to some extent directly conditioned through differential reinforcements administered initially by external agents. In this learning process the agent adopts a criterion of what constitutes a worthy performance and consistently rewards the subject for matching or exceeding the adopted criterion level, while performances that fall short of it are nonrewarded or punished. When subsequently the subject is given full control over the self-administration of reinforcers, he is likely to utilize the rewards in a contingent manner, with achieved performance levels serving as the primary discriminative stimuli.

Some recent evidence for the direct conditioning of self-reinforcing responses is provided by Kanfer and Marston (1963a) who found that when subjects were generously rewarded on an ambiguous noncontingent task they not only increased their rate of self-reinforcement, but also rewarded themselves frequently on a new learning task; in contrast, when subjects participated with an agent who grudgingly parted with limited token rewards and cautioned against excessive self-reward, the subjects exhibited considerably less self-reinforcement on both the training and generalization tasks. In addition, the incidence of self-reinforcement has been found to be partly dependent on the correctness of the subjects' responses, and on the similarity between training and generalization tasks (Kanfer, Bradley, & Marston, 1962; Kanfer & Marston, 1963b; Marston & Kanfer, 1963).

While the studies quoted above demonstrate the role of direct reinforcement in the acquisition of self-rewarding tendencies, it is doubtful that people receive much direct training in self-reinforcement on the majority of tasks they encounter, nor can performances in most situations be evaluated meaningfully independent of the accomplishments of others. Consequently, a person's self-evaluations may be importantly dependent upon the degree to which he matches the behavior of models whom he has chosen for comparison, and the self-reinforcement schedules which the models have adopted with respect to their own achievements. Some evidence for the influential role of vicarious learning is provided in recent demonstrations that social behavior may be rapidly acquired or modified as a function of observing the behavior and attitudes exhibited by models (Bandura, 1962). The present experiment, therefore, studied self-reinforcing responses as products of imitative learning.

Children participated in a task with an adult or a peer model, the scores being controlled by the experimenter. Under one experimental condition the model set a high criterion for self-reinforcement; on trials in which the model obtained or exceeded the standard he rewarded himself, while on trials in which he failed to meet the adopted standard he displayed self-denial and self-critical behavior. In a second experimental condition the model displayed a similar pattern of self-reward and self-disapproval, but adopted a relatively low self-reinforcement criterion. After exposure to their respective models the children received a wide range of scores and the performances for which they rewarded themselves were recorded.

It was predicted that children would imitate the self-reinforcement patterns exhibited by their respective models, whereas control-group subjects who were not exposed to the models would display no consistent pattern of self-reinforcement. On the assumption that children are apt to have been repeatedly positively reinforced for imitating models of the same sex and nonrewarded or negatively reinforced for opposite-sex imitation, it was also predicted that the subjects would match the self-reinforcement patterns of a same-sex model to a greater degree than that of a model of the opposite sex.

Finally, the relative effectiveness of models in shaping self-reinforcing responses may vary as a function of their prestige, competence, age status, or social power (Bandura, Ross, & Ross, 1963; Jakubczak & Walters, 1959; Miller & Dollard, 1941; Rosenbaum & Tucker, 1962). Because of differential competencies, adults are likely to exhibit more successful and rewarding responses than peers and, therefore, to the extent that children are differentially rewarded for matching adult and peer models, adults would eventually become the more powerful modeling stimuli. On the other hand, it might be argued that children would view adults as too divergent in ability to serve as meaningful models for self-evaluation (Festinger, 1954), whereas the self-reinforcement patterns exhibited by peers would be considered more realistic and, therefore, would be adopted more readily. In the present experiment, however, the adults displayed considerable variability in performance and a given subject would readily notice, from his own similarly wide range of scores, that there were little or no adult-child ability level differences on the particular task employed. Consequently, it was predicted that children would match the self-reinforcement patterns of adult models more closely than those of peer models.

METHOD

Subjects

The subjects were 80 boys and 80 girls ranging in age from 7 to 9 years. The children were drawn from six public schools participating in the Los Angeles Board of Education summer recreation program.

A male and female adult and two 9-year-old children served in the role of models. None of the subjects was acquainted with either the adult or the peer models.

Experimental Design

The children were subdivided into male and female subjects and randomly assigned to 16 experimental subgroups of 8 subjects each, and a control group consisting of 16 boys and 16 girls. Half the experimental children observed adult models, and half were exposed to peer models. In addition, half the children in both the adult and peer model conditions observed same-sex models, while the remaining children in each group witnessed models of the opposite sex. The control children had no prior exposure to the models and were tested only on the self-reinforcement task.

Procedure

A male assistant to the experimenter contacted the children individually on the playground and invited them to participate in the study. The assistant escorted each child to the experimental room and introduced him to the female experimenter and to the model, who supposedly had arrived early and was waiting for the session to commence.

In order to enhance the credibility of the experimental situation, the instructions were given to both the child and the model simultaneously, thus creating the set that the model was simply another naive subject. The experimenter explained that the purpose of the study was to collect normative data on the psychomotor abilities of a large sample of people. In the adult-model conditions, the experimenter added that data from adults as well as from children were desired, and that it was more convenient to test the adults in school than to transport the test apparatus from place to place. The experiment further explained that subjects were being tested in pairs so as to expedite collection of the normative data. The same explanations were given to children in the peer-model condition, except the subjects were led to believe that their partner was selected at random from the participants in the recreation program. Following these preliminary instructions, the child and the model were introduced to the bowling task that provided a means for modeling self-reinforcement responses.

Apparatus

The bowling apparatus used in this experiment was the one employed by Gelfand (1962). The equipment consisted of a miniature bowling alley with a 3-foot runway at the end of which there were three upright doweled target markers. The middle marker was labeled 10 points while the two adjacent ones were each labeled 5 points. The subjects were informed that whenever a bowling ball hit a target; the corresponding marker would drop. The target area, however, was carefully screened from view by fiber-board shields which covered the end-zone area of the runway and encircled the targets; consequently, the children had no knowledge of whether or not the bowling balls were in fact striking the targets. The experimenter further explained that occasionally the balls might bounce off the sides of the alley and, therefore, there may at times be little correspondence between the observed route of the bowling balls and the markers that drop. Actually, the experimenter sat behind the apparatus and controlled the scores by pulling appropriate strings that dropped the point markers. The models thus obtained identical scores with each subject and, similarly, all children received the same pattern of performance scores. Since the experimenter had to reset the markers after each trial and to return the bowling balls to the children from the back of the apparatus via an inclined trough, her position and activities appeared quite natural and justified.

After acquainting the child and the model with the bowling apparatus, the experimenter explained the rules of the game. The subjects would be allowed three balls per game and each would have a chance to play quite a few games. In the adult-model condition, the experimenter asked the child if he would mind letting the model take the first turn since he had to return to his work shortly, while in the peer-model condition, the experimenter's decision to let the model perform first appeared to be arbitrary.

The experimenter then called the subject's attention to a large bowl of M & M candies positioned beside the starting point of the alley within easy reach of the bowler. The subjects were given highly permissive instructions to help themselves to the candy whenever they wished, but if they did not feel like eating all the M & Ms during the session they could save them in the containers provided. M & M candies were selected as reinforcers because of their high attractiveness value and low satiation properties.

Before commencing the trials, the subjects were asked to treat themselves to some candy while the experimenter set the targets. This procedure, in addition to enhancing permissiveness for self-reward, was primarily designed to identify those children who would refuse to take candy because of parental prohibitions or for other reasons. If a child refused to take any candy he was, therefore, excluded from subsequent phases of the experiment. This occurred very infrequently, affecting only approximately 5% of the children.

Patterns of Self-Reinforcement

The model performed for 10 trials of three balls each and obtained scores ranging from 5 to 30 points.

In the *high criterion for self-reinforcement* condition the model rewarded himself with candy and positive self-evaluative verbalizations only when he obtained or exceeded a score of 20. On such trials the model took one or two M & Ms and commented approvingly, "I deserve some M & Ms for that high score." "That's great! That certainly is worth an M & M treat." In contrast, on trials in which he failed to meet the adopted criterion of 20, the model denied himself candy and remarked self-critically, "No M & Ms for that." "That does not deserve an M & M treat."

In the *low criterion for self-reinforcement* condition the model, while exhibiting a similar pattern of self-reward and self-disapproval, adopted a criterion of 10 points, a relatively low level of performance. On trials in which he obtained or exceeded a score of 10, he rewarded himself with candy and made self-approving comments, while on trials in which he failed to meet the adopted standard he took no candy and criticized himself.

There was some minor variation in the magnitude of self-reinforcement; the model generally took one M & M when he performed at or slightly above criterion, and two M & Ms when he scored well above the adopted minimum level.

While the model performed his trials the child, seated next to the bowling apparatus, was engaged to help in the scoring process. The assistant stood at a nearby blackboard, recorded the appropriate number whenever a marker dropped, totaled the scores at the end of each game, and then announced them to the bowler. The child was asked to call out the number each time the marker dropped. His participation was solicited in this manner for two reasons: First, to reinforce the three-balls-per-game set so that his scores would be meaningful to him, and second, to insure that he was attending to the model's performances and self-reinforcing responses.

After completing his 10 trials the model departed, the assistant generously refurnished the candy supply, and the experimenter asked the child to take his turns. The postexposure test was conducted with the models absent in order to remove any situational pressures on the children to adopt the model's patterns of self-reinforcement.

The child then performed 15 trials of three balls each. He received scores similar to those of the model, ranging from 5 to 30 points, according to a prearranged program.

It was found during pretesting that children occasionally forgot their subscores or made errors in addition. Therefore, in the experiment proper the assistant recorded the scores on the blackboard for the child and announced the total number of points at the completion of each trial.

For the purpose of testing our hypotheses the scores were divided into three critical levels: 5, 10–15, and 20–30. Since even the model who adopted a low criterion for self-reinforcement had to reach a minimum level of 10 points before rewarding himself, and since pretest data revealed that children rewarded themselves relatively infrequently when they obtained the lowest possible score, only two 5-point trials were included. Similarly, it was not expected that scores of 20 or higher would elicit differential self-reinforcing behavior from control and experimental children since all subjects would be inclined to reward themselves for such commendably high levels of performance. For this reason, in only 5 of the 15 programed trials did children receive scores of 20 or higher. It was assumed that the 10–15 performance level would be the most crucial one in differentiating the groups and, therefore, the children obtained a score of 10 or 15 on approximately half of the total trials.

Measures of Self-Reinforcement

The assistant recorded on data sheets the trials for which the child rewarded himself with candy and the total number of M & Ms taken in each self-reinforced trial. The frequency of positive and negative self-evaluative remarks by the child that matched precisely the model's verbal responses was also recorded.

RESULTS

In order to provide a picture of the children's distribution of self-reinforcement as a function of treatment conditions, the number of times each child rewarded himself with candy for 5, 10–15, and for 20–30 point performances, respectively, was divided by his total number of self-reinforced trials. The mean percentages of self-reinforcing responses displayed by the experimental and control groups at each of the three performance levels are shown in Table 49-1 and summarized graphically in Figures 49-1 and 49-2.

It should be noted that compared to the programed distribution the control children and those exposed to low-criterion models engaged in a slightly disproportionate frequency of self-reinforcement at the low or intermediate performance levels. The reason for this discrepancy is that some of the children displayed midtrial self-reinforcement; e.g., on a 20-point trial in which a child secured a score of 10 on the first roll, he might reward himself immediately rather than wait until he had completed the trial by rolling the two remaining bowling balls. In such cases the children were scored as having rewarded themselves for a 10-point performance and thus some children accumulated more 5- and 10-point trials than had been intended in the original programing.

Midtrial self-reinforcement occurred relatively frequently in the control group (23% of the total self-reinforced trials), but rarely in groups of

TABLE 49-1. Distribution of Mean Percentage of Self-Reinforcement as a Function of Sex of Subjects, Sex and Age of Models, and the Self-Reinforcement Criteria Exhibited by the Models

	Performance level					
	Adult models			Peer models		
Experimental treatment	5	10–15	20–30	5	10–15	20–30
High criterion						
Male model						
Boys	0	0	100	0	11	89
Girls	0	13	87	8	25	67
Female model						
Boys	0	8	92	0	23	77
Girls	0	5	95	6	16	78
Total	0	7	93	4	19	77
Low criterion						
Male model						
Boys	3	59	38	7	57	36
Girls	0	67	33	2	58	40
Female model						
Boys	0	75	25	3	67	30
Girls	0	60	40	7	60	33
Total	1	66	33	5	61	34
No model control	24	47	28			
Programed distribution	14	53	33			

children who observed a model exhibit either high (5%) or low (9%) standards for reinforcement. The difference between percentages of mid-trial self-reinforcement for the control children and those in the combined-model conditions is highly significant ($Z = 2.53$, $p < .02$). Considering that the models consistently postponed self-reward until the completion of a trial, these intergroup differences provide some evidence that the behavior of models is influential in transmitting self-control in the utilization of readily available rewarding resources.

Evaluation of Group Differences

The fact that the majority of children seldom rewarded themselves following performances that fell short of their models minimum criteria precluded the use of parametric tests of significance. Consequently, in group comparisons where the obtained frequencies of self-reinforcing responses were relatively low, chi-square tests were employed based on the number of children in a condition who reinforced themselves at all after a given level of performance. The median test was utilized to evaluate the signifi-

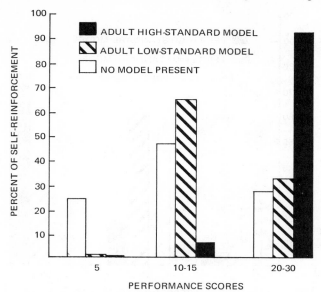

Figure 49-1. The distribution of self-reinforcement as a function of performance level by control children and those exposed to adult models adopting high and low criteria for self-reinforcement.

cance of differences at performance levels that resulted in a higher incidence of self-reward.

Since the results failed to reveal any significant sex-of-model or sex-of-subject influences on self-reinforcing responses, the data yielded by these subgroups were combined in testing the principal hypotheses.

Age Status of the Model

As predicted, children matched the self-reinforcement patterns of the adult models more precisely than their peer counterparts. Relative to the children who observed the high-criterion adult model, children in the high-criterion peer condition displayed a slightly greater tendency to reward themselves for 10–15 point performances ($\chi^2 = 7.06$, $p < .01$). The corresponding percentages of children in these two groups were 10% and 37%, respectively.

For the high-criterion subjects a score of 5 points fell well below the model's minimum standard. Consequently, very few of these children rewarded themselves at this performance level and no significant differences between peer- and adult-model conditions were obtained. On the other

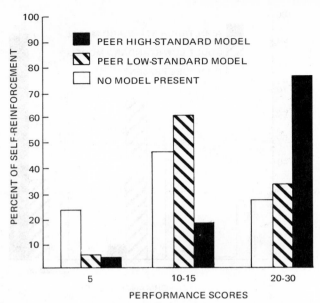

Figure 49-2. The distribution of self-reinforcement as a function of performance level by control children and those exposed to peer models adopting high and low criteria for self-reinforcement.

hand, in the low-criterion condition, where a score of 5 approached but did not quite reach the model's minimum criterion, more of the children who observed the peer model rewarded themselves at least once for a 5-point performance (37%) than did children who were exposed to the adult model (3%). This difference yielded a chi-square value of 11.68 that is significant beyond the .001 level. At the high performance levels, of course, the children engaged in frequent self-reinforcement regardless of the age status of the model.

Because of the differential influence of the adult and peer models, data from these treatment groups were analyzed separately.

Influence of Modeled Self-Reinforcement Patterns

In order to test the statistical significance of the obtained differences attributable to modeling, separate chi-square analyses were obtained for each of the three performance levels. The chi-square values and their corresponding level of significance appear in Table 49-2.

These group differences may be summarized as follows: Children exposed to models adopting either low or high standards for self-reinforcement

TABLE 49-2. Significance of the Differences in Self-Reinforcing Responses between Children in the Modeling Conditions and Those in the Control Group

Performance level	Adult-model condition χ^2	Peer-model condition χ^2
5 points	36.50*	15.79*
10–15 points	63.21*	33.33*
20–30 points	49.95*	40.53*

* $p < .001$.

rarely rewarded themselves when performing at the lowest possible level, whereas a relatively high proportion of the control children engaged in self-reinforcement after obtaining identically low scores. At the intermediate performance level most of the children in the control and the low-criterion groups rewarded themselves, while self-reinforcement by children exposed to high-criterion models was relatively infrequent. Finally, at the high performance level children who observed the high-criterion model engaged in an exceedingly high proportion of self-reward relative to the controls and to the low-criterion model groups.

Imitation of Self-Approving and Self-Critical Verbal Responses

Since the incidence of imitative verbal self-reinforcement was essentially the same irrespective of the sex, age status, and criterion level of the models, the experimental subgroup data were combined in the statistical analysis.

Twenty-seven percent of the experimental children reproduced precisely the models' self-approving or self-critical verbalizations in response to their own performances. In contrast, not a single child in the control group expressed any positive or negative self-evaluative statements, imitative or otherwise. This difference yielded a chi-square value of 8.12, which is significant beyond the .01 level.

Magnitude of Self-Reinforcement

The children displayed some variability in the mean number of candies taken per self-reinforced trial. Chi-square analyses revealed that generosity in self-reward was not attributable to sex-of-subjects, sex-of-models, or to differential modeling treatments. The age status of the model, however, appeared to be a significant source of variance ($\chi^2 = 10.10$, p < .01). On the average, a higher percentage of the children in the peer-model condition (41%) rewarded themselves in excess of their model's maximum of two candies, than did either the control children 31%) or those who observed adult models (16%).

It will be recalled that the models rewarded themselves with two candies when they obtained high scores relative to their adopted standard, but took only one candy for criterion-level performances. In order to test for any modeling effects in the distribution of magnitude of self-reinforcement the mean number of M & Ms taken per trial after scores of 20 or lower were compared by the Wilcoxon test with the means for scores of 25 and 30 points.

While the control-group children did not engage in differential amounts of self-reinforcement as a function of performance level, subjects in each of the experimental subgroups, irrespective of whether they observed adults or peers modeling high or low standards, displayed greater self-reinforcement at the higher achievement levels. In each experimental condition the Z value was significant well beyond the .01 level.

DISCUSSION

The overall results of this experiment provided strong support for the hypothesis that patterns of self-reinforcement can be acquired imitatively through exposure to models without the subjects themselves being administered any direct differential reinforcement by external agents.

This is shown clearly by the fact that children in the experimental conditions made self-reinforcement contingent on their achieving performance levels that matched the self-reward criteria of their respective models, whereas children in the control group administered rewards to themselves more or less independently of their task accomplishments. The influence of models is further reflected in the finding that a number of children reproduced precisely the content of their model's self-approving and self-critical verbal behavior. Not only did the children adopt the model's self-rewarding standards and verbal reinforcements, but they even matched the minor variations in magnitude of self-reinforcement exhibited by the models.

There are several possible reasons for the surprisingly precise matching of the models' self-reinforcing response patterns. First, the bowling task scores did not have much absolute value, consequently they provided the subjects little basis for judging what might constitute an inadequate or a superior performance independent of some reference norm. Even if relevant normative data were available, since the subjects' performances varied widely and unpredictably the children still had no basis for evaluating their own abilities. Thus the combination of performance ambiguity and instability would tend to enhance the patency of the model's standard-setting and self-reinforcing behavior. On the other hand, had the subjects' performances been consistently low and markedly discrepant from the model's achievements, the children might very well have rejected the model's relatively high self-reinforcement standards. In order to investigate this variable systematically, a study of imitative learning of self-reinforcement patterns is planned in which groups of children will obtain relatively stable scores at varying degrees of discrepancy from the performance levels and self-reinforcement criteria displayed by the models.

In accord with prediction and findings from other investigations cited earlier, adults served as more powerful modeling stimuli than peers in transmitting both standards and magnitude of self-reinforcement. Contrary to hypothesis, however, the study failed to yield any significantly Sex-of-Model × Sex-of-Subject interaction effects. This is particularly surprising since bowling might be considered a partially masculine-typed activity and, therefore, boys should at least be more prone than girls to imitate the male model (Bandura, Ross, & Ross, 1961). While the data from the high-standard condition suggest such a trend, the differences are not of statistically significant magnitude, perhaps because of the small number of cases in the cells.

Although the children acquired positive and negative self-reinforcing responses without the mediation of direct external reinforcement, it is probable that the evaluative properties of performances which fall short of, match, or exceed a reference norm are the resultant of past discriminative reinforcements. Through the repeated pairing of performance deficits with aversive consequences and successfully matched behavior with rewards, differential achievement levels per se eventually acquired positive and negative valence. It should be noted, however, that performance-produced cues have relatively little evaluative significance apart from a selected reference norm. Once the evaluative properties of differential accomplishments are well established, adequate or inadequate matches are likely to elicit similar self-evaluative responses irrespective of the specific behavior being compared. At this stage the whole process becomes relatively independent of external reinforcement and the specific contingencies of the original training situations. As demonstrated in the present experiment, subjects will adopt the particular criteria for self-reinforcement exhibited by a reference model, evaluate their own performances relative to that standard, and then serve as their own reinforcing agents.

Theory and research relating to the process of internalization and self-control have generally focused on *resistance to deviation* and the occurrence of *self-punitive responses* following transgression. Perhaps, an even more prevalent and important behavioral manifestation of self-control is the manner in which a person regulates the self-administration of highly rewarding resources. Thus in the experiment rewarding resources were readily available and their use was socially permissible; nevertheless, the groups of children differed markedly in the extent to which they utilized the reinforcers to obtain self-gratification. Children presented with low-criterion models were highly self-indulgent, rewarding themselves on the average more than twice as frequently as children in the high-criterion condition who displayed considerable self-denial. In the case of the control children, self-rewards were apparently freely dispensed and not made contingent on meeting or surpassing any minimum standard of achievement. These group patterns may be regarded as prototypic of cultures in which the majority of adults consistently display self-denying (Eaton & Weil, 1955) or self-indulgent (Hughes, Tremblay, Rapoport, & Leighton, 1960) behavior and, having limited opportunity to observe other behavioral examples, the children tend to model themselves after the prevalent self-reinforcement patterns.

In discussions of psychopathology and psychotherapy attention is frequently directed to the presence of behavioral deficits or to anxiety- and guilt-motivated inhibitory tendencies. A large proportion of the clients seeking psychotherapy, however, present relatively competent repertoires and are not excessively inhibited in their social behavior. These clients experience a great deal of self-generated aversive stimulation and self-imposed denial of positive reinforcers stemming from their excessively high standards for self-reinforcement, often supported by comparisons with historical or contemporary models noted for their extraordinary achievement. This process frequently gives rise to depressive reactions, a lessened disposition to perform because of the unfavorable work to self-reinforcement ratio, and efforts to escape the self-generated aversive stimulation through alcoholism, grandiose ideation, and other modes of avoidant behavior. In these cases, the modification of standards for self-reinforcement would clearly constitute a principal psychotherapeutic objective (Bandura, 1969).

REFERENCES

Bandura, A. Social learning through imitation. In M.R. Jones (Ed.), *Nebraska symposium on motivation: 1962.* Lincoln: Univer. Nebraska Press, 1962. Pp. 211–269.

Bandura, A. *Principles of behavioral modification.* New York: Holt, Rinehart, & Winston, 1969.

Bandura, A., Ross, Dorothea, & Ross, Sheila A. Transmission of aggression through imitation of aggressive models. *J. abnorm. soc. Psychol.,* 1961, 63, 575–582.

Bandura, A., Ross, Dorothea, & Ross, Sheila A. A comparative test of the status envy, social power, and secondary reinforcement theories of identificatory learning. *J. abnorm. soc. Psychol.,* 1963, 67, 527–534.

Eaton, J. W., & Weil, R. J. *Culture and mental disorders.* Glencoe, Ill.: Free Press, 1955.

Ferster, C. B. Reinforcement and punishment in the control of human behavior by social agencies. *Psychiat. res. Rep.,* 1958, *12,* 101–118.

Festinger, L. A theory of social comparison processes. *Hum. Relat.,* 1954, *7,* 117–140.

Gelfand, Donna M. The influence of self-esteem on rate of verbal conditioning and social matching behavior. *J. abnorm. soc. Psychol.,* 1962, *65,* 259–265.

Hughes, C. C., Tremblay, M., Rapoport, R. N., & Leighton, A. H. *People of cove and woodlot: Communities from the viewpoint of social psychiatry.* New York: Basic Books, 1960.

Jakubczak, L. F., & Walters, R. H. Suggestibility as dependency behavior. *J. abnorm. soc. Psychol.,* 1959, *59,* 102–107.

Kanfer, F. H., Bradley, Marcia A., & Marston, A. R. Self-reinforcement as a function of degree of learning. *Psychol. Rep.,* 1962, *10,* 885–886.

Kanfer, F. H., & Marston, A. R. Conditioning of self-reinforcing responses: An analogue to self-confidence training. *Psychol. Rep.,* 1963, *13,* 63–70. (a)

Kanfer, F. H., & Marston, A. R. Determinants of self-reinforcement in human learning. *J. exp. Psychol.,* 1963, *66,* 245–254. (b)

Marston, A. R., & Kanfer, F. H. Human reinforcement: Experimenter and subject controlled. *J. exp. Psychol.,* 1963, *66,* 91–94.

Miller, N. E., & Dollard, J. *Social learning and imitation.* New Haven: Yale Univer. Press, 1941.

Rosenbaum, M. E., & Tucker, I. F. The competence of the model and the learning of imitation and nonimitation. *J. exp. Psychol.,* 1962, *63,* 183–190.

Skinner, B. F. *Cumulative record.* New York: Appleton-Century-Crofts, 1961.

50

Influence of Models'
Reinforcement Contingencies on the
Acquisition of Imitative Responses

ALBERT BANDURA

It is widely assumed that the occurrence of imitative or observational learning is contingent on the administration of reinforcing stimuli either to the model or to the observer. According to the theory propounded by Miller and Dollard (1941), for example, the necessary conditions for learning through imitation include a motivated subject who is positively reinforced for matching the rewarded behavior of a model during a series of initially random, trial-and-error responses. Since this conceptualization of observational learning requires the subject to perform the imitative response before he can learn it, this theory evidently accounts more adequately for the emission of previously learned matching responses, than for their acquisition.

Mowrer's (1960) proprioceptive feedback theory similarly highlights the role of reinforcement but, unlike Miller and Dollard who reduce imitation to a special case of instrumental learning, Mowrer focuses on the classical conditioning of positive and negative emotions to matching response-correlated stimuli. Mowrer distinguishes two forms of imitative learning in terms of whether the observer is reinforced directly or vicariously. In the former case, the model performs a response and simultaneously rewards the observer. If the modeled responses are thus paired repeatedly with positive reinforcement they gradually acquire secondary reward value. The observer can then administer positively conditioned reinforcers to himself simply by reproducing as closely as possible the model's positively valenced behavior. In the second, or empathetic form of

From A. Bandura, Influence of Models' Reinforcement Contingencies on the Acquisition of Imitative Responses. *Journal of Personal and Social Psychology*, 1965, *1*, 589–595. Copyright 1965 by the American Psychological Association, and reproduced by permission of publisher and author.

This investigation was supported by Research Grant M-5162 from the National Institutes of Health, United States Public Health Service.

The author is indebted to Carole Revelle who assisted in collecting the data.

imitative learning, the model not only exhibits the responses but also experiences the reinforcing consequences. It is assumed that the observer, in turn, experiences empathetically both the response-correlated stimuli and the response consequences of the model's behavior. As a result of this higher-order vicarious conditioning, the observer will be inclined to reproduce the matching responses.

There is some recent evidence that imitative behavior can be enhanced by noncontingent social reinforcement from a model (Bandura & Huston, 1961), by response-contingent reinforcers administered to the model (Bandura, Ross, & Ross, 1963b; Walters, Leat, & Mezei, 1963), and by increasing the reinforcing value of matching responses per se through direct reinforcement of the participant observer (Baer & Sherman, 1964). Nevertheless, reinforcement theories of imitation fail to explain the learning of matching responses when the observer does not perform the model's responses during the process of acquisition, and for which reinforcers are not delivered either to the model or to the observers (Bandura et al., 1961, 1963a).

The acquisition of imitative responses under the latter conditions appears to be accounted for more adequately by a contiguity theory of observational learning. According to the latter conceptualization (Bandura, in press; Sheffield, 1961), when an observer witnesses a model exhibit a sequence of responses the observer acquires, through contiguous association of sensory events, perceptual and symbolic responses possessing cue properties that are capable of eliciting, at some time after a demonstration, overt responses corresponding to those that had been modeled.

Some suggestive evidence that the *acquisition* of matching responses may take place through contiguity, whereas reinforcements administered to a model exert their major influence on the *performance* of imitatively learned responses, is provided in a study in which models were rewarded or punished for exhibiting aggressive behavior (Bandura et al., 1963b). Although children who had observed aggressive responses rewarded subsequently reproduced the model's behavior while children in the model-punished condition failed to do so, a number of the subjects in the latter group described in postexperimental interviews the model's repertoire of aggressive responses with considerable accuracy. Evidently, they had learned the cognitive equivalents of the model's responses but they were not translated into their motoric forms. These findings highlighted both the importance of distinguishing between learning and performance and the need for a systematic study of whether reinforcement is primarily a learning-related or a performance-related variable.

In the present experiment children observed a film-mediated model who exhibited novel physical and verbal aggressive responses. In one treatment condition the model was severely punished; in a second, the model was generously rewarded; while the third condition presented no response consequences to the model. Following a postexposure test of imitative behavior, children in all three groups were offered attractive incentives contingent on their reproducing the models' responses so as to provide a more accurate index of learning. It was predicted that reinforcing consequences to the model would result in significant differences in the performance of imitative behavior with the model-rewarded group displaying the highest number of different classes of matching responses, followed by the no-consequences and the model-punished groups, respectively. In accordance with previous findings (Bandura et al., 1961, 1953a) it was also expected that boys would perform significantly more imitative aggression than girls. It was predicted, however, that the introduction of positive incentives would wipe out both reinforcement-produced and sexlinked performance differences, revealing an equivalent amount of learning among children in the three treatment conditions.

METHOD

Subjects

The subjects were 33 boys and 33 girls enrolled in the Stanford University Nursery School. They ranged in age from 42 to 71 months, with a mean age of 51 months. The children were assigned randomly to one of three treatment conditions of 11 boys and 11 girls each.

Two adult males served in the role of models, and one female experimenter conducted the study for all 66 children.

Exposure Procedure

The children were brought individually to a semi-darkened room. The experimenter informed the child that she had some business to attend to before they could proceed to the "surprise playroom," but that during the waiting period the child might watch a televised program. After the child was seated, the experimenter walked over to the television console, ostensibly tuned in a program and then departed. A film of approximately 5 minutes duration depicting the modeled responses was shown on a glass lenscreen in the television console by means of a rear projection arrangement, screened from the child's view by large panels. The televised form of presentation was utilized primarily because attending responses to televised stimuli are strongly conditioned in children and this procedure would therefore serve to enhance observation which is a necessary condition for the occurrence of imitative learning.

The film began with a scene in which the model walked up to an adult-size plastic Bobo doll and ordered him to clear the way. After glaring for a moment at the noncompliant antagonist the model exhibited four novel aggressive responses each accompanied by a distinctive verbalization.

First, the model laid the Bobo doll on its side, sat on it, and punched it in the nose while remarking, "Pow, right in the nose, boom, boom." The model then raised the doll and pommeled it on the head with a mallet. Each response was accompanied by the verbalization, "Sockeroo . . . stay down." Following the mallet aggression, the model kicked the doll about the room, and these responses were interspersed with the comment, "Fly away." Finally, the model threw rubber balls at the Bobo doll, each strike punctuated with "Bang." This sequence of physically and verbally aggressive behavior was repeated twice.

The component responses that enter into the development of more complex novel patterns of behavior are usually present in children's behavioral repertoires as products either of maturation or of prior social learning. Thus, while most of the elements in the modeled acts had undoubtedly been previously learned, the particular pattern of components in each response, and their evocation by specific stimulus objects, were relatively unique. For example, children can manipulate objects, sit on them, punch them, and they can make vocal responses, but the likelihood that a given child would spontaneously place a Bobo doll on its side, sit on it, punch it in the nose and remark, "Pow . . . boom, boom," is exceedingly remote. Indeed, a previous study utilizing the same stimulus objects has shown that the imitative responses selected for the present experiment have virtually a zero probability of occurring spontaneously among preschool children (Bandura et al., 1961) and, therefore, meet the criterion of novel responses.

The rewarding and punishing contingencies associated with the model's aggressive responses were introduced in the closing scene of the film.

For children in the model-rewarded condition, a second adult appeared with an abundant supply of candies and soft drinks. He informed the model that he was a "strong champion" and that his superb aggressive performance clearly deserved a generous treat. He then poured him a large glass of 7-Up, and readily supplied additional energy-building nourishment including chocolate bars, Cracker Jack popcorn, and an assortment of candies. While the model was rapidly consuming the delectable treats, his admirer symbolically reinstated the modeled aggressive responses and engaged in considerable positive social reinforcement.

For children in the model-punished condition, the reinforcing agent appeared on the scene shaking his finger menacingly and commenting reprovingly, "Hey there, you big bully. You quit picking on that clown. I won't tolerate it." As the model drew back he tripped and fell, the other adult sat on the model and spanked him with a rolled-up magazine while reminding him of his aggressive behavior. As the model ran off cowering, the agent forewarned him, "If I catch you doing that again, you big bully, I'll give you a hard spanking. You quit acting that way."

Children in the no-consequences condition viewed the same film as shown to the other two groups except that no reinforcement ending was included.

Performance Measure

Immediately following the exposure session the children were escorted to an experimental room that contained a Bobo doll, three balls, a mallet and pegboard, dart guns, cars, plastic farm animals, and a doll house equipped with furniture and a doll family. By providing a variety of stimulus objects the children were at liberty to exhibit imitative responses or to engage in nonimitative forms of behavior.

After the experimenter instructed the child that he was free to play with the toys in the room, she excused herself supposedly to fetch additional play materials. Since many preschool children are reluctant to remain alone and tend to leave after a short period of time, the experimenter reentered the room midway through the session and reassured the child that she would return shortly with the goods.

Each child spent 10 minutes in the test room during which time his behavior was recorded every 5 seconds in terms of predetermined imitative response categories by judges who observed the session through a one-way mirror in an adjoining observation room.

Two observers shared the task of recording the occurrence of matching responses for all 66 children. Neither of the raters had knowledge of the treatment conditions to which the children were assigned. In order to provide an estimate of interscorer reliability, the responses of 10 children were scored independently by both observers. Since the imitative responses were highly distinctive and required no subjective interpretation, the raters were virtually in perfect agreement (99%) in scoring the matching responses.

The number of different physical and verbal imitative responses emitted spontaneously by the children constituted the performance measure.

Acquisition Index

At the end of the performance session the experimenter entered the room with an assortment of fruit juices in a colorful juice-dispensing fountain, and booklets of sticker-pictures that were employed as the positive incentives to activate into performance what the children had learned through observation.

After a brief juice treat the children were informed, that for each physical or verbal imitative response that they reproduced, they would receive a pretty sticker-picture and additional juice treats. An achievement incentive was also introduced in order to produce further disinhibition and to increase the children's motivation to exhibit matching responses. The experimenter attached a pastoral scene to the wall and expressed an interest in seeing how many sticker-pictures the child would be able to obtain to adorn his picture.

The experimenter then asked the child, "Show me what Rocky did in the TV program," "Tell me what he said," and rewarded him immediately following each matching response. If a child simply described an imitative response he was asked to give a performance demonstration.

Although learning must be inferred from performance, it was assumed that the number of different physical and verbal imitative responses reproduced by the children under the positive-incentive conditions would serve as a relatively accurate index of learning.

RESULTS

Figure 50-1 shows the mean number of different matching responses reproduced by children in each of the three treatment conditions during the no-incentive and the positive-incentive phases of the experiment. A

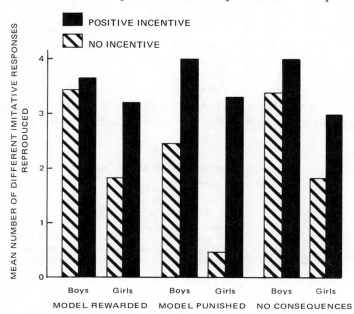

Figure 50-1. Mean number of different matching responses reproduced by children as a function of positive incentives and the model's reinforcement contingencies.

TABLE 50-1.   Analysis of Variance of Imitative Performance Scores

Source	df	MS	F
Treatments (T)	2	1.21	3.27*
Sex (S)	1	4.87	13.16**
T × S	2	.12	<1
Within groups	60	.37	

* $p < .05$.
** $p < .001$.

square-root transformation $(y = \sqrt{f + \frac{1}{2}})$ was applied to these data to make them amenable to parametric statistical analyses.

Performance Differences

A summary of the analysis of variance based on the performance scores is presented in Table 50-1. The findings reveal that reinforcing consequences to the model had a significant effect on the number of matching responses that the children spontaneously reproduced. The main effect of sex is also highly significant, confirming the prediction that boys would perform more imitative responses than girls.

Further comparisons of pairs of means by tests (Table 50-2) show that while the model-rewarded and the no-consequences groups did not differ from each other, subjects in both of these conditions performed significantly more matching responses than children who had observed the model experience punishing consequences following the display of aggression. It is evident, however, from the differences reported separately for boys and girls in Table 50-2, that the significant effect of the model's rein-

TABLE 50-2.   Comparison of Pairs of Means between
Treatment Conditions

	Treatment conditions		
Performance measure	Reward versus punishment	Reward versus no consequences	Punishment versus no consequences
	t	t	t
Total sample	2.20**	0.55	2.25**
Boys	1.05	0.19	1.24
Girls	2.13**	0.12	2.02*

* $p < .05$.
** $p < .025$.

forcement contingencies is based predominantly on differences among the girl's subgroups.[1]

Differences in Acquisition

An analysis of variance of the imitative learning scores is summarized in Table 50-3. The introduction of positive incentives completely wiped out the previously observed performance differences, revealing an equivalent amount of imitative learning among the children in the model-rewarded, model-punished and the no-consequences treatment groups. Although the initially large sex difference was substantially reduced in the positive-incentive condition, the girls nevertheless still displayed fewer matching responses than the boys.

Acquisition-Performance Differences

In order to elucidate further the influence of direct and vicariously experienced reinforcement on imitation, the differences in matching responses displayed under nonreward and positive-incentive conditions for each of the three experimental treatments were evaluated by the t-test procedure for correlated means. Table 50-4 shows that boys who witnessed the model either rewarded or left without consequences performed all of the imitative responses that they had learned through observation and no new matching responses emerged when positive reinforcers were made available. On the other hand, boys who had observed the model punished and girls in all three treatment conditions showed significant increments in imitative behavior when response-contingent reinforcement was later introduced.

DISCUSSION

The results of the present experiment lend support to a contiguity theory of imitative learning; reinforcements administered to the model influenced the observers' performance but not the acquisition of matching responses.

It is evident from the findings, however, that mere exposure to modeling stimuli does not provide the sufficient conditions for imitative or observational learning. The fact that most of the children in the experiment failed to reproduce the entire repertoire of behavior exhibited by the model,

---

[1] Because of the skewness of the distribution of scores for the subgroup of girls in the model-punished condition, differences involving this group were also evaluated by means of the Mann-Whitney U test. The nonparametric analyses yield probability values that are identical to those reported in Table 50-2.

even under positive-incentive conditions designed to disinhibit and to elicit matching responses, indicates that factors other than mere contiguity of sensory stimulation undoubtedly influence imitative response acquisition.

Exposing a person to a complex sequence of stimulation is no guarantee that he will attend to the entire range of cues, that he will necessarily select from a total stimulus complex only the most relevant stimuli, or that he will even perceive accurately the cues to which his attention is directed. Motivational variables, prior training in discriminative observation, and the anticipation of positive or negative reinforcements contingent on the emission of matching responses may be highly influential in channeling, augmenting, or reducing observing responses, which is a necessary precondition for imitative learning (Bandura, 1962; Bandura & Walters, 1963). Procedures that increase the distinctiveness of the relevant modeling stimuli also greatly facilitate observational learning (Sheffield & Moccoby, 1961).

In addition to attention-directing variables, the rate, amount, and complexity of stimuli presented to the observer may partly determine the degree of imitative learning. The acquisition of matching responses through observation of a lengthy uninterrupted sequence of behavior is also likely to be governed by principles of associate learning such as frequency and recency, serial order effects, and other multiple sources of associative interference (McGuire, 1961).

Social responses are generally composed of a large number of different

TABLE 50-3. Analysis of Variance of Imitative Learning Scores

Source	df	MS	F
Treatments (T)	2	0.02	<1
Sex (S)	1	0.56	6.22*
T × S	2	0.02	<1
Within groups	60	0.09	

* $p < .05$.

TABLE 50-4. Significance of the Acquisition-Performance Differences in Imitative Responses

	Treatment conditions		
Group	Reward t	Punishment t	No consequences t
Total sample	2.38*	5.00***	2.67**
Boys	0.74	2.26*	1.54
Girls	3.33**	5.65***	2.18*

* $p < .025$.
** $p < .01$.
*** $p < .001$.

behavioral units combined in a particular manner. Responses of higher-order complexity are produced by combinations of previously learned components which may, in themselves, represent relatively complicated behavioral patterns. Consequently, the rate of acquisition of intricate matching responses through observation will be largely determined by the extent to which the necessary components are contained in the observer's repertoire. A person who possesses a very narrow repertoire of behavior, for example, will, in all probability, display only fragmentary imitation of a model's behavior; on the other hand, a person who has acquired most of the relevant components is likely to perform precisely matching responses following several demonstrations. In the case of young preschool children their motor repertoires are more highly developed than their repertoires of verbal responses. It is, perhaps, for this reason that even in the positive-incentive condition, children reproduced a substantially higher percentage (67%) of imitative motor responses than matching verbalizations (20%). A similar pattern of differential imitation was obtained in a previous experiment (Bandura & Huston, 1961) in which preschool children served as subjects.

It is apparent from the foregoing discussion that considerably more research is needed in identifying variables that combine with contiguous stimulation in governing the process of imitative response acquisition.

It is possible, of course, to interpret the present acquisition data as reflecting the operation of generalization from a prior history of reinforcement of imitative behavior. Within any social group, models typically exhibit the accumulated cultural repertoires that have proved most successful for given stimulus situations; consequently, matching the behavior of other persons, particularly the superiors in an age-grade or prestige hierarchy, will maximize positive reinforcement and minimize the frequency of aversive response consequences. Since both the occurrence and the positive reinforcement of matching responses, whether by accident or by intent, are inevitable during the course of social development, no definitive resolution of the reinforcement issue is possible, except through an experiment utilizing organisms that have experienced complete social isolation from birth. It is evident, however, that contemporaneous reinforcements are unnecessary for the acquisition of new matching responses.

The finding that boys perform more imitative aggression than girls as a result of exposure to an aggressive male model, is in accord with results from related experiments (Bandura et al., 1961, 1963a). The additional finding, however, that the introduction of positive incentives practically wiped out the prior performance disparity strongly suggests that the frequently observed sex differences in aggression (Goodenough, 1931; Johnson, 1951; Sears, 1951) may reflect primarily differences in willingness to exhibit aggressive responses, rather than deficits in learning or "masculine-role identification."

The subgroups of children who displayed significant increments in imitative behavior as a function of positive reinforcement were boys who had observed the aggressive model punished, and girls for whom physically aggressive behavior is typically labeled sex inappropriate and nonrewarded or even negatively reinforced. The inhibitory effects of differing reinforcement histories for aggression were clearly reflected in the observation that boys were more easily disinhibited than girls in the reward phase of the experiment. This factor may account for the small sex difference that was obtained even in the positive-incentive condition.

The present study provides further evidence that response inhibition and response disinhibition can be vicariously transmitted through observation of reinforcing consequences to a model's behavior. It is interesting to note, however, that the performance by a model of socially disapproved or prohibited responses (for example, kicking, stricking with objects) without the occurrence of any aversive consequences may produce disinhibitory effects analogous to a positive reinforcement operation. These findings are similar to results from studies of direct reinforcement (Crandall, Good, & Crandall, 1964) in which nonreward functioned as a positive reinforcer to increase the probability of the occurrence of formerly punished responses.

Punishment administered to the model apparently further reinforced the girls' existing inhibitions over aggression and produced remarkably little imitative behavior; the boys displayed a similar, though not significant, decrease in imitation. This difference may be partly a function of the relative dominance of aggressive responses in the repertoires of boys and girls. It is also possible that vicarious reinforcement for boys, deriving from the model's successful execution of aggressive behavior (that is, overpowering the noncompliant adversary), may have reduced the effects of externally administered terminal punishment. These factors, as well as the model's self-rewarding and self-punishing reactions following the display of aggression, will be investigated in a subsequent experiment.

REFERENCES

Baer, D. M., & Sherman, J. A. Reinforcement control of generalized imitation in young children. *Journal of Experimental Child Psychology*, 1964, *1*, 37–49.

Bandura, A. Social learning through imitation. In M. R. Jones (Ed.), *Nebraska symposium on motivation: 1962*. Lincoln: University Nebraska Press, 1962. Pp. 211–269.

Bandura, A. Vicarious processes: A case of no-trial learning. In L. Berkowitz (Ed.), *Advances in experimental social psychology*. Vol. 2. New York: Academic Press, 1965.

Bandura, A., & Huston, Aletha C. Identification as a process of incidental learning. *Journal of Abnormal and Social Psychology*, 1961, *63*, 311–318.

Bandura, A., Ross, Dorothea, & Ross, Sheila A. Transmission of aggression through imitation of aggressive models. *Journal of Abnormal and Social Psychology*, 1961, 63, 575–582.

Bandura, A., Ross, Dorothea, & Ross, Sheila A. Imitation of film-mediated aggressive models. *Journal of Abnormal and Social Psychology*, 1963, 66, 3–11. (a)

Bandura, A., Ross, Dorothea, & Ross, Sheila A. Vicarious reinforcement and imitative learning. *Journal of Abnormal and Social Psychology*, 1963, 67, 601–607. (b)

Bandura, A., & Walters, R. H. *Social learning and personality development.* New York: Holt, Rinehart, & Winston, 1963.

Crandall, Virginia C., Good, Suzanne, & Crandall, V. J. The reinforcement effects of adult reactions and non-reactions on children's achievement expectations: A replication study. *Child Development*, 1964, 35, 385–397.

Goodenough, Florence L. *Anger in young children.* Minneapolis: Unver. Minnesota Press, 1931.

Johnson, Elizabeth Z. Attitudes of children toward authority as projected in their doll play at two age levels. Unpublished doctoral dissertation, Harvard University, 1951.

McGuire, W. J. Interpolated motivational statements within a programmed series of instructions as a distribution of practice factor. In A. A. Lumsdaine (Ed.), *Student response in programmed instruction: A symposium.* Washington, D.C.: National Academy of Sciences, National Research Council, 1961. Pp. 411–415.

Miller, N. E., & Dollard, J. *Social learning and imitation.* New Haven: Yale Univer. Press, 1941.

Mowrer, O. H. *Learning theory and the symbolic processes.* New York: Wiley, 1960.

Sears, Pauline S. Doll play aggression in normal young children: Influence of sex, age, sibling status, father's absence. *Psychological Monographs*, 1951, 65(6, Whole No. 323).

Sheffield, F. D. Theoretical considerations in the learning of complex sequential tasks from demonstration and practice. In A. A. Lumsdaine (Ed.), *Student response in programmed instructions: A symposium.* Washington, D. C.: National Academy of Sciences, National Research Council, 1961. Pp. 13–32.

Sheffield, F. D., & Maccoby, N. Summary and interpretation on research on organizational principles in constructing filmed demonstrations. In A. A. Lumsdaine (Ed.), *Student response in programmed instruction: A symposium.* Washington, D. C.: National Academy of Sciences, National Research Council, 1961. Pp. 117–131.

Walters, R. H., Leat, Marion, & Mezei, L. Inhibition and disinhibition of responses through empathetic learning. *Canadian Journal of Psychology*, 1963, 17, 235–243.

FACTOR ANALYTIC TYPOLOGIES | XII

A VAST MAJORITY of personality theories —major and minor, historically and currently—have been based primarily on the relatively subjective observations of the theorist, sometimes supplemented by small amounts of objective data. The biases of the theorist are maximized, and often the relationship of the theory to empirical data is tenuous. At nearly the opposite extreme among personality theories are the factor analytic typologies. These theoretical orientations are based largely on a mathematical system of data analysis plus the penetrating interpretation and reportage of an astute observer. Instead of beginning with a general theory, based on relatively few, relatively subjective, observations, the factor theorist begins, ideally, with no theory and collects large numbers of observations upon which he may then base theoretical conclusions.

No attempt will be made here to provide a detailed understanding of the procedures of factor analysis, since the topic consumes entire volumes. It should be noted, however, that factor analysis is basically a statistical technique which serves to provide relatively parsimonious accounts of relatively complicated sets of data. More specifically, the factor analytic solution, and the interpretation which follows it, provide a smaller number of variables (i.e., factors) to describe a larger variable set. The factors are generally viewed as dimensions which underlie the larger variable set. As an example, we might select from the literature of personality psychology a set of thirty personality variables, each measured by a separate personality scale. Suspecting that the thirty variables are not entirely independent (i.e., that there is considerable overlap among certain variables), we could carry out a factor analysis in order to determine the underlying dimensions of this variable set. To do this, we would simply give all thirty of the scales, under appropriately controlled conditions, to each of a large number of subjects, score each scale for each subject, and factor analyze the results. We might find, for example, that five major factors were adequate to describe the set of thirty variables, and if these factors are supported in further studies, we might hypothesize that they represent major dimensions of the personality.

It must be emphasized that this example represents only one of many types of applications of factor analysis. In addition, the example is necessarily oversimplified in a number of ways. For instance, factor analysis is not unitary; there are a number of different methods. There are also a variety of procedures (methods of rotation) for treating the factors, once they have been initially derived. And the interpretation of factor analytic solutions is generally a far more subjective procedure than factor analysts would prefer.

The major proponents of factor typologies of personality have for some time been Raymond B. Cattell and Hans J. Eysenck. Both are prolific and careful researchers, and both have made major contributions to personality psychology. The first article chosen for inclusion here is an important Cattell paper in which is outlined a "Theory of Situational, Instrument, Second Order, and Refraction Factors in Personality Structure Research." While the title may sound complex, the concepts are not. Before reading this paper, it will be helpful to note that Cattell had earlier proposed a theoretical distinction between two types of personality traits, which he termed surface traits and source traits. The surface trait is a set of observable, behavioral variables that appear to be associated with each other and hence to constitute a superficial trait. Source traits, clearly the more important in Cattell's viewpoint, are underlying variables or dimensions which are identified through factor analysis. Cattell had further proposed that source traits are of such a general nature as to operate across three major media of experimental observation: L data, collected from life records and in naturalistic settings; Q data, from self-evaluation inventories, interviews, and the like; and T data, from situational tests, objective assessments, and tests not involving self-evaluation.

In the article reprinted here, Cattell replies to a critique by Becker, in which the latter accepts as disproof of Cattell's theory of source traits the fact that correlations between L-data and Q-data determinations of the same variables are sometimes less than perfect. Cattell's reply points to the operation of certain complicating, "perturbing" influences which operate in the factor analytic study and tend to obscure source trait relationships.

The second Cattell article serves as an example of one application of factor analysis, the determination of factors underlying numerous variables, each measured by a personality subscale. The article also familiarizes the reader with two major factor-analytically derived personality questionnaires and provides discussions of some major issues and examples of important techniques in factor analysis.

The present section is completed by two articles by Eysenck. For many years, Eysenck has reported the existence of two major factors, extraversion (E) and neuroticism (N), which occur in many factor analyses, cutting across a wide variety of subject populations and variables. More recently a third dimension, psychoticism (P) has been introduced, and it is with this factor that the first Eysenck article included here is concerned. The concluding article reflects Eysenck's relatively recent interest in a particular type of psychotherapy, behavior therapy. He provides here a straightforward discussion of major issues, a careful review of relevant literature, and a statement of his own theoretical viewpoint.

51

Theory of Situational, Instrument, Second Order, and Refraction Factors in Personality Structure Research

RAYMOND B. CATTELL

Exploration of personality by multivariate experimental methods, as a means of objectively determining personality structure, has revealed, on the one hand, an array of stable, meaningful, cross-checking structures (Cattell, 1946, 1957; French, 1953), and on the other, some baffling inconsistencies. The latter have recently been pointed out by Becker (1960), apparently in criticism of the present writer's personality theory, but have been known for several years, and were, in fact, first brought to light by Cattell and Saunders (1950). Nevertheless, Becker does a service to advertise these facts; for psychologists have greatly neglected the solution of the problems revealed in this field.

The present writer's theoretical position is that it is conceptually correct to speak of the same unique source trait, e.g., cyclothymia-schizothymia, anxiety, ego-strength, surgency-desurgency, as something expressing itself (in terms of recognizable, replicable factor patterns) across all three possible media of experimental observation. That is to say, the same influence should appear in L data (life record, behavior *in situ*), Q data (questionnaire, consulting room, verbal self-evaluation), and T data (objective, laboratory, miniature situational, non-self-evaluative test performances).

In the article (Becker, 1960) to which I reply the fact that the actual correlation between the L-data and Q-data estimates of what are apparently equivalents in the two media, sometimes falls far short of perfection, is accepted as disproof of this theory. This theoretical conclusion is unsubtle; and the thesis of my reply is that countless threads of evidence contribute to the view that the same abstract personality source trait commonly operates across different media. However, certain "perturbations" have to be

From R. B. Cattell, Theory of Situational, Instrument, Second Order, and Refraction Factors in Personality Structure Research. *Psychological Bulletin*, 1961, 58, 160–174. Copyright 1961 by the American Psychological Association, and reproduced by permission of publisher and author.

recognized which prevent the simple relation appearing on the surface, and these need to be taken into account in understanding psychological measurement generally.

In this area of scientific investigation, Becker has not asked the right question. Unexpected, but systematically evaluated perturbations of existing laws have often led to new discoveries, not so much by rejecting a law as by extending it, e.g., in astronomy in the discovery of Neptune through observed perturbations in the expected orbit of Uranus. So here, it is argued that there is no reason to abandon the notion of unitary source traits (Cattell, 1946) but that one must recognize certain new concepts, which we have introduced under the terms situational, instrument, and refraction factors. These are supported partly by marshaling existing evidence, but also by experiments undertaken ad hoc, but which, through an editorial veto on space to reply, have been reported in a separate publication (Cattell, 1960).

THE DEFINITION OF INSTRUMENT FACTORS

The first and major source of perturbation in transmedia factor matching arises from what may be called *instrument factors*. Apparently, the first explicit recognition and demonstration of an instrument factor occurred in a structural analysis of a very widely selected set of objective personality tests, by Cattell and Gruen (1955), where a factor appeared literally produced by diurnal variations of sensitivity of a brass instrument (GSR). This purely instrumental influence created a factor by throwing common variance into all types of personality measures in which it was used. Such factors have appeared since in publications by Holzmann and Bitterman (1956), F. L. Damarin, D. T. Campbell, and L. Berwyn (unpublished), and several other unpublished studies known to the writer. Indeed, wherever questionnaire variables are mixed with ratings, attitude scales with questionnaires, or, sometimes, even one type of answer form with another, one or more factors may generally be found covering *all variables having formal similarity*.

The difficulty factors of Wherry and Gaylord (1944), and Dingman (1958), should definitely be regarded as a subspecies of instrument factor. Recently, in a study of the Music Preference Test of Personality (Cattell & Anderson, 1953) by Mayeske (1961) an instrument factor appeared even separating all items resting on one form of musical recording from those based on another technique. Instrument factors have become better understood in the last couple of years through extensive studies of their appearance in objective motivation structure analyses (Cattell, Radcliffe, & Sweney, 1960; R. B. Cattell & J. Horn, unpublished). There they appear

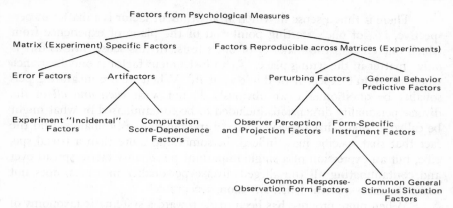

Figure 51-1. The place of instrument factors in a taxonomy of factors.

as "vehicle factors" covering all objective devices using the same vehicle, e.g., information, autism, for the objective measurement of motivation strength. In this, and many similar contexts, it has been shown that instrument factors can be fairly clearly eliminated by ipsative scoring (R. B. Cattell & J. Horn, unpublished, see Table 51-1).

Before proceeding beyond this introduction by illustrations, to a more comprehensive definition of the concept of instrument factor, it is desirable, however, to make clear which peripheral factors are *not* to be included. This can be done most compactly by Figure 51-1, presenting a hierarchy which will be clear to multivariate experimentalists. Incidentally, the term "artifactors" is due to Roberts (1959), and has been sharpened by additional conditions here to make their separation from instrument factors cleaner.

The justification for the labels of the three forms of "perturbing" factors reproducible across experiments (matrices) will be given as we proceed. Concentrating first on instrument factors, let us note that they are definable, initially, only in terms of intention and perspective. Later, the definition can be made more satisfactory as we develop precise concepts indicating various universes of variables. For a quality which persists across the differences of content of a series of opinionnaires of similar form, and which perhaps consists of response to a particular form inherent in this instrument, though irrelevant to the content interest of the experimenter may yet represent behavior dependent on a real personality trait. For example, what comes as an instrument factor covering the variables of similar form, $a_1 \ldots a_n$, may well load (when $a_1 \ldots a_n$ are condensed to a single variable a, set in the new context of variables b, c, d, etc.) some important general personality factor.[1]

---

[1] Incidentally, it is the failure to recognize this perspective which, in the present writer's opinion, has made so much recent work on response sets a rather uneconomical

There is thus a sense in which an instrument factor is a matter of perspective, i.e., of one's starting point and of the plane of experience from which one chooses the majority of one's tests. In this sense, just as dirt is only "matter in the wrong place," so an instrument factor is only "variance where we didn't expect it or don't want it." When we are measuring personality by questionnaire we obviously do not want *each and all* of the diverse personality dimensions included to be contaminated by what might be called a "generalized specific," i.e., a specific to questionnaires. And the fact that that specific may, indeed, be something more than a trivial specific, but an expression of a single important personality factor spread over and contaminating all the alleged diverse personality measures, does not make the measurement harsh any more acceptable!

When more progress has been made toward a systematic taxonomy of tests, on some such objective basis as that worked out by Cattell and Warburton (1967), it would become possible to set up also a relatively objective classification of instrument factors, according to the types of personality approach to which they are tangential. For "form" and "content" are quite subjective categories, and, in any case, by no means exhaust the possible planes of experiment to which instrument factors can be orthogonally intrusive. For the time being, however, we must take a relativistic position, and one centered in "content." On this basis we shall contingently define an instrument factor as any uniquely (simple structure) rotated factor which covers a whole set of diverse variables having formal resemblance in presentation, mode of permitted response, or scoring, and which does not extend to tests of the same psychological content when couched in other modes of formal presentation, response, etc.

THEORY OF SOURCES OF PERTURBATION AFFECTING TRAIT ALIGNMENT

It should be noted that there are two distinct, though related senses in which a source trait can be said to be the same or not the same in two different media:

---

use of psychological research time. Whereas educational psychometrists during the late 1950s "discovered," in their opinionnaire tests, response sets (Cronbach, 1950), social desirability sets (Edwards, 1957), extremity of response sets (Berg, 1955), and acquiescence—tendency to agree, yes-vs.-no (Messick & Jackson, 1961)—these had already been employed by designers of objective personality tests in the late 1940s and early 1950s (Cattell, 1946; Cattell & Gruen, 1955). In the context of broader personality theories, and varied behavioral measures involved, it had already become clear that what itemetrists, without knowledge of the literature in this area, later treated merely as "flaws" in their paper-and-pencil tests, were actually expressions of well defined personality factors, e.g., anxiety or UI 24, comention or UI 20, superego rigidity or UI 29, as well as UI 31 (Cattell, 1957).

1. An estimate of the factor from the variables in one medium may correlate less than unity with its estimate from variables in another medium, even when attenuation-corrected for (*a*) unreliability of measurement, and (*b*) imperfection of estimate.

2. It may not be possible to discover a trait, when factoring both media together, which has simple structure across both media and also possession of the hypothesized, similar-meaning salient loadings in both media. (Whether one also means that the simple structure position in one medium will not project into the other we shall discuss below.)

Becker has been concerned with the first of these, denying alignment without first checking that Corrections *a* and *b* could not restore the correlation to unity. In any case, the second meaning is more important. If unity is this sense holds, personality theory is profoundly simplified, and it is only a matter of the mechanics of statistics to produce weighted measures from the two media that *will* approach a correlation of unity.[2]

In the larger collation of data and new experimental work (Cattell, 1960), from which the present article abstracts, it has been shown that the presence of unrecognized instrument factors in the two media will prevent alignment either in Sense 1 or 2, unless special new techniques are used. Before devoting a section to closer inspection of this result, however, it is desirable to set out a clear theory about more general sources of perturbation. For, in principle, one can see that there are some six possible origins of the failure to find a one-to-one alignment of primary personality factors measured in one medium with those measured in another. Some of these will produce instrument factors; others will contribute to other kinds of nonalignment to be described.

Sources of Nonalignment

Human transmission (perception, evaluation, projection, memory) of score values. Largely this means rating and self-rating (L and Q data). This is too subtle and complex a field—hitherto handled too simply in terms of "halo"—for the present abstract summary to be illustrated in available space (see Cattell, 1960). Theoretically, the pattern of correlations, and therefore of obtained factors, could be distorted by, and only by, properties of the individual and his relation to the recorder which affect the recording of *all* his behavior variables, and by properties of the perceiving recorder. The former can be divided into (*a*) value relationships, of which

---

[2] Such a procedure should be sharply distinguished from what Becker (1960) appears to advocate, and describes Gough as doing, namely, to force a Q scale to align itself with an L factor by assiduous item selection. Any such procedure contributes nothing to our knowledge of structure, but only hides the problem. If it succeeds, and if our theory is correct that L-data factors are the most heavily contaminated of any medium with irrelevant factors, this is forcing a poorly oriented measure to agree with a still poorer one.

liking-disliking (a constituent in halo) is only one; and (b) perspicacity or visibility effects, e.g., extraversion making the ratee more known, position effects making certain behaviors more clear. The latter can be divided into projections of (a) stereotypes or cultural clichés,[3] and (b) refraction factors, discussed below, peculiar to one medium. In all the "perceiving recorder effects" a correlation is produced by "projection" of a (perhaps quite unconscious) conviction that certain variables go together. Some of these may produce typical instrument factors, uniformly and about equally loading all variables in the medium; but others may load only *some* variables, producing what are perhaps best described as "perception-evaluation" projection factors, and which are not true instrument factors.

Communality of variables in respect to some trait required for handling a similar formal performance in all of them (or for registering in an observation situation). This is essentially one of the two main sources (see following paragraph) of instrument factors only. The countless possibilities may be illustrated by e.g. the use of 30 scales in all of which the score (in one direction or the other) depends on an ability to read, or on information or skill of expression, or tendency to say yes rather than no, etc.

Communality of variables in respect to scoring or scaling applied after administration. Quite apart from common demands on the subject's actual performance as in the previous paragraph, anything in the formal *scoring* procedure which tends to give similar sigmas, and skewedness (and in some cases means) throughout one class of tests will tend to create higher correlation among them and a common factor. That is to say, if the matrix of correlations of tests a_1 through a_n were just the same, on a rank formula, as that for b_1 through b_n, but if all the a's, on the one hand, and all b's, on the other, have similar distribution, then basing the matrix afresh on a product-moment formula will tend to give an instrument factor for the a's and/or the b's separately.

Coincidence of different global stimulus situations with different test media alministrations. If a person answered one set of questionnaires in private, and another orally and publicly (which is akin to the interview or behavior rating situation), we should expect real differences in response due to the actual stimulus situation, covering the occasion on which all items of one test were answered, being different from that covering the other test-taking setting. A priori this could create both an instrument factor, conterminous with each medium-situation, and also a change in loading of the same items on the same personality factors in the two situations.

Habitual broad area differences in actual trait development and expression. Among children, for example, we should expect the particular behav-

---

[3] Since sociologists have ruined "stereotype," by applying it equally to a widespread concept which either (a) does or (b) does not, correspond to statistical reality, I suggest "cultural cliché" explicitly for a widespread cultural concept which is significantly different from any externally existing pattern.

ior variables representing, say, the dominance factor, to be expressed to different degrees in the home environment and in the school environment. This is analogous to the point in the above paragraph, except that the influence is expressly conceived not to lie in the temporary measurement situation itself, but in the prolonged life situation, leading to real differences of actual habit strength, i.e., of the trait itself. Factor analytically, this might produce a home dominance factor and a school dominance factor, representing the relative impact of home and school, respectively, or alternatively, one factor modified by two other factors, each peculiar to one broad area. If the former proves to be more characteristic, then we can confidently predict that the two first-order factors will correlate highly and yield a single second-order dominance factor. Even if the former is true it would be possible, in a rough factoring to perceive the structure as that of a home and school instrument factor (as in the second possibility) but psychologically, the interpretation, if the proper structure is obtained, would now be different from an instrument factor effect. The area differences would then be interpreted as *real* structure differences, and the concept of a single dominance trait would be discovered and justified *only* at the second-order factor level.

Differences among media in density of representation of variables. If in sampling variables in the ability field an experimenter accidentally took one variable for each of Thurstone's primary abilities and factored, he would obtain, straightaway, i.e., as a first-order factor, that general ability factor which, in any "dense" representation of variables, appears only as a second-order factor (Thurstone, 1938). This concept of density of variable representation has been developed further elsewhere(Cattell, 1957, pp. 808–817), but it is easy to see that if there were really large differences of density unrecognized between media we should obtain no correlational alignment of the primaries in the two fields. Only on exploring the second order would the possibility arise of discovering that a second order in one medium is the same as a first order in the other.

Actually, a soon as systematic exploration of second-order structure in questionnaires reached to six factors (Cattell, 1957; Cattell & Scheier, 1961; Cattell & Warburton, 1967), it became evident that four second-order *questionnaire* factors aligned with four first-order *objective test* factors (UI 19, 20, 24, and 32); and in two of these, UI 24 (anxiety) and UI 32 (extraversion), the agreement is perfect within small limits of experimental error. An instance from a different realm, but amounting to a correlation of only 0.80 between the two media, exists in Tollefson's demonstration (1961) that the second-order extraversion factor in the questionnaire is a first-order factor in the Humor Test of Personality. These alignments (from the earlier, 1954–1957, publications above) are not mentioned in Becker's article (1960), perhaps because his comments are all on L- and Q- (rather than T-) data alignments. But the findings are highly relevant as showing that there does exist a corner of the intermedia jigsaw puzzle which is beginning to fit in place. These five experimental instances alone are surely sufficient to encourage us in that rejection of nihilism which this article undertakes.

To risk a prediction in the little explored field of "density," one might judge that variables in Q data will prove somewhat more "dense" than L data. But substantially, as the above evidence shows, one can conclude only that variables as commonly chosen are much more dense in Q than T data. This is understandable; e.g., in the T-data anxiety factor, we test startle response by a single cold pressor test (Cattell & Scheier, 1961) whereas in most anxiety questionnaires there are a dozen items asking in different ways how easily the person startles. Cronbach (1960), Comrey, and others who criticize low homogeneity when reviewing factor scales, are perhaps unwittingly driving their flocks toward the more serious danger of using personality scales heavily loaded in spurious "specific" variance of this latter kind, instead of watching that their scales deal with personality factors having broad psychological relevance and effectiveness.

If the above search for sources of perturbation has been truly exhaustive, our summary must include three other forms of distortion besides instrument factors, constituting four in all, as follows (beginning with instrument factors):

1. Test instrument factors, including common test form (response-observation-score) factors, and common test general stimulus situation factors.

2. Modification of actual trait by influences peculiar to one area of expression, producing primaries for each area and requiring conceptual unity to be sought at a higher order level.

3. Difference of density of representation of variables, as commonly unconsciously chosen by experimenters, in their different media, resulting in a higher order in one medium matching a lower order in another.

4. Perception-evaluation or projection factors, which trespass on the variance of the variables used to estimate personality factors, *not* by uniformly loading all in one medium (as does an instrument factor) but having each a characteristic form, and, when restricted to one medium, having the properties of refraction factors described below.

THE PRACTICAL PROBLEM OF REACHING
PERSONALITY STRUCTURE DESPITE DISTORTIONS

If the above theoretical analysis is correct the manifest correlational picture of personality structures will be less like Whistler's portrait of his mother than the cubist's rendering of the same, fractured into surprising new supernumerary planes and facets. To translate from the latter to the former, it is necessary that research, first, check the hypotheses about the forms of distortion at work and, second, find experimental and statistical means for isolating and setting aside these various perturbing influences.

One cannot do more than glance at these tasks here. As to the first, our initial examination of data shows definitely that form-specific instrument factors exist, while my colleagues and I have also begun to give evidence for the Sources 2, 3, and 4. The source of nonalignment labeled 2—local area modification of real traits—has been more fully illustrated elsewhere (Cattell, 1960) but must be left to others systematically to investigate. Source 3, changing density with changing medium, has already been substantiated.

As to the second task—segregating the distorting influences to arrive at essential structure—the unraveling of Effects 2 and 3 above is straightforward, by second-order factoring, though the possibility has been mooted above that Source 2 could produce two instrument factors, beyond a single first-order factor, instead of two first orders resolving into a second.

Setting 2 and 3 aside, therefore, we shall devote the present section to unraveling the effect of instrument factors, 1 above, and the following section to perception-evaluation-project phenomena, 4 above.

The special experiments with instrument factors described elsewhere (Cattell, 1960) proceeded first to find what happens when one factors correlation matrices derived from known, numerically stated factor models, and secondly, to experiment with varieties of solution in actual psychological data where the existence and boundaries of an instrument factor were well known beforehand. These experiments showed that:

1. Where the instrument factor covers *all* variables, i.e., where they are not embedded in a larger matrix, with other media to constitute a hyperplane and determine unique rotation, the typical investigator and procedure will not find or be aware of the instrument factor.

2. If the instrument factor is not found then either: (*a*) the correlations among the primaries will be distorted (if it is positive on all and they are all positively correlated, it will increase their correlations); or, (*b*) the simple structure which really exists among the primaries will not be found, or found only in very impaired form. Commonly *b* will predominate, but both will operate.

After this demonstration of the effect of an instrument factor in a single medium we proceeded to models and real instances containing blocks of variables uniformly from each of two or three media. Herein each medium was covered by *one* instrument factor but where *true* personality factors existed in the sense of having a simple structure position with salient loadings on variables of similar meanings in *both* media. Here it was shown:

1. If one obtains the best possible simple structure (perhaps imperfect because of mixed-in instrument factor) among variables separately in

TABLE 51-1. Psychological and Instrument Factors as Found in Objective, Dynamic Trait Simple Structure

	Factor Matrix				
	Psychological Factors			Instrument Factors	
Attitude Variable and Device Measurement	Escape Erg	Sentiment to Parents	Self-Sentiment	Information Device Factor	Autism Device Factor
1 Desire for good self-control. Information measure	00	—02	26	54	03
2 Wish to know oneself. Information measure	03	—05	31	27	19
3 Wish to never become insane. Information measure	—06	12	22	43	04
4 Readiness to turn to parents for help. Information measure	—02	35	09	28	—01
5 Feeling proud of one's parents. Information measure	—06	28	—01	24	01
6a Desire to avoid fatal disease and accidents. Information measure	16	04	13	65	—02
7a Wish to get protection from A bomb. Information measure	14	—08	03	14	—05
8 Desire for good self-control. Autism measure	01	—04	30	02	22
9 Wish to know oneself. Autism measure	—08	07	37	—01	31
10 Wish never to become insane. Autism measure	00	—01	16	00	25
11 Readiness to turn to parents for help. Autism measure	—08	18	09	—08	42
12 Feeling proud of one's parents. Autism measure	—03	14	01	06	14
13a Desire to avoid fatal disease and accidents. Autism measure	26	20	01	04	17
14a Wish to get protection from A bomb. Autism measure	23	13	09	15	10

Note: The theoretically required salients to define the factors are boxed in, and except for two values at the bottom of the parental sentiment factor column, the salients are high (above .09) where, and only where, they are theoretically required to be.

a Attitudes 13 and 14 are the same as 6 and 7, but in a different medium, and similarly, for the other cross-media personality factors.

each medium, the same simple structures cannot usually be found when the media are put together.

2. One reason for this is that if one projects the simple structure position satisfactorily obtained in one medium into the second,[4] it definitely does not give simple structure within the second.

3. If, however, one first admits the existence of, and locates by simple structure in the combined matrix, the instrument factors (which can now have determinate hyperplanes), then the true personality factors, operating across both media, can be located (in blind simple structure rotation). A successful example of this in real data—objective motivation measurement (R. B. Cattell & J. Horn, unpublished)—is shown in Table 51-1 here, and in other models elsewhere (Cattell, 1960). Our ignorance of this principle in 1948 was presumably responsible for the chaotic outcome of the first extensive transmedium factor analyses (Cattell & Saunders, 1950, 1955).

Incidentally, it will be obvious that missing the instrument factor, failing to rotate it correctly if one does not miss it, and encountering the subsequent distortion are due respectively to (a) the lack of a test for factor extraction that will decide, to within less than an error of two or three factors, how many should be extracted; (b) having no variables from other media to give a hyperplane for it; and (c) the variance that should have been in the instrument factor being pushed into the personality factors, destroying the clarity of their hyperplanes. The remedy which worked in the above cases was to give good technical attention to these issues.

ON ISOLATING TRANSMEDIUM PERSONALITY FACTORS AND REFRACTION FACTORS

Our final step consisted in returning to the actual L and Q data from which Becker infers that personality factors are unmatchable across media, and showing that when examined by more penetrating concepts, as above, uniquely determinate, psychologically meaningful, factor patterns appear, expressing themselves appropriately in both media for each factor. This has theoretical interest in giving additional substance to Point 3 above, by introducing the notion of refraction factors, and in producing some order in that L-Q frontier which has hitherto been the most hopelessly obscure of the transmedia relationships. Nevertheless, this approach does no more than reveal *some* order, and at the same time opens the door on a lot of problems, particularly in the field of behavior rating, which will now demand systematic investigations.

---

[4] This cannot be done, of course, simply by applying the same discovered transformation (λ) matrix to the centroids, because the latter begin at different positions. One first discovers by the Procrustes program the λ most nearly reproducing the first medium simple structure from the joint medium centroid.

It is not easy to find in any published study of the past 20 years (ever since personality structure research began in earnest) an experiment really adequate in reaching the technical conditions necessary to get anywhere on this question. One needs, among other things, an experiment: (*a*) on a sufficient sample for sampling errors not to be intrusive; (*b*) where the subjects had a long testing period in which they were simultaneously rated *in situ* and subjected to questionnaires, comprehensive, reliable, and valid enough to define several factors clearly; (*c*) where ratings and questionnaire variables were strategically chosen to represent psychologically *familiar* factors, already vouched for by earlier researches; and (*d*) where ratings were carried out by peers and under the requisite conditions described elsewhere (Cattell, 1946, 1957). Probably the most satisfactory data available is that in which the experimental work was broadly conceived and painstakingly carried out by Coan, on 7.8-year-old children (Cattell & Coan, 1957, 1958). It suffers only with respect to *d*, in that ratings were made by teachers instead of peers, and perhaps in reduced homogeneity of sample through equal inclusion of boys and girls.

Taking the data of this experiment we find that 24 rating variables have already been factored and blindly rotated into 12 very definite simple structure factors, each represented by two markers (see Table 5 in Cattell, 1960). Similarly, 24 variables in Q data, each consisting of a scale of about eight items, have been resolved as 12 well known simple structure factors, each marked essentially by two salient variables. However, on psychological inspection of these resolutions, the hypothetical position was taken that only 10 of the 12 factors were common to the two matrices, the remaining 4 being special, 2 to each matrix.

The two sets of 24 variables were now combined and intercorrelated in a cross-medium, L-Q matrix of 48 variables, which, by Tucker's test, yielded 16 factors. (With the hypothesis of matching, above, one would expect 14, but it is usual to find some new factor created by the mixture when two matrices are pooled.) The structure of this new factor space proved to be complex. Projection of simple structure obtained in one into the other, as described earlier (Footnote 4), would not yield a good combined simple structure. Attempts to force simple structure by varimax, oblimax, or other "analytical" programs failed because these rigid programs could not recognize and uniquely rotate the instrument factors, which, on the basis of the above principles and findings, we knew must be present. Only a patient and comprehensive exploratory visual rotation (aided by the photographic Rotoplot program on Illiac), over 22 rotations, yielded a position of such stability that one could repeatedly return to it. In reaching this position we found that the hyperplanes in the data were noticeably a little broader (about $\pm.13$ instead of $\pm.10$) than those existing in one medium alone.

On examining the solution, set out in Table 51-2,[5] we found that we had essentially an instrument factor for L data and another for Q data (not set out at the *end* of the matrix, but marked In$_L$ and In$_Q$, in Table 51-2). There are also two other factors, which we would guess might be projected "clichés," numbered 13 and 16. The interesting fact is that when this debris is set aside, patterns for the well known personality dimensions C (Ego strength), D (Excitability), F (Surgency), and H (Parmia), appear, with the appropriate four markers (2L and 2Q) on each, though the hyperplanes are pierced by one or two random appreciable loadings on other factors. (Counting within $\pm.13$ they reach acceptable percentages of 65, 73, 77, and 54 in the hyperplane.)

However, a hitherto undescribed phenomenon is encountered here, namely, the appearance of factors restricted to one medium, *and appearing in one or both of the separate media alongside, and simultaneous with, the appearance of the joint medium factor having the same personality meaning*. This is illustrated by C and C$_L$, D and D$_Q$ (Table 51-2), wherein the real psychological factor (C or D), loading the four essential variables across both media, carries alongside it an incomplete image of itself in each medium. The incomplete image loads only the two variables which belong in one medium. To these patterns, occurring simultaneously with the combined pattern, I have tentatively given the name "refraction factors," since they are analogous to what would be seen if one looked at an object both directly and refracted through a prism of another medium, one on each side of the line of vision.

Actually Table 51-2 does not simultaneously present *all* refraction factors for all real factors, but this should not disturb us any more than the failure of a single archeological digging to provide all the bones of a skeleton or all cultural elements for a given period. For, as it has been argued elsewhere (Cattell, 1958) any matrix typically has strictly as many dimensions as variables, and probably even more hyperplanes, i.e., one is always taking a selection in simple structure among more possible hyperplanes than one has chosen to extract factors. Further search should be made for refraction factors, therefore.

A vital empirical question affecting further inference at this point concerns the correlations among the real and refraction factors for a given psychological dimension. We had expected them to be positively correlated, but the best estimate from existing data is that they are only slightly correlated, if at all. It is possible, however, that if more dimensions

[5] The matrix containing the correlations among factors, the lambda matrix, and the centroid for Table 51-2 have been deposited with the American Documentation Institute. Order Document No. 6570 from ADI Auxiliary Publications Project, Photoduplication Service, Library of Congress; Washington 25, D.C., remitting in advance $1.75 for microfilm or $2.50 for photocopies. Make checks payable to: Chief, Photoduplication Service, Library of Congress.

TABLE 51-2.

Simple Structure Rotation of Combined L and Q Data, with Regard for Instrument Factors
(Primary Factor Pattern)

		C	D	F	H	InL	Inq	Aq	GL	Gq	Jq	CL	O40	13	Oq	Dq	16
L	A	+20	−03	+05	+06	+44	+09	−10	−07	−16	+04	−20	+06	−48	+02	−01	−25
	C	[+45]	−13	−15	−03	+04	−01	−19	−04	+05	+04	−64	−11	−16	−08	+00	−03
	D	+07	[+45]	+00	−12	+67	−03	−11	−10	−03	+15	+02	+04	+07	−03	−10	−10
	E	+13	−31	[−08]	+30	+43	+03	+09	−10	+01	−09	−16	+21	+04	+04	−04	+22
	F	+39	−05	[+50]	−09	−22	−01	+10	+06	+07	+04	+14	+08	+07	−01	−07	−25
	G	−19	−09	+01	[+08]	−19	+01	−05	[+66]	+00	−01	−01	−11	+05	−04	+04	+00
	H	+10	−03	−07	[+48]	−11	−06	−01	+50	+08	−01	−01	−04	+06	−22	+04	−07
	I	−14	+10	−01	+05	−56	−21	−10	−13	−11	+00	+06	+40	−07	+00	−10	+19
	J	−04	+31	−20	+09	+45	+09	−35	−04	+00	−08	+00	−33	−04	−09	−10	+05
	L	+00	+19	+00	+14	+60	−02	+00	−03	+09	+05	−12	−65	+02	−04	+13	+08
	M	+10	−08	−07	−17	−22	−03	+16	+70	+01	−01	+06	+19	−02	+06	+13	−09
	O	−19	−09	+07	−44	−11	−18	+11	−38	+12	−09	−02	−10	−53	+03	−12	+15
	A	+03	−28	+15	+53	+18	+15	+06	+00	+11	+04	−02	−08	−10	+03	−19	−02
	C	[+49]	−12	+19	+19	−22	+03	+09	+07	−01	+08	−56	+08	+11	+10	+04	−06
	D	+00	[+20]	+00	−14	+84	+00	−05	−10	+09	+04	+12	−06	+07	−07	−13	−13
	E	+00	+05	+01	+48	+71	+02	+07	+19	+03	+05	+10	+18	−10	+08	−19	−01
	F	−13	+03	[+46]	+27	−21	−10	+06	−65	−04	−09	+10	−01	+02	+02	−07	+08
	G	+12	+12	+07	+25	−19	+07	−01	[+76]	−04	−05	−08	−04	+13	+00	+06	+11
	H	−07	−09	+04	[+55]	−21	+02	+06	+22	+07	−02	−04	−08	+08	−08	−23	+01
	I	+32	−01	−07	+09	+05	+12	+05	−22	+03	−05	−07	+84	+13	+01	−03	+05
	J	−06	+12	−04	−41	+84	+07	+04	+07	+01	−05	−10	−03	−02	+02	−27	−10
	L	+10	+06	−11	+00	+67	−03	+07	+10	+00	−13	−35	−06	+02	−01	−24	−14
	M	+12	+01	−07	+44	+40	+03	−05	+37	+04	+04	+12	+04	−42	−02	+27	+01
	O	−03	−22	+07	−48	−34	+07	−14	+13	+07	−07	+20	−00	−16	−01	+13	+30

TABLE 51-2. (Continued)

	C	D	F	H	In_L	In_Q	A_Q	G_L	G_Q	J_Q	C_L	O_{40}	13	O_Q	D_Q	16
A	−03	+06	−19	+06	+10	+01	[+58]	−74	+07	−13	−10	−51	+01	+03	+10	−09
C	[+36]	+28	+07	+20	+05	−03	+12	+07	+03	−06	+24	−17	+04	+04	−12	+06
D	+01	[+65]	+00	+20	−11	+08	+02	−04	+36	−05	−12	+06	−10	+03	−49	−05
E	−27	+14	+00	−03	−01	−07	+02	−18	−51	+01	+04	−04	−3.3	−03	−26	+10
F	+00	+10	[+49]	−03	+15	+45	+04	−06	+04	−07	−14	−17	−13	−11	+00	+29
G	−16	−01	−05	+03	+11	−31	+00	−04	[+58]	+02	+06	+03	−04	−17	−04	−01
H	−10	−06	−09	[+36]	−12	+03	+06	+10	+01	+06	+02	−04	−10	+37	+58	−07
I	−17	−13	−07	+02	−01	+72	+00	+00	+08	+12	+13	−11	+00	−07	+00	−07
J	−12	+10	−05	+05	−07	−07	+10	+01	+05	[+66]	+02	−06	+05	−34	+03	−10
N	+19	−09	−27	−17	−22	−26	[−47]	−25	+05	−07	−13	+12	−15	−02	−14	+02
O	−04	+04	+03	+09	+03	−64	−16	+04	−08	+05	−01	−00	+08	+30	−04	+06
Q_t	−29	+06	−01	+09	−08	−12	+10	−03	+04	−05	+02	[+40]	+01	−12	+03	−3.3
A	+14	+06	−35	−08	−01	+01	[+51]	+04	−08	−07	−16	−18	+00	−01	−12	+06
C	[+55]	+06	−01	−05	+04	+02	+05	−04	−05	+05	+08	−04	−11	+03	+00	+03
D	+12	[+60]	+04	−05	−26	−12	+10	+09	+44	+02	−18	+19	+11	+10	−42	+11
E	+04	+40	−04	−14	−01	−03	+05	−16	+00	−29	+10	−07	−23	+02	−58	−03
F	−07	+15	[+39]	−25	+10	+06	−02	+03	−07	−04	−07	+08	+04	+02	−12	+08
G	+09	+17	−03	−11	−05	+30	−06	−06	[+80]	+06	+04	−18	−11	−03	−12	−06
H	−06	+08	+11	[+69]	−11	−06	−02	−09	+01	−07	−04	−04	+01	−04	+52	+06
I	−06	−01	+01	+06	−11	+70	+19	+13	+49	−12	+05	−10	+05	+12	+06	+05
J	+12	+09	+07	+05	+07	+01	+00	−06	−03	[+45]	−05	+01	−10	+21	−12	+17
N	+13	+04	+07	+06	+05	−18	[−42]	−03	+16	−05	−10	−04	+12	+15	+06	−02
O	−17	+03	−08	+03	+12	−31	+01	−01	+13	+13	+13	−12	−01	+46	−17	−31
Q_t	−06	+00	+04	+03	+01	−06	+01	−06	+11	+01	−11	[+57]	−07	+02	+17	−37

had been taken out their correlations would have been increased (see Diagram 5, Cattell, 1958).

Exploration and evaluation of possible hypotheses to account for refraction factors would require at least an article to itself. One does not go too far in interpretation, however, to say that they imply that each individual, in addition to his assessment on the real factor, gets a "bonus" on the variables peculiar to each medium, which is substantially unrelated to his status on the real factor. Our hypothesis is that these refraction factors belong to the perceptual class (Class 4 on page 166 above) and arise from the behavior in question being differently perceived in the two media. In self-rating a varying sensitivity and self-awareness—only in special cases a function of the trait being rated—could provide the differing "bonus" from person to person. The differing visibilities of these individuals from the position of the rater, giving the L-data refraction, would be expected to be quite unrelated to the order of their individual sensitivities in self-rating.

If this is correct one might also expect the lesser loadings, on variables other than the two salients, to be systematically different on the two refraction factors. For example, the rating by others, in the case of a factor much concerned in delinquency, might impart something of the stereotype of a scoundrel, where the Q-data refraction factor might convey more of a good person in difficulties. Since our main concern is with the order which emerges little has been said of the "debris" factors notably 13 and 16 in Table 51-2. But our conclusion, tentatively, is that "evaluative" and "visibility" factors other than refraction factors are at present run together in the insufficient factor space so far used, and that, especially in the L data, these "halo" and related factors are substantial. They do not appear to be any known second-order factors, which can sometimes appear in inadequate first-order factorings. It has sufficed for our present investigation simply to set them aside. But if closer research scrutiny in this heap shows that our present indications are correct that these Class 4 perturbers are much larger in L than Q data, then the practice of trying to force questionnaire factors to align with rating "criteria" comes still more in question than it is today.

That the reader may more directly evaluate the nature and quality of the simple structure in Table 51-2 we have set out in Figure 51-2 a plot of two psychological ("real") factors therefrom.

SUMMARY AND CONCLUSION

1. Correlations among primary personality factors in different media do not provide a simple pattern of one-to-one relations, and fall decidedly short of unity between two factors of the same apparent psychological meaning.

2. The theoretical possibilities and the natural occurrences of perturb-

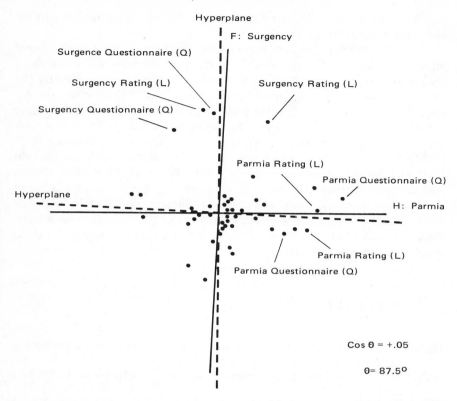

Figure 51-2. Simple structure appearing between cross-media personality factors. (Marker variables labeled)

ing influences hiding true alignment have been discussed and demonstrated. They have been classified as (*a*) test instrument factors; (*b*) actual trait modification by differing experience in subareas, requiring unity to be sought at a higher order level; (*c*) differences of density of representation of variables in different media; and (*d*) perceptual-evaluation-projection factors, occurring where human transmission of observations is involved.

3. Experimenters, especially when leaving rotation decisions to falsely founded analytical computer programs, commonly miss instrument factors, but when these are properly isolated and set aside by careful experiment it is possible to find the well known primary personality factors, each appearing as a single factor expressing itself in both L and Q media.

4. Regard for instrument and second-order-first-order factor relations is already producing clarity and consistency in personality structure research; but much remains to be explored regarding at least four forms of distortion which apparently occur where human transmission is involved,

i.e., in L and Q data. The new phenomenon of refraction factors particularly calls for intensive research.

5. One must distinguish between the question "Does a single simple structure factor exist loading variables of the same meaning on both media?" and "Can one get a perfect correlation between estimates of apparently (by meaning) the same factor, made in the two media?" Even when the answer to the first, so important for personality theory, is "Yes," as this paper claims to have shown, the answer to the second remains "No." The variance due to instrument factors, refraction factors, and any evaluation-perceptual factors peculiar to one medium will remain with and confound the estimate of a factor from that medium. Possibilities exist, by ipsative scoring and discriminant function methods of improving the correlation between estimates of the same factor made in two different media, and a path has been opened above toward a proper estimation of the correction for attenuation that can be applied to see if the correlation could be unity. But these developments await research.

REFERENCES

Becker, W. C. The matching of behavior rating and questionnaire personality factors. *Psychol. Bull.*, 1960, 57, 201–212.

Berg, I. A. Response bias and personality: The deviation hypothesis. *J. Psychol.*, 1955, 40, 61–72.

Cattell, R. B. *Description and measurement of personality.* New York: World Book, 1946.

Cattell, R. B. *Personality and motivation structure and measurement.* New York: World Book, 1957.

Cattell, R. B. Extracting the correct number of factors in factor analysis. *Educ. psychol. Measmt.*, 1958, 18, 791–838.

Cattell, R. B. *Experiments on sources of perturbation in factor analytic resolution of traits.* (Advanced Publication No. 11) Urbana, Illinois: Laboratory of Personality Assessment and Group Behavior, University of Illinois, 1960.

Cattell, R. B., & Anderson, J. C. *The IPAT Music Preference Test of Personality.* Champaign, Illinois: Institute for Personality and Ability Testing, 1953.

Cattell, R. B., & Coan, R. W. Child personality structure as revealed in teachers' behavior ratings. *J. clin. Psychol.*, 1957, 13, 315–327.

Cattell, R. B., & Coan, R. W. Personality dimensions in the questionnaire responses of six and seven year olds. *Brit. J. educ. Psychol.*, 1958, 28, 232–242.

Cattell, R. B., & Gruen, W. The primary personality factors in eleven year old children by objective tests. *J. Pers.*, 1955, 23, 460–478.

Cattell, R. B., Radcliffe, J., & Sweney, A. The objective measurement of motivation structure in children. *J. clin. Psychol.*, 1960, *16*, 227–232.

Cattell, R. B., & Saunders, D. R. Interrelation and matching of personality factors from behavior rating, questionnaire and objective test data. *J. soc. Psychol.*, 1950, *31*, 243–260.

Cattell, R. B., & Saunders, D. R. Beiträge zur Faktoren-Analyse der Personlichkeit. *Z. exp. angew. Psychol.*, 1955, *7*, 319–343.

Cattell, R. B., & Scheier, I. H. *The meaning and measurement of neurosis and anxiety.* New York: Ronald, 1961.

Cattell, R. B., & Warburton, W. W. *A compendium of objective tests in personality.* Urbana: Univer. Illinois Press, 1967.

Cronbach, L. J. Further evidence on response sets and test design. *Educ. psychol. Measmt.*, 1950, *10*, 3–31.

Cronbach, L. J. *Essentials of psychological testing.* (2nd ed.) New York: Harper, 1960.

Dingman, H. F. The relation between coefficients of correlation and difficulty factors. *Brit. J. Statist. Psychol.*, 1958, *9*, 13–18.

Edwards, A. L. *The social desirability variable in personality assessment and research.* New York: Dryden, 1957.

French, J. W. *The description of personality measurement in terms of rotated factors.* Princeton: Educational Testing Service, 1953.

Holzmann, W. H., & Bitterman, M. E. A factorial study of adjustment to stress. *J. abnorm. soc. Psychol.*, 1956, *52*, 179–185.

Mayeske, G. Some associations of musical preference dimensions of personality. Unpublished doctoral thesis, University of Illinois, 1961.

Messick, S., & Jackson, D. N. Acquiescence and the factorial interpretation of the MMPI. *Psychol. Bull.*, 1961, *58*, 299–304.

Roberts, A. O. H. "Artifactor" analysis: Some theoretical background and practical demonstrations. *J. Nat. Inst. Personnel Res., Johannesburg,* 1959, *7*, 168–188.

Thurstone, L. L., *Primary mental abilities.* Chicago: Univer. Chicago Press, 1938.

Tollefson, D. Response to humor in relation to other measures of personality. Unpublished doctoral thesis, University of Illinois, 1961.

Wherry, R. J., & Gaylord, R. H. Factor pattern of test items and test as a function of the correlation coefficient: Content, difficulty, and constant error factors. *Psychometrika,* 1944, *9*, 237–244.

52

Personality Factor Structure of the Combined Guilford and Cattell Personality Questionnaires

RAYMOND B. CATTELL
& B. D. GIBBONS

THE ISSUE OF ORTHOGONAL OR OBLIQUE PERSONALITY SOURCE TRAITS

Practicing psychologists are puzzled by being presented with two major, but different, systems of well-factored personality-measurement scales in the questionnaire medium. On the one hand, there is an othogonal series (at the adult level only) by Guilford and his co-workers (Guilford, 1940; Guilford & Guilford, 1936; Guilford & Martin, 1943; Guilford & Zimmerman, 1956) now principally embodied in the Guilford-Zimmerman scale (1949). On the other, there is the oblique series constituted by the 16 PF (Cattell & Eber, 1966), the HSPQ (Cattell, et al., 1967; Cattell, Coan, & Beloff, 1958), the CPQ (Porter, Schaie, & Cattell, 1966), and the ESPQ (Baker, Cattell, & Coan, 1965), by Cattell and his co-workers, aiming to measure the same unitary traits in steps over the developmental age range.

It is not surprising that many have asked "Which factor in the Cattell series corresponds to which in the Guilford-Zimmerman?" and that many correlation matrices have been developed empirically to discover what the relationships may be. For example, French (1953) has attempted a decision at an inspectional level, and Becker (1961) found large correla-

From R. B. Cattell, and B. D. Gibbons, Personality Factor Structure of the Combined Guilford and Cattell Personality Questionnaires. *Journal of Personality and Social Psychology*, 1968, 9, 107–120. Copyright 1968 by the American Psychological Association, and reproduced by permission of publisher and author.

This investigation was supported in part by Public Health Service Research Grant MH1733.09 from the National Institute of Mental Health. The writers wish to record their thanks to research assistant Jack Ford for many computational checks.

tions of Cattell's H, F, and Q4 with Guilford's S, R and N, respectively, while Michael, Barth, and Kaiser (1961) found much space in common to Cattell's 16 PF and Thurstone's Temperament Schedule (derived from Guilford's factors). However, with the exception of the last study (which aimed at second-order structure), these psychologists have unfortunately thought fit to ask a question which, in the simple form posed, has no systematic answer. This quickly becomes even empirically apparent in the above correlational studies, wherein the Cattell-Guilford-Zimmerman scale correlation matrix can never be arranged as a simple diagonal of near-unity correlations.

While this may be disappointing to anyone seeking an immediate convenient practical translation, in terms of supporting basic principles it is a satisfying and edifying conclusion. For it is exactly what would be expected from the obvious geometrical principle that a system of orthogonal and truly oblique factors can *never* become mutually aligned! The practitioner's demand for some kind of conceptual harmony thus compels psychometrists to face the larger issue which they should have faced before, namely, the theoretical problem of whether simple structure factor resolutions should be orthogonal or oblique. That the importance of this issue for all personality theory is now becoming more widely realized is evidenced by the recently arranged debate on the topic between Guilford and Cattell.[1]

On behalf of the orthogonal factor position, it is argued that all calculations are simpler, and that scales are—at least theoretically, though not in practice—maximally independent. On the other hand, the argument for allowing simple structure to go oblique, if required by the data, goes back to one's possible preference for the scientific model which claims that the greatest simple structure alone will yield *invariant* unitary source traits. This model rests also on the arguments: (*a*) that unitary influences operating in a common universe would be *expected* to have some interrelation and correlation; (*b*) that in empirical fact, the ideal of simple structure per se is simply not achievable, when evaluated as total hyperplane count, when pursued with the orthogonal restriction as when pursued freely (obliquely) as the sole principle of rotation; (*c*) that even if simple structure factors happened to be orthogonal in one population or sample, statistical laws would cause the same factor scales to be oblique in all others (whence it is inconsistent as a generally sought goal); (*d*) that the practical calculation simplicities hoped for from orthogonal factors are, in practice, never gained, because even if the pure factors *are* made orthogonal, the actual scales, which can never be developed as pure measures, remain oblique, and (*e*) that if the obliquity of the natural structure is accepted, a new explanatory domain of higher order factors is opened up in which we already have evidence of well defined, replicated structure.

---

[1] J. P. Guilford and R. B. Cattell, "Oblique or Orthogonal Factors?" Annual Meeting of the Society for Multivariate Experimental Psychology, University of Colorado, Boulder, 1963.

Regarding the last, that is, ignoring the higher order, by maintaining what seems to us the fiction of orthogonal factors, "personality psychology" is in fact denied a domain of scientific meaning in which many, for example, Cattell and Scheier (1961), Eysenck (1953), Thurstone (1938), have already found useful predictive concepts. For example, extraversion and anxiety are two well-replicated (Cattell & Scheier, 1961) higher order factors scorable from the 16 PF and also from the High School Personality Questionnaire, etc. (HSPQ—Cattell, 1965; Cattell & Nuttall, 1967), which would never be perceived in the orthogonal resolution.

Some of the above issues, notably the argument of essential incompatibility of orthogonality and simple structure, have been pursued within the technical realm of factor analysis *per se* elsewhere (Cattell, 1966). But in the present article, it is planned simply to carry out a first adequate, though not exhaustive, factor analysis jointly upon the Cattell 16 PF and the Guilford-Zimmerman scales to see what simple structure yields. The questions asked are: (*a*) In correlation matrices jointly from scales originally fitted to orthogonal and oblique factorings, can a good, unique, simple structure resolution actually be attained? (*b*) If so, are the natural source traits thus revealed those conceived in the G-Z or in the 16 PF? (*c*) Quite apart from whatever factor resolution is indicated, do the two series of scales *occupy* the same or a different personality space? (For if the answer to the last is that there is considerable overlap, it would at least be possible to supply practicing psychologists with multiple regression equations for predicting scores on Guilford factors from Cattell factors and vice versa.) (*d*) Can any meaning, perhaps distinct from either scale concepts, be given to any extra dimensions that may be found?

DESIGN OF THE EXPERIMENT

The Guilford scales, which we shall generically call the G-Z scales for short, are actually spread over four sources labelled in Table 52-1, the GAMIN (Guilford & Martin, 1943), the DFOS (Guilford & Zimmerman, 1956), the STDCR (Guilford, 1940), and the GZTS Guilford & Zimmerman, 1949). It is helpful to give a brief historical resume of the origins of this work. Guilford's interest began with an attempt to define Extraversion-Introversion, in which he and R. B. Guilford selected 35 questionnaire items which represented recognized qualities in that area. These items were administered to a large sample of 302 subjects and tetrachoric correlations were calculated. The centroid factor analysis revealed 5 meaningful factors, named by them, social introversion, emotionality, masculinity, thinking introversion, and rhathymia (Guilford & Guilford, 1936). Two additional studies by the Guilfords resulted in the identification of four additional factors: Depression, Alertness, Nervousness, and General Drive (Guilford & Guilford, 1939a, 1939b).

Using the information from these early studies on Introversion-Extraversion, Guilford (1940) developed the *Inventory of Factors STDCR*, and collaborating with Martin, developed the *Inventory of Factors GAMIN* (Guilford & Martin, 1943). Finally, in order to consolidate factors into a single inventory for obtaining a comprehensive picture of individual personalities, Guilford and Zimmerman selected factors from the Guilford and Guilford-Martin inventories and developed the *Guilford-Zimmerman Temperament Survey* (1949).

By contrast, the 16 PF was based on the concept of a total *personality sphere* of variables, which at first had to rest on the dictionary and therefore on factors found in ratings (Cattell, 1946). A systematic survey of all factors found in questionnaires up to that date showed that they occupied only a corner—and largely a clinical corner—of the personality sphere space (Cattell, 1946), so their items were balanced, in the hundreds of items from which the 16 PF was developed, by such rating dimension equivalents as dominance-submission, radicalism, premsia, autia, the self-sentiment, etc. The succession of factor analysis since then (Cattell, 1950, 1956; Cattell & Eber, 1966; Cattell, Pichot, & Rennes, 1961; Cattell & Tsujioka, 1965) have checked the structure, here and abroad, and have extended the measurement basis. However, this work has always recognized (Cattell, 1957) that some 10 further factors need inclusion, some of them in the psychotic behaviors area. On historical origins, therefore, one might except the 16 PF to reach out into somewhat broader space (notably beyond the *exvia-invia* area using exvia for the second order factor at the core of the popular "extraversion" notion), yet still not to be entirely comprehensive of a normal and abnormal personality sphere.

Because only 1.5–2 hours of student time were available, the full Guilford and Cattell scales could not be used, but instead two or three sufficiently representative "packages" of items from each of the Guilford scales and each of the 16 PF scales (1962 edition: see Cattell & Eber, 1966) were made up, of the size and nature shown in Table 52-1. The plan called for each hypothesized factor to be represented by at least two packages—the theoretically requisite minimum number for marking a common or broad factor—in the case of both the Guilford and the Cattell systems. In some cases, however, the supply of items made it possible to introduce three, and in a few instances, perhaps unfortunately, only one marker was introduced. When the latter was done, it was justified on the high probability, from psychological meaning ("content"), that other packages existed elsewhere in the series to bring out that factor.[2]

[2] From the standpoint of the senior author, it would have been more satisfactory here not to omit Factor N from the 16 PF or to rest the definition of A on only one marker. In explaining this slight difference of valuation it may be helpful to the reader

As far as representation of the hypotheses inherent in the G-Z scales and the 16 PF is concerned, the 40 markers averaging five items each from the former and 28 averaging six each from the latter, as shown in Table 52-1, would seem to be adequate. Incidentally, the above slight discrepancy in items representing the 14 of the 16 PF marked and the 15 G-Z factors cannot be said to give any really heavier representation to one than the other in determining the final common factors, since there is a certainty from

TABLE 52-1. Brief Identification of 69 Variables: Personality Factor Scale Packages Used in This Analysis

Variable no.	Name	No. items in package	Personality test	Factor symbol	Variable no.	Name	No. items in package	Personality test	Factor symbol
1	Male-Female dichotomy	—	—	—	15	Persistent effort	5	16 PF	Q_3
2	Social interest	5	16 PF	H	16	Emotional immaturity	5	16 PF	Q_4
3	Social poise	5	16 PF	H	17	Social interest	5	16 PF	A
4	Artistic refinement	5	16 PF	I	18	Ascendance (face-to-face)	5	16 PF	E
5	Refinement vs. practicality	5	16 PF	I	19	Liking activity and change	5	16 PF	F
6	Refinement vs. practicality	5	16 PF	I	20	Lack of moral restraint	5	16 PF	F
7	Cultural interests	5	16 PF	M	21	Rhathymia vs. restraint	5	16 PF	F
8	Inferiority vs. confidence	5	16 PF	O	22	Confidence vs. inferiority	5	16 PF	G
9	Emotional immaturity	5	16 PF	O	23	Moral restraint	5	16 PF	G
10	Meditative thinking	5	16 PF	Q_1	24	Confidence vs. inferiority	5	16 PF	H
11	Disliking activity with others	5	16 PF	Q_2	25	Criticalness	5	16 PF	L
12	Disliking activity with others	5	16 PF	Q_2	26	Criticalness	5	16 PF	L
13	Lack of impulsiveness	5	16 PF	Q_3	27	Resentment	5	16 PF	L
14	Lack of impulsiveness	5	16 PF	Q_3	28	Cultural sensitivity	5	16 PF	M
					29	Cultural sensitivity	5	16 PF	M
					30	Inferiority vs. confidence	5	16 PF	O

to be informed that the junior author had the "third person" role, highly desirable in a research of this kind, of working on the one hand closely with J. P. Guilford on the thesis designed in this area and on the other, with R. B. Cattell, as a research associate, experimenting with rotational methods.

TABLE 52-1. (continued)

Variable no.	Name	No. items in package	Personality test	Factor symbol	Variable no.	Name	No. items in package	Factor symbol Personality test
31	Lack of social interest	5	16 PF	Q_2	50	Maintain one's rights	6	GAMIN A
32	Inferiority vs. confidence	5	16 PF	Q_4	51	Feelings of acceptance	6	GAMIN I
33	Nervousness vs. composure	5	16 PF	Q_4	52	Lack of restlessness	6	GAMIN N
34	Moral sensitivity	5	16 PF	C	53	Lack of nervousness–jumpiness	6	GAMIN N
35	Moral sensitivity	5	16 PF	C	54	Lack of fatigueability	6	GAMIN N
36	Lack of hypochondriasis	5	16 PF	C	55	Lack of gregariousness	6	STDCR S
37	Ascendance (Leadership)	5	16 PF	E	56	Physical depletion	6	STDCR D
38	Confidence vs. inferiority	5	16 PF	E	57	Carefreeness vs. restraint	6	STDCR R
39	Ascendance	5	16 PF	H	58	Unconcern vs. seriousness	6	STDCR R
40	Radicalism vs. conservatism	5	16 PF	Q_1	59	Lack of social poise	6	STDCR S
41	Radicalism vs. conservatism	5	16 PF	Q_1	60	Liking for serious thinking	6	STDCR T
42	Rapid pace	6	GAMIN	G	61	Analysis for self and others	6	STDCR T
43	Drive for activity	6	GAMIN	G	62	Emotional depression	6	STDCR D
44	Masculine vocational preference	6	GAMIN	M	63	Tolerance	6	GZTS P
45	Masculine avocational preference	6	GAMIN	M	64	Thickskinned	6	GZTS O
46	AA–Graphic arts	6	DFOS	AA	65	Lack of hostility	6	GZTS F
47	AA–Drama	6	DFOS	AA	66	Liking social affairs	6	GZTS S
48	AA–Literature	6	DFOS	AA	67	Friends and acquaintances	6	GZTS S
49	Cultural conformity–conformity	6	DFOS	CC	68	Optimism	6	GZTS E
					69	Even mood	6	GZTS E

previous research that a great deal of common space will emerge so that most markers will do duty in defining the factors of both series of scale.

A factor analysis of the final battery of 424 items, representing the 68 variables of Table 52-1 (plus a masculine-feminine sex variable), seemed to require a minimum of 250 subjects on Tucker's rule that subjects outnumber variables at least 3 to 1, and the empirical finding of Cattell (1966) and Cattell, Rican, and Jaspers (1968) that with studies of their general size the loadings stabilize with numbers between 250 and 500. Accordingly, a sample of 302 undergraduate students, roughly evenly divided between the sexes, and ranging in age from 17 to 25, were given the whole battery in a single session of 1½ to 1¾ hours.

STATISTICAL ANALYSIS

Scores on the 69 scales (parcels) were intercorrelated by the tetrachoric correlation coefficient by use of the cosine-pi approximation. To decide on the number of factors, both a Kaiser-Guttman (Kaiser, 1960) and a Scree (Cattell, 1966b) test were applied. Both required that a principal axis factoring with unities in the diagonal first be performed. Since the number of factors is an important issue here, the result of these tests is shown in Figure 52-1.

The Scree test definitely indicates either 17 or 18 factors, while the Kaiser-Guttman suggests 23 or 24 factors. As shown elsewhere (Cattell, 1966a), the latter test tends to underestimate with few variables and overestimate with many (say, over 50), so the former is supported. In any case, rather than risk factor fission in the rotation, the authors preferred the disadvantage of possibly missing a factor and having somewhat blurred hyperplanes. Accordingly, we compromised on 18 and returned to the computer

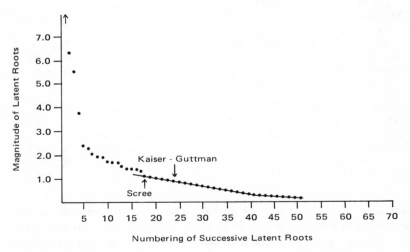

Figure 52-1. Application of tests for the number of factors.

to interate the communalities to exact values for this number of factors. The resulting unrotated V_0 matrix is preserved and available from the senior author while the original correlation matrix is obtainable from a thesis (Gibbons, 1966).

Two different rotational solutions, one restricted to orthogonal position and one not so restricted, were tried. The first, using varimax, obtained a total $\pm.10$ hyperplane count of 48%. By Bargmann's test (1954), this gives a nonsignificant simple structure of $p > .20$. It has accordingly not been reported in detail here, but is available for inspection elsewhere (Gibbons, 1966). The second analysis, for oblique simple structure, used the new topological computer program Maxplane,[3] followed by a very thorough pursuit of simple structure by 11 shifts on the Rotoplot program (Cattell & Foster, 1963). The latter showed the usual climb to a steady hyperplane maximum (plateau on curve), and achieved a hyperplane count ($\pm.10$ hyperplane) of 63.6%. This reaches a Bargmann significance of $p > .20$, emphatically better than for the alternative orthogonal resolution above, yet not so good as the 81% obtained for the 16 PF alone (Cattell & Eber, 1966). However, regardless of the absolute significance, the very extensive trial and error exploration of the space by the 11 Rotoplot shifts makes it extremely improbable that any substantially better position exists to be found, and that we are close to the unique maximum.

This highest achieved simple structure position is definitely oblique, the correlations among the factors being shown in Table 3. The reference vector solution obtained is shown in Table 52-2, where the numbers of the variables are the same as in Table 52-1.

Two of the factors in Table 52-2, namely 16 and 18, can be written off as practically formless residuals (we believed we had overextracted by one factor to allow for such error factors). Also, from a personality standpoint, we can set aside 17 which picks out clearly the interest factor in arts, in Variables 46, 47, and 48 in DFOS. As an interest-motivation factor it is not of the same species as the personality factors. Of the remaining 15 factors, 11 (Numbers 1–7, 9, 10, 12, and 13) turn out to have the markers for the 16 PF factors appearing upon them just as the theory regarding these personality source traits would require, the highest loading of the 16 PFs being higher than for any other variable. In two other factors, 8 and 11, both the 16 PF markers again appear just as they should, as to sign and significance, and the simple structure is good, but a slightly higher loading than that of the legitimate markers is achieved by some seemingly erratic variable, adequate for marking neither a Guilford nor a Cattell factor in terms of its marker "company." The remaining two factors are relatively obscure: 15 is a split off "half" of Guilford's E factor; 14 has

---

[3] R. B. Cattell, J. Ford, and A. Wagner. The flexible and prescribed Maxplane topological program for oblique simple structure. Manuscript in preparation.

TABLE 52-2.

Primary Factor Pattern: Rotated Factor Matrix

Indent. by 16 PF Variable No. (Table 52-1)	1 A	2 C	3 E	4 F	5 G	6 H	7 I	8 L	9 M	10 O	11 Q_1	12 Q_2	13 Q_3	14 (New) Q_4	15 Resid.	16 Resid.	17 (AA)	18 Resid.	(Old) 14 Q_4
Catell Markers:																			
1	19	00	20	-04	-03	-00	-67	13	-07	-02	26	10	08	-07	07	-08	13	08	-07
2	01	-10	-11	-02	-12	62	16	02	-10	-07	-01	-00	07	-02	-04	-13	25	04	01
3	-02	-40	30	-07	04	58	17	-06	-05	-12	12	01	01	-04	-00	41	07	29	01
4	-26	15	15	-03	11	-11	37	01	10	06	-06	08	-02	-05	06	07	06	18	-08
5	02	-11	03	18	05	01	76	-18	12	07	-01	-03	-08	05	-01	04	-17	-05	03
6	16	09	-21	21	01	-08	60	-05	11	01	03	07	06	-01	06	02	07	19	-01
7	03	03	-00	12	-11	-07	47	03	24	02	-06	22	06	04	-04	01	05	-01	-03
8	-02	-10	04	-04	15	-26	10	-09	03	30	-25	-11	15	08	-02	-29	-08	22	-03
9	-04	-14	12	08	-03	08	-02	-09	13	49	-29	-02	00	14	-03	01	-04	09	-05
10	24	03	12	06	15	-06	-25	15	04	-12	19	-05	-11	-19	38	-10	-10	-05	-16
11	-23	02	-07	24	-13	-10	66	-47	03	05	01	67	04	16	-00	15	17	12	15
12	-33	-02	-04	-01	14	05	-23	-00	-01	-10	20	45	-03	-14	02	-16	06	-06	-11
13	11	-19	-09	-13	21	-11	-19	-05	-11	-22	32	-04	10	-10	28	-02	-11	-05	-02
14	18	09	-24	09	04	-30	-06	-01	03	-35	-00	-04	21	32	-00	13	-09	05	-01
15	13	-02	06	-11	-06	07	-11	01	-03	-01	-05	07	59	44	-17	00	09	04	35
16	00	01	17	-09	12	-05	03	07	21	43	-43	00	-09	-03	-05	04	06	03	24
17	54	03	-01	09	15	07	04	15	-11	03	-07	-23	01	11	02	-20	10	03	-04
18	03	-03	16	16	-10	42	-01	-30	29	34	33	07	-14	15	-01	-05	05	15	-02
19	-11	10	15	04	19	40	02	27	-16	21	-12	00	-11	21	03	36	-01	02	08
20	01	-08	-07	85	05	03	14	-07	13	-03	03	03	03	10	02	-00	-08	54	-22
21	01	-00	01	11	02	49	06	09	03	13	-01	-07	-02	-08	-05	06	-07	04	06
22	07	05	-18	-12	49	-01	10	00	-08	-12	03	11	-02	01	05	28	-01	-11	-04
23	17	11	-08	01	33	-06	-66	30	-08	-05	-12	-03	32	-17	-01	-01	-07	06	03
24	00	-17	-02	-18	05	47	-09	36	41	-18	-01	-02	06	06	07	02	-03	-05	-11
25	-01	-12	03	-09	28	00	-26	14	19	13	-12	04	-13	22	-04	01	-05	-13	01
26	03	-10	11	-02	-07	03	-03	42	06	45	-08	02	-01	10	23	03	06	05	06
27	-04	-03	-08	-18	09	26	10	01	44	29	04	08	02	11	-33	06	14	07	-01
28	-02	-03	-03	14	06	-03	27	02	45	25	-06	00	52	-03	30	11	09	05	02
29	-03	-06	-06	-18	-08	04	28	-01	50	-09	-04	01	-10	34	-12	32	02	07	00
30	06	-03	03	03	-04	-19	23	05	-04	61	-05	02	03	-04	-21	15	09	07	12
31	-25	-01	-17	-01	32	-36	-05	06	-02	-02	-24	17	-05	23	-03	-00	05	05	03
32	08	-17	-06	-07	05	06	13	-30	12	49	-09	-06	09	22	05	32	13	-14	05
33	-04	09	-03	-05	07	-05	20	-04	-08	60	05	12	01	-10	12	15	05	-07	00
34	11	43	-02	20	23	-07	-21	-03	04	-43	-07	-03	01	14	03	-24	-07	-10	06
35	-02	28	-05	-12	10	00	11	-04	-02	-32	-09	-03	-03	01	12	05	-03	06	28
36	-05	35	11	-09	04	-09	-04	-03	-21	-26	-07	-01	-08	01	33	07	10	07	12

TABLE 52-2. (Continued)

Indent. by 16 PF Variable No. (Table 52-1)	1 A	2 C	3 E	4 F	5 G	6 H	7 I	8 L	9 M	10 O	11 Q_1	12 Q_2	13 Q_3	14 Q_4 (New)	15 Resid.	16 Resid.	17 (AA)	18 Resid.	14 Q_4 (Old)
37	-01	02	30	12	-12	27	-01	15	01	09	-03	02	-02	09	29	-01	11	-00	06
38	09	09	51	01	-01	05	-06	-08	03	-01	11	20	-05	00	02	01	12	01	00
39	-04	-01	19	-01	44	70	09	-06	06	13	06	29	01	16	04	06	13	10	12
40	-14	-24	17	-09	-04	-01	09	-26	-02	-04	33	13	02	02	-06	19	-12	-01	04
41	-08	04	06	21	-12	-06	-17	-17	21	04	29	-09	07	37	10	07	01	01	38
Guilford Markers:																			
42	09	-10	-02	20	-09	37	-02	02	05	-02	08	-06	-02	37	01	-02	-25	-02	41
43	01	-09	03	-06	05	46	-00	-08	-15	07	-04	28	-06	54	01	-02	-09	-03	55
44	30	08	32	-04	-02	-18	-70	16	-05	-02	09	-07	11	02	08	-06	24	-01	03
45	-07	11	23	-06	05	08	-42	23	-09	01	-09	-12	-02	00	-06	-20	-03	-04	-00
46	-04	03	26	08	-04	03	59	-05	06	02	08	06	09	04	07	11	42	-10	04
47	00	08	-08	04	03	15	57	-12	-01	03	-01	04	-01	-04	-03	-13	51	02	-05
48	22	-13	-00	06	-04	-02	49	02	04	01	-04	06	-04	-01	09	-12	54	13	01
49	-14	-22	11	-13	02	12	32	11	-10	-01	-10	-05	25	22	-02	-14	-04	06	24
50	-06	-19	11	-02	-03	12	-04	-00	20	-13	00	-15	-04	15	-01	13	10	-06	21
51	10	04	08	07	-04	04	-03	-05	10	-31	-10	-00	06	09	05	28	03	08	22
52	02	-09	02	11	-03	-40	03	-10	07	-41	-09	-04	39	-13	-00	02	02	10	02
53	-03	-01	28	05	-08	-10	-05	-00	06	-46	-11	08	13	-14	-20	-08	-03	-06	03
54	01	-04	08	-00	06	-07	-07	-09	08	-55	-08	-08	-12	-12	03	-17	-03	21	09
55	07	-01	-05	04	-11	-40	-28	04	05	-15	-33	04	03	-03	01	-15	-01	-01	03
56	-06	-01	19	-01	-11	-03	-04	07	-27	50	01	-03	11	18	-03	21	19	-11	-01
57	-11	02	00	12	02	12	-12	-04	-06	04	07	-27	13	09	06	08	07	34	08
58	-44	-06	04	09	-14	-02	-05	-06	-03	-13	-36	-25	-03	-46	-30	-02	02	-05	-44
59	05	-13	-09	01	03	-34	06	-03	-06	30	-07	-01	-06	29	-03	-22	08	-03	19
60	-06	-02	-01	18	-08	-01	51	03	30	-07	25	-05	-05	22	-02	09	13	-07	27
61	00	39	01	22	03	-04	47	-07	45	04	03	-31	-00	30	02	05	-02	-40	31
62	-07	-12	09	05	06	-03	22	-01	-12	49	-02	-06	06	-12	-26	11	20	-02	07
63	-07	-06	-14	19	-09	-25	-04	-12	-19	-47	-21	-22	-10	-03	01	-02	09	10	16
64	01	09	-03	18	-04	-00	-10	-03	04	-37	-02	-08	18	-14	12	01	12	05	04
65	01	02	-02	-05	-09	-25	18	01	00	03	-30	07	-02	-20	31	08	02	03	07
66	02	-30	04	04	16	64	31	-02	-13	-28	06	-09	04	05	04	00	28	00	04
67	01	-01	-06	01	-05	39	05	-06	06	-53	-12	-30	02	-04	06	01	14	10	07
68	00	07	-11	05	12	03	-01	-08	20	-53	03	-27	-09	-18	37	-03	00	-02	02
69	-16	-03	-02	-11	06	07	-12	-06	01	-59	-10	-05	-05	-35	17	-10	03	-06	-14

Note: All decimal points have been omitted. ☐ Around loadings fitting final interpretation by these markings. ⌐⌐⌐ Around loadings not fitting final interpretation by these markings.

some loading on the 16 PF Ergic Tension (Q_4) and consistently on the two Guilford markers for his General Activity (42, Rapid Pace, and 43, Drive for Activity), but also some seemingly erratic loading on 47 and 58. If the latter could be reconciled it could be reasonably interpreted as a factor combining the meaning of Cattell's Ergic Tension (Q_4) and Guilford's General Activity, which are psychologically consistent in conceptualization.

By contrast with the above extent of consistency, shown by 13 of the 15 submitted 16 PF factors having turned up with their markers on, and essentially *only* on, a given factor here, the G-Z factor markers are mainly scattered. For example, the markers for GAMIN G, though substantially homogeneous (by the verdict of the correlation matrix) split in rotation evenly between the simple structure Factors 6 and 14; the markers for R split between 1 and 12; those for Guilford's T straddle 7 and 9 evenly; those for the G-Z E divide between 10 and 15; while conversely, those for D, P, O and F (Numbers 62–65) lose their independent identity by landing on one and the same factor.

On the other hand, three G-Z factors, M, N, and S, show good consistency both as to consistency of marker placement and goodness of simple structure property. However, they do so by landing on factors already more highly marked by 16 PF factors. Thus M (Masculinity) is seemingly identical with the 16 PF factor I (−) (Harria), while N (Nervousness— 52, 53, 54) aligns with 16 PF O, Guilt Proneness, and S Sociability (Variables 59, 66, 67) coming out clearly in company with Cattell's H factor, Parmia-vs.-Threctia. Since the last is only one of four distinct components in sociability (i.e., in the second order FI, Exvia-vs.-Invia, in the 16 PF), the restricted technical (autonomic) definition given by the term Parmia-vs.-Threctia is perhaps preferable in precise psychological analysis to "Sociability."

Description of the total resolution in Table 52-2 would require some reference also to minor, more detailed points, only briefly discussable in this space. As far as support for the 16 PF factors is concerned, the main weakness here lies in the comparatively poor definition of the Ergic Tension (Q_4) factor, and the absorption of part of its variance, as well as some of C(−), Ego Weakness, into O factor. We suspect that if anyone cares to carry the notational exploration still further he may find some improvement of the relative positions of these factors which would exclude the trespass of C and Q_4 on O and of O slightly on Q_1. Since the above table was set up, in fact, a new position was found by a research assistant for Q_4 (Factor 14). It has the original loadings shown at the right of Table 52-2, as 14, and this position, having slightly better simple structure, has been used in further work in Table 52-3 and in the mean simple structure count. This slight mutual entanglement of C(−), O, and Q_4, which are normally clearly separate, yet productive by their characteristic positive correlations of a common second order factor (Anxiety), will be discussed below.

Since the parcels of items were cut to rather few items each to get into the total 1½ hours of testing, Table 52-2 shows the defects of some unreliability of loadings (including the random erratics mentioned) and of uneven communalities. Bringing all variables to the same, unit communality as in Alpha factor analysis (Kaiser & Caffrey, 1965) might be a useful step to throw a little light on one question—the estimated degree of factor purity. However, any estimate of what would happen with increased marker reliability simultaneously introduces other errors, so we have not pursued analysis in this direction on the present sample. However, the issue needing to be explored is whether such alternative analyses raise loadings of markers where a true factor match has been asserted without raising their loadings on other, nonrelevant factors beyond the hyperplane level.

The main upshot of the analysis to this point may therefore be described as the appearance, at the maximum simple structure position, of: (*a*) all but possibly one of the 16 PF factors; (*b*) the alignment of three G-Z factors with three of them; M(−) with I in the 16 PF, N with O, and S with H; (*c*) the almost even splitting, as if they were complex variables of four Guilford factors: G, R, T, and E, between just two 16 PF factors in that, reciprocally to the above splitting, there is coherence of five absence of evidence of the full supposed dimensionality in the Guilford factors in that, reciprocally to the above splitting, there is coherence of fiive supposed independent factors—D, P, O, F, and N upon one factor, O in the 16 PF (This could be—except in the case of N—for lack of second markers, i.e., they might have factor dimensionality if split again, but correlate strongly with 16 PF O.); (*e*) a small number of random unexpected projections, not nearly enough to upset simple structure, but indicating that a precise answer on issues above will require scales of longer item count. One hopes that these uncertainties will be cleared up in the larger scale study by Sells (1966) now in progress.

THE HIGHER STRATUM STRUCTURE

It is now generally recognized that the matching and identification of factors is not to be settled by primary factor loading pattern alone, but also by factor variance size, etc. (Cattell, 1962), and, particularly, by the structure which emerges at the higher order (Cattell, 1962). Accordingly, the present analysis was next carried to the second order, to compare with the now numerous and concordant results on second-order structure in this realm (Cattell, 1956, 1957; Cattell & Eber, 1966; Cattell & Tsujioka, 1965; Gorsuch & Cattell, in press; Karson & Pool, 1958.)

The Scree test (Cattell, 1966b), applied to the latent roots from Table 52-2, and similarly calculated to that shown in Figure 52-1 at the first order, showed 9 factors, which, when extracted and rotated by Max-

TABLE 52-3.   Structure at the Second Order: Rotated Factor Matrix

Factors by 16PF symbols	Primary No.	Second-stratum numbers								
		1 Exvia	2 Anxiety	3 Cortertia	4 Indep.	5	6	7	8	9
A	1	16	−01	35	−25	−05	10	−06	−16	00
C	2	07	−49	−03	−03	01	−01	13	12	−19
E	3	32	−05	14	46	33	06	05	−00	−13
F	4	41	−02	−10	19	−03	−09	−04	02	01
G	5	51	37	−09	09	16	−22	−03	04	01
H	6	10	−46	−12	−12	08	−14	−03	19	06
I	7	02	01	58	−08	08	−08	−01	05	06
L	8	−04	−01	−12	−02	71	14	01	01	−09
M	9	−07	03	−05	63	−01	19	29	−34	−04
O	10	−61	04	−12	−28	−41	01	03	−29	−19
Q_1	11	−46	−02	11	16	09	01	−08	−19	−28
Q_2	12	−20	03	02	10	−13	87	01	02	03
Q_3	13	−02	−21	00	−01	−20	−03	01	78	−00
Q_4	14	09	41	−50	−04	06	−00	01	06	05
(?)	15	−03	−03	−01	02	−03	01	−00	−01	64
(?)	16	34	−31	06	−03	−07	−10	−08	−10	−01
(AA)	17	09	03	−24	38	−02	04	−11	−08	06
(?)	18	02	−01	02	−00	01	−03	77	−01	04

Note: All decimal points have been omitted.

plane plus 10 Rotoplot shifts, finished with the highest attainable simple structure (63.5%) shown in Table 52-3.

The agreement with the central tendency of other studies is on the whole good, but weak on Factor I, Exvis-vs.-Invia. Characteristically this loads A+, E+, F+, H+, and Q_2−, as here, but in the present instance, Factor I also has some substantial loadings on G, O, and Q_1. Factor II is an excellent anxiety pattern, except perhaps for insufficient loading on O.

TABLE 52-4. $R_{f_{II}}$: Correlations Among Second-Order Factors

	1	2	3	4	5	6	7	8	9
1	100	−18	−02	−28	−20	32	−07	−15	−03
2	−18	100	10	−08	04	00	−06	05	−23
3	−02	10	100	−11	−04	10	08	07	09
4	−28	−08	−11	100	−22	−31	−21	09	20
5	−20	04	−04	−22	100	08	01	16	−37
6	32	00	10	−31	08	100	−05	−08	−10
7	−07	−06	08	−21	01	−05	100	−06	−07
8	−15	05	07	09	16	−08	−06	100	−06
9	−03	−23	09	20	−37	−10	−07	−06	100

Note: All decimal points have been omitted.

Factors II and IV behave just as Cortertia and Independence patterns typically do, except here for the large loading on Q_4, while the later smaller factors are compatible with the alternatives which normally arise in rotations of the remainder. The second order thus supports what was suggested at the first: (a) that the main 16 PF factors are identifiable, but (b) that there is something amiss in the rotation positions of O and Q_4. (Incidentally, the new primary—"graphic arts interest," No. 17—is shown to be partly a combination of Pathemia, No. 3 ($-$), opposite of Corteria, and Independence, No. 4, which suggests a promising psychological hypothesis for those concerned with the roots of artistic interest.)

A third, but slighter check on the present identification of the primaries comes from the sex correlation—Row I in Table 52-2. These again are congruent with the 16 PF source trait findings generally, the associations of masculinity with Dominance ($E+$), with Harria (I), again and with Radicalism (Q_1), being those typically found. However, again O and Q_4 seem to be poorly located, for the usual correlation of higher score with feminine sex does not appear. For those wishing to examine yet higher orders the correlations of the secondaries are set out in Table 52-4.

DISCUSSION AND SUMMARY

The vital issues which this factor analytic study raises for further discussion turn less on any technical procedures employed in determining number of factors, communalities, etc., which are those ordinarily used and leave little room for dispute, than on the precision of the particular resolution research by simple structure. A reliable verdict in any simple structure resolution needs to be based on (a) use of a sufficiently large and comprehensive (stratified or random) sample of variables; (b) blind pursuit of a maximum hyperplane count without regard to subjective ideas of meaning or the preservation of orthogonality; (c) demonstration that the position reached is statistically significant or unimprovable. Parenthetically, it is neither a necessary nor a sufficient condition that the position reached by an *automatic* computer program! For most analytic programs are inadequate, and blind rotation, pursued for example by Rotoplot (Cattell & Foster, 1963), can practically invariably reach more significant hyperplane counts than any automatic program.

Elsewhere (Cattell, Coan, & Beloff, 1958) the senior author has pointed out that though rotation by putting axes through homogeneous clusters can very easily be biased by choice of items, it is difficult, by similar artificial choice of items, to create an n dimensional hyperplane "cluster," that is, to modify rotation by deliberate choice of items. However, in the *orthogonal* case only, a collection of variables *can* be relatively easily manufactured in which hyperplanes fit an a priori system. It can be done by starting with enough items and retaining, as each factor marker is set up in the next research in the area, just those high on other factors (in the orthogonal matrix) which have zero loading on the vector one has arbitrarily chosen to consider a factor. Thus one "purifies" the orthogonal matrix, in favor of items having only highs and zeroes as required, and this could be done even from the first, principal axis unrotated matrix.[4]

If one's aim, as in the philosophy of "structured psychological measurement" (Cattell, 1957) is to construct scales which follow the forms of nature, each factor scale or battery being aimed at some meaningful psychological concept which is invariant across experiments, then simple structure has to be found in a random sample of variables, not made. By contrast, the argument for orthogonal scales being functional is akin to that of a forester who lops off from his trees all branches that are not horizontal and then preceeds with his forestry science on the definition of branches as horizontal projections.

Once artificial scales have been set up with certain restrictions (be they, in our analogy, horizontal branches, or, say, only all oblique branches left exactly at 45 degrees to the vertical), simple structure is likely to pull out of research what was put in. Factor analysis so conducted is vulnerable to all the old criticism that "it only gets out what it puts in." There is some gleam of possible discovery, however, even in such procedures, since the fallible human experimenter, despite himself, in injecting his own a priori structure, may have forgotten to remove some more subtle structure which he failed to see, and which remains as an alternative to his imposed structure. Consequently, when as here, one puts together a set of variables possessing an imposed orthogonal structure, with a set claiming to represent the natural oblique structure originally found in nature in a far larger sample of items representing the personality sphere, it is not a foregone conclusion that the artificial orthogonal structure will determine the rotation. But, almost certainly, problems will arise in the rotation which do not arise in rotating a broad sample of variables for the first time from the personality sphere.[5]

Since a predominance of scales from an artificial orthogonal construc-

[4] Scientifically the procedure is no more defensible than was Spearman's "purification" of a correlation matrix by rejecting whatever broke the hierarchy of his general factor, yet oddly enough it has not so far incurred the same criticism. Indeed, Guilford has actually set up this notion of purification as an ideal in scale construction, and practiced it in producing his scales. As pointed out, any corresponding attempt at artificial hyperplane construction with oblique structures would be far more difficult, and it would also (on an arbitrary basis) be pointless, so that as far as the authors know, it has never been invoked.

[5] This was clearly evident in our Rotoplots, which had an unmistakably abnormal appearance relative to those we have seen in several dozens of experiments with representative or random samples of variables. The oddity consisted mainly of an unusual number of variables of high communality (long vectors) fanning out about the central hyperplane tendency instead of settling into reasonably narrow hyperplanes.

tion could swamp the natural position, it would seem that in cases of this kind the salvation of the natural resolution lies in (*a*) the fact that those who attempt to construct scales along a priori orthogonal vectors (which are not factor source traits) will fail to get orthogonality in the scales themselves, and the regression from orthogonality will be toward the zones where items are more readily obtained (the hyperplanes); (*b*) attention to the experimental design's retaining a predominance of scales which have not been tampered with, that is, which simply reflect the simple structure found in a far larger sample of variables, and (*c*) the inclusion not just of *one* experimenter's selection of orthogonal scales but of such orthogonals from at least three or four independent subjective choices of orthogonal systems. For unless the investigators all happen to be bewitched by the same concepts in the Zeitgeist, prejudices will tend to cancel and the scales will make the same approach to a comprehensive random sampling of behavior as originally occurred in items. However, even then there will be *some* false concentrations of variables at right angles to the positions in which the concentrations naturally occur, that is, the true obliquity will tend to be reduced.

Fortunately, the solution to this problem is helped here, even with the unusually good workmanship of the Guilford scales, by the above regression of constructed scales from the orthogonality aimed at in the theoretical scales. For the actual G-Z scales, as is well known (see Guilford & Zimmerman, 1963), do not preserve the mutual zero correlation specified in the ideal orthogonal scales of the original factor analysis from which the blue prints were constructed. Whatever natural tendencies there were to concentrate in certain planes which existed in the large sample of original items will to some extent get through. However, our experience with the distortion of the second-order realm here (where slight deviations, as in the O and Q_4 factors, can cause appreciable upset) strongly supports the above theoretical argument that any attempt to decide between factor structures of two scales had best (*a*) include other sources of items carefully chosen as a stratified sample from a representative defined total personality sphere, and (*b*) break down the scales under examination ideally into single items or, if economy forbids this, into a fair number—at least three or four—non-overlapping, random "parcels" from each scale.

The present study has introduced *a* only to a minor degree, and has gone only a moderate way toward a sufficiency of *b*. As a pilot study its results suggest that the conditions chosen are perhaps only just within the limits of successful handling of the problem. Certainly a definitive study will need to go further in the direction indicated for ideal conditions.

Meanwhile, our results on the present basis may be summarized:

1. That the simple structure obtainable in a joint sample of variables by oblique resolution, even where one of the two systems has constructed

its scales to be orthogonal, is decidedly better than for the corresponding orthogonal resolution.

2. This resolution confirms, by the two or three markers for the hypothesized factor appearing consistently together on one factor, and not saliently on any other, all 14 of the 16 PF factors included (Intelligence, B, and Shrewdness, N, were not used).

3. Further evidence of the present resolution being correct exists, (a) in the sex differences on the factors appearing, where they appear, as previously found and, (b) more crucially, in the second order structure being consistent in its major features with that usually obtained.

4. Nevertheless, the same criteria agree in suggesting that Factor O, Guilt Proneness, Q_4, Ergic Tension, and C, Ego Strength, suffer from some distortion of their usual rotation position here.

5. Three Guilford factors align as simple structure factors clearly with Cattell factors (M with I; N with O, and S with H). Four (like C, O, and Q_4 above), namely E, G, R, and T, split their loadings and would be considered, by the 16 PF and this analysis, as test-homogeneous–factor-heterogeneous scales. Five G-Z factors seem to be expressions of only one factor here; that usually identified as Guilt Proneness, O.

6. No broad dimensionality not common to the two series can be clearly recognized except in the "arts interest" factor. It is not easy to make an unqualified condensed quantitative statement of the percentage of space common to the two systems of personality scales. But if we project to a space in which all factors clearly located here could be assumed to be measured with full validity, the extent of overlap could be expressed by saying that the 14 Cattell dimensions and 15 Guilford scales have eight dimensions in common: namely, A, H, I, M, O, Q_2, and Q_4, and less clearly, Q_1 in their 16 PF labels. The 14 dimensions used from the 16 PF retain a dimensionality of 14, while the 15 from the G-Z yield 9. Consequently 6 dimensions—C, E, F, G, L, and Q_3—remain essentially outside the G-Z, and one dimension in the G-Z—AA, Arts' interest—remains outside the 16 PF. On the eight common dimensions mutual multiple regression coefficients could be set up giving tolerably efficient mutual estimations between the scales of the two series.

7. From a methodological standpoint this pilot study indicates that present experimental design conditions stand within the limits of tolerable effectiveness, but discussion is given to further conditions desirable in a definitive study. These indicate the need to include more than one independent orthogonal choice of scales, and, especially, the need for more numerous "packages," approaching perhaps only two or three items in each, so that sampling is adequate for naturally occurring hyperplanes clearly to express themselves.

REFERENCES

Baker, R., Cattell, R. B., & Coan, R. B. The Early School Personality Questionnaire. Champaign, Ill.: Institute for Personality and Ability Testing, 1968.

Bargmann, R. Signifikanzuntersuchungen der Einfachen Struktur in der Faktoren Aanalyse. Mitteilungsblatt für Mathematische Statistik. Sonderdruck. Wurzburg: Physica-Verlags, 1954.

Becker, W. C. A comparison of the factor structure and other properties of the 16 P.F. and the Guilford-Martin Personality Inventories. *Educational and Psychological Measurements*, 1961, 21, 393–404.

Cattell, R. B. *Description and measurement of personality*. Yonkers-on-Hudson, N.Y.: World Book, 1946.

Cattell, R. B. The main personality factors in questionnaire, self-estimate material. *Journal of Social Psychology*, 1950, 31, 3–38.

Cattell, R. B. *Factor analysis*. New York: Harper, 1952.

Cattell, R. B. Validation and intensification of the Sixteen Personality Factor Questionnaire. *Journal of Clinical Psychology*, 1956, 12, 205–214.

Cattell, R. B. *Personality and motivation structure and measurement*. New York: Harcourt, Brace & World, 1957.

Cattell, R. B. The basis of recognition and interpretation of factors. *Educational and Psychological Measurements*, 1962, 22, 667–697.

Cattell, R. B. A cross-cultural check on second stratum personality factor structure—notably of anxiety and exvia. *Australian Journal of Psychology*, 1965, 17, 12–23.

Cattell, R. B. The meaning and strategic use of factor analysis. In R. B. Cattell (Ed.), *Handbook of multivariate experimental psychology*. Chicago: Rand McNally, 1966. (a)

Cattell, R. B. The Scree Test for the Number of Factors. *Multivariate Behavioral Research*, 1966, 1, 78–98. (b)

Cattell, R. B., Coan, R., & Beloff, H. A reexamination of personality structure in late childhood, and development of the High School Personality Questionnaire. *Journal of Experimental Education*, 1958, 27, 73–88.

Cattell, R. B., & Eber, H. W. The Sixteen Personality Factor Questionnaire. (3rd ed.) Champaign, Ill.: Institute for Personality and Ability Testing, 1966.

Cattell, R. B., & Foster, M. J. The Rotoplot program for multiple, single plane, visually guided rotation. *Behavioral Science*, 1963, 8, 156–165.

Cattell, R. B., & Nuttall, R. The High School Personality Questionnaire. Champaign, Ill.: Institute for Personality and Ability Testing, 1967.

Cattell, R. B., Pichot, P., & Rennes, P. Constance inter-culturelledes facteurs de personalite measures par le test 16 P.F. II. Comparison franco-americaine. *Revue de Psychologie Applique*. 1961, 11, 165–196.

Cattell, R. B., & Jaspers, J. A general plasmode (No. 30-10-5-2) for factor analytic exercises and research. *Multivariate Behavioral Research Monographs*, 1967, No. 67-3, 211 p.

Cattell, R. B., & Scheier, I. H. *The meaning and measurement of anxiety and neuroticism*. New York: Ronald Press, 1961.

Cattell, R. B., & Tsujioka, B. A cross cultural comparison of second stratum questionnaire personality factor structure—anxiety and exvia—in America and Japan. *Journal of Social Psychology*, 1965, *65*, 205–219.

Eysenck, H. J. *The structure of human personality*. London: Methuen, 1953.

French, J. W. *The description of personality measurements in terms of rotated factors*. Princeton, N.J.: Educational Testing Service, 1953.

Gibbons, B. D. A study of the relationships between factors found in Cattell's 16 PF questionnaire and factors found in the Guilford personality inventories. Unpublished doctoral dissertation, University of Southern California, 1966.

Gorsuch, A. L., & Cattell, R. B. Second strata personality factors defined in the questionnaire medium by the 16 PF. *Multivariate Behavioral Research*, 1967, *2*, 211–224.

Guilford, J. P. *Inventory of factors STDCR*. Beverly Hills, California: Sheridan Supply, 1940.

Guilford, J. P. When not to factor analyze. *Psychology Bulletin*, 1952, *49*, 26–37.

Guilford, J. P. *Personality*. New York: McGraw-Hill, 1959.

Guilford, J. P., Christensen, P. R., & Bond, N. A. *The DF Opinion Survey: Manual of instructions and interpretations*. Beverly Hills, Calif.: Sheridan Supply, 1956.

Guilford, J. P., & Guilford, R. B. Personality factors S, E, and M and their measurement. *Journal of Psychology*, 1936, *2*, 109–127.

Guilford, J. P., & Guilford, R. B. Personality factors D, R, T, and A. *Journal of Abnormal and Social Psychology*, 1939, *34*, 21–36. (a)

Guilford, J. P., & Guilford, R. B. Personality factors N, G, and D. *Journal of Abnormal and Social Psychology*, 1939, *34*, 239–248. (b)

Guilford, J. P., & Martin, H. G. *An inventory of factors GAMIN*. Beverly Hills, Calif.: Sheridan Supply, 1943.

Guilford, J. P., & Martin, H. G. *Personnel inventory*. Beverly Hills, Calif.: Sheridan Supply, 1943.

Guilford, J. P., & Zimmerman, W. S. *The Guilford-Zimmerman temperament survey*. Beverly Hills, Calif.: Sheridan Supply, 1949.

Guilford, J. P., & Zimmerman, W. S. Fourteen dimensions of temperament. *Psychological Monographs*, 1956, *70*(10, Whole No. 417).

Guilford, J. P., & Zimmerman, W. S. Some variable-sampling problems in the rotation of axes in factor analysis. *Psychology Bulletin*, 1963, *60*, 289–301.

Hammond, S. Personality factors in ratings. In R. B. Cattell (Ed.), *Handbook of modern personality theory*. Chicago: Aldine, 1968, in press.

Kaiser, H. F. Comments on communalities and the number of factors. Unpublished manuscript, University of Illinois, 1960.

Kaiser, H. F., & Caffrey, J. Alpha factor analysis. *Psychometrika*, 1965, *30*, 1–14.

Karson, S., & Pool, K. B. Second order factors in personality measurement. *Journal of Consulting Psychology*, 1958, 22, 299–303.

Michael, W. B., Barth, G., & Kaiser, H. F. Dimensions of temperament in three groups of music teachers. *Psychological Reports*, 1961, 9, 601–704.

Porter, R., Schaie, W., & Cattell, R. B. The Child Personality Questionnaire. Champaign, Ill.: Institute for Personality and Ability Testing, 1967.

Sells, S. B. Personal communications on planning of factor study across the Q-data realm, 1966. Texas Christian University, Fort Worth, Texas.

Thurstone, L. L. *Primary mental abilities*. Chicago: Chicago University Press, 1938.

Tupes, E. C., & Cristal, R. C. Stability of personality-trait rating factors obtained under diverse condition. USAF, WADC, Technical Note, 1958, No. 58–61.

53

A Factorial Study of Psychoticism
as a Dimension of Personality

H. J. EYSENCK
& SYBIL B. G. EYSENCK

INTRODUCTION

This paper reports some work done in order to make possible the measurement, by way of personality questionnaires, of the hypothesized personality dimension of "psychoticism." Its main interest is probably substantive, although we believe that there are also some interesting features relating to its procedural aspects. Any proper evaluation must of course consider both aspects together, but for the purpose of clarification it may be useful to separate them in the following discussion which precedes the experimental report. It seems likely that the substantive part will incur a more critical reception by clinical readers, while the procedural part is more likely to receive such a critical reception by psychometric readers. In both respects our approach is sufficiently different from that current in American psychology to justify the comments made below.

Substantive aspects. The background for the present article has been provided in detail elsewhere (Eysenck, 1968). Briefly, the system suggested there stresses the superiority of a dimensional over a categorical approach to psychodiagnostics, emphasizing that the carry-over of the medical disease concept with its categorical principle of classification was essentially ill adapted to the data derived from psychological and psychiatric work with neurotic and psychotic patients. It is further suggested that three main higher-order factors (dimensions, concepts) may account for a large proportion of the observed variance, viz. extraversion-introversion (E), neuroticism-stability (N), and psychoticism (P). Psychiatric diagnoses of the categorical type are conceived of as referring to certain parts of the three-

From H. J. Eysenck and S. B. G. Eysenck, A Factorial Study of Psychoticism as a Dimension of Personality. *Multivariate Behavioral Research*, 1968, Special Issue, 15–31. Reprinted by permission of authors and publisher.

This study was supported by a grant from the Maudsley and Bethlem Royal Hospital Research Fund.

dimensional space generated by this framework. Thus the diagnosis "psychopathy" refers to individuals who are high on neuroticism and high on extraversion; "anxiety state" refers to individuals who are high on neuroticism and high on introversion; "process" and "reactive" schizophrenics are high on psychoticism and respectively high and low on introversion (Armstrong et al., 1967); and so forth. The diagnoses do not refer to a group of individuals qualititatively differentiated from all other individuals in any particular respect; rather, they refer to a core group which shades gradually into other groups without any particular boundary which could be drawn on any but an arbitrary basis.

The two dimensions of E and N have been previously discussed many times and no more will be said here, except to point out that higher-order factors corresponding very closely to E and N emerge from the work of Guilford and Cattell and many other writers (Eysenck, 1960a); in a recent study involving the factor-analysis of over three hundred items chosen by Cattell and Guilford as having the highest loadings on their various primary factors, as well as the items of the Eysenck Personality Inventory (Eysenck & Eysenck, 1965), it was found for both men and women that practically identical factors of E and N emerged from the analyses of questions furnished by these three groups of investigators (Eysenck & Eysenck, 1968). The far-reaching relevance and significance of these two factors is now widely recognized, and the situation has certainly changed considerably since Eysenck (1947) originally put forward some evidence suggesting the importance of these two dimensions of personality.

A curious contrast is presented by the hypothesis that there exists a set of correlated behavior variables indicative of predisposition to psychotic breakdown, demonstrable as a continuous variable in the normal population, and independent of E and N. Although several studies using discriminant function analysis (Lubin, 1951; Eysenck, 1952a, 1955; Sybil Eysenck, 1956; Devadasan, 1964), factor analysis (Trouton and Maxwell, 1956; Eysenck, 1960b), and criterion analysis (Eysenck, 1952b) have given support to the hypothesis, no criticism or appraisal of it appears to have come forth from psychiatrists or clinical psychologists, and no use has been made of this concept by other researchers. Occasional experiments from the outside have supported one or the other of the views stated above; thus Cattell & Scheier (1961, p. 369) state, on the basis of their experimental work, that "psychoticism is a direction of abnormality distinct from neuroticism and anxiety. As a rule, neurotic-contributory factors are not psychotic-contributory, that is, the neurotic-contributory factors discriminate between neurotics and normals, and between neurotics and psychotics, but they do not discriminate between psychotics and normals." Other support comes from genetic studies such as those of Cowie (1961) who failed to find higher neuroticism in the children of psychotic parents. The evidence, then, is comparatively strong, but what has been missing hitherto has been a measuring device of the questionnaire type; the series of studies of which this is the first to be reported, was designed to supply this want.

Procedural aspects.   Thurstone (1947, p. 55) pointed out that "when a particular domain is to be investigated by means of individual differences, one can proceed in one of two ways. One can invent a hypothesis regarding the processes that underlie the individual differences, and one can then set up a factorial experiment . . . to test the hypothesis. If no promising hypothesis is available, one can represent the domain as adequately as possible in terms of a set of measurements or numerical indices and proceed with factorial experiment. The analysis might reveal an underlying order which would be of great assistance in formulating the scientific concepts covering the particular domain. In the first case we start with a hypothesis that determines the nature of the measurements that enter into the factorial analysis. In the second case we start with no hypothesis, but we proceed, instead, with a set of measurements or indices that cover the domain, hoping to discover in the factorial analysis the nature of the underlying order." Most, if not all of the well-known psychometric psychologists have followed the second of these paths; the Maudsley group is perhaps almost unique in having largely followed the first. Instead of taking random (or what passes hopefully as random) samples of the population of tests, questions, or indices and applying these to a random (or what passes hopefully as random) sample of the population of subjects, hoping that in this way the major dimensions would be revealed, we have, on the contrary, started with more or less well developed hypotheses, structured the selection of samples (both of tests and of subjects) around these hypotheses, and used factor analysis to support or disconfirm the hypotheses in question. If properly carried out, both paths should meet, rather like the two sections of a tunnel driven into a mountain from opposite sides; it is noteworthy that in the case of E and N the work of Cattell and Guilford, using Thurstone's second method, has led to findings essentially identical with those of Eysenck & Eysenck (1968) using Thurstone's first method. Many of the criticisms made in the past, e.g. by Cattell, can be seen to be unjustified when it is realised that we are pursuing a method of analysis which makes different assumptions, and uses a different paradigm, than does his own. Hence also our insistence on such techniques as criterion analysis, and the use of outside criterion groups to identify the correct position of factors. To the purist using Thurstone's second method, such devices will no doubt appear lacking in elegance and even relevance, but when it is realised that an effort is being made to test a theory which extends beyond the tests or indices used to the position of certain social or clinical groups on the hypothesised factors, then a rather less critical view may be taken.

In our work with psychoticism too we have followed this method, starting with an hypothesis as explicit as the existing knowledge in this field permitted; we then attempted to collect inventory items which appeared relevant to our hypothesis, and tried these out on groups (normals, neurotics, psychotics of various kinds) which could be predicted to have certain scores on these items. At no stage did we attempt to work with random samples of items, nor were we interested in factors other than P, and the two other second-order factors, E and N, which we wanted to keep as far as possible orthogonal to P. Thus our task was *not* to analyse large numbers of randomly selected inventory items, from which in due course there might or might not emerge something akin to a P factor. Our hypothesis was that there existed a set of items, independent of E and N, correlating positively together, which would define a factor which would be found both in normal and in abnormal groups, and which would discriminate between normal, neurotic, and psychotic populations. The existence of such a set of items dos not of course *prove* the correctness of our theories regarding psychoticism, just as failure to find such a set would not prove our theories to be fallacious. Possibly individuals high on this hypothetical P factor are characterised by an inability to introspect and recognise their personality traits sufficiently well to answer the questions in such a way as to demarcate themselves appropriately. Nevertheless, the discovery of the existence of such a set of items would give welcome support to our hypothesis, while failure would certainly make further work along these lines less inviting. Nothing more can be claimed for the outcome of our preliminary studies. Nor, of course, would we wish to reify the P factor, should it emerge; its nature and function are purely heuristic and its scientific and clinical usefulness can only be assessed in terms of theories and experiments going beyond the factorial field.

SELECTION OF ITEMS

It is well known that on the MMPI there is a "neurotic triad" as well as a "psychotic triad," i.e. two sets of three scales each of which shows high scores for neurotic and psychotic patients respectively. We selected a number of items from the "psychotic triad" of scales, frequently re-writing these in order to make them more "normal"; in our experience with English subjects the MMPI is too "abnormal" in many of its questions to be tolerated well by non-patient subjects. Other items were found in the published scales of Cattell, Guilford, and others, or written specifically by ourselves, on the basis of such scant "clinical experience and intuition" as we could lay claim to, and on the basis of a fairly wide reading of the psychiatric literature. The total number of items so obtained was much too large to even consider the possibility of using them all in a factor analysis, and consequently the following method of selection was adopted.

A member of the staff of the Department is associated with a commercial market research organisation which holds weekly "parties" to which random samples of the population are invited; they are shown films, given presents, take part in competitions, and answer questions regarding products and advertisements which are of interest to the firm concerned. We were allowed to introduce into this "party" a short questionnaire of some 24 questions; the questions varied from week to week, but each questionnaire was answered by a group of some 300 subjects who were a reasonably random sample of the total population. Each week we introduced 6 E questions and 6 N questions; we have a large stock of such questions with known factor ladings on E and N. We also introduced a dozen of our P questions, in order to test whether these were independent of E and N, and also whether they correlated together to form a separate factor. Each set of questions was then factor analysed by the principal components method, and three factors extracted; two of these were always clearly E and N, while the third was usually made up of several of the hypothetical P items. Some of these hypothetical items had no P loadings, others had high N loadings, or more rarely, high E loadings. Items having high P loadings and low E and N loadings were retained and included again on another occasion, together with a new batch of prospective P items; if they proved themselves again they were considered for our final scale. This process of selection was continued over a lengthy period of time, until we had accumulated a sufficient number of items to make possible the next stage of testing.

It would take too much space, and would not be of any great scientific interest, to reprint the outcome of all these preliminary studies. However, Table 53-1 has collected together items having high P loadings and

TABLE 53-1.

Number of questions in Table 53-2	Number of experiment	First Occasion			Second Occasion		
		N	E	P	N	E	P
18	01	−.06	.30	−.40			
29	01	−.09	.28	.48	.41	.07	.33
10	01	−.01	.23	−.58	−.04	.05	−.57
35	01	.10	.11	.24	.11	.26	.25
47	01	.00	.05	−.39	−.16	.06	−.48
58	01	.13	.01	.21	.02	.25	.55
	01	−.33	.07	.54			
19	02	−.03	.09	.60	.04	−.13	.39
30	02	−.06	−.15	.65	.15	−.36	.24
12	02	−.23	.11	.47	.06	.19	.04
36	02	.21	.03	.33	.40	.15	.21
59	02	.04	−.32	.57	.16	−.09	.64
20	03	.19	−.10	.55	.27	−.28	−.18
105	03	−.21	.16	.57	.04	−.00	−.54
38	03	.11	−.01	.66	−.06	−.12	−.16
13	03	−.02	.07	.18	.04	−.01	−.77
21	04	.07	.04	.64	.38	−.12	.24

TABLE 53-1.   (continued)

Number of questions in Table 53-2	Number of experiment	First Occasion			Second Occasion		
		N	E	P	N	E	P
3	04	.01	.00	.66	.37	.13	.49
15	04	−.23	.07	.44	−.09	.32	.45
39	04	.19	.11	.47	.31	.02	.20
52	04	.10	.04	−.33	−.01	.09	−.32
23	05	.11	.16	−.44	−.12	.36	−.24
4	05	.07	−.11	.40	.03	−.06	.61
16	05	.05	.22	.60	.23	.04	.31
40	05	.18	.06	.62	−.05	.12	.63
102	06	−.07	.18	−.33	−.48	−.04	.12
101	06	.02	.12	.54	.23	−.10	.25
104	06	.05	−.03	.28	.33	−.34	−.21
41	06	.08	−.16	.47	.22	−.26	.18
53	06	.29	.18	−.32	.09	.28	−.28
50	06	−.17	.00	.44	−.19	.10	.14
25	07	.29	−.02	.39	.26	.13	.44
7	07	−.01	.05	.66	−.02	.16	.71
32	07	−.10	.04	.71	.29	.02	.42
44	07	−.03	.04	.72	.11	−.11	.56
55	07	.15	.06	.44	.08	.28	.52
26	08	−.19	−.03	−.46	−.32	.03	−.63
8	08	.14	.24	.57	.25	.05	−.46
27	09	.01	.22	.66	.38	−.15	.27
9	09	.13	.11	.61	.07	−.04	.54
33	09	−.06	−.03	.70	−.09	−.06	.70
45	09	.12	.17	−.43	.07	−.01	−.66
56	09	.20	.17	.53	.14	−.04	.55
62	09	−.05	−.10	.62	−.12	.06	.69
70	10	−.08	.18	.64			
98	10	−.11	.09	−.48			
67	10	.15	.11	.48			
72	11	−.11	−.04	.38			
74	11	.10	.25	−.50			
77	11	.11	.01	.45			
80	11	.23	.20	.41			
82	11	−.04	−.24	.46			

low E and N loadings. Column 1 gives the item number in Table 53-2, which prints in full the text of all the items used in our large-scale factor analysis; column 2 gives the number of the experimental session in which the responses were obtained for the analysis, the results of which are reported in this Table. Column 3 gives the loadings of the selected items for N, E and P, obtained on the first occasion that these items were used. Column 4 gives the loadings of the same items for N, E, and P on the second occasion that each item was used, i.e. in conjunction with a quite different set of items than the first time. Not all the items were tried out a third time, and hence no figures are given for the third testing. It will be seen that there are quite a few rather high loadings on the factor prematurely and hopefully called "P" and it is, of course, realized that it is quite possible that the factors so-called in each of the different experiments may in fact be a quite independent factor having no relation to all the others. This is perhaps unlikely in view of the fact that most of the items retained high loadings when re-analyzed in a different collection of items, but in any case this was of course only a preliminary exercise to find promising items for a larger and more inclusive analysis; no evidential value is attributed to the findings so far. All that can be claimed, perhaps, is that there do seem to exist sets of items which cohere together while having low loadings on N and E; whether or not these sets measure our hypothetical variable P must be decided on other grounds.

TABLE 53-2.

1. Are you more distant and reserved than most people?	Yes	No
2. Do you find it hard to get going some mornings?	Yes	No
3. Have you ever been afraid of losing your mind?	Yes	No
4. Do most things taste the same to you?	Yes	No
5. Can you get a party going?	Yes	No
6. Can you usually make up your mind easily?	Yes	No
7. Do you enjoy hurting people you love?	Yes	No
8. Do you often wonder why people do the things they do?	Yes	No
9. Do you find it hard to look people straight in the eye?	Yes	No
10. Are you generally in good health?	Yes	No
11. Do you do much day dreaming?	Yes	No
12. Do you agree that everything is turning out just like the Prophets of the Bible said it would?	Yes	No
13. Was your mother a good woman?	Yes	No
14. Would you consider yourself as efficient as most others?	Yes	No
15. Do you drink unusually much water?	Yes	No
16. Have you had more trouble than most?	Yes	No
17. Would you do almost anything for a dare?	Yes	No
18. Do you do many things that interest you?	Yes	No
19. Have you had an awful lot of bad luck?	Yes	No
20. Do you go to church about once a week?	Yes	No
21. Do you worry a lot about catching diseases?	Yes	No
22. Do you find it hard to keep your mind on what you are doing?	Yes	No
23. Did you love your mother?	Yes	No
24. Do you often feel fed up?	Yes	No
25. Do you get depressed in the mornings?	Yes	No
26. Would you enjoy hunting, fishing and shooting?	Yes	No
27. Are there several people who keep trying to avoid you?	Yes	No
28. Would you blame anyone for taking advantage of someone who lays himself open to it?	Yes	No
29. Is there someone who is responsible for most of your troubles?	Yes	No
30. Do you let your dreams warn or guide you?	Yes	No
31. Do you nearly always have a "ready answer" when people talk to you?	Yes	No

TABLE 53-2. (continued)

32. Do people generally seem to take offence easily?	Yes	No
33. Would you take drugs which may have strange or dangerous effects?	Yes	No
34. Do you have thoughts too bad to talk about?	Yes	No
35. Do you believe that people are only honest for fear of being caught?	Yes	No
36. Do you often feel that you have been punished without cause?	Yes	No
37. Are you rather lively?	Yes	No
38. Do you believe in the second coming of Christ?	Yes	No
39. Do you seem clumsier than most people?	Yes	No
40. Do you have enemies who wish to harm you?	Yes	No
41. Would you refuse to play a game because you are no good at it?	Yes	No
42. Are you ever "off your food"?	Yes	No
43. Are you full of energy at times?	Yes	No
44. Do your friendships break up easily without it being your fault?	Yes	No
45. Do you like to be busy most of the time?	Yes	No
46. Does your mood often go up and down?	Yes	No
47. Was your father a good man?	Yes	No
48. Do you like plenty of bustle and excitement around you?	Yes	No
49. Do you ever keep on at a thing until others lose their patience with you?	Yes	No
50. Would you say that you have never been in love?	Yes	No
51. Do you like mixing with people?	Yes	No
52. Is your weight more or less steady over the years?	Yes	No
53. Have you had any peculiar or strange experiences?	Yes	No
54. Do you sometimes feel you don't care what happens to you?	Yes	No
55. Do people mean to say and do things to annoy you?	Yes	No
56. Are you ever bothered by the idea that someone is reading your thoughts?	Yes	No
57. Do you ever feel 'just miserable' for no good reason?	Yes	No
58. Would you have been more successful if people had not put difficulties in your way?	Yes	No
59. Do you feel sad most of the time?	Yes	No
60. Would you call yourself happy-go-lucky?	Yes	No
61. Are you often troubled about feelings of guilt?	Yes	No
62. When you are in a crowded place like a bus do you worry about dangers of infection?	Yes	No
63. Do you find it hard to show your feelings?	Yes	No
64. Do you feel self-pity now and again?	Yes	No
65. Can you usually let yourself go and enjoy yourself a lot at a gay party?	Yes	No
66. Do you suffer from sleeplessness?	Yes	No
67. Have people sometimes thought your ideas a bit odd?	Yes	No
68. Would you call yourself tense or 'highly strung'?	Yes	No
69. Do you like people around you?	Yes	No
70. Do you quite enjoy doing things that are a little frightening?	Yes	No
71. Do you worry a lot about your looks?	Yes	No
72. Do you think you enjoy spicey foods more than your friends do?	Yes	No
73. Has anyone ever tried to influence your mind?	Yes	No
74. Are you always careful to make sure your doors are locked at night?	Yes	No
75. Do you like practical jokes?	Yes	No
76. Do you often feel very weak all over?	Yes	No
77. Do you enjoy gossiping about people you know very well?	Yes	No
78. Do you sometimes feel uneasy indoors?	Yes	No

TABLE 53-2. (continued)

79. Do you normally prefer to be alone?	Yes	No
80. Do people ever talk about you secretly?	Yes	No
81. Do you feel as well now as ever you did?	Yes	No
82. Have you always thought of yourself as different to others?	Yes	No
83. Do you enjoy stretching and yawning?	Yes	No
84. Do you like going out a lot?	Yes	No
85. Do you believe in life after death?	Yes	No
86. Does your voice change without you having a cold?	Yes	No
87. Do you prefer to try new places to go on your holidays?	Yes	No
88. Have you ever wished you were dead?	Yes	No
89. Do you make friends easily with members of your own sex?	Yes	No
90. Do you get depressed in the evenings?	Yes	No
91. Do you usually work by fits and starts?	Yes	No
92. Do you often rush even when you have a lot of time?	Yes	No
93. Do you wake very early in the mornings and find it hard to get back to sleep?	Yes	No
94. Would you call yourself talkative?	Yes	No
95. Did you love your father?	Yes	No
96. Do things sometimes seem as if they were not real?	Yes	No
97. When you were a child did you often like a rough and tumble game?	Yes	No
98. Do you prefer loud to soft music?	Yes	No
99. Would it upset you a lot to see a child or animal suffer?	Yes	No
100. Do you like telling jokes or funny stories to your friends?	Yes	No
101. Do you often worry about whether you have locked your front door?	Yes	No
102. Do you get as much sympathy from people as you need?	Yes	No
103. When you make new friends do you usually make the first move?	Yes	No
104. Do you mistrust people who are too friendly?	Yes	No
105. Are you most careful to do what you consider your duty at all times?	Yes	No
106. Do you have trouble getting to sleep at bedtime?	Yes	No

RESULTS: THREE-FACTOR SOLUTION

Our final list of items for analysis is given in Table 53-2. The items were administered to groups selected in the same way as before, in the same sequence, with instructions emphasising speed, the necessity to answer every question, and the fact that there were no right or wrong answers. Subjects appeared to enjoy, or at least not to resent, the experience, and happily completed the inventory in between seeing their television shows and competing for prizes in various games. If the conditions under which the inventory was administered seem less than optimal, it should be remembered that we are dealing with a cross-section of the population, not with the very exceptional populations usually tested in this connection, i.e. sophomores. Conditions which might appear somewhat odd to university students are much more acceptable to ordinary people than would be the sterilized atmosphere of the psychological laboratory or clinic. Furthermore, the attitudes of students must be assumed to be far less naive than those of the "guests" of the market research organisation, put at their ease at considerable expense and not suspecting that their answers would be used in psychological experiments. Other groups of normals, as well as

TABLE 53-3.

| | Three Factor Solution | | | | | | Third Order Solution | | | | | |
| | M n = 512 | | | F n = 821 | | | M n = 512 | | | F n = 821 | | |
Item No.	N	E	P	N	E	P	N	E	P	N	E	P
1	.16	−.41	−.13	.15	−.41	.04	.04	−.18	.12	.06	−.31	.01
2	.43	−.03	−.15	.42	−.08	−.21	.12	.04	.19	.21	−.02	−.01
3	.40	−.04	.06	.35	−.03	.17	.40	−.02	.04	.19	−.05	.37
4	.07	−.08	.19	−.06	.02	.27	.30	−.00	−.05	.15	−.20	.01
5	−.01	.51	.20	−.18	.53	.12	.14	.27	−.06	−.25	.48	.33
6	−.26	.19	.01	−.38	.19	.14	−.09	.29	−.18	−.38	.23	.23
7	−.04	.05	.45	.12	.08	.22	.19	.01	.16	.02	.00	.30
8	.17	.05	−.21	.11	.07	−.21	.18	.10	−.11	.03	.19	−.09
9	.29	−.18	.07	.30	−.11	.04	.05	−.21	.23	.43	−.20	−.21
10	−.07	.18	−.27	.04	.14	−.38	−.20	.21	−.01	.01	.27	−.32
11	.37	−.04	−.01	.57	−.05	−.21	.16	−.09	.20	.36	.00	−.02
12	−.07	.02	.13	−.13	−.02	.14	.15	−.06	−.21	−.19	−.06	.12
13	−.01	−.01	−.50	.12	.07	−.34	−.02	−.03	−.30	−.02	.27	−.15
14	−.13	.24	−.20	−.15	.14	−.12	−.12	.17	−.15	−.09	.27	−.15
15	.26	.08	−.05	.07	.04	.23	−.01	.09	.17	.12	.03	.21
16	.28	.05	.23	−.05	.08	.53	.69	−.08	−.24	−.00	−.08	.50
17	.08	.42	.28	.13	.39	.16	.23	.53	.09	.15	.26	.21
18	−.01	.39	−.08	−.11	.31	−.11	−.16	.24	.03	.00	.36	−.18
19	.34	.08	.18	−.05	.05	.49	.75	.10	−.24	.13	−.12	.32
20	−.04	.04	.18	−.02	−.04	−.05	.00	.15	.12	−.12	.01	−.02
21	.37	−.04	.06	.20	−.08	.26	.21	.05	.19	.25	−.20	.10
22	.43	−.02	.14	.49	−.10	.06	.29	.05	.23	.37	−.19	.10
23	.01	.05	−.60	.06	.06	−.26	−.08	.04	−.34	−.06	.25	−.07
24	.60	−.12	−.20	.56	−.17	.02	.47	−.10	.01	.41	−.13	.07
25	.59	−.01	−.05	.53	−.12	−.03	.30	.02	.24	.45	−.04	.01
26	.13	.29	−.06	.02	.24	.09	.15	.22	−.06	.10	.11	.08
27	.20	.00	.17	.20	.02	.36	.18	.13	.15	.37	−.17	.11
28	−.09	−.17	.04	.01	−.16	−.10	.02	−.05	−.04	−.16	−.13	−.01
29	.27	.10	.14	.12	.06	.29	.20	.13	.24	.20	−.09	.13
30	.24	−.04	.14	.07	.14	.32	.10	−.12	.22	.22	−.01	.12
31	−.06	.35	.09	−.22	.36	.13	−.05	.30	.07	−.34	.39	.36
32	.36	−.04	.17	.14	.04	.23	.26	−.02	.27	.16	−.01	.11
33	.15	.01	.44	.02	.09	.30	.01	.04	.53	.09	−.09	.23
34	.40	.05	.10	.37	.13	.07	.05	−.13	.37	.35	.13	.10
35	.15	.15	.04	.13	.16	.21	.25	.13	−.01	.20	.04	.08
36	.49	.17	.07	.24	.13	.32	.46	.11	.03	.38	.00	.12
37	.12	.57	−.05	−.10	.57	.01	.14	.50	−.11	−.00	.46	.01
38	−.14	.03	.21	.02	−.05	−.04	−.06	−.03	.01	−.04	.01	−.02
39	.30	−.15	.04	.32	−.02	.06	.27	−.10	.01	.32	−.08	.07
40	.30	.11	.27	−.12	.07	.36	.30	.05	.18	.10	−.17	.09

TABLE 53-3. (continued)

| | Three Factor Solution | | | | | | Third Order Solution | | | | | |
| | M n = 512 | | | F n = 821 | | | M n = 512 | | | F n = 821 | | |
Item No.	N	E	P	N	E	P	N	E	P	N	E	P
41	.18	−.26	.08	.20	−.28	.02	.01	.24	.25	.15	−.21	−.11
42	.34	−.10	−.15	.21	−.05	.04	.21	−.16	−.01	.24	−.03	−.04
43	.14	.28	−.23	.01	.29	−.22	−.06	.24	.02	.02	.28	−.16
44	.30	−.07	.23	.18	−.06	.35	.28	−.17	.12	.32	−.13	.15
45	−.01	.18	−.14	−.15	.21	−.01	.19	.14	−.33	−.01	.22	−.12
46	.57	.02	−.17	.60	−.10	−.14	.31	.03	.14	.39	.01	−.02
47	.03	−.02	−.47	.06	.01	−.34	−.11	−.07	−.22	.05	.00	−.37
48	.17	.54	.03	.11	.50	−.04	.11	.37	−.00	.27	.42	−.07
49	.21	.05	.06	.34	.07	.07	−.04	.07	.29	.27	.11	.10
50	.16	.06	.22	.04	.04	.17	.06	.03	.20	.14	−.07	.06
51	−.07	.49	−.03	−.04	.49	−.10	.09	.26	−.33	.12	.41	−.12
52	−.16	−.02	−.11	−.09	.07	−.13	−.24	.01	.06	−.09	.11	−.17
53	.30	.26	.04	.25	.23	.14	.09	.21	.21	.14	.21	.31
54	.52	.07	.05	.47	.07	.17	.46	.10	.09	.43	.04	.28
55	.48	.16	−.08	.24	.09	.22	.25	.17	.14	.44	−.02	−.03
56	.47	.06	.06	.42	.08	.02	.10	.12	.38	.47	.05	−.06
57	.51	−.14	−.17	.58	−.13	−.14	.18	−.12	.20	.40	.01	−.01
58	.32	.09	.03	.05	.08	.46	.33	.09	−.02	.16	−.08	.26
59	.32	−.26	.27	.03	−.09	.44	.23	−.26	.32	.07	−.22	.38
60	.01	.43	.03	−.17	.42	.02	.17	.41	−.19	−.06	.25	−.02
61	.40	.00	.05	.34	−.02	.02	.26	−.00	.20	.24	−.00	.09
62	.23	−.03	.23	−.03	−.01	.26	.18	−.04	.21	.08	−.09	.10
63	.15	−.35	−.07	.11	−.32	.10	.08	−.31	−.02	.17	−.34	−.06
64	.53	−.04	−.20	.52	−.10	−.13	.17	−.11	.19	.33	.01	.04
65	.03	.58	−.03	−.02	.59	.02	.15	.35	−.23	.08	.43	.08
66	.38	−.10	.05	.07	−.08	.40	.30	−.10	.11	.15	−.21	.32
67	.44	.17	−.11	.48	.15	−.11	.18	.20	.17	.27	.18	.08
68	.25	−.24	.21	.24	−.10	.19	.26	−.25	.24	.08	−.02	.27
69	−.11	.42	−.19	−.02	.45	−.15	.03	.22	−.46	.13	.41	−.17
70	.28	.37	−.01	.24	.39	.04	.01	.43	.27	.23	.33	.11
71	.35	.11	.05	.42	.18	−.07	−.04	.14	.43	.41	.17	−.06
72	.12	.12	.06	.09	.17	.10	.12	.07	.04	.00	.16	.24
73	.30	.11	.02	.33	.25	.03	.05	−.04	.20	.27	.21	.11
74	−.02	−.03	−.24	−.07	−.02	−.03	−.05	−.06	−.20	.05	.04	−.17
75	.18	.46	.07	.09	.38	.06	.07	.50	.12	.19	.30	.01
76	.56	−.09	−.21	.35	−.08	.17	.35	−.15	−.01	.34	−.09	.19
77	.25	.00	.02	.34	−.06	−.18	−.10	−.05	.31	.22	.06	−.12
78	.52	.06	.04	.38	.02	.12	.28	.06	.27	.44	.00	.05
79	.30	−.29	.04	.02	−.32	.31	−.01	−.12	.47	−.11	−.33	.37
80	.37	.17	−.06	.28	.15	.06	.24	.14	.06	.35	.21	.05
81	−.14	.23	−.06	.03	.29	−.24	−.23	.25	.07	.11	.36	−.26
82	.46	.06	.03	.33	.05	.05	.15	.20	.41	.11	.16	.23
83	.18	.14	−.16	.22	.14	−.24	.01	.03	−.07	.31	.24	−.19
84	.11	.49	.04	.11	.44	−.06	.01	.31	.03	.24	.36	−.12
85	−.08	.08	.24	.00	.00	−.15	−.07	−.01	.12	−.15	.09	−.03
86	.39	.09	.03	.20	−.04	.15	.17	.15	.25	.15	−.10	.20

TABLE 53-3. (continued)

	Three Factor Solution						Third Order Solution					
	M n = 512			F n = 821			M n = 512			F n = 821		
Item No.	N	E	P	N	E	P	N	E	P	N	E	P
87	.04	.23	−.13	.14	.17	−.20	−.06	.22	−.03	.21	.18	−.17
88	.39	−.04	.09	.42	.05	.11	.51	−.11	−.08	.31	.06	.36
89	−.17	.44	−.09	−.11	.26	−.15	−.22	.46	−.05	.08	.24	.07
90	.50	−.16	−.10	.41	−.12	.14	.34	−.07	.14	.44	−.02	.13
91	.29	−.08	.02	.49	−.11	−.12	−.11	−.02	.41	.27	−.04	.11
92	.28	−.05	−.18	.13	.01	.05	.21	.05	.07	.26	.05	−.05
93	.19	−.23	−.18	−.09	−.03	.37	.41	−.20	−.30	.04	−.16	.23
94	.08	.39	.22	.14	.36	−.02	.07	.37	.19	.01	.38	.19
95	.00	.01	−.51	.04	.06	−.34	−.08	.01	−.30	.06	.02	−.40
96	.57	.15	−.18	.48	.14	−.09	.37	.06	.03	.41	.17	.03
97	.00	.26	−.25	.08	.32	−.08	−.03	.25	.23	.15	.22	−.07
98	.26	.24	.14	.24	.28	.11	−.02	.39	.36	.38	.18	.04
99	−.06	.15	−.32	.13	.04	.44	−.14	.07	−.21	−.05	.24	−.25
100	.07	.43	−.16	.17	.32	−.10	−.10	.30	−.09	.16	.29	−.04
101	.30	.02	−.16	.14	−.06	.07	.25	.08	−.07	.25	−.04	−.10
102	−.38	.05	−.06	−.17	.02	−.25	−.35	.09	−.08	−.17	.11	−.17
103	.01	.40	.07	.01	.31	.06	.11	.28	−.12	−.02	.34	.27
104	.24	−.11	−.12	.13	−.13	−.02	.25	−.18	−.12	−.07	−.06	.06
105	−.08	−.00	−.07	−.33	−.05	.14	.28	.05	−.39	−.23	−.08	−.03
106	.41	−.10	.02	.13	−.13	.28	.23	.00	.21	.11	−.21	.28

neurotics and psychotics, were also tested, under more usual conditions but this article is concerned only with the results obtained from our "market research" samples.

Eight hundred and ninety-four women and 550 men were tested in all, but of these a number failed to complete the questionnaire, so that the numbers forming part of the analysis were 821 women and 512 men. Table 53-3 gives the loadings of the three principal components factors extracted from the respective matrices of product-moment matrices and rotated to simple structure by PROMAX in the order N, E and P; again we have denoted the third factor "P" somewhat prematurely, because complete proof of its nature is of course not yet obtainable; our main reason must be simple convenience of labelling, and if the reader rejects the interpretation of this factor as "psychoticism" he may conveniently simply regard the letter "P" as an indeterminate symbol. It is certainly notable that nearly all the items having high loadings on P are in fact items which in previous work with the MMPI and other inventories have successfully distinguished clinically diagnosed psychotics (of different types) from neurotics and normals; nevertheless, this may be taken only as suggestive, and certainly not as proof of the identity of this factor.

Coefficients of factor comparison (Eysenck & Eysenck, 1968) were calculated between sexes to determine the degree to which the factors in one sex were replicable in the other. The figures are all reasonably high: N = .960; E = .979; P = .948. The figure for the P factor is lower than those for either N or E, but the differences are trifling. We may conclude that similar if not identical factors can be derived in separate samples, distinguished by sex; it should be noted that it cannot be assumed without proof that sex does not influence factor identities—much evidence on this point is given in Eysenck & Eysenck (1968). The fact that sex does not seem to distort the factors extracted suggests that they have considerable stability from sample to sample.

The factors are not independent in either sample; the correlations for the women are: NE = .15; NP = .34; EP = −.05, and for the men: NE = .14; NP = .30; EP = −.13. Of these, the only correlation which is of any interest is that between N and P; in both sexes, there is an overlap between factors amounting to about 10%. This is not only statistically significant but sufficiently substantial to call for an explanation; it may be suggested that possibly the possession of high P by a person living in our culture pattern imposes a considerable stress on him which in turn results in higher strain. This higher strain, in turn, may lead to a slight increase in N scores; it is well known that N scores are responsive to strain in this fashion (Eysenck & Eysenck 1968). This tentative explanation may of course not be the true one; the correlation states a problem which requires an experimental solution.

RESULTS: PRIMARY FACTOR SOLUTION

Cattell (1965) has opposed the type of analysis typified in the preceding section, calling it "resolution into pseudo-second orders" which he also calls "*space-deformed.*" "When closely examined, the imitation, in loading pattern, of the true second orders by these pseudo-second orders is poor. This is because in one case the missing variance is a series of centroid factors, each a mixture of everything, while in the other it is the specific factor variance of the primaries, i.e. that part of the primaries which does not come into the second order common space." Eysenck & Eysenck (1968) have shown that, in at least one case, Cattell's argument does not appear to be universally true; they actually compared by way of indices of factor similarity "pseudo-second orders" and proper second order factors extracted from the same matrix, and obtained very high indices indeed—so high that they suggested virtual identity of the E and N factors extracted. We cannot, therefore, agree with Cattell that "pseudo-second order factors" are of necessity inferior to "proper second-order factors"; there are certain conditions when the two may be identical. We would suggest that the clue to this riddle lies in another sentence of Cattell's, taken from the same paper: "The guesswork involved in deciding how many second orders exist *before* one has taken out the primaries, and the inelegance of seeking a solution in short, deformed space, combine to make this "pseudo second-order" approach scientifically indefensible." When what is involved is truly guesswork, then Cattell is undoubtedly right; remembering what we said in the section devoted to *procedural aspects*, we would agree that his objurgations apply to Thurstone's second case. They do not, however, apply to his first case, particularly when much theoretical and experimental work precedes the use of the factorial method. In the study by Eysenck & Eysenck referred to, dozens of previous analyses left very little doubt in our minds as to the number of (important) second order factors to expect, or their nature; hence our "guess" was perhaps a little more than a guess, and turned out to be correct. Similarly in the present case; we would argue that there are three main factors to be expected at the second order level, and hence that we are justified in extracting and rotating three "pseudo-second orders." The analysis through primary to second order factors to be reported in this section may help to illustrate our position. It should be said again that we do not wish to generalise our argument and state that Cattell's argument is erroneous under all circumstances; we would expect him to be right in the majority of cases, but we would be prepared to say that under special circumstances, involving Thurstone's first case, "pseudo-second orders" and proper second orders may be virtually identical.

Twenty primary factors were extracted from the original matrices of correlations, and rotated by Promax, separately for men and women. These primary factors will not be given in detail here or discussed, as they are not relevant to our main point. From the intercorrelations of the primaries, 7 second-order factors were extracted for each sex and again these will not be discussed. Finally, 3 third-order factors were extracted for both groups, and it is these factors which are to be compared with our 'pseudo-second order." The criterion for ceasing to extract second and third factors was the usual one of extracting factors with latent roots of unity or above. For the sake of comparison, the third-order factors are given in Table 53-3. To avoid subjectivity in these comparisons, indices of factor comparison (Eysenck & Eysenck, 1968) were calculated between the factors, for men and women separately. For the men, the indices were as follows: Neuroticism .98; Extraversion .99; Psychoticism .91. For the women they were: Neuroticism .99; Extraversion .97; Psychoticism .96. While these values differ from unity, they are sufficiently close to unity to give us confidence that our "pseudos" are good approximations to the third-order factors to make their use permissible. For all practical purposes, it may be said that the choice between the two solutions is arbitrary when interest is in the higher-order factors; the simple three factor solution is at a disadvantage, of course, when interest is in the primaries.

Cattell would argue, perhaps, that where there are differences between the two solutions the third-order factors are in principle preferable, because they give a more accurate picture of underlying reality. We are sceptical of this argument. "Underlying reality" is a slippery concept, and we would find it difficult to suggest any practical way of testing such a statement. Further than that, however, we believe that the superiority of the third-order solution would be apparent only with perfect samples of infinite size. With the usually small and imperfect samples we work with, there is an inevitable chance error in the original correlations which is magnified when angles between successive higher-order factors are being determined; the hypothetical superiority of higher-order factors may in fact turn to inferiority through these cumulative and inevitable errors. We do not want to insist on the actual superiority of the original three-factor solution; we merely wish to state that we do not consider it as necessarily inferior to the third-order solution. Fortunately the argument is an academic one in the present case as the indices of factor similarity are so high as to suggest virtual identity.

DISCUSSION AND CONCLUSION

The data presented in this paper suggest that it is possible to extract from carefully selected questions a sub-sample which is (a) relatively independent of N and E and which (b) relates in its content to psychotic abnormality. For the sake of convenience we have labelled this factor one of psychoticism, although recognising that the evidence so far given is not sufficient to establish the name as appropriate. As will be shown in future papers, the same factors here found in normal subjects also recur in samples of neurotic and psychotic patients, and the frequency of endorsement of P questions is considerably higher in psychotic patients than in normals or neurotics. It should be possible to go on from this demonstration to an experimental demonstration of similarities in behaviours in experimental situations of psychotics as compared with normals and neurotics, and of high-P scorers as compared with low-P scorers. Only by weaving a reasonably firm nomological network of this kind will it be possible to substantiate the hypothesis embodied in our choice of nomenclature for this factor.

Further research should also be concerned with the exact nature and cause of the correlation observed between N and P. This has been found in many samples tested since completion of this research, including the neurotic and psychotic ones mentioned in the last paragraph, and must be taken as probably constituting an established fact. It would be pointless to speculate at length about possible causes at this point, ranging from response sets to emotional stress produced by pre-psychotic or psychotic incapacity; the problem needs an empirical attack and will no doubt be resolved in time.

We may conclude that within the limits set by any purely factorial approach, our investigation has succeeded in supporting our original hypothesis about the existence of a third higher-order factor to take its place beside E and N. The actual choice of items for making up a scale, the testing of the reliability of that scale, and its application to various normal and abnormal samples will be reported in subsequent articles.

REFERENCES

Armstrong, H. G., Johnson, M. H., Ries, V. J., & Holmes, D. S. Extraversion-introversion and process-reactive schizophrenia. *British Journal of Clinical Psychology*, 1967, 6, 69.

Cattell, R. B. Higher order factor structures and reticular-vs-hierarchical formulae for their interpretation. In C. Beech & G. L. Broadhurst (Eds.), *Studies in Psychology*. London: University Press, 1965.

Cattell, R. B., & Scheier, I. H. *The meaning and measurement of neuroticism and anxiety*. New York: Ronald Press, 1961.

Cowie, V. The incidence of neurosis in the children of psychotics. *Acta Psychologica Scandinavia*, 1961, 37, 37–87.

Devadasan, K. Cross-cultural validity of twelve clinical diagnostic tests. *Journal of Indian Academy of Applied Psychology*, 1964, 1, 55–57.

Eysenck, H. J. *Dimensions of personality*. New York: Praeger, 1947.

Eysenck, H. J. *The scientific study of personality*. New York: Praeger, 1952. (a)

Eysenck, H. J. Schizothymia-cyclothymia as a dimension of personality. *Journal of Personality*, 1952, 20, 345–384. (b)

Eysenck, H. J. Psychiatric diagnosis as a psychological and statistical problem. *Psychological Reports*, 1955, 1, 3–17.

Eysenck, H. J. *The structure of human personality*. New York: Macmillan, 1960. (a)

Eysenck, H. J. Classification and the problem of diagnosis. In H. J. Eysenck (Ed.), *Handbook of Abnormal Psychology*. New York: Basic Books, 1960. (b)

Eysenck, H. J. A dimensional system of psychodiagnostics. In A. R. Mahrer (Ed.), *New approaches to psychodiagnostic systems*. New York: Aldine, 1968, in press.

Eysenck, H. J., & Eysenck, S. B. G. *Personality, structure and measurement*. San Diego: R. Knapp, 1969.

Eysenck, S. B. G. Neurosis and psychosis: an experimental analysis. *Journal of Mental Science*, 1956, 102, 517–529.

Eysenck, S. B. G., & Eysenck, H. J. *The Eysenck Personality Inventory*. San Diego: Educational and Industrial Testing Service, 1965.

Lubin, A. Some contributions to the testing of psychological hypotheses by means of statistical multivariate analysis. Unpublished doctoral dissertation, University of London, 1951.

Thurstone, L. L. *Multiple-factor analysis*. Chicago: University Press, 1947.

Trouton, D. S., & Maxwell, A. E. The relations between neurosis and psychosis. *Journal of Mental Science*, 1956, 102, 1–21.

54

New Ways of Curing the Neurotic

H. J. EYSENCK

For the past fifty years there has been virtually unanimous agreement that neurotic disorders can best be understood and treated in terms of some form of dynamic system, stemming in various ways from Freud and his colleagues. Theory and practice stressed the origins of neurotic disorders in early childhood, repression of these early incidents into the unconscious, reactivation through some event in adult life, and the need for therapy to uncover the unconscious motives, interpret actions, dreams and thoughts in the light of these unconscious complexes, and give the patient insight into them. Under these conditions, and only under these conditions, would a cure follow; all other types of therapy were merely symptom-oriented, and getting rid of the symptom without curing the underlying complex would only make matters worse, and lead to relapse or symptom substitution. Without treatment, neurotic disorders would either remain in their original state or get worse; possibilities of spontaneous remission were discounted. Treatment along psychoanalytic lines might be lengthy, but it was thorough; eventually it would lead to a cure, and once accomplished, the cure was permanent—relapses after psychotherapy were not seriously considered as a possibility. These general beliefs were hardly ever contested, and even nowadays they still constitute the daily diet on which many psychiatrists, particularly in the United States, are brought up. The casual reader of modern textbooks of psychiatry or clinical psychology, particularly American ones, would hardly be aware that none of the beliefs listed above has in fact any evidence to support it, and that in many cases there is considerable evidence to show that the belief is definitely false.

I shall only deal very briefly with studies directed at disproving earlier dogmas, and concentrate rather on recent work of a more positive kind which offers an effective alternative, both theoretically and practically, to psychoanalysis. In the first place, then, let us note that one of the most striking features about neurotic disorders is the fact that they are subject to spontaneous remission. Figure 54-1 shows a curve drawn to illustrate the percentage improvement of severely neurotic patients not given any form of

From Eysenck, H. J. New Ways of Curing the Neurotic. *Psychological Scene*, 1967, 26, 383–390. Reprinted by permission of author and publisher.

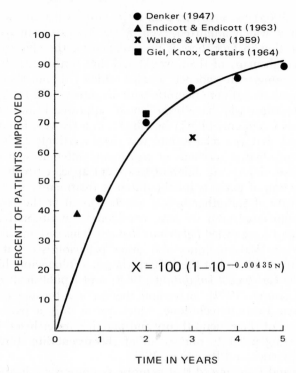

● Denker (1947)
▲ Endicott & Endicott (1963)
✗ Wallace & Whyte (1959)
■ Giel, Knox, Carstairs (1964)

$$X = 100 \, (1-10^{-0.00435\,N})$$

PERCENT OF PATIENTS IMPROVED

TIME IN YEARS

Figure 54-1.   Spontaneous remission as a function of time. In the formula, X denotes percentage improvement, and N denotes number of weeks.

psychiatric treatment, as well as a formula which was derived to fit the data; the data come from several studies dealing with quite a large number of cases followed up over various periods of time, as indicated in the Figure. While the formula is of course only a rough and ready first approach to a genuine quantitative treatment of spontaneous remission, it is nevertheless a reasonable approximation to the data (most of which had not been published when the formula was derived), and the literature leaves little doubt that spontaneous remission of neurotic symptoms occurs on a massive scale.

When we turn to the efficacy of psychotherapy, it is surely clear that it must surpass the spontaneous remission rate; if after two years of treatment only 70% of patients are cured, when the treatment has added precisely nothing to the spontaneous remission rate. In 1952 I analyzed published figures of the effects of psychotherapy, and concluded that they did not in any way differ from those obtained without treatment, i.e. through spontaneous remission. Later reviews (Eysenck, 1960), including much larger bodies of data, have reinforced this conclusion for adult patients, and

Levitt (1957, 1963) has analysed data for children with precisely the same result. It is now widely admitted, even by leading psychoanalysts and psychotherapists, that in fact there is no evidence for the efficacy of psychotherapy, although many of them would add that further search might succeed in discovering such evidence, a belief which I do not share. Not only does psychoanalysis not cure neurotic patients in excess of the spontaneous remission rate; those who have been "cured" appeared to have a very large relapse rate, as Cremerius (1962) has shown in a ten-year follow-up study. He also found that the relapse rate was disconcertingly high with other widely used psychiatric methods of treatment; differences in relapse rate between groups undergoing different treatment appeared to be due to differential selection of patients for the different treatments.

The falsity of the other beliefs which I listed at the beginning can only be demonstrated after we have considered the alternative system of therapy, which I have called *behaviour therapy*. This system has its roots in early studies of Watson, Jones and other behaviourists, but it may be said to date from the end of the 1950's, when J. Wolpe wrote his book *Psychotherapy by Reciprocal Inhibition* (1958) and I published my paper on *Behaviour Therapy* (1959). Behaviour therapy is a broader concept than Wolpe's desensitization technique, which forms only a part; though an important one, of the general theory and practice; nevertheless it makes an excellent starting point to our survey of the recent literature (Eysenck, 1960, 1964; Eysenck and Rachman, 1965).

Wolpe and I are agreed that neurotic symptoms are learned, i.e. they are neither innate nor are they due to lesions in the nervous system; consequently any explanation of neurotic behaviour ought to proceed from the firm basis of our knowledge of learning and conditioning, gained in the laboratory. Furthermore, theories so generated should throw light on possible methods for extinguishing the neurotic behaviour. In other words, we argued that psychiatry is simply a discipline for the application of fundamental psychological knowledge, particularly in the fields of learning and conditioning, to the practical problems presented by the symptoms and general malfunctioning of neurotic patients. In this way, psychology was merely following the usual path of the applied sciences where fundamental scientific discoveries preceded their application to practical problems. Freud has tried to reverse this process, by basing his "dynamic" psychology on the alleged discoveries made during his attempts to cure patients; he then attempted to universalize these notions by applying them to all human beings, and base a whole new psychology on them. His failure clearly points to the dangers of such attempts to short-circuit the ordinary processes of scientific progress.

Desensitization was developed by Joseph Wolpe in the early 1950's. He arrived at this method, which may be described as a gradual deconditioning of anxiety responses, in the following manner. Dissatisfied with the results which he was obtaining with the prevailing forms of psychotherapy, Wolpe returned to an examination of experimentally-induced neurotic disturbances. At the time, two promising leads were those provided by the work of Pavlov and his successors on artificial neuroses, and the early but neglected work of Watson (1920) and Jones (1924) on the genesis and elimination of children's fears. Wolpe carried out a series of experiments on the artificial induction of neurotic disturbances in cats, and came to the conclusion that the most satisfactory way of treating these neurotic animals was by gradual deconditioning along the lines proposed by Jones in 1924. He started off by feeding the neurotic cats in an environmental situation which was distinctly dissimilar from the original traumatic environment. Wolpe then proceeded gradually, through a series of carefully worked out stages, to situations which approximated more and more to the original traumatic situation. He found that in this way he was able to overcome the animal's neurotic reactions and restore them to apparent normality. It was obvious, however, that feeding responses would not be particularly effective in the treatment of adult neurotic patients. His search for responses which would be antagonistic to anxiety led him to the work of Jacobson (1938), who recommended the use of relaxation as a treatment for neurotic disorders. Wolpe decided to substitute relaxation for feeding as the major incompatible response which would dampen the anxiety reactions.

At first he attempted to relax his patients in the presence of the actual anxiety-provoking objects. This method, he soon discovered, was both tedious and impractical, as it involved amassing a large collection of objects for the treatment of each patient. Furthermore, as some patients did not experience anxiety in the presence of discrete and tangible objects, it meant that he would either have to refuse such patients treatment or develop some new method. He then began experimenting with the imaginary evocation of the anxiety-producing stimuli and soon found that it provided a very effective substitute for the real object. In other words, instead of attempting to treat a patient complaining of a phobia of dogs with an accumulation of photographs and models of dogs, he simply asked the patient to imagine these objects while relaxing in the consulting room. This method produced results and was easy to manipulate in the consulting room. It also allowed the therapist a high degree of flexibility in the planning of treatment.

Very simply, this is how the method of desensitization works: The patient is requested to imagine the anxiety-producing stimuli in a very mild and attenuated form. When the image is obtained vividly the therapist relaxes the patient causing the small amount of anxiety which the image had produced to dissipate. This process is repeated with the same stimulus or with a stimulus which is slightly more disturbing. The patient is again relaxed and the next stimulus is then presented and anxiety dissipated. With each evocation and subsequent dampening of the anxiety response, conditioned inhibition is built up. Eventually the patient is able to imagine even the most anxiety-provoking stimulus with tranquility which then generalizes to the real-life situation. The transfer of improvements from the consulting room to real-life situations usually accompanies each stage of the treatment programme in a regular, temporal fashion. When the person is able to envisage the previously disturbing stimulus in the consulting room without anxiety, he generally finds that he is able to cope with the actual stimulus in the real-life situation without difficulty. Naturally, before the systematic desensitization proper commences, various preliminary steps have to be taken. In the first place a full history of the patient's current disorder and his general history are obtained. Secondly, an attempt is made to reduce or eliminate any conflicts or anxiety-provoking situations which prevail at the time of treatment. Thirdly, the patient is trained in the methods of progressive relaxation as described by Jacobson. Fourthly, hierarchy, or group of hierarchies containing the anxiety-producing stimuli is established by the therapist and patient as a result of detailed therapeutic discussions. In these discussions the therapist, with the aid of the patient, builds up a series of situations which might produce anxiety in the patient. The patient is then required to rank them from the most disturbing to the least disturbing situation. When all these steps have been completed, the desensitization itself may proceed. Accounts of the actual technique are provided by Wolpe (1958), Eysenck and Rachman (1965) and Wolpe and Lazarus (1966) and a selection of cases is available in Eysenck (1960, 1964).

The method of desensitization and the other therapeutic procedures used by Wolpe are all based on the following general principle, as stated by him: "If a response antagonistic to anxiety can be made to occur in the presence of anxiety-provoking stimuli so that it is accompanied by a complete or partial suppression of the anxiety responses, the bond between the stimuli and the anxiety responses will be weakened."

This process is illustrated in Figure 54-2. There is a gradient of fear responsivness as the real or imagined fear-producing object is further and further removed from the patient. At a sufficient distance, where only very little anxiety is generated, the object is produced bodily, or a mildly fear-producing image is called up by the patient, at the same time as fear responses are reciprocally inhibited by relaxation. Thus relaxation responses are now conditioned to the fear-producing stimulus, and the whole gradient lowered; we can now present an object, or an image, which originally produced a strong fear (B), and again counteract this with relaxation. In this manner we can proceed until the gradient has disappeared altogether, and the patient is cured of this particular symptom.

Is this method clinically effective? Wolpe claimed that it was *much more* effective than psychotherapy, and also that it was much *quicker*. In his unselected series of over 300 cases he found it effective in 90% of his patients, with a mean of 30 sessions. Other reports by students and followers

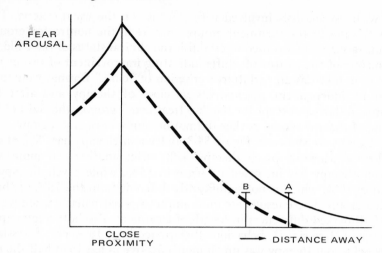

Figure 54-2.   Principle of desensitization therapy. The fear gradient
(solid line) exists along a real or ideational continuum.
At point A, where fear arousal is minimal, experimental
desensitization can be undertaken and if successful will
lower the whole gradient to the position indicated by the
broken line. Now desensitization can be carried out at
point B, again lowering the gradient if successful and
enabling the therapist to come closer and closer to the
most strongly felt arousing stimulus.

of his have been summarized in Eysenck and Rachman's book *Causes and
Cures of Neurosis* (1965): some report even better results, others slightly
worse ones. However, none of these many clinical studies contain proper
controls to enable us to answer such questions as: "Is desensitization superior to psychotherapy?" or: "Is desensitization shorter than psychotherapy?"
in a proper quantitative manner. A recent experiment carried out in my
department by Mr. J. Humphery furnishes us with some relevant data.

The point of the research was the comparison of the effects of psychotherapy with those of behaviour therapy, carried out on matched groups of
children in a child guidance clinic; there was also a "no treatment" group.
Cases embodied all the disorders common in a child guidance clinic, with
only psychotic and brain damaged cases excluded. All children were assessed
before and after treatment by experienced psychiatrists who were not aware
of the treatment received or planned for each child. Treatment was carried
out by Mr. Humphery, who is a psychotherapist of many years' experience,
and who used to be in charge of a child guidance clinic; he was trained in
behaviour therapy in our Department specifically for the purpose of this
experiment. Cessation of treatment was decided upon by him in consulta-

tion with psychiatrists involved with the case on the usual criteria. There were 37 cases in the treatment groups, and 34 in the nontreated group. A 5-point rating scale was used to establish the clinical status of the child, and the success of the treatment; shifts indicating improvement of two or more steps were taken as an (arbitrary) criterion of "cure." Ratings were undertaken by independent psychiatrists at close of therapy and after a 10 months' follow-up, except for the "no treatment" group, who did not have a close of therapy rating, as they did not of course have any therapy.

Results are shown in Figure 54-3. Behaviour therapy has 75% of cures at close of therapy, psychotherapy 35%; after another ten months behaviour therapy has increased its score to 85%, while psychotherapy has fallen to 29%, which is not significantly different from the 18% of the untreated group. These results are quite impressive, particularly when we bear in mind marked differences in length of treatment. Psychotherapy required 31 weeks (21 sessions); behaviour therapy required 18 weeks (9 sessions). Thus behaviour therapy was much more effective in less than half the number of sessions. It may also be mentioned that the behaviour therapy cases happened (by accident of sampling) to be more seriously ill than the psychotherapy cases; this too would militate against the success of behaviour therapy. All the differences to which attention has been drawn are of course

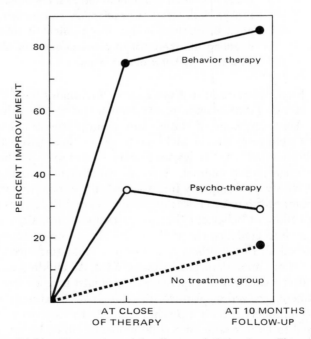

Figure 54-3.   Comparison of effects of Behaviour Therapy, Psychotherapy, and no treatment.

fully significant statistically, and it will be remembered that the ratings were made by independent psychiatric judges in ignorance of the method of treatment employed. And lest it be thought that the therapist did not try particularly hard with the psychotherapy cases, let it be added that his success rate was superior to the average success rate achieved by experienced psychotherapists in the child guidance clinics in question. The results on the whole confirm similar work with adults, as for instance the well-known experiment of Lazarus (1961).

Interesting as this study may be, it is undoubtedly possible to criticise it on various grounds. It assumes, for instance, that the crucial therapeutic element in the treatment is the conjunction of desensitization and relaxation; other theories may be put forward. Thus we may be dealing simply with a process of extinction due to a failure to reinforce the conditioned stimulus; the feared object is evoked without any aversive consequences following, and it is to be expected according to the laws of conditioning that extinction should take place. According to this theory desensitization without relaxation would be expected to be equally effective as desensitization with relaxation. An alternative hypothesis might be put forward, to the effect that relaxation lowers drive level, and that this in itself would reduce the conditioned fear response and might bring about a cure. On this hypothesis relaxation without desensitization would be adequate for achieving a cure. A third alternative hypothesis might be that the curative element is the attention of a sympathetic person in a position of authority; this view has often been expressed by psychotherapists who feel that behaviour therapy embodies certain psychotherapeutic procedures. We clearly require more formally experimental studies than the "clinical trial" type of investigation reported by Humphery, Lazarus and others, and fortunately the last few years have seen a whole series of such studies.

Some of the most important experimental work on this subject has been carried out by Lang and Lazovik. In 1963 they reported on the results of an experiment carried out on non-psychiatric subjects who suffered from an excessive fear of snakes. This pioneer experiment was carefully and elaborately prepared, and the experimental design and execution were of a high quality. The stringent controls which they applied enhanced the significance of their findings.

They chose to study snake phobias because of their common occurrence and also because of the assumed symbolic sexual significance attached to this disorder. Twenty-four subjects participated in the research. They were all college student volunteers and were selected by a combination of interview, questionnaire, and direct exposure to a non-poisonous snake. Only those subjects who rated their fears as intense and whose behaviour in the presence of the snake confirmed this subjective report, were used in the experiment. The subjects were divided into two matched groups, an experimental group consisting of 13 subjects and a control group comprising 11 subjects. The experimental treatment comprised two essential parts, training and desensitization proper. The training procedure consisted of five sessions of 45 minutes duration during which an anxiety hierarchy consisting of 20 situations involving snakes was constructed. The subjects were then trained in deep relaxation and taught how to visualize the feared scenes vividly while under hypnosis.

Following this training period, the experimental subjects were given 11 sessions of systematic desensitization during which they were hypnotized and instructed to relax deeply. The anxiety items from the hierarchy were then presented, starting with the least frightening scenes and working up the scale to the most frightening scenes. (As the experimental design demanded that each treated subject received only 11 treatment sessions, some of the subjects were not desensitized to all the items in the hierarchy. In order to assess the effectiveness of reality training, half of the experimental subjects were exposed to the snake before treatment on a number of occasions.) The control subjects did not participate in desensitization, but they were evaluated at the same time as their opposite numbers in the experimental series and their behaviour in the presence of the snake was ascertained at the beginning and end of the experiment. All of the available subjects were seen and evaluated six months after the completion of therapy.

The authors summarized their results in the following way. "The results of this present experiment demonstrate that the experimental analogue of desensitization therapy effectively reduces phobic behavior. Both subjective rating of fear and overt avoidance behaviour were modified and these gains were maintained or increased at the six months follow up. The results of objective measures were in turn supported by extensive interview material. Close questioning could not persuade any of the experimental subjects that their desire to please the therapist had been a significant factor in their change. Furthermore, in none of these interviews was there any evidence that other symptoms appeared to replace the phobic behaviour. The fact that no significant change was associated with the pre-therapy training argues that hypnosis and general muscle relaxation were not in themselves vehicles of change. Similarly, the basic suggestibility of the subject must be excluded . . . clearly the responsibility for the reduction in the phobic behaviour must be assigned to the desensitization process itself."

Lang and Lazovik also found a very close connection between the degree of improvement and the amount of progress made in the desensitization of hierarchy items within the 11 sessions provided by the experiment. They also make three general points on the basis of their results. Firstly, as has been argued on previous occasions (see Eysenck and Rachman, 1965), it is not necessary to "explore with the subject, the factors contributing to the learning of a phobia or its unconscious meaning in order to eliminate the fear behaviour." Secondly, they were not able to find any evidence to support the presumed claim that symptom substitution will arise if the symptoms are treated directly. Thirdly, they point out that in reducing phobic behaviour, it is not necessary to alter the basic attitudes, values or personality of the subject.

Lang, Lazovik and Reynolds (1966) recently reported further developments with this experimental procedure. They have now completed a study which included the experimental treatment of 23 subjects by systematic desensitization, 11 untreated controls and a further 10 subjects who participated in "pseudo-therapy." This last group of subjects is a particularly important addition as they received the same preliminary training as the desensitization group and participated in the same number of interview sessions. The major difference was that the pseudo-therapy group were relaxed in the interview sessions but not desensitized—instead, the therapist carefully avoided presenting any anxiety-provoking stimuli. The subjects were under the impression that they were given a form of dynamic or interpretative therapy. The essential difference in the treated and pseudo-therapy groups lay then in the use of systematic desensitization. Consequently any difference in the treatment outcome must be attributed to the use of this behaviour therapy technique. The results were clearcut and indicated that the subjects treated by systematic desensitization showed significant reductions in phobic behaviour. The untreated subjects and the subjects who participated in pseudo-therapy showed no improvement whatever. Among the subsidiary observations made by these research workers the following are of particular interest. None of the successfully treated subjects showed signs of developing substitute symptoms. Again, it was found to be unnecessary to delve into the presumed basic causes of their fear of snakes. Simply having a therapeutic relationship with the therapist was not capable of effecting changes in the phobia. Successful behaviour therapy is completely independent of the subject's basic suggestibility (as assessed on the Stanford scale). The systematic desensitization of the specific fear generalizes positively to other fears and an all-round improvement is observed.

Substantially confirmatory results were also reported in an experiment by Paul (1966). He investigated the effectiveness of desensitization in reducing interpersonal performance anxiety (actually, fear of public speaking). Five groups of carefully matched students were randomly allotted to the following groups: 1. Systematic desensitization; 2. insight therapy; 3. attention placebo (i.e. a dummy treatment); 4. no-treatment control; 5. no contact. Each of the 56 students comprising the first four groups was assessed before and after the completion of the experiment on three different types of scale. These measures included a number of self-report questionnaires, physiological measures (pulse rate and palmar sweating) and a rating of their behaviour in a real-life stress situation (which involved speaking in public). Five experienced therapists participated in the study;

they had been specifically trained in a short course to use behaviour therapy, although their personal preference was of course for psychotherapy. Each therapist was allotted patients from the three treatment groups (i.e. desensitization, insight, attention placebo). On the completion of a comparatively short period of treatment all the subjects, including the no-treatment controls, were retested. The results indicate that the subjects who had received desensitization treatment showed a significantly better response to treatment than any of the other subjects. This superiority was evident on all three types of measurement—subjective report, physiological arousal and reaction to stress. The superiority of the desensitized group was maintained at the six week follow-up period. Like the experiments conducted by Lang and Lazovik, the work of Paul indicates that it is possible to bring about significant reductions in fear, even long-standing fears, by the use of systematic desensitization. It also indicates that fears can be eliminated without any exploration in depth.

Paul and Shannon (1966) have since reported an another similar experiment, in which they added to their other experimental groups one which was given group behaviour therapy, rather along the lines introduced by Lazarus in a clinical experiment mentioned previously. Five patients were treated at a time, and the results were excellent. Group desensitization was as effective as individual desensitization. It was further found that the academic performance of subjects treated by behaviour therapy improved greatly, indicative of a general lowering of anxiety in these patients.

A very well controlled investigation of the effect of desensitization was recently carried out by Davison (1965). He had two main aims in designing his study. First, he wanted to examine the overall effect of desensitization treatment when compared with a no-treatment control group. Secondly, he was interested in teasing out the effective elements of desensitization treatment. He used 28 non-psychiatric female subjects all of whom complained of, and demonstrated, excessive fear of snakes. Subjects were divided into four matched groups on the basis of their behaviour in the presence of real snakes. The four groups were treated in the following manner. Group No. 1 received desensitization under relaxation, in the usual manner. The second group received relaxation training, but during the treatment sessions these subjects were given irrelevant images to consider while under deep relaxation. The third group of subjects was given desensitization without either receiving training in relaxation or being relaxed in the actual treatment sessions. The fourth group of subjects received no active treatment, but was merely assessed prior to and after the completion of the experiment. The subjects in groups 2 and 3 were "yoked" to the systematic desensitization subjects thereby ensuring that all of the girls who received treatment of any kind received the same number and durations of exposure to imaginary stimuli. The same therapist acted for all the subjects. At the completion of treatment the retest avoidance exposures showed that the desensitization under relaxation group showed greater improvements than the other three groups, which did not differ. It was also observed that the subjects who were asked to imagine the anxiety-evoking stimuli without first being relaxed signalled anxiety far more often during treatment sessions than the other subjects. The importance of this study, apart from providing another demonstration of the undoubted effectiveness of desensitization in eliminating or reducing fears, is that it helps to isolate the mechanisms which produce the reductions in fear. Davison has demonstrated in this experiment that it is neither relaxation alone nor desensitization alone which produces the improvements. Rather it is the combination of desensitization *and* relaxation which reduces fear. Apart from its practical importance this experimental result goes some way towards confirming Wolpe's theoretical account of his treatment procedure. One would predict on the basis of his ideas of reciprocal inhibition that neither desensitization nor relaxation would in themselves be adequate procedures for eliminating fear.

A very similar result was also reported by Rachman (1965) from our own laboratories. In this study four small groups of spider phobic, non-psychiatric subjects were allocated to the following experimental groups: desensitization with relaxation, desensitization without relaxation, relaxation only, no-treatment controls. The purpose of the experiment was "further to explore the effective mechanism contained in the treatment called 'systematic desensitization' based on relaxation." What are the necessary parts of the treatment procedure? Three specific questions were framed: is the treatment more effective than no treatment? Is the treatment more effective than relaxation alone? Is the treatment more effective than desensitization without relaxation? The effects of treatment were assessed by subjective reports, avoidance tests and fear estimates. Marked reductions in fear were obtained only in the desensitization-with-relaxation group and it was concluded that the combined effects of relaxation and desensitization are greater than their separate effects. Results are shown in Figure 54-4. Commenting on the results Rachman said that "neither relaxation nor desensitization are effective in their own right. The combined effect of the two procedures is greater than their separate actions. It means also that the learning process involved is probably conditioned inhibition rather than extinction. This is not meant to imply that extinction is never responsible for the reduction of fear. In the present context, however, inhibition is the more effective process." Like Davison, Paul, and Lang and Lazovik, Rachman could adduce no evidence of symptom substitution. Moreover the improvements in phobic behaviour were found to be reassuringly stable over a three month follow-up period. Rachman (1966) also tested another technique, which he called "flooding"; this consisted of exposing the subjects to intensively disturbing imaginal stimuli involving spiders. Although strong emotional reactions were provoked by this pro-

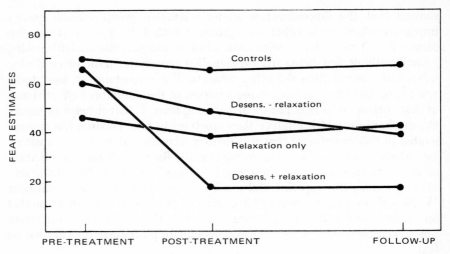

Figure 54-4.   Mean fear estimates obtained on the pre-treatment, post-
treatment and follow-up avoidance tests for each group
of subjects. (From S. Rachman, 1965)

cedure it did not produce a reduction in fear of the phobic object. Results
are shown in Figure 54-5.

Cooke (1966) compared the relative effectiveness of the two types of
desensitization treatments—imaginal desensitizing vs. real life desensitizing.
He employed three groups of non-psychiatric subjects with excessive fears
of rats. Each group consisted of four subjects and their fear reactions were
ascertained by avoidance tests in the usual manner. The first group was
relaxed and then exposed in a graded and gradual manner to real rats,
while the second group was relaxed and desensitized to similar items in
imagination only. The third group consisted of a no-treatment control.
Cooke found no overall difference between the two types of treatment, both
of which produced significant decreases in fear. He showed, however, that
highly anxious subjects showed more fear reduction when treated in the
Wolpeian fashion with imaginal stimuli. Some other findings to emerge
from Cooke's study and which are of interest include the following. No
symptom substitution was observed nor were any increases in anxiety noted
after treatment. Cooke also remarks on the consistency and reliability of
the avoidance test scores and subjective fear estimates.

Two other aspects of desensitization treatment which have received
recent attention are the distribution of treatment sessions and the speed of
generalization from imaginal desensitization to real-life behaviour. Ramsay
et al. (1966) compared the effectiveness of massed and spaced treatment
sessions. Twenty non-psychiatric subjects with fears of various animals were
given desensitization treatment under conditions of massed and spaced

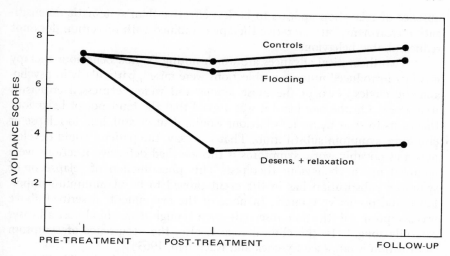

Figure 54-5.   Mean avoidance scores obtained under pre-treatment,
post-treatment and follow-up tests for each group of subjects. (From S. Rachman, 1966a)

practice. In the spaced practice condition each subject was given four fear-
hierarchy stimuli to imagine in a 20-minute period. Four such treatment
sessions were given. For the massed practice group, each treatment session
contained eight items and the session lasted for 40 minutes. Two of these
prolonged sessions were administered. In this way the subjects in the two
groups received the same amount of time in treatment and the same number of item presentations. The results showed a highly significant drop in
fear due to the treatment, and the learned reductions in fear were more
efficiently induced under the distributed practice condition. Ramsay et al.
comment in passing, on the ease with which the experimental therapists
(with no previous experience of desensitization) acquired the necessary skill
in successfully administering the treatment.

The present state of the experimental evidence on desensitization
permits the following conclusions. Desensitization therapy effectively reduces phobic behaviour. The elimination of phobic behaviour is analogous
to the elimination of other responses from the subject's repertoire. It is not
necessary to ascertain the origin of the phobia in order to eliminate it.
Neither is it necessary to change the subject's basic attitudes or to modify
his personality. The elimination of a phobia is not followed by symptom
substitution. The response to treatment is not related to suggestibility.
Relaxation or hypnosis alone do not reduce the phobia. Relaxation and
hypnosis accompanied by pseudotherapeutic interviews do not reduce the
phobia. The establishment of a therapeutic relationship with the patient
does not of itself reduce the phobia. Desensitization administered in the

absence of relaxation appears to be less effective than systematic desensitization treatment. Interpretative therapy combined with relaxation does not reduce phobic behaviour.

Two theoretical advances are worth noting. When behaviour therapy was first introduced numerous objections were raised, particularly in psychoanalytic circles. Two of the most serious and widely expressed criticisms were these. On the one hand it was argued that the tendency of behaviour therapists to treat neurotic behaviour would, if successful, lead to relapse or else some symptom substitution. That is to say, the patient would develop new and possibly worse symptoms if the so-called defensive reactions were removed by the behaviour therapist. This phenomenon of relapse or of symptom substitution has in the event proved to be of minimum importance and occurs very rarely. In none of the experiments described above was symptom substitution observed—even though it was in almost all cases carefully sought. In the clinical reports also, the occurrence of symptom substitution is rare (see Eysenck and Rachman, 1965).

A second objection which was raised was that it is impossible to bring about the reduction or elimination of neurotic symptoms and behaviour unless one first eliminated the presumed basic causes of the illness. It was said that behaviour therapy could not succeed because it was directing its attention to the wrong area. This objection too has now been firmly eliminated. In the experimental investigations and the clinical reports there is overwhelming evidence that substantial improvements in neurotic behaviour can be obtained by systematic desensitization (and other methods of behaviour therapy) even when little or no attention is paid to the possible or presumed underlying causes of the illness. There is no evidence in all our experimental material of unconscious complexes "causing" abnormal behaviour. As I once rather paradoxically expressed it, "the symptom *is* the illness"; in other words, symptoms are not really symptomatic of anything. They are simply conditioned autonomic and skeletal responses, which are maladaptive and require to be extinguished.

We are now able to answer some of the questions we put at the beginning of this paper and to put forward a rather different theory to account for the existence of neurotic disorders. From this theory also emerges an answer to the question which may appear rather puzzling, namely the reasons for spontaneous remission. It is often said that "time is the great healer," but clearly it is not time itself which provides the cure of neurotic disorder, but *events occurring in time,* and it is essential to pinpoint the precise events which have this effect. In 1965 I put forward the theory that we are dealing here with experimental extinction pure and simple. If phobic and other dysthymic symptoms are in fact conditioned responses, then the occurrence of the conditioned stimulus with the occurrence of an unconditioned stimulus, i.e. a traumatic or aversive event which originally gave rise to the symptoms, should produce an increment of extinction; gradually further increments should be added until remission (extinction) was complete. This may not happen in certain cases because the patient refuses to encounter the conditioned stimulus, i.e. the fear-producing stimulus; by thus running away from it he experiences reinforcement for all evasive type of reaction which is now in turn becoming conditioned, thus making "reality testing" impossible; this may account for those cases where no spontaneous remission takes place. Consider a woman we have recently treated (Freeman and Kendrick, 1960), who suffered from a severe cat phobia, which forced her to stay in her room in case she should meet a cat outside. The phobia developed when as a young girl her father drowned her favourite kitten in front of her eyes; the kitten is the conditioned stimulus, the fear the conditioned response. Seeing cats without any similar traumatic event following should effectively extinguish the conditioned fear response. However, she developed a habit of running away whenever she saw a cat; this running away was followed by a reduction in anxiety, which was reinforcing and thus led to a conditioned avoidance habit which ultimately led to her being immured in her room. Behaviour therapy completely restored her to a normal life within a few weeks, without relapse or symptom substitution.

It is now time to formulate some conclusions. I have concentrated in this paper on desensitization methods, but behaviour therapy is of course much more extensive than that, including aversion therapy for enuresis, fetishism, homosexuality, alcoholism and other sexual deviations and addictive practices; negative practice or conditioned inhibition, applied to tics and other muscular-skeletal dysfunctions; operant conditioning, applied with much success to psychotic disorders, autistic children, and mentally defective children and adults. Concentration has been focused on desensitization because it illustrates best the main contribution which behaviour therapy, and the learning theories of neurotic disorders have made to psychiatry and clinical psychology. This contribution does not lie, in my opinion, in the practical improvement of methods of treatment, real though these improvements may be, or even in the better understanding of neurotic disorders which we now have, thanks to the link forged between them and the laboratory facts of learning and conditioning. I would like to suggest that the main contribution of behaviour therapists has been the insistence that all theoretical formulations and clinical claims should be subjected to an experimental test, and the actual working out of methods for conducting such tests. It is possible, although perhaps unlikely, that all the theoretical formulations mentioned in this paper are in fact erroneous; yet the scientific method of experimental testing of theories would guarantee that these errors would in due course be exposed, and new facts be adduced on which new and better theories could be based.

One objection to psychoanalysis and its allied psychotherapeutic theories and practices is not based on purely theoretical grounds, but rather on two facts which rule the Freudian approach out of court as far as science is concerned. In the first place, theories are not formulated in a manner which permits of falsification; it is difficult if not impossible to think of ways in which Freudian theories can be experimentally tested. In the second place, no efforts have ever been made by psychotherapists to carry out the empirical sort of work which alone could give us the facts on which a proper evaluation of their efforts should be based. They demand belief, but do not offer proof; this is the negation of the scientific approach. Behaviour therapists offer proof, and ask for suspension of judgment until the proof is conclusive; this, as I see it, is nothing more nor less than the introduction, long delayed, of scientific method into this murky and passion-ridden field. If the experiments are subject to criticism, then on the basis of such criticism better experiments will be designed. If the theories are found to be lacking when submitted to experimental test, then better theories will be designed on the basis of the established facts. Only in this way will progress be made, and the subject matter of this paper become truly scientific, after over fifty years in the twilight zone of unverified claims, unjustified beliefs and passionately held dogma.

REFERENCES

Cooke, G. (1966). The efficacy of two desensitization procedures: an analogue study. Behaviour Research and Therapy, 4, 17–24.

Cremerius, J. (1962). Die Beurteilung des Benhandlungserfolges in der Psychotherapie. Berlin: Springer.

Davison, G. (1965). The influence of systematic desensitization, relaxation, and graded exposure to imaginal stimuli in the modification of phobic behaviour. Unpublished doctoral dissertation, Stanford University.

Denker, P. G. (1957). Results of treatment of psychoneuroses by the general practitioner: a follow-up study of 500 cases. Arch. Neurol. Psychiat., 57, 504–505.

Endicott, E. G. & Endicott, J. (1963). "Improvement" in untreated psychiatric patients. Arch. Gen. Psychiat., 9, 575–585.

Eysenck, H. J. (1952). The effects of psychotherapy: an evaluation. J. Consult. Psychol., 16, 319–324.

Eysenck, H. J. (1959). Learning theory and behaviour therapy. J. Ment. Sci., 105, 61–75.

Eysenck, H. J. (1960). The effects of psychotherapy. In: H. J. Eysenck (Ed.) Handbook of Abnormal Psychology. London: Pitmans.

Eysenck, H. J. (Ed.) (1960). Behaviour Therapy and Neuroses. Oxford: Pergamon.

Eysenck, H. J. (1963). Behaviour, spontaneous remission and transfer in neurotics. Amer. J. Psychiat., 119, 867–871. Reprinted: Eysenck, 1964.

Eysenck, H. J. (Ed.) (1964). *Experiments in Behaviour Therapy*. Oxford: Pergamon.

Eysenck, H. J. & Rachman, S. (1965). *The Causes and Cures of Neurosis*. London: Routledge and Kegan Paul.

Freeman, H. L. & Kendrick, D. C. (1960). A case of cat phobia. *Brit. Med. J.*, 2, 497–502. Reprinted Eysenck, 1964.

Giel, R., Knox, R. S. & Carstairs, G. M. (1964). A five year follow-up of 100 neurotic out-patients. *Brit. Med. J.*, 2, 160–163.

Jacobson, E. (1938). *Progressive relaxation*. Chicago: University of Chicago Press.

Jones, M. C. (1924). A laboratory study of fear: the case of Peter. *Ped. Sem.*, 31, 308–315. *Reprinted in Eysenck*, 1960.

Lang, P. & Lazovik, G. D. (1963). The experimental desensitization of a phobia. *J. Abnorm. Soc. Psychol.*, 66, 519–525. Reprinted in Eysenck, 1964.

Lang, P., Lazovik, A. D. & Reynolds, D. J. (1965). Desensitization, suggestibility and pseudo-therapy. *Journal of Abnormal Psychology*, 70, 395–402.

Lazarus, A. G. (1961). Group therapy of phobic disorders by systematic desensitization. *J. Abnorm. Soc. Psychiat.*, 63, 504–510. Reprinted in Eysenck, 1964.

Levitt, G. G. (1957). Results in psychotherapy with children: an evaluation. *J. Consult. Psychol.*, 21, 189–196.

Levitt, G. G. (1963). Psychotherapy with children: a further evaluation. *Behav. Res. Ther.*, 1, 45–51.

Paul, G. L. (1966). *Insight vs. desensitization in psychotherapy*. Stanford: University Press.

Paul, G. L. & Shannon, D. T. (1966). Treatment of anxiety through systematic desensitization in therapy groups. *J. Abnorm. Psychol.*, 71, 124–135.

Rachman, S. (1965). Studies in desensitization—I: The separate effects of relaxation and desensitization. *Behav. Res. Ther.*, 3, 245–251.

Rachman, S. (1966). Studies in desensitization—II: Flooding. *Behav. Res. Ther.* 4, 1–6.

Rachman, S. (1966). Studies in desensitization—III: Speed of generalization. *Behav. Res. Ther.*, 4, 7–15.

Ramsay, R., Barends, J., Breuker, J. and Kruseman, A. (1966). Massed versus spaced desensitization of fear. *Behav. Res. Ther.* 4, 3, 205–208.

Wallace, N. E. R., & Whyte, M. P. H. (1959). Natural history of the psychoneuroses. *Brit. Med. J.*, 1, 144–148.

Watson, J. B. & Rayner, R. (1920). Conditioning emotional responses. *J. Exp. Psychol.*, 3, 1–14. Reprinted in Eysenck, 1960.

Wolpe, J. (1958). *Psychotherapy by reciprocal inhibition*. Stanford: University Press.

Wolpe, J. & Lazarus, G. G. (1966). *Behaviour Therapy Techniques*. Oxford: Pergamon.

Name Index

785

Subject Index

Abasement: 249, 250, 252, 253, 255, 256

Abnorm: 291

Abnormality: 291, 292, 297, 751. *See also* Normality

Abstract Apparatus Test (A.A.): 400

Abstraction and Abstraction capacity: 296, 409, 509, 510, 513, 551, 556, 573

Academic achievement: 776; birth order study, 149–57

Achievement: 352, 353, 670, 679; academic, 149–57, 776; Jastak-Bijou test, 60; motivation, 443; need, 666. *See also* Striving

Act completion experiments: 208, 536–43

Activation: 306, 308, 312, 574. *See also* Arousal

Active imagination *see* Creative imagination

Adam and Eve: 180, 602–03

Adaptability: 293

Adaptation: 229, 231, 425, 478, 510, 589, 592; impeded, 96–99; social, 442, 444

Adaptation level theory: 670, 675

Adjustment: 142, 210, 293, 378, 478, 507, 508; and client-centered counseling, 385–86, 388–89; concepts, 289, 290, 292; ego as organ of, 199, 202, 203; role of need attitudes, 347–53

Adlerian psychology: 144–67, 368, 392, 396; applied to civil rights, 143, 158–67; birth-order study, 149–57; compared to other theories, 142, 236; *Gemeinsinn* concept, 145; inferiority, 76, 159–60, 161; influence on Jung, 72, 76–78; power theory, 144–48. *See also* Neoanalytic theory

Adolescence and Adolescents: 147, 201, 215–16, 230–32, 242, 245, 421, 657; identity crisis, 222–25

Affect and affectivity: 61, 64, 68, 305, 556, 561, 563–64, 572, 594

Affirmation: 173–75, 570, 574

Age and aging: 169, 329, 469; Jungian approach, 77–78; organismic view, 513–15

Aggression: 51, 162–63, 256, 330, 333, 335, 496, 666; adolescent, 227, 657; anxiety and, 169–72, 174, 674; Freudian theory, 168–69, 171–75, 177; Horney's theory, 169–77, 180, 181–82; model reinforcement study, 695–704; as need attitude, 347–53; and psychic structure formation, 206–08, 214, 215. *See also* Hostility

Alchemy: 73

Alcoholics and Alcoholism: 145, 274, 275, 348, 349, 351–52, 494, 570, 692, 781

Alienation: 181, 448, 462–63

Allport-Vernon-Lindzey Scale of Values (A-V-L): 490n, 492, 494, 495

Alpha rhythm: 561

Ambiguity tolerance: 563, 659

Ambivalence: 16, 50, 206, 214, 226, 415; transcending, 430

Anabolic functions: 296, 298

Anality: 207, 209, 663

Anal-compulsives: 221

Analysis *see* Psychoanalysis and Psychotherapy

Analysts *see* Therapists

Analytical Psychology: 72–139; personality inventories, 111–16, 118–38; psychotherapeutic aims, 75–88; use of spontaneous art, 84–87; word association method, 73, 89–109. *See also* Jungian theory

Anamnesis: 527–28; data, 663

Anger: 221, 411, 423, 507; definitions, 330; personological study, 323–37

Angst: 457n. *See also* Care

Animals: 174, 289, 297, 679, 769; anxiety in, 587n, 589–90; instincts, 202–03; power drive, 147; visceral learning experiments, 608–32

794